INTERDISCIPLINARY RESEARCH

Case Studies from Health and Social Science

Edited by

Frank Kessel

Patricia L. Rosenfield

Norman B. Anderson

OXFORD

UNIVERSITY PRESS

2008

OXFORD
UNIVERSITY PRESS

Oxford University Press, Inc., publishes works that further
Oxford University's objective of excellence
in research, scholarship, and education.

Oxford   New York
Auckland   Cape Town   Dar es Salaam   Hong Kong   Karachi
Kuala Lumpur   Madrid   Melbourne   Mexico City   Nairobi
New Delhi   Shanghai   Taipei   Toronto

With offices in

Argentina   Austria   Brazil   Chile   Czech Republic   France   Greece
Guatemala   Hungary   Italy   Japan   Poland   Portugal   Singapore
South Korea   Switzerland   Thailand   Turkey   Ukraine   Vietnam

Published by Oxford University Press, Inc.
198 Madison Avenue, New York, New York 10016

www.oup.com

Library of Congress Cataloging-in-Publication Data
Interdisciplinary research: case studies from health and social science / edited by Frank Kessel,
Patricia L. Rosenfield, and Norman B. Anderson.
p. ; cm.
New ed. of: Expanding the boundaries of health and social science. 2003.
Includes bibliographical references and index.
ISBN 978-0-19-532427-3   1. Medicine—Research.   2. Social sciences—Research.   3. Interdisciplinary re-
search.   I. Kessel, Frank S.   II. Rosenfield, Patricia L.   III. Anderson, Norman B.   IV. Expanding the
boundaries of health and social science.
[DNLM: 1. Health Occupations.   2. Interdisciplinary Communication.   3. Research Personnel.
4. Public Health.   5. Research. W 20.5 I5144 2008]
R853.I53E955 2008
610.72—dc22   2007036471

9 8 7 6 5 4 3 2 1
Printed in the United States of America
on acid-free paper

CONTENTS

Preface to the New Edition   *ix*
Frank Kessel and Patricia L. Rosenfield

Foreword   *xxi*
Craig Calhoun and Cora Marrett

Contributors   *xxv*

Introduction: Approaching Interdisciplinary Research   *3*
John W. Rowe

PART I: HOME IS WHERE THE HEART IS:
THE SOCIAL WORLD AND CARDIOVASCULAR
HEALTH AND DISEASE

1.   Domain Introduction   *13*
    Postscript   *16*
    John T. Cacioppo

2.   A Contemporary Perspective on Multilevel Analyses and
    Social Neuroscience   *21*
    Postscript   *39*
    Gary G. Berntson and John T. Cacioppo

3. Risk of Hypertensive Heart Disease: The Joint Influence
    of Genetic and Behavioral Factors   44
    Postscript   65
    Kathleen C. Light, Susan S. Girdler, and Alan L. Hinderliter

4. Status, Stress, and Heart Disease: A Monkey's Tale   74
    Postscript   94
    Jay R. Kaplan and Stephen B. Manuck

PART II: MIND MATTERS: AFFECTIVE
AND COGNITIVE NEUROSCIENCE

5. Domain Introduction   105
    Postscript   108
    Richard J. Davidson

6. Affective Neuroscience: A Case for Interdisciplinary Research 111
    Postscript   127
    Richard J. Davidson

7. Visual Mental Imagery: A Case Study in
    Interdisciplinary Research   135
    Postscript   154
    S. M. Kosslyn

8. Plasticity and Health: Social Influences on Gene Expression
    and Neural Development   160
    Postscript   182
    Michael J. Meaney

PART III: POSITIVE HEALTH: WHAT NOURISHES
WHO FLOURISHES?

9. Domain Introduction   193
    Postscript   196
    Carol D. Ryff

10. Thriving in the Face of Challenge: The Integrative Science
    of Human Resilience   198
    Postscript   217
    Carol D. Ryff and Burton Singer

11. Integrating Psychosocial Factors with Biology: The Role
    of Protective Factors in Trajectories of Health and Aging   228
    Postscript   246
    Teresa E. Seeman

12. Religion, Spirituality, and Health: The Duke Experience   255
     Postscript   274
     Linda K. George

     PART IV: IN SEARCH OF METHUSELAH: POPULATION
                PERSPECTIVES ON HEALTH AND LONGEVITY

13. Domain Introduction   287
     Postscript   289
     Linda Waite

14. Social Resources and Health   292
     Postscript   316
     Michael Marmot

15. A Journey through the Interdisciplinary Landscape
     of Biodemography   322
     Postscript   340
     S. Jay Olshansky and Bruce A. Carnes

     PART V: A TALE OF TWO CITIES: PREVENTION
               AND MANAGEMENT OF HIV/AIDS

16. Domain Introduction   351
     Postscript   354
     Neil Schneiderman

17. Learning to Cope with HIV/AIDS   358
     Postscript   383
     Neil Schneiderman and Michael Antoni

18. The Evolution of HIV Prevention in San Francisco:
     A Multidisciplinary Model   393
     Postscript   419
     Margaret A. Chesney and Thomas J. Coates

     Closing Commentary: Fostering Interdisciplinary Research:
     The Way Forward   429
     Patricia L. Rosenfield and Frank Kessel

     Index   465

PREFACE TO THE NEW EDITION

Interdisciplinary team science has emerged as the defining feature of the scientific endeavor in the twenty-first century. Moving beyond lip service and fashion, scholars, scientists, practitioners, and funders recognize that scientists working largely alone in their labs and within a unidisciplinary framework are no longer best equipped to address the complex problems facing global society, whether these arise from climate change, social change, or challenges to human health.

Such understanding and acceptance were not widespread when the first edition of this book was published. Now distinctly different conditions exist, shaping the work of many scientists, including those who have contributed to this collection. In the health domain, for example, interdisciplinary team research has benefited from consistent increases in funding and innovative funding mechanisms at the U.S. National Institutes for Health. And as indicated by the current strategic plan of the European Science Foundation (2005), European countries are equally committed to interdisciplinary approaches in a wide range of fields.

As co-editors of this volume we are convinced that these developments represent a significant trend rather than a fad on the scientific funding and practice horizon. Science is crossing a threshold of innovation in interdisciplinary research that should yield valuable new findings and understanding. These, in turn, bode favorably for addressing current conditions and mobilizing new approaches to prevention and for stimulating proactive approaches to emerging problems. As a central corollary, the experiences of the scientific collaborators described here and the consequential lessons learned about the process of building and sustaining interdisciplinary teams are even more salient for those eager to embark on research that brings together the health and social sciences. Indeed, these cases may be of value to researchers and practitioners in other fields seeking to draw together diverse disciplines around a common theme.

In this preface we build briefly on our original closing commentary by providing a rapid review of interdisciplinary initiatives and signaling aspects of the continuing collaborative efforts contained in the updates reported on in this new edition.[i] We end with some suggested next steps for further interdisciplinary research and related institutional innovation.

Recognition of the Value of Interdisciplinary Team Science: Complementary Initiatives

Since this volume was originally published two salient efforts in the United States have produced significant publications, one undertaken by The National Academies of Science (NAS) and the other by the National Institutes of Health (NIH).

Building on a decade of work supported by the W. M. Keck Foundation, the NAS Committee on Science, Engineering and Public Policy has been addressing ways to conduct interdisciplinary research as well as to train and educate scientists and engineers via its *Futures Initiative,* "a program designed to realize the full potential of interdisciplinary research" (Committee on Facilitating Interdisciplinary Research, 2005, p. ix). As emphasized in the Preface to *Facilitating Interdisciplinary Research,* "science and engineering research continually evolves beyond the boundaries of single disciplines and offers employment opportunities that require not only depth of knowledge but also breadth of knowledge, integration, synthesis and an array of skills. . . . Greater emphasis on interdisciplinary research and training would be consistent with those findings" (p. ix). The NAS volume is therefore an invaluable review of "the state of interdisciplinary research and education in science and engineering and recommend(s) ways to facilitate them" (p. x).

The second signal initiative was also a function of almost nearly 10 years of support, in this case from the Behavioral Research Program of the NIH/National Cancer Institute (NCI) Division of Cancer Control and Population Sciences. On October 30–31, 2006 the NCI held a watershed meeting in Bethesda, Maryland devoted to "The Science of Team Science: Assessing the Value of Transdisciplinary Research." The conference brought together a wide range of social scientists, health scientists, medical practitioners, and health research funders at NIH and elsewhere to discuss the potential and the challenges of undertaking research across disciplines.[ii]

Consistent with the case study themes and findings in this volume, many of the NCI conference participants underlined the increased interest in interdisciplinary research linking the health and social sciences, particularly around issues related to smoking, nutrition, and physical activity. They also emphasized the importance of appropriate scientific training so that team members drawn from different disciplines can collaborate around a common problem.[iii] Publication of part of the conference proceedings will undoubtedly be of value to any scientists wishing to undertake interdisciplinary research. In particular, we draw attention to Stokols, Taylor, Hall, and Moser's (2006) introduction of an ecological framework for analyzing both team building and collaborative research practice, Nash's (2006) discussion of the development of innovative training programs, and Klein's (2006) theoretical analysis.

Viewing the NAS and NIH/NCI initiatives from the perspective of this collection of case studies, it seems worth highlighting the consistency across different analyses of the factors that facilitate and constrain interdisciplinary team science. What we presented in Table 3 of our original commentary (pp. 452–458) is thus encouragingly echoed in the NAS volume and several of the NIH/NCI conference papers. We highlight particularly the continuing need to design new approaches that reduce the range of institutional barriers to interdisciplinary research in academic settings. As a corollary, there is ongoing concern about how discipline-driven promotion and tenure criteria still inhibit cross-boundary work on the part of young scientists, and about continuing challenges regarding the funding and publication of team-oriented interdisciplinary efforts. Nevertheless, the NAS report concludes that interdisciplinary research "plays an essential and growing role in permitting researchers to venture beyond the frontiers of their own disciplines and address questions of ever-increasing complexity and societal urgency" (p. xii).

Paralleling the growing United States' commitment to interdisciplinary research, in 2006 the European Science Foundation introduced a paradigm-shifting strategic plan covering the rest of this decade. (European Science Foundation, 2006) That plan identifies and endorses the import of interdisciplinary efforts across the Foundation's many committees, including the medical sciences, the social sciences and humanities, as well as the physical and life sciences. The Foundation emphasizes that "many research questions are so complex or so broad that they cannot be solved by a single brilliant researcher, a single institute, or even a single country, because of the need for critical mass of both competencies and resources. The critical mass of competences may be disciplinary in nature but the requirement for interdisciplinary modern research is increasing" (European Science Foundation, p. 19). For example, consistent with the affective and social cognitive science case studies in this volume (Chapters 2 and 6), the Foundation endorses "bringing together researchers from the molecular neurosciences, psychology, learning, logic, philosophy, computer sciences . . . creating conditions for new research in the cognitive sciences."

Foreshadowing the European emphasis, in 2005 the Academy of Finland issued a significant publication, *Promoting Interdisciplinary Research.* (Bruun, Hukkinen, Huutoniemi, and Klein, 2005). This publication details how the Academy examined new theoretical perspectives and the changing nature of scientific production in order to find ways to overcome the variety of barriers impeding interdisciplinary research. The review covers approaches for both conducting integrative research and applying the resulting findings.

In a similar spirit, when Canada reorganized its national research institutions in 2000 and the Canadian Institutes for Health Research (CIHR) was established as the primary successor to the Medical Research Council (MRC), two initiatives were given high priority—the Interdisciplinary Health Research Team (IHRT) program and the Community Alliances for Health Research (CAHR) program. Funded on the order of CAN$80 million over five years, both were seen as marking an important departure in Canada's funding of health research.[iv] The IHRT program, in particular, was designed to encourage health researchers from multiple disciplines to work together on programmatic research that formed an integrated entity, to go beyond the traditional single-researcher, single-laboratory model. A formative evaluation of the two programs,[v] identified concerns similar to those reported in both our first edition and the NAS volume, e.g., institutional barriers to conducting interdisciplinary research and implications for promotion and tenure. Nevertheless, it appears that the programs succeeded in stimulating interdisciplinary work—most of the Canadian researchers reported that they had contributed "to the design and execution of research that actively involves other disciplines over a substantial period of time at each stage of the research." The evaluation also suggests that the grants may have led to University-based changes such as the creation of new courses and the introduction of increased flexibility in existing programs.

Based on such results and other analyses, the CIHR is in the process of establishing a next-generation "Team Grant" program that folds the IHRT and CAHR programs into a single framework clearly consistent with the NIH/NCI initiative mentioned above. More broadly, the Team Grant program is an expression of a CIHR "Blueprint" which recognizes that "the complexity and scale of today's research challenges increasingly require that researchers and countries reach out beyond their own areas of expertise and that we experiment with new models to bring people and sectors together . . . [The Blueprint] commits CIHR to continue to catalyze and encourage the convergence of disciplines that underlie the most exciting and important discoveries in health research, and to resolve ever-more complex health problems."[vi]

Finally, before turning to a sampling of new findings and reflections from our case study authors, we also want to draw attention to a textbook that not only complements the kinds of initiatives mentioned above, but also will be of considerable value for student courses and for interdisciplinary team development and practice. In *Health Social Science: A Transdisciplinary and Complexity Perspective*, Higginbotham, Albrecht and Connor (2001) have drawn on their extensive work in promoting and conducting cross-disciplinary research in Asia and Pacific countries. They review in detail the conceptual basis for transdisciplinary research (with case studies on, *inter alia,* heart disease and pharmaceuticals), along with the role of research teams and the function of research in the community.

This publication is complemented by a collection of case studies edited by Higginbotham, Briceno-Leon, and Johnson (2001). *Applying Health Social Science: Best Practices in the Developing World* not only presents best research practices, but also reflectively highlights the challenges addressed by interdisciplinary teams in

African, Asian, and Latin American countries. Given that these challenges are reminiscent of many faced in North America, an initiative that brings together teams from such diverse settings to share best practices and ways of transcending obstacles in the path of innovative, interdisciplinary research would have much merit. (See our suggestions for "Next Steps" below.)

Case Study Updates

Roughly four years after the publication of our original volume, the case study groups are not only still intact but flourishing. Moreover, as Cacioppo (Chapter 1) suggests, consistent with the emerging pattern of scientific practice described above, in at least some instances these teams have become even more interdisciplinary in character. Our review of the Postscripts suggests that two primary, mutually reinforcing factors are at work in this continued pattern of productivity. In effect, because the teams are recognized as having a major impact on their substantive fields, funding and institutional support for such research have increased significantly. (See Waite, Chapter 13.)

The interaction of these central factors—substantive impact and continuous support—serves to minimize or circumvent the kinds of significant constraints on cross-boundary collaboration that emerged in our first edition (Rosenfield and Kessel, 2003, pp. 390–393; Table 19.3). Thus, unlike Sewell's (1989) cautionary tale of the 25 years of interdisciplinary social psychology, these teams have succeeded in ensuring continuity and sustainability in their collaborative research. In the following paragraphs, we briefly highlight what seem to us significant features of the updated postscript material.

New methods, techniques, and findings

Working across disciplines, many of the research teams are developing new methods for combining social and biological measures. Several of the teams are finding new ways to combine data drawn from brain imagery and genetic analyses with social and behavioral analyses; this, in turn, sometimes involves drawing on and blending both qualitative and quantitative approaches. In addition to the pioneering work of Berntson and Cacioppo, Davidson, and Ryff and Singer mentioned above, Light (Chapter 3), Manuck and Kaplan (Chapter 4), Kosslyn (Chapter 7), Meaney (Chapter 8), and Seeman (Chapter 11) are demonstrating how new techniques from basic biological sciences can be combined with behavioral science approaches to deepen understanding of gene–mind–behavior interactions. For their part, Olshansky and Carnes (Chapter 15) discuss how they have continued to sharpen methodological approaches that combine population science and biology in order to study the biodemography of aging. Similarly, Schneiderman and Antoni (Chapter 17) describe how their approach combining multiple pathways and multiple disciplines in the development of cognitive behavioral stress management (CBSM) intervention is highly effective in producing adherence to medication for HIV/AIDS and thereby reducing viral load. Indeed, in some cases behavioral interventions in the form of stress reduction may be needed in addition to adherence training

These new methods and techniques, embedded in creative conceptual frameworks, have enabled the teams to achieve a rich range of empirical advances. These advances can be seen as significant "signposts of interdisciplinary innovation." (See our original commentary, pp. 434–443 and Table 19.1.) While such advances warrant far more space than can be provided in a Preface, three examples illustrate the appreciable enlarging of the scope of scientific findings resulting from all of these integrative efforts: First, the powerful presence of neural plasticity and related understanding of how social experiential interventions can affect not only mental and physical functioning, but also genomic function (Cacioppo, Chapter 1; Davidson, Chapter 5; Meaney, Chapter 8). Second, the significance of oxytocin in a range of biobehavioral interactions involving mother–infant bonding, emotions and stress sensitivity, relationships that, in turn, have implications for understanding how loving support and close physical and emotional contact among family members can have multiple health benefits (Light et al., Chapter 3; Ryff and Singer, Chapter 10; Seeman, Chapter 11). And third, Marmot's research—which he frames in terms of the social determinants of health—suggesting that Americans are less healthy than the British, a finding that has predictably captured much media attention (Cowell, 2006; Marmot, Chapter 14, 2005).

New integrative fields

Like the vibrancy of modern molecular science that emerged in the mid-twentieth century and led to the development of interdisciplinary fields such as molecular biology and molecular genetics, many of these teams have laid the groundwork for, and are now successfully sustaining, interdisciplinary fields that intrinsically integrate the social and biological sciences. As Berntson and Cacioppo (Chapter 2) and Davidson (Chapter 6) point out, the fields of Affective and Social Neuroscience are now fully institutionalized in the academic curriculum as generative areas of interdisciplinary research. In a related vein, Berntson and Cacioppo note (Chapter 2) that a new organization, the Society of Heart Brain Medicine, serves as an institutional representation of the intricate links that have now been established—via the power of multilevel, multilayer interdisciplinary analyses—between psychological processes and physiological functions, autonomic and immune regulation, and cardiovascular health. Meaney (Chapter 8), in turn, underlines the continuing vitality of developmental psychobiology as an inherently interdisciplinary endeavor. Similarly, Ryff and Singer (Chapter 10) and Seeman (Chapter 11) describe how their teams are deepening, often in cross-collaboration, the biopsychosocial basis of the science of Positive Psychology. More generally, Cacioppo (Chapter 1) emphasizes how the new forms of neuroscience embody and express a fundamentally different metaphor for understanding the human mind.

Research networks

In the United States the work of Ryff and Singer, Seeman, and Davidson is being extended through the National Institute of Aging, the MacArthur Foundation and other networks to include a wide range of centers and partners. For example, Ryff and Singer (Chapter 10) are now working with over 40 other teams around the country and in Puerto Rico to conduct interdisciplinary work as part of their leadership of the Midlife-in-the-United States (MIDUS) network, a network of investigators representing health psychology, psychophysiology, neuroscience, sociology, epidemiology, and medicine. A member of MIDUS, Seeman (Chapter 11) has also initiated a variety of other projects with colleagues from an array of disciplines.

Three teams have become increasingly international in nature, i.e., they are now collaborating with complementary teams in many countries, in the first case on the issue of understanding how socio-economic circumstances affect the health gradient, especially as populations age, and in the second, on the prevention and melioration of the HIV/AIDS epidemic.

In his Postscript, Marmot (Chapter 14) describes not only new research findings and studies, but also an unanticipated institutional effect of his team's interdisciplinary initiatives. By becoming home to the World Health Organization's Commission on Social Determinants of Health, his Institute has become the host of a global activity. This Commission will extend the impact of Marmot and his colleagues' work by developing health policies around the world based on interdisciplinary research.

Chesney and Coates' Center for AIDS Prevention Studies (CAPS) is having comparable global impact. As Stephen Morin (the new CAPS Director) notes in their Postscript (Chapter 18), the Center is connecting new centers around the country with groups in Argentina, Brazil, China, Croatia, India, Peru, Uganda, Vietnam, and Zimbabwe. This work extends internationally the importance of integrative research in the field of HIV/AIDS with the goal of building the basis for a global response that is grounded in interdisciplinary understanding and thus likely to achieve greater impact on affected and at-risk populations and communities. And Schneiderman (Chapter 16) notes the enlarged focus of University of Miami's AIDS and TB Training and Research Program to include collaboration with colleagues in Colombia, the Dominican Republic, Guyana and Peru.

Institutional leadership, training, and curriculum development

As a consequence of the dynamic interaction of important research findings and continued outside funding, administrators on the campuses where these teams are based have continued to recognize the import of support and flexibility for interdisciplinary centers. There has thus been continued support for such centers at the University of California, San Francisco, Duke, the University of Illinois at Chicago, the University of Miami, the University of Oklahoma Health Sciences, Pittsburgh, the Wake Forest School of Medicine, and Wisconsin. Such support for the case study authors has come via encouragement of new training programs, faculty appointments, cross-department linkages, and even cross-university connections. As one example, Duke University has extended its support for George and her colleagues (Chapter 12), enabling closer ties with both the Divinity and Medical Schools, continued analysis of large data sets, and greater involvement in translational research related to both medical care and religious practices, and as both a signal and symbol of such support, the Center has become Center for the Study of Spirituality, Theology and Health.

To build the basis for the next generation of interdisciplinary scholars and researchers, many of the case study teams are engaged in active training programs. Olshansky and Carnes (Chapter 15), for example, have moved to a significant level of curriculum innovation by developing interdisciplinary programs linking demography and biology, as well as a wide range of other fields, in the emerging field of population biomedical science. More generally, in his Domain Introduction and Chapter Postscripts, Davidson (Chapters 5 and 6) points to the success of institutional investment in centers, programs and training in creating "a new generation of highly interdisciplinary, well-trained young scientists [who] for the first time in history, they possess the multidisciplinary skills to make genuine progress on important problems that eluded scientific analysis (pp. 128–129)." We can only endorse his conclusion that, with continued support for training and associated curriculum development, interdisciplinary research will flourish and make even more substantial contributions to improving human health.

Publications

In his Chapter Postscript (Chapter 6), Davidson also notes that the establishment of a new journal of *Social, Cognitive and Affective Neuroscience* has provided a new outlet for interdisciplinary teams that may have had previous difficulty publishing cross-boundary research. In a similar spirit, Light et al. (Chapter 3) underline the continued importance of publishing in clinical journals, where she and her team have had greater acceptance and therefore greater impact on clinician understanding of the complex impact of a wide range of social and biological factors on blood pressure as a precursor to cardiovascular distress. Light notes how critical it is to reach clinicians and has made significant inroads doing so. This point is reinforced by the work of Schneiderman and Antoni (Chapter 17) and CAPS (Chapter 18) in fostering understanding on the part of clinicians and policymakers of how particular interventions can bring about greater adherence to HIV-AIDS medication regimens.

Funding

Sustained institutional support is generally acknowledged as the major limiting factor affecting interdisciplinary research. Thus the most encouraging development over the past four years has been continued funding by the National

Institutes of Health for such research, notably at the intersection of the biological, behavioral, and social sciences. Seeman (Chapter 11), for example, notes how many, large NIH-funded studies have been adding biological assessments to their range of sociological and psychological protocols, thus increasing the likelihood of greater understanding of how bio–psycho–social relationships affect trajectories of health and well-being across the life course.

Equally important, as Olshansky and Carnes point out (Chapter 15), NIH's acceptance of the merit of multiple principal investigators on grant proposals and its provision of support through a variety of center, program and training initiatives has done much to insure that interdisciplinary research can thrive in the United States.[vii] As a corollary, NIH's leadership is critical in shaping changes in university promotion and tenure criteria. In particular, the National Institute of Aging has maintained its leadership commitment to innovative interdisciplinary research. Schneiderman (Chapter 16) highlights the institutional support for interdisciplinary research centers on HIV/AIDS at both the University of Miamai and University of California, San Francisco from the National Institute of Allergy and Infectious Diseases. And as exemplified by the work under the auspices of the National Cancer Institute referred to above, others are solidifying the support for such research through a variety of creative funding mechanisms.

In complementary fashion, the MacArthur Foundation has maintained a leading non-governmental role via its interdisciplinary research networks— "research institutions without walls"—on topics related primarily to human and community development. Moreover, Marmot (Chapter 14) identifies a similar growing level of funding for such initiatives in the United Kingdom. All of which suggests that a golden era of imaginative interdisciplinary research in the health and social sciences will surely be extended well into the twenty-first century.

Next Steps

The new edition of this volume further elucidates the key factors in sustaining the kind of paradigm shift that interdisciplinary research represents—talented investigators, supportive institutions, and sustained funding, along with a variety of dissemination outlets for reaching the widest range of the public, policymakers, practitioners, and patients (Rosenfield and Kessel, 2003, pp. 386–394).

Celebrating and reflecting on the breadth and depth of the increasing institutionalization of interdisciplinary research in the health and social sciences, we hope that NIH will remain in a position to encourage other foundations and government agencies to join this exhilarating intellectual endeavor (in and beyond the United States). More specifically, we suggest that a consistent, ongoing process is needed to bring research teams together across disciplines as well as geographic boundaries. As a first step, possibly within the framework of the NIH Roadmap, a gathering of generative teams supported by NIH and various foundations such as MacArthur, along with those associated with the European Science Foundation and Australian and Canadian initiatives, could lead to a consolidation and extension of such networks. That, in turn, could help build the basis for increased understanding of the importance of such research in designing and implementing health programs on the part of global policymakers. Naturally such a "gathering" and such consolidation and extension of networks would take creative advantage of current and emerging communications technology.

What might be a fruitful way to conceptualize such sustained networking across boundaries, disciplinary and otherwise? Amplifying a concluding comment in our original commentary), we have sought to extend further the ideas of Berntson and Cacioppo (Chapter 2) and Crumley (2005, 2007) by applying the notion of *heterarchy* to the study of inter- and trans-disciplinary research in the health and social sciences (Kessel and Rosenfield, 2007). The goal of that extension is to move heterarchy from analysis of complex social systems *per se* to the realm of organizational arrangements that can enhance the capacity to conduct and sustain team science around multi-level, multi-layered health issues located in dynamic social and cultural contexts. Drawing from the field of management science, where heterarchy is widely used as an analytical concept for research on corporate effectiveness (Fairtlough, 2005), and prompted by CAPS and other case studies in this volume, we have proposed some initial guidelines for the understanding and assessment of team science capacity. (For example, "Establish degrees of flexibility in ranking of leaders, disciplines and topics in the conduct, sequencing and re-sequencing of research activities.") Beyond that, as we explored recent writings on heterarchy, we discovered an extension of the idea in the field of international relations, *viz., panarchy.*[viii] Thus our final 'next step' suggestion is that panarchy, emerging as a meta-frame for networking networks, could be relevant to further development of the theory and practice of interdisciplinary team science.

Finally, we hope that the ideas and findings reported in this second edition will demonstrate how effectively and imaginatively the challenges to cross-boundary research are being overcome. That said, university and funding leaders will need to continue to heed the call to take actions that will facilitate and support new approaches to interdisciplinary research, in the health area and beyond. Allied to such imaginative actions, the second edition of this volume may help stimulate even further excitement and greater understanding of the value *and* the increasing necessity of interdisciplinary, if not transdisciplinary, research linking the health and social sciences in integrative efforts to improve human and social well-being in the twenty-first Century.[ix]

Frank Kessel and Patricia L. Rosenfield

July 2007

NOTES

i. These updates take the form of end-of-chapter "Postscripts" in which the authors offer reflections on substantive and organizational developments since the original edition.

They have also provided recent references that are cited both in the postscripts and at appropriate points in their original chapters.

ii. How to demarcate "transdisciplinary" from "interdisciplinary" (and "multidisciplinary") is obviously a significant analytic and research-praxis issue. Since that lies beyond the scope of this preface, and as a form of continuity with the first edition, we primarily speak here of "interdisciplinary research." (See Kessel and Rosenfield, 2007.)

iii. "The problematics of the problem," i.e., how researchers from different disciplinary perspectives come to agree on what constitutes "a common problem," is one of a number of issues introduced in our original commentary that we suggest warrant continuing attention.

iv. http://www.cihr-irsc.gc.ca/publications/funding/decisions/2001/jan2001_e.shtml

v. CIHR-IRSC, Interim Evaluative Study of the Interdisciplinary Health Research Team Program and the Community Alliance for Health Research Program: Extended Executive Summary, 2006. http://www.cihr-irsc.gc.ca/e/34743.html

vi. http://www.irsc.gc.ca/e/24791.html

vii. This is not to say that the issue of appropriate, and appropriately briefed, review panels for interdisciplinary proposals has been completely resolved.

viii. See Hartzog (nd), von Goldammer, Paul and Newbury(2003), and Gunderson and Holling (2002), the latter a volume produced by the "Sustainability Scale Project" of the Resilience Alliance. Only recently discovering such intellectual explorations and programmatic initiatives, we are forcefully reminded, yet again, of the inertial boundaries between different domains that could be creatively complementary. As a final example—among other writings on collaboration in the arts and humanities, John-Steiner's (2000) work could provide insights for funders, administrators and researchers seeking generative space at the intersection of the health and social sciences.

ix. We are grateful to several people at Oxford University Press for their care in sheperding this volume to completion – Nicholas Liu, Lynda Crawford, and Mary Rodriguez, and especially Catharine Carlin for her constant commitment to editorial excellence.

REFERENCES

Bruun, H., Hukkinen, J., Huutoniemi, K., and Klein, J.T. (2005). *Promoting Interdisciplinary Research: The case of the Academy of Finland.* Helsinki: Academy of Finland.

Committee on Facilitating Interdisciplinary Research, National Academy of Sciences, National Academy of Engineering, Institute of Medicine. (2005). *Facilitating Interdisciplinary Research.* Washington, D.C.: The National Academies Press.

Cowell, A. (2006). Study says older Americans less healthy than British. *The New York Times.* May 3.

Crumley, C.L. (2005). Remember how to organize: Heterarchy across disciplines. In C.S. Beekman and W. W. Baden (Eds.), *Nonlinear Models for Archeology and Anthropology: Continuing the Revolution.* Hampshire, U.K. and Burlington, VT: Ashgate.

Crumley, C.L. (2007). Historical ecology: Integrated thinking at multiple temporal and spatial scales. In A. Hornborg and C.L. Crumley (Eds.), *The World System and the Earth System: Global Socioenviromental Change and Sustainability Since the Neolithic.* Walnut Creek, CA: Left Coast Press.

European Science Foundation. (2005). Strategic Plan 2006–2010. Strasbourg, France: European Science Foundation.

Fairclough, G. (2005). *The Three Ways of Getting Things Done: Hierarchy, Heterarchy and Responsible Autonomy in Organizations.* Devon, U.K.: Triarchy Press.

Gunderson, L.H., and Holling, C.S. (Eds.). (2002). *Panarchy: Understanding Transformations in Human and Natural Systems.* Washington, D.C.: Island Press.

Hartzog, P. (nd). Panarchy: Governance in the network age. www.panarchy.com

Higginbotham, N., Albrecht, G. and Connor, L. (2001). *Health Social Science: A Transdisciplinary and Complexity Perspective.* Melbourne: Oxford University Press.

Higginbotham, N., Briceno-Leon, R., and Johnson, N. (Eds.). (2001). *Applying Health Social Science: Best Practice in the Developing World.* London: Zed Books.

John-Steiner, V. (2000). *Creative Collaboration.* New York: Oxford University Press.

Kessel, F., and Rosenfield, P.L. (2007). Toward a framework for transdisciplinary research: Challenges and opportunities. *American Journal of Preventive Medicine* (under review).

Kessel, F., Rosenfield, P.L., and Anderson, N.B. (Eds.). (2003). *Expanding the Boundaries of Health and Social Science: Case Studies of Interdisciplinary Innovation.* New York: Oxford University Press.

Klein, J. T. (2006). Evaluation of interdisciplinary and transdisciplinary research collaboration: An international review of the state of the art. Paper presented at National Cancer Institute conference on "The science of team science: Assessing the value of transdisciplinary research," October 30–31, 2006. Bethesda, Maryland.

Marmot, M. (2005). *The Status Syndrome: How Social Standing Affects Our Health and Longevity.* New York: Henry Holt & Co.

Nash, J.M. (2006). Trandisciplinary training programs: Key components and prerequisites for success. Paper presented at National Cancer Institute conference on the science of team science: Assessing the value of transdisciplinary research; October 30–31, 2006. Bethesda, Maryland.

Stokols, D., Taylor, B., Hall K., and Moser, R. (2006). The science of team science: Overview of the conference and the field. Paper presented at National Cancer Institute conference on "The science of team science: Assessing the value of transdisciplinary research," October 30–31, 2006. Bethesda, Maryland.

von Goldammer, E., Paul, J., and Newbury, J.(2003). Heterarchy-hierarchy: Two complementary categories of description. www.vordenker.de

FOREWORD

CRAIG CALHOUN and CORA MARRETT

It has long been established wisdom that a disproportionate number of major scientific discoveries and innovations involve crossing the boundaries of established disciplines. It has also probably escaped few observers that a range of new interdisciplinary fields has formed in recent decades or that the interfaces among biological, behavioral, social, and health sciences have been perhaps the most fertile ground for their development. In the early twenty-first century, medical research would simply be inconceivable within the traditional disciplinary boundaries of the early twentieth century. Yet, there has been precious little research into how interdisciplinary fields form, what makes them succeed or fail, or how they—and through them, intellectual creativity—can best be nurtured. Of course, interdisciplinarity in itself is no panacea. Many an interdisciplinary field, once somewhat institutionalized, becomes as protective of its turf and its conventional wisdom as older disciplines are. Many an interdisciplinary project has turned out to be more fashionable than fruitful. Quite simply, interdisciplinarity can be an excuse for lack of discipline. Nonetheless, it seems clear that the advancement of science in the twenty-first century depends on effective collaboration across disciplinary boundaries. This is so, first and foremost, because of the complexity of issues that must be addressed and, second, because of the degree to which the primary disciplines were forged in relation to particular historical and social contexts, intellectual problems and achievements, and available methodologies. In significant respects, then, the organization of disciplines reflects the form and level of knowledge achieved in earlier periods and not necessarily the greatest promise for understanding contemporary research issues and social problems. Conversely, the rise of interdisciplinary research reflects new questions and new technologies, as well as new intellectual orientations.

The Social Science Research Council (SSRC) is an appropriate institution to sponsor research into creative interdisciplinary work across the biological, behavioral, and social sciences. The first recorded use of the word "interdisciplinary" came in the discussions that led to SSRC's creation in 1923. Promoting effective interdisciplinary collaboration has always been central to the council's mission. In addition, the council has always included psychology among the social sciences and sought greater integration between behavioral and social sciences. So, too, the SSRC has helped to sponsor links—of which more are needed—between biomedical and social science researchers. At times, these links have served to bring together different theoretical perspectives and, at other times, have resulted in new research networks. Indeed, on the council's current agenda is an effort to explore how interdisciplinary training might help produce researchers better able to draw simultaneously and with equal sophistication on the behavioral, social, and biomedical sciences. Such training would contrast with the more frequent current practice in which specialists in distinct disciplines—such as psychology, sociology, epidemiology, and behavioral medicine—are brought together around a common topic in a somewhat ad hoc way.

Interdisciplinary research always involves a learning process, whether this is rooted in interdisciplinary graduate or postdoctoral training, in the mutual learning that marks the best collaborations, or in individual study of a new field. As the studies reported in this volume reveal, successful interdisciplinary projects depend generally on both a sense of need for some nontraditional skills or intellectual content and a willingness to learn. Successful collaboration is not simply a matter of appropriation but requires mutual transformation. This is the difference between simply transporting a technique from one field to another, or citing research across disciplinary boundaries, and actually forging integrative interdisciplinary research projects.

New, interdisciplinary fields sometimes emerge because of new phenomena that become prominent within the scientific community, as well as within the wider public. Research into HIV/AIDS is a clear example. The development and spread of AIDS challenges disciplines as far flung as immunology and anthropology; and the public health crisis that results from this spread provides an imperative for the crossing of disciplinary boundaries. The rise of new collaborations can also reflect the growing importance of a problem that has eluded solution—as in the case of cardiovascular disease. In other cases, an analytic approach or method opens up new lines of research—as in the way population thinking reshaped studies of health generally and of aging in particular. In still other cases, changes in intellectual perspective prompt different research needs. Thus research on positive health has turned attention to health as more than simply the absence of disease, resulting in a reframing of questions previously shaped by a discourse of disease or of their decline and their absence.

CONTRIBUTORS

NORMAN B. ANDERSON
Chief Executive Officer
American Psychological Association
750 First Street NE
Washington, DC 20002
nanderson@apa.org

MICHAEL ANTONI
Professor
Department of Psychology and Behavioral Medicine Research Center
University of Miami
P.O. Box 248185
Coral Gables, Florida 33124-2070
mantoni@miami.edu

GARY G. BERNTSON
Professor
Department of Psychology, Psychiatry, and Pediatrics
Ohio State University
1835 Neil Avenue
Columbus, OH 43210
Berntson.2@osu.edu

JOHN T. CACIOPPO
Tiffany and Margaret Blake Distinguished Service Professor and Director
Center for Cognitive and Social Neuroscience
The University of Chicago
5848 S. University Avenue
Chicago, IL 60637
Cacioppo@uchicago.edu

CRAIG CALHOUN
President
Social Science Research Council
810 Seventh Avenue
New York, NY 10019
calhoun@ssrc.org

BRUCE A. CARNES
Reynolds Department of Geriatric Medicine
University of Oklahoma Health Sciences Center
921 13th Street N.E. (11G)
Oklahoma City, OK 73104
Bruce-Carnes@ouhsc.edu

MARGARET A. CHESNEY
Professor in Residence
Center for AIDS Prevention Studies
University of California, San Francisco
50 Beale Street, Suite 1300
San Francisco, CA 94105
ChesneyM@mail.nih.gov

THOMAS J. COATES
Michael and Sue Steinberg Professor of Global AIDS Research
Director
UCLA Program in Global Health
David Geffen School of Medicine
University of California, Los Angeles
37-121 CHS, MC-168817
Los Angeles, CA 90095
tcoates@mednet.ucla.edu

RICHARD J. DAVIDSON
William James and Vilas Research Professor of Psychology and Psychiatry
Director
W.M. Keck Laboratory for Functional Brain Imaging and Behavior, Laboratory for Affective
    Neuroscience, Wisconsin Center for Affective Science
University of Wisconsin-Madison
1202 West Johnson Street
Madison, WI 53706
rjdavids@wisc.edu

Finally, as we noted, new technologies can also be important catalysts for work across disciplinary lines. As a noteworthy example, the rise of modern cognitive and affective neuroscience would be inconceivable without computer technology, which has changed research within specific disciplines as it has also called forth new interdisciplinary collaborations. In no case, however, did interdisciplinary collaboration simply happen. Intellectual breakthroughs were encouraged by institutional support; field development depended on funding.

This carries a lesson for the future: It is not enough simply to call for scientists to overcome their tendencies to work too narrowly within their disciplines. It is not enough simply to declare the virtues of consilience or to propound integrative theories. Rather, it is crucial to create institutional contexts and funding mechanisms that will foster interdisciplinary work. Doing this is a special challenge because it obliges administrators, funders, and project reviewers to judge research at the boundaries of intellectual fields—research that precisely breaks with established ways of doing things and is not owned by any one discipline.

The case studies in this book provide a basis for better understanding the conditions and interventions that promote successful interdisciplinary collaboration. Accordingly, they should be of value not only to scientists but also to decision makers in universities, institutes, and funding agencies. Offering prominent researchers' actual experiences, they are contributions to the history of science with a possible practical bearing on its continuing advancement. In an important sense, they are also exemplars. Every study in this book has been improved by interdisciplinary discussion among the group of researchers who joined in the intellectual project that produced it. Over a period of several years they examined and compared the trajectories and internal logics of different fields.

Not only is this book itself a result of interdisciplinary collaboration, but also it is a product of effective intervention and a conducive institutional context. It was conceived from the beginning as a partnership between the Social Science Research Council and the National Institutes of Health (NIH), with the NIH Office of Behavioral and Social Science Research (OBSSR) playing the leading role. The organizations deserve recognition for creating a setting in which ideas about interdisciplinary collaboration could be developed and examined. Similarly, the contributors to the volume warrant acknowledgment for generating the ideas and bringing the project to fruition. Norman Anderson, then the director of OBSSR, played an important role in initiating the project and also became a significant intellectual contributor to it. Anderson approached Kenneth Prewitt, then president of the SSRC, who brought Frank Kessel into the design of the project; Kessel continued as program director. Patricia Rosenfield of the Carnegie Corporation of New York served superbly as chair. It is thus appropriate that the three partners who shaped this project throughout have joined in editing this important book. As is often the case in successful interdisciplinary projects, though, there is also a hidden collaborator and stimulator. Richard Suzman of the National Institute of Aging gave this project crucial support. We are grateful to all of the institutions and individuals involved, as, we think, all who value creative science should be.

Linda K. George
Professor
Center for the Study of Aging and Human Development
Duke University Medical Center
Box 3003
Durham, NC 27710
lkg@geri.duke.edu

Susan S. Girdler
Stress and Health Research Program
Department of Psychiatry
School of Medicine
University of North Carolina
CB 7175, Medical Building A
University of North Carolina
Chapel Hill, NC 27599-7175
Susan_Girdler@med.unc.edu

Alan L. Hinderliter
Professor
Department of Medicine
School of Medicine
University of North Carolina
CB 7075, Burnett Womack Bldg
University of North Carolina
Chapel Hill, NC 27599-7075
hinderli@med.unc.edu

Jay R. Kaplan
Professor and Head of Comparative Medicine and Professor of Anthropology
Director
Comparative Medicine Clinical Research Center
Wake Forest University School of Medicine
Medical Center Boulevard
Winston-Salem, NC 27157-1040
jkaplan@wfubmc.edu

Frank Kessel
Professor
Early Childhood Multicultural Education
Department of Individual, Family and Community Education
College of Education
MSC05 3040
1 University of New Mexico
Albuquerque, NM 87131-0001
fkessel@unm.edu
kesfam@pdq.net

STEPHEN M. KOSSLYN
John Lindsley Professor of Psychology
Harvard University
Department of Psychology
33 Kirkland Street
Cambridge, MA 02138
smkosslyn@wjh.harvard.edu

KATHLEEN C. LIGHT
Stress and Health Research Program
Department of Psychiatry
School of Medicine
University of North Carolina
CB 7175, Medical Building A
University of North Carolina
Chapel Hill, NC 27599-7175
Kathy_Light@med.unc.edu

STEPHEN B. MANUCK
Director
Behavioral Physiology Laboratory
Department of Psychology
University of Pittsburgh
506 EH
4015 O'Hara Street
Pittsburgh, PA 15260
manuck+@pitt.edu

CORA MARRETT
Assistant Director
Directorate for Education and Human Resources
National Science Foundation
4201 Wilson Boulevard
Arlington, VA 22230
cmarrett@nsf.gov

MICHAEL MARMOT
Director
International Institute for Society and Health
Department of Epidemiology and Public Health
University College London
1-19 Torrington Place
London WC1E 6BT
UNITED KINGDOM
michael@public-health.ucl.ac.uk

Michael J. Meaney
Professor
McGill Program for the Study of Behavior, Genes and Environment
Douglas Hospital Research Centre
McGill University
Montreal
CANADA H4H 1R3
michael.meaney@mcgill.ca

Stephen F. Morin
Director
Center for AIDS Prevention Studies and
AIDS Policy Research Center
University of California, San Francisco
50 Beale Street, Suite 1300
San Francisco, CA 94105
Steve.Morin@ucsf.edu

S. Jay Olshansky
Professor
School of Public Health
University of Illinois at Chicago
1603 West Taylor Street, Room 885
Chicago, IL 60612
sjayo@uic.edu

Patricia L. Rosenfield
Program Director
Carnegie Scholars
Carnegie Corporation of New York
437 Madison Avenue
New York, NY 10022
plr@carnegie.org

John W. Rowe
Professor of Health Policy and Management
Department of Health Policy and Management
Columbia University Mailman School of Public Health
600 West 168th Street
Room 614
New York, NY 10032
jwr2108@columbia.edu

Carol D. Ryff
Director
Institute on Aging
University of Wisconsin
2245 Medical Science Center
Madison, WI 53706
cryff@facstaff.wisc.edu

Neil Schneiderman
Professor
Department of Psychology and Behavioral Medicine Research Center
University of Miami
P.O. Box 248185
Coral Gables, FL 33124-2070
nschneid@miami.edu

Teresa E. Seeman
Professor
Divisons of Geriatrics and Epidemiology
UCLA Schools of Medicine & Public Health
10945 Le Conte Avenue, Suite 2339
Los Angeles, CA 90095-1687
TSeeman@mednet.ucla.edu

Burton Singer
Professor
Office of Population Research
Princeton University
245 Wallace Hall
Princeton, NJ 08544, and
Institute on Aging
University of Wisconsin
1300 University Avenue, Rm. 2245 MSC
Madison, WI 53706
singer@princeton.edu

Linda Waite
Lucy Flower Professor of Sociology
Department of Sociology
University of Chicago
Chicago, IL 60637
L-Waite@uchicago.edu

Interdisciplinary Research

Introduction

Approaching Interdisciplinary Research

JOHN W. ROWE

At first glance, this volume may appear to be an eclectic mix of essays on issues that vary from affective and cognitive neuroscience, cardiovascular disease, and population perspectives on health and longevity to HIV/AIDS and the psychobiology of wellness. But, as the domain introductions and the closing commentary indicate, the reports in this volume all have one critical thing in common: they report the life histories and results of the best kind of interdisciplinary research on health.

Why do we care so much about interdisciplinary research? Because it represents a critical natural step in the evolution of research on complex issues related to human biology and health. The absurdity of trying to solve problems with inadequate tools is increasingly driving science, and scientists, to engage in integrated efforts. The tools of individual disciplines, whether they be biologic, physiologic, psychologic. or sociologic, are no longer adequate by themselves to fully address the complex problems that we are facing. As Kahn and Prager (1994) observed, "The myth of the solitary scientist in search of truth is a romantic notion whose continued existence serves as the major barrier to progress in bringing the collective weight of the sciences to bear on the problems of human kind. And the idea that all scientific progress takes place within the boundaries of current disciplines is historically invalid and currently counter-productive" (p. 12).

Our thesis is that the pressing problems in human biology and health *require* the intrinsic power of an interdisciplinary approach. While interdisciplinary work is hardly a new idea, our increasing reliance on it urges a detailed analysis of how it is most effectively organized, along with a detailed consideration of the factors that facilitate and impede it.

In considering how to advance interdisciplinary research beyond its current prolonged developmental period, we thought it would be valuable to have scholars involved in successful interdisciplinary efforts describe the impediments and facilitating factors they encountered in their work. This strategy has some limitations. Our selection of projects and scholars was not random; we intentionally selected largely successful cases of interdisciplinary collaboration, rather than failures, to illustrate best practices across a range of health domains (some well established, others emerging). While this selection provides a partial picture, we believe the collective experience reflected in these case studies will be informative for investigators, academic administrators, and funders of research who wish to enter this important and neglected arena.

First, a definition: By "interdisciplinary research," we refer to a true collaboration—a melding of disciplines—not just the addition of techniques and technology from one field to research in another. In addition, we generally refer to collaborations *across* major disciplinary boundaries (such as combinations of physiology and social sciences) as opposed to the more common, and also powerful, combinations within broad disciplinary boundaries (such as addition of anatomical studies—i.e., electron microscopy—to efforts in basic cellular biology).

Interdisciplinary work implies that the various approaches are generally applied simultaneously over a substantial period of time rather than sequentially, which is more commonly termed *multidisciplinary*. I will draw on my clinical background for an example that distinguishes these two common and important forms of collaboration. In the management of a hospitalized patient, a multidisciplinary approach entails separate encounters of the patient with his or her primary physician, one or more specialists, a social worker, several nurses, and perhaps a physical therapist—each writing a separate note in the patient's record, adding their findings to the growing body of information and opinion regarding the patient's condition. In a truly interdisciplinary approach, the various clinicians would meet together as a team to examine and interview the patient, review test results, share opinions and perspectives, and develop a unified plan that might be reflected in a single note in the patient's record. Neither approach is intrinsically superior to the other, nor is either superior to a standard unidisciplinary approach. It all depends on the question being asked and the problem being solved (see Chapter 7, by Kosslyn).

Interdisciplinary research collaborations take many forms. They often involve a pair of investigators—one from the cognitive, social, or behavioral sciences and another from the biological or physiological side—joined in an effort to identify the biological correlates or mechanisms through which contextual factors influence the underlying biological substrate. Obvious examples ripe for such collaboration and discussed in this volume include the psychosocial predictors of successful aging (Chapter 10, by Ryff and Singer), the relationship between professional status and health, particularly as elucidated in the Whitehall Studies (Chapter 14, by Marmot), the effect of psychosocial stress on development of cardiovascular disease (Chapter 2, by Berntson and Cacioppo, and other chapters in Part II, and the entire arena of mind-body interactions (Chapter 6, by Davidson; Chapter 11, by Seeman, and Chapter 12, by George). The most common biological measures employed in such collaborations include measures of the autonomic nervous system, immune system, and endocrine function; measures of inflammation; genetic measures; and functional imaging of the central nervous system, such as PET scanning. The nonbiological measures vary widely across social, behavioral, and cognitive levels and often include epidemiological studies, as well as detailed measures in individual study participants.

Increasingly over the past decades, interdisciplinary research has been reflected in dyads research, as well as in a broader model in which a large team of investigators are brought around a central set of questions, study population, or database. Prominent examples include the mental health and human development networks of the MacArthur Foundation and the interdisciplinary research teams that have conducted a number of significant longitudinal studies, such as the Framingham Study and the Baltimore Longitudinal Study of Aging, an intramural effort of the National Institute of Aging (Shock et al., 1984). HIV/AIDS is another domain in which large multidisciplinary teams of investigators have produced new knowledge with broad implications (see Chapter 17, by Schneiderman and Antoni, and Chapter 18, by Chesney and Coates). Disciplines often represented in these large teams include epidemiology, psychology, sociology, anthropology, cell biology, immunology, endocrinology, and clinical specialties including cardiovascular medicine, neurology, and psychiatry. In addition, interdisciplinary groups of scientists working at the human level often find it advantageous to partner with colleagues who work on animal models, as hypotheses generated at the epidemiological or clinical research level can often be pursued in greater detail at the animal level (see Chapter 4, by Kaplan and Manuck, and Chapter 8 by Meaney).

Some research efforts undergo a gradual transition from being unidisciplinary or multidisciplinary to becoming truly interdisciplinary. While most efforts are interdisciplinary by design from the outset (such as the MacArthur Networks), others—such as the Whitehall Studies, as related in Chapter 14, by Marmot, or the Wisconsin Longitudinal Study, as described in Chapter 10, by Ryff and Singer, become interdisciplinary over time, not necessarily by intention, but through the development of an interdisciplinary audience and the emergence of questions in an ongoing research project that require additional disciplines, concepts, and methods. This pathway, which might be termed "interdisciplinary by secondary intention," is inherently slower but just as rewarding and productive as research projects that are interdisciplinary by primary intention.

Determinants of the Success of Interdisciplinary Research

Factors that determine the success of interdisciplinary research can be divided into three groups: investigator-specific, project-specific, and external factors.

The first group of *investigator-specific factors* includes:

1. Passion for the work, including a true openness to the approach, perspectives, and attitudes of scientists from other disciplines
2. Mutual respect of scientists in the team
3. Complementary skills and knowledge
4. Ability of scientists to develop a common language
5. Ability of scientists to meet together on a regular basis (Geographic dispersion of members of an interdisciplinary team is often a major inhibiting factor.)

A second group of factors, relating to the *communal research project,* include:

1. *Data sources.* Data sources such as longitudinal samples and established research populations, such as twin registries, are especially valuable to interdisciplinary inquiry and analysis. Many such sources have biological specimens, as well as longitudinal data and ongoing access to the study population.

2. *New integrative concepts.* Many large interdisciplinary research efforts are organized around an overriding concept (e.g., successful aging) or problem domain (e.g., HIV/AIDS) that are specific enough to permit approaches by different investigators, yet general enough to provide a meaningful focus for the group. Lack of such an integrative concept or organizing problem is often a limiting factor in the development of effective interdisciplinary team research.

3. *Emergence of new technologies.* Methods of analysis and research tools that represent a synthesis of inputs from different disciplines are often effective cohesive elements in interdisciplinary research team. For instance, the MacArthur Foundation Research Network on Successful Aging developed an interdisciplinary research tool known as the MacArthur Battery (i.e., MacBat) that was applied in its work. Use of this tool was very effective in bringing about enhanced cohesion of the research group (Berkman et al., 1993).

The third group of factors, relating to *external issues,* includes:

1. *Funding.* Funding is of major significance and often is the limiting factor in the development of successful interdisciplinary research. Traditional research funding, especially from NIH, focuses on investigator-initiated awards, which generally reward relatively narrow projects to be conducted over a short period of time. Interdisciplinary research has none of these characteristics and is thus at a major disadvantage for this form of external funding. Nevertheless, certain NIH funding mechanisms—including program projects, centers, and special emphasis research career awards—have been especially effective in fostering interdisciplinary research. In addition, enlightened academic administrators are increasingly providing support from institutional funding for this work. And a number of foundations have been very important supporters of the development of integrated interdisciplinary research efforts in both the United States and its collaborators in developed and developing countries. These have included the MacArthur Foundation's mental health and human development networks, the Rockefeller Foundation's health sciences program, the Ford Foundation's international forum for

social sciences and health, and the McDonnell Foundation's support of the development of cognitive neuroscience.

2. *Institutional flexibility and freedom.* The general organization of academic institutions into discipline-specific departments inhibits the natural development of interdisciplinary research. A number of universities have developed interdisciplinary research centers and institutes in an attempt to foster interdisciplinary research, but in many cases, the funding of these has been less secure than that of traditional individual departments.

3. *Career advancement issues.* Promotion and attainment of tenure is generally related to research productivity, as measured by number of research publications, especially those with a single author. By their very nature, interdisciplinary publications, have multiple authors, often take longer to develop, and are less likely to lead to promotion. In addition, it is often more difficult to publish truly interdisciplinary research in the finest journals since most journals are discipline-specific. To mitigate this effect, traditional academic views must change, and interdisciplinary research must develop a truly interdisciplinary audience.

4. *Attitudes toward interdisciplinary research.* Unfortunately, interdisciplinary research is often viewed as not including elements that are at the cutting edge of any individual discipline. The prevalent emphasis on "methodological purity" in research may represent a subtle bias against development of interdisciplinary research, since many individuals feel that, by definition, it is methodologically impure. We, of course, hold the opposite view that interdisciplinary research represents a methodological advancement in many cases over research that focuses solely on one discipline.

The Importance of Time

Time is an additional factor critical in productive interdisciplinary research. It is often the case that things must go slowly. Development of a true interdisciplinary collaboration requires continuous involvement of at least two and often many more investigators over a substantial period of time. Time is needed for individuals to listen to each other and to learn to work together with the goal of developing a common language and a common, or at least correlated, approach to individual questions. In analyzing the experience of the MacArthur Mental Health and Human Development Networks, Prager and Kahn (1994) identified these four phases in the development of interdisciplinary group research:

1. Listening across the interdisciplinary gulf
2. Conceptual translation
3. Onset of collaboration
4. Development of joint projects

Each of the case studies in this volume can be viewed through the lens of such stages.

In a large-scale interdisciplinary research project, scientists from one discipline are made aware of research findings at another level of organization, such as epidemiological data, and are able to apply these findings to their own research much more quickly than if they had relied on the usual communication mechanisms of requiring publication in journals. Having the investigators in different disciplines meet frequently enhances communication and facilitates and quickens the pace of discovery.

Approaches to Interdisciplinary Training

A closing comment about forms of interdisciplinary training: to date, the effectiveness of interdisciplinary research programs has generally been characterized by a collaboration of individuals who are already based in different disciplines. Such effectiveness might be enhanced by the development of a cadre of more genuinely interdisciplinary scientists, each of whom possesses a knowledge base and skills from more than one discipline. The traditional approach to developing this enhanced expertise has been for individuals who are fully trained in one specialty to then train in an additional area, either immediately after their initial doctoral work or at some later point in their career. Mindful of the value of such crossover training, the National Institutes of Health has established a special program, the Special Emphasis Research Career Award (SERCA). This approach has been exceptionally helpful in many instances and is specifically cited by both Olshansky and Carnes (Chapter 15) and Seeman (Chapter 11) in this volume as being instrumental in their development of interdisciplinary perspectives.

However, a second approach to interdisciplinary training also deserves consideration: an individual's doctoral training may be inherently interdisciplinary. Such training would include substantial simultaneous exposure from the outset to more than one discipline. Such programs might be somewhat longer in duration and best located in a trans-university interdisciplinary research institute or program. When exactly should this occur? While one might think such a trainee might be properly based in a large multi-investigative institutional program, my experience suggests that individuals who have not yet completed their doctoral degree cannot actively participate in these programs. I suggest, therefore, that it would be more appropriate to limit such experience to immediate postdoctoral efforts. That said, as interdisciplinary research on health grows and more universities develop programs in this area, a range of additional interdisciplinary training models will no doubt emerge.

Researchers engaging questions requiring an interdisciplinary approach are certain to face significant obstacles. While this introduction provides a general context, clues to effective strategies for dealing with specific problems will be found in the following chapters. These analyses of successful interdisciplinary initiatives are replete with valuable lessons, and the broad variety of studies presented increases the likelihood that individual investigators will find useful insights relevant to their work. That is our goal.

REFERENCES

Berkman, L. F., Seeman, T. E., Albert, M., Blazer, D., Kahn, R., Mohs, R., Finch, C., Schneider, E., Cotman, C., McClearn, G., Nesselroade, J., Featherman, D., Garmezy, N., McKhann, G., Brim, G., Prager, D., and Rowe, J. W. (1993). High, usual and impaired functioning in community-dwelling older men and women: Findings from the Mac-Arthur Foundation Research Network on Successful Aging. *Journal of Clinical Epidemiology, 46*(10), 1129–1140.

Kahn, R. L., and Prager, D. L. (1994). Interdisciplinary collaborations are a scientific and social imperative. *Scientist,* July 11, p. 12.

Shock, N. W., Greulich, R. C., Andres, R., Arenberg, D., Costa, P. T., Lakatta, E. G., and Tobin, J. D. (1984). *Normal Human Aging: The Baltimore Longitudinal Study of Aging.* NIH Publication No. 84–2450. Washington, DC: U.S. Department of Health and Human Services.

HOME IS WHERE THE HEART IS

The Social World and Cardiovascular Health and Disease

Domain Introduction

JOHN T. CACIOPPO

Imagine that a killer is loose and that not only is it the number one cause of death in the United States but also that it has been the number one killer every year since 1900, except one. Imagine that this killer stalks Americans over the course of many years, striking on average every 33 seconds and accounting for more deaths than the next seven leading causes of death combined! And imagine that social and behavioral factors are the major determinants of where this voracious killer strikes. It's not imaginary; it's true. The identity of this killer is cardiovascular disease (Wright, 1997).

Dealing with this killer is also financially ruinous. At the twilight of the twentieth century, there were approximately 60.2 million physician office visits and 4.5 million hospital emergency room visits with a principal diagnosis of cardiovascular disease (Slusarcick and McCaig, 2000). During approximately the same period, hospital expenses for cardiovascular problems totaled $26.1 billion—or 33.3% of all hospitalization expenditures (Frankenfield, Marciniak, Drass, and Jencks, 1997). Persons with cardiovascular disease rank first among all disease categories in numbers of hospital discharges.

The National Heart, Lung, and Blood Institute was one of the first at the National Institutes of Health (NIH) to complement biological levels of analysis with social, psychological, and behavioral levels because the evidence for their contributions to the development and course of cardiovascular disease was undeniable. For instance, about one in five deaths from cardiovascular diseases is attributable to smoking. The risk of myocardial infarction is highest at lower levels of high-density lipoprotein (HDL) cholesterol levels and higher total cholesterol levels, both of which are affected by diet and exercise (e.g., Day, 2001; Keil, 2000). Individuals who do not feel socially connected show larger age-related increases in blood pressure and are less likely to survive cardiovascular disease than are individuals who do feel socially connected (House, Landis, and Umberson, 1988; Seeman, 2000; Uchino, Cacioppo, and Kiecolt-Glaser, 1996). A sedentary lifestyle and emotional reactivity (e.g., hostility) have also been identified as major predictors of cardiovascular disease and death (e.g., Gump, Matthews, and Raikkonen, 1999). Overweight (body mass index of 25–30) and obese (body mass index over 30) individuals also are at greater risk for cardiovascular disease (Melanson, McInis, Rippe, Blackburn, and Wilson, 2000). Overall, the relative risk of coronary heart disease associated with a sedentary lifestyle ranges from 1.5 to 2.4, an increase that is comparable to smoking, high blood pressure, or high blood cholesterol (e.g., Beilin, 1999).

Although social, psychological, and behavioral factors have been linked to cardiovascular disease, the mechanisms underlying these associations have received less attention. The chapters in Part I illustrate the important contributions of multilevel integrative analyses to the understanding of these basic mechanisms and to the delineation of the etiology of cardiovascular disease (Cacioppo, Berntson, Sheridan, and McClintock, 2000). Although the specific subject populations, methods, focus, and cardiovascular endpoint differ across these chapters, they share several features. First, each chapter represents a program of research that exemplifies scientific synergism, extending beyond the technical or scientific capacity of a single investigator. Each considers not only predisease pathways within the brain, genetic heritage, or cardiovascular system but also contextual (e.g., social, cognitive, behavioral) factors. Each also uses new and emerging methods and technologies that require multidisciplinary collaborations (e.g., biomedical engineers, cardiologists, biopsychologists, health psychologists). And each, in quite different ways, illustrates that cardiovascular regulation and dysregulation and, ultimately, the development and effective treatment of cardiovascular disease demands a consideration of social and behavioral, as well as physiological and genetic, levels of representation—levels that deal, for example, with individual differences, stress appraisal and reactivity, and social context.

Gary Berntson and John Cacioppo (Chapter 1) review work on the heterarchical organization of the nervous system, with multiple but interactive levels of processing that may manifest differently as one moves from rostral (higher) to caudal (lower) levels of the central nervous system. For example, Berntson and colleagues used pharmacological manipulations in humans to map the range and topography of the neural control of the heart in response to both nonpsychological stressors (orthostasis) such as postural variation and psychosocial stressors such as active coping (e.g., mental arithmetic). The neural control of the heart's response to orthostasis is regulated primarily by mechanisms in the brain stem, whereas the neural control of the heart's response to active coping tasks involves more rostral (e.g., cortical) mechanisms. The neural control of the heart is communicated generally through the sympathetic (excitatory) and parasympathetic (inhibitory) branches of the autonomic nervous system. Berntson and colleagues measured the sympathetic and parasympathetic contributions to cardiac responses based on autonomic blockade studies.

The traditional dogma is that sympathetic and parasympathetic innervations of the heart are reciprocally activated. This principle was evident in nomethetic (group) analyses for both the orthostatic and the active coping tasks. At the group level, both the orthostatic stressor and the psychosocial stressors yielded an essentially equivalent pattern of heart rate increase, with the underlying mechanism appearing to be sympathetic activation and parasympathetic withdrawal. Idiographic (individual difference) analyses revealed a different pattern, however. For the orthostatic (nonpsychological) stressor, the cardiac response reflected a relatively tight reciprocal central control of the autonomic branches, as suggested by the nomethetic analyses. But the cardiac response to psychosocial stressors showed considerable individual differences in the pattern of autonomic response and virtually no correlation between responses of the two branches of the autonomic nervous system. Furthermore, the idiosyncratic patterns of neural control were highly reliable across different psychological stressors, with some individuals showing primarily sympathetic activation, some showing reciprocal sympathetic activation and parasympathetic withdrawal, and others primarily parasympathetic withdrawal. These results suggest that cardiovascular regulation (and dysregulation) is more flexible and idiosyncratic as more central neurobehavioral mechanisms become involved. These studies also point to the need for more sophisticated conceptualizations of stress and cardiovascular disease, with a special emphasis on social and psychological characteristics that lead to risky patterns of sympathetic activation due to natural life demands.

Kathy Light, Susan Girdler, and Alan Hinderliter (Chapter 3) have similarly focused on cardiovascular reactivity, but they have examined its relationship to hypertension and predisease indicators of hypertension (such as left ventricular mass). They report, for instance, that the magnitude of blood pressure responses during laboratory stressors and natural life demands were stronger predictors of left ventricular mass index and relative vascular wall thickness than was either clinical blood pressure or baseline blood pressure. These and related studies by Light and colleagues indicated that cardiovascular responses to the demands of everyday life add prognostic information to that obtained from clinical blood pressure levels. Consistent with the work of Berntson and his colleagues, such identification of the social and psychological processes responsible for high reactivity (e.g., cognitive appraisal processes) will further advance our understanding of the etiology and prevention of cardiovascular disease.

As a significant example of such studies, Light and colleagues have shown that the risk of hypertension varies with family history, but family history per se does not doom one to life with hypertension. To test whether stress reactivity to the demands of everyday life would increase the risk of later blood pressure elevation in those individuals with a genetic susceptibility to develop hypertension, Light et al. conducted a 10-year follow-up study of young men. The results revealed that men with a positive family history of hypertension had a twofold increase in risk of elevated blood pressure over 10 years than had men with a negative family history. However, men with a positive family history who also were in the top quartile in cardiovascular reactivity (as measured 10 years earlier) had a sevenfold increase in risk. In addition, in the high reactors, high exposure to stress fostered increases in blood pressure at the follow-up visit. This research not only suggests substantial plasticity in the relationship between genetic factors and the development of cardiovascular disease but also attributes a major role to social and psychological influences on cardiovascular function.

In a series of studies in cynomolgus monkeys, Jay Kaplan and Stephen Manuck (Chapter 4) demonstrate that social disruptions and instability promote coronary atherogenesis, a form of cardiovascular disease. Animals that exhibited a heightened cardiac reactivity to stress were found to develop the most extensive coronary lesions. But β-adrenergic blockade, which eliminates the effects of sympathetic activation, diminished the behavioral exacerbation of atherosclerosis. This result points to sympathetic activation as a major contributor to coronary atherogenesis.

To study the effects of a stressful social environment, social groups were repeatedly reorganized in the Kaplan and Manuck studies. Macaque males responded antagonistically to the presence of strangers and reasserted their hierarchic relationships. Even in the absence of an atherosclerosis-inducing diet, disruptions of social connections increased the formation of coronary disease (in the form of endothelial lesions). This result was eliminated by β-adrenergic blockade, again implicating sympathetic activation as a major contributor to coronary disease, at least in males. The story for Macaque females is somewhat different but helps explain the differential susceptibility of males and females to atherosclerosis before menopause and then the similarities after menopause.

Given that all of these pioneering programs of research have had to overcome funding issues that typically hinder interdisciplinary research, the authors address both the obstacles to such research they encountered and the means by which they overcame them. We hope that their stories—the trials and tribulations, as well as successes—will offer some guidance and encouragement to others who are contemplating multilevel integrative research so that we might better understand, prevent, and ameliorate the effects of what has been the leading killer in the United States for more than a century.

Postscript

The dominant metaphor for the scientific study of the human mind during the latter half of the twentieth century has been the computer — a solitary device with massive information processing capacities. So powerful was the grip of this metaphor on the field that the first published reference to the term "social neuroscience" in 1992 required an accompanying explanation of why the term was not an oxymoron (Cacioppo and Berntson, 1992). Computers today are massively interconnected devices with capacities that extend far beyond the resident hardware and software of a solitary computer. It has become apparent that the tele-receptors (e.g., eyes, ears) of the human brain have provided wireless broadband interconnectivity to humans for millennia. Just as computers today have capacities and processes that are transduced through but extend far beyond the hardware of a single computer, the human brain has evolved to promote social and cultural capacities and processes that are transduced through but that extend far beyond a solitary brain. To understand the full capacity of humans—and the full range of pathogenic stimuli contributing to human disease—one needs to appreciate not only the memory and computational power of the brain but also its capacity and predilection for representing, understanding, and connecting with other individuals.

Indeed, humans are irrepressibly social, and their connections with one another extend beyond time and space. These effects are evident in the updates by Light, Girdler, and Hinderliter (Chapter 3), who have built on their earlier collaboration to investigate the salubrious effects of social contacts that extend beyond the presence of significant others. In studies of loving spouses and loving mothers and infants, Light and colleagues have found that meaningful social connections buffer the effects of stress even when the other is absent, that these effects are not only palpable but are large and replicable, and that specific, neurohormonal mechanisms are responsible for these effects. Rigorous scientific advances have come forth so quickly, it seems inconceivable that fewer than 20 years ago one had to justify the scientific validity of social neuroscience.

Berntson and Cacioppo (Chapter 2) have extended their studies of the effects of social isolation on mind, brain, neuroendocrine activity, genetics, and health in a population-based longitudinal study of middle-aged and older adults from the Chicago metropolitan area. The size and interdisciplinary breadth of their collaboration have increased as the nature and complexity of the questions that were asked and the methods that were incorporated stretched their collective expertise. Where measures of the internal workings of the brain and body in the recent past required invasive procedures, often limited a short time ago to patient and animal studies, imaging procedures are now safe and available to study predisease processes in normal, waking individuals. Where a decade ago, single gene transcripts were assayed with difficulty, assays for tens of thousands of gene transcripts are now readily available. Using functional magnetic resonance imaging, Berntson, Cacioppo, and colleagues recently found that the ventral striatum, an area associated with reward, is down-regulated in people lacking meaningful social connections when viewing pleasant pictures involving people. This finding provides a mechanistic explanation for the stress buffering effects enjoyed by individuals who have satisfying social connections but not by individuals who feel socially isolated. In the early 1990s, Williams, Kaplan, Manuck and colleagues found that disrupted social environments were associated with endothelial dysfunction in cynomolgus monkeys (Williams, Kaplan, and Manuck, 1993). Thirty-six monkeys were given an atherogenic diet for 36 months in one of three experimental conditions: *(1)* "stable" social environment group, *(2)* "early stress" group characterized by unstable social environment in the first half of the study followed by stable social environment in the second half, and *(3)* "late stress" group characterized by stable social environment in the first half of the study followed by unstable social environment in the second half. Among monkeys in the "late stress" group, vasodilation to acetylcholine was decreased compared to the stable group, indicating a decrease in endothelial function. In recent work, Kaplan and Manuck (Chapter 4) have found greater endothelial dysfunction in subordinate than dominant female animals, and this effect did not depend on diet. Their results indicate that social stressors may have a greater effect on endothelial function in female animals. rather than on changes in plasma lipid profiles, The association between mental stress and endothelial function has also been observed in humans, and underscores the importance of the social environment as a pathogenic agent.

Finally, biological systems are particularly prone to variation, and to bridge the gap between psychological phenomena and their underlying biological substrata such variation can be regarded as important data in its own right (Kosslyn et al., 2002). All three collaborative teams featured here combine nomethetic and idiographic factors to identify the transduction pathways through which the social world promotes or protects against cardiovascular disease.

In sum, the scientific teams whose work was highlighted in the first edition have continued their collaborations and in each case their work has grown more interdisciplinary. Multidisciplinary research is characterized by the aggregation of the work of different experts—i.e., by investigators coming together with their different expertises to solve problems, and then returning, largely unchanged by the collaboration, to their own disciplines. Interdisciplinary research, by contrast, is characterized by synergies among experts that can transform. Interdisciplinary scientific research can be riskier than multidisciplinary research because multidisciplinary research requires only that one share an established procedure with an investigator in another field. Interdisciplinary research, however, often requires innovation at the conceptual and operational levels of research. The success of interdisciplinary efforts rest on interactions among group members—it is a group product rather than the simple sum of its individual products. Accordingly, interdisciplinary teams are more subject to failure than solitary and multidisciplinary scientific efforts. But with this higher risk also comes the potential for higher payoffs in the form of innovation and comprehensiveness.

Although obstacles remain, there is an increasing dominance of interdisciplinary teams in the production of scientific knowledge, and an increasing impact of scientific discoveries that reflect the work of teams relative to individuals (e.g., Wuchty, Jones, and Uzzi, 2007). The contextual conditions that have fostered the current momentum are manifold. The twentieth century saw a growth and maturation of psychological science and relevant disciplines to the point that they now provide a solid base from which to launch successful interdisciplinary expeditions. Advances in mathematical tools for dealing with large and complex data structures have helped the psychological sciences bridge to other disciplines. At the same time, the development of new and powerful methods and measurement tools promoted productive interdisciplinary research across the neurosciences, cognitive sciences, behavioral sciences, and social sciences. As the postscripts to this new edition testify and as detailed analyses have verified (e.g., Wuchty, Jones, and Uzzi, 2007), the landscape of science is changing and the notion of the solitary genius advancing knowledge is being replaced by teams of scientists asking big questions that are no longer constrained by traditional disciplinary boundaries. The recent abandonment of the metaphor of the solitary computer in favor of the metaphor of the internet with its massively interconnected computers may be as applicable to the scientific enterprise as to the mind.

REFERENCES

Beilin, L. J. (1999). Lifestyle and hypertension: An overview. *Clinical and Experimental Hypertension, 21*, 749–762.

Cacioppo, J. T., and Berntson, G. G. (1992). Social psychological contributions to the decade of the brain: Doctrine of multilevel analysis. *American Psychologist, 47*, 1019–1028.

Cacioppo, J. T., Berntson, G. G., Sheridan, J. F., and McClintock, M. K. (2000). Multi-level integrative analyses of human behavior: The complementing nature of social and biological approaches. *Psychological Bulletin, 126*, 829–843.

Day, D. (2001). Population-based screening with the coronary heart disease risk factor calculator. *Advances in Therapy, 18*, 21–32.

Frankenfield, D. L., Marciniak, T. A., Drass, J. A., and Jencks, S. (1997). Quality improvement activity directed at the national level: Examples from the health care financing administration. *Quality Management in Health Care, 5*, 12–18.

Gump, B. B., Matthews, K. A., and Raikkonen, K. (1999). Modeling relationships among socioeconomic status, hostility, cardiovascular reactivity, and left ventricular mass in African American and White children. *Health Psychology, 18*, 140–150.

Hawkley, L. C., Masi, C. M., Berry, J. D., & Cacioppo, J. T. (2006). Loneliness is a unique predictor of age-related differences in systolic blood pressure. *Psychology and Aging, 21*, 152–164.

Keil, U. (2000). Coronary artery disease: The role of lipids, hypertension and smoking. *Basic Research in Cardiology, 95 Suppl 1*, I52–158.

Kosslyn, S. M., Cacioppo, J. T., Davidson, R. J., Hugdahl, K., Lovallo, W. R., Spiegel, D., and Rose, R. (2002). Bridging psychology and biology: The analysis of individuals in groups. *American Psychologist, 57*, 341–351.

Melanson, K. J., McInnis, K. J., Rippe, J. M., Blackburn, G., and Wilson, P. F. (2000). Obesity and cardiovascular disease risk: Research update. *Cardiology in Review, 9*, 202–207.

Seeman, T. E. (2000). Health promoting effects of friends and family on health outcomes in older adults. *American Journal of Health Promotion, 14*, 362–370.

Slusarcick, A. L., and McCaig, L. F. (2000). National hospital ambulatory medical care survey: 1998 outpatient department summary. *Advance Data, 317*, 1–23.

Williams J. K., Kaplan, J.R., and Manuck, S.B. (1993). Effects of psychosocial stress on endothelium-mediated dilation of atherosclerotic arteries in cynomolgus monkeys. *The Journal of Clinical Investigation, 92,* 1819–1823.

Wright, R. O. (1997). *Life and Death in the United States: Statistics on Life Expectancies, Diseases and Death Rates for the Twentieth Century.* New York: McFarland.

Wuchty, S., Jones, B. F., and Uzzi, B. (2007). The increasing dominance of teams in production of knowledge. *Science, 316,* 1036–1039.

2

A Contemporary Perspective
on Multilevel Analyses and
Social Neuroscience

GARY G. BERNTSON and JOHN T. CACIOPPO

The nervous system is organized in a heterarchical fashion, with multiple but interactive levels of processing that may differentially manifest at divergent levels of analysis. Consequently, a comprehensive understanding of neurobiological mechanisms, and their health implications, will require interdisciplinary approaches that entail integrative multilevel analyses. This chapter overviews a collaborative interdisciplinary effort to elucidate the links and underlying mechanisms of psychophysiological relations and their implications for health.

A fundamental organizational feature of the nervous system lies in the basic hierarchical structure of multiple processing levels. This is not a strict hierarchy in the formal sense, but a more complex set of interacting levels, with parallel and serial processing elements, and with both direct and indirect interactions between proximate as well as remote levels—what has been referred to as a *heterarchy* (see Berntson, Boysen, and Cacioppo, 1993). Although distinguishable levels and components of this system can be identified, they are highly interactive. Consequently, an understanding of a given level of functional organization, as gleaned from a single level of analysis, may be accurate but is likely to be incomplete.

Our collaborative program has fostered integrative analyses across levels of organization that range from the social to the neural, and this emphasis on diversity has been critical to the progress we have made on brain-behavior relationships and health. Before we began this collaboration, each of us had established programs that entailed multiple levels of analysis. For one of us (Cacioppo) that extended from the social to the psychophysiological level; and for the other (Berntson), from the psychophysiological to the psychobiological/neural level.

Consequently, we had a common perspective and approach, and the overlap in psychophysiology afforded a grounding for a broader joint effort that would extend from the social to the neural levels of analysis. Important in this venture has been a deep mutual intellectual respect, mirrored in the quality of the collaboration, which has driven perspectives from different levels equally, without one level of analysis being subservient to another.

Multiple Levels of Organization and Processing

The nineteenth-century neurologist John Hughlings Jackson, in his essay "Evolution and Dissolution of the Nervous System," emphasized the hierarchical structure of the brain and the *re-representation* of functions at multiple levels within this neural hierarchy (Jackson, 1884). Implicit in his message was the fact that information is processed at multiple levels of organization within the nervous system. Primitive protective responses to aversive stimuli are organized at the level of the spinal cord, as is apparent in flexor (pain) withdrawal reflexes to noxious stimuli. These primitive protective reactions are expanded and embellished at higher levels of the nervous system (see Berntson et al., 1993). The evolutionary development of higher neural systems, such as the limbic system, endowed organisms with an expanded behavioral repertoire, including escape reactions, aggressive responses, and even the ability to anticipate and avoid aversive encounters. Evolution not only endowed us with primitive, lower-level adaptive reactions, but also it sculpted the awesome information-processing capacities of the highest levels of the brain. At progressively higher levels of organization, there is a general expansion in the range and relational complexity of contextual controls and in the breadth and flexibility of discriminative and adaptive responses (Berntson et al., 1993).

Adaptive flexibility of higher-level systems has costs, however, given the finite information-processing capacity of neural circuits. Greater flexibility implies a less rigid relationship between inputs and outputs, a greater range of information that must be integrated, and a slower serial-like mode of processing. Consequently, the evolutionary layering of higher processing levels onto lower substrates has adaptive advantage in that lower and more efficient processing levels may continue to be expressed. For example, pain withdrawal reflexes, mediated by inherent spinal circuits, can manifest in rapid protective responses to pain stimuli. At the same time, however, ascending pain pathways convey information to higher levels of the brain that mediate more complex affective, cognitive, and behavioral reactions such as fear, anxiety, avoidance, and aggression.

Although reflex responses provide a rather rigidly organized prepotent response, they are not immutable, as higher neurobehavioral processes can come to suppress or bypass pain withdrawal reflexes (e.g., self-injecting insulin or recovering a billfold from a fire). These multilevel organizational features are not limited to somatic systems but apply to the autonomic nervous system as well

(Berntson, Sarter, and Cacioppo, 1998). Thus, brainstem baroreceptor reflexes represent fundamental mechanisms for the regulation of blood pressure, but they also can be inhibited, modulated, or bypassed by higher neurobehavioral substrates during stress (see Berntson et al., 1998). This has important implications for cardiovascular control and cardiovascular disorders, and a common theme of our collaborative work has been the links between behavioral processes and cardiovascular functions and health.

Affect, stress, and autonomic control

The multiplicity of processing levels does not reflect a simple redundancy. Because the capacity for stimulus processing differs across levels of the neuraxis, these mechanisms may be sensitive to distinct or only partially overlapping features of the behavioral context and may have differential access to response systems. Pain stimuli can evoke a spinally mediated withdrawal reflex and may also trigger higher-level reactions such as anger or aggression, or acquired anticipatory reactions that may permit avoidance or control of the aversive stimulus. Even associative processes, however, are represented at multiple levels of the neuraxis. Research by LeDoux (1995) and colleagues on conditioned fear reactions to acoustic stimuli, for example, indicates that projections from the auditory thalamus to the amygdala constitute a sufficient subcortical route for simple fear conditioning. In contrast, less-specific contextual conditioning, or pseudoconditioning, which is more akin to anxiety, appears to be critically dependent on the cortex (see Berntson, Sarter and Cacioppo, 1998; LeDoux, 1995).

Although the multiple levels of organization entail partially independent processing substrates, they are typically integrated, with systems at one level able to control, modulate, or bias processing at other levels of organization. An important thesis of our research program is that the heterarchical structure of the brain permits both top-down and bottom-up biases and, in some cases, the complete bypassing of other levels. This is a concept of consequence, because it implies that a comprehensive understanding of neurobehavioral processes and their relation to health will require multilevel analyses. This is illustrated by our studies on stress, anxiety, and autonomic control of the heart (see "Key Findings and Perspectives" below).

Historically, the sympathetic and parasympathetic controls of the heart have been viewed as reciprocally organized, with increases in activity of one branch associated with decreases in the other (Berntson, Cacioppo and Quigley, 1991). This concept arose largely through work on basic autonomic reflexes, however, and does not adequately reflect the greater range of autonomic control that can be exerted by rostral neural systems. Our collaborative work has documented that higher neurobehavioral systems are far more flexible in their pattern of autonomic control over the cardiovascular system and may be evidence of notable individual differences (Berntson et al., 1994). This is important because distinct patterns of autonomic control may have important health implications (Berntson et al., 1998; Bigger and Schwartz, 1994; Cacioppo, 1994). As we and others (e.g., see Chapters 3 and 4 in this volume) have shown, sympathetic activation in response to psychological stressors may be associated with the development of disease, and we have found relatively stable individual differences in modes of autonomic cardiac control that vary with the type of stressor (e.g., active vs. passive coping tasks or orthostatic stressors; e.g., Berntson et al., 1994; Berntson, Cacioppo, and Fieldstone, 1996). In this regard, sympathetically driven increases in heart rate, but not similar cardiac responses associated with vagal withdrawal, were found to predict reduced immune responses to influenza vaccine (Cacioppo, 1994).

Of relevance to these psychophysiological relationships is our emerging neurobiological model of the brain systems that underlie fear and anxiety, which emphasizes potential ascending routes by which sympathetic outflow and associated visceral feedback may bias or color processing by rostral systems, including cortical systems that mediate the higher-level cognitive functions. The further elucidation of these systems is important because they represent fundamental links between behavioral processes, autonomic control, and health outcomes. For example, further understanding of these systems and their ascending influences may clarify the physiological and cognitive/attentional bases for the vicious cycle between sympathetic outflow and anxiety in panic attacks and may suggest meaningful treatment strategies.

Personal ties and well-being

Our research program takes an interdisciplinary, multilevel approach to elucidating psychophysiological processes and their relations to health. This ranges from psychophysiological studies in humans to neural and physiological investigations in animals. As outlined in this chapter, some of this work focuses on lower-level neural, physiological, and immune processes. These efforts, however, are seen in the service of explicating more complex psychobiological relations. Work on basic patterns of autonomic control has helped clarify psychophysiological relationships, their links to multiple levels of functional organization, and their implications for health. Additional studies of brain mechanisms have revealed important neural systems and processes that likely underlie cognitive contributions to anxiety and autonomic control. But our collaborative efforts do not stop there, as understanding the mediating and moderating effects of social processes and personal ties on mental and physical functioning is equally important if we are to elucidate fully the mechanisms that underlie health and disease.

The social world has tended to be ignored in the neurosciences because it is complex, falls outside the physical bounds of the body, and operates on biological processes through multifarious and to date poorly specified mechanisms. Personal ties, however, are a ubiquitous part of life, serving important social, psychological, and behavioral functions across the lifespan (e.g., Gardner, Gabriel, and Diekman, 2000). People form personal ties with others from the moment they are born, as the very survival of newborns depends on their attachment to and nurturance by others over an extended period of time (cf. Baumeister and Leary, 1995). Indeed, evolution has heavily sculpted the human genome to be sensitive to and succoring of contact and relationships with others (Cacioppo, Berntson, Sheridan, and McClinock, 2000). The need to belong does not stop at infancy; rather; affiliation and nurturant social relationships are essential for physical and for psychological well-being across the lifespan (see Gardner et al., 2000). People who report having contact with five or more intimate friends in the prior six months are 60% more likely to report that their lives are "very happy," as compared to those who do not report such contact (Burt, 1986). Disruptions of personal ties—whether through ridicule, discrimination, separation, divorce, or bereavement—are among the most stressful events people must endure (Gardner et al., 2000). The restriction of social contact during infancy and childhood has dramatic effects on psychopathology across the lifespan. For instance, blood pressure tends to increase with age in America; this trend is evident in individuals with low levels of social support but is weakened or absent in individuals with high levels of social support (Uchino, Cacioppo, Malarkey, Glaser, and Kiecolt-Glaser, 1995; Uchino, Kiecolt-Glaser, and Cacioppo, 1992).

Epidemiological research has further found that social isolation is a major risk factor for morbidity and mortality from widely varying causes, including cardiovascular diseases. This relationship is evident even after statistically controlling for known biological risk factors, social status, and baseline measures of health. The negative health consequences of social isolation are particularly strong among some of the fastest growing segments of the population: the elderly, the poor, and minorities. Astonishingly, the strength of social isolation as a risk factor is comparable to high blood pressure, obesity, sedentary lifestyles, and possibly even smoking (for review, see House, Landis, and Umberson, 1988).

Our collaborative program is actively exploring the effect of social factors on autonomic, cardiovascular, and immune functions. The autonomic and immune systems have traditionally been viewed as distinct functional domains, with only remote or tangential links and associations. This view is rapidly changing. It is now apparent that substantial two-way communications exist between the brain and immune tissues, and that this reciprocal interaction impacts substantially on behavior and autonomic control (see Maier and Watkins, 1998). Consequently, a comprehensive understanding of cardiovascular health and disease will require an understanding of the heterarchical structure of the brain (Berntson and Cacioppo, 2000), including the integral and reciprocal contributions of the immune system. The effect of social factors on cardiovascular and immune functions, along with the potential links and mediators of these relations, represents an important component of our current research focus (see the following section, "Key Findings and Perspectives").

Interim summary

The overarching perspective of our collaborative program is that the links between psychological and biological processes, and their implications for health, cannot be comprehended fully by a single level of analysis or by investigations at a single level of organization. An integrative, interdisciplinary approach across levels of organization and analysis can add unique perspectives because different levels of analysis can reveal distinct patterns of order in data, and because different levels of organization are known to interact. There remains a need for research with a more restricted focus, and it is not necessary that all researchers pursue multilevel analyses. It is important, however, to include a multilevel perspective if we are to understand the various mechanisms by which the social world gets under the skin.

Key Findings and Perspectives

Multiple levels of processing and bottom-up influences

Multiple levels of processing in neurobehavioral systems are inherent in the heterarchical structure of the brain and help clarify aspects of cognition and behavior. The cerebral cortex is a crucial neural substrate for higher-level social and cognitive processes, and it is tempting to consider lower levels of the neuraxis as fundamentally subservient to higher-level influences. It is clear that higher-level systems can powerfully modulate lower-level regulation of autonomic, neuroendocrine, and immune functions. An important feature of the heterarchical pattern of neural organization, however, is that there are ample routes by which lower systems may modulate or bias processing of the highest levels of the nervous system. It is increasingly recognized that central and peripheral processes constitute reciprocally linked dimensions of neurobehavioral function. One aspect of our research program examines the role of ascending neural systems in anxiety and autonomic control. Anxiogenic or fear-eliciting contexts are often associated with robust autonomic responses, and abnormal autonomic control and visceral reactivity is a common feature of anxiety disorders. These are important issues because anxiety represents a clear risk factor for cardiovascular disease and sudden cardiac death (Hayward, 1995; Kawachi et al., 1994) and because they bear on the fundamental nature of anxiety and the underlying neural mechanisms that link behavioral processes and autonomic function.

As mentioned earlier in this chapter, research by LeDoux (1975) and colleagues on conditioned fear reactions reveals at least two circuits through which affective learning can occur. Simple fear conditioning to an acoustic stimulus can be mediated by a subcortical circuit that is composed of a direct projection from the auditory thalamus to the amygdala, which, in turn, projects to lower mechanisms for behavioral, autonomic, and neuroendocrine expression. Although an adequate subcortical mechanism exists for simple fear conditioning, more complex contextual conditioning and pseudoconditioning appear to depend on a cortical link (Berntson et al., 1998; LeDoux, 1995). In this regard, cortical and cognitive processes are increasingly recognized to contribute to anxiety states in humans. Figure 2.1 illustrates some interconnected components of the descending systems that have been implicated in fear and anxiety (see Berntson et al., 1998). One likely contribution of cortical systems is in the attentional and evaluative processing of anxiety-related stimuli and associations.

Cortical processing is modulated by ascending neural circuits. Among these is cholinergic projection from the basal forebrain to the cerebral cortex, which appears to generally enhance cortical processing (Figure 2.1; Berntson et al., 1998). Consequently, the degree and efficiency of cortical processing of anxiety-related stimuli and associations would be expected to be a function of activity of this basal forebrain cholinergic system (Sarter and Bruno, 1997). Consistent with this view are the cognitive deficits and dementia associated with the degeneration of this system in Alzheimer's disease. Findings from our collaborative research program (with Martin Sarter) suggest that the basal forebrain cholinergic system also is an important site of action for the antianxiety actions of benzodiazepine receptor (BZR) agonists, such as chlordiazepoxide (Librium) and diazepam (Valium). By enhancing inhibitory actions on basal forebrain cholinergic neurons, BZR agonists can reduce cortical acetylcholine release. The resulting attenuation of cortical processing likely underlies in part the known cognitive-impairing effects of these agents and, we have hypothesized, also mediates the antianxiety actions of these compounds (see Berntson et al., 1998). That is, it appears that the antianxiety actions of compounds like Librium and Valium are due at least in part to the reduction in the attentional focus on, and cognitive processing of, anxiety-related stimuli.

An important feature of the ascending pathways of Figure 2.1 is that they provide relatively direct routes through which sympathetic activation and the associated visceral afferent activity can drive the basal forebrain cholinergic system and thereby potentiate cortical processing. A major excitatory input to the basal forebrain cholinergic system is the noradrenergic projection from the locus coeruleus, which is highly sensitive to emotional states and sympathetic activation (Aston-Jones, Rajkowski, Kubiak, Valentino, and Shipley, 1996; Berntson et al., 1998). A major input to the locus coeruleus originates from a region in the medullary reticular formation (the nucleus paragigantocellularis, or PGi), a region that directly innervates sympathetic motor neurons and receives input from a variety of sources, including visceral afferent activity. Collectively, these considerations suggest that PGi projections to the locus coeruleus transmit information that reflects the state of sympathetic control and associated visceral afference (see Aston-Jones et al., 1996; Berntson et al., 1998). Because PGi neurons activate both the locus coeruleus and sympathetic motor neurons, they appear to modulate both the autonomic and cognitive aspects of emotional activation.

Although the precise role of these ascending pathways in anxiety and cardiovascular control remains to be clarified, they generally appear to enhance or prime cortical processing of anxiogenic stimuli. Consistent with this suggestion is the finding that visceral afference can enhance emotional memories in both humans and animals (see Clark, Naritoku, Smith, Browning, and Jensen, 1999). The

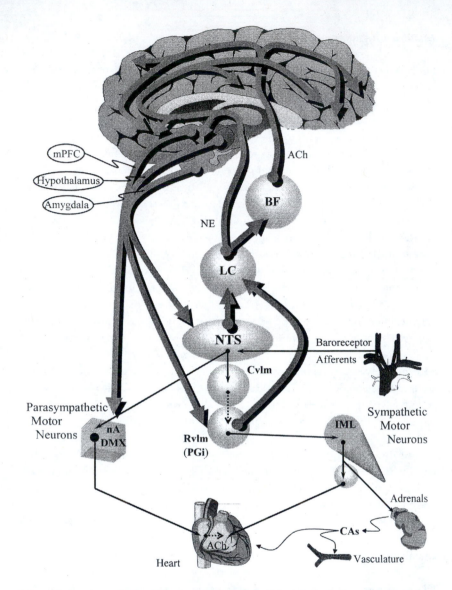

Figure 2.1. Ascending and descending branches of the anatomical model of neuronal substrates by which cortical and cognitive processes may contribute to the development and expression of anxiety and its autonomic features. The model is not intended to present an anatomically complete description of relevant circuits and transmitters; rather, it is conceptually driven and focuses on hypotheses derived in part from experimental evidence (see Berntson et al., 1998). Abbreviations: ACh, acetylcholine; BF, basal forebrain cortical cholinergic system; CAs, catecholamines; Cvlm, caudal ventrolateral medulla; DMX, dorsal motor nucleus of the vagus; IML, sympathetic preganglionic neurons of the intermediolateral cell column; LC, locus coeruleus; mPFC, medial prefrontal cortex; nA, nucleus ambiguous; NE, norepinephrine; NTS, nucleus tractus solitarius; PGi, nucleus paragigantocellularis; Rvlm, rostral ventrolateral medullary "pressor" area. Adapted from Berntson and Cacioppo (2000), with permission of Cambridge University Press.

latter finding may underlie the vivid and seemingly indelible traumatic memories of posttraumatic stress disorder, as well as the exaggerated autonomic reactivity and feedback that prime and underlie the "vicious cycle" of visceral and emotional responses in panic disorder. In any event, the available findings suggest an important modulatory role for visceral afferent information on central information processing. There is an emerging recognition of a symmetry in the reciprocal interplay among levels of organization, entailing both direct and indirect mutual interactions (top-down and bottom-up) that impact both biological and psychological processes. This interplay could not be appreciated from approaches that focus on a single level of organization or a single level of analysis.

Top-down influences on autonomic, neuroendocrine, and immune functions

Important in the further integration of the biological and the social psychological perspectives in the study of cardiovascular disease is the ability to relate constructs at one level of analysis to those of another. This is not a one-way process, as the scientific value of multilevel efforts accrues to both higher and lower levels of analysis. Illustrative of this issue is the traditional view of the sympathetic and parasympathetic branches of the autonomic nervous system as being subject to reciprocal central control, with activation of one branch associated with inhibition of the other. This is a conception that arose from the early physiological literature and continues to the present, although qualifications are increasingly recognized (see Berntson et al., 1991). Although lower autonomic reflexes, such as the baroreceptor-heart rate reflex, display this reciprocal pattern of organization, our collaborative work has documented that autonomic control arising from higher neurobehavioral systems is not so tightly obligated (Berntson et al., 1991, 1994). In behavioral contexts, activities of the two autonomic branches may show reciprocal, concordant (coactive), or independent changes. These findings, arising from the psychophysiological literature, mandate an expansion and calibration of biological conceptions of autonomic control. This is important because it illustrates how organizational principles derived from lower levels of analysis may not be applicable to higher-level behavioral systems and, in fact, may obscure psychophysiological relations that are crucial in understanding cardiovascular control in health and disease.

An illustration comes from our study of the autonomic responses of human subjects to orthostatic stress (assumption of an upright posture) and to social and cognitive stressors (Berntson et al., 1994; Cacioppo et al., 1994). Quantitative estimates of the sympathetic and parasympathetic contributions to cardiac responses were derived from single and dual autonomic blockade studies. At the group level, the orthostatic and psychological stressors yielded an essentially equivalent pattern of heart rate increase, associated with sympathetic activation and parasympathetic withdrawal. For the orthostatic stressor, the cardiac response reflected a relatively tight reciprocal central control of autonomic outflows, as evidenced by the

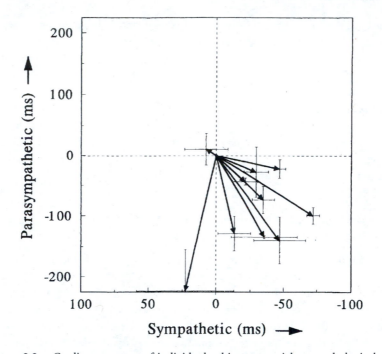

Figure 2.2. Cardiac responses of individual subjects to social or psychological stressors, depicted as changes in sympathetic and parasympathetic control derived from autonomic blockades. The arrows represent individual autonomic responses (from baseline) along the sympathetic and parasympathetic axes, expressed in ms of heart period. Each arrow vector represents the mean response of a given subject, across three separate tasks. The horizontal and vertical error bars at each arrowhead depict the standard errors of the sympathetic and parasympathetic responses, respectively, across the three tasks for that subject. As is apparent, there were large and stable individual differences in the amplitude and direction of the response vectors. Adapted from Berntson et al. (1994), with permission of Cambridge University Press.

significant negative correlation between the responses of the autonomic branches across subjects. Although the overall group response to psychological stressors was similar, there were considerable individual differences in the pattern of autonomic reaction, and there was no significant correlation between responses of the two branches across subjects. Although the individual modes of response were highly reliable over different psychological stressors, subjects differed considerably in their pattern of response (Figure 2.2). Some subjects showed primarily sympathetic activation, some showed reciprocal sympathetic activation together with parasympathetic withdrawal, and still others displayed primarily parasympathetic withdrawal. These are significant findings because individual patterns of response are likely to reflect distinct psychological states and have differential implications for health.

These studies point to the need for more sophisticated conceptualizations of stress. Mason (1972) and Selye (1973) and made seminal contributions to the scientific study of stress by demonstrating that physical and psychological stressors serve similarly to activate the sympathetic adrenomedullary (SAM) and hypothalamic pituitary adrenocortical (HPA) axis. In our own research, nomethetic (group) analyses have indeed revealed very similar levels of SAM and HPA activation as a function of physical (e.g., orthostatic) and psychological (e.g., mental arithmetic) stressors. Idiographic (individual) analyses, however, have revealed very different organizations in these data. Importantly, individual differences in the pattern of autonomic response to psychological stress were distinct from responses to physical stressors, and it was the former (but not the latter) that were predictive of immunological status (Berntson et al., 1994; Cacioppo et al., 1998). Similarly, the clinical outcome after myocardial infarction appears to be a function in part of the specific pattern of autonomic cardiac autonomic control (Bigger and Schwartz, 1994). Stress has often been recognized as a contributor to disease. Current findings, however, suggest that identification of the underlying mechanisms of stress effects, their clinical implications, and the development of meaningful treatment strategies may all benefit from a differentiation of subtypes of stress and somatovisceral response.

In sum, researchers often seek general laws, universal patterns, and common mechanisms, with individual differences treated as error variance. The health implications of individual differences may be important to consider as well, however. Accordingly, reliable individual differences should be treated more as a crucible for refining conceptual models, and for theory construction and testing, than as error variance per se. Toward this end, multilevel research on stress that considers both the heterarchical organization of the brain and individual differences in the construal of the social world is clearly needed (Berntson et al., 1998).

Social factors in health

Our interdisciplinary research (which has involved psychologists, immunologists, endocrinologists, and molecular biologists) indicates that social factors mediated by higher neurobehavioral systems can exert especially potent modulatory effects on cardiovascular, neuroendocrine, and immune functions. A meta-analytic review of the extant human literature revealed that perceived social isolation is associated with a variety of altered physiological functions, such as blood pressure regulation, catecholamine levels, and immune reactions (Uchino, Cacioppo, and Kiecolt-Glaser, 1996). A causal link in these relations is suggested by findings of improved physiological functioning after interventions that served to reduce social isolation (Uchino et al., 1996). The role of psychological variables in these relations is indicated by the fact that subjective indices of social isolation are often better predictors of stress and health than are objective indices (Seeman, 1996; Uchino et al., 1996). These findings in humans are supported by studies on animals, which document the important of social factors in cardiovascular and immune function (see Cacioppo et al., 2002b).

Kaplan and Manuck (this volume) review evidence that social reorganization contributes to cardiovascular disease in primates, and Padgett et al. (1998) found that social reorganization can reactivate herpes-simplex virus in mice. Importantly, social reorganization has effects above and beyond what might be expected from traditional models of stress and disease. For example, Padgett et al. (1998) demonstrated that physical stressors yielded comparable elevations in glucocorticoid levels but had much less potent effects on disease; thus, psychosocial stress was selectively transduced into physiological signals that modulated the expression and effect of virally transmitted host/pathogen genes. Importantly, the immunological consequences of social stress also appear to be modulated by individual differences in social relations, as dominant mice were more likely to show reactivation than submissive mice—a finding that again is mirrored in research on social reorganization and cardiovascular disease in primates (Kaplan and Manuck, this volume).

The influence of social factors on cardiovascular and immune functions is not limited to animals. Parallel findings of stress effects on cardiovascular function (e.g., Uchino et al., 1996) and susceptibility to viral infections and other markers of immune function have also been reported for humans, with social stressors being particularly potent (Cohen, Frank, Doyle, Skoner, Rabin, and Gwaltney, 1998; Kiecolt-Glaser, Malarkey, Cacioppo, and Glaser, 1994). These examples demonstrate the potent influence of social relations on autonomic and immunological function, and they illustrate how the order in physiological, pharmacological, or immunological data may not be fully understandable from the vantage of a single level of analysis. Rather, comprehensive accounts of psychophysiological relations will likely require multiple analyses across distinct levels of functional organization. As described in this chapter, we have found that autonomic response patterns can predict immune reactions. An obvious question arises as to the mechanism of this association. Some insights into these mechanisms are beginning to emerge from the literature, but their ultimate elucidation will require even more integrative, interdisciplinary research.

As discussed here, a particularly significant insight has recently emerged concerning the bidirectional interactions between the brain and the immune system, and the associated links between immune, autonomic, neuroendocrine, and behavioral mechanisms (Maier and Watkins, 1998). It is now clear that cardiovascular regulation is not isolated from immune function. Indeed, an infection (or an injection of lipopolysaccaride—a component of bacterial membranes) triggers a centrally orchestrated sickness response, mediated in part by vagal afferents, and entailing behavioral (e.g., inactivity and a decrease in appetite and food intake), as well as autonomic and neuroendocrine, components (Maier and Watkins, 1998). The immune system cannot be viewed as a functional domain independent of the brain or autonomic nervous system. Indeed, it would be most surprising if the immune system was functionally isolated from behavioral and autonomic mechanisms, given the early evolutionary emergence of immunological functions and the adaptive significance of these processes. Clearly, a comprehensive under-standing of cardiovascular health and disease will require an understanding of the heterarchical structure of the brain, as well as the contributions of the immune system to this heterarchical regulation. An important aspect of our collaborative research is directed toward the identification of the critical signaling mechanisms and molecules that mediate the interactions between the immune systems and autonomic control. This research represents a particularly important emerging focus that will likely contribute to the understanding of relations between behav-ioral, autonomic, neuroendocrine, and immune processes.

As noted, social isolation and loneliness have been shown to be major risk factors for morbidity and mortality from widely varying causes and are comparable to smoking, hypertension, and obesity (House et al., 1988). Differences in health behaviors represent a partial but incomplete explanation of these relations. Our recent work in humans, therefore, sought to identify pathways and signals that link higher neurobehavioral processes to immune functions and health. In a recent laboratory and ambulatory study, chronically lonely college students (matched on other factors) were found to have altered sympathoadrenal and hypothalamic-pituitary-adrenal (HPA) functions. The enhanced HPA activity and elevated ad-renal corticosteroid levels of lonely subjects may represent one mechanism by which social factors, including the stress of social isolation, can affect immune functions. A potentially related pathway may be via lymphocyte growth hormone (L-GH), which is secreted by peripheral blood lymphocytes. The social isolation of care-giving spouses of Alzheimer's patients was associated with markedly suppressed L-GH levels, which were negatively correlated with ACTH and norepinephrine (Wu et al., 1999). Moreover, lymphocytes from caregivers displayed a blunted L-GH response to an influenza vaccine, and this attenuated response may con-tribute to a reduced lymphocyte proliferation and cytokine production (Wu et al., 1999). Thus, it appears that L-GH may enhance immune reactions to a foreign antigen and that the L-GH response may be diminished by social stress.

Finally, lonely and nonlonely college students were found to engage in gen-erally comparable health behaviors, but the salubrity of restorative behaviors such as sleep was found to be less in lonely individuals. Although these studies are still in early stages, they offer promise for the ultimate elucidation of the routes by which higher neurobehavioral processes can affect the autonomic, neuroendocrine, and immune systems, and they may suggest important approaches to intervention.

Life History of the Program

Our interdisciplinary research effort was enabled by the availability and efforts of a large number of highly competent researchers with broad vision and profound dedication. The rapidly advancing state of knowledge within specialized disci-plines, and their distinct levels and methods of analysis, impose limits on the ability of a single investigator to pursue multilevel research, except across relatively proximate levels of analysis. A broad, integrative, multilevel approach increasingly requires an interdisciplinary team of researchers with specialized knowledge of the methods, data, and concepts of their respective fields. The composition of our research group has often been dynamic, being reshaped based on the issues at hand. In fact, it is not composed of a single coherent group but of various consortia. The crucial feature of our collaborative venture lies not in the particular set of individuals who make up the research group but in key principals who share a common recognition of the need for multilevel analyses.

The important feature of our interdisciplinary research has been the continued involvement of two individuals, the authors of this chapter, Bernston and Cacioppo, who constitute the "glue" for the effort, who maintain the overall focus, and who organize the disparate and often changing constituents of the program. Our collaborative effort began in 1989, when Cacioppo joined the faculty at Ohio State. There was an immediate compatibility between us, both personally and professionally. Both of us had a long history of efforts to bridge at least proximate levels of analysis. Cacioppo was formally trained as a social psychologist but had also emerged as a leading contributor to the field of psychophysiology. Berntson was trained in psychobiology and behavioral neuroscience, with an abiding interest in basic neurobiological mechanisms and their implications for psychophysiological processes. The fit was natural, as each of us bridged distinct levels, and the confluence afforded the opportunity for a broader bridge—that between social psychology and neurobiological mechanisms.

The resulting collaboration, although initially limited primarily to the two of us, proved to be a highly synergistic and productive intersection. In part, the success of our effort lies in the dissatisfaction and frustration each of us had felt (independently) over the limitations of single levels of analysis. An additional cohering force was the mutual respect that we shared over each other's prior multilevel research efforts. This led to a natural intellectual synergy, rather than an instrumentality, in the collaboration. That is, neither of the principals was overly concerned about personal benefits from a joint venture, and both saw the opportunity to continue individual efforts with the added intellectual and scientific benefits accrued from the collaborative component. Indeed, in addition to the ongoing collaborative effort, each of us continued to pursue independent links to higher and lower levels of analysis, and these partially independent efforts ultimately led to the broader interdisciplinary program of research. But that broader effort would take additional time to fully develop.

Further development involved a gradual coalescence of our mutual program with our other, relatively independent collaborative ventures. Those included the work of Cacioppo with the psychoneuroimmunology group at Ohio State, and the collaborative work of Berntson with neuroscientists in examining neural and neurochemical systems involved in anxiety and autonomic control. Initially, that coalescence was at the conceptual level, which ultimately developed into an integrated research program. There were impediments to this effort, including a degree of disciplinary isolationism that existed even within the subdisciplines of psychology.

Historical impediments

Social psychology and psychobiology have shared a richly intertwined history. The Darwinian revolution had immense impact on psychology, as it focused attention on the biological origins of behavior and emphasized the continuity between the human and the animal mind. This perspective fostered a view of psychology as a biological science, despite its historical roots in philosophy, and promoted a conceptual evolution toward biological models of psychological processes. Among the benefactors of the Darwinian movement were instinct theorists, who consequently had a mechanism for their views on the nature and origins of "purposive" behavior. Instinct models struck an intellectual chord with both social psychologists and psychobiologists and held out the promise of an integrated psychology. Instinct theories collapsed, however: in part, because of their teleological focus, but also because of their devolution into massive instinct "lists" and their failure to mature into predictive, explanatory, and hypothesis-generating theoretical systems.

The instinct adventure was a failure for both social psychology and for psychobiology, and both disciplines sought alternative paradigms, models, and theories. Behaviorism, with its emphasis on learning, offered some hope for a conceptual link between the subdisciplines, and learning models continue as salient features of both areas. But there developed a growing chasm between the areas. Both psychobiology and social psychology were hampered by the straitjacket of behaviorism. Especially pernicious was the radical behaviorism of Skinner, which eschewed scientific explanations of behavior that appeal to "something going on in another universe, such as the mind or the nervous system" (Skinner, 1968, p. 88). This perspective effectively excluded meaningful accounts of behavior in terms of biology, and it failed to admit emerging concepts from social and cognitive psychology. Psychobiology and social psychology pursued separate paths. Social psychology increasingly focused on the cognitive bases of behavior, whereas psychobiology increasingly embraced the emerging neuroscience perspective. For many, these were seen as incompatible, or at best inharmonious, directions (Scott, 1991).

Contemporary impediments

There remain impediments to the initiation of interdisciplinary research. There are residual disciplinary boundaries between departments and programs, often including those of physical location, administrative structure, and differences in language and perspectives. Biopsychology often focuses on neural substrates and production mechanisms for behavior, whereas social psychology generally emphasizes multivariate systems and situational influences in studies of the effect of human association on mind and behavior. Human biology is anchored in concrete anatomy and genetics, providing fundamental elements from which to draw interconnections and with which to construct theory. In contrast, the social world is a complex set of abstractions, representing the actions and influences of the relationships among individuals, groups, societies, and cultures. The differences in levels of analysis have resulted in distinct histories, research traditions, and technical demands, which constitute an impediment to truly integrative research across social and biological levels of analysis. An additional impediment arises in grant review. Even when programs are interested in supporting interdisciplinary research, the gateway to these programs is the initial review process, which may involve review panels that "represent" more traditional disciplines and perspectives. Consequently, the initial stages of the collaborative effort were maintained by grant support to each of the principles for more limited and focused research. Ultimately, broader support for aspects of the interdisciplinary program were obtained in the form of program project grants, center grants, and funding from private foundations.

Positive developments

Current developments in both social psychology and neuroscience, however, are shifting the paths of these disciplines toward an intersection that is based on a more solid scientific foundation in both disciplines. That intersection, which has been termed *social neuroscience*, is based on integrative multilevel analyses that seek to integrate information derived from levels of analysis ranging from social psychology to molecular biology. This perspective is now increasingly embraced by the rapidly developing fields of behavioral neuroscience, cognitive neuroscience, behavioral neurology, behavioral medicine, behavior genetics, and psychoneuroimmunology. The explosive developments in these fields are attributable to the recognition of the value of multilevel analyses and the inclusion of both social and biological perspectives.

Conclusions and Implications

Changes in medical science, worldwide health problems (e.g., AIDS, chronic disease), and U.S. demographics have helped fuel basic social and biological research on societal problems. Many of the most pressing contemporary health problems—cardiovascular disease, drug or alcohol abuse, HIV/AIDS, chronic obstructive pulmonary disease, cancer, diabetes, sleep disorders, and affective disorders—are social as well as biological phenomena. The etiology and course of these chronic health conditions have biological substrates, but these biological substrates and the efficacy of treatments are influenced profoundly by the social world. The complementarity of biological and social approaches to human behavior were not readily apparent when research methods were limited primarily to descriptions of the behavior of animals, to observations of patients with localized disorders of the brain, and to postmortem examinations. As a consequence, biological approaches tended to be viewed by social psychologists as uselessly reductionistic, while social approaches tended to be viewed by biopsychologists as more literary than scientific.

The complementarity of biological and social approaches also was not readily apparent from either traditional or contemporary training programs. The collaboration between the coauthors, for instance, began by accident rather than by design and was accompanied by skepticism and a certain amount of suspicion by colleagues in our respective programs. Multiple factors led the collaboration to flourish, however: foremost among them were personal factors, such as a deep respect for and trust in one another; institutional factors, such as the freedom to explore new ground without preconceptions about what the collaboration had to yield or become; and intellectual factors, such as the order in the data that emerged when working collaboratively on theoretical analyses, experimental designs, and empirical data. These factors promoted interdisciplinary research representing the union rather than the intersection of our respective fields.

Although serendipity and personal dispositions will likely play a large role in the establishment of successful interdisciplinary collaborations, their establishment need not be left completely to chance. Our own experiences suggest that support for the following would promote interdisciplinary work on health:

1. Most laboratories and funding opportunities support single or limited levels of analysis. Investigations of individual mechanisms (e.g., social, neural) in isolation, however, can hinder discovery of associations and interactions among these mechanisms. Because health outcomes across the lifespan tend to be multiply determined, research would ideally be multivariate and multilevel (cutting across multiple levels of organization). Initiatives that foster integrative interdisciplinary analyses (e.g., centers, PO1s) are therefore important if the diverse expertise required in research that cuts across multiple levels of organization is to coalesce.

2. To the extent that accrued stress and the associated allostatic load contribute to the development of disease, cross-sectional and complementary longitudinal studies should be promoted. Longitudinal research that cuts across multiple levels of analysis is especially needed.

3. The effect of social relationships on physiological responses has typically been studied either in animal models or in the laboratory. The extent to which these snapshots generalize to what people do or how they actually respond in their daily lives is an open question. Advances in ambulatory recording procedures and experience in sampling methods now make it possible to address this question. Given the complementing strengths of laboratory and ambulatory research (and the feasibility of now performing ambulatory behavioral along with physiological and endocrinological assessments), it is now possible and fruitful to extend traditional laboratory studies by using the experience in sampling methodologies and the corresponding ambulatory physiological assessments.

4. Identifying associations between concepts in the social sciences and neurosciences is important but does little to illuminate any underlying mechanisms or to advance effective interventions. Unfortunately, much of the prior research has been correlational, leaving open the question of causal factors. Animal studies offer

a valuable complement, although significant limits exist here, too, as, for instance, when studying the effects of norms and cultures. One of the greatest challenges is to go beyond correlational data to reveal the psychological and physiological mechanisms and causal (including reciprocal) structures involved.

5. As noted here, nomethetic and idiographic analyses reveal different organizations in the data. The latter is often treated as error variance but more often should be treated as a crucible for theory construction and testing.

6. Finally, scientific inquiries require that individual investigators specialize and focus. Interdisciplinary research teams provide a means of overcoming this limitation, but disciplinary training, departmental reward contingencies, and institutional policies tend to foster parochialism and work against the establishment of such teams. Parochialism, however, ignores the distinction between levels of explanation, the organization in the data that may become evident from research across levels of organization, the theoretical insights about the nature and timing of the relationships among variables that can be derived from descriptions of phenomena from multiple scales or perspectives, and the economy of thought that can be gained by using the form of representation most appropriate for the task. Parochialism also alienates scientists who are working at a different level of organization and who might otherwise contribute relevant theory and data, and it renders it acceptable to ignore relevant research simply because it was not born from one's own level of analysis. Because there are phenomena that derive from events at one level of analysis that are only or distinctly observable at other or broader levels of analysis, multilevel integrative analyses may contribute to the empirical data and theoretical insight needed for a comprehensive understanding of human behavior.

Recent research has provided growing evidence that multilevel analyses spanning neural and social perspectives can foster more comprehensive accounts of cognition, emotion, behavior, and health. Social and biological approaches are complementary rather than antagonistic. Together, these perspectives are helping to illuminate questions about cardiovascular function and disease by examining how organismic processes are shaped, modulated, and modified by social factors, and vice versa. Rather than viewing social sciences and the neurosciences as alternative approaches to understanding health and disease, we see the potential for more comprehension of these problems and their underlying mechanisms through research that cuts across these distinct but equally important levels of organization.

To summarize, it is increasingly apparent that problems and issues in both the neurosciences and the social sciences will not be fully understood by studies restricted to a single level of analysis, regardless of the specific level selected (Anderson, 1998; Cacioppo and Berntson, 1992). A process or event at one level of organization may have antecedents and determinants both within and across organizational levels, as encapsulated in what has been termed the *principle of multiple determinism* (Cacioppo and Berntson, 1992). Neither social scientists nor neuroscientists can, or should, directly concern themselves with all possible levels of analysis. A corollary to the principle of multiple determinism is that mapping relationships across levels of organization becomes more complex as the number of intervening levels increases. Although it is certainly worthwhile to adopt a broad scientific perspective, specific research programs would probably achieve maximal benefit by attention to more proximate levels of analysis (both higher and lower). If this perspective was embraced generally by those pursing distinct levels of analysis, it may be sufficient to ensure the ultimate integration among disciplines.

An important trend in neuroscience is toward more molecular levels of analysis. There remains a need for higher-level analyses as well, because the properties of more basic elements at lower levels of organization may only become apparent when these elements interact with others, at a higher level of organization. Although the whole may not be greater than the sum of its parts, the properties of its parts may only, or more readily, be knowable by the properties of the whole. This has been articulated as the *principle of nonadditive determinism* (Cacioppo and Berntson, 1992). There are efficiencies in higher-level organizations of information. For example, the essential features of Beethoven's Ninth Symphony may be fully captured by the digital data on a CD, and analysis of that data set may be sufficient to identify the piece; alternatively, it may be easier and more enjoyable to simply play it out acoustically. The esthetic organization of the data is more efficiently processed by auditory perceptual mechanisms, and identification of the relevant digital patterns that correspond to specific perceptual qualities could not be derived readily from the digital data stream alone.

A final principle that characterizes the relations among heterarchical levels of organization is the *principle of reciprocal determinism,* which asserts that there can be mutual influences among higher and lower levels of organization in the determination of behavior. To the extent to which both top-down and bottom-up processes contribute to anxiety and autonomic regulation, for example, an account of these processes based on a single level of analysis is necessarily incomplete.

Postscript

Since this volume was originally published, social neuroscience has continued to generate important insights. Recent findings regarding social influences on health are illustrative.

The first set of findings underlines how social factors mediated by higher neurobehavioral systems can exert especially potent modulatory effects on cardiovascular, neuroendocrine, and immune functions. Lonely, compared to nonlonely, young adults were characterized by higher vascular resistance (Cacioppo et al., 2002a; Hawkley et al., 2003), which over time can lead to elevated blood pressure. Consistent with this reasoning, lonely older adults were found to be characterized by higher blood pressure than nonlonely older adults (Cacioppo et al., 2002a; Hawkley et al., 2006). Moreover, the mechanisms and mediators of the immunological and health effects of social stress are being clarified by recent research. Social stress, for example, has been shown to mobilize specific subsets of lymphocytes that may selectively traffic to, and exacerbate, sites of inflammatory reactions associated with atherosclerotic plaque (Bosch et al., 2003; Quan et al., 2003). In contrast, positive social connections may serve to buffer stressors. Cacioppo, Berntson and colleagues (2004), for example, have recently found that the ventral striatum, an area associated with reward, shows greater activation in people with higher social connectedness, when they are viewing pleasant pictures involving people. This may represent a mechanistic explanation for the stress-buffering effects of satisfying social connections.

Increasingly, multilevel interdisciplinary approaches are clarifying the relations between neurobiological processes and cardiovascular functions, as well as the autonomic, immunological, and endocrinological mechanisms that underlie these relations. An illustration of the recognition of these interactions is the recent establishment of a new society—the Society of Heart Brain Medicine. The proceedings of the first summit of this society document the multiple and intricate links between psychological processes and physiological functions, autonomic and immune regulation, and cardiovascular health (see *Cleveland Clinic Journal of Medicine*, 2007, 74:suppl. 1). Such integrative research, cutting across disciplinary boundaries and levels of organization and analysis, is truly one of the important emerging developments in the study of mind–body relations.

ACKNOWLEDGMENTS

Preparation of this paper was support in part by a grant from the MacArthur Foundation, and by a grant from the National Heart, Lung and Blood Institute (HL 54428).

RECOMMENDED READINGS

Anderson, N. B., and Scott, P. A. (1999). Making the case for psychophysiology during the era of molecular biology. *Psychophysiology, 36,* 1–13.

Cacioppo, J. T., Berntson, G. G., Sheridan, J. F., and McClintock, M. K. (2000). Multi-level integrative analyses of human behavior: The complementing nature of social and biological approaches. *Psychological Bulletin, 126,* 829–843.

REFERENCES

Anderson, N. B. (1998). Levels of analysis in health science: A framework for integrating sociobehavioral and biomedical research. *Annals of the New York Academy of Science, 840,* 563–576.

Aston-Jones, G., Rajkowski, J., Kubiak, P., Valentino, R. J., and Shipley, M. T. (1996). Role of the locus coeruleus in emotional activation. *Progress in Brain Research, 107,* 379–402.

Baumeister, R. F. and Leary, M. R. (1995). The need to belong: Desire for interpersonal attachment as a fundamental human motivation. *Psychological Bulletin, 117,* 497–529.

Berntson, G. G., and Cacioppo, J. T. (2007). Integrative physiology: Homeostasis, allostasis and the orchestration of systemic physiology. In Cacioppo, J. T., Tassinary, L. G., and Berntson, G. G. (eds.). *Handbook of Psychophysiology*, 3rd edition, (433–452). Cambridge, UK: Cambridge University Press.

Berntson, G. G., Boysen, S. T., and Cacioppo, J. T. (1993). Neurobehavioral organization and the cardinal principle of evaluative bivalence. *Annals of the New York Academy of Science, 702,* 75–102.

Berntson, G. G., Cacioppo, J. T., Binkley, P. F., Uchino, B. N., Quigley, K. S., and Fieldstone, A. (1994). Autonomic cardiac control: III. Psychological stress and cardiac response in autonomic space as revealed by pharmacological blockades. *Psychophysiology, 31,* 599–608.

Berntson, G. G., Cacioppo, J. T., and Fieldstone, A. (1996). Illusions, arithmetic, and the bidirectional modulation of vagal control of the heart. *Biological Psychology, 44,* 1–17.

Berntson, G. G., Cacioppo, J. T., and Quigley, K. S. (1991). Autonomic determinism: The modes of autonomic control, the doctrine of autonomic space, and the laws of autonomic constraint. *Psychological Review, 98,* 459–487.

Berntson, G. G., Sarter, M., and Cacioppo, J. T. (1998). Anxiety and cardiovascular reactivity: The basal forebrain cholinergic link. *Behavioural Brain Research, 94,* 225–248.

Berntson, G. G., Sarter, M. and Cacioppo, J. T. (2003). Ascending visceral regulation of cortical affective information processing. *European Journal of Neuroscience, 18,* 2103–2109.

Bigger, J. T., and Schwartz, P. J. (1994). Markers of vagal activity and the prediction of cardiac death after myocardial infarction. In M. N. Levy and P. J. Schwartz (Eds.), *Vagal Control of the Heart: Experimental Basis and Clinical Implications* (pp 481–508). Armonk, NY: Futura.

Bosch, J. A., Berntson, G. G., Cacioppo, J. T., Dhabhar, F. S., and Marucha, P. T. (2003). Acute stress evokes selective mobilization of T cells that differ in chemokine receptor expression: a potential pathway linking immunologic reactivity to cardiovascular disease. *Brain, Behavior and Immunity, 17,* 251–259.

Burt, R. S. (1986). Strangers, friends, and happiness. GSS Technical Report No. 72. National Opinion Research Center. Chicago: University of Chicago.

Cacioppo, J. T. (1994). Social neuroscience: Autonomic, neuroendocrine, and immune responses to stress. *Psychophysiology, 31,* 113–128.

Cacioppo, J. T., and Berntson, G. G. (1992). Social psychological contributions to the decade of the brain: Doctrine of multilevel analysis. *American Psychologist, 47,* 1019–1028.

Cacioppo, J. T., and Berntson, G. G. (1994). Relationship between attitudes and evaluative space: A critical review with emphasis on the separability of positive and negative substrates. *Psychological Bulletin, 115,* 401–423.

Cacioppo, J. T., Berntson, G. G., Binkley, P. F., Quigley, K. S., Uchino, B. N., and Fieldstone, A. (1994). Autonomic cardiac control: II. Basal response, noninvasive indices, and autonomic space as revealed by autonomic blockades. *Psychophysiology, 31,* 586–598.

Cacioppo, J. T., Berntson, G. G., Sheridan, J. F., and McClintock, M. K. (2000). Multi-level integrative analyses of human behavior: The complementing nature of social and biological approaches. *Psychological Bulletin, 126,* 829–843.

Cacioppo, J. T., Ernst, J. M., Burleson, M. H., McClintock, M. K., Malarkey, W. B., Hawkley, L. C., Kowalewski, R. B., Paulsen, A., Hobson, J. A., Hugdahl, K., Spiegel, D., and Berntson, G. G. (2000). Lonely traits and concomitant physiological processes: The MacArthur Social Neuroscience Studies. *International Journal of Psychophysiology, 35,* 143–154.

Cacioppo, J. T., Gardner, W. L., and Berntson, G. G. (1999). The affect system has parallel and integrative processing components: Form follows function. *Journal of Personality and Social Psychology, 76,* 839–855.

Cacioppo, J. T., Hawkley, L. C., Berntson, G. G., Ernst, J. M., Gibbs, A. C., Stickgold, R., and
    Hobson, J. A. (2002a). Lonely days invade the nights: Social modulation of sleep
    efficiency. *Psychological Science, 13,* 384–387.
Cacioppo, J. T., Hawkley, L. C., Crawford, L. E., Ernst, J. M., Burleson, M. H., Kowalski,
    R. B., Malarkey, W. B., VanCauter, E., and Berntson, G. G. (2002b). Loneliness and
    health: Potential mechanisms. *Psychosomatic Medicine, 64,* 407–417.
Clark, K. B., Naritoku, D. K., Smith, D. C., Browning, R. A., and Jensen, R. A. (1999).
    Enhanced recognition memory following vagus nerve stimulation in human subjects.
    Nature Neuroscience, 1, 94–98.
Cohen, S., Frank, E., Doyle, W. J., Skoner, D. P., Rabin, B. S., and Gwaltney, J. M. (1998).
    Types of stressors that increase susceptibility to the common cold in adults. *Health
    Psychology, 17,* 214–223.
Crites, S. L., Cacioppo, J. T., Gardner, W. L., and Berntson, G. G. (1995). Bioelectric echoes
    from evaluative categorization: II. A late positive brain potential that varies as a
    function of attitude registration rather than attitude report. *Journal of Personality and
    Social Psychology, 68,* 997–1013.
Gardner, W. L., Gabriel, S., and Diekman, A. B. (2000). Interpersonal processes. In J. T.
    Cacioppo, L. G. Tassinary, and G. G. Berntson (Eds.), *Handbook of Psychophysiology*
    (pp. 643–664). New York: Cambridge University Press.
Glaser, R., and Kiecolt-Glaser, J. K. (1994). *Handbook of Human Stress and Immunity.* San
    Diego: Academic Press.
Hawkley, L. C., Bosch, J. A., Engeland, C. G., Marucha, P. T., and Cacioppo, J. T. (in press).
    Loneliness, dysphoria, stress and immunity: A role for cytokines. In N. P. Plotnikoff,
    R. E. Faith, and A. J. Murgo (Eds.), *Cytokines: Stress and immunity* (2nd ed.). Boca
    Raton, LA: CRC Press.
Hawkley, L. C., Burleson, M. H., Berntson, G. G., and Cacioppo, J. T. (2003). Loneliness in
    everyday life: Cardiovascular activity, psychosocial context, and health behaviors.
    Journal of Personality and Social Psychology, 85, 105–120.
Hawkley, L. C., Masi, C. M., Berry, J. D., and Cacioppo, J. T. (2006). Loneliness is a unique
    predictor of age-related differences in systolic blood pressure. *Psychology and Aging, 21,*
    152–164.
Hayward, C. (1995). Psychiatric illness and cardiovascular disease risk. *Epidemiological
    Review, 17,* 129–138.
House, J. S., Landis, K. R., and Umberson, D. (1988). Social relations and health. *Science,
    241,* 123–140.
Jackson, J. H. (1884). Evolution and dissolution of the nervous system (Croonian Lectures).
    Reprinted in J. Taylor (Ed.), 1958, *Selected writings of John Hughlings Jackson.* New
    York: Basic Books.
Kawachi, I., Colditz, G. A., Ascherio, A., Rimm, E. B., Giovannucci, E., Stampfer, M. J., and
    Willett, W. C. (1994). Prospective study of phobic anxiety and risk of coronary heart
    disease in men. *Circulation, 89,* 1992–1997.
Kiecolt-Glaser, J. K., Malarkey, W. B., Cacioppo, J. T., and Glaser, R. (1994). Stressful
    personal relationships: Endocrine and immune function. In R. Glaser and J. K. Kiecolt-
    Glaser (Eds.), *Handbook of Human Stress and Immunity* (pp. 321–339). San Diego:
    Academic Press.
LeDoux, J. E. (1995). Emotion: Clues from the brain. *Annual Review of Psychology, 46,*
    209–235.

Maier, S. F., and Watkins, L. R. (1998). Cytokines for psychologists: Implications of bidi-rectional immune-to-brain communication for understanding behavior, mood, and cognition. *Psychological Review, 105,* 83–107.

Malarkey, W. B., Lipkus, I. M., and Cacioppo, J. T. (1995). The dissociation of catechol-amine and hypothalamic-pituitary-adrenal responses to daily stressors using dexa-methasone. *Journal of Clinical Endocrinology and Metabolism, 80,* 2458–2463.

Padgett, D. A., Sheridan, J. F., Dorne, J., Berntson, G. G., Candelora, J., and Glaser, R. (1998). Social stress and the reactivation of latent herpes simplex virus-type 1. *Pro-ceedings of the National Academy of Sciences, 95,* 7231–7235.

Quan, N., Avitsur, R., Stark, J. L., He, L., Lai, W., Dhabhar, F., Sheridan, J. F. (2003). Molecular mechanisms of glucocorticoid resistance in splenocytes of socially stressed male mice. *Journal of Neuroimmunology, 137,* 51–58.

Sarter, M., and Bruno, J. P. (1997). Cognitive functions of cortical acetylcholine: Toward a unifying hypothesis. *Brain Research Reviews, 23,* 28–46.

Scott, T. R. (1991). A personal view of the future of psychology departments. *American Psychologist, 46,* 975–976.

Seeman, T. E. (1996). Social ties and health: The benefits of social integration. *Annals of Epidemiology, 6,* 442–451.

Selye, H. (1973). Homeostasis and heterostasis. *Perspectives in Biology and Medicine, 16,* 441–445.

Skinner, B. F. (1968). *The Man and His Ideas.* New York: E. P. Dutton.

Uchino, B. N., Cacioppo, J. T., and Kiecolt-Glaser, J. K. (1996). The relationship between social support and physiological processes: A review with emphasis on underlying mechanisms and implications for health. *Psychological Bulletin, 119,* 488–531.

Uchino, B. N., Cacioppo, J. T., Malarkey, W. B., Glaser, R., and Kiecolt-Glaser, J. K. (1995). Appraisal support predicts age-related differences in cardiovascular function in wo-men. *Health Psychology, 14,* 556–562.

Uchino, B. N., Kiecolt-Glaser, J. K., and Cacioppo, J. T. (1992). Age-related changes in cardiovascular response as a function of a chronic stressor and social support. *Journal of Personality and Social Psychology, 63,* 839–846.

Wu, H., Wang, J., Cacioppo, J. T., Glaser, R., Kiecolt-Glaser, J. K., and Malarkey, W. B. (1999). Chronic stress associates with spousal caregiving of patients with dementia is associated with downregulation of B-lymphocyte GH mRNA. *Journal of Gerontology: Medical Sciences, 54,* M212–215.

3

Risk of Hypertensive Heart Disease

The Joint Influence of Genetic and Behavioral Factors

KATHLEEN C. LIGHT, SUSAN S. GIRDLER,
and ALAN L. HINDERLITER

Behavioral Contributions to Hypertension Development: Key Hypotheses

The belief that behavioral factors may contribute to the pathogenesis of hypertension is almost as old as the earliest methods of measuring blood pressure (BP). (For reviews, see Henry and Grim, 1990; Light, 2000; Pickering, 1997.) One group of candidates for increasing hypertension risk may be termed "indexes of environmental exposure." In etiologic models of hypertension, the most frequently mentioned environmental exposure factors are high dietary salt intake and high life stress. High salt intake seems like an area where little new research is needed because our public health messages have emphasized that it has well-documented negative health effects, but the story is not nearly as simple as this implies. Laboratory studies indicate that less than half of the population is salt sensitive, and salt restriction has been associated in at least one major investigation with increased rather than decreased risk of morbidity (Alderman et al., 2000). Stress is also something that the lay public is very familiar with, and most people believe it is well established that stress helps "cause" high BP, heart attack, and stroke, yet physicians and scientists continue to debate among themselves about whether and how stress may play any role (see Manuck, 1994; Pickering and Gerin, 1990).

The linchpin for our research group holding together the apparently contradictory findings on behavior and hypertensive heart disease is this:

Individuals may be high or low in their own susceptibilities—including susceptibility to salt, to stress, and to manifest their physiological responses in ways that promote hypertension and cardiovascular disease. The same behavior (i.e., eating lots of salty food or dealing frequently with high stress at work or at home) that enhances risk in one person may decrease risk or have no effect in his or her neighbor.

The premise that some individuals or groups will show signs of greater sensitivity than others to behavioral factors with the potential to contribute to hypertension is part of what made our research group (and others in the relatively young field of cardiovascular behavioral medicine) think in nontraditional ways about these issues. Our approach has allowed us over the past two decades to look at many types of individual and group differences, including gender and racial group; family history of hypertension; personality and psychosocial traits like hostility, pessimism, and low social resources; and high versus low cardiovascular and renal responders to lab stressors. This chapter is intended to reflect on the history of this research under Light's leadership. This format allows the selective presentation of the accomplishments of one group among many active teams contributing to this field, with the underlying aim of giving more personal viewpoints than are conventional. (For more comprehensive reviews of the literature on individual differences, behavioral factors, and hypertensive heart disease, see Anderson, McNeilly, and Myers, 1992; Berkman, 1985; Frankenhaeuser, 1983; Houston, 1992; Julius et al., 1995; Kaplan and Keil, 1993; Light, 2000; Pickering, 1997, Smith, 1992.)

Our studies of differences in potential risk related to racial group and gender have been less controversial than other studies, since it is well accepted that men have a higher risk of hypertension through the fifth decade of life, when they are surpassed by women, and that black Americans develop hypertension more often than white Americans (Anderson et al., 1992; Light, Girdler, West, and Brownley, 1998). Other traits that are now firmly accepted risk factors but where the underlying physiological changes have been obscure include behavioral and psychosocial traits like depression, pessimism, low and high anger expression, and hostility (Houston, 1992; Smith, 1992). Another individual trait that is still very controversial in relation to hypertension risk is high cardiovascular or neuroendocrine responsivity to stressors. This trait is typically defined as exceeding some group mean response in the magnitude of BP, heart rate (HR), or "stress hormones" like norepinephrine or cortisol, whether individually or as a composite cardiovascular response score, to one or more behavioral tasks, such as reaction time, speech, mental arithmetic, and cold pressor tests. High stress responsivity is typical in patients with established hypertension and those with borderline hypertension, but inconsistency in findings from longitudinal research in persons with initially normal BP has led to skepticism about whether it is a consequence rather than a causal factor in hypertension (Pickering and Gerin, 1990; Manuck, 1994). Greater stress responses may not be truly separate from the other factors described above, for one hypothesized pathway by male gender or being black or lacking social support may contribute to hypertension is through exaggerated responsivity to stress or slow recovery after stress. Lastly, it has recently been at least as exciting to examine factors that reduce or buffer against the adverse physiological and psychological effects of stress exposure, thereby decreasing hypertension risk. This "stress buffers" category includes access to social support, particularly emotional support. Another factor that has been included, but which may also have other beneficial actions, is physical exercise. More recently, religiosity and spirituality have been cited in this category as well. Like the behavioral traits, these stress buffers may potentially influence physiologic stress responsivity, but they may also improve recovery after stress and ability to relax between life demands, thus influencing resting or mean 24-hour BP.

The major findings by our group addressed in this chapter are summarized in Table 3.1. The majority of the investigations described will highlight the interaction between genetic and behavioral traits. In early work, subjects with a genetic predisposition for hypertension, indexed by a positive family history, more frequently showed high BP and HR increases, and those with both a family history and high HR response showed greater slowing of sodium excretion during stress. Recently, a 10-year follow-up study in 103 young men indicated that both high cardiovascular stress responsivity and high current life stress exposure are significant predictors of later BP elevation in men with a positive family history but not in those with no family history of hypertension. These results led to the conclusion that potential behavioral risk factors should be studied in combination with markers of genetic risk for hypertension. Other recent findings to be described include (1) social support buffers the adverse effects of hostility on BP; (2) increasing potassium intake can lower BP levels in salt-sensitive individuals without lowering salt intake; and (3) in postmenopausal women, six months of oral estrogen replacement leads to lower BP and decreased vascular resistance during stress and rest, as well as to decreases in left ventricular mass. We also discuss the factors that encouraged this interdisciplinary research (including access to medical school colleagues and resources and NIH support) and the factors that impeded this work (such as increasing paperwork burden, the trend toward requiring all grants to undergo multiple revisions before funding, and communication barriers). Future goals include efforts to translate these findings into efficient assessments used in routine clinical visits and to work toward increased cross-talk with primary care physicians, with the aim of increasing the effect of this research on preventive efforts and clinical management of hypertension.

Key Elements of Our Interdisciplinary Research Program

Of the numerous investigations our research team has completed over the years, those that have had the greatest influence on behavioral medicine, perhaps, are those in which the behavioral components were not studied alone but were examined in the context of key biomedical risk factors. The most critical of these factors is genetic susceptibility, an area that is now on the verge of breakthroughs in which risk may be defined by the presence of gene variants that are associated with

Table 3.1. Summary of Major Findings on Genetic and Behavioral Risks for Hypertension from UNC Stress and Health Research Program, 1981 to 2001

Date	First author	Findings
1981	Obrist	Men with family history of hypertension show greater heart rate and blood pressure increases to reaction time and other stressful tasks.
1983	Light	Men with family history and/or borderline hypertension with high heart rate response to stress have slow excretion of sodium and water, prolonging the blood pressure increase.
1989	Light	Black men, especially with borderline hypertension, show less cardiac output and greater vasoconstriction responses than white men; β-blockade unmasks an apparently greater α-adrenergic activity.
1989	Sherwood	Aerobic exercise training leads to decreased stress responsivity in type A men.
1992	Light	In a 10-year follow-up study, young men who are high heart rate or systolic blood pressure responders to a reaction time task have higher clinic, work, and home blood pressure at follow-up.
1992	Hinderliter	Left ventricular structure and function is altered in men vs. women and in blacks vs. whites, controlling for blood pressure level.
1992	Light	Slow sodium and water excretion with stress is more common in young black men.
1992	Light	Job strain is related to higher blood pressure at work in young adult men but not women.
1993	Light	Black men and women show greater vasoconstriction than whites during many stressors; men show greater systolic blood pressure increases than women and slower recovery after stressors. Lab stress blood pressure is moderately predictive of blood pressure during real-life events.
1993	Girdler	β-blockade and combined α + β-blockade confirms greater adrenergic activity mediating blood pressure increases in males vs. females.
1995	Girdler	Phase of the menstrual cycle influences gender differences in cardiovascular stress responses, with greater differences when estrogen/progesterone are high.
1995	Light	Women and blacks with high-status jobs have increased work blood pressure if they use a high-effort coping style (John Henryism).
1996	Brownley	In black and white adults, hostile persons with low emotional support from others show higher 24-hour blood pressure, while hostile persons with high support have blood pressure as low as low hostile groups.
1996	Brownley	In sedentary persons with borderline hypertension, blood pressure decreases at work for up to six hours after a single bout of exercise."

(continued)

Table 3.1. (*continued*).

Date	First author	Findings
1996	Hinderliter	In black and white men and women, greater blood pressure response to the cold pressor test predicts increases in left ventricular mass index.
1996	Girdler	In a small biracial sample, greater blood pressure response to the cold pressor was the strongest predictor of clinic systolic blood pressure two years later.
1997	Hinderliter	Blacks show decreased maximal vasodilatory capability even when blood pressure is normal.
1999	Broadwell	Married partners with high social support from partner and family show lower blood pressure and vasoconstriction before, during, and after marital conflict discussions.
1999	West	Among black and white adults who are salt sensitive, increasing potassium intake while maintaining high salt intake lowers blood pressure, similar to restricting salt intake.
1999	Light	In another 10-year follow-up study of 103 men, high-stress responsivity predicted greater incidence of borderline and stage 1 hypertension, but only in those with a family history of hypertension.
2001	Light	In postmenopausal women, six months of conjugated estrogen replacement results in lower resting and stress vasoconstriction and blood pressure levels and decreased left ventricular mass index.

specific physiological alterations—for example, abnormal epithelial sodium channel function or angiotensinogen production or function or faster β-2 adrenergic receptor downregulation (Corvol, Persu, Gimenez-Roquelplo, and Jeunemaitre, 1999; Gratze et al., 1999). During the term of these behavioral investigations, however, the broadest and most common clinical index of genetic susceptibility, positive parental history of hypertension, was the best measure available. Another biomedical risk factor that was highlighted in these studies was ethnic group—specifically, being a black American, a risk factor that reflects some genetic but also important stress exposure components. Incorporating in our models other key biomedical factors, including body mass index, smoking, age, and (in women) menopausal status, has also been important.

Our research team is not a large one. Over the years, the key players have changed, but the makeup of the group has usually been two to three behavioral scientists, a collaborating cardiologist, and another clinician (dental researcher, gynecologist, etc), plus two to three graduate students or other trainees. Teaching and mentoring have been important factors in our success. The graduate students and postdoctoral fellows who have been part of our team during their training years were a truly gifted group of individuals, and they have first-authored many of our group's most influential papers, reflecting both the strength of their ideas and the effort they put into testing them. The opportunity to compete for and receive support from both individual NIH National Research Service predoctoral fellowships and predoctoral training grants in neurobiology and biopsychology were important in facilitating this student-initiated research and further encouraged interdisciplinary work. In several cases, including coauthor Girdler, the mentored students and fellows returned to our group later as independent research scientists, with their own grants and areas of special expertise. Fostering the symbiotic relationships between mentors and trainees has always been a priority in our research group, and we have been conscious that this commitment to mentoring has not competed with but enhanced our productivity.

Our researchers and program enjoyed a number of important advantages that allowed our research to make steady progress in this focused research area. First, our research team always included investigators who did not perceive boundaries between fields and disciplines (such as between psychophysiology and renal physiology, or between cardiology and social psychology) as barriers, but instead saw them as bridges. This required the behavioral scientists in our group to become more knowledgeable about cardiovascular control systems and renal physiology, the physicians to learn about behavioral stressors and physiological responsivity or reactivity, and all team members to learn a common technical language. As the psychologists learned about preload and afterload, renal tubular reabsorption, and so on, the cardiologists and other physicians learned about rapid cardiovascular changes during active and passive coping stressors, about individual differences in sympathetically mediated responses, and about repeated measures of analysis of variance. Second, we were fortunate in maintaining good continuity of extramural research support over many years. Third, the medical school setting in which our research group worked permitted and encouraged interdepartmental collaborations, allowing psychologists to enlist cardiologists and other physicians as co-investigators. This setting also gave us access to the resources of the NIH-supported General Clinical Research Center, which helped underwrite costs of routine blood and urine tests, provided nurse and lab staff support in doing volunteer medical screening and high-level HPLC assays, and provided irreplaceable services such as designing diets and providing all meals for subjects on many days of controlled electrolyte intake. Fourth, our studies were assisted by our having access to then novel and important technological advances, including specialized equipment developed specifically for our purposes by a departmentally supported bioengineer. Fifth and finally, our research advanced in great part because of beneficial critiques and discussions with clinical and basic hypertension researchers worldwide, through their invited visits to our university and their invitations to us to participate in national and international symposia.

In any research history like ours that spans several decades, it is a challenge to be comprehensive yet focused about describing our program's development, to highlight some successes, and also to save some space to comment on what we still must strive to achieve. Thus, we cannot address all areas of our collaborative work, including our recent exciting research on women's health and psychiatric illness. Instead, this review will focus on the history of our research on behavioral factors in hypertension. The overview that begins below describes our transition from basic psychophysiological work to cross-sectional and then longitudinal efforts to establish associations between behavioral factors and BP elevation. This overview also summarizes many of the diverse findings that accrued over this long period, including findings on stress, salt intake, and sodium excretion rates; on ethnic group, gender, and female reproductive hormone-related differences in stress responses; on personality and environment interactions associated with increased ambulatory BP; and on stress buffers, including social support and exercise; as well as on the work leading up to our focus on the combination of genetic and cardiovascular stress responsivity factors. Finally, we provide our insights about barriers that may have impeded our progress or limited the theoretical and clinical impact of our work to date, offering some suggestions for ways that we and others active in this area of research can respond to current needs in this field.

Transition to Focus on BP Control

The Stress and Health Research Program at the University of North Carolina was originally labeled the UNC Psychophysiology Research Laboratory. This change of name reflects the transition in research objectives that occurred over a period of years. Initially, the majority of research projects performed were directed at clarifying basic psychophysiological relationships between cardiovascular activity changes and attentional and motor processes involved in reaction time tasks. Volunteers tested were all healthy young adults, and there was no specific focus on health or disease models.

With the collaborative assistance of physicians from the departments of psychiatry, anesthesiology, and medicine providing critical medical supervision, it was possible to administer autonomic antagonists during behavioral protocols to help clarify the role of sympathetic and parasympathetic activity in mediating the increases and decreases in HR and indirect measures of contractile force. Pharmacological blockade in these early psychophysiology studies showed that the brief phasic changes in HR and cardiac contractile force (occurring in seconds) that Obrist and his colleagues (see Obrist, 1981; Obrist et al., 1978) were initially studying were superimposed on much larger and more sustained increases in these measures (lasting for several minutes) that were related to enhanced cardiac sympathetic activity. Parallel studies performed in chronically instrumented dogs revealed other intriguing results. When the animals moved and struggled and also when they learned to be still except to press a panel to avoid a signaled shock, they demonstrated BP increases that were due to increased cardiac output, while animals who became immobile and passively endured the shocks showed BP increases with no rise in cardiac output. Subsequently, a series of studies in healthy men confirmed that behavioral tasks encouraging sustained active coping or mental effort typically resulted in greater and more sustained HR and cardiac output increases, while tasks that involved passively enduring the stressor led to BP increases with much less cardiac activation.

In early studies employing the β-antagonist propranolol and later studies comparing propranolol with the α-antagonists phentolamine, phenoxibenzamine, and prazosin, and with combined α and β blockade, evidence accumulated supporting the interpretation that the HR and systolic blood pressure (SBP) increases during active coping and mental effort were primarily due to increased β-adrenergic activity that resulted in greater cardiac output (Light, 1981; Obrist, 1981). Diastolic pressure (DBP) typically increased very little or fell during active coping, due to decreases in vascular resistance. In contrast, the BP increases during passive coping and helpless distress involved lesser β-adrenergic and greater α-adrenergic activity, resulting in enhanced vascular constriction.

Early Efforts to Relate Cardiovascular Stress Responses to Hypertension

The transition in to a greater focus on stress-related physiological alterations that could contribute to hypertension pathogenesis had just begun when Light joined the UNC Psychophysiology research team in 1976. Fresh from her doctoral research, which involved evaluation of cognitive and performance deficits in nearly 500 hypertensive and normotensive subjects, Light brought a more clinical perspective and (just as important) a second source of grant support for clinically relevant studies with larger sample sizes. With the imperative desire to understand the current major theories about BP control mechanisms, the works of Bjorn Folkow and Arthur Guyton, as well as other authorities in hypertension were read and discussed. Then Obrist and Light, stimulated and assisted by an exceptional group of students and fellows, began collaborating on several projects concurrently, each directed at examining a different potential physiological alteration induced by stress.

One project led by Light (Light and Obrist, 1980) demonstrated that, during a variety of lab stressors and during home self-determinations, men with borderline hypertension had greater HR and SBP responses than normotensive men had, thus showing both a connection to early pathology and a temporal stability of stress responses. Another line of research led by Obrist with major contributions by Andrew Sherwood, Rick Turner, and Alan Langer, focused on verifying the different hemodynamic states associated with active versus passive coping, and on determining whether high cardiac output responsivity and high vascular responsivity were stable characteristics of individuals (Obrist et al., 1978; Sherwood, Dolan, and Light, 1990; Sherwood et al., 1997). From examining the research of Per Lund-Johansen and Stevo Julius, clear parallels were noted between the high cardiac output state during active coping tasks and that which characterizes early borderline hypertension. The high vascular resistance state during passive coping tasks more closely resembles the hemodynamic pattern associated with fixed essential hypertension.

Noting that premenopausal women have a lower risk of becoming hypertensive, and concerned that women were generally understudied in cardiovascular research, another series of investigations by Light and Girdler focused on gender and menstrual cycle differences in cardiovascular responses to stress (see Light, Girdler, et al., 1998). Influenced by Guyton's position that hypertension pathogenesis must at some point involve an alteration in the body's long-term BP control system—that is, renal sodium and water excretion—a third series of studies examined whether behavioral stress and the sympathetic activity it elicits may lead to slowed excretion in animal models and in humans. This type of slowed excretion was first demonstrated during shock-avoidance stress in saline-loaded dogs. In humans, Light and colleagues (Light, Koepke, Obrist, and Willis, 1983) replicated this pattern of stress-induced slowing of sodium and fluid excretion, but only in high-stress responders with risk factors for later hypertension. In fact, exposure to continuous behavioral stressors for 40 to 60 minutes elicited two distinct response patterns: *(1)* faster excretion in subjects who were low-stress responders or who had no risk factors for hypertension (which is normal in view of the rise in BP serving as a force to increase both filtration and excretion), or *(2)* slower excretion in high-stress responders with hypertensive parents or borderline hypertension (a response that is maladaptive in terms of magnifying the size and duration of the stress-related BP increase).

During the period of this initial switch to focusing on behavioral tasks that alter the function of several physiological systems involved in BP control, the research group benefited from direct feedback by several of the physician researchers whose work had influenced the shift. Julius and Folkow, as well as two leaders in animal research on stress-induced hypertension, James Henry and David Anderson, all visited the laboratory and consulted with the research team on future research directions. Julius in particular played a strong role by also inviting Obrist and later Light to participate in international symposia on borderline hypertension, where our findings and those of clinical researchers in that special research field could be compared and integrated. With the helpful insights of these pioneers, known for their ability to extrapolate and synthesize, as well as to complete seminal investigations, and those of other behavioral scientists like Steve Manuck (see Manuck, 1994) whose research was in many ways operating along similar tracks with our own, certain messages and problems became clear.

First, providing direct evidence of the linkage of any hemodynamic, renal, and adrenergic patterns of responses during active or passive coping to essential hypertension in humans would not be easy. Hypertension pathogenesis may require decades, as reflected by Lund-Johansen's prospective work on the hemodynamic shift associated with moving from borderline to fixed essential hypertension (Lund-Johansen, 1979). Second, chronic stress exposure can be directly manipulated in animal models but not humans, and furthermore there were no well-established methods of assessing total stress burden over a period of years in humans. Third, even though prospective research would provide the most definitive evidence in humans of any relationships between physiologic stress response patterns and later onset of hypertension, such research is very time-consuming and costly, tends to outlast the careers of individual researchers (as was true for Obrist), and thus requires extensive justification before it is undertaken.

Cross-Sectional Research to Reinforce the Plausible Link to Hypertension

The first efforts to establish links between behavioral stress response patterns and hypertension focused on individual differences in these responses. Some individuals showed much greater HR and BP increases than others to the same tasks. Also, as described, some individuals demonstrated faster sodium and water excretion rates during stress while others showed slowing of excretion. Following medical models, which employ family history of hypertension and current borderline hypertension as two of the better established risk factors for later fixed hypertension, cardiovascular and renal responses of individuals with and without hypertensive parent(s) and with and without borderline hypertension were compared (Light, 1981; Light et al., 1983; Obrist, Light, James, and Strogatz, 1987). In support of the hypothesized link, the high-risk groups demonstrated greater HR and BP increases to the behavioral stressors than did the low-risk groups. Also, men with a positive family history or current borderline hypertension tended to show slowing of sodium and water excretion during stress, if they were also in the group showing above-average HR and BP increases. This was our first strong signal that it is the combination of a high cardiovascular stress response with a genetic susceptibility that is most strongly related to alterations in BP control systems that may eventually lead to hypertension. It was a forerunner of the same combination that would relate to BP increases over time in our later follow-up investigation.

Other research efforts focused on establishing that high cardiovascular stress responsivity is a stable trait of some individuals. These studies examined the relationship of systolic (SBP) and diastolic (DBP) pressure, HR, cardiac output, and vascular resistance responses across different stressors within the same session and in a test-retest format over time. The stability of HR and SBP and both hemodynamic measures were consistently high in these investigations, even over intervals as long as 10 years (see Turner, Sherwood, and Light, 1994; Sherwood et al., 1997). Actual levels of HR and BP were more stable than reactivity scores (stress-induced changes from baseline levels). In contrast, DBP responses were far less stable. Likewise, there was some evidence that cardiovascular responses to active coping tasks were somewhat more stable than responses to the painful cold pressor test. With the development of new technology for noninvasive ambulatory BP monitoring, including a system whose prototype was developed by our bioengineer, another test of the stability of stress responses was examined. This test examined the relationship of lab cardiovascular stress responses with BP responses obtained during natural life events (Light, Turner, Hinderliter, and Sherwood, 1993b). Relationships obtained in this test were only modestly supportive of the importance of the relationship of lab stress responses; that is, correlations were significant in many cases, particularly when levels rather than reactivity scores were used, but relationships were not much stronger than seen between resting baseline levels and ambulatory levels. This created a significant credibility issue, particularly for clinicians, since it was during this same time frame when ambulatory BP levels were shown to be better predictors of left ventricular hypertrophy than were clinic BP determinations (see Pickering and Gerin, 1990).

Echocardiography and Impedance Cardiography as Critical Tools

As the technology for 24-hour ambulatory BP monitoring was progressing and becoming an integral part of the research group's investigations, cardiologist Alan Hinderliter joined the department of medicine at the University of North Carolina. Earlier in his training, Hinderliter had been mentored by Stevo Julius and was familiar with both our prior research and the related perspective of clinical practitioners on the autonomic and hemodynamic patterns seen in borderline versus fixed essential hypertension. In addition to augmenting our team's strengths relating to the clinical side of hypertensive heart disease, Hinderliter provided critical skill in echocardiographic assessment of left ventricular structure and function. The importance of this type of noninvasive assessment was that increased left ventricular mass had been shown to be the strongest predictor of subsequent cardiac morbidity and mortality other than increasing age; in fact, it was a stronger predictor than hypertension was (Levy, Garrison, Savage, Kannel, and Castelli, 1990). Further, other studies indicated that changes in left ventricular mass considered clinically important were detectable with interventions after only a few months. Thus, much shorter term prospective research was possible with this as the key outcome variable than would be true with hypertension onset as the central outcome.

At this same time, through dedicated efforts of our bioengineer J. Stanford Hutcheson and Dr. Andrew Sherwood, noninvasive assessment of stroke volume and cardiac output during behavioral activities estimated by impedance cardiography was also added to our arsenal of technologies (Sherwood, Allen, et al., 1990). When cardiac output was obtained concurrently with BP, total vascular resistance could be calculated from a standard formula, thus permitting our first solid look at behavioral effects on whole-body vasoconstriction and vasodilatation. Another important factor that influenced the course of our research at this time was an NIH request for applications (RFA) to study stress and BP in African Americans. We were aware of findings by Anderson (Anderson, Lane, Monou, Williams, and Houseworth, 1988) indicating that forearm blood flow (an index of skeletal muscle dilatation) failed to increase as much in black men as in white men during mental arithmetic. Our own initial study (Light and Sherwood, 1989) with borderline hypertensive and normotensive black and white men examining impedance-derived cardiac output and vascular resistance response to active coping stressors before and after β-blockade indicated that cardiac output responses were reduced and vasoconstriction was enhanced in the black men. Also, β-receptor blockade caused a marked rise in vascular resistance during the stressor, suggesting that an ⟨-adrenergic effect had been unmasked and that this effect was greater in the black men. This RFA provided the impetus for us to formalize a previously informal relationship with social epidemiologist Sherman James, then on the faculty at the UNC School of Public Health. James is best known for his development of the John Henryism Active Coping Scale, which assessed the preference for high-effort coping as a trait measure of certain individuals. His insights provided the first stimulus for our group to study interactive effects of behavioral traits with each other and with education, income, and job status.

Our proposal in response to the RFA was funded both initially and later, and this support over more than a decade led to a series of investigations. In terms of gaining clinical credibility, it led to work demonstrating that there is evidence of greater thickening in the walls of the left ventricle in nonhypertensive young black adults compared with age- and BP-matched whites, and in men relative to age-matched premenopausal women, as well as increased left ventricular mass in those subjects with borderline hypertension (Hinderliter, Light and Willis, 1991, 1992a, b). This research also reconfirmed in a much larger sample ($n = 155$) our prior finding that black subjects demonstrate greater vasoconstriction (or blunted vasodilatation) during behavioral stressors than do white subjects. A later investigation, led by Hinderliter, of maximal forearm vasodilatory capacity showed that black subjects had evidence of vascular structural changes (hypertrophy) that occur concurrently with their cardiac hypertrophy (Hinderliter et al., 1997). Other studies directed by Girdler and by Sherwood using sympathetic antagonists and agonists suggested that another factor relating to these vascular response differences between blacks and whites was the increased ratio of ?-adrenergic to β-adrenergic activity within the body's resistance vessels (Girdler, Hinderliter, and Light, 1993; Sherwood, Hinderliter, and Light, 1995). This grant also supported a comparison of the contribution of circulating epinephrine and norepinephrine to the different responses of high-cardiac reactors, high-vascular reactors, and low reactors to behavioral stress (Light, Turner, Hinderliter, Girdler, and Sherwood, 1994).

One of the most important papers resulting from this research employed a sample of 133 healthy black and white men and women, but the findings did not focus on ethnic group or gender differences. In this study, Hinderliter and associates (Hinderliter, Light, Girdler, Willis, and Sherwood, 1996) demonstrated that SBP responses during laboratory stressors and during natural life demands (mean ambulatory levels at work) were stronger predictors of increased left ventricular mass index and relative wall thickness than was either clinic BP or baseline BP.

Consistent with work by Treiber and colleagues (Treiber, McCaffrey, and Pflieger, 1993) in a biracial sample of children, in our study in adults greater SBP response to the cold pressor test was the strongest predictor of greater left ventricular mass index, even after adjusting for baseline BP. Similarly, in a subset of 40 of these subjects, SBP during the cold pressor was the strongest predictor of SBP clinic levels two years later, even after adjusting for baseline levels (Girdler et al., 1996). These results indicate that responses to lab and natural life demands do provide additional prognostically important information beyond that which can be obtained from clinic BP levels.

Salt and Potassium Intake, Hemodynamics, and Salt Sensitivity

Out studies of ethnic group differences were expanded to look at salt intake and elimination interacting with stress, based on prior work showing that black men and women are more frequently salt sensitive than are other ethnic groups. In addition to support from research grants awarded to our investigators through the National Institutes of Health (NIH), the UNC General Clinical Research Center (GCRC) fostered this research project in many ways. The GCRC director and staff facilitated our work by encouraging interdepartmental input and review, by providing medical staff to assist with blood drawing and screening physicals, by underwriting the cost of routine clinical blood tests, and particularly by setting up an HPLC system for performing catecholamine assays. The GCRC Research Kitchen also made possible other studies involving many days of controlled salt and potassium intake by our research group, which was focusing on ethnic groups' differences in salt sensitivity and stress-related changes in excretion.

Our first study (Light and Turner, 1992) focused on salt elimination and stress in ethnic groups, but only young black men and white men were included. Our results confirmed our hypothesis that black men were more likely to demonstrate slow sodium and water excretion during stress. Because a larger proportion of the black men had hypertensive parents, this again suggested a connection to genetic susceptibility. An additional study in which urinary clearance measures during stress were assessed with and without β-receptor blockade (propranolol) suggested that tubular reabsorption was increased in slow sodium excreters, but that this effect was unchanged after β-blockade. Together, these findings suggested a link to α-adrenergic activity and enhanced vasoconstriction during stress.

Our most recent investigation of sodium and stress (led by Light, with major contributions from Hinderliter and fellow Sheila West) attempted to clarify the effects of high and low salt and potassium (K) intake, as well as stress, in black and white men and women. Each volunteer was asked to complete a sequence of four different dietary regimens, each lasting a full 8 to 10 days. One diet was their own usual free-intake diet, but each of the others required the subject to eat and drink only foods and fluids provided by the GCRC kitchen, including a low-salt/low-K diet, a high-salt/low-K diet, and a high-salt/high-K diet. Even with 5-hour lab studies and 24-hour ambulatory BP assessments on each diet, we were able to obtain complete data on 67 working men and women, aged 22 to 48, including 32 black individuals.

Our first reports from this study emphasized two things. First, in these short-term interventions, only about half the sample showed BP increases on the high-salt versus the low-salt diet (that is, were salt sensitive). Adverse increases in total and LDL cholesterol and in circulating catecholamines were seen in response to the low-salt diet, and these effects were consistent with a number of previous metabolic investigations of salt restriction. In the salt-resistant individuals, these effects were seen together with increases, not decreases, in BP (West et al., 1997). These findings suggest that clinicians should be aware that recommending salt restriction may have adverse health consequences for some individuals, and that it might be best to limit this recommendation to those whose BP can be shown to fall with a low-salt diet. Second, our results showed that the majority (76%) of the salt-sensitive subjects tested demonstrated the same beneficial reduction in BP seen with salt restriction simply by increasing their potassium intake while maintaining the same high-salt diet (West, Light, et al., 1999). The similar decreases in BP with low salt intake and with potassium supplementation was maintained during baseline, during both active and passive coping stressors, and during post-stress recovery. Because more black subjects than whites subjects are salt sensitive, these results are especially relevant to preventive clinical strategies for African Americans. Other findings from this study are that slow sodium excretion during stress is minimized after combined α- and β- receptor blockade. Premenopausal women are also less likely than men to show such slowed excretion during stress.

Initial Studies of Life Stress Exposure in Relation to BP

The effect of the leap in the complexity of our model was as large as the leaps in technology after we began to use stress exposure and cardiovascular stress responsivity as independent measures in our studies. Our first efforts with this approach were relatively simple. First, we divided college student subjects into those who were high and those who were low in two coping styles that were potentially maladaptive: keeping to yourself and blaming yourself when stress happens. The high-self-focused students had higher ambulatory BP throughout the events of a high-stress exam day, including late that night hours after the test was over, while no group differences were observed in BP on a non-exam day (Dolan, Sherwood, and Light, 1992). Second, we studied working young men and women and found that men reporting high job strain had higher BP throughout an eight-hour workday than other men but that job strain was not related to high BP in women (Light, Turner, and Hinderliter, 1992).

Next, our approach became slightly more complex. Guided by James's hypothesis (James, Hartnett, and Kalsbeek, 1983; James, Strogatz, Wing, and Ramsey,

1987) that BP would be increased in persons who are high-effort copers in an adverse environment, we examined the effect of John Henryism in black and white men and women with high-status jobs versus those with lower-status jobs (Light et al., 1995). Because our sample was young, healthy, and highly educated and all were employed, it was markedly different from the rural black population in which John Henryism was first related to higher BP. In our sample, ambulatory BP at work was higher in women and in blacks with high-status jobs if they were high in John Henryism. We interpreted these results as reflecting the effect of chronic active coping in a highly demanding work environment, one where women and blacks have few peers and less peer support, plus where they may feel under additional scrutiny and pressure to succeed because of their minority status.

Behavioral Buffers against Adverse Cardiovascular Effects of Stress

The first potential stress buffer that drew our attention was exercise. Again, this was based on the medical model of hypertension, in which increasing aerobic exercise is one of the first behavioral recommendations made by clinicians in cases of high normal or borderline hypertension. Our initial study (Sherwood, Light, and Blumenthal, 1989) compared cardiovascular stress responses in borderline hypertensive men before and after a three-month intervention focusing either on aerobic fitness or strength training. BP responses to stress were attenuated after aerobic training but not after strength training. This finding was not easy to replicate, however, which led us to consider that the benefits of extended exercise training may be difficult to separate from short-term benefits of a single bout of exercise. Our subsequent work focused on documenting the type and duration of potential reductions in cardiovascular stress responses after a single bout of exercise. Sedentary individuals were tested after 20 minutes of controlled, moderate-intensity exercise and, on a separate day, after a similar period of rest, in counterbalanced order. In this work (led by predoctoral trainees Brownley and West), first we found that exercise led to marked reductions in total vascular resistance during the postexercise period (West, Brownley, and Light, 1999). Peak BP responses to controlled laboratory stressors were modestly reduced during the first hour after exercise. When the 31 subjects left the lab and went to their workplaces, wearing our ambulatory BP monitor, some subjects continued to show BP decreases after exercise (Brownley, West, Hinderliter, and Light, 1996). In the 11 subjects with elevated BP but not those with normal BP, pressure levels during the demands of their jobs were significantly lower on the exercise day than on the control day for five hours after the exercise. Thus, in sedentary men and women, all subjects benefited from one bout of moderate exercise by having a brief reduction in peak BP response to stress, and this was associated with lower vascular resistance. Those sedentary persons with higher BP levels showed more enduring BP reductions, which appeared to blunt BP responses to the natural stress of job-related activities.

The second stress buffer whose benefits have been supported by our research findings is social support (see Cohen, 1988). Support from family and friends has been prospectively related to decreased cardiovascular morbidity and mortality in both patients with confirmed coronary heart disease and in initially healthy older adults. Health benefits of social support can come from its direct effects (help getting to the doctor, help adhering to treatment recommendation, social contact to encourage health-promoting behaviors like losing weight and quitting smoking). Separating these effects from potential stress-buffering effects of support is a challenge. In our first investigation (Brownley, Light, and Anderson, 1996), clinic and workday ambulatory BP levels were examined in 129 black and white men and women. Those subjects scoring high in hostility were assumed to be more susceptible to stress. Emotional (appraisal) support was examined as a potential stress buffer. Subjects who scored high in hostility but reported low emotional support, as expected, had significantly higher SBP and DBP in the clinic, at work, and at home than had subjects low in hostility. In contrast, high-hostile subjects reporting high emotional support had BP levels as low as low-hostile men and women; their support appears to buffer them against the adverse BP effects of their hostile outlook. These results have a parallel in the literature on Type A. For example, Orth-Gomer and Unden (1990) found that Type A men with high social support had a much lower mortality rate than those with low social support and, in fact, did not differ from Type B men. Other studies by our group have indicated that low social support is associated with subclinical depressive symptoms and high sympathetic nervous system activity in women (Light, Kothandapani, and Allen, 1998), and that high family and partner support is associated with reduced cardiovascular responses during conflict discussion among married couples (Broadwell and Light, 1999). Altogether, evidence is building that social support, especially emotional support, may be an effective buffer reducing adverse cardiovascular effects that occur during stress.

The Use of Longitudinal Approaches in a Small Research Group

Despite their drawbacks, the value of the data obtained from following high and low cardiovascular stress responders over periods as long as 10 years and reevaluating their BP level led us to attempt a number of such studies. Unlike multicenter or large-scale epidemiological investigations, the biggest drawbacks to these studies were the smaller number of subjects making up the initial test group, the use of samples of convenience rather than population representative samples, and (due to lack of financial support for formal subject retention efforts), a relative high rate of loss to follow-up studies. In our first 10- to 15-year follow-up study (Light, Dolan, Davis, and Sherwood., 1992), the findings indicated that high HR and SBP level during an active coping task and high HR increases from baseline (reactivity) were each associated with higher clinic and ambulatory BP levels at follow-up. However, the sample sizes were very small, and the study did not differentiate subjects who had high BP at both initial test and follow-up from those who developed increased BP over time.

The second 10-year follow-up study (Light et al., 1999) involved a similar population of young men, but the sample retrieved at follow-up was larger ($n = 103$) and was more representative of the original sample. The second investigation also had several distinct advantages over the first. The primary advantage was in the greater completeness of the model to be tested, and the direct connections between the model and clinical models of hypertension risk. Instead of examining the relationship of high cardiovascular stress responsivity by itself or after adjustment for traditional predictors, the new model tested a hypothesized interaction between stress responsivity and family history of hypertension, the clinician's preferred index of hypertension risk. The rationale was that high stress responsivity would increase risk of later BP elevation more in those individuals with than without a genetic susceptibility to develop hypertension. This position was based in large part on animal models of stress-induced hypertension, which have demonstrated that hypertension development depends as much on the animal's genetic strain as on the chronic stress exposure. Thus, as posited by Harshfield and Grim (1997), it is the combination of the "wrong genes in the wrong environment" that leads to high likelihood of hypertension, whether that environment is high-salt intake or high in stress exposure. A second important advantage to the second follow-up study was that a measure of stress exposure, the Daily Stress Inventory score, was also available. Thus, the model tested the effects of stress responsivity in both high and low genetic susceptibility groups and in high and low stress exposure groups. Finally, the study focused on clinic BP, the gold standard measure for family physicians and clinic practitioners.

The results of this second follow-up study are especially encouraging. The findings indicate that although men with a positive family history, the traditional clinical predictor, had a modestly increased risk of a rise in BP over 10 years, the men who had both a family history and were in the top quartile in cardiovascular stress responsivity had a much greater increase in risk. There was over a sevenfold increase in risk associated with the combination of these factors, as opposed to a less than twofold risk associated with family history alone. In addition, high stress exposure also enhanced change in BP level at follow-up in the more susceptible groups. High daily stress was associated with greater BP increases among high stress reactors after controlling for effects of family history, and among low stress reactors if they also had a positive family history. The findings indicate strongly that there is substantial plasticity in the relationship between genetic factors and hypertension development. The outcome (hypertension development or not) in those with high genetic susceptibility (family history) is environmentally modifiable, influenced by both level of exposure to environmental stress and by the individuals' characteristic responsivity to stress, which may itself have both genetic and past experiential determinants. On the basis of these observations, we asserted that the original so-called Reactivity Hypothesis was oversimplified and needed to be updated. Its suggested replacement, the Gene and Environment Modulated Reactivity Hypothesis, states that cardiovascular stress responses will be related to greater risk of later BP elevation if they occur in individuals with high genetic susceptibility and/or those with high daily stress exposure.

A consistent theme in our collaborative research was to clarify both behavioral and physiological gender differences in responses to stress (e.g., Girdler, Hinderliter, and Light, 1993; Girdler and Light, 1994; Light, Girdler, et al., 1998; Light, Turner, Hinderliter, and Sherwood, 1993a). These findings, together with other observations suggesting that estrogen has vasodilatory effects, led us to hypothesize that estrogen may protect women against adverse vascular responses evoked by sympathetic activity during behavioral stress. Recently, our medical school collaborations expanded by inclusion of gynecologists John Steege and Ellen Wells, permitting us to compete for RFA funds focusing on collaborative studies of women's health. For this project, a shorter seven-month prospective design was used to examine the benefits of oral estrogen replacement on cardiovascular stress responses and left ventricular structure and function in a randomized, double-blind, placebo-controlled design. This investigation (jointly directed by all three authors) involved a pretest, with retesting after three months and six months of treatment with either conjugated estrogens or placebo. The findings showed that BP and vascular resistance during baseline but especially during behavioral stressors in the lab were reduced after six months of estrogen replacement (both with and without progestin replacement) but showed a tendency to increase after six months with placebo (Light et al., 2001). Equally important, left ventricular mass index was reduced after six months of estrogen replacement but not after placebo. Given the recent findings of greater—not less—cardiovascular risk in long-term users of HRT in the Womens Health Initiative (WHI), it is important to note that our study showed greater benefits in women who, unlike the large majority of WHI participants, were less than five years since onset of menopause (Light et al., 2001), and in women who were nonsmokers (Girdler et al., 2000). Finally, ambulatory BP was reduced in hypertensive but not normotensive women after six months of estrogen replacement, while vascular resistance reductions were significantly greater in hypertensive women, indicating the importance of susceptibility to hypertension in this model as well (Adamian et al., 1999). This type of shorter-term intervention is a striking example of both the value of interdisciplinary collaboration and the clinical relevance of findings from behavioral approaches in augmenting the understanding of previously undiscerned effects of common treatments like estrogen replacement.

Factors Impeding Interdisciplinary Interactions or Limiting Impact on the Field

Despite the relative success of our research program and that of other similar programs focusing on behavioral factors, for many years the effect on the clinical cardiology research field was modest. There has been a notable change in our field's impact on clinical research in the recent past, as reflected in major multicenter trials such as the NIH-sponsored ENRICHD trial (Enhancing Recovery in Coronary Heart Disease), which will test whether interventions aimed at ameliorating depression and social isolation may improve survival after myocardial infarction. However, the effect of the findings of our field on preventive or therapeutic practices in hypertension is still relatively limited. A number of factors have contributed to these limitations.

One factor is that the majority of the publications from this research appeared in behavioral journals. In this era of specialization, behavioral journals (even those most widely read by other scientists in behavioral medicine) are rarely read by physicians who manage the care of patients with hypertension or more serious cardiological disorders. Physicians in family practice or general medicine who are not researchers but clinicians have little access to these journals, and their findings are not often synopsized in the major reviews appearing in journals they have access to. It is often difficult to get papers with a behavioral focus published in clinical hypertension journals, in part because the reviewers may not be sophisticated in regard to behavioral issues, and in part because the complexity of the design, procedures, and analytic strategies employed in many behavioral studies are difficult to package in the limited length preferred by most clinical journals. Among our publications and those of our colleagues at other institutions, those appearing in *Hypertension* or other clinical journals have had the widest impact on physicians. Recently, more behavioral papers are appearing in these journals, indicating an enhanced receptiveness to such work. Thus, while continuing to publish in our own specialty journals, further efforts to publish in journals widely read by clinical practitioners in hypertension are vital.

A related issue is the current need for research focusing on behavioral factors that is specifically designed for ready translation to clinical practice. In the past, our central goal was to demonstrate relationships between biobehavioral measures and abnormal physiological adjustments or development of disease, but we should now be ready to step beyond this boundary to try to show that this relationships we established can be useful in developing prevention and treatment strategies. However, this era is one of extreme consciousness about the cost-effectiveness of each minute spent by a physician or practitioner with the patient. Adding even 10 minutes to the average preventive clinic visit or initial examination must be strongly justified. In sharp contrast is the time it takes to obtain the complex array of information gained from our laboratory studies (which typically involve 2–5 hours of psychophysiological stress testing plus 30–60 minutes of questionnaire completion and/or clinical interviews plus 24-hour ambulatory monitoring per subject). As researchers, our compulsiveness (a trait strongly selected for in getting grants funded) causes us to prefer greater completeness over greater efficiency. Also, in one case where our cardiologist and behavioral scientists worked together to develop a grant aimed at designing and validating a salt sensitivity test that could be used by clinicians with no access to research kitchens or special facilities, using the new widely available frozen meals that specify sodium and potassium content, the reviewers found these aims of the grant less compelling than others focusing on biological pathways. The position underlying this grant, namely that salt restriction is not a totally benign intervention for everyone and that its use might best be restricted to persons confirmed as salt sensitive, is a politically sensitive issue in the United States, where for decades physicians and patients alike have been targets of the public health message that you should lower salt intake to lower your BP.

Another factor that has burdened research in this field in general is that over time, our researchers have been spending more and more of their time writing grant applications, and less and less time is available for writing papers. One reason for this is the current theme of accountability, which has increased the paperwork burden for everyone and has made it less politically correct for departments to underwrite support for time spent on research-related activities. Salary support for our bioengineer whose talents were so important in our group's advances would now be required to come entirely from grants. A second very important factor is the fact that virtually all new NIH grants and even competing renewal applications from established investigators must be submitted for review two or even three times to receive funding. The climate for research funding has been so competitive that it has created a mind set among reviewers that no grant for which they can devise any improvements should be funded until the investigators commit to those improvements by resubmitting. This increases burden on both the investigators and the reviewers. It also creates the imperative of having two or more active grants in any research group that wants to maintain continuity of staff, because with only one grant there would always be a hiatus in funding during resubmission.

Our future progress will also be accelerated if we are able to develop tools to assess "total stress burden." Researchers have traditionally focused on one aspect of life stress, such as job strain, marital/family dynamics, caretaker burden, or personality traits. For the strongest clinical impact, it would be more efficient to employ brief but effective methods for assessing multiple stress-exposure variables and stress buffers. The fact that hypertension develops over considerable time, and therefore that these stress-exposure and stress-buffer variables change over time, makes this task more challenging.

Other factors that created obstacles in performing interdisciplinary work include recent changes in clinical duties and expectations in medical schools. In teaching departments like psychology, pharmacology, and cell biology, obtaining grant support increases research responsibilities, but this is typically balanced by decreasing other responsibilities. In clinical departments, there is often no re-duction in clinical responsibilities or only a token reduction relative to the time and effort required by the research. When the physician is only a co-investigator rather than the principal investigator, as is often true on behavioral investigations, and both the prestige and the indirect costs dollars will go to another department, this type of disincentive to collaboration is especially common. Interdisciplinary research frequently requires that five or more co-authors share the credit on important papers. Sometimes the second and third author will have contributed almost as much time to the project as the first author, yet the recognition for first authorship remains far greater. A trade-off factor that our research group has valued is that most of our large interdisciplinary projects have led to separate first-authored papers for all major investigators.

More Interdisciplinary Studies Linking Behavior to Hypertension Are Still Needed

The progress that social science researchers have made in the area of hypertension over the past two decades is tremendous. Both patients and physicians are now more aware of the need to address behavioral factors in patient care. The stage has been set, and now the challenge for us is to make our research increasingly relevant to these groups. In terms of future research, it will be more important than ever for behavioral researchers to consider the clinician's views and restrictions in their planning. Most BP assessments will continue to be made in a few minutes during a clinic visit, and most decisions about hypertension prevention and treatment will be handled by primary-care physicians and health-care providers under continuing pressure to streamline and prove the cost-effectiveness of any tests or interventions. The clinicians' needs and priorities have not been much considered in our prior investigations, and if we are to have an expanded impact on decisions made in the clinic, future research tailored to fit clinical priorities represents a new and important opportunity for social scientists focusing on hypertension.

One interdisciplinary study that is a good first step in this process is to develop and test a composite assessment battery including an array of stress-exposure variables, stress-susceptibility factors (including cardiovascular responsivity to stress), and stress buffers. The battery should be designed with maximum efficiency in regard to clinic visit time, and with consideration of limiting patient burden at home as well. This will require developing brief but valid assessment methods for hostility, anger expression, depression, and other key psychosocial measures, as well as social support and habitual exercise patterns. We have already developed a model for a home test of salt sensitivity of BP that could be evaluated for feasibility and effectiveness.

Another interdisciplinary study that would be highly desirable would be a larger multisite prospective study modeled after our recent 10-year follow-up study, which is designed to examine stress responsivity as a composite index determined based on several cardiovascular measures and responses to multiple stressors. Most importantly, stress responsivity will be evaluated in combination with genetic susceptibility to hypertension, and with stress exposure and access to stress buffers as expected modulators of any relationships to later hypertension. It would be ideal if, in addition to family history of hypertension, genetic profiling can be done to clarify which subjects show particular gene variants related to altered sodium channel function, to angiotensinogen function, or to adrenergic receptor distribution, function, or regulation.

Thus, without changing the focus of our current and planned investigations, there are still certain steps that we as researchers can take to increase our visibility across disciplines and our impact on the field of research and clinical care in hypertension:

1. We can make an effort to submit more often to clinical hypertension, cardiology, and general medicine journals.
2. We can encourage the leaders in our field to prepare reviews written to be comprehensible for primary-care physicians about the implications of recent behavioral research.
3. We can increase our efforts to interact directly with primary-care physicians by attending and giving presentations at the meetings of their national and international societies and by seeking advice from their members at our own institutions.

Our past and current preclinical research documenting biobehavioral contributions to health and disease, which will also continue, may serve as both the foundation and the impetus for this expected era of new developments in our field. It is our expectation that the era of biobehavioral research in hypertension and cardiovascular health is only beginning, and the promise of the future is brighter than ever.

Postscript

Since 2003, we have greatly expanded our interdisciplinary research focused on the biobehavioral processes linked to the multiple health benefits of loving support from spouses and partners, and of close physical and emotional contact with them and with other family members. We have been able to show that for both men and women, 10 minutes of sitting next to their husbands or wives, holding hands and talking about how they first became attached to each other, has a powerful stress buffering effect that lasts even when the spouse is no longer present. Men and women who had this warm partner contact prior to separating and then performing a speech stressor showed a 50% reduction in their SBP and HR increases to this task compared to others who simply rested alone prior to the task (Grewen, Anderson, Girdler and Light, 2003).

Similarly, in mothers of infants who performed the same speech task on two occasions, once after 10 minutes of cuddling their infants and once after leaving their babies at home and resting alone, SBP increases were lower after baby holding (Light, Smith, Johns, Hofheimer, and Amico, 2000). When we examined whether this stress-buffering effect was greater in mothers or couples who showed greater plasma levels of oxytocin (a neuropeptide associated in animal models with both onset of maternal behavior and pair-bonding), we found that higher oxytocin was not associated with decreases in BP reactivity to the speech task, but was linked to lower baseline, recovery and overall BP levels in mothers and other women. This, however, was not true in men (Light, Smith, Johns, Hofheimer and Amico, 2000; Light, Grewen and Amico, 2005; Grewen, Girdler, Amico and Light, 2005). We were also able to link greater oxytocin levels to stronger partner-relationship quality in both men and women, and to more frequent hugs in women.

Oxytocinergic neurons extend from the paraventricular nucleus of the brain to contact many of the major regulatory areas of the CNS (e.g., the noradrenergic, opioidergic, and serotonergic pathways), but is integrated particularly with the dopaminergic reward pathways, presumably making contact between spouses and between mothers and infants rewarding (Carter, 1998; Uvnas-Moberg, 2003, Insel and Young, 2001). Oxytocinergic activity has also been linked to lower central alpha adrenergic tone, which appears to be responsible for long-term BP decreases that occur when daily systemic administration of oxytocin is given to animals (Petersson, Lundeberg, and Uvnas-Moberg, 1999). Our own findings in mothers of infants suggest that increased BP (both during lab and home monitoring) and higher negative affect is seen in mothers with low plasma oxytocin responsivity. In these studies, oxytocin responses in high-responder mothers were enhanced after 10 minutes of baby holding and play compared to responses of the same women on another day after 10 minutes resting alone without their babies. Similarly, waking BP levels at home were lower in these high oxytocin-responding mothers than in low oxytocin responders. Together, these observations suggest that baby holding and cuddling can increase oxytocin activity in more responsive mothers, and this may be associated with decreases in BP and more positive mood states. Conversely, low oxytocin responses may be related to increased maternal BP, negative emotions and stress sensitivity.

These findings build on research in monogamous species of mammals such as prairie voles, where oxytocin has previously been shown to play a major role in the development of pair-bonds especially in females; a sister peptide, vasopressin, plays a more major role in formation of pair-bonds in male voles (Carter, 1998). We suggest that some of the cardiovascular benefits of loving family relationships and recent warm contact with a loved one may be mediated via oxytocin, particularly in women, but that decreases in BP reactivity during stress after warm contact may involve other mediating pathways.

Preliminary evidence from human mothers suggests that oxytocin helps modulate their affective state, and this may, in turn, influence their stress responses. In mothers who both breast- and bottle-feed their infants, the act of breast- feeding (which typically elicits greater rises in plasma oxytocin) is associated with less perceived stress, depression and anxiety than bottle-feeding Further, women who are breast feeders also report less anxiety than bottle-feeding women and show lower BP before and during stress (Modahl and Newton, 2000; Mezzacappa and Katkin, 2002). Uvnas-Moberg (2003) has proposed that although the sympathetic–adrenomedullary and hypothalamic–pituitary–adrenocortical (HPA) systems are key pathways mediating integrated stress responses, exemplified by the classic "fight or flight" pattern, there are complementary integrated patterns she has labeled the "relaxation and growth" response and the "calm and connection" response; oxytocin is one of the central components integrating these responses.

In addition to its anti-stress role, oxytocin has positive effects, by being linked to the dopaminergic reward pathways. As a result, oxytocin influences many behaviors that we as humans value most: attachment to family, friends, and other members of our social groups; desire for physical closeness; and both maternal and sexual responses. Oxytocin–knock-out mice, lacking the gene to produce oxytocin, have an abnormal inability to recognize a formerly familiar conspecific despite having no deficits in underlying learning or sensory functions. This lack of social recognition disappears if oxytocin is administered to the medial amygdala, and can be mimicked in normal mice by administering an oxytocin antagonist to the same region (Winslow, Hearn, Ferguson, Young, Matzuk and Insel, 2000; Ferguson, Aldag, Insel and Young, 2001). Abnormal social interactions begin during early life and carry over to adulthood. As infants, these oxytocin–knock-out mice vocalize less during separations from their dams, eliciting less licking, close contact, and other maternal behavior when separation ends. As adults, the females show less maternal behavior and the males show increased aggression (Winslow, Hearn, Ferguson, Young, Matzuk, and Insel, 2000; Ferguson, Aldag, Insel, and Young, 2001; Pedersen and Boccia, 2002). Oxytocin plays a critical role in lactation, and female knock-out mice are unable to nurse their offspring. Another maternal behavior enhanced by oxytocin is massage-like licking. Increased maternal pup licking (known to increase pup oxytocin and to decrease HPA activity) has diverse benefits that endure into adulthood: decreased stress behaviors and HPA activity, decreased BP particularly in females that were stressed prenatally, and increased next-generation maternal behavior in the female pups as adults (Champagne and Meaney, 2001; Pedersen and Boccia, 2002).

The study of the health benefits of oxytocinergic activity as enhanced by close contact with human loved ones is still in its early days, but recent studies in animal models have confirmed that this process contributes to slowing the formation of atherosclerotic plaques in genetically susceptible rabbit strains (McCabe et al., 2002; Paredes et al., 2006) and to faster wound healing in other monogamous mammals (Glasper and Devries, 2005; Devries, Craft, Glasper, Neigh and Alexander, 2007). We are encouraged by these exciting findings to continue to pursue this new research direction, both because of its potential importance to mental and physical health, and because loving family ties are among the few things that we all universally long for and cherish.

RECOMMENDED READINGS

Grewen, K. M., Girdler, S. S., and Light, K. C. (2005). Relationship quality: influence on ambulatory blood pressure in a multiracial sample of men and women. *Blood Pressure Monitoring*, 10, 117–124.

Hinderliter, A. L., Light, K. C., Girdler, S. S., Willis, P. W., and Sherwood A. (1996). Blood pressure responses to stress: Relation to left ventricular structure and function. *Annals of Behavioral Medicine, 18,* 61–66.

Light, K. C., Girdler, S. S., Sherwood, A., Bragdon, E. E., Brownley, K. A., West, S. G., and Hinderliter, A. L. (1999). High stress responsivity predicts later blood pressure only in combination with positive family history and high life stress. *Hypertension, 33,* 1458–1464.

Light, K. C., Grewen, K. M., and Amico, J.A. (2005). More frequent partner hugs and higher oxytocin levels are linked to lower blood pressure and heart rate in premenopausal women. *Biological Psychology, 6,* 5–21.

Turner, J. R., Sherwood, A., and Light, K. C. (1992). *Individual Differences in Cardiovascular Response to Stress.* New York: Plenum.

REFERENCES

Adamian, M. S., Girdler, S. S., West, S. G., Grewen, K. M., Chung, S. H., Koo, J., Hinderliter, A., and Light, K. C. (1999). Hormone replacement reduces lab and 24-hour blood pressure in hypertensive postmenopausal women. Presented at the 57th Annual Scientific Meeting of the American Psychosomatic Society in Vancouver, Canada, March 17–20, 1999. (Abstract).

Alderman, M. H. (2000). Salt, blood pressure, and human health. *Hypertension, 36,* 890–893.

Anderson, N. B., Lane, J. D., Monou, H., Williams, R. B. Jr, and Houseworth, S. J. (1988). Racial differences in cardiovascular reactivity to mental arithmetic. *International Journal of Psychophsyiology, 6,* 161–164.

Anderson, N. B., McNeilly, M., and Myers, H. (1992). Toward understanding race difference in autonomic reactivity. In J. R. Turner, A. Sherwood, and K. C. Light (Eds.), *Individual Differences in Cardiovascular Response to Stress* (pp. 125–145). New York, Plenum.

Berkman, L. F. (1985). The relationship of social networks and social support to morbidity and mortality. In S. Cohen and S. L. Syme (Eds.), *Social Support and Health* (pp. 241–262). New York: Academic Press.

Brady, S. S., and Matthews, K. A. (2006). Chronic stress influences ambulatory blood pressure in adolescents. *Annals of Behavioral Medicine, 31,* 80–88.

Broadwell, S., and Light, K. C. (1999). Family support and cardiovascular responses during conflict and other interactions. *International Journal of Behavioral Medicine, 6,* 40–63.

Brownley, K. A., Light, K. C., and Anderson, N. B. (1996). Social support and hostility interact to influence clinic, work and home blood pressure in Black and White men and women. *Psychophysiology, 33,* 434–445.

Brownley, K. A., West, S. G., Hinderliter, A. L., and Light, K. C. (1996). Acute aerobic exercise reduces ambulatory blood pressure in borderline hypertensive men and women. *American Journal of Hypertension, 9,* 200–206.

Carter, C. S. (1998). Neuroendocrine perspectives on social attachment and love. *Psychoneuroendocrinology, 23,* 779–818.

Champagne F., and Meaney, M. J. (2001). Like mother, like daughter: evidence for non-genomic transmission of parental behavior and stress responsivity. *Progress in Brain Research, 133:* 287–302.

Cohen, S. (1988). Psychosocial models of the role of social support in the etiology of physical disease. *Health Psychology, 7,* 269–297.

Corvol, P., Persu, A., Gimenez-Roquelplo, A-P., and Jeunemaitre, X. (1999). Seven lessons from two candidate genes in human essential hypertension: Angiotensinogen and epithelial sodium channel. *Hypertension, 33,* 1324–1331.

Das, S., and O'Keefe, J. H. (2006). Behavioral cardiology: recognizing and addressing the profound impact of psychosocial stress on cardiovascular health. *Current Athero-sclerosis Reports, 8,* 111–118.

Devries, A. C., Craft, T. K., Glasper, E. R., Neigh, G. N., and Alexander, J. K. (2007). Social influences on stress responses and health. *Psychoneuroendocrinology, 32,* 587–603.

Dolan, C. A., Sherwood, A., and Light, K. C. (1992). Cognitive coping strategies and blood pressure response to real-life stress. *Health Psychology, 11,* 233–240.

Ferguson, J. N., Aldag, J. M., Insel, T. R., Young, L. J. (2001). Oxytocin in the medial amygdala is essential for social recognition in the mouse. *Journal of Neuroscience, 21,* 8278–8285.

Flaa, A., Mundal, H. H., Eide, I., Kjeldsen, S. and Rostrup, M. (2006). Sympathetic activity and cardiovascular risk factors in young men in the low, normal and high blood pressure ranges. *Hypertension, 47,* 396–402.

Frankenhaeuser, M. (1983). The sympathetic-adrenal and pituitary-adrenal response to challenge: Comparison between the sexes. In T. M. Dembroski, T. H. Schmidt, and G. Blumchen (Eds.), *Biobehavioral Bases of Coronary Heart Disease* (pp. 91–105). Basel: Karger.

Girdler, S. S., Hinderliter, A. L., Brownley, K. A., Turner, J. R., Sherwood, A., and Light, K. C. (1996). The ability of active versus passive coping tasks to predict future blood pressure levels in normotensive men and women. *International Journal of Behavioral Medicine, 3,* 233–250.

Girdler, S. S., Hinderliter, A. L., and Light, K. C. (1993). Peripheral adrenergic receptor contribution to cardiovascular reactivity: influence of race and gender. *Journal of Psychosomatic Research, 37,* 177–193.

Girdler, S. S., Hinderliter, A. L., West, S. G., Grewen, K., Steege, J., and Light, K. C. (2000). Postmenopausal smokers show reduced hemodynamic benefit from oral hormone replacement. *American Journal of Cardiology 86,* 590–592.

Girdler, S. S., and Light, K. C. (1994). Hemodynamic stress responses in men and women examined as a function of female menstrual cycle phase. *International Journal of Psychophysiology, 17,* 233–248.

Glasper, E. R., and Devries, A. C. (2005). Social structure influences effects of pair-housing on wound healing. *Brain, Behavior and Immunity, 19,* 61–68.

Gratze, G., Fortin, J., Labugger, R., Binder, A., Kotanko, P., Timmerman, B., Luft, F. C., Hoehe, M. R., and Skrabal, F. (1999). -2 adrenergic receptor variants affect resting blood pressure and agonist-induced vasodilation in young adult Caucasians. *Hypertension, 33,* 1425–1430.

Grewen, K. M., Anderson, B. J., Girdler, S. S., and Light, K. C. (2003). Warm partner contact is related to lower cardiovascular reactivity. *Behavioral Medicine, 29,* 123–130.

Grewen, K. M., Girdler, S. S., Amico, J. A., and Light, K. C. (2005). Effects of partner support on oxytocin, cortisol, norepinephrine and blood pressure before and after warm partner contact. *Psychosomatic Medicine, 67,* 531–538.

Grewen, K. M., Girdler, S. S., and Light, K. C. (2005). Relationship quality: influence on ambulatory blood pressure in a multiracial sample of men and women. *Blood Pressure Monitoring, 10,* 117–124.

Harshfield, G. A., and Grim, C. E. (1997). Stress hypertension: The wrong genes in the wrong environment. *Acta Physiologica Scandinavica, 161* (suppl 640), 129–132.

Henry, J. P., and Grim, C. E. (1990). Psychosocial mechanisms of primary hypertension: Editorial Review. *Journal of Hypertension, 8,* 783–793.

Hinderliter, A. L., Light, K. C., Girdler, S. S., Willis, P. W., and Sherwood, A. (1996). Blood pressure responses to stress: Relation to left ventricular structure and function. *Annals of Behavioral Medicine, 18,* 61–66.

Hinderliter, A. L., Light, K. C., and Willis, P. W. IV (1991). Left ventricular mass index and diastolic filling: Relation to blood pressure and demographic variables in a healthy biracial sample. *American Journal of Hypertension, 4,* 579–585.

Hinderliter, A. L., Light, K. C., and Willis, P. W. IV (1992a). Gender differences in left ventricular structure and function in young adults with normal or marginally elevated blood pressure. *American Journal of Hypertension, 5,* 32–36.

Hinderliter, A. L., Light, K. C., and Willis, P. W. IV (1992b). Racial differences in left ventricular structure in healthy young adults *American Journal of Cardiology, 69,* 1196–1199.

Hinderliter, A. L., Sager, A., Sherwood, A., Light, K. C., Girdler, S. S., and Willis, P. W. (1997). Ethnic differences in forearm vasodilator reserve. *American Journal of Cardiology, 78,* 208–211.

Houston, B. K. (1992). Personality characteristics, reactivity and cardiovascular disease. In J. R. Turner, A. Sherwood, and K. C. Light (Eds.), *Individual Differences in Cardiovascular Response to Stress* (pp. 103–123). New York: Plenum.

Insel, T. R, and Young, L. J. (2001). The neurobiology of attachment. *Nature Rev (Neurosci), 2,* 129–136.

James, S. A., Hartnett, S. A., and Kalsbeek, W. D. (1983). John Henryism and blood pressure differences among black men. *Journal of Behavioral Medicine, 6,* 259–278.

James, S. A., Strogatz, D. S., Wing, S. B., and Ramsey, D. L. (1987). Socioeconomic status, John Henryism and hypertension in blacks and whites. *American Journal of Epidemiology, 126,* 664–673.

Julius, S., Amerena, J., Smith, S., and Petrin, J. (1995). Autonomic and behavioral factors in hypertension. In J. H. Laragh and B. M. Brenner (Eds.), *Hypertension: Pathophysiology, Diagnosis and Management* (pp. 2557–2570). New York: Raven.

Kaplan, G. A., and Keil, J. E. (1993). Socioeconomic factors and coronary heart disease: A review of the literature. *Circulation, 88,* 1978–1998.

Levy, D., Garrison, R. J., Savage, D. D., Kannel, W. B., and Castelli, W. D. (1990). Prognostic implications of echocardiographically determined left ventricular mass in the Framingham Heart Study. *New England Journal of Medicine, 322,* 1561–1566.

Light, K. C. (1981). Cardiovascular responses to effortful active coping: Implications for the role of stress in hypertension development. *Psychophysiology, 18,* 216–225.

Light, K. C. (2000). Environmental and psychosocial stress in hypertension onset and progression. In S. Oparil and J. Weber (Eds.), *Hypertension* (pp. 59–70). Philadelphia: W.B. Saunders.

Light, K. C., and Obrist, P. A. (1980). Cardiovascular reactivity to behavioral stress in young males with and without marginally elevated casual systolic pressures: A comparison of clinic, home and laboratory measures. *Hypertension, 2,* 802–808.

Light, K. C., and Sherwood, A. (1989). Race, borderline hypertension, and hemodynamic responses to behavioral stress before and after β-adrenergic blockade. *Health Psychology, 8,* 577–595.

Light, K. C., and Turner, J. R. (1992). Stress-induced changes in the rate of sodium excretion in healthy Black and White men. *Journal of Psychosomatic Research, 36,* 497–508.

Light, K. C., Brownley, K. A., Turner, J. R., Hinderliter, A. L., Girdler, S. S., Sherwood, A., and Anderson, N. B. (1995). Job status and high-effort coping influence work blood pressure in women and blacks. *Hypertension, 25,* 554–559.

Light, K. C., Dolan, C. A., Davis, M. R., and Sherwood, A. (1992). Cardiovascular responses to an active coping challenge as predictors of blood pressure patterns 10 to 15 years later. *Psychosomatic Medicine, 54,* 217–238.

Light, K. C., Girdler, S. S., Sherwood, A., Bragdon, E. E., Brownley, K. A., West, S. G., and Hinderliter, A. L. (1999). High stress responsivity predicts later blood pressure only in combination with positive family history and high life stress. *Hypertension, 33,* 1458–1464.

Light, K. C., Girdler, S. S., West, S, and Brownley, K. A. (1998). Blood pressure responses to occupational challenges and laboratory stress in women. In K. Orth-Gomer, M. A. Chesney, and N. Wenger (Eds.), *Women, Stress and Heart Disease* (pp. 237–261). Mahwah, NJ: Lawrence Erlbaum.

Light, K. C., Grewen, K. M., and Amico, J. A. (2005). More frequent partner hugs and higher oxytocin levels are linked to lower blood pressure and heart rate in premenopausal women. *Biological Psychology, 6,* 5–21.

Light, K. C., Hinderliter, A. L., West, S. G., Grewen, K. M., Steege, J. F., Sherwood, A., and Girdler, S. S. (2001). Hormone replacement improves hemodynamic profile and left ventricular geometry in hypertensive and normotensive postmenopausal women. *Journal of Hypertension, 19,* 269–278.

Light, K. C., Koepke, J. P., Obrist, P. A., and Willis, P. W. (1983). Psychological stress induces sodium and fluid retention in men at risk for hypertension. *Science, 220,* 429–431.

Light, K. C., Kothandapani, R. V., and Allen, M. T. (1998). Enhanced cardiovascular and catecholamine responses in women with depressive symptoms. *International Journal of Psychophysiology, 28,* 157–166.

Light, K. C., Smith, T. E., Johns, J. M., Hofheimer, J. A., and Amico, J. A. (2000). Oxytocin responsivity in mothers of infants: relationships to laboratory and home blood pressure, affect and perceived support. *Health Psychology 19,* 560–567.

Light, K. C., Turner, J. R., and Hinderliter, A. L. (1992). Job strain and ambulatory blood pressure in healthy young men and women. *Hypertension, 20,* 214–218.

Light, K. C., Turner, J. R., Hinderliter, A. L., Girdler, S. S., and Sherwood, A. (1994). Comparison of cardiac versus vascular reactors and ethnic groups in plasma epinephrine and norepinephrine responses to stress. *International Journal of Behavioral Medicine, 3,* 229–246.

Light, K. C., Turner, J. R., Hinderliter, A. L., and Sherwood A. (1993a). Race and gender comparisons: I. Hemodynamic responses to a series of behavioral stressors. *Health Psychology, 12,* 354–365.

Light, K. C., Turner, J. R., Hinderliter, A. L., and Sherwood, A. (1993b). Race and gender comparisons: II. Predictions of work blood pressure from laboratory baseline and cardiovascular reactivity measures. *Health Psychology, 12,* 366–375.

Lund-Johansen, P. (1979). Spontaneous changes in central hemodynamics in essential hypertension. In G. Onesti and C. R. Klimt (Eds.), *Hypertension: Determinants, Complications and Interventions* (pp. 201–209). NewYork: Grune and Stratton.

Manuck, S. B. (1994). Cardiovascular reactivity in cardiovascular disease: Once more unto the breach. *International Journal of Behavioral Medicine, 1,* 4–31.

McCabe, P. M., Gonzales, J. A., Zaias, J., Szeto, A., Kumar, M., Herron, A. J., and Schneiderman, N. (2002). Social environment influences the progression of atherosclerosis in the Watanabe Heritable Hyperlipidemic rabbit. *Circulation, 105,* 354–359.

Mezzacappa, E. S., and Katkin, E. (2002). Breast-feeding is associated with reduced perceived stress and negative mood in mothers. *Health Psychology, 21,* 187–193.

Modahl, C., and Newton, N. (2000). Mood state differences between breast and bottle-feeding mothers. In L. Carenza and L. Zinchella (Eds.), *Emotions and reproduction: Proceedings of the Serrano Symposium* (Vol 20B, pp. 81–92), New York: Academic Press.

Nazarro, P., Seccia, T., Vulpis, V., Schirosi, G., Serio, G., Battista, L., and Pirelli, A. (2005). Measures of total stress-induced blood pressure responses are associated with vascular damage. *American Journal of Hypertension, 18,* 1226–1232.

Obrist, P. A. (1981). *Cardiovascular Psychophysiology: A Perspective.* New York: Plenum.

Obrist, P. A., Gaebelein, C. J., Teller, E. S., Langer, A. W., Grignolo, A., Light, K. C., and McCubbin, J. A. (1978). The relationships among heart rate, carotid dP/dt, and blood pressure in humans as a function of the type of stress. *Psychophysiology, 15,* 102–115.

Obrist, P. A., Light, K. C., James, S. A., and Strogatz, D. S. (1987). Cardiovascular responses to stress: I. Measures of myocardial response and relationship to high resting systolic pressure and parental hypertension. *Psychophysiology, 24,* 65–78.

Orth-Gomer, K., and Unden, A. (1990). Type A behavior, social support and coronary risk: Interaction and significance for mortality in cardiac patients. *Psychosomatic Medicine, 55,* 37–43.

Paredes, J., Szeto, A., Levine, J. E., Zaias, J., Gonzales, J. A., Mendez, A. J., Llabre, M. M., Schneiderman, N., and McCabe, P. M. (2006). Social experience influences hypothalamic oxytocin in the WHHL rabbit. *Psychoneuroendocrinology, 31,* 1062–1075.

Pedersen, C. A., and Boccia, M. L. (2002).Oxytocin links mothering received, mothering bestowed and adult stress responses. *Stress, 5,* 259–267.

Petersson, M., Lundeberg, T., and Uvnas-Moberg, K. (1999). Short-term increase and long-term decrease of blood pressure in response to oxytocin-potentiating effect of female steroid hormones. *Journal of Cardiovascular Pharmacology; 33:* 102–108.

Pickering, T. G. (1997). The effects of environmental and lifestyle factors on blood pressure and the intermediary role of the sympathetic nervous system. *Journal of Human Hypertension, 11* (suppl 1), S9–S18.

Pickering, T. G., and Gerin, W. (1990). Cardiovascular reactivity in the laboratory and the role of behavioral factors in hypertension: A critical review. *Annals of Behavioral Medicine, 12,* 3–16.

Sherwood, A., Dolan, C. A., and Light, K. C. (1990). Hemodynamics of blood pressure responses during active and passive coping. *Psychophysiology, 27,* 656–668.

Sherwood, A., Girdler, S. S., Bragdon, E. E., West, S. G., Brownley, K. A., Hinderliter, A. L., and Light, K. C. (1997). Ten year stability of cardiovascular responses to laboratory stressors. *Psychophysiology, 34,* 185–191.

Sherwood, A., Hinderliter, A. L., and Light, K. C. (1995). Physiological determinants of hyperreactivity to stress in borderline hypertension. *Hypertension, 25,* 384–390.

Sherwood, A., Light, K. C., and Blumenthal, J. A. (1989). Effects of aerobic exercise on hemodynamic responses during psychosocial stress in normotensive and borderline hypertensive Type A men: A preliminary report. *Psychosomatic Medicine, 23,* 89–104.

Sherwood, A., Allen, M. T., Fahrenberg, J., Kelsey, R. M., Lovallo, W. R., and Doornen, L. J. (1990). Methodological guidelines for impedance cardiography. *Psychophysiology, 27,* 1–23.

Smith, T. W. (1992). Hostility and health: Current status of a psychosomatic hypothesis. *Health Psychology, 11,* 139–150.

Treiber, F. A., McCaffrey, F., and Pflieger, K. (1993). Determinants of left ventricular mass in normotensive children. *American Journal of Hypertension, 6,* 505–513.

Turner, J. R., Sherwood, A., and Light, K. C. (1994). Intertask consistency of hemodynamic responses to laboratory stressors in a biracial sample of men and women. *International Journal of Psychophysiology, 17,* 159–164.

Uvnas-Moberg K. (2003). *The Oxytocin Factor: Tapping the Hormone of Calm, Love and Healing.* (Translation by R. Francis, 204 pp.). Boston: Da Capo/Perseus Press.

West, S. G., Brownley, K. A., and Light, K. C. (1999). Postexercise vasodilation reduces diastolic blood pressure responses to stress. *Annals of Behavioral Medicine, 20,* 77–83.

West, S. G., Light, K. C., Hinderliter, A. L., Stanwyck, C. L., Bragdon, E. E., and Brownley, K. A. (1999). Potassium supplementation induces beneficial cardiovascular changes during rest and stress in salt sensitive individuals. *Health Psychology, 18,* 229–240.

West, S. G., Stanwyck, C. L., Brownley, K. A., Bragdon, E. E., Hinderliter, A. L., and Light, K. C. (1997). Salt restriction increases norepinephrine and cholesterol in Blacks more than in Whites. Presented at the Eighteenth Annual Meeting of the Society of Behavioral Medicine, San Francisco, April 1997. (Abstract).

Winslow, J. T., Hearn, E. F., Ferguson, J., Young, L. J., Matzuk, M. M., and Insel, T. R. (2000). Infant vocalization, adult aggression, and fear behavior of an oxytocin null mutant mouse. *Hormones and Behavior, 37,* 145–155.

Zhu, H., Poole, J., Lu, Y., Harshfield, G. A., Treiber, F. A., Snieder, H. and Dong, Y. (2005). Sympathetic nervous system, genes, and human essential hypertension. *Current Neurovascular Research, 2,* 303–317.

4

Status, Stress, and Heart Disease

A Monkey's Tale

JAY R. KAPLAN and STEPHEN B. MANUCK

This chapter describes the history of the scientific collaboration between the two of us, Jay Kaplan and Steve Manuck. We are behavioral scientists whose collaboration reflects a common interest in the role behavior may play in the development of heart disease. Our relationship has spanned more than two decades and encompasses virtually our entire careers. We begin by describing the interdisciplinary features of the collaboration, then identify the research findings that we believe comprise our principal collaborative contribution; we also speculate on the public health relevance of these findings. The final sections recount our history as a team, with an aim toward identifying factors that contributed most to our productivity. However, before beginning the narrative of our collaboration, it is worth introducing the phenomenon that has been the focus of our research efforts, namely atherosclerosis. It is also useful to mention the central element that brought us together, the availability of the crab-eating monkey (*Macaca fascicularis*) as an animal model suited to the study of behavioral influences on atherosclerotic heart disease.

Atherosclerosis refers to the development of fatty deposits (lesions) within the inner lining of arteries. Although all arteries are prone to such development, atherosclerosis is particularly pernicious when it affects the arteries that supply the heart (where it causes heart disease) and the brain (where it may culminate in stroke). Atherosclerotic lesions begin developing when the cells lining the artery wall, called endothelial cells, become damaged by risk factors such as high blood cholesterol concentrations, high blood pressure, and, perhaps, behavioral stress

(Henderson, 1996; Skantze et al., 1998). In turn, damaged endothelial cells allow entry into the artery of cholesterol-containing particles and cell types (smooth muscle cells, monocytes, lymphocytes) that are usually excluded. These infiltrating cells and particles release growth factors that stimulate further lesion development and encourage the accumulation of fat and the abnormal growth of extracellular material (Henderson, 1996; Libby, 1996). Over time, the progressing lesion often becomes complicated by mineral deposits, dead tissue, and internal bleeding, and it is subject to rupture and subsequent clot formation. The early and later stages of this process are depicted in Figure 4.1.

In addition to structural damage, the atherosclerotic artery also undergoes functional alterations, losing its ability to widen or narrow appropriately in response to changes in blood flow or the release of hormones. Usually, decades pass before the sum of these changes culminate in the various signs of heart disease. The latter include instances where blocked or functionally compromised coronary arteries reduce blood flow to the heart. If they are transient, such reductions can result in temporary oxygen starvation and associated pain ("ischemia"); however, severe and prolonged interruptions of blood flow to the heart may cause tissue death (a "heart attack" or "myocardial infarction"). Atherosclerotic coronary arteries also contribute to an increased susceptibility to heartbeat irregularities and sudden death. The long-term objective of our research has been to clarify the role of behavior in the preclinical processes of heart disease, such as atherosclerosis and resulting changes in arterial function.

Regarding the choice of an animal model to study atherosclerosis, it is reasonable to ask why it was necessary to use monkeys at all for this purpose. The answer relates, in part, to the difficulty of studying the development of heart disease in people. First, the protracted nature of atherogenesis requires that, to be informative, studies in humans must extend over many years, even decades. In addition, atherosclerosis and coronary disease are thought to be influenced by numerous—and difficult to control—genetic, demographic, and environmental factors (diet, age, sex, living conditions), as well as by what were, at the time our collaboration began, poorly understood individual differences in behavior and physiology. Also, ethical considerations prevent the application of invasive techniques to the evaluation of disease in "normal" individuals—that is, those in whom the presence of atherosclerotic disease is not yet suspected. The use of animal models in this context offers many advantages to the study of disease, including experimental control over relevant environmental variables, manipulation of suspected risk factors, relatively rapid development of lesions, and a more precise characterization of disease than is possible in human studies.

Importantly, not all animal models are equally useful for investigating atherosclerosis and heart disease. We have argued that the most suitable models are those that most closely approximate human beings in the location of lesions, the timing of lesion development, the response to risk factors such as sex and dietary

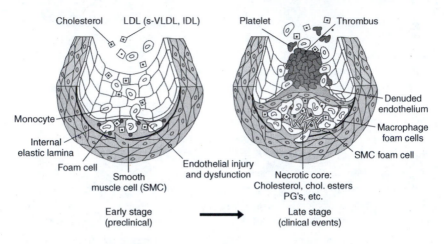

Figure 4.1. Cartoon depiction of the development of atherosclerosis from an initial lesion to a complicated plaque, a process that proceeds over decades.

fats and cholesterol, and the expression of functional alterations representative of clinical events (e.g., ischemia, infarction, impaired ability of the coronary arteries to alter diameter in response to changes in blood flow). While the perfect animal model does not exist, the foregoing requirements are reasonably approximated by macaque monkeys. Macaques are a genus of Old World monkey, native to parts of North Africa and most of South and Southeast Asia. Of the dozen or so macaque species, rhesus and crab-eating monkeys have been most widely used in biomedical research. The smaller size and greater availability of the crab-eating macaque make it somewhat more useful than the rhesus, and our group therefore chose to focus on this species. An additional advantage provided by these group-living monkeys is that their behavior, in both expression and pattern, is arguably more similar to our own than is that of most other primates and all nonprimates (see Box 4.1). The most prominent characteristic of the macaque social group is the arrangement of the animals in a pecking order (social status hierarchy), ultimately based on the outcome of competition over space, food, and preferred social partners. Within a social group, identifying the relative status of individual monkeys is not difficult, even to the most casual observer.

Lest the reader wonder how two behavioral scientists could establish a program for the study of atherosclerosis and heart disease, we did not. All of our work has a history that predates the collaboration, based on the studies of our colleagues at the Bowman Gray School of Medicine (now Wake Forest University School of Medicine). Prominent among these colleagues was Tom Clarkson, who was largely responsible for developing the crab-eating monkey as a suitable model for the study of atherosclerosis and its risk factors. However, he did more than

> Box 4.1. Our Animal Model: The Cynomolgus Macaque
> (*Macaca fascicularis*)
>
> This medium-sized (2–4 kg females, 5–8 kg males) Old World monkey approximates human beings in susceptibility to atherosclerosis and the response to risk factors such as male sex and dietary fats. Their behavior is similar to our own in expression, pattern, and evolutionary origin. A prominent feature of their social groups is the formation of a pecking order (social status hierarchy), based on the outcome of fights. Finally, females of this species resemble women in reproductive hormones and in the presence of a 30-day menstrual cycle.

provide us with an animal model appropriate for the study of behavioral influences on atherosclerosis. He also gave us our dependent variable, the vascular pathology—which was outside the expertise of either of us—and our basic understanding of the natural history of heart disease. Perhaps most important, Tom found the hypothesis that behavior could influence atherosclerosis plausible. At the time our program began (1979), such ideas were not widely held among investigators doing experimental studies on heart disease. Tom not only held such ideas, he had already done investigations in pigeons, squirrel monkeys, and crab-eating macaques that provided initial data suggesting that behavior may contribute to the development of atherosclerotic lesions (Kaplan, Manuck, Clarkson, and Prichard, 1985). In fact, these data, were used to obtain funding for studies that were already in progress when the two of us (Kaplan and Manuck) came to Wake Forest. In all ways, Tom was the mentor who provided the expertise, infrastructure, and encouragement to begin a formal program dedicated to evaluating behavioral influences on heart disease. Without the support and expertise of the investigators at Bowman Gray (Wake Forest), it would not have been possible for us to build a research program in cardiovascular behavioral medicine. It is to this program, and our individual as well as collaborative contributions, that we now turn.

Interdisciplinary Features and a Brief Description of the Collaborative Enterprise

Our collaboration represents the pairing of two disciplines—physical anthropology (primatology) (Kaplan) and psychology (Manuck). For one of us (Kaplan), knowledge regarding the potential influence of behavior on disease came not from studies of people but from a larger literature describing the effect of social interactions on the physiology of small mammal populations (e.g., Calhoun, 1963; Christian, 1980). The observations reported in these studies encouraged us to

investigate the role that social environment and individual behavioral characteristics might play in the disease susceptibility of monkeys—the natural history of
which one of us (Kaplan) studied intensively as a graduate student. In contrast,
Manuck had training in health psychology, psychophysiology, and experimental
design and had already studied the heart rate and blood pressure effects of psychological stress in persons thought to be at risk for heart disease because of
their behavioral attributes (e.g., Type A behavior). More definitive tests of the
hypothesis that behavior could promote heart disease and identification of the
underlying physiologic processes were not possible in symptom-free human
subjects for the reasons already stated. This favored collaboration to exploit a
suitable animal model. Fortunately, we were both at Wake Forest University at the
same time (1979), although we did not yet know each other. On first meeting,
however, we realized that together we could build a research program that neither
of us could initiate alone.

The core of our research program is comprised of two major collaborators and
is focused on behavioral variables that promote the development of coronary artery
atherosclerosis. However, no progress would have been made had it not been for
the early support provided by Tom Clarkson. His funding support and pathobiological expertise were crucial ingredients in the initiation of our work. After
several years, our program expanded to include two additional academic veteri-
narians: Michael Adams, whose expertise relates to the pathobiology of atherosclerosis in females, and Koudy Williams, a veterinary "cardiologist" focusing on
hormonal and behavioral factors influencing coronary vasomotion (as measured
both in vivo and in vitro). The program also grew to include several scientists
associated with the University of Gothenburg (Goran Bondjers, Knut Pettersson,
and Harriet Skantze), who provided expertise in the biology of the artery wall and
the role of the sympathetic nervous system in atherogenesis. Together, our collaborators in pathobiology not only aided the initiation of our program but
throughout have helped steer us toward those behavioral questions of most relevance to the natural history of coronary disease and its clinical consequences.

As described earlier, both of us were located initially at the Wake Forest
University School of Medicine. Within one year, however, Manuck moved to
the University of Pittsburgh to further develop his research program focusing
on the psychological and physiological risk factors for heart disease in humans.
As the program at Pittsburgh grew, considerable cross-fertilization took place between studies involving human subjects and those done on monkeys. This cross-
fertilization resulted in several individual NIH research grants and program projects
that were shared to some extent between the two institutions. The collaboration has
thus entailed expansion of expertise by both of us under the primary mentorship of
Clarkson, the recruitment of a small number of additional investigators (Adams,
Williams), and the development of a formal, cross-institutional relationship between Wake Forest University and the University of Pittsburgh. In addition to this
core program, interactions with Swedish investigators prompted a group of studies
relating specifically to early events in atherogenesis.

New Findings Generated by the Collaboration

We believe the major contribution of our research program has been to demonstrate that stressful circumstances and an individual's social position (status) within a group influence coronary artery atherosclerosis, the pathologic process that produces vulnerability to heart disease. This series of studies, undertaken in socially housed female, as well as male, crab-eating monkeys, documents behavioral effects on atherosclerosis and reveals how hormones may figure in this process.

In the paragraphs that follow, we review the three sets of findings generated by our research since the early 1980s: *(1)* the interactive effects of social status and social environment on coronary artery atherosclerosis in males; *(2)* the effect of social status on the coronary artery atherosclerosis of females; and *(3)* the effect of exaggerated heart rate reactivity to stress on the coronary artery atherosclerosis of both males and females. There are commonalties across all of these studies. The monkeys, for example, were all housed in social groups of four to six animals each. As described earlier, each group forms a dominance or status hierarchy in which some individuals ("dominants") predictably defeat others ("subordinates") in competitive encounters. We found that social status measured in this way is the primary factor associated with coronary artery atherosclerosis in monkeys housed under these conditions, regardless of sex. Interestingly, though, the relationship between status and disease differs in important respects between males and females.

An additional feature of our studies is that animals are usually fed a cholesterol-containing diet designed to mimic that typically consumed by North Americans. This diet results in plasma cholesterol concentrations somewhat higher than those usually seen in humans (e.g., 350–450 mg/dl), although some people exhibit such values. In response to these diets, the monkeys develop substantial atherosclerotic lesions in approximately two years, allowing us to observe the effect of various behavioral risk factors within a relatively compressed time period. Finally, in order to gain insight into the variables controlling the beginning as well as progressing stages of atherosclerosis, we have also evaluated the effect of status and environment on the arteries of socially housed monkeys in the absence of a cholesterol-containing diet. Such studies provide evidence that behavioral factors can, independently of dietary cholesterol, injure arteries and make them vulnerable to the development of atherosclerotic lesions.

Status and atherosclerosis in males

In our first experiment we evaluated the effects of both a stressful social environment and individual differences in social status (i.e., whether monkeys were dominant or subordinate in their groups). To create a stressful social environment, we repeatedly reorganized the membership of particular social groups, taking advantage of the fact that macaque males respond aggressively to the presence of social strangers and under such circumstances are forced to reassert their status,

relative to other individuals. Furthermore, because male monkeys frequently encounter strangers—they typically leave their groups of birth at adolescence and
thereafter tend to wander from group to group—repeated social reorganization
represents a "real life" stressor. Other, unstressed animals were housed in groups
of fixed membership for the length of the study. We refer to the monkeys in the
reorganized groups as "unstable," while those in the groups of constant membership are labeled "stable." Interestingly, we observed in this first experiment that
dominant animals tended to remain dominant and subordinates tended to remain
subordinate, even when social groups were repeatedly reorganized. Our primary
observation was that at study's end, dominant monkeys had developed markedly
worse atherosclerosis than their subordinate counterparts, but only among the
animals housed in unstable social groups. In the stable groups, dominant and
subordinate monkeys developed equivalent atherosclerosis, and indistinguishable
in extent from that of subordinates in the unstable groups (Kaplan, Manuck,
Clarkson, Lusso, and Taub, 1982).

The more extensive atherosclerosis of the dominant monkeys in the unstable
social setting could not be explained by variation in blood cholesterol or blood
pressure, the two usual risk factors applicable to this animal model. In trying to
identify a mechanism that might underlie the greater disease of unstable dominant
monkeys, we were intrigued by the pioneering studies of J. P. Henry (Henry and
Stephens, 1977); results of these investigations, involving mice, suggested that
attempts by dominant animals to maintain social control in the face of challenge
(e.g., as by our dominant males in an unstable setting) are accompanied by metabolic changes and by increases in heart rate and blood pressure that indicate
arousal of the sympathetic nervous system (one of the body's primary systems for
responding to emergencies); such animals also have an increased risk of arterial disease. In contrast, Henry suggested that social subordination was preferen-
tially associated with activation of a different emergency hormone system—that
involving the hypothalamus, anterior pituitary, and adrenal cortex—without appreciable adverse effects on blood vessels.

If the excessive atherosclerosis seen in our males that retained dominant
status in an unstable social environment resulted from excessive arousal of the
sympathetic nervous system, it follows that these animals might be protected by
administration of a drug that could "block" effects of such arousal on the heart.
We tested this hypothesis in a subsequent experiment by exposing all animals to
repeated social reorganization, but treating half of these monkeys with propranolol, a sympathetic nervous system blocking agent that was commonly prescribed
as an antihyptertensive in the 1980s. As in the unstable condition of our first
experiment, we again found that untreated dominant animals developed about
twice the atherosclerosis of their subordinate counterparts. However, sympathetic blockade completely eliminated the excess atherosclerosis otherwise seen in
dominant animals, thereby removing all difference in lesion development between
dominant and subordinate monkeys. These observations thus suggest that the

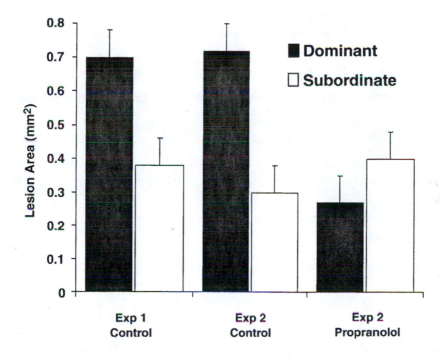

Figure 4.2. Atherosclerosis extent in the coronary arteries of dominant and subordinate animals living in unstable groups. Here are depicted data representing animals from the initial experiment (Exp 1), as well as those that were either treated or not treated with the sympathetic blocker propranolol (Exp 2). Atherosclerosis was pronounced in untreated dominant animals from both experiments; treatment with propranolol inhibited atherosclerosis in dominant animals but did not affect subordinates ($p < .05$). Adapted from Kaplan, Manuck, Adams, Weingand, and Clarkson (1987).

behavioral risk associated with dominant status in an unstable social environment is due to activation of the sympathetic nervous system. It is not entirely clear why dominant animals are selectively affected by social instability, but it may be noted that it is the status of these monkeys alone that is contested in times of group formation (Kaplan, Manuck, Adams, Weingand, and Clarkson, 1987). Figure 4.2 illustrates this finding and depicts, for comparison, the atherosclerosis of dominant and subordinate monkeys from the unstable condition of the first study described here (i.e., showing the relative exacerbation of disease in dominants, compared to subordinates).

Our initial results indicated that behavioral factors influence the progression of atherosclerosis in the presence of a diet high in fat and cholesterol. We observed a similar pattern of behavioral influence on atherosclerosis among monkeys eating

Box 4.2. Primary Findings: Male Macaques

- Atherosclerosis is worsened among individuals that retain dominant status in social groups that were disrupted by frequent changes in composition; in contrast, lesions are equivalently small in dominant and subordinate animals living in groups of stable composition.
- The excessive atherosclerosis of dominants in disrupted social groups is prevented by propranolol, a drug that inhibits the stress-induced increases in heart rate and blood pressure that are generally associated with arousal of the sympathetic nervous system.
- The behavioral effects on atherosclerosis begin within days and culminate in adverse changes in the way arteries respond and constrict to changes in blood flow.

a low-cholesterol diet (although lesions here were considerably smaller), suggesting that behavior can damage arteries even in animals that are otherwise well protected (Kaplan et al., 1983). To address this question more directly, we focused our next studies on the cells of the endothelium, the inner lining of the coronary arteries. Thus, we conducted a series of acute experiments in which normal-diet monkeys were placed into a new social grouping for a few days. We then evaluated the endothelial surfaces of their arteries for the presence of a biological marker indicating the presence of endothelial damage and cell death (immunoglobulin G), both of which are among the first signs of atherosclerosis. Here, we found that social disruption caused significant damage to the arterial endothelium, and, importantly, that a sympathetic blocking drug again prevented such injury. These observations further underscore the role that sympathetic nervous system activation plays in mediating behavioral influences on atherosclerosis in this animal model—at least in males (Skantze et al., 1998; Strawn et al., 1991).

Finally, the ability of the coronary arteries to widen (dilate) and constrict in response to hormonal stimulation and changes in blood flow provides another marker of endothelial health. The compound acetylcholine, for example, stimulates the healthy endothelium to widen. If the endothelium is damaged, however, the artery fails to dilate and may even constrict in response to acetylcholine. To the extent that stress damages the endothelium, the artery wall of an affected individual might not widen when exposed to substances such as acetylcholine. Consistent with this hypothesis, we found that chronic exposure to the stress of social reorganization significantly impairs acetylcholine-induced coronary dilation, and does so regardless of diet that animals may have consumed or even the degree of atherosclerosis that may have accumulated (Williams, Vita, Selwyn, Manuck, and Kaplan, 1991; Williams, Kaplan, and Manuck, 1993). These studies provide further evidence that behavioral factors can adversely affect the earliest, as well as the later, stages of atherosclerosis. A summary of our findings in male cynomolgus monkeys is listed in Box 4.2.

Status and atherosclerosis in females

A great mystery in the natural history of heart disease is that premenopausal females are relatively spared from atherosclerotic lesions and consequent heart disease in comparison to similarly aged males. Because of this, so-called female "protection," research relating to atherosclerosis and heart disease has traditionally emphasized male subjects. In the 1970s, however, investigators at Wake Forest University began using crab-eating macaques to explore factors contributing to female protection and to determine whether such protection was, in fact, uniformly distributed among premenopausal animals. Fortuitously, female macaques in general, and crab-eating monkeys in particular, share many reproductive characteristics with women—a 30-day menstrual cycle, qualitatively and quantitatively similar circulating levels of sex hormones, and the occurrence of a natural menopause (Jewett and Dukelow, 1972; Williams and Hodgen, 1982). Furthermore, unlike rhesus monkeys, crab-eating macaques engage in reproductive activity the year round (Mahone and Dukelow, 1979). Most important, one previous study demonstrated that premenopausal crab-eating monkeys, like young women, are relatively protected from the development of atherosclerosis in comparison to males (Rudel and Pitts, 1978).

Having identified a suitable model, we then began to study the behavioral and hormonal correlates of lesion development (and its retardation). We began by housing premenopausal females together in groups of four to six animals each. Like males, females form stable status hierarchies in which some animals habitually defeat others in competitive encounters. In our first study, we also routinely monitored the animals' menstrual cycles for length and hormonal profile. As expected, we found that females developed significantly less coronary artery atherosclerosis than similarly housed males, but, interestingly, only if they were socially dominant; subordinate females and males were indistinguishable in extent of atherosclerosis (Kaplan, Adams, Clarkson, and Koritnik, 1984). This was our first clear evidence that female protection did not extend to all premenopausal animals.

We next tried to understand the physiology underlying this status-dependent variation in atherosclerosis among females. First, blood cholesterol concentrations could not explain the outcome. Our hormonal studies showed, however, that subordinate monkeys, in comparison to dominants, had fewer ovulatory cycles, a greater percentage of hormonally deficient menstrual cycles, and reduced production of estrogen at ovulation than did dominants. They were thus relatively estrogen deficient (Adams, Kaplan, and Koritnik, 1985). We should note that subordinate monkeys are not unique in experiencing such behaviorally induced ovarian abnormalities. Social subordination, and social stress in general, are commonly associated with reproductive impairment in female mammals (Christian, 1980).

Could the relative estrogen deficiency and ovarian impairment of socially subordinate females *explain* their loss of "female protection"? And, if it did, what might be the implications for women? In a related experiment we found that dominant and subordinate females that had had their ovaries removed and then consumed a fat-containing diet did not differ in extent of atherosclerosis; moreover, lesion extent in both groups was approximately equivalent to that observed in subordinates with intact ovaries. This result indicates that surgical induction of estrogen deficiency (by removal of the ovaries) essentially eliminates the "protection" from diet-induced atherosclerosis that is typically experienced by dominant monkeys (Adams, Kaplan, Clarkson, and Koritnik, 1985). We also observed that repeated pregnancy, a condition of "high" estrogen, almost completely inhibits the development of atherosclerosis, irrespective of social status (Adams, Kaplan, Koritnik, and Clarkson, 1987). Together, these findings suggested that reproductive condition governs female vulnerability to atherosclerosis. They also provided the rationale for our next study. Specifically, if ovarian impairment accelerates lesion development in premenopausal females, estrogen supplementation might prove protective, and especially so for monkeys most predisposed to estrogen deficiency—namely, socially subordinate animals.

To test this hypothesis, we randomized a large number of premenopausal animals to one of two experimental conditions: (1) a high-fat diet alone, or (2) a high-fat diet plus an oral contraceptive containing an estrogen (ethinyl estradiol) and a progestin (levonorgestrel). We predicted that untreated subordinates would develop more atherosclerosis than either dominants (contraceptive-treated or not) or contraceptive-treated subordinates. After two years of diet and treatment, a biopsy was taken from an artery in the left leg of each animal. Previous studies had shown that atherosclerosis at this site strongly predicts the amount of coronary artery atherosclerosis in the same monkeys. Use of this artery as a surrogate for the coronary in this experiment allowed us to subsequently study the same animals in a second experiment, immediately following the first. Thus, following biopsy, all monkeys had their ovaries removed and then were randomly assigned to one of three postmenopausal treatment conditions: (1) a soy-based diet devoid of plant estrogens (i.e., "isoflavones"); (2) a soy-based diet with plant estrogens intact; or (3) a soy-based diet devoid of plant estrogen but containing mammalian estrogens (Clarkson, Anthony, and Morgan, 2001). The data from the premenopausal biopsy are shown in Figure 4.3 (Kaplan et al., 1995). It can be seen from this figure that contraceptive treatment was indeed protective, and selectively so for the subordinate animals; in the untreated condition, the subordinate females developed (as previously) considerably more atherosclerosis than did the dominants. This outcome supports our hypothesis that social subordination causes acceleration of atherosclerosis by virtue of estrogen deficiency.

More recently, we were able to examine the coronary arteries of these same animals after three years of postmenopausal treatment as described above. These data provided us with the unique opportunity to determine whether premenopausal hormonal and behavioral conditions (social subordination, estrogen treatment) would affect the extent of coronary artery atherosclerosis postmenopausally, even in the face of postmenopausal hormone replacement. In particular, we wanted

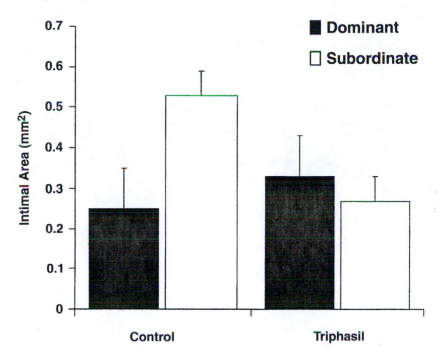

Figure 4.3. Atherosclerosis extent in the leg (iliac) arteries of dominant and subordinate females treated or not with an oral contraceptive. Untreated (control) subordinates had more atherosclerosis than untreated dominants and more atherosclerosis than treated (triphasil) animals, regardless of status ($p < .05$). Adapted from Kaplan et al. (1995).

to look at the fate of those animals that were at high risk (i.e., untreated subordinates) compared to those at low risk (all others). We first divided the animals according to their premenopausal social status (dominant or subordinate) and then analyzed the effects of pre- and postmenopausal hormone treatments on atherosclerosis. Our analysis of these data indicates that premenopausal dominance status and contraceptive treatment interact to predict extent of coronary artery atherosclerosis in postmenopausal monkeys, just as they had predicted atherosclerosis in a leg artery biopsy taken from the same monkeys premenopausally (Kaplan, Manuck, Anthony, and Clarkson, 2002). The foregoing life course study suggests three conclusions: *(1)* social subordination places premenopausal females at high risk for development of atherosclerosis; *(2)* estrogen treatment (with oral contraceptives) provides selective protection to high-risk animals, indicating that estrogen deficiency underlies their heightened risk; and *(3)* the elevated risk associated with social subordination and the selective protection offered by oral contraceptives persist postmenopausally, and do so irrespective of

Box 4.3. Primary Findings: Female Macaques

• Premenopausal monkeys that are subordinate in their social groups are at high risk
  for early acceleration of atherosclerosis.
• Subordinate females also experience moderate ovarian impairment and are thus
  generally deficient in estrogen.
• Estrogen treatment (e.g., contraceptive hormones) provides selective protection to
  these high-risk individuals, suggesting that estrogen deficiency underlies their risk.
• Both the excessive risk associated with social subordination and the protection
  provided by estrogen treatment persist into the postmenopausal period, irrespective
  of postmenopausal treatment.

postmenopausal exposure to estrogen replacement. The experimental results derived from the females are summarized in Box 4.3.

Individual differences in cardiovascular responsivity to stress

Studies have long shown that individuals vary considerably in their cardiovascular
responses to behavioral stress—some persons show marked increases in heart rate
or blood pressure, for instance, when exposed to the same stimulus (stressor) that
provokes little or no response in others. It is also widely believed that individuals
experiencing the largest cardiovascular responses to stress are at greatest risk for
heart disease and stroke (Manuck, 1994). To test this hypothesis in relation to
atherosclerosis, we evaluated animals' heart rate responses to a distinctly stressful
stimulus, the threat of capture and handling. As among human subjects, monkeys
varied greatly in the degree of their cardiac (heart rate) response to this stressor,
and repeated testing showed these reactions to be reproducible. Most important,
animals that exhibited the largest heart rate responsivity also developed the most
extensive atherosclerosis of the coronary and carotid arteries. We have now observed this association in males, in premenopausal females, and in females lacking
ovaries but given hormone replacement therapy (Manuck, Adams, McCaffry, and
Kaplan, 1997; Manuck, Kaplan, Adams, and Clarkson, 1989; Manuck, Kaplan, and
Clarkson, 1983). Data from this latter population are depicted in Figure 4.4. The
primary findings describing the association between high heart rate reactivity and
extensive atherosclerosis are summarized in Box 4.4.

Monkey Models and Human Disease

As we suggest in the preceding discussion, the reason for using monkeys to study
behavioral influences on atherosclerosis relates to the many similarities in disease
development that exist between certain monkey species and people. Furthermore,
the social behavior of monkeys in many respects resembles our own in both its

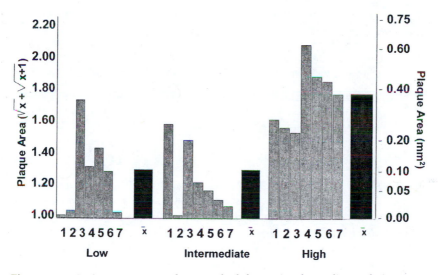

Figure 4.4. Lesion area averaged across the left anterior descending and circumflex arteries among low, intermediate, and high heart rate (HR) reactive animals. Animals are ranked in order of HR reactivity within each grouping. Solid bars denote mean atherosclerosis for each group. The left ordinate is scaled to the square root transformation of plaque measurements; corresponding values for lesion area, in mm^2, are indicated on the right ordinate.

physical appearance (posture, facial expression) and pattern of occurrence (the existence of status hierarchies). Finally, we can obtain data from primate models that cannot be derived in symptom-free human populations because of our inability to apply procedures and controls that would be unethical, impractical, or virtually interminable in people. These characteristics allowed us to design experiments that, by extrapolation, may have implications for human health and well-being. We address these implications first with respect to our studies of male crab-eating monkeys and then in relation to our studies of females.

Implications for men

The studies of male crab-eating monkeys suggest two major conclusions: *(1)* atherosclerosis is worsened among individuals that are habitually dominant in competition with social strangers; and *(2)* the increased risk of atherosclerosis experienced by such animals is related, in part, to the physiologic arousal that we presume is produced by the demands of retaining dominant status in an unstable social environment. Our experimental manipulation (social perturbation) forced males to confront strangers repeatedly, and each animal responded in its habitual way to this challenge—engaging and winning such contests (i.e., the eventual dominants) or either withdrawing or engaging, but losing, competitive interactions

Box 4.4. Primary Findings: Heart Rate Responsivity in Macaques

• Male and female monkeys, like their human counterparts, vary in their heart rate
  responses to stressful stimuli.
• Male and female monkeys that exhibit an exaggerated heart rate response to a
  standard laboratory stressor (fear of capture) also develop excessive atherosclerosis,
  in comparison to their less responsive counterparts.

(i.e., the eventual subordinates). Our results suggest that behavioral risk in males
does not reside alone in either a temperamental trait relating to being dominant or
in the degree of stress (e.g., instability) associated with the social environment but,
rather, in the interaction of these two factors. Regarding other findings, the deleterious effects of stress on the earliest stages of atherosclerosis (endothelial injury)
in males implies that adolescents and young adults may be susceptible to behavioral
influences on lesion development. Although it has been known at least since the
Korean War that significant lesion development occurs in some men by the age of
20 (and thus must begin even earlier), our data are among the first to suggest that
behavioral factors could be responsible, at least in part, for this phenomenon. At
the other end of the disease time line, our data relating behavioral stress to abnormalities in the functional properties of arteries—their ability to dilate and
constrict—suggest that behavioral factors contribute to the symptomatic expression of heart disease (e.g., interruptions in blood flow or ischemia), as well as to the
development of atherosclerosis.

Finally, we would suggest that our observations support a popular hypothesis
explaining how behavior influences atherosclerosis. It has often been suggested
that chronic stress causes arousal of the sympathetic nervous system, which contributes to the development of atherosclerosis and heart disease. Our observation
that chronic administration of the sympathetic-blocking drug propranolol pre-
vents the behavioral exacerbation of atherosclerosis provides an initial, direct
test of the hypothesis that sympathetic activation mediates behavioral influences
on lesion development, at least in the monkeys. Our findings also suggest that
sympathetic blocking agents ("antagonists") may confer a degree of protection
against heart disease among behaviorally predisposed individuals.

Implications for women

As informative as the male studies were with respect to the onset, expression, and
physiologic mediation of behavioral influences on atherosclerosis, our experiments involving females are potentially more interesting, as they may have unmasked a previously unrecognized risk factor for atherosclerosis in premenopausal
women—ovarian impairment and relative estrogen deficiency. In monkeys, this

state is associated with social subordination, possibly as part of a stress response (e.g., subordinate females also have enlarged adrenal glands and produce large amounts of the stress hormone, cortisol). As a result of estrogen deficiency, subordinate females develop worse atherosclerotic disease than dominants, an effect that is reversed by estrogen supplementation.

Based on our findings, we believe that behavioral factors may lead similarly to ovarian impairment in some young women, and that such impairment may, in turn, predispose to the early or accelerated development of atherosclerosis. In fact, ovarian dysfunction and estrogen deficiency are relatively common in women of reproductive age (Prior, Vigna, Schechter, and Burgess, 1990; Prior et al., 1996), with behavioral stress generally believed to be the most frequent cause (Berga, Daniels, and Giles, 1997; Cameron, 1997). What about atherosclerosis and heart disease in premenopausal women? Although conventional wisdom suggests that women are uniformly spared in their reproductive years, the recently published Pathologic Determinants of Atherosclerosis in Youth (PDAY) study demonstrates that a third of women have significant coronary artery atherosclerosis by age 35 (Strong et al., 1999). Regarding the role of estrogen in this process, a markedly increased risk of heart disease is observed in relatively young women in association with surgical removal of the ovaries and early menopause. Furthermore, there is at least one study showing that premenopausal women with confirmed heart disease are relatively estrogen deficient in comparison to control subjects (Hanke et al., 1997). Together, these observations are consistent with the speculation that some young women experience an early development of atherosclerosis that reflects, in part, behavioral and hormonal factors similar to those observed in our premenopausal monkeys. These factors may become particularly important as women move into the perimenopausal period (the three to five years prior to menopause) and begin to experience a more widespread decline in ovarian hormone production (Speroff, 2000). The monkey data suggest further that such pre- and perimenopausal conditions significantly influence postmenopausal disease and do so irrespective of postmenopausal hormonal intervention. This latter finding implies that primary prevention of heart disease should begin in the premenopausal years, when significant disease-related changes first occur.

One final speculation in this regard is that behavioral factors may be less relevant for lesion progression in postmenopausal women than among their premenopausal counterparts. This is because behaviorally induced ovarian dysfunction—the primary phenomenon mediating behavioral influences on atherosclerosis susceptibility in female monkeys—is not a relevant risk factor following menopause (when ovarian function is substantially reduced in all individuals). Consistent with this suggestion, postmenopausal dominant and subordinate monkeys do not differ in atherosclerosis extent if exposure to an atherogenic diet (and thus the process of atherogenesis) does not begin until after removal of the ovaries. Of course, behavioral factors may be just as relevant to clinical events among postmenopausal women as men, since they more closely resemble men hormonally at this stage of life.

Cardiovascular responsivity to stress in males and females

An additional arena in which our findings may be relevant to people concerns individual differences in heart rate and blood pressure responses to behavioral provocation. Independently of variation in social environment, we have observed that crab-eating monkeys, similar to humans, differ in the magnitude of their heart rate reactions to behavioral challenge. Specifically, animals (males, and both pre-menopausal and postmenopausal females) in which heart rates increase most appreciably in response to stress develop more extensive coronary and carotid artery atherosclerosis than do animals that show a less pronounced cardiac (heart rate) responsivity. This observation provided support for the hypothesis that coronary disease risk is elevated in persons whose physiologic reactions to stress involve marked elevations in heart rate, blood pressure, or other markers of circulatory response (e.g., elevated cardiac output) (Manuck, Kaplan, and Clarkson, 1983). It also gave impetus to parallel studies in human subjects as technologies became available in the past several years for noninvasive evaluation of atherosclerotic disease. For instance, heightened blood pressure reactions to stress have now been shown to correlate significantly with extent of carotid artery atherosclerosis (as assessed by ultrasonography) in population samples of both men and women (Barnett, Spense, Manuck, and Jennings, 1997; Kamarck et al., 1997; Matthews et al., 1998).

Conclusion

Our studies with monkeys demonstrate that behavioral factors influence susceptibility and resistance to atherosclerotic disease, and they suggest some of the biological mechanisms by which such influences are mediated. In addition, the data described here for both male and female monkeys are generally consistent with epidemiological observations derived from studies of people. This consistency in outcome suggests that our studies are relevant for understanding the etiology and development of atherosclerosis and coronary disease among human beings. Our results also suggest intervention strategies (sympathetic blockade in males and estrogen supplementation in females) that might be applied to inhibit or prevent the behavioral worsening of atherosclerosis and coronary disease in high-risk populations.

Origins and Life Course of the Collaboration

Our collaboration developed serendipitously, as we were unknown to each other before meeting at Wake Forest University during Manuck's first, and only, year in residence. However, both of us were interested in heart disease. One of us (Kaplan) had the opportunity to test the hypothesis that the behavioral and hormonal disruptions induced by reorganizing groups of socially housed monkeys might cause a worsening of atherosclerosis. The other's (Manuck's) initial interest was directed toward understanding the relationship between individual differences in cardiovascular responsivity to stress and the development of hypertension and heart disease. When Manuck discovered that Kaplan had ongoing studies investigating behavioral influences on atherosclerosis, he initiated a meeting and suggested that individual differences in behaviorally evoked cardiovascular responsivity could be assessed in the ongoing monkey experiments and might provide an informative adjunct to those studies.

Manuck's suggestion was implemented, along with a much closer evaluation of individual differences in behavior, particularly social status. Furthermore, Manuck was able to contribute a new perspective regarding experimental design and control, as Kaplan had been trained as an observational scientist studying the natural (unmanipulated) history of monkeys. As the first year ended, Manuck moved to Pittsburgh but, nonetheless, remained in close contact with the emerging research program. At about this time, it became apparent that we were not involved in a single study but rather, in the development of an integrated, multidisciplinary program of research. As a result, decisions regarding publications and grant applications typically have been framed in terms of programmatic contributions.

Although we obviously discussed the order in which the manuscripts should be published and the arrangement of authorship, neither of us recalls any contentiousness over issues of publication or authorship. Probably, our first few meetings set the tone for subsequent interactions, which we like to think have been characterized by cooperation rather than competition with regard to publication. Like any investigators, we do argue, but such arguments invariably relate to the conduct of studies, the interpretation of results, and the stylistic aspects of the manuscripts submitted for publication.

The collaboration between us began in 1979 and continues to the present. In the beginning, the major intellectual effort involved applying concepts from cardiovascular behavioral medicine to the design and implementation of studies that used monkeys in experimental investigations allowing the study of disease and disease mechanisms not feasible in people. Upon interpreting and publishing the results of these studies, however, it became apparent that some of the hypotheses thus generated nonetheless might profitably be tested in human subjects. The resulting studies in people then led to yet further investigations in monkeys, and so forth. For example, Manuck's initial work in humans suggested monkey studies that could evaluate the consequences of an exaggerated heart rate responsivity to stress. As noted in the discussion in this chapter, the results of these investigations demonstrated that high heart rate reactive animals did develop more extensive coronary and carotid artery atherosclerosis than did their less responsive counterparts. In turn, these data enhanced the rationale for more ambitious epidemiological and clinical studies in humans. Newly developed ultrasound technologies for noninvasive assessment of the carotid arteries made such studies feasible in symptom-free individuals.

Sometimes, an observation made initially in monkeys has been extended to a human study. In one instance, for example, we observed that during initial (and stressful) periods of new group formation, the heart rates of monkeys were lower while they were passively in physical contact with their neighbors than while they were sitting alone (an asocial state). This observation suggests that social support might reduce the adverse cardiovascular responses evoked by social instability. This hypothesis was tested in Pittsburgh by investigators who showed that blood pressure reactions to stress were less pronounced in individuals who maintained physical contact with a friend during testing procedures than when the friend was either absent or present, but not in physical contact (Kamarck, Manuck, and Jennings, 1990).

Factors That Facilitated and Constrained the Work

We believe two major factors facilitated our collaboration: *(1)* our complementary intellectual traditions, and *(2)* the support and intellectual contributions of our colleagues with expertise in atherosclerosis pathology. With regard to the former, Manuck's expertise in health psychology, psychophysiology, and experimental design seemed to perfectly complement Kaplan's background in mammalian and primate natural history. Kaplan's knowledge about species-typical patterns of social behavior helped identify those factors, both individual and situational (for example, dominance status, an antipathy to social strangers, susceptibility to socially induced reproductive dysfunction) that might be both relevant to the real life of the animals and pertinent to studies of disease susceptibility and resistance. The incorporation of such information into the design of relevant experiments, and later the rigorous assessment and interpretation of results emerging from such studies, comprised Manuck's equally important and complementary contribution to the joint research program.

With regard to facilitating factors, it is not possible to overstate the contributions made by our colleagues in the department of comparative medicine at Bowman Gray School of Medicine (Wake Forest University). This department was started in the 1950s with the mission of investigating atherosclerosis and heart disease by using animals as clinical surrogates. Pigeons were initially a major focus in this endeavor, as some strains are naturally susceptible to atherosclerosis. However, the anatomy of pigeons and their pattern of atherosclerosis differ in substantial ways from what is observed in people. As a result, beginning in the 1960s, pigeons were replaced as a primary model, first by squirrel monkeys and later by African green monkeys and macaques (including rhesus and crab-eating monkeys). Tom Clarkson and his colleagues played a major role in establishing the usefulness of all of these animals in modeling various aspects of atherosclerosis. Furthermore, these investigators helped develop the techniques still used in the measurement of atherosclerosis extent and severity.

Almost from its inception, our collaboration has been cross-institutional, with the primate studies conducted entirely at Wake Forest University. Surprisingly, this physical separation has not been a particular impediment to the conduct of our collaborative research. Technological advances in communication have provided us with the means of staying in daily contact and transferring data, analyses, and manuscripts. In fact, such communication has become so routine that we probably spend as much or more time in contact with each other as either of us does with most colleagues at our respective institutions. From a personal standpoint, therefore, the collaboration has been relatively easy to maintain. Nevertheless, there have been some minor institutional impediments to the collaboration that have had to be overcome. These impediments primarily involve institutional infrastructures that are not designed to interact well with their complementary components elsewhere.

Concluding Musings: The Makings of a Successful Collaboration

We have enjoyed doing collaborative science and believe that we have been more productive as a team than we could have been individually. If such collaborations are indeed viewed as a good thing, it might be asked whether there are training programs that could be designed to produce investigators willing and able to collaborate across scientific disciplines. In our case, the training that provided a basis for collaboration was *not* interdisciplinary. One of us was trained as a psychologist with a research interest in psychophysiology and health, while the other was trained as a physical anthropologist, with specialty training in primate behavior, biology, and evolution. The success of this collaboration probably relates in large part to the *non*-interdisciplinary aspects of our training, as these provided us with the complementary expertise that ultimately were used to create a program greater than the sum of its parts. Thus, the lesson to be derived from our collaboration in relation to training is that individuals should be provided with specific skills relating to a particular body of knowledge. Only then will they have something of potential complementary value to bring to a collaborative table. We have also gained, however, from overlapping scientific interests broader than our own disciplines. As a result, we have had an appreciation of, if not expertise in, each other's areas of training as well as those larger domains (e.g., social status, individual differences, and adaptation) that encompass our research. In this sense then, parochial training regarding disciplinary expertise can facilitate collaboration; parochial scientific interests, however, would likely be anathema.

In this context, we believe that the actions of institutions, funding agencies, and training programs are of secondary importance in the creation of successful, long-term, interdisciplinary collaborations. Rather, such collaborations ultimately emanate from the interests of the investigators themselves and depend on a willingness of these investigators to invest a level of energy in research collaboration comparable to that expended on behalf of other strong, interpersonal relationships. In this sense, in our experience, the successful collaboration more closely resembles a happy marriage than an impersonal, scientific endeavor.

Postscript

Extending studies of premenopausal precursors of postmenopausal disease

Our recent work has focused on early pathobiological changes in premenopausal females and their association with social status and ovarian function. In advance of describing these investigations, it is worth restating the hypothesis that has driven them, i.e., that although premenopausal women are usually thought to be protected from atherosclerosis and the resulting coronary disease, *emerging clinical and animal model data indicate that the atherosclerosis and clinical events observed among postmenopausal women have their origins in the premenopausal years.* Related data suggest, further, that a history of clinical or subclinical ovarian impairment may by responsible for initiating those processes (such as abnormal vascular function and accelerated development of atherosclerosis) leading to an increased risk of later coronary disease (Kaplan and Manuck, 2004). Notably, premenopausal ovarian abnormalities are also associated with osteoporosis and hence increased risk of future fracture. As reviewed previously, our studies with premenopausal cynomolgus monkeys suggest that psychosocial stress secondary to social subordination (affecting about half of the animals in both naturally constituted and captive groupings) may be a primary factor contributing to ovarian impairment and placing monkeys—and by extension women—on a high-risk trajectory for the development of postmenopausal disease.

Our latest studies used premenopausal female monkeys to investigate the etiology of endothelial dysfunction, a condition in which there is impaired arterial dilation in response to coronary blood flow and that ultimately contributes to clinical events. The overall objectives were to determine whether psychosocial stress or ovarian impairment could initiate endothelial dysfunction and to establish the extent to which any such dysfunction might be dependent on the presence of concomitant atherosclerosis or an elevation in plasma lipids. Two lines of evidence provided the basis for these questions. First, we demonstrated previously among monkeys consuming an atherogenic (i.e., fat- and cholesterol-containing) diet that psychosocial stress could adversely affect endothelial function independently of variability in atherosclerosis extent (Williams, Kaplan, and Manuck, 1993). Also, we showed in such monkeys that chronic exercise could alter endothelial function beneficially without affecting atherosclerosis and, again, independently of individual differences in atherosclerosis extent (Williams, Kaplan, Suparto, Fox, and Manuck, 2003). In two other further experiments we demonstrated that psychosocial stress could initiate endothelial cell death (the first stage in athero-genesis) as well as cause development of atherosclerotic lesions *in the absence* of an atherogenic diet or abnormal elevations in plasma lipids (Kaplan, Manuck, Clarkson, Lusso, Taub, and Miller, 1983; Skantze et al., 1998). The foregoing investigations were all conducted in male monkeys, and further, did not determine whether psychosocial stress in the absence of a lipid-containing diet or athero-sclerosis can cause endothelial dysfunction. Hence, the current studies not only employed females but also evaluated the effect of an atherogenic diet and ath-erosclerosis on endothelial dysfunction.

The first of these investigations compared coronary artery vascular respon-sivity to infused acetylcholine among socially dominant (i.e., nonstressed, typi-cally ovarian normal—Figure 4.5A) and subordinate (stressed, typically ovarian impaired—Figure 4.5B) monkeys consuming for three months diets that were either relatively high or low in saturated fat and cholesterol. The major result was that the arteries of subordinate animals constricted to a significantly greater extent than those of their dominant counterparts, indicating greater endothelial dys-function (Figure 4.6). Importantly, there were *no* significant differences in pattern between monkeys consuming atherogenic or nonatherogenic diets. This result indicated that endothelial dysfunction can occur in the absence of either athero-sclerosis or elevated plasma lipids.

Our second study was limited to the monkeys consuming an atherogenic diet and assessed vascular function on a second occasion, 15 months following the initiation of diet. Again, the coronary arteries of subordinate monkeys tended to constrict more than those of dominant individuals. Furthermore, the absolute amount of constriction did not increase from the first to the second vascular de-termination, nor were there significant correlations between atherosclerosis extent (regardless of how measured) and vessel dilation. These latter results suggest that progressing atherosclerosis, at least insofar as observed over the initial 15 months of consuming an atherogenic diet, does not influence patterns of endothelial responsivity. Taken together, our recent observations indicate that, stress-induced endothelial dysfunction occurs among premenopausal females, it varies indepen-dently of pre-existing atherosclerosis, and notably, it can initiate and progress in the absence of an atherogenic diet. These findings were unanticipated in that we did not expect that social factors would overshadow changes in plasma lipid profiles or progression of early atherosclerotic lesions as correlates of adverse changes in vascular responsivity. One potential implication of these observations is that psychological stress and accompanying ovarian impairment might also occasion adverse changes in vascular responsivity among premenopausal women. If so, physicians would do well to consider pursuing primary prevent of coronary disease in this population, using both behavioral interventions to ameliorate predisposing psychosocial factors as well as traditional risk-factor management.

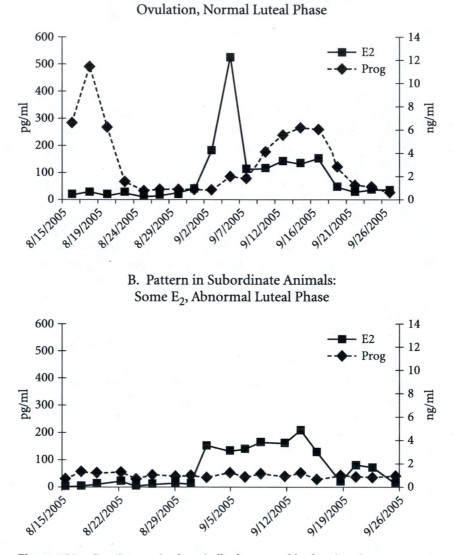

A. Pattern in Dominant Animals: Normal Ovulation, Normal Luteal Phase

B. Pattern in Subordinate Animals: Some E$_2$, Abnormal Luteal Phase

Figure 4.5A. Dominant animals typically show monthly elevations in progesterone as well as an ovulatory surge in estradiol. **4.5B.** Subordinate animals often show suppressed production of progesterone across the cycle with a variable amount of estradiol but no evidence of normal ovulation or formation of a corpus luteum.

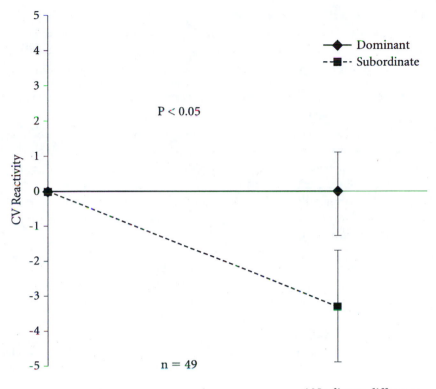

Figure 4.6. Vascular responses following intracoronary infusion of acetylcholine in comparison to vehicle. Subordinate monkeys constricted to a significantly greater extent than dominants, an effect that was independent of elevations in plasma lipids.

The final frontier: Do women provide a good model for cynomolgus monkeys?

The menopausal loss of cyclic ovarian function is believed to contribute to coronary heart disease (CHD) and osteoporosis, conditions comprising a major portion of the health burden of older women. We are coming to appreciate, however, that ovarian function varies in quality throughout the premenopausal years, with women experiencing disruptions in cyclic hormonal activity that range from mild to profound. Because they often occur among individuals that continue to cycle spontaneously, such disruptions are likely far more common than is generally recognized. Based on our aggregate work in female monkeys, we now propose that to the extent cyclic ovarian function affords protection against CHD and osteoporosis, ovulatory abnormalities in young women—even if mild and subclinical—will correspondingly accelerate development of these two diseases of aging and may affect risk of other chronic conditions such as diabetes and dementia. While affected individuals might not manifest the aforementioned diseases clinically during their premenopausal years, they may be at greatly increased risk post-menopausally. Importantly, the degree to which subclinical ovarian dysfunction accelerates premenopausal atherosclerosis and bone loss and thus affects post-menopausal health depends in part on the prevalence of such abnormalities among women of reproductive age. Functional hypothalamic anovulatory syndrome and polycystic ovarian syndrome are the most likely contributors to such impairment. While clinically obvious manifestations of these syndromes together affect ap-proximately 10% of premenopausal women, a much larger but as yet unknown number may experience subclinical dysfunction that nonetheless adversely influ-ences chronic disease risk (e.g., Berga, 1996; Reindollar, Novak, Tho, and McDo-nough, 1986; Carmina, Rosato, Janni, Rizzo, and Longo, 2006). Hence, the research program we have planned for the future will address two major gaps in knowledge concerning premenopausal women: *(1)* the prevalence of subclinical reproductive deficits in an unselected ("normal") population of spontaneously cycling women; and *(2)* the extent to which vulnerability to such abnormalities is a reliable indi-vidual trait that can be evaluated in relation to postmenopausal disease. The objective of this research is not only to determine whether common, subclinical reproductive abnormalities contribute to the postmenopausal health burden, but also to identify the point along the continuum of reproductive abnormality at which disease risk begins to accelerate. Our hope is that the resulting data will provide the rational basis for programs aimed at preventing or greatly delaying the onset of chronic disease in older women.

Conclusion

The most recent investigations described here reflect the continuing multidisci-plinary characteristics of the collaboration between Manuck and Kaplan. As with our previous studies, the current effort was supported by a program project that spanned the University of Pittsburgh and Wake Forest University School of Medicine. The nonhuman primate phase of this research program has ended for the time being to allow translation of these new data to studies of premenopausal women. Moving forward into this arena, we anticipate continued multidisciplinary collaboration as Kaplan's interests in reproductive medicine are complemented by Manuck's expertise in the genetic and environmental factors underlying suscep-tibility and resistance to chronic disease.

RECOMMENDED READINGS

Kaplan, J. R., and Manuck, S. B. (1999). Status, stress, and atherosclerosis: The role of environment and individual behavior. *Annals of the New York Academy of Science, 896,* 145–161.

Kaplan, J. R., Adams, M. R., Anthony, M. S., Morgan, T. M., Manuck, S. B., and Clarkson, T. B. (1995). Dominant social status and contraceptive hormone treatment inhibit atherogenesis in premenopausal monkeys. *Arteriosclerosis, Thrombosis and Vascular Biology, 15,* 2094–2100.

Kaplan, J. R., Adams, M. R., Clarkson, T. B., Manuck, S. B., Shively, C. A., and Williams, J. K. (1996). Psycho-social factors, sex differences, and atherosclerosis: Lessons from animal models. *Psychosomatic Medicine, 58,* 598–611.

Kaplan, J. R., Manuck, S. B., Adams, M. R., Weingand, K. W., and Clarkson, T. B. (1987). Inhibition of coronary atherosclerosis by propranolol in behaviorally predisposed monkeys fed an atherogenic diet. *Circulation, 76,*1364–1372.

Kaplan, J. R., Manuck, S. B., Anthony, M. S., and Clarkson, T. B. (2002). Premenopausal social status and hormone exposure predict postmenopausal atherosclerosis in female monkeys. *Obstetrics and Gynecology, 99*(3), 381–388.

Manuck, S. B., Adams, M. R., McCaffery, J. M., and Kaplan, J. R. (1997). Behaviorally elicited heart rate reactivity and atherosclerosis in ovariectomized cynomolgus monkeys (*Macaca fascicularis*). *Arteriosclerosis, Thrombosis and Vascular Biology, 17,*1774–1779.

Rozanski, A., Blumenthal, J. A., and Kaplan, J. R. (1999). Impact of psychological factors on the pathogenesis of cardiovascular disease and implications for therapy. *Circulation, 99,* 2192–2217.

Skantze, H. B., Kaplan, J., Pettersson, K., Manuck, S., Blomqvist, N., Kyes, R., Williams, K., and Bondjers, G. (1998). Psychosocial stress causes endothelial injury in cynomolgus monkeys via â1-adrenoceptor activation. *Atherosclerosis, 136,* 153–161.

REFERENCES

Adams, M. R., Kaplan, J. R., Clarkson, T. B., and Koritnik, D. R. (1985). Ovariectomy, social status, and atherosclerosis in cynomolgus monkeys. *Arteriosclerosis, 5,* 192–200.

Adams, M. R., Kaplan, J. R., and Koritnik, D. R. (1985). Psychosocial influences on ovarian endocrine and ovulatory function in *Macaca fascicularis. Physiology and Behavior, 35,* 935–940.

Adams, M. R., Kaplan, J. R., Koritnik, D. R., and Clarkson, T. B. (1987). Pregnancy-associated inhibition of coronary artery atherosclerosis in monkeys. Evidence of a relationship with endogenous estrogen. *Arteriosclerosis, 7,* 378–384.

Barnett, P. A., Spence, J. D., Manuck, S. B., and Jennings, J. R. (1997). Psychological stress and the progression of carotid artery disease. *Journal of Hypertension, 15,* 49–55.

Berga, S. L. (1996). Functional hypothalamic chronic anovulation. In E.Y. Adashi, J.A. Rock, Z. Rosenwaks (Eds.), *Reproductive Endocrinology, Surgery, and Technology* (Vol 1, pp. 1061–1075). Philadelphia PA: Lippecott-Rowen.

Berga, S. L., Daniels, T. L., and Giles, D. E. (1997). Women with functional hypothalamic amenorrhea but not other forms of anovulation display amplified cortisol concentrations. *Fertility and Sterility, 67,* 1024–1030.

Calhoun, J. (1963). The social use of space. In W. Mayer and R Van Gelder (Eds.), *Physiological Mammalogy* (Vol 1, pp. 2–188). New York: Academic Press.

Cameron, J. L. (1997). Stress and behaviorally induced reproductive dysfunction in primates. *Seminars in Reprodroduction and Endocrionology, 15,* 37–45.

Carmina, E., Rosato, F., Janni, A., Rizzo, M., and Longo, R. A. (2006). Relative prevalence of different androgen excess disorders in 950 women referred because of clinical hyperandrogenism. *Journal of Clinical Endocrinolonological Metabolism, 91,* 22–26.

Christian, J. J. (1980). Endocrine factors in population regulation. In N. N. Cohen, S. Malpass, and H. G. Klein (Eds.), *Physiological Mammalogy: Biosocial Mechanisms of Population Regulation* (pp. 55–116). New Haven: Yale University Press.

Clarkson, T. B., Anthony, M. S., and Morgan, T. M. (2001). Inhibition of postmenopausal atherosclerosis progression: A comparison of the effects of conjugated equine estrogens and soy phytoestrogens. *Journal of Clinical Endocrinology and Metabolism, 86*(1), 41–47.

Hanke, H., Hanke, S., Ickrath, O., Lange, K., Bruck, B., Muck, A. O., Seeger, H., Zwirner, M., Voisard, R., Haasis, R., and Hombach, V. (1997). Estradiol concentrations in premenopausal women with coronary heart disease. *Coronary Artery Disease, 8,* 511–515.

Henderson, A. (1996). Coronary heart disease: overview. *Lancet, 348,* S1–S4.

Henry, J. P., and Stephens, P. M. (1977). *Stress, Health and the Social Environment: A Sociobiological Approach to Medicine.* New York: Springer-Verlag.

Jewett, D. A., and Dukelow, W. R. (1972). Cyclicity and gestational length of *Macaca fascicularis. Primates, 13,* 327–330.

Kamarck, T. W., Everson, S. A., Kaplan, G. A., Manuck, S. B., Jennings, J. R., Salonen, R., and Salonen, J. T. (1997). Exaggerated blood pressure responses during mental stress are associated with enhanced carotid atherosclerosis in middle-aged Finnish men: Findings from the Kuopio Ischemic Heart Disease Study. *Circulation, 96,* 3842–3847.

Kamarck, T. W., Manuck, S. B., and Jennings, J. R. (1990). Social support reduces cardiovascular reactivity to psychological challenge: A laboratory model. *Psychosomatic Medicine, 52,* 42–58.

Kaplan, J. R., Adams, M. R., Anthony, M. S., Morgan, T. M., Manuck, S. B., and Clarkson, T. B. (1995). Dominant social status and contraceptive hormone treatment inhibit atherogenesis in premenopausal monkeys. *Arteriosclerosis, Thrombosis and Vascular Biology, 15,* 2094–2100.

Kaplan, J. R., Adams, M. R., Clarkson, T. B., and Koritnik, D. R. (1984). Psychosocial influences on female "protection" among cynomolgus macaques. *Atherosclerosis, 53,* 283–295.

Kaplan, J. R., and Manuck, S.,B. (2004). Ovarian dysfunction, stress, and disease: A primate continuum. National Research Council: *Institute of Laboratory Animals Resources (ILAR) Journal. 45,* 89–115.

Kaplan, J. R., Manuck, S. B., Adams, M. R., Weingand, K. W., and Clarkson, T. B. (1987). Inhibition of coronary atherosclerosis by propranolol in behaviorally predisposed monkeys fed an atherogenic diet. *Circulation, 76,* 1364–1372.

Kaplan, J. R., Manuck, S. B., Anthony, M. S., and Clarkson, T. B. (2002). Premenopausal social status and hormone exposure predict postmenopausal atherosclerosis in female monkeys. *Obstetrics and Gynecology, 99*(3), 381–388.

Kaplan, J. R., Manuck, S. B., Clarkson, T. B., Lusso, F. M., Taub, D. M., and Miller, E. W. (1983). Social stress and atherosclerosis in normocholesterolemic monkeys. *Science, 220,* 733–735.

Kaplan, J. R., Manuck, S. B., Clarkson, T. B., Lusso, F. M., and Taub, D. M. (1982). Social status, environment and atherosclerosis in cynomolgus monkeys. *Arteriosclerosis, 2,* 359–368.

Kaplan, J. R., Manuck, S. B., Clarkson, T. B., and Prichard, R. W. (1985). Animal models of behavioral influences on atherogenesis. *Advances in Behavioral Medicine, 1,* 115–163.

Libby, P. (1996). Atheroma: more than mush. *Lancet, 348,* S4–S7.

Mahone, J. P., and Dukelow, W. R. (1979). Seasonal variation of reproductive parameters in the laboratory-housed male cynomolgus macaque (*Macaca fascicularis*). *Journal of Medical Primatology, 8,* 179–183.

Manuck, S. B., Adams, M. R., McCaffery, J. M., and Kaplan, J. R. (1997). Behaviorally elicited heart rate reactivity and atherosclerosis in ovariectomized cynomolgus monkeys (*Macaca fascicularis*). *Arteriosclerosis, Thrombosis and Vascular Biology, 17,* 1774–1779.

Manuck, S. B., Kaplan, J. R., Adams, M. R., and Clarkson, T. B. (1989). Behaviorally elicited heart rate reactivity and atherosclerosis in female cynomolgus monkeys (*Macaca fascicularis*). *Psychosomatic Medicine, 51,* 306–318.

Manuck, S. B., Kaplan, J. R., and Clarkson, T. B. (1983). Behaviorally induced heart rate reactivity and atherosclerosis in cynomolgus monkeys. *Psychosomatic Medicine, 45,* 95–108.

Manuck, S. B. (1994). Cardiovascular reactivity in cardiovascular disease: "Once more unto the breach." *International Journal of Behavioral Medicine, 1,* 4–31.

Matthews, K. A., Owens, J. F., Kuller, L. H., Sutton-Tyrrell, K., Lassila, H. C., and Wolfson, S. K. (1998). Stress-induced pulse pressure change predicts women's carotid atherosclerosis. *Stroke 8,* 1525–1530.

Prior, J. C., Vigna, Y. M., Barr, S. I., Kennedy, S., Schulzer, M., and Li, D. K. B. (1996). Ovulatory premenopausal women lose cancellous spinal bone: A five year prospective study. *Bone, 18,* 161–167.

Prior, J. C., Vigna, Y. M., Schechter, M. T., and Burgess, A. E. (1990). Spinal bone loss and ovulatory disturbances. *New England Journal of Medicine, 323,* 1221–1227.

Reindollar, R. H., Novak, M., Tho, S. P., and McDonough, P. G. (1986). Adult-onset amenorrhea: a study of 262 patients. *American Journal of Obstetric Gynecology, 155,* 5315–5343.

Rudel, L. L., and Pitts, L. L. (1978). Male-female variability in the dietary cholesterol-induced hyperlipoproteinemia of cynomolgus monkeys (*Macaca fascicularis*). *Journal of Lipid Research, 19*(8), 992–1003.

Skantze, H. B., Kaplan, J., Pettersson, K., Manuck, S., Blomqvist, N., Kyes, R., Williams, K., and Bondjers, G. (1998). Psychosocial stress causes endothelial injury in cynomolgus monkeys via a1-adrenoceptor activation. *Atherosclerosis, 136,* 153–161.

Speroff, L. (2000). The perimenopausal transition. *Annals of the New York Academy of Science, 900,* 375–392.

Strawn, W. B., Bondjers, G., Kaplan, J. R., Manuck, S. B., Schwenke, D. C., Hansson, G. K., Shively, C. A., and Clarkson, T. B. (1991). Endothelial dysfunction in response to psychosocial stress in monkeys. *Circulation Research, 68,* 1270–1279.

Strong, J. P., Malcom, G. T., McMahan, C. A., Tracy, R. E., Newman W. P. III, Herderick, E. E., and Cornhill, J. F. (1999). Prevalence and extent of atherosclerosis in adolescent and young adults. Implications for prevention from the Pathobiological Determinants of Atherosclerosis in Youth Study. *Journal of the American Medical Association, 281,* 727–735.

Williams, J. K., Kaplan, J. R., and Manuck, S. B. (1993). Effects of psychosocial stress on endothelium-mediated dilation of atherosclerotic arteries in cynomolgus monkeys. *Journal of Clinical Investigation, 92,* 1819–1823.

Willliams, J. K., Kaplan, J. R., Suparto, I., Fox, J. L., and Manuck, S. B. (2003). Effects of exercise on cardiovascular outcomes in monkeys with risk factors for coronary heart disease. *Arteriosclerosis Thrombosis Vascular Biology, 23,* 8648–8671.

Williams, J. K., Vita, J. A., Selwyn, A. P., Manuck, S. B., and Kaplan, J. R. (1991). Psychosocial factors impair vascular responses of coronary arteries. *Circulation, 84,* 2146–2153.

Williams, R. F., and Hodgen, G. D. (1982). The reproductive cycle in female macaques. *American Journal of Primatology* Supplement 1, 181–192.

MIND MATTERS

Affective and Cognitive Neuroscience

Domain Introduction

RICHARD J. DAVIDSON

How is it that feelings and thoughts can affect our bodies and influence our health? The mind/brain is quite literally housed within a body and causally exerts an influence over it. This relationship is decidedly not unidirectional but, rather, operates reciprocally. We are truly on the dawn of a new understanding of this relationship that is both breathtaking in range and focused on mechanism or process. The role of mental events such as emotions, moods, and attitudes in physical health and illness is becoming a tractable problem because we have new tools for interrogating brain function, new concepts of how the brain gets molded by experience, and new data that illustrate the powerful role that the central circuitry of emotion and cognition can play in modulating autonomic, endocrine, and immune function. The data and conceptual frameworks that are emerging from this new work offer the potential for developing new interventions that target emotion and behavior change to facilitate health-promoting activity. In addition, this body of research is providing new insights into the way social and psychological factors appear to be associated with health outcomes. For the first time, we are able to go from the brain to the periphery and begin to characterize the detailed mechanisms by which central events influence bodily systems. And we have now begun to amass evidence and theory on the reverse pathway in this complex feedback system: the mechanisms by which bodily processes (including endocrine, immune, and autonomic processes) feed back on the brain and influence its functioning.

Although the interaction between brain and body has been a part of certain theoretical models of emotion for more than 100 years (e.g., James, 1890), it is only recently that the requisite conceptual and methodological advances have been made that underscore the importance of these interactions for health and disease. For example, we now know that central events regulate autonomic and endocrine function. The stress hormone cortisol is strongly influenced by activity in the hippocampus and amygdala, two of the important structures that make up the central circuitry of emotion. In turn, cortisol, through systemic circulation, feeds back on the brain. We also know that the hippocampus is a site with a high density of glucocorticoid receptors and is part of the regulatory pathway for cortisol.

Over the past several decades much evidence has accrued on central controls over autonomic function. Every level of the neuraxis, from the brainstem to the cortex, contributes to autonomic regulation. In turn, the autonomic nervous system feeds back on the brain through projections from the periphery back to the multiple regions within the brain and influences activity in these regions. And we are learning about the neural contributions to immune function. One mechanism through which central activity influences immune function is via the sympathetic nervous system. A growing corpus of evidence is establishing the critically important feedback role played by certain peripheral cytokines that cross the blood–brain barrier and influence brain activity. Thus, for each of the three peripheral systems implicated in health, we now know that there are two-way connections between the brain and these bodily systems. These are the mechanisms of mind-body interaction.

Each of the chapters in Part II tells a story about a successful interdisciplinary outcome that is focused on certain aspects of these issues. Each chapter embraces the view that psychological constructs are best addressed by simultaneously considering behavioral and biological levels of analysis. Each chapter discusses the brain mechanisms that are implicated in cognition or emotion, or both, and each illustrates the power that such an interdisciplinary approach provides. New ways of parsing psychological and behavioral constructs emerge from a consideration of the underlying brain processes that may be at work. And a deeper understanding of how environmental events might impinge on health is provided by a consideration of how the brain is shaped by environmental influence that, in turn, may influence the bodily systems that are implicated in health and disease.

The chapters span a range of levels; they review research that extends from molecular approaches in animals to brain imaging in humans. Each chapter spans neuroscience and psychology. In addition, one of the chapters ranges from molecular genetics to behavior (Chapter 8, by Meaney), while the others include brain-imaging methods that themselves require an extraordinary confluence of disciplines, including psychology, neuroscience, physics, and radiology. In addition to the presentation of basic, normative phenomena, each chapter also features the study of individual differences. The power of examining individual differences as a strategy for theory-based hypothesis testing is exemplified in several different ways. These presentations underscore the fact that the study of individual differences, once relegated to the "softer" sides of psychology, can now be approached with extraordinary rigor and with an emphasis on the underlying mechanisms that give rise to the behavioral expression of these individual differences.

In Chapter 6, Davidson presents an overview of recent findings on the neural substrates of emotion. He illustrates the confluence between findings at the animal level, recent studies of humans using noninvasive brain-imaging methods, and the study of patients with localized brain lesions. The development of noninvasive imaging methods has provided an extraordinary window on the study of neural circuitry in intact people and has catalyzed an unusual hybrid of disciplines working collaboratively, most notably physics, neuroscience, and psychology. The implications of this new interdisciplinary hybrid for scientific training are enormous since graduate education must keep pace with the rapid blurring of disciplinary boundaries. Some examples of how this might occur are offered.

In Chapter 7, Kosslyn presents the story of how visual mental imagery has progressed from a time of introspective analysis alone to the examination of the brain circuitry that underlies it. Imagery has been an important topic in the history of psychology since its beginning. In the early days of psychology, however, the sole method available for the study of mental imagery was introspection. Not surprisingly, little consistency emerged from such an analysis. In contemporary work, Kosslyn has been a major leader in the development of the view that the mechanisms underlying mental imagery draw on the same circuitry as that required for perception. In the case of visual mental imagery, this has meant the visual systems of the brain. Using a combination of clever experimental tasks that were developed on the basis of clearly articulated theory, along with sophisticated brain-imaging methods, he has systematically examined the contribution of different cortical territories to various aspects of visual mental imagery.

A major aid to the development of Kosslyn's theory was computational modeling. The combination of behavioral methods, computational modeling, and brain imaging provided the requisite tools for a detailed analysis of the mechanisms that underlie mental imagery. Two other aspects of this work are noteworthy. First, Kosslyn has studied the role of individual differences in activation levels in particular components of the visual system and has demonstrated that such differences predict individual differences in specific aspects of visual mental imagery ability. These findings again highlight the new ways in which differences among people in cognitive and emotional characteristics can now be studied. Second, Kosslyn shows how the cognitive restructuring of emotional visual imagery has predictable consequences for peripheral autonomic measures. While only preliminary, this work is the basis for a mechanistic explanation of how mental events—in this case, visual mental imagery—can affect the autonomic nervous system and thereby, possibly, influence health.

Meaney (Chapter 8) presents a breathtaking view of the effect of parental care on the psychology and biology of offspring. This elegant program of research, conducted with rodents, provides a detailed model of how early environmental influences can induce profound changes in the biology of the offspring at the level of gene expression. These changes in gene expression then have a cascading effect and alter the physiology of the offspring in ways that are enduring, probably lifelong. Meaney's work thus tackles the issue of nature and nurture and powerfully illustrates how, in light of modern molecular evidence, asking about the relative contributions of each is problematic. In particular, the expression of genes is so powerfully influenced by the environments in which they reside that the question loses its significance.

More generally, Meaney's research provides a molecular model of non-genomic transmission of psychological characteristics through maternal behavior toward her offspring. And, like the other two chapters in Part II, Meaney's chapter offers an extraordinary view of the power of analysis of individual differences. In this case, individual differences in maternal licking and grooming influence the development of neural systems in the pup that mediate behavioral and hypothalamic-pituitary adrenal responses to stress.

Each of the three examples featured in Part II illuminates the power of an interdisciplinary approach and shows how phenomena that were previously treated in a monodisciplinary way now have been tremendously enriched through inter-disciplinary analysis. It is also worth recognizing that, in the development of his research program, each author has had to overcome many obstacles. The description of these obstacles and the anticipation of the problems that lie ahead, particularly those pertaining to the training of the next generation of scientists, will hopefully inspire the continued cultivation of these approaches. The mechanisms by which emotion and cognition are instantiated in the brain, and the impact of these brain events on peripheral biology, offer great promise in both understanding psychological influences on health and in developing new methods for influencing the brain and behavior to promote better mental and physical health.

Postscript

In re-reading the material in this section for the new edition of this volume what is most striking is how firmly established this general area has become. When the phrase "affective neuroscience" was first used in a scientific journal article in 1995, it was inconceivable to me that in a mere 10 years, there would advertisements from the top psychology departments in the country recruiting for faculty in affective neuroscience. Moreover, the general trend presaged by these chapters—namely the importance of interdisciplinary research for addressing important and novel questions, has become very firmly grounded in much of the academy today where there appears to be generally increased interest in establishing interdisciplinary research centers and in hiring faculty who cross between two or more units on campus and who can talk with a broad range of colleagues.

There has also been remarkable progress in research methods that enable this work to mature and evolve. Brain imaging methods have evolved considerably so that tools are now available to interrogate both the structural and functional connections among different brain regions. These methods provide powerful opportunities to study circuits and not centers in the brain. The detailed connections between the brain and the periphery have begun to be delineated so that much more is known about the signaling systems and pathways that enable the bidirectional communication between the brain and the autonomic, endocrine, and immune systems. There are also methods now available that permit the transient perturbation of localized cortical function in humans (e.g., transcranial magnetic stimulation, TMS) and these offer the possibility of making causal inferences about the role of particular cortical regions in processes of interest. This strategy is particularly powerful when used in combination with brain imaging given that imaging methods are inherently correlational and in themselves, do not permit strong causal inferences to be made about the role of particular brain regions in specific psychological processes. TMS was used effectively by Kosslyn and his colleagues (1999) in research where they were able to transiently disrupt neural activity in visual cortex (where the imaging data suggested an important contribution) and observe behavioral changes on a mental imagery task that was putatively controlled by neural activity in visual cortex. Molecular biological methods have exploded in growth and the ability to study localized changes in gene expression in the brain for thousands of genes simultaneously is now possible. All of these developments have resulted in a plethora of new data that still very much requires integration and digestion and will be the focus of intensive scholarship over the next decade.

Another significant trend in research in this area is the general importance of neuroplasticity. This term refers to the fact that the brain can change in response to experience and training. The brain is the key organ that is built to change in response to experience, more so than any other organ. This provides an important clue to understanding how both deleterious and salubrious environments might alter brain function (and possibly brain structure) and then exert downstream effects on the body that impact health. It also implies that one of the intervention targets for at least certain physical diseases might be the mind–brain. And it provides a scientifically rigorous theoretical framework for understanding the mechanisms by which interventions at the level of mind can impact our physical health. As the reader will note from the postscript by Michael Meaney, his work has probed more deeply into the underlying molecular mechanisms changes through which environmental experience is transduced. The hybrid field of epigenetics refers to modifications in the genome that do not sequence changes but do involve alterations in genomic function. His work has shed important light on the molecular pathways through which epigenetic change occurs.

Finally, an important trend in this area of interdisciplinary research is the combination of field and laboratory research in the same group of subjects. To understand the brain mechanisms that are implicated in health, it is ultimately necessary to study people both in the laboratory and in the field, and this practice is becoming increasingly more prevalent. There are several current examples where laboratory protocols are being selectively added to longitudinal field studies. One example is the Midlife in the United States (MIDUS) sample that is currently being funded by the National Institute on Aging. This began as a field study and the current wave of data collection includes laboratory measures taken at several sites around the country. The opportunity to combine the fine-grained biological measures collected in the lab with the survey and interview-based measures of well-being and other psychological characteristics obtained over a many-year span will provide an unparalleled and rich dataset to begin to make meaningful connections between the brain, body, and the social world. These trends bode well for the next chapter in this interdisciplinary research adventure.

REFERENCES

Damasio, A. R. (1994). *Descartes' Error.* New York: Avon Books.

Davidson, R. J. (2000). Affective style, psychopathology and resilience: Brain mechanisms and plasticity. *American Psychologist, 55,* 1196–1214.

Davidson, R. J., Jackson, D. C., and Kalin, N. H. (2000). Emotion, plasticity, context and regulation: Perspectives from affective neuroscience. *Psychological Bulletin, 126*(6), 890–906.

James, W. (1890). *Principles of Psychology.* New York: Holt.

Kosslyn, S. M., Pascual-Leone, A., Felician, O., Camposano, S., Keenan, J. P., Thompson, W. L., Ganis, G., Sukel, K. E., and Alpert, N. M. (1999). The role of area 17 in visual imagery: Convergent evidence from PET and rTMS. *Science, 284,* 167-170.

McEwen, B. S. (1998). Protective and damaging effects of stress mediators. *New England Journal of Medicine, 338,* 171–179.

Sapolsky, R. M. (1996). Why stress is bad for your brain. *Science, 273,* 749–750.

6

Affective Neuroscience

A Case for Interdisciplinary Research

RICHARD J. DAVIDSON

> In nature hybrid species are usually sterile, but in science the reverse is often true. Hybrid subjects are often astonishingly fertile, whereas if a scientific discipline remains too pure it wilts.
>
> Francis Crick, *What Mad Pursuit*

Why is it that some people can handle stress effectively, while others exhibit more intense and prolonged reactions and sometimes even develop psychiatric or physical ailments when they are confronted with aversive events? Are the factors that determine these differences among people the same as those that govern why one toddler is exceedingly wary and shy and another is outgoing and bold? Are we born with these characteristics? What is the extent to which these characteristics change over time and in response to specific types of experiences? What are the brain mechanisms responsible for these emotional styles? These are a few of the many questions the new interdisciplinary area of affective neuroscience is considering.

Questions about the nature of emotion have been prominent in philosophy and psychology since these disciplines first emerged as domains of scholarly inquiry. For example, William James (1981[1890]) in his now famous chapter in *The Principles of Psychology* considers some of the origins of our subjective experience of emotion and suggests that our feelings arise as a consequence of specific patterns of bodily and visceral action. He argued that the commonly assumed causal sequence that eventuates in an emotional experience was incorrect. James explained that it is not the result of our experience of fear that our heart beats more strongly and quickly but, rather, it is just the reverse—namely, that we feel fear *because* our heart beats strongly and quickly. While the details of these two proposals continue to be debated today (for discussion, see Davidson, Jackson, and Kalin, 2000), both views helped to focus attention on the fact that emotion is a biobehavioral process, one that requires an accounting of both mental and physical attributes.

This view of emotion as a fundamentally psychobiological process is endorsed by nearly every theoretical camp in affective science today (Ekman and Davidson, 1994). It has also helped to focus attention on the brain mechanisms that support emotion and the circuitry that underlies different aspects of emotional or affective style. Over the past five years, a remarkable convergence has occurred that has led to the emergence of affective neuroscience as a new interdisciplinary effort. Four major strands can be identified that have played an important role in shaping this emerging area.

First is the trend already noted that holds emotion to be fundamentally a psychobiological process, one that demands interaction between the mind and body.

Second is a long tradition of research in animals that has delineated some of the key components of circuitry that subserves at least rudimentary components of emotional processes.

Third is a growing literature on the effects of discrete localized brain lesions on emotional behavior.

Fourth, there are the remarkable advances made possible by the advent of modern neuroimaging, particularly functional magnetic resonance imaging (fMRI).

The classic literature of what was then called "physiological psychology" in the 1950s and 1960s concerned the neural substrates of emotion and related constructs such as motivation. However, it has been only recently that strong connections between this research tradition and the study of emotion in humans has been made (Berridge, 2002). While the emotional consequences of human brain injury have been a focus of clinical inquiry from the early days of neuropsychology and behavioral neurology, little systematic work on this topic was performed before the past two decades. However, during this recent past, a growing literature has accumulated that suggests different roles for the left and right prefrontal regions in different aspects of emotion, as well as specific roles for subcortical regions such as the amygdala, hippocampus, and ventral sriatum (for review, see Davidson and Irwin, 1999b). The circuitry identified in the animal and human lesion literature can now be probed by using completely noninvasive imaging in humans. It was not until 1995 that the very first article to use fMRI to study emotion was published, but since then an enormous corpus of literature has been generated (see Davidson and Irwin, 1999a). This work is still very much in its infancy, although it promises to dramatically change how we study emotion and affective style.

Some of the important findings from this collective body of work will be summarized in Part III of this volume, but for now, these four strands underscore the wide range of disciplines that have played a role in the creation of affective neuroscience. In addition to neuroscience and psychology, neurology, psychiatry, psychophysiology, radiology, and physics have assumed important roles. The latter two disciplines have been involved because of their interest and expertise in neuroimaging. As increasingly sophisticated experimental designs and image-processing requirements come on the scene, neuroimaging research is also attracting computer scientists, mathematicians, and statisticians. In my own laboratory, there are currently three Ph.D. physicists working on various aspects of neuroimaging and image analysis. These are physicists who are conversant in psychology and neuroscience, a combination that was not even imagined a mere decade earlier.

Reaching even further across traditional disciplinary divides is new work that seeks to integrate our understanding of the brain mechanisms that support emotion and determine individual differences in affective style with other research on bodily systems implicated in health and disease such as the endocrine and immune systems. We are now beginning to understand how the brain communicates with these systems and how the chemical products produced by these systems can influence the brain through systemic circulation. These new levels of integration have required immunologists and endocrinologists to enter the mix to promote new understanding of how the brain influences these systems and vice versa (see, e.g., McEwen, 1998). For the first time, this work is revealing the detailed mechanisms by which emotions, as instantiated in the brain, can have downstream effects on biological systems that are directly implicated in health and disease. These new insights have profound implications for understanding the role of behavioral factors in health. They also necessitate a radical re-thinking of how graduate training should be conducted to harness the power of such interdisciplinary effort.

The Circuitry of Emotion and Affective Style

Two areas of the brain that have been identified as playing an especially important role in affective processes are the prefrontal cortex (PFC) and the amygdala. Figure 6.1 displays these brain regions. In the first two parts of this section, I provide some of the key concepts and findings that link different territories of the PFC and the amygdala to affective processes. In the third part of this section, I consider the issue of affective style. One of the most salient characteristics of emotion is that the same emotionally challenging event will frequently elicit very different reactions across different individuals. Affective style refers to a broad range of differences among individuals in emotional reactivity and affective processing.

The prefrontal cortex

Although it approaches the topic from very different perspectives, a growing body of literature is converging on the idea that there exist two fundamental systems that underlie approach- and withdrawal-related emotion and motivation, or positive and negative affect (Cacioppo and Gardner, 1999; Davidson and Irwin, 1999b; Gray, 1994; Lang, Bradley, and Cuthbert, 1990; Schnierla, 1959). The precise description of these systems differs somewhat across investigators, as does the anatomical circuitry that is featured, but the essential elements are quite similar in each proposal. The approach system has been described by Davidson and Irwin (1999b)

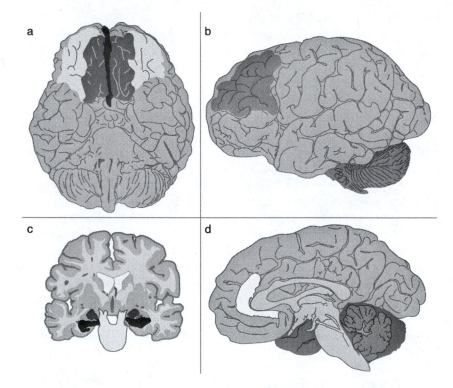

Figure 6.1. Key structures in the circuitry underlying affective processing and emotion regulation. (a) Orbital prefrontal cortex (lightest areas) and ventromedial prefrontal cortex (darkest areas); (b) dorsolateral prefrontal cortex (dark area at left); (c) hippocampus (darkest areas) and amygdala (darkened areas above hippocampus); (d) anterior cingulate cortex (lightest area). Each of these interconnected structures plays a role in different aspects of emotion and emotion regulation. Abnormalities in one or more of these regions or in the interconnections among them (or both) are associated with failures of emotion regulation. From Davidson, Marshall, Tomarken, and Henriques (2000).

as facilitating appetitive behavior and generating particular types of positive affect that are approach-related, such as the emotion occurring as an organism moves closer toward a desired goal. The withdrawal system, in contrast, facilitates the withdrawal of an organism from sources of aversive stimulation or organizes appropriate responses to cues of threat. This system also generates withdrawal-related negative emotions such as disgust and fear. A variety of evidence indicates that these systems are implemented in partially separable circuits, and it is to this evidence that we now turn. My focus here is on two key components of this circuitry: the prefrontal cortex (PFC) and the amygdala. For more extensive discussion of this entire circuitry, including other regions not considered here, see Davidson and Irwin (1999b).

A large corpus of data at both the animal and human levels implicate various sectors of the PFC in emotion. The PFC is not a homogeneous zone of tissue but, rather, has been differentiated on the basis of both cytoarchitectonic and functional considerations. The three subdivisions of the primate PFC that have been consistently distinguished include the dorsolateral, ventromedial, and orbitofrontal sectors. In addition, there appear to be important functional differences between the left and right sides within each of these sectors.

The case for the differential importance of left and right PFC sectors for emotional processing was first made systematically in a series of studies on patients with unilateral cortical damage (Gainotti, 1972; Robinson, Starr, and Price, 1984; Sackeim et al., 1982). Each of these studies compared the mood of patients with unilateral left- or right-sided brain damage and found a greater incidence of depressive symptoms after left-sided damage. The general interpretation that has been placed on these studies is that depressive symptoms are increased after left-sided anterior PFC damage because this brain territory participates in a circuit that underlies certain forms of positive affect; damage to this region leads to deficits in the capacity to experience positive affect, which is a hallmark feature of depression (Watson et al., 1995). Although most of the extant lesion data are consistent with this general picture (for a review, see Robinson and Downhill, 1995), some inconsistencies have also appeared (e.g., Gainotti, Caltagirone, and Zoccolotti, 1993; House et al., 1990). I have reviewed in detail these studies and addressed a number of critical methodological and conceptual concerns in this literature (see Davidson, 1993).

A growing corpus of evidence in normal intact humans is consistent with the findings derived from the lesion evidence. We (Davidson, Ekman, Saron, Senulis, and Friesen, 1990) and others (e.g., Ahern and Schwartz, 1985; Jones and Fox, 1992; Tucker, Stenslie, Roth, and Shearer, 1981) have reported that induced positive and negative affective states shift the asymmetry in prefrontal brain activation in lawful ways.

Other investigators have used clinical groups to induce a stronger form of negative affect in the laboratory than is possible with normal controls. One common strategy for evoking anxiety among anxious patients in the laboratory is to present them with specific types of stimuli that are known to provoke their anxiety (e.g., pictures of spiders for spider phobics; making a public speech for social phobics). In a study using brain electrical activity measures, my colleagues and I recently found that when social phobics anticipate making a public speech, they show large increases in right-sided anterior activation (Davidson, Marshall, Tomarken, and Henriques, 2000). Pooling across data from three separate anxiety-disordered groups, Rauch, Savage, Alpert, Fischman, and Jenike (1997) found two regions of the PFC that were consistently activated across groups: the right inferior PFC and the right medial orbital PFC.

The ventromedial PFC has been implicated in the anticipation of future positive and negative affective consequences. Bechara and his colleagues (Bechara, Damasio, Damasio, and Anderson, 1994) have reported that patients with bilateral lesions of the ventromedial PFC have difficulty anticipating future positive or negative consequences, although immediately available rewards and punishments do influence their behavior. Such patients show decreased levels of electrodermal activity in anticipation of a risky choice compared with controls, while controls exhibit such autonomic change before they explicitly know that it is a risky choice (Bechara, Damasio, Damasio, and Lee, 1999; Bechara, Damasio, Tranel, and Damasio, 1997; Bechara, Tranel, Damasio, and Damasio, 1996).

The findings from the lesion method when effects of small unilateral lesions are examined and from neuroimaging studies in normal subjects and patients with anxiety disorders converge on the conclusion that increases in right-sided activation in various sectors of the PFC are associated with increased negative affect. Less evidence is available for the domain of positive affect, in part because positive affect is much harder to elicit in the laboratory.

Systematic studies designed to disentangle the specific role played by various sectors of the PFC in emotion are lacking. Many theoretical accounts of emotion assign it an important role in guiding action and organizing behavior toward the acquisition of motivationally significant goals (e.g., Frijda, 1994; Levenson, 1994). This process requires that the organism have some means of representing affect in the absence of immediately present rewards and punishments and other affective incentives. Such a process may be likened to a form of affective working memory. It is likely that the PFC plays a key role in this process (see, e.g., Watanabe, 1996). Damage to certain sectors of the PFC impair an individual's capacity to anticipate future affective outcomes and consequently result in an inability to guide behavior in an adaptive fashion. Such damage is not likely to disrupt an individual's responding to immediate cues for reward and punishment, only the anticipation before and sustaining after an affective cue is presented. With regard to the different functional roles of the dorsolateral and ventromedial sectors of the PFC, Davidson and Irwin (1999a, b), on the basis of considering both human and animal studies, suggested that the latter sector is most likely involved in the representation of elementary positive and negative affective states in the absence of immediately present incentives, while the former sector is most directly involved in the representation of goal states toward which these more elementary positive and negative states are directed.

The amygdala

A large corpus of research at the animal—mostly rodent—level has established the importance of the amygdala for emotional processes (e.g., Aggleton, 1993; Cahill and McGaugh, 1998; LeDoux, 1996). Since many reviews of the animal literature have appeared recently, a detailed description of these studies will not be presented here. LeDoux and his colleagues have marshaled a large body of compelling evidence to suggest that the amygdala is necessary for the establishment of conditioned fear. Whether the amygdala is necessary for the expression of that fear following learning and whether the amygdala is the actual locus of where the learned information is stored are still matters of some controversy (see Cahill Weinberger, Roozendaal, and McGaugh, 1999; Faneslow and LeDoux, 1999). Also not resolved is the extent to which the amygdala participates in all learning of stimulus-incentive associations, both negative and positive, and whether there are functional differences between the left and right amygdala (Davidson and Irwin, 1999b). The classic view of amygdala damage in nonhuman primates resulting in major affective disturbances as expressed in the Kluver-Bucy syndrome—where the animal exhibits abnormal approach, hyper-orality and sexuality, and little fear—is now thought to be a function of damage elsewhere in the medial temporal lobe. When very selective excitotoxic lesions of the amygdala are made that preserve fibers of passage, nothing resembling the Kluver-Bucy syndrome is observed (Kalin, Shelton, Davidson, and Kelley, 2001). The upshot of this diverse array of findings is to suggest a more limited role for the amygdala in certain forms of emotional learning, even though the human data imply a more heterogeneous contribution.

While the number of patients with discrete lesions of the amygdala is small, they have provided unique information on the role of this structure in emotional processing. A number of studies have now reported specific impairments in the recognition of facial expressions of fear in patients with restricted amygdala damage (Adolphs, 2002; Broks et al., 1998; Calder et al., 1996). Recognition of facial signs of other emotions was found to be intact. In a study that required subjects to make judgments of trustworthiness and approachability of unfamiliar adults from facial photographs, patients with bilateral amygdala damage judged the unfamiliar individuals to be more approachable and trustworthy than did control subjects (Adolphs, Tranel and Damasio, 1998). Other researchers (Bechara et al., 1995) have demonstrated that aversive autonomic conditioning is impaired in a patient with amygdala damage, despite the fact that the patient showed normal declarative knowledge of the conditioning contingencies. Collectively, these findings from patients with selective bilateral destruction of the amygdala suggest specific impairments on tasks that tap aspects of negative emotion processing. Most of the studies have focused on the perceptual side where the data clearly show the amygdala to be important for the recognition of cues of threat or danger. The conditioning data also indicate that the amygdala may be necessary for acquiring new implicit autonomic learning of stimulus-punishment contingencies.

Since 1995, a growing number of studies using positron emission topography (PET) and fMRI to investigate the role of the amygdala in emotional processes have begun to appear. Many studies have reported more activation of the amygdala detected with either PET or fMRI when anxiety-disordered patients have been exposed to their specific anxiety-provoking stimuli than when they were exposed to control stimuli (e.g., Breiter et al., 1996). When social phobics were exposed to neutral faces, they showed activation of the amygdala comparable to what was observed in both the phobics and controls in response to aversive versus neutral odors (Birbaumer et al., 1998). Consistent with the human lesion data, a number of studies have now reported more activation of the amygdala in response to facial expressions of fear than in response to neutral, happy, or disgust control faces (e.g., Adolphs, 2002; Breiter et al., 1996). In a recent study, Whalen and his colleagues (Whalen et al., 1998) observed activation of the amygdala in response to masked fear faces that were not consciously perceived. Unpleasant pictures have also been found to activate the amygdala more than neutral and pleasant pictures did (Irwin et al., 1996; Lane et al., 1997). Finally, a number of studies have reported activation of the amygdala during early phases of aversive conditioning (Buchel et al., 1998; Morris, Ohman, and Dolan, 1998).

The findings from both the lesion and neuroimaging studies on the role of the amygdala in affective processes raise a number of important questions about the functional significance of amygdala activation and the precise role this structure may play in human emotion. One key question is whether the amygdala is implicated in all emotion—negative affect in particular—or fear most specifically. Most neuroimaging studies that have induced actual emotion find greater amygdala activation to negative than to positive elicitors. Of the studies that have examined amygdala activation in response to facial expressions, all have consistently found greater activation in response to fear than to other emotional faces, although a complete range of other emotions has not been sampled. Whalen (1999) has interpreted these data within a model that assigns a primary role to the amygdala for the detection of ambiguity. According to this model, preferential activation of the amygdala is observed in response to fear than to anger faces because the former convey threat, even though the source of the threat is ambiguous, while angry faces convey an unambiguous threat.

Finally, an issue left unaddressed in the human data is whether the amygdala is required for the ongoing expression of negative affect, or whether it is specifically involved in only the initial acquisition of aversive learning. The fact that amygdala activation is present during early phases of conditioning and then appears to rapidly habituate (Buchel et al., 1998) is consistent with the idea that the amygdala may be required only in the initial stages of learning. These findings imply that the amygdala may be crucial for learning new stimulus-threat contingencies but may not be necessary for the expression of already acquired individual differences in temperament or affective style.

Affective style

I have used the term *affective style* to refer to the broad range of individual differences in subcomponents of affective reactivity and dispositional mood (see Davidson, 1992, 1998). This is a very global term, and it is imperative to specify with more precision which particular system one is measuring affective reactivity in, and which subcomponent of reactivity is being targeted for study. For example, one could measure affective reactivity by using startle magnitude, magnetic resonance (MR) signal change in the amygdala, or ratings on a self-report scale as the measure. Each of these obviously reflects activity in very different systems, and activation in these systems will not necessarily cohere. What is meant by "subcomponent of reactivity" has been articulated in detail previously (Davidson, 1998) and includes the following parameters: tonic level, threshold to respond, peak or amplitude of response, rise time to peak of response, and recovery time. These are not meant to necessarily reflect an exhaustive list of subcomponents; they are merely offered as examples. Each of these subcomponents potentially can be studied in different response systems, leading to many parameters of affective style. We know virtually nothing about the psychometric characteristics of measures of these different parameters, except for self-report measures (for two recent efforts examining different subcomponents of affective style in two different physiological response systems, see Tomarken, Davidson, Wheeler, and Kinney, 1992; Larson, Ruffalo, Nietert, and Davidson, 2000), although this information is crucial if we are to develop rigorous measures of these constructs. In this section, I review data on the contributions of individual differences in prefrontal and amygdala function to affective style.

In two decades of previous research, we have performed a large number of studies designed to examine the role of activation asymmetries in prefrontal cortex and other anterior cortical zones in aspects of affective style. This work has been reviewed recently (Davidson, 1995, 1998), so that here only highlights are presented. Using measures of scalp-recorded brain electrical activity, we found that indices of activation asymmetry based on power spectral measures were stable over time and exhibited excellent internal consistency reliability (Tomarken, Davidson, Wheeler, and Kinney, 1992), thus fulfilling a number of important psychometric criteria for an index of a trait-like construct. In a series of studies, we found that there are large individual differences in the magnitude and direction of baseline asymmetric activation in brain electrical activity measures obtained from prefrontal scalp regions in both infants (Davidson and Fox, 1989) and adults (Davidson and Tomarken, 1989). We found that 10-month-old infants with greater relative right-sided prefrontal activation in prefrontal scalp regions were more likely to cry in response to a brief period of maternal separation than were their left-activated counterparts (Davidson and Fox, 1989). We observed that toddlers and young children with greater relative right-sided prefrontal activation showed more behavioral inhibition and wariness (measured through laboratory-based behavioral observation) (Davidson and Rickman, 1999). In adults, we found that individual differences in such measures predict dispositional mood (Tomarken, Davidson, Wheeler, and Doss, 1992), self-report measures of behavioral activation and inhibition (Sutton and Davidson, 1997), repressive defensiveness (Tomarken and Davidson, 1994), reactivity to positive and negative emotion elicitors (Tomarken, Davidson, and Henriques, 1990; Wheeler, Davidson, and Tomarken, 1993) baseline immune function (Kang et al., 1991), and reactivity of the immune system to emotional challenge (Davidson, Coe, Dolski, and Donzella, 1999). In recent work (Larson et al., 1998) we found that individual differences in electrophysiological measures of prefrontal asymmetry predicted the magnitude of recovery following a negative affective stimulus. These data suggest that the prefrontal cortex may play a role in regulating the time course of emotional responding or in the active inhibition of negative affect.

We also found that individual differences in these brain electrical measures of anterior asymmetry are associated with mood and anxiety disorders. In particular, we found that depressed subjects and individuals who are currently euthymic but have a history of past depression exhibit less left prefrontal activation than do never-depressed controls (Henriques and Davidson, 1990). We also found that when social phobics anticipate making a public speech, they show large increases in right-sided prefrontal activation, although they do not differ from controls at baseline (Davidson et al., 2000).

In a series of studies with Kalin (Davidson, Kalin, and Shelton, 1992, 1993; Kalin, Larson, Shelton, and Davidson, 1998), we have demonstrated that similar activation asymmetries can be measured in rhesus monkeys and that they predict similar types of behavior and biology as we observe in humans. In the most recent effort of this kind, we (Kalin et al., 1998) found that animals with greater relative right-sided prefrontal activation exhibit higher basal levels of the stress hormone cortisol. Similar data have recently been reported in humans (Buss, Dolski, Malmstadt, Davidson, and Goldsmith, 1997)

The data from the Larson et al. (1998) study referred to above indicated that individuals with greater relative left-sided prefrontal activation at baseline have greater recovery of startle potentiation following the offset of a negative stimulus. Moreover, the measure of asymmetric prefrontal activation accounted for more variance in the magnitude of startle post-negative-stimulus offset (i.e., startle recovery) than it did during the stimulus. These findings imply that individual differences in prefrontal activation asymmetry may play a role in regulating the time course of emotional responding and that those individuals with more left-sided prefrontal activation may recover more quickly than their right-activated counterparts from negative affect or stress.

A clue to the mechanism that may underlie this consequence of left prefrontal activation is provided by a study from LeDoux's laboratory, where they found that rats with lesions of the medial prefrontal cortex show dramatically slower extinction of a learned aversive response than do sham-operated controls (Morgan, Romanski and LeDoux, 1993; but see Gewirtz, Fall, and Davis, 1997). These findings imply that there is a descending pathway between the medial PFC and the amygdala (Amaral, Price, Pitkanen, and Carmichael, 1992) that is inhibitory and thus represents an active component of extinction. In the absence of this normal inhibitory input, the amygdala remains unchecked and continues to stay activated.

The two key features of the circuitry underlying positive and negative affect highlighted in this essay are the prefrontal cortex and the amygdala. Earlier, I detailed studies on the basic function of the amygdala in affective behavior. Here I ask the question about individual differences in amygdala function and its relation to affective style. Using magnetic resonance imaging (MRI)-guided regions of interest to extract glucose metabolic rate measured with PET, we (Abercrombie et al., 1998) found that individual differences in metabolic activity in the right amygdala predicts dispositional negative affect on the Positive and Negative Affect Schedule (PANAS; Watson, Clark, and Tellegen, 1988) in a group of depressed patients. Using the same measure of negative affect, we (Irwin, Davidson, Kalin, Sorenson, and Turski, 1998) also found MR signal changes in the amygdala in response to negative versus neutral stimuli accounts for a substantial amount of variance in PANAS trait negative affect scores ($r = .63$).

The fact that there exist reliable individual differences in baseline metabolic rate in the amygdala also requires comment, in light of the earlier discussion about the amygdala's role in phasic affective processes. There is clearly intrinsic neural activity in the amygdala, even during sleep. As a number of studies have now shown, baseline nontask ("resting") levels of activation in the amygdala are associated with dispositional negative affect (Abercrombie et al., 1998) and depression (Drevets et al., 1992). Whether these baseline differences in amygdala activation reflect activation in response to the PET environment or whether such differences predict the magnitude of task-induced activation in the amygdala in response to emotion elicitors are questions that must be addressed in future research.

The findings presented in the preceding section highlight the role of the prefrontal cortex and the amygdala in affective processing. What is most significant about this research is that information about the neural systems underlying affect led to new insights about the mechanisms of emotion and emotion regulation. The distinctions between pre-goal and post-goal attainment positive affect, between the initial learning of affective associations and their subsequent expression, and between emotional reactivity and emotion regulation were all informed by knowledge of the brain circuitry involved. The amygdala appears to play a crucial role in alerting other brain systems that a stimulus of biological significance, usually a threat, is occurring. The prefrontal cortex is crucially involved in the representation of affective states in the absence of environmental stimuli. In particular, the PFC is crucial for the anticipation of upcoming affective challenges and for the maintenance of affect following the offset of an emotional elicitor. In addition, the PFC appears to play an important role in emotion regulation, in part by modulating the reactivity of the amygdala. Of most importance for the research described here is the fact that there are reliable individual differences in the activation levels in this circuitry and that such differences are systematically related to affective style. These individual differences play a key role in determining personality and vulnerability to psychopathology. They also appear to be related to endocrine and immune function and, as such, likely will be important in our developing understanding of the mechanisms by which emotions influence physical health.

Origins of Interdisciplinary Collaboration

My own quest for interdisciplinarity began as a graduate student at Harvard where the faculty were especially receptive to my fledgling efforts to reach across vast disciplinary boundaries that rarely had been previously connected. While pursuing graduate work in personality and experimental psychopathology, it was clear to me from the outset that a biological approach to these topics would afford a level of precision that was not possible to achieve if one remained exclusively within the behavioral sciences. Moreover, as new findings were becoming available on the functional specialization of the human brain, it was apparent that this information provided useful constraints on theory at the psychological level and also provided unique insights into how to best parse domains that were previously categorized only on the basis of descriptive phenomenology. Accordingly, during those graduate school years, I took courses in neuroanatomy with Walle Nauta at MIT and in behavioral neurology with Norman Geschwind at Harvard Medical School. These two great scientists provided a critical complement to the traditional courses I was taking in the psychology department. Harvard is one of those rare institutions that imposes minimal formal requirements on its students and permits them great freedom in sculpting their own graduate curriculum. This permissive environment was a key factor in nurturing my early yearnings for the interdisciplinary quest that now has come to define my career.

Immediately after graduate school, I was able to continue some of the interdisciplinary work that I began to conceive in graduate school because of two separate opportunities. One involved continuing my training in brain electrophysiology with a world-class neuroscientist in New York—Roy John, who helped me to appreciate the possibility of using electrophysiological measures to address questions about higher mental function. The second began by a chance encounter with a former graduate student friend and colleague—Nathan Fox, then a developmental psychologist in New York City. As we began to interact, it quickly became apparent that Fox and I shared an interest in individual differences in emotional reactivity or temperament, although we approached them from totally different perspectives. Our interactions led to collaborative work that eventuated in our first joint publication in 1982, in *Science* (Davidson and Fox, 1982), and reported the first demonstration of differentiation between positive and negative affect in human infants on the basis of prefrontal brain electrical asymmetries. The collaboration with Fox was a very fruitful one, leading to a series of publications that helped define an important developmental component to our ongoing work in affective neuroscience. This developmental work continues today.

Once I moved to Wisconsin in 1985, a series of other opportunities were available. One of the strengths of Wisconsin lies in the Harlow Primate Laboratory. It soon became apparent that an important extension of the work I had been conducting with humans would be to develop a nonhuman primate model that would enable us to investigate some of the underlying biological mechanisms in ways that were not possible in humans. With Ned Kalin, we embarked on a major program of work that has led to an extremely fruitful collaboration in both monkeys and humans. This work continues today and has resulted in the securing of two large grants from NIH for the newly secured center for the study of mind–body interaction.

In addition to the collaboration with Kalin, there were other extremely fortunate collaborative opportunities at Wisconsin. While I had a long-standing interest in the possible health implications of variations in affective style, I had little opportunity to examine the mechanisms by which such interactions might occur. That variations in affective style might be connected with health was an idea that was beginning to receive widespread acceptance in both the lay and scientific communities. However, the search for underlying mechanisms was embryonic at best. I had the opportunity to collaborate with Chris Coe, a psychoneuroimmunologist, to begin a series of studies that focused on relations between individual differences in brain function in the circuitry of emotion and immune function. The opportunity to continue this line of research will expand with our new NIH center.

As the importance of examining the circuits (including both cortical and subcortical components) that subserve affective style became more apparent, so did the need for better tools to examine regional brain function. This need has driven a major new initiative at Wisconsin that I have directed to establish new and better facilities for functional neuroimaging. During the period from about 1990 to 1995, I initiated a set of collaborations throughout the country to begin to study emotion with modern neuroimaging methods, both PET and fMRI. It was through these initial collaborations that I learned many of the basics of these procedures. In response to my urging, and following the receipt of a substantial foundation grant, Wisconsin decided to invest heavily in new neuroimaging facilities. Our ability to marshal a convincing case was in large measure a function of the successful interdisciplinary integration that we have been able to achieve among a remarkably diverse group of faculty and staff that include members of the departments of psychology, psychiatry, medical physics, and radiology.

A significant major catalyst for interdisciplinary work over the past decade originated in my membership in the MacArthur Foundation Research Network for the Study of Mind-Body Interaction. This group, comprising approximately 12 scholars, including psychologists, psychiatrists, immunologists, an endocrinologist, and a historian of science, met regularly together for about eight years, with a focus on understanding the mechanisms by which mental events, as they are instantiated in the brain, can have downstream effects on the body that may affect health and disease. Participation in this group was a remarkable privilege and deeply affected each of us. Moreover, I think it is fair to say that we all learned an enormous amount and, over time, felt more comfortable talking each other's language and thus laying the foundation for more meaningful interdisciplinary research. My participation in the MacArthur network was a seminal stimulus for launching a collaboration with Carol Ryff, a colleague at Wisconsin and a member of another MacArthur network, and Burt Singer of Princeton, a member of the MacArthur Health and SES Network. Together we have begun to examine connections between life histories and biology in the context of the Wisconsin Longitudinal Study (WLS) described above. Along with the primate collaboration, this work with Ryff and Singer provided a crucial foundation for us to compete successfully for the NIH Center for Mind-Body Interaction.

Constraints and Facilitating Factors

Many formidable forces constrain interdisciplinary work. Perhaps the most difficult to overcome is the dominant zeitgeist in the scientific community that strongly
dictates the questions that are worth examining and possible to study. In the late
1970s, when I completed graduate school, there was no field of inquiry called affective neuroscience, and the very idea of studying emotion and the brain in people
was looked at askance. Obtaining grant funds for this type of research in those days
was a difficult and frustrating process since reviewers competent in both the biological measures and the substantive area of emotion research were exceedingly
rare. This is all quite different today, and it is heartening to see that so much has
changed in 20 years.

Many factors can be identified that facilitated this work. The culture changed
during the 1990s, and today the notion that emotions can affect our health is
generally well accepted among citizens, even though the mechanisms by which
such interaction occurs remains elusive. This transformation in the cultural milieu
created pressure nationally to recalibrate scientific priorities so that they are more
in line with the dominant cultural view. Federal granting agencies now take affective neuroscience more seriously and fund proposals that seek to examine the
mechanisms by which emotions may influence our health. The NIMH recently
joined with the Library of Congress to host a very well publicized meeting for
congressional staffers and media representatives on the new "Biology of Emotion."
Tipper Gore was one of the keynote speakers at this meeting. And, at the first
White House Conference on Mental Health that was held in June 1999, research
on the brain mechanisms underlying emotion and the downstream consequences
of emotional dysfunction for physical disease were featured prominently. All of
this high-profile attention to affective neuroscience has helped legitimize this area
and establish its presence as an important, even necessary, component of our collective attempt to understand mental and physical health and well-being.

A second major factor that has facilitated the development of this interdisciplinary work is the rapid developments that have occurred in the technologies for
human brain imaging. The import of this development is difficult to overestimate.
Functional magnetic resonance imaging (fMRI) was first developed in 1991 and
became more widely available in about 1994. fMRI is the first noninvasive imaging
tool we had to examine localized regional brain activation with excellent spatial
and temporal resolution. Since it involves no exposure to ionizing radiation, fMRI
is safe to use with children, so that a large segment of the age distribution that had
been off-limits to more invasive methods can now be studied. Most important, the
ability to examine in humans the functional activity of circuits, composed of a set
of interconnected structures, allows scientists to make meaningful comparisons
between more invasive animal studies, where these circuits have been more in-
vasively probed, and human research. Prior to this development, the large corpus
of research in animals made little contact with the physiological studies of emotion

in humans because the latter work was mostly restricted to research using peripheral physiological measures whose underlying neural substrates were not clearly known. Today we can seamlessly go back and forth between the animal and human studies and use data from each to inform the other domain.

The development of fMRI has underscored another issue that plays an important role in shaping interdisciplinary work of this kind: the institutional barriers and opportunities for psychologists and neuroscientists to use technology that is typically controlled by departments of radiology. This is a complex problem that varies tremendously across different institutions. There are a few general principles related to this problem that I've gleaned from my experience at Wisconsin in creating a major new brain imaging laboratory over the past five years:

First is the advantage conferred by having a medical school and school of arts and sciences on the same campus. The geographic proximity helps to foster the types of interdisciplinary collaboration that is key to making this type of work successful.

Second is the importance of fostering a very good relationship between departments of psychology and psychiatry. Historically, such departments have not had much to do with one another. Yet I have found from my experience at Wisconsin that having these departments collaborate and move forward together to create opportunities for functional brain imaging is helpful. Faculty from schools of arts and science will have a much tougher time going at it alone.

Third is the importance of not rigidly adhering to disciplinary origins in hiring new faculty. Research in affective neuroscience and related interdisciplinary areas is creating genuinely hybrid scientists who were originally trained in one discipline and, while using their original disciplinary expertise, are moving into other substantive domains. As an example, we recently hired an individual with a Ph.D. in physics for a position as assistant professor of psychiatry. This young scientist does neuroimaging research and is now playing a key role in the development of our new facilities for neuroimaging.

Fourth and finally, it is worth noting that as the use of MRI by psychologists and neuroscientists becomes increasingly more common and extensive, creating a demand for more extensive access, the creation of new facilities that are independent of departments of radiology will become more common. Our facility at Wisconsin will not be directed by radiology. And, at least two universities are currently installing MRI scanners in their psychology buildings (Princeton and Dartmouth).

This section would be incomplete if it did not pay tribute to the importance that private funding agencies can play in fostering new interdisciplinary initiatives. Foundations are less encumbered by the dominant scientific zeitgeist and are typically more flexible in the funding mechanisms that they can offer. Two recent examples are particularly pertinent. One example is the major initiative in cognitive neuroscience undertaken by the McDonnell Foundation. This initiative, which included the funding of several large centers (along with many smaller grants, fellowships, summer institutes, and a new journal), was instrumental in launching this as a major domain of interdisciplinary inquiry. Virtually all major departments

of psychology now have some cognitive neuroscience representation, and some of
the top 10 departments feature cognitive neuroscience as their intellectual cen-
terpiece. The other example is the interdisciplinary research networks pioneered
by the MacArthur Foundation. These networks bring together scholars from diverse disciplines with the mandate to collaborate. While not all of such networks
have been successful, as inferred from the impact of their collective products, many
have been. It is my conjecture that the members of the more successful networks
have their scientific careers irrevocably transformed as a result of their participation
in the network. The opportunity for intensive immersion in the language and
thought of other disciplines creates ripe conditions for nurturing novel work and
provides the requisite expertise to use the tools of the contributing disciplinary
approaches.

Implications

Two important implications of modern research in affective neuroscience that were
not formally addressed earlier in this chapter are mentioned here. The first concerns plasticity in the central circuitry of emotion and the implications of such
plasticity for therapy, education, and social policy. While the topic of plasticity will
be examined in detail in another essay, it is important to note here the impressive
array of new findings at the animal level that demonstrate the dramatic influences
of environmental events, particularly early in life, in shaping the functional properties of the neural circuitry that controls emotion. These new findings are beginning to provide a detailed mechanistic understanding of how experientially
induced changes in patterns of affective reactivity are produced. The data also
provide a rationale for examining the brain bases of changes in emotion and health
produced by both traditional and nontraditional psychological interventions such
as psychotherapy and meditation, respectively. With support from the MacArthur
Foundation Network on Mind-Body Interaction, we recently completed a study on
the effects of an eight-week program in mindfulness-meditation on brain and
immune function. We found evidence of reliable shifts in patterns of anterior brain
activation, which we previously linked with affective style, toward a more positive
direction. We also found that subjects assigned to the meditation group showed a
larger rise in antibody titers in response to influenza vaccine than did a wait-list
control group. Moreover, the magnitude of change in brain activity predicted the
magnitude of change in immune function. This initial study provides encouragement for a more detailed examination of the biological effect of such interventions and a careful analysis of the possible consequences of such biological
change for physical health and disease.

Finally, I end this essay by considering the importance of training as a key
component required to foster interdisciplinary scholarship in this area into the
next century. Affective neuroscience and other similar hybrid areas of science
require unusual training programs that demand flexibility and access to a wide

range of course offerings and laboratory opportunities across many departments. All of my graduate students in psychology take courses in neuroanatomy and neurophysiology in the medical school. In addition, those using fMRI take at least one course in MR physics in the department of medical physics. For this type of training to work, it is imperative that flexibility be granted in the home department so that some required psychology courses be waived in place of taking courses elsewhere in the university. We have implemented such a program at Wisconsin where we waive all requirements except for statistics and have a faculty committee decide on an individual specialized set of course offerings for a particular student's needs. We only exercise this option when the interdisciplinary nature of the student's intended work demands such flexibility.

Students pursuing such interdisciplinary research also benefit enormously from having a mentoring committee rather than a single faculty member serving in this capacity. The committee might be composed of scientists from a number of diverse disciplines who could provide the student with a breadth that is unattainable through any single individual. Formal NIH-supported training programs that involve faculty from many different departments are a particularly effective vehicle for achieving a number of the goals described in this chapter. Such a training program can help faculty overcome the usual institutional barriers to cross-department collaboration and can dramatically improve the training environment and mentoring opportunities for students who are pursuing interdisciplinary research. I direct such a program at Wisconsin focused on emotion research that supports eight predoctoral and two postdoctoral trainees per year. Trainees are exposed to a much broader range of faculty than they would ordinarily be in a traditional graduate program. Already, a number of graduates of earlier versions of this training program are assuming positions of leadership in first-rank universities throughout the country.

As we closed the twentieth century and the decade of the brain, it became apparent that the pace of discovery and technological innovation will continue to accelerate in many areas of science. Recently formed interdisciplinary hybrids such as affective neuroscience, while still extraordinarily early in their development, are sure to benefit from these successes. Unifying themes and concepts are beginning to emerge that effectively integrate research at the molecular, animal-organismic, and human integrative levels in ways that were not even dreamed about a mere five years ago. It is an exciting time in this area of science. With a new cohort of interdisciplinary students coming on the scene, we have much to look forward to in this area of research in the coming century.

Postscript

In the approximately five years since the original version of this chapter was written, affective neuroscience has been blossoming and flourishing. There is now a new journal with the title *Social, Cognitive and Affective Neuroscience* and there are literally hundreds of publications each year in the best journals in science and neuroscience focused on this topic. Of particular importance to this volume and to the work reviewed in this chapter is new research on specific physical diseases in which psychological factors have been documented to be of importance in modulating the course of the illness. I am part of a network that represents the next stage of the Research Network on Mind–Body Interaction that was originally supported by the MacArthur Foundation and that I described in the original chapter. A number of the scientists who were part of that network and some new scholars have formed a new network that we refer to as the Mind–Brain–Behavior and Health Initiative. The Initiative is now funded by an NIH grant, itself an important statement. In its first year of existence, our group considered which physical disorder would provide good traction for making progress on understanding how social and mental events as they are instantiated in the brain could impact the course of illness in the body. We eventually settled on asthma. We wanted to choose a physical disorder that was a significant public risk problem and that had clearly defined and objectively measurable biological endpoints. Asthma nicely meets these criteria. It provides a potentially important and novel opportunity for highly interdisciplinary research that can span from psychological factors to the brain and to the body, down to the level of gene expression in sputum sampled from the lung.

This problem has been extremely rich in the opportunity it affords. We have published an initial article (Rosenkranz et al., 2005) in which asthmatic subjects were scanned on three separate occasions and exposed to a saline challenge, a methacholine challenge that produces broncoconstriction, and then an antigen challenge that provokes airway inflammation. Following these challenges, participants were presented with an asthma stroop task that we designed. The critical condition in this task consisted of asthma-relevant words (e.g., wheeze, suffocate) that were printed in different colors. The subjects' task was to press one of four buttons to indicate the color in which the word was presented. The main finding from this study was that in response specifically to the antigen challenge, asthmatic subjects showed very strong correlations between activation in the anterior cingulate cortex and insula and measures of lung function and airway inflammation, including the number of eosinophils in sputum. Apart from the specific findings from this study, the experiment represents a proof-of-concept where we could take patients with asthma and measure brain function in response to a peripheral challenge and obtain a very strong signal in regions of the brain that are intimately associated with emotional processing. In addition to providing mechanistic clues regarding mind–body interaction in asthmatics, this study also provides novel therapeutic targets for interventions at the level of the central nervous system in asthma.

The work on asthma as well as other recent research is beginning to emphasize the important role of the body in the neural circuitry of emotion and will help to make affective neuroscience even broader and more interdisciplinary than it has been in the past. Of particular concern to the themes of this volume, there is now a new generation of highly interdisciplinary well-trained young scientists who are interested in these questions and for the first time in history, they possess the multidisciplinary skills to make genuine progress on important problems that eluded scientific analysis. The next decade is likely to be associated with even more rapid progress than the previous decade and we have much to look forward to in this vibrant research area.

ACKNOWLEDGMENTS

The research described in this essay was supported over the years primarily by a series of grants from the National Institute of Mental Health. Most recently, this work has been supported by NIMH grants MH43454, MH40747, P50-MH52354, and K05-MH00875. In addition, some of the recent studies described herein have been supported by a grant from the Research Network on Mind-Body Interaction from the John D. and Catherine T. MacArthur Foundation. Essay prepared for the SSRC/NIH Working Group on Bio-Behavioral-Social Perspectives on Health.

RECOMMENDED READINGS

Damasio, A. R. (1994). *Descartes' Error: Emotion, Reason, and the Human Brain.* New York: Avon Books.

Davidson, R. J. (2000). Affective style, psychopathology and resilience: Brain mechanisms and plasticity. *American Psychologist, 55,* 1193–1214.

Davidson, R. J., and Irwin, W. (1999). The functional neuroanatomy of emotion and affective style. *Trends in Cognitive Sciences, 3,* 11–21.

LeDoux, J. (1996). *The Emotional Brain: The Mysterious Underpinnings of Emotional Life.* New York: Touchstone Press.

McEwen, B. S. (1998). Protective and damaging effects of stress mediators. *New England Journal of Medicine, 338,* 171–179.

REFERENCES

Abercrombie, H. C., Schaefer, S. M., Larson, C. L., Oakes, T. R., Lindgren, K. A., Holden, J. E., Perlman, S. B., Turski, P. A., Krahn, D. D., Benca, R. M., and Davidson, R. J. (1998). Metabolic rate in the right amygdala predicts negative affect in depressed patients. *Neuroreport, 9,* 3301–3307.

Adolphs, R. (2002). Recognizing emotion from facial expressions: Psychological and neurological mechanisms. *Behavioral and Cognitive Neuroscience Reviews, 1,* 21–62.

Adolphs, R., Tranel, D., and Damasio, A. R. (1998). The human amygdala in social judgment. *Nature, 393,* 470–474.

Aggleton, J. P. (1993). The contribution of the amygdala to normal and abnormal emotional states. *Trends in Neurosciences, 16,* 328–333.

Ahern, G. L., and Schwartz, G. E. (1985). Differential lateralization for positive and negative emotion in the human brain: EEG spectral analysis. *Neuropsychologia, 23,* 745–755.

Amaral, D. G., Price, J. L., Pitkanen, A., and Carmichael, S. T. (1992). Anatomical organization of the primate amygdaloid complex. In J. P. Aggleton (Ed.), *The Amygdala: Neurobiological Aspects of emotion, Memory and Mental Dysfunction* (pp. 1–66). New York: Wiley-Liss.

Bechara, A., Damasio, A. R., Damasio, H., and Anderson, S. (1994). Insensitivity to future consequences following damage to human prefrontal cortex. *Cognition, 50,* 7–12.

Bechara, A., Damasio, H., Damasio, A. R., and Lee, G. P. (1999). Different contributions of the human amygdala and ventromedial prefrontal cortex to decision-making. *Journal of Neuroscience, 19,* 5473–5481.

Bechara, A., Damasio, H., Tranel, D., and Damasio, A. R. (1997). Deciding advantageously before knowing the advantageous strategy. *Science, 275,* 1293–1294.

Bechara, A., Tranel, D., Damasio, H., Adolphs, R., Rockland,C., and Damasio, A. R. (1995). Double dissociation of conditioning and declarative knowledge relative to the amygdala and hippocampus in humans. *Science, 269,* 1115–1118.

Bechara, A., Tranel, D., Damasio, H., and Damasio, A. R. (1996). Failure to respond autonomically to anticipated future outcomes following damage to prefrontal cortex. *Cerebral Cortex, 6,* 215–225.

Berridge, K. C. (2002). Comparing the emotional brain of humans to other animals. In R. J. Davidson, H. H. Goldsmith, and K. Scherer (Eds.), *Handbook of affective science* (pp. 25–51). New York: Oxford University Press.

Birbaumer N., Grodd, W., Diedrich, O., Klose, U., Erb, M., Lotze, M., Schneider, F., Weiss, U., and Flor, H. (1998). fMRI reveals amygdala activation to human faces in social phobics. *Neuroreport, 9,* 1223–1226.

Breiter, H. C., Rauch, S. L., Kwong, K. K., Baker, J. R., Weisskoff, R. M., Kennedy, D. N., Kendrick, A. D., Davis, T. L., Jiang, A., Cohen, M. S., Stern, C. E., Belliveau, J. W., Baer, L., O'Sullivan, R. L., Savage, C. R., Jenike, M. A., and Rosen, B. R. (1996). Functional magnetic resonance imaging of symptom provocation in obsessive-compulsive disorder. *Archives of General Psychiatry, 53,* 595–606.

Broks, P., Young, A. W., Maratos, E. J., Coffey, P. J., Calder, A. J., Isaac, C. L., Mayes, A. R., Hodges, J. R., Montaldi, D., Cezayirli, E., Roberts, N., and Hadley, D. (1998). Face processing impairments after encephalitis: Amygdala damage and recognition of fear. *Neuropsychologia, 36,* 59–70.

Buchel, C., Morris, J., Dolan, R. J., and Friston, K. J. (1998). Brain systems mediating aversive conditioning: An event-related fMRI study. *Neuron, 20,* 947–957.

Buss, K., Dolski, I. V., Malmstadt, J. R., Davidson, R. J. and Goldsmith, H. H. (1997). EEG asymmetry, salivary cortisol, and affect expression: An infant twin study. *Psychophysiology, 34,* S25.

Cacioppo, J. T., and Gardner, W. L. (1999). Emotion. *Annual Review of Psychology, 50,* 191–214.

Cahill, L., and McGaugh, J. L. (1998). Mechanisms of emotional arousal and lasting declarative memory. *Trends in Neuroscience, 21,* 294–299.

Cahill, L., Weinberger, N. M., Roozendaal, B., and McGaugh, J. L. (1999). Is the amygdala a locus of "conditioned fear"? Some questions and caveats. *Neuron, 23,* 227–228.

Calder, A. J., Young, A. W., Rowland, D., Perrett, D. I., Hodges, J. R., and Etcoff, N. L. (1996). Facial emotion recognition after bilateral amygdala damage: Differentially severe impairment of fear. *Cognitive Neuropsychology, 13,* 699–745.

Crick, F. (1988). *What Mad Pursuit.* New York: Basic Books.

Davidson, R. J. (1992). Emotion and affective style: Hemispheric substrates. *Psychological Science, 3,* 39–43.

Davidson, R. J. (1993). Cerebral asymmetry and emotion: Conceptual and methodological conundrums. *Cognition and Emotion, 7,* 115–138.

Davidson, R. J. (1995). Cerebral asymmetry, emotion and affective style. In R. J. Davidson and K. Hugdahl (Eds.), *Brain Asymmetry* (pp. 361–388). Cambridge, MA: MIT Press.

Davidson, R. J. (1998). Affective style and affective disorders: Perspectives from affective neuroscience. *Cognition and Emotion, 12,* 307–330.

Davidson, R. J., and Fox, N. A. (1982). Asymmetrical brain activity discriminates between positive versus negative affective stimuli in human infants. *Science, 218,* 1235–1237.

Davidson, R. J., and Fox, N. A. (1989). Frontal brain asymmetry predicts infants' response to maternal separation. *Journal of Abnormal Psychology, 98,* 127–131.

Davidson, R. J., and Irwin, W. (1999a). Functional MRI in the study of emotion. In C. T. W. Moonen and P. A. Bandetti (Eds.), *Functional MRI* (pp. 487–499). Berlin: Springer-Verlag.

Davidson, R. J., and Irwin, W. (1999b). The functional neuroanatomy of emotion and affective style. *Trends in Cognitive Sciences, 3,* 11–21.

Davidson, R. J., and Rickman, M. (1999). Behavioral inhibition and the emotional circuitry of the brain: Stability and plasticity during the early childhood years. In L. A. Schmidt and J. Schulkin (Eds.), *Extreme Fear and Shyness: Origins and Outcomes* (pp. 67–87). New York: Oxford University Press.

Davidson, R. J., and Tomarken, A. J. (1989). Laterality and emotion: An electrophysiological approach. In F. Boller and J. Grafman (Eds.), *Handbook of Neuropsychology* (pp. 419–441). Amsterdam: Elsevier.

Davidson, R. J., Coe, C. C., Dolski, I., and Donzella, B. (1999). Individual differences in prefrontal activation asymmetry predicts natural killer cell activity at rest and in response to challenge. *Brain, Behavior, and Immunity, 13,* 93–108.

Davidson, R. J., Ekman, P., Saron, C., Senulis, J., and Friesen, W. V. (1990). Approach/withdrawal and cerebral asymmetry: Emotional expression and brain physiology, I. *Journal of Personality and Social Psychology, 58,* 330–341.

Davidson, R. J., Jackson, D. C., and Kalin, N. H. (2000). Emotion, plasticity, context and regulation: Perspectives from affective neuroscience. *Psychological Bulletin, 126,* 890–906.

Davidson, R. J., Kalin, N. H., and Shelton, S. E. (1992). Lateralized effects of diazepam on frontal brain electrical asymmetries in rhesus monkeys. *Biological Psychiatry, 32,* 438–451.

Davidson, R. J., Kalin, N. H., and Shelton, S. E. (1993). Lateralized response to diazepam predicts temperamental style in rhesus monkeys. *Behavioral Neuroscience, 107,* 1106–1110.

Davidson, R. J., Marshall, J. R., Tomarken, A. J., and Henriques, J. B. (2000). While a phobic waits: Regional brain electrical and autonomic activity in social phobics during anticipation of public speaking. *Biological Psychiatry, 47,* 85–95.

Drevets, W. C., Videen, T. O., Price, J. L, Preskom, S. H., Carmichael, S. T., and Raichle, M. E. (1992). A functional anatomical study of unipolar depression. *Journal of Neuroscience, 12,* 3628–3641.

Ekman, P., and Davidson, R. J. (Eds.). (1994). *The Nature of Emotion: Fundamental Questions.* New York: Oxford University Press.

Fanselow, M. S., and LeDoux, J. E. (1999). Why we think plasticity underlying Pavlovian fear conditioning occurs in the basolateral amygdala. *Neuron, 23,* 229–232.

Frijda, N. H. (1994). Emotions are functional, most of the time. In P. Ekman and R. J. Davidson (Eds.), *The Nature of Emotion: Fundamental Questions* (pp. 112–122). New York: Oxford University Press.

Gainotti, G. (1972). Emotional behavior and hemispheric side of the lesion. *Cortex, 8,* 41–55.

Gainotti, G., Caltagirone, C., and Zoccolotti, P. (1993). Left/right and cortical/subcortical dichotomies in the neuropsychological study of human emotions. *Cognition and Emotion, 7,* 71–93.

Gewirtz, J. C., Falls, W. A., and Davis, M. (1997). Normal conditioned inhibition and extinction of freezing and fear-potentiated startle following electrolytic lesions of medial prefrontal cortex in rats. *Behavioral Neuroscience, 111,* 712–726.

Gray, J. A. (1994). Three fundamental emotion systems. In P. Ekman and R. J. Davidson (Eds.), *The Nature of Emotion: Fundamental Questions* (pp. 243–247). New York: Oxford University Press.

Henriques, J. B., and Davidson, R. J. (1990). Regional brain electrical asymmetries discriminate between previously depressed subjects and healthy controls. *Journal of Abnormal Psychology, 99,* 22–31.

Henriques, J. B., and Davidson, R. J. (1991). Left frontal hypoactivation in depression. *Journal of Abnormal Psychology, 100,* 535–545.

House, A., Dennis, M., Mogridge, L., Hawton, K., (1990). Life events and difficulties preceding stroke. *Journal of Neurology, Neurosurgery, and Psychiatry, 53,* 1024–1028.

Irwin, W., Davidson, R. J., Lowe, M. J., Mock, B. J., Sorenson, J. A., and Turski, P. A. (1996). Human amygdala activation detected with echo-planar functional magnetic resonance imaging. *NeuroReport, 7,* 1765–1769.

Irwin, W., Davidson, R. J., Kalin, N. H., Sorenson, J. A., and Turski, P. A. (2001). Relations between human amygdala activation and self-reported dispositional affect. *Journal of Cognitive Neuroscience, Suppl. S,* 109.

James, W. (1981). *The Principles of Psychology.* Cambridge: Harvard University Press. (Original work published in 1890.)

Jones, N. A., and Fox, N. A. (1992). Electroencephalogram asymmetry during emotionally evocative films and its relation to positive and negative affectivity. *Brain and Cognition, 20,* 280–299.

Kalin, N. H., Larson, C., Shelton, S. E., and Davidson, R. J. (1998). Asymmetric frontal brain activity, cortisol, and behavior associated with fearful temperament in Rhesus monkeys. *Behavioral Neuroscience, 112,* 286–292.

Kalin, N. H., Shelton, S. E., Davidson, R. J., and Kelley, A. E. (2001). The primate amygdala mediates acute fear but not the behavioral and physiological components of anxious temperament. *Journal of Neuroscience, 21,* 2067–2074.

Kang, D., Davidson, R. J., Coe, C. L., Wheeler, R. E., Tomarken, A. J., and Ershler, W. B. (1991). Frontal brain asymmetry and immune function. *Behavioral Neuroscience, 105,* 860–869.

Lane, R. D., Reiman, E. M., Bradley, M. M., Lang, P. J., Ahern, G. L., Davidson, R. J., and Schwartz, G. E. (1997). Neuroanatomical correlates of pleasant and unpleasant emotion. *Neuropsychologia, 35,* 1437–1444.

Lang, P. J., Bradley, M. M., and Cuthbert, B. N. (1990). Emotion, attention, and the startle reflex. *Psychological Review, 97,* 377–395.

Larson, C. L., Davidson, R. J., Abercrombie, H. C., Ward, R. T., Schaefer, S. M., Jackson, D. C., Holden, J. E., and Perlman, S. B. (1998.) Relations between PET-derived measures of thalamic glucose metabolism and EEG alpha power. *Psychophysiology, 35.* 162–169.

Larson, C. L., Ruffalo, D., Nietert, J. Y., and Davidson, R. J. (2000). Temporal stability of the emotion-modulated startle response. *Psychophysiology, 37,* 92–101.

LeDoux, J. (1996). *The Emotional Brain: The Mysterious Underpinnings of Emotional Life.* New York: Touchstone Press.

Levenson, R. W. (1994). Human emotion: A functional view. In P. Ekman and R. J. Davidson (Eds.), *The Nature of Emotion: Fundamental Questions* (pp. 123–126). New York: Oxford University Press.

McEwen, B. S. (1998). Protective and damaging effects of stress mediators. *New England Journal of Medicine, 338,* 171–179.

Morgan, M. A., Romanski, L., and LeDoux, J. E. (1993). Extinction of emotional learning: Contribution of medial prefrontal cortex. *Neuroscience Letters, 163,* 109–113.

Morris, J. S., Ohman, A., and Dolan, R. J. (1998). Conscious and unconscious emotional learning in the human amygdala. *Nature, 393,* 467–470.

Rauch, S. L., Savage, C. R., Alpert, N. M., Fischman, A. J., and Jenike, M. A. (1997). The functional neuroanatomy of anxiety: A study of three disorders using positron emission tomography and symptom provocation. *Biological Psychiatry, 42,* 446–452.

Robinson, R. G., and Downhill, J. E. (1995). Lateralization of psychopathology in response to focal brain injury. In R. J. Davidson and K. Hugdahl (Eds.), *Brain Asymmetry* (pp. 693–711). Cambridge, MA: MIT Press.

Robinson, R. G., Starr, L. B., and Price, T. R. (1984). A two-year longitudinal study of mood disorders following stroke: Prevalence and duration at six months follow-up. *British Journal of Psychiatry, 144,* 256–262.

Rosenkranz, M. A., Busse, W. W., Johnstone, T., Swenson, C. A., Crisafi, G. M., Jackson, M. M., Bosch, J. A., Sheridan, J. F., and Davidson, R. J. (2005). Neural circuitry underlying the interaction between emotion and asthma symptom exacerbation. *Proceedings of the National Academy of Sciences, 102,* 133191–133324.

Sackeim, H. A., Greenberg, M. S., Weiman, A. L., Gur, R., Hungerbuhler, J. P., and Geschwind, N. (1982). Hemispheric asymmetry in the expression of positive and negative emotions: Neurologic evidence. *Archives in Neurology, 39,* 210–218.

Schnierla, T. C. (1959). An evolutionary and developmental theory of biphasic processes underlying approach and withdrawal. *Nebraska Symposium of Emotion,* 1–42.

Sutton, S. K., and Davidson, R. J. (1997). Prefrontal brain asymmetry: A biological substrate of the behavioral approach and inhibition systems. *Psychological Science, 8,* 204–210.

Tomarken, A. J., and Davidson, R. J. (1994). Frontal brain activation in repressors and nonrepressors. *Journal of Abnormal Psychology, 103,* 339–349.

Tomarken, A. J., Davidson, R. J., and Henriques, J. B. (1990). Resting frontal brain asymmetry predicts affective responses to films. *Journal of Personality and Social Psychology, 59,* 791–801.

Tomarken, A. J., Davidson, R. J., Wheeler, R. E., and Doss, R. C. (1992). Individual differences in anterior brain asymmetry and fundamental dimensions of emotion. *Journal of Personality and Social Psychology, 62,* 676–687.

Tomarken, A. J., Davidson, R. J., Wheeler, R. W., and Kinney, L. (1992). Psychometric properties of resting anterior EEG asymmetry: Temporal stability and internal consistency. *Psychophysiology, 29,* 576–592.

Tucker, D. M., Stenslie, C. E., Roth, R. S., and Shearer, S. L. (1981) Right frontal lobe activation and right hemisphere performance: Decrement during a depressed mood. *Archives of General Psychiatry, 38,* 169–174.

Watanabe, M. (1996). Reward expectancy in primate prefrontal neurons. *Nature, 382,* 629–632.

Watson, D., Clark, L. A., and Tellegen, A. (1988). Development and validation of brief measures of positive and negative affect: The PANAS scales. *Journal of Personality and Social Psychology, 54,* 1063–1070.

Watson, D., Clark, L. A., Weber, K., Assenheimer, J. S., Strauss, M. E., McCormick, C. M., et al. (1995). Testing a tripartite model: I. Evaluating convergent and discriminant validity of anxiety and depression symptom scales. *Journal of Abnormal Psychology, 104,* 3–14.

Whalen, P. (1999). Fear, vigilance and ambiguity: Initial neuroimaging studies of the human amygdala. *Current Directions in Psychological Science.*

Whalen, P. J., Rauch, S. L., Etcoff, N. L., McInerney, S. C., Lee, M. B., and Jenike, M. A. (1998). Masked presentations of emotional facial expressions modulate amygdala activity without explicit knowledge. *Journal of Neuroscience, 18,* 411–418.

Wheeler, R. E., Davidson, R. J., and Tomarken, A. J. (1993). Frontal brain asymmetry and emotional activity: A biological substrate of affective style. *Psychophysiology, 30,* 82–89.

Visual Mental Imagery

A Case Study in Interdisciplinary Research

S. M. KOSSLYN

What shape are Snoopy's ears? Which is darker green, a Christmas tree or a frozen pea? If you were driving to the airport and the road was blocked halfway there, what would be the shortest detour? When most people try to answer questions like these, they report visualizing the objects or scene, for example "seeing" Snoopy's head and droopy ears. Visual mental imagery is "seeing" in the absence of the appropriate immediate sensory input; perception is the registration of physical present stimuli, whereas imagery is the perceiving of patterns that arise from memory.

As the examples illustrate, visual mental imagery plays a role in memory and spatial reasoning. It also aids linguistic comprehension, learning motor skills (visualizing oneself practicing a new skill will actually improve one's later performance of it), and even symbolic reasoning (as many mathematicians and physicists, including Albert Einstein, have attested). These functions of imagery require the brain to reconstruct, to present for "recognition," and to put to further use information stored from past, first-hand experience.

If mental images are, in fact, "simulations" of possible encounters in the real world, then they can be used to help one relax in the face of stress (as was so convincingly demonstrated by the founders of "systematic desensitization" behavioral therapy, so many years ago). Moreover, imagery may play a role in the placebo effect, which allows the mind to affect various aspects of bodily function (e.g., Harrington, 1998). Thus, the basic research that informs our knowledge of the nature of imagery, in turn, can provide the foundations for studies of the role of imagery in health.

My own research program was born when I was a first-year graduate student at Stanford University in 1970, and some of my subjects made mistakes. At the time, I was testing a model of semantic memory by asking subjects to evaluate whether statements were true or false. One of the statements was "A flea can bite." As it happened, two people answered "No." Having had many cats as pets, I was amazed. When I interviewed them after the study, one said, "I looked for a mouth, but couldn't find one," and the other said, "I looked, but couldn't see any teeth." What was this talk about "looking" and "seeing"? I then called up the other subjects and asked them whether they tended to visualize or not, and analyzed the data separately for each group. As it turned out, if people reported visualizing, they took more time to evaluate small properties of the objects (such as whiskers for a mouse, compared to its back); if they didn't use imagery, they took more time to evaluate less associated properties (such as a mouse's back). At about the same time, I was taking a computer programming class (using punch cards!), and had to write a program for displaying graphic patterns based on subroutines that printed basic geometric forms. It occurred to me that this could be the beginnings of a model for human mental imagery, and thus began a line of research that continues to this day.

This research program has been interdisciplinary from its very start. It began as a project in "cognitive science," a blend of experimental psychology and computer science, making use of distinctions from philosophy and linguistics (for a more detailed discussion of the origins and early goals of the project, see Kosslyn, 1980). Over time, the kinds of questions we were asking led us to take advantage of emerging facts about the brain. Indeed, our efforts to answer questions about imagery were an early effort in the emerging field of cognitive neuroscience, and this work in turn helped to shape a part of that field (Gazzaniga, Ivry, and Mangun, 1998). Thus, in its present form, the work is highly interdisciplinary, drawing on findings and theory from psychology, neuroscience, philosophy, computer science, and linguistics, as well as neurology and psychiatry.

My research program has been driven in large part by issues that have been present since the inception of research on mental imagery in particular, and on the mind in general. Thus, I will frame the present research program by briefly putting it in historical context (based on discussions in Kosslyn, 1980, 1994); it is sobering how many of the issues raised hundreds of years ago are still with us today. Next we will consider the evolution of the research program over time, which will lead us to a brief summary of its present status. This will set the stage for a discussion of the possible relevance of imagery research for health. Finally, I conclude with some reflections on the process of doing this research, on the work of doing the work itself.

A Checkered Past

Mental imagery has a long and checkered past, but research and discussion about it never seems to stay away, nor does it remain uncontroversial, for long. Plato moved imagery to center stage with his famous wax tablet metaphor. He believed that mental images are like patterns etched in wax, and individual differences could be understood in terms of properties of the wax—such as its temperature, purity, and so forth. The notion that information is represented as images was common throughout the history of philosophy, perhaps finding its heyday during the eighteenth century with the British Associationists. Imagery played a major role in theories of mental events up until psychology and philosophy parted ways; indeed, it held sway during the infancy of scientific psychology, with both Wilhelm Wundt and William James devoting much energy toward understanding it.

But imagery soon fell prey to what has been characterized as "physics envy." The early experimental psychologists were highly aware that they were starting a new science, and they were intent that it be a genuine science; this apparently sometimes led them to be obsessed with methodological purity. As Popper (1959) and other philosophers have instructed us, the scientific method rests on being able to disprove hypotheses to everyone's satisfaction, which requires that the subject matter be publicly observable. Mental images—like all mental events—are notoriously difficult to put on public display, and so the topic is sometimes greeted with a raised eyebrow by scientists. But electrons, quarks, and black holes are also difficult to put on public display, and so this cannot be the only reason imagery is not always regarded as a proper topic for scientific study.

The problem is that, unlike with electrons and their brethren, psychologists could not even point to the tracks or the spoor left behind by mental images. Subatomic particles cause certain effects that can be measured, and these measurements are publicly observable. But how does one measure a mental image? This methodological problem was exacerbated by deeper conceptual problems: psychologists did not know how to characterize the nature of imagery. Clearly, mental images are not actual pictures in the head (there is no light up there, and besides, who would look at them?), but if not actual pictures, what are they?

These problems made imagery a ripe target for the behaviorists. All manner of mental events, and imagery in particular, were not generally considered proper subject matter for scientific psychology from roughly 1913, with Watson's famous article attacking the very existence of mental imagery, to the early 1960s.

Imagery returned to the scene for a number of good reasons. First, the radical behaviorism of Watson and his ideological descendants ran out of steam. If that program had lived up to its early promise, scientists may never have strayed from its path. But, as many others have documented (e.g., see Gardner, 1985), the radical behaviorist program fell short when it was applied to the most central human faculties, such as language and reasoning. Second, as the limits of behaviorism became obvious, many researchers interested in "verbal learning" suddenly became cognitive psychologists. The transition often consisted simply of a shift from studying factors that affect acquisition to those that affect retention; in the present context, however, the important thing is that mental events were once again acceptable components of psychological theories. Third, the need for internal events was highlighted by Chomskian linguistics and, perhaps more important for the majority of psychologists, by the advent of artificial intelligence (AI; for a review of these developments, see Gardner, 1985). It is clear that one needs to understand what goes on in a computer to alter its behavior, but one does not need to know the state of every circuit or piece of memory. Rather, one needs to understand the computer at a slightly more abstract level, at the level of its function—as can be schematized by a flowchart. Psychologists such as Newell, Shaw, and Simon (1958) realized that the "functional language" of flowcharts could be applied as easily to brains as to electronic machines. And so did philosophers, who attempted to buttress the conceptual foundations of the "new" approach (e.g., see Fodor, 1968).

Just as imagery was swept out with the receding tide of the early mentalistic psychology of James, Wundt, and their followers, it was swept back in with the rise of cognitive psychology. Alan Paivio, in particular, deserves enormous credit for spearheading the return of theorizing about imagery during the 1960s. Paivio began his research squarely in the tradition of verbal learning and quickly discovered that one's ability to learn a set of words was predicted well by how easily one could visualize their referents (e.g., see Paivio, 1971). He forced hard-nosed experimental psychologists to take imagery seriously by playing by their rules; he showed that factors affecting imagery accounted for empirical results. This work opened the way for more daring investigations (including some by Paivio himself; see Paivio, 1991).

Perhaps the most dramatic example of the new wave of research on imagery is that of Roger Shepard, Lynn Cooper, and their colleagues (see Shepard and Cooper, 1982). This research demonstrated conclusively that complex properties of imagery could be studied scientifically—and lent credence to the existence not only of mental images but also of complex operations that could transform them in various ways. For example, these researchers showed that people can mentally rotate objects in images and that this rotation operation is incremental: People require additional time for every additional amount that they must mentally rotate an imaged object. Indeed, they demonstrated that "mentally rotating" an object moves it along a trajectory, showing that one could "catch the image on the fly." They computed the rate of rotation and asked subjects to imagine a pattern rotating, and then they showed a stimulus that should line up or not line up with the mental image. The presence of the imaged object at a specific orientation was neatly demonstrated by showing that subjects could compare the imaged object to the perceived stimulus fastest if the two were aligned than if additional rotation were necessary (see Cooper, 1976; Shepard and Metzler, 1971). Similar experiments demonstrated that people can "mentally fold" objects in images and otherwise transform them (e.g., Shepard and Feng, 1972). These experiments gave life to the idea that images are internal representations, which in some sense "stand in" (re-present) the corresponding objects.

Three Waves of Controversy

The systematic results obtained in imagery experiments convinced most researchers that there was something to the idea that humans have "mental images." Theories about the role of imagery in information processing moved forward when researchers began to think about how one could program a computer to produce specific types of behavior. To program a computer to mimic imagery, one must specify an image representation with specific properties; a representation is a type of code, a way of specifying information. Hence, this approach forces one to think clearly about the nature of such representations. This soon resulted in a series of debates about the nature of mental imagery representations (for detailed reviews, see Kosslyn, 1980, 1994).

In the first phase, the focus was highly constrained by concepts of alternative types of mental representations that might underlie imagery. This phase consisted of an interplay of philosophical exchanges and empirical research; indeed, professional philosophers played a key role in these discussions (e.g., see Block, 1981). The discussion focused rather tightly on ways that computer models could be developed to mimic imagery. At this phase, there was essentially no interest in how the brain might actually give rise to imagery (e.g., Kosslyn, 1980; Pylyshyn, 1973).

In the second phase, the focus shifted to the nature of the empirical results collected during the first phase, and the arguments concerned possible methodological problems with the experiments (e.g., Intons-Peterson, 1983; Kosslyn, 1981; Pylyshyn, 1981). These debates served the useful role of forcing researchers to refine their methods.

In the third phase, researchers responded to the possible methodological and conceptual problems with the earlier purely behavioral research by turning to facts about brain function. This phase involves collaborations between neuroscientists and psychologists; although computer models still play an important role, they are now heavily shaped by facts about the brain. Similarly, although philosophers still provide useful criticism, the issues are no longer at the abstract level that characterized the first phase of the debate. My laboratory was one of the first in cognitive science to draw heavily on cutting-edge findings from neuroscience, making use of facts about neuroanatomy and neurophysiology. Our efforts were distinct from much of those in neuropsychology in that we absorbed neuroscientific data into a cognitive science approach (emphasizing computer models and distinctions from philosophy and linguists; see Kosslyn, 1980, 1994). Initially, the efforts to inject neuroscientific facts and theories into our theories met with resistance (I recall more than one scowl from traditional experimental psychologists as I spoke about the new approach), and some researchers went so far as to tell me I was wasting my time (and some still do, I should add!). Nevertheless, it has been gratifying to see that the vast majority of my colleagues now see the value of paying attention to the brain. This third phase of research is still under way, and I will focus here on this phase.

Developing a Theory: Mental Images in the Brain

Virtually all researchers who study mental imagery assume that imagery shares at least some mechanisms with like-modality perception. In this section, I provide a very brief overview of the major features of our initial neuroscience-based theory of visual mental imagery, which is grounded in this assumption. The theory posits that different parts of the brain do different things. Specifically, we posit six major components, as schematized in Figure 7.1. Each of these "components" is a coarsely described system of processes in its own right; each accepts input and transforms it in specific ways to produce output. Each component is assumed to store information, as well as to transform it (in fact, the stored information plays crucial roles in performing the transformations). In my 1994 book I referred to the theory outlined in Figure 7.1 as a "protomodel" because it is simply the bare bones of a theory. In that book I attempted to refine these major components, typically by dividing each into more specialized subcomponents, but I am no longer convinced that such a fine level of detail can be justified. Thus, I will stick to the broad strokes here. The motivation for positing each component rests in large part on findings about the neurophysiology and neuroanatomy of visual perception. (The following summary has been adapted from that of Kosslyn et al., 1994.)

Visual buffer

Introspectively, images appear to embody the spatial layout of shapes. This sort of introspection suggests that visual mental images reconstruct the spatial geometry of objects. In fact, numerous areas of cerebral cortex are spatially organized; patterns of activity within these areas make explicit the spatial organization of the planar projection of a stimulus. Neuroanatomical studies of nonhuman primates have revealed that at least 32 distinct cortical areas are involved in vision, and about half of these are retinotopically organized, including Areas 17 and 18 (see Felleman and Van Essen, 1991; Van Essen, 1985; Van Essen and Maunsell, 1983). During visual perception, these areas represent images by preserving (roughly) the spatial layout of the pattern of activation on the retina, and hence these areas are called retinotopically organized (e.g., for a 2-deoxyglucose study in the macaque, see Tootell, Silverman, Switkes, and DeValois, 1982). Fox et al. (1986) used positron emission tomography (PET) to demonstrate that Area 17 (also known as primary visual cortex, striate cortex, area OC, and area V1) is retinotopically organized in humans. Kosslyn et al. (1993, 1999; Kosslyn, Thompson, Kim, and Alpert, 1995) used PET to produce evidence that this area (among others) is active during visual mental imagery. We group the retinotopically mapped areas of cortex into a single functional structure, which we call the "visual buffer."

As suggested by the philosopher Tye (1991), at each location in the retinotopically organized representation are a set of "symbolic" codes that indicate information such as the color and luminance at that point. Thus, the depictive

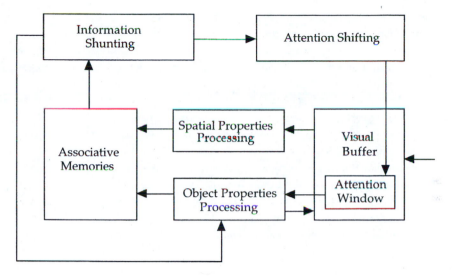

Figure 7.1.   The "protomodel."

aspect of imagery relies on the visual buffer. By "depictive," I mean that each part of the representation corresponds to a representation of part of the object such that the distances among the parts on the object are reflected (albeit not perfectly) by the distances among the representations of the parts (see Kosslyn, 1980). In addition to this "picture-like" aspect of the representation, the visual buffer specifies information that is interpreted as nonspatial properties associated with each location. Finally, the visual buffer is not a passive screen but, rather, serves to organize input in various ways, such as delineating figure from ground.

Attention window

There is far more information in the visual buffer than can be processed in detail. Thus, an "attention window" operates within this structure, which selects a region of the buffer and sends the pattern of activation in it to other areas for further processing (cf. Moran and Desimone, 1985; Treisman and Gelade, 1980). The attention window can be covertly shifted, allowing one to scan over patterns in the visual buffer without moving one's eyes.

Processing object properties versus spatial properties

The information within the attention window is further processed along two pathways. One goes from the occipital lobe ventrally to the inferior temporal lobe, while the other goes dorsally to the posterior parietal lobe. In order to investigate the function of each pathway, Ungerleider and Mishkin (1982; see also Pohl, 1973) trained macaque monkeys to use either object properties or spatial information to find food. Different parts of the animal's brain were removed after the task was learned, and the behavioral deficits were observed. Removal of the inferior temporal lobes and posterior parietal lobes resulted in a double dissociation: Ablating the inferior temporal lobes drastically impaired an animal's ability to encode shape, but had little effect on its ability to encode location; in contrast, ablating the posterior parietal lobes had the opposite effect.

These results have suggested to many that the dorsal pathway acts as a spatial-properties-processing system (the "where" system), whereas the ventral pathway acts as an object-properties-processing system (the "what" system; see also Maunsell and Newsome, 1987; Ungerleider and Haxby, 1994). Neuroimaging research suggests that the middle temporal gyrus, inferior temporal gyrus, and fusiform gyrus may be the locus of visual memories in humans; see Haxby et al., 1991; Kosslyn et al., 1994; Sergent, Ohta, and MacDonald, 1992); these areas are selectively activated when one must recognize a stimulus.

In addition, findings of Tanaka and colleagues (e.g., Fujita, Tanaka, Ito, and Cheng, 1992; Tanaka, Saito, Fukada, and Moriya, 1991) suggest that information is stored in the object-properties-processing system using a "population code" that, essentially, compresses the information. Shapes are stored by coding the presence or absence of each of a large set of attributes (which are not themselves interpretable in simple ways). Visual mental images, in contrast, appear to depict spatial information (for reviews, see Kosslyn, 1980, 1994). If this is correct, then images (i.e., spatial representations in the visual buffer) would be formed by activating the stored memories in such a way that the implicit spatial information is "unpacked" (for a detailed theory of how this may occur, see Kosslyn, 1994). Indeed, virtually every area involved in vision that has an afferent (forward) connection to another area also receives an efferent (backward) connection from that area, and the forward and backward projections are of comparable size (e.g., Van Essen, 1985). These features of the anatomy imply that a great deal of information flows backward in the system, from "higher-level" areas to the "lower-level," retinotopically organized areas. In fact, Douglas and Rockland (1992) have found direct connections from area TE (in the anterior inferior temporal lobe) to Area 17 in the macaque (see also Rockland, Saleem, and Tanaka, 1992). Such direct cortico-cortico connections from the higher-level areas to the lower-level areas are consistent with the hypothesis that visual mental images are formed by using stored information to reconstruct spatial patterns in retinotopically organized cortical areas. Similar ideas have long been popular (e.g., cf. Damasio, Damasio, Tranel, and Brandt, 1990; Hebb, 1968; James, 1890).

As a test of the sufficiency of our ideas, we have always implemented computer models and used these models as heuristic guides to help us formulate research questions. For example, in Kosslyn, Flynn, Amsterdam, and Wang (1990), we showed that the effects of various kinds of strokes could be mimicked by damaging a computer model. In this model, we adopted the conventional wisdom that the major visual pathway implemented in the inferior temporal lobes deals with object recognition ("what") and the one implemented in the posterior parietal lobes deals with spatial processing ("where").

Associative memory

One of the advances of research on memory is the finding that different types of memories can be stored in different regions of the brain (e.g., Schacter, 1996; Squire, 1987). We can infer that there must be a long-term memory structure that associates object properties with spatial properties; the mere fact that people can recall where furniture is located in their homes indicates that the two sorts of information must have been cross-indexed in memory. Associative memory stores multimodal information, associating not only visual object properties and spatial properties but also auditory, tactile, and other sorts of information. Many complex objects are encoded over the course of numerous eye movements. In this case, parts may be encoded separately, and a representation of the structure of the object (indicating how parts are spatially organized) would be entered into associative memory.

Associative memory is implemented in multiple loci in the brain. The dorsolateral prefrontal lobes appear to retain short-term memories that associate, at the minimum, information about what an object is and where it is located; Goldman-Rakic and her colleagues (e.g., Goldman-Rakic, 1987; Wilson, Scalaidhe, and Goldman-Rakic, 1993) have shown in the monkey that the object properties processing and spatial properties processing systems send projections directly to regions of the frontal lobe, and Rao, Rainer, and Miller (1997) have shown that about half of the relevant neurons actually code for the conjunction of shape and location. According to the theory of Kosslyn (1994), long-term associative memory stores descriptions that indicate how parts of objects are arranged, as well as how objects are arranged in scenes (i.e., collections of separate objects). If this theory is correct, then when such an object is visualized, the representation of the object's structure would be accessed in order to look up the locations where parts and characteristics should be visualized. We hypothesize that long-term associative memory relies on "association cortex" in the region of the angular gyrus and part of Area 19.

Information shunting

The frontal lobes can be viewed, in large part, as a shunting device, sending information from one part of the brain to another in an effort to further one's goals. The locus of short-term associative memory in the frontal lobes is convenient, allowing representations in the more posterior areas to be "written over" by new input, while at the same time briefly retaining the information they previously registered. Moreover, having this information "on tap" provides the information-shunting processes easy access to key facts about the current environment.

A key role of the frontal lobes during perception occurs when one cannot identify an object at first glance; the information encoded in a single eye fixation is not sufficient to match a stored representation (cf., Neisser, 1967). However, the input provides some indication of what is being viewed, and the partial match to stored representations in associative memory may serve as a hypothesis. In this case, additional information is needed to identify the input. Frontal lobe processes apparently access information in associative memory, both short-term and long-term, and use this information to guide further encodings. Such processing allows one to seek a particularly diagnostic part or characteristic. Many researchers have found that damage to the frontal lobe disrupts systematic search (e.g., Damasio, 1985; Luria, 1980). In addition, Kosslyn, Thompson, Kim, and Alpert (1995) found that the frontal lobes are in fact active when one must access information in memory (see also Tulving and Markowitsch, 1997).

It has long been known that the frontal lobes are crucially involved in planning (e.g., Berthoz, 2000). As part of the planning process, motor programs can be set up and "instructions" sent to low-level motor cortex to prepare one to move (see Chapter 7 of Kosslyn and Koenig, 1992/1995). Kosslyn (1994) argues that part of the process of motor control involves priming the visual system to encode the expected consequences of making a movement. This priming mechanism also underlies the process of forming an image, as noted in the following section.

Attention shifting and top-down priming

Finally, according to this theory, an attention-shifting system actually shifts attention to the location of a possibly distinctive part, which allows one to encode it. This system apparently includes a subsystem that disengages attention from its current location and guides positioning of the attention window, as well as the eyes, head, and body; in addition, the frontal eye fields (Area 9) and superior colliculus may play a role in actually shifting attention, and the thalamus (particularly the pulvinar nucleus) and possibly the anterior cingulate gyrus (cf. LaBerge and Buchsbaum, 1990) may play a role in reengaging attention once it is shifted (for evidence, e.g., see Corbetta, Miezin, Shulman, and Petersen, 1993; Posner and Petersen, 1990).

And here is a crucial idea for the theory of imagery: At the same time that attention is shifted to the location of an expected part or characteristic, the representation of that part or characteristic is primed in the object-properties processing system. Such priming allows one to encode the sought part or property more easily (for evidence of such priming, see Kosslyn, 1994, pp. 287–289; McDermott and Roediger, 1994).

According to the theory, in order to create an image representation on the basis of stored information, frontal lobe processes access the stored representation of the structure of an object in associative memory and then send information to the inferior temporal lobes to activate a representation of visual properties. This activation process is identical to the priming that occurs during top-down hypothesis testing in perception, only now the priming is so strong that activation propagates backward and an image representation is formed in the visual buffer. According to the theory of Kosslyn (1994), if an image of a single object is formed, the global shape is visualized first. Following this, if necessary to perform the task, the same process is repeated to activate images of individual parts or characteristics to form a more detailed image; the same process is also used when a scene (not an object) is visualized, but now images of individual objects (not parts) are formed. Kosslyn, Cave, Provost, and Von Gierke (1988) provide evidence that images are generated by building them up part-by-part over time. Indeed, the segments of letters are placed in the image in the same order that they typically are drawn when block letters are printed.

Summary of theory of information processing during visual imagery

According to the present theory, visual mental image representations are generated by first looking up a "visual index" in long-term associative memory, which, in turn, activates a description of the shape of an object or composition of a scene. This representation is then used to activate the visual memory of either the global shape of an object or the central object in a scene. These modality-specific visual memories are stored in the object-properties-processing system (implemented in the middle temporal, inferior temporal, and fusiform gyri). The image itself corresponds to activation in the visual buffer, which is implemented in retinotopically organized regions in the occipital lobe. If images of details are required, the information shunting process accesses long-term associative memory (which relies on the angular gyrus and Area 19) and looks up the most distinctive part or property, as well as its location if an object is being visualized, or other objects in a scene if a scene is being visualized; attention is then shifted (using the frontal eye fields, superior parietal lobe, and subcortical structures) to the appropriate location (using posterior parietal structures to register the sought location). As soon as attention is properly positioned, the part or property is visualized. This process is repeated for each additional part (or object in a scene), which explains why there is a linear increase in time to generate images of objects with more parts (e.g., Kosslyn, 1980; Kosslyn et al., 1988).

Once an image is present in the visual buffer, one can inspect the imaged pattern by shifting the attention window over it; this allows one to encode previously unconsidered properties (e.g., the shape of an animal's ears). However, most image scanning involves sequentially substituting a series of images in the visual buffer (thus, most scanning is like watching a TV screen when the camera pans across a scene—the image shifts across the screen). Imaged patterns are recognized by matching the input to stored visual memories in the object-properties-processing system, just as is done during perceptual encoding. Similarly, spatial relations are encoded using the spatial-properties-processing system, just as is in perception.

When is imagery used? One reason people may use imagery is that when parts are encoded separately from objects, the spatial relations of the parts are specified relative to specific origins. Objects are stored in memory with a certain organization; for example, you store the Star of David as two overlapping triangles, so when I ask whether there is a hexagon in the middle, you need to reconstruct the shape and reexamine the image. Similarly, the parts of an object are organized relative to a single origin. Although the visual memories of parts are stored in the object-properties-processing system, the description of spatial relations among the parts is stored in long-term associative memory (in part because spatial relations can be described using categorical relations, such as above/below, inside/outside). If you need to consider how a part is positioned relative to another one, and neither of them is the origin of the description, you will need to form an image. For example, if I ask whether a cat's ears protrude above the top of its skull, you will probably visualize the animal's head to decide. But if I ask you whether its nose is further forward than its ears, you may incidentally form an image but probably don't need the image to answer the question—this one can be answered using simply the stored description. It is only when you need to break up or otherwise reorganize the description that you need to form an image.

Finally, one also can transform an imaged pattern by shifting the pattern in the visual buffer. In my view, image scanning is a type of imagery transformation. One way to transform images is to anticipate what one would see if the object were physically manipulated in some way, such as being rotated. This anticipation leads to priming (in the same way that generating an image relies on mechanisms used in priming), but now an existing image is transformed in accordance with one's expectations. You can imagine what you would see if you transformed the object yourself, or if some external force transformed it (see Kosslyn, DiGirolamo, Thompson, and Alpert, 1998; Wexler, Kosslyn, and Berthoz, 1998).

Testing the theory of processing components

I have found a deep resistance to theorizing in much of psychology, perhaps as a holdover from the behaviorist orientation that was prevalent for so long. Thus, many researchers are uncomfortable with theories of the sort we developed—and funding through the usual National Institute of Health (NIH) and National Science Foundation (NSF) channels has sometimes been difficult to obtain. Fortunately for us, the Office of Naval Research, Air Force Office of Scientific Research, and foundations (particularly the John D. and Catherine T. MacArthur Foundation and James S. McDonnell/Pew Charitable Trust alliance) have supported us at crucial junctures. Such support allowed us to perform one of the first (if not the first—this isn't clear) neuroimaging studies of imagery. After a considerable struggle to get this work published (which took over two years), we succeeded in 1993. Why the resistance? This study produced a surprising result: the first cortical visual areas to receive input from the eyes, Areas 17 and 18, were activated during visual mental imagery. The visual buffer included structures much "lower" in the system than we had expected. To this day, debate rages about the significance of this finding. (Fortunately, at about the same time Denis LeBihan and his colleagues independently used functional magnetic resonance imaging [fMRI] to obtain the same result, which has been repeated many times now; for a review, see Thompson and Kosslyn, 2000.) We found evidence not only for a visual buffer but also for the other processes summarized in this chapter.

The earlier results were sufficiently encouraging that Kosslyn et al. (1994) decided to test directly the theory outlined in the block diagram of Figure 7.1. (The theory we tested was slightly different, but only in assumptions about connectivity, not about the nature of the processes.) We scanned the brains of participants while they performed three tasks, each in a separate block of trials. They decided whether words named pictures of objects viewed from a canonical perspective, decided whether words named pictures of objects viewed from a noncanonical (unusual) perspective, or saw random patterns of lines and pressed a pedal when they heard the word (this was a baseline condition). We expected the entire system to be used more when objects seen from noncanonical points of view were presented. And, in fact, areas that we took to implement the functions outlined in Figure 7.1 were activated more in the noncanonical condition than in the canonical condition. Dorsolateral prefrontal cortex (in the region we assumed implements the information-shunting subsystem) was activated when participants identified objects seen from noncanonical perspectives, as expected if this region is involved in looking up stored information to guide top-down perceptual processing. In addition, areas in the occipital, temporal, and parietal lobes were selectively activated when participants identified objects seen from noncanonical perspectives.

The inference that either the angular gyrus or Area 19 (or both) plays a role in implementing long-term associative memory was supported by results reported by Kosslyn, Thompson, Kim, and Alpert (1995), who asked participants to decide whether words named accompanying pictures while undergoing PET scanning. In one condition, the names were at the "entry" level (i.e., the level spontaneously named, "bird" for a robin), in another condition they were at a superordinate level (e.g., "animal"), and in another they were at a subordinate level (e.g., "robin"). Jolicoeur, Gluck, and Kosslyn (1984) showed that people spontaneously name objects at the entry level and, hence, must search memory to evaluate a superordinate term. For example, when shown a picture of a robin, they name it as "bird." If they were asked whether it is an animal, they then must look up in memory the fact that birds are animals before they can respond. We found that masking a stimulus (i.e., showing it briefly and then presenting a nonsense pattern that disrupts the afterimage, ensuring that the stimulus can be encoded for only a brief period) did not disrupt evaluating superordinate names any more than it disrupted evaluating entry-level names, even though more time was taken for superordinates (as expected if an additional processing step was required). In contrast, masking greatly disrupted evaluating a subordinate name, as expected if participants had to encode additional perceptual information to evaluate these terms. Hence, by subtracting cerebral blood flow when participants evaluated entry-level terms from cerebral blood flow when participants evaluated superordinates, we expected to find activation in the angular gyrus or in Area 19, if these areas in fact implement associative memory. And this is what we found. In another condition the participants saw written words that named the entry-level term and decided whether the named object could appropriately be named by a specific superordinate term. Similar activation was observed as was found when participants evaluated superordinate terms for pictures, as expected if the same associative memory structure was accessed in both cases.

In addition, Kosslyn, Thompson, and Alpert (1997) compared the pattern of brain activation in a perceptual task and an imagery task. We used the picture verification task of Kosslyn et al. (1994), in which participants evaluated names of canonical and (in another condition) noncanonical pictures. We compared the additional activation that arises when one evaluates noncanonical pictures with that in the grids-and-X imagery task used in our original PET imagery experiments. In this task, subjects see a 4 by 5 grid that contains a single X mark in one cell, and they are asked to decide whether a specific block letter (memorized prior to the task) would have covered the X mark if it were in the grid (this is an imagery task first developed by Podgorny and Shepard, 1978). We intentionally chose two tasks that appear on the surface to be very different, but for which our theory led us to expect that common underlying processing would be used to perform. Fourteen areas were activated in common by both tasks, all of which could be organized in terms of the functions outlined in Figure 7.1; in addition, two areas were activated in perception but not imagery, and five were activated in imagery but not perception. Thus, two-thirds of the activated areas were activated in common.

More specifically, Kosslyn et al. (1997) found strong correspondence between visual imagery and perception in areas that implement the visual buffer and information-shunting systems. The areas that we interpreted as implementing the other processes were less often precisely the same in the two functions, which may suggest that the functions may play slightly different roles in imagery and perception. Our finding that about one-third of the areas activated during imagery and perception were not shared allows us to understand why lesions can disrupt imagery but not perception, and vice versa (see Behrmann, Winocur, and Moscovitch, 1992; Jankowiak, Kinsbourne, Shalev, and Bachman, 1992). Depending on which of the areas that are not shared is damaged, a patient can have difficulties with imagery or perception independently.

In short, most of the brain areas activated by imagery were also activated during perception, and vice versa. This fact supports that idea that images can "stand in" for percepts, and it has intriguing implications for the possible roles of imagery in health—as discussed here shortly.

Revising the theory

The protomodel illustrated in Figure 7.1 has been revised in three ways. First, we have reconceptualized the role of the spatial-properties-processing system. As noted in this chapter, the conventional wisdom is that the major visual pathway implemented in the inferior temporal lobes deals with object recognition ("what") and the one implemented in the posterior parietal lobes deals with spatial processing ("where"). But as stated, this idea cannot explain the data. Although monkeys cannot learn to discriminate locations when they have lesions in the parietal system, they do reach correctly in this task (just for the wrong object). Thus, they must be registering location. Similarly, monkeys cannot learn to discriminate shapes when they have lesions in the inferior temporal system, and this is true even if shapes are checkerboards versus stripes—which differ in the number of locations (black areas) that are defined. The traditional view that parietal system registers "where" can't explain why the monkey fails to notice that there are more locations defined by one pattern than another; if it does register such information, why can't it make the discrimination?

Our recent designs for models suggest a different slant—namely, that the parietal system represents locations of objects in order to perform coordinate transformations. We begin by organizing the world relative to our heads (which serve as the origin of the coordinate space), but for many purposes we need to represent objects relative to other parts of the body, such as the hands (as when we reach). Moreover, we often need to represent objects or parts relative to each other (e.g., the rock is to the left of the tree, or is three feet from it). The type of coordinate system must be altered, typically in three-dimensions. In my view, the key function performed by the spatial-properties-processing system is to reconstruct three-dimensional layout relative to a given point of origin (fixed on one's body, a part of the body, or on an object) and to shift coordinate systems as necessary for specific tasks. Given this notion, it is not surprising that mental rotation activates the posterior parietal lobes (e.g., Kosslyn et al., 1998). The available results make more sense if we view this as the function of the relevant portions of the parietal lobes, instead of simply registering "where" objects are.

The revised view has the potential to solve some puzzles in the imagery literature. For example, in 1978 my colleagues and I found that it takes the same amount of time to scan between two "visible" locations on an image as to scan from a visible location to one that initially was "off screen" (Kosslyn, Ball, and Reiser, 1978). In this task, the participant is asked to focus on a given location (e.g., the hut drawn on a map of the island), and then to scan to another location. If the subjects always started from a single location, they soon could learn the angle and distance of each other object, and then use this information simply to visualize the target location without scanning. This is a kind of "ballistic" shifting, with no intermediate corrections. However, if the point of focus is shifted, the subjects would not have such polar coordinates memorized and thus would need to scan to monitor their progress as they traversed the map. This is a kind of "guided" shifting. The need to observe the intermediate material to correct the scan would require representations in the visual buffer.

This shift operation causes the image to scroll through the visual buffer, and this scroll process operates at the same rate, regardless of whether points are "visible." In addition, if one has looked at points on an object relative to many other points, and thus has stored many separate representations of the structure of the object in associative memory (where parts are associated via spatial relations), depictive imagery will not be necessary to perform many tasks. This notion may explain why some neuroimaging studies of visual mental imagery have not found activation of structures that make up the visual buffer (e.g., see Mellet, Petit, Mazoyer, Denis, and Tzourio, 1998; Thompson and Kosslyn, 2000). During its next phase, our research project will focus on this notion in detail.

In addition, in an earlier version of the theory, the information-shunting system was labeled the "information-lookup" system, which is based on a meta-phor to conventional computer programs. That notion emphasizes the idea that this frontal-lobe-based process serves to direct information from one part of the brain to another. We think of the frontal lobe as a large collection of special-purpose "filters," which transform input and send it elsewhere. Reverberating circuits among these filters can accomplish many serial tasks, as well as provide temporary short-term memory stores.

Third, we take seriously neuroantomical evidence that both the ventral and dorsal streams project directly to the dorsolateral prefrontal lobes (e.g., Rao et al., 1997; Wilson et al., 1993). Neurons in the parts of the frontal lobes that receive these projections are activated when input must be retained over time before the animal can make a response (such as moving the eyes to a previous location or noticing a repeated pattern; e.g., Cohen et al., 1997; Goldman-Rakic, 1992; Rao et al., 1997; Wilson et al., 1993). In my view, short-term associative memory maintains "pointers" back to the structures that encode the information, which serves to keep this information "on line" to be used in performing a task. If struc-tures usually used to store memories must be used immediately after to encode another stimulus (as in the "n-back" task of Cohen et al.), the frontal structures can "protect" these memories from being disrupted.

These modifications preserve the power of the original protomodel to predict and explain the observed findings, but they also lead us to design new studies—both behavioral and neuroimaging—to test new distinctions directly.

Implications for Health

Turning to the brain allows us to dispel an age-old conundrum: Who (or what) "looks" at an object in a mental image? Given that parts of the brain that are activated during early stages of perception are also activated in imagery, there is no puzzle: the brain processes signals, and if imagery engenders the same kind of signals as perception, they can be processed the same way in both cases. This perspective certainly helps to resolve long-standing issues, but looking at the neural substrate of imagery also puts us in a position to consider how imagery could affect the body and health.

Mental simulation of aversive events

The idea that mental images can "stand in" for actual objects suggests that images can evoke some of the same emotions as the corresponding objects. In one study, we asked subjects to visualize pictures of neutral or aversive stimuli (primarily from the Lang set), and then to determine whether auditorially presented statements were true or false of the stimuli. Kosslyn et al. (1996) used PET to record cerebral blood flow while they performed the task. Imagery of negative stimuli enhanced cerebral blood flow, relative to imagery of neutral stimuli, in Areas 17 (left) and 18 (bilateral), as well as in the anterior insula (bilateral) and middle frontal cortex (left). Areas 17 and 18 have been identified as supporting the representations that underlie the experience of imagery, and the anterior insula is the major cortical recipient of input from the autonomic nervous system. The activation in the anterior insula is particularly intriguing: it suggests that imagery may affect the body, which, in turn, feeds back to affect the brain. If this is correct, then manipulating imagery could affect the body in profound ways, such as regulating the effects of stress. We next discuss one way this could occur.

Imagery and cognitive restructuring

Recent work by Sapolsky and his colleagues (e.g., Sapolsky, 1992) has shown that persistent stress can cause cortisol secretions that not only compromise the immune system but also can damage the hippocampus (and thereby, presumably, disrupt memory). One question we asked was whether imagery could mitigate some of the effects of stress, which would thus have direct implications for health. In particular, we wanted to know whether imagery could be used to "cognitively restructure" a stimulus or event, so that it was no longer so stress-inducing.

Psychotherapists have demonstrated that, in fact, restructuring therapies, which alter how people interpret and organize events and the consequences of behavior, can modify behavior and feelings of emotional discomfort. For example, cognitive restructuring has been shown to reduce anxiety in socially anxious people (Kanter and Goldfried, 1979); increase assertiveness and decrease anxiety in submissive people (Linehan, Goldfried, and Goldfried, 1979); reduce anger (Hazaleus and Deffenbacher, 1986); and can attenuate anxiety in arachnophobes (O'Donohue and Szymanski, 1993). We wanted to know whether cognitive restructuring is an effective way for members of nonclinical populations to dampen emotional responses to aversive events.

Kosslyn and Koenig (1992/1995) treat emotion as a process that modulates one's goals and information processing; specifically, it leads one to select specific goals over others, while at the same time priming some processes and inhibiting others. According to this view, emotion serves to promote behaviors that will achieve a goal, and emotion tends to push one until the goal is reached. If this is true, we reasoned, then one way to reduce emotion would be to help one reach closure, so that one is not impelled to behave in a certain way. We operationally define positive resolution as completion of an emotionally aversive situation in a way that both produces a positive outcome and removes any need to act further in the situation. We theorize that restructuring events that lead to positive resolution of an aversive situation will subsequently attenuate one's emotional response to that situation. In contrast, when the context surrounding an aversive situation is left unresolved, we expect no subsequent attenuation of the participant's emotional response to the situation.

In our first study on this topic (still in progress), David Hurvitz, Ingrid Dombrower, and I measured changes in skin conductance response (SCR) when people reinterpreted the meanings of visualized aversive stimuli in ways that did or did not "put the emotion to bed." We selected SCR as a measure of change in autonomic processing because previous research has shown that the form of an SCR is sensitive to the evaluated significance value of a stimulus (Barry, 1981). Furthermore, Geen and Rakosky (1973) used SCR to demonstrate differences in emotional reactivity to alternative interpretations (e.g., fictional versus real) of the same complex stimuli (e.g., a film of a fight). Moreover, researchers have found that SCRs are sensitive to emotional aspects of mental images (Dadds, Cutmore, Bovbjerg, and Redd, 1997; Deschaumes-Molinaro, Dittmar, and Vernet-Maury, 1992; Lang, Kozak, Miller, Levin, and McLean, 1980; Lichstein and Lipshitz, 1982; Yaremko and Butler, 1975).

The skin conductance responses of participants were recorded as they visualized aversive stimuli before and after reading scripts that contextualized the stimulus. For each participant, six of the scripts resolved the depicted situation and six left the situation unresolved. Comparisons of the response magnitudes between the resolved and unresolved conditions were used to determine whether cognitive resolution can modify physiological components of emotional responses to visualized scenes. The preliminary results showed a difference between the magnitude of skin conductance responses when the stimulus was visualized after reading the resolved versus the unresolved contextualizing script. However, responses actually increased after the unresolved scripts, and the effect of the resolved scripts was to prevent this increase. This unexpected finding leads to a host of additional questions (for example, is what's important closure, or is it positive closure?).

In short, our just-being-born work on health-related uses of imagery has grown directly out of our more general framework for understanding imagery. By thinking of imagery as a computational system that is implemented in the brain, we have been able to conceptualize how images in the mind could affect the body.

Imagery and mind-body interactions

Imagery has been implicated in much grander roles, such as in curing cancer (I've seen admonitions to visualize tiny knights on horseback spearing cancer cells). Imagery has also been implicated in the placebo effect, which is nontrivial in a wide range of illnesses (e.g., see Harrington, 1998). Imagery has also been treated as a method of curing a wide range of mental illnesses. The data are not overwhelmingly supportive for any of these claims, so the first job is to establish the effect conclusively. If it turns out that imagery really does play a role in such effects, we now know enough to begin to formulate detailed hypotheses about how imagery may have its effects. In many cases, simply being able to ask the question clearly gets us halfway toward answering it.

Reflections on a 30-Year Research Program

As should be clear, the research program summarized here has been driven in part by responses to criticisms and suggestions, and in part because of the availability of new kinds of data and new techniques for testing hypotheses. Because of the varied combination of skills necessary to do the work that has emerged during the most recent phase of our research, I as the principal investigator have continually had to become familiar with new methods and techniques (most recently, PET; fMRI; and transcranial magnetic stimulation, TMS). Moreover, this learning has invariably taken place in the context of collaborations with an ever-expanding group of colleagues. The collaborations have all grown naturally out of the questions that needed to be answered and have faded away when the questions were answered to our level of satisfaction. Many of the collaborations began with the availability of new research tools (e.g., neuroimaging and TMS), which opened the possibility of answering old questions in new ways or of approaching new questions altogether.

Although funding has always been available, it often has been secured only after a struggle. As the work has become progressively more cumulative and focused, some reviewers have apparently felt that it was not innovative enough to deserve continued support. This has been particularly frustrating at the National Institutes of Health, where if even one review panel member feels strongly negatively toward a proposal, it is unlikely that the panel will vote to support the work. It is unfortunate that there are so few models for how to conduct a long-term research project on a single topic; if more models were available, perhaps reviewers and agencies would be able to put in context the kind of research that seeks to refine and expand on previous work, not simply by spinning off a related idea but rather by further articulating a theory.

The kind of framework we are developing is valuable in part because it can serve as a foundation for additional research. For example, one particularly intriguing direction returns us to the very beginnings of the scientific study of imagery: individual differences. The standard approach to individual differences is to put people in categories (e.g., visualizer vs. verbalizer, visile vs. audile). The current approach invites us instead to treat each person as a unique "point in a space," where each dimension corresponds to a different type of processing. By assessing enough different processes, a profile can be obtained—with each score being equivalent to a position on a dimension in a high-dimensional space. Thus, no two people are likely to be exactly alike, and their use of imagery to perform specific tasks should be slightly different. One of the great promises of cognitive neuro-science is the ability to use basic findings to tailor practices and treatments for particular individuals.

Postscript

As of the new edition of this book, I find myself in an interesting situation: My closest collaborators and I just published *The Case for Mental Imagery* (Kosslyn, Thompson, and Ganis, 2006), which summarizes the imagery debate and the lines of our work that bear directly on it. This book was published almost exactly 30 years after my first paper on the imagery debate was actually written. I find that I don't have much more to say on the topic, and wonder whether I will have deep or innovative ideas about imagery in the future. My work has been cumulative and programmatic, and has gradually produced a coherent (to my eyes, anyway) story. I've tried to keep an open mind, and consider other alternatives—but this is becoming increasingly difficult as time goes on, and the story seems to become more firmly rooted in a diverse set of data. Thus, I think it's best for me to move on to something else, something different. I'm sure I'll draw on my earlier work (how could I not?), but will try to carve out an entirely new line of theory and research. As of this writing, several new topics and ideas are bumping up against each other in my head, and I'll just have to see which ones bear fruit. As in the previous research, I will seek unnoticed intersections among different fields, where scholars regard similar questions from different perspectives—and try to discover whether there's something lurking in the interstitial spaces, something testable. A key to making this happen will be finding the right people, who are open-minded, willing to exchange ideas (as opposed to simply stating prior positions), and interested in stretching beyond familiar boundaries. I consider myself extraordinarily lucky still to have the time to try something new!

ACKNOWLEDGMENTS

Preparation of this article was supported by NIH grant 1 R01 MH60734–02 and NSF grant REC-0106760. Portions of this article were adapted from Kosslyn (1994) and Kosslyn et al. (1994), with permission of the publishers.

RECOMMENDED READINGS

Gardner, H. (1985). *The Mind's New Science: A History of the Cognitive Revolution.* New York: Basic Books.

Kosslyn, S. M. (1994). *Image and Brain: The Resolution of the Imagery Debate.* Cambridge, MA: MIT Press.

Paivio, A. (1991). *Images in Mind: The Evolution of a Theory.* London: Harvester Wheat-sheaft.

Shepard, R. N., and Cooper, L. R. (1982). *Mental Images and Their Transformations.* Cambridge, MA: MIT Press.

REFERENCES

Barry, R. J. (1981). Signal value and preliminary processes in OR elicitation. *Pavlovian Journal of Biological Science, 16,* 116–150.

Behrmann, M., Winocur, G., and Moscovitch, M. (1992). Dissociation between mental imagery and object recognition in a brain-damaged patient. *Nature, 359,* 636–637.

Berthoz, A. (2000). *The Sense of Movement.* Cambridge, MA: Harvard University Press.

Block, N. (Ed.) (1981). *Imagery.* Cambridge, MA: MIT Press.

Cohen, J. D., Peristein, W. M., Braver, T. S., Nystrom, L. E., Noll, D. C., Jonides, J., and Smith, E. E. (1997). Temporal dynamics of brain activation during a working memory task. *Nature, 386,* 604–608.

Cooper, L. (1976). Demonstration of a mental analogy of an external rotation. *Perception and Psychophysics, 19,* 296–302.

Corbetta, M., Miezin, F. M., Schulman, G. L., and Petersen, S. E. (1993). A PET study of visuospatial attention. *Journal of Neuroscience, 13,* 1202–1226.

Dadds, M., Cutmore, T., Bovbjerg, D., Redd, W. (1997) Imagery in human classical conditioning. *Psychological Bulletin, 122,* 89–103.

Damasio, A. R. (1985). The frontal lobes. In K. M. Heilman, and E. Valenstein (Eds.), *Clinical Neuropsychology* (pp. 339–402). New York: Oxford University Press.

Damasio, A. R., Damasio, H., Tranel, D., and Brandt, J. P. (1990). Neural regionalization of knowledge access: Preliminary evidence. *Cold Spring Harbor Symposia on Quantitative Biology, 55,* 1039–1047.

Deschaumes-Molinaro C., Dittmar, A., and Vernet-Maury, E. (1992). Autonomic nervous system response patterns correlate with mental imagery. *Physiology and Behavior, 51,* 1021–1027.

Douglas, K. L., and Rockland, K. S. (1992). Extensive visual feedback connections from ventral inferotemporal cortex. *Society of Neuroscience Abstracts, 18,* 390.

Felleman, D. J., and Van Essen, D. C. (1991). Distributed hierarchical processing in primate cerebral cortex. *Cerebral Cortex, 1,* 1–47.

Fodor, J. A. (1968). *Psychological Explanation: An Introduction to the Philosophy of Psychology.* New York: Random House.

Fox, P. T., Miezin, F. M., Allman, J. M., Van Essen, D. C., and Raichle, M. E. (1987). Retinotopic organization of human visual cortex mapped with positron emission tomography. *Journal of Neuroscience, 7,* 913–922.

Fox, P. T., Mintun, M. A., Raichle, M. E., Miezin, F. M., Allman, J. M., and Van Essen, D. C. (1986). Mapping human visual cortex with positron emission tomography. *Nature, 323,* 806–809.

Fujita, I., Tanaka, K., Ito, M., and Cheng, K. (1992). Columns for visual features of objects in monkey inferotemporal cortex. *Nature, 360,* 343–346.

Gardner, H. (1985). *The Mind's New Science.* New York: Basic Book.

Gazzaniga, M.S., Ivry, R. B., and Mangun, G. R. (1998). *Cognitive Neuroscience: The Biology of the Mind.* New York: Norton.

Geen, R., and Rakosky, J. (1973) Interpretations of observed aggression and their effects on GSR. *Journal of Experimental Research in Personality, 6,* 289–292.

Goldman-Rakic, P. S. (1987). Circuitry of primate prefrontal cortex and regulation of behavior by representational knowledge. In F. Plum (Vol. Ed.) and V. B. Mountcastle (Sec. Ed.), *Handbook of Physiology, Section 1: The Nervous System, Volume 5: Higher Functions of the Brain.* Bethesda, MD: American Physiological Society.

Goldman-Rakic, P. (1992). Working memory and the mind. *Scientific American, 267,* 110–117.

Harrington, A. (Ed.) (1998). *The Placebo Effect: An Interdisciplinary Exploration.* Cambridge, MA: Harvard University Press.

Haxby, J. V., Grady, C. L., Horowitz, B., Ungerleider, L. G., Mishkin, M., Carson, R. E., Herscovitch, P., Schapiro, M. B., and Rapoport, S. I. (1991). Dissociation of object and spatial visual processing pathways in human extrastriate cortex. *Proceedings of the National Academy of Sciences of the United States of America, 88,* 1621–1625.

Hazaleus, S. L., and Deffenbacher, J. L. (1986). Relaxation and cognitive treatments of anger. *Journal of Consulting and Clinical Psychology, 54,* 222–226.

Hebb, D. O. (1968). Concerning imagery. *Psychological Review, 75,* 466–477.

Intons-Peterson, M. J. (1983). Imagery paradigms: How vulnerable are they to experimenters' expectations? *Journal of Experimental Psychology: Human Perception and Performance, 9,* 394–412.

James, W. (1890). *Principles of Psychology.* New York: Holt.

Jankowiak, J., Kinsbourne, M., Shalev, R. S., and Bachman, D. L. (1992). Preserved visual imagery and categorization in a case of associative visual agnosia. *Journal of Cognitive Neuroscience, 4,* 119–131.

Jolicoeur, P., Gluck, M. A., and Kosslyn, S. M. (1984). Pictures and names: Making the connection. *Cognitive Psychology, 16,* 243-275.

Kanter, N. J., and Goldfried, M. R. (1979). Relative effectiveness of rational restructuring and self-control desensitization in the reduction of interpersonal anxiety. *Behavior Therapy, 10,* 472–490.

Kosslyn, S. M. (1980). *Image and Mind.* Cambridge, MA: Harvard University Press.

Kosslyn, S. M. (1981). The medium and the message in mental imagery: A theory. *Psychological Review, 88,* 46–66.

Kosslyn, S. M. (1994). *Image and Brain: The Resolution of the Imagery Debate.* Cambridge, MA: MIT Press.

Kosslyn, S. M., Thompson, W. L., and Ganis, G. (2006). *The case for mental imagery.* New York: Oxford University Press.

Kosslyn, S. M., and Koenig, O. (1992/1995). *Wet Mind: The New Cognitive Neuroscience.* New York: Free Press.

Kosslyn, S. M., Alpert, N. M., Thompson, W. L., Chabris, C. F., Rauch, S. L., and Anderson, A. K. (1994). Identifying objects seen from different viewpoints: A PET investigation. *Brain, 117,* 1055–1071.

Kosslyn, S. M., Alpert, N. M., Thompson, W. L., Maljkovic, V., Weise, S. B., Chabris, C. F., Hamilton, S. E., Rauch, S. L., and Buonanno, F. S. (1993). Visual mental imagery activates topographically organized visual cortex: PET investigations. *Journal of Cognitive Neuroscience, 5,* 263–287.

Kosslyn, S. M., Ball, T. M., and Reiser, B. J. (1978). Visual images preserve metric spatial information: evidence from studies of image scanning. *Journal of Experimental Psychology: Human Perception and Performance, 4,* 47–60.

Kosslyn, S. M., Cave, C. B., Provost, D., and Von Gierke, S. (1988). Sequential processes in image generation. *Cognitive Psychology, 20,* 319–343.

Kosslyn, S. M., DiGirolamo, G., Thompson, W. L., and Alpert, N.M. (1998). Mental rotation of objects versus hands: Neural mechanisms revealed by positron emission tomography. *Psychophysiology, 35,* 151–161.

Kosslyn, S. M., Flynn, R. A., Amsterdam, J. B., and Wang, G. (1990). Components of high-level vision: A cognitive neuroscience analysis and accounts of neurological syndromes. *Cognition, 34,* 203–277.

Kosslyn, S. M., Pascual-Leone, A., Felician, O., Camposano, S., Keenan, J. P., Thompson, W. L., Ganis, G., Sukel, K. E., and Alpert, N. M. (1999). The role of Area 17 in visual imagery: Convergent evidence from PET and rTMS. *Science, 284,* 167–170.

Kosslyn, S. M., Thompson, W. L., and Alpert, N. M. (1995). Identifying objects at different levels of hierarchy: A positron emission tomography study. *Human Brain Mapping, 3,* 107–132.

Kosslyn, S. M., Thompson, W. L., and Alpert, N. M. (1997). Neural systems shared by visual imagery and visual perception: A positron emission tomography study. *NeuroImage, 6,* 320–334.

Kosslyn, S. M., Thompson, W. L., Kim, I. J., and Alpert, N.M. (1995). Topographical representations of mental images in primary visual cortex. *Nature, 378,* 496–498.

Kosslyn, S. M., Shin, L., Thompson, W., McNally, R., Rauch, S., Pitman, R., and Alpert, N. (1996). Neural effects of visualizing and perceiving aversive stimuli: A PET investigation. *NeuroReport, 7,* 1569–1576.

LaBerge, D., and Buchsbaum, M. S. (1990). Positron emission tomography measurements of pulvinar activity during an attention task. *Journal of Neuroscience, 10,* 613–619.

Lang, P., Kozak, M., Miller, G., Levin, D., and McLean, A. (1980) Emotional imagery: Conceptual structure and pattern of somato-viseral response. *Psychophysiology, 17,* 179–192.

Lichstein, K., and Lipshitz, E. (1982). Physiological effects of noxious imagery: prevalence and prediction. *Behavioral Research Therapy, 30,* 339–345.

Linehan, M. M., Goldfried, M. R., and Goldfried, A. P. (1979). Assertion therapy: Skill training or cognitive restructuring. *Behavior Therapy, 10,* 372–388.

Luria, A. R. (1980). *Higher Cortical Functions in Man.* New York: Basic Books.

Maunsell, J. H. R., and Newsome, W. T. (1987). Visual processing in monkey extrastriate cortex. *Annual Review of Neuroscience, 10,* 363–401.

McDermott, K. B., and Roediger, H. L. (1994). Effects of imagery on perceptual implicit memory tests. *Journal of Experimental Psychology: Learning, Memory, and Cognition, 20,* 1379–1390.

Mellet, E., Petit, L., Mazoyer, B., Denis, M., and Tzourio, N. (1998). Reopening the mental imagery debate: Lessons from functional neuroanatomy. *NeuroImage, 8,* 129–139.

Metzler, J., and Shepard, R. N. (1974). Transformational studies of the internal representation of three-dimensional objects. In R. L. Solso (Ed.), *Theories of Cognitive Psychology: The Loyola Symposium* (pp. 147–202). Potomac, MD: Erlbaum.

Moran, J., and Desimone, R. (1985). Selective attention gates visual processing in the extrastriate cortex. *Science, 229,* 782–784.

Neisser, U. (1967). *Cognitive Psychology.* New York: Appleton-Century-Crofts.

Newell, A., Shaw, J. C., and Simon, H. A. (1958). Elements of a theory of human problem solving. *Psychological Review, 65*(3), 151–166.

O'Donohue, W., and Szymanski, J. (1993). Change mechanisms in cognitive therapy of a simple phobia: Logical analysis and empirical hypothesis testing. *Journal of Rational-Emotive and Cognitive Behavior Therapy, 11,* 207–222.

Paivio, A. (1971). *Imagery and Verbal Processes.* New York: Holt, Rinehart and Winston.

Paivio, A. (1991). *Images in Mind: The Evolution of a Theory.* London: Harvester Wheatsheaf.

Podgorny, P., and Shepard, R. N. (1978). Functional representations common to visual perception and imagination. *Journal of Experimental Psychology: Human Perception and Performance, 4,* 21–35.

Pohl, W. (1973). Dissociation of spatial discrimination deficits following frontal and parietal lesions in monkeys. *Journal of Comparative and Physiological Psychology, 82,* 227–239.

Popper, K. R. (1959). *The Logic of Scientific Discovery.* New York: Basic Books.

Posner, M. I., and Petersen, S. E. (1990). The attention system of the human brain. *Annual Review of Neuroscience, 13,* 25–42.

Pylyshyn, Z. W. (1973). What the mind's eye tells the mind's brain: A critique of mental imagery. *Psychological Bulletin, 80,* 1–24.

Pylyshyn, Z. W. (1981). The imagery debate: Analogue media versus tacit knowledge. *Psychological Review, 87,* 16–45.

Rao, S. C., Rainer, G., and Miller, E. K. (1997). Integration of what and where in the primate prefrontal cortex. *Science, 276,* 821–824.

Rockland, K. S., Saleem, K. S., and Tanaka, K. (1992). Widespread feedback connections from areas V4 and TEO. *Society for Neuroscience Abstracts, 18,* 390.

Sapolsky, R. M. (1992). *Stress, the Aging Brain, and the Mechanisms of Neuron Death.* Cambridge, MA: MIT Press.

Schacter, D. L. (1996). *Searching for Memory: The Brain, the Mind, and the Past.* New York: Basic Books.

Sergent, J., Ohta, S., and MacDonald, B. (1992). Functional neuroanatomy of face and object processing: A positron emission tomography study. *Brain, 115,* 15–36.

Shepard, R. N., and Cooper, L. R. (1982). *Mental Images and Their Transformations.* Cambridge, MA: MIT Press.

Shepard, R. N., and Feng, C. (1972). A chronometric study of mental paper folding. *Cognitive Psychology, 3,* 228–243.

Shepard, R. N., and Metzler, J. (1971). Mental rotation of three-dimensional objects. *Science, 171,* 701–703.

Squire, L. R. (1987). *Memory and Brain.* New York: Oxford University Press.

Tanaka, K., Saito, H., Fukada, Y., and Moriya, M. (1991). Coding visual images of objects in the inferotemporal cortex of the macaque monkey. *Journal of Neurophysiology, 66,* 170–189.

Thompson, W. L., and Kosslyn, S. M. (2000). Neural systems activated during visual mental imagery: A review and meta-analyses. In J. Mazziotta and A. Toga (Eds.), *Brain Mapping II: The Systems* (pp. 535–560). New York: Academic Press.

Tootell, R. B. H., Silverman, M. S., Switkes, E., and De Valois, R. L. (1982). Deoxyglucose analysis of retinotopic organization in primate striate cortex. *Science, 218,* 902–904.

Treisman, A. M., and Gelade, G. (1980). A feature integration theory of attention. *Cognitive Psychology, 12,* 97–136.

Tulving, E., and Markowitsch, H. J. (1997). Memory beyond the hippocampus. *Current Opinion in Neurobiology, 7,* 209–216.

Tye, M. (1991). *The Imagery Debate.* Cambridge: The MIT Press.

Ungerleider, L. G., and Haxby, J. V. (1994) "What" and "Where" in the human brain. *Current Opinion in Neurology, 4,* 157–165.

Ungerleider, L. G., and Mishkin, M. (1982). Two cortical visual systems. In D. J. Ingle, M. A. Goodale, and R. J. W. Mansfield (Eds.), *Analysis of Visual Behavior* (pp. 549–586). Cambridge, MA: MIT Press.

Van Essen, D. C. (1985). Functional organization of primate visual cortex. In A. Peters and E. G. Jones (Eds.), *Cerebral Cortex* (pp. 259–329). New York: Plenum Press.

Van Essen, D. C., and Maunsell, J. H. (1983). Hierarchical organization and functional streams in the visual cortex. *Trends in Neurosciences, 6,* 370–375.

Watson, J. B. (1913). Psychology as the behaviorist views it. *Psychological Review, 20,* 158–177.

Wexler, M., Kosslyn, S. M., and Berthoz, A. (1998). Motor processes in mental rotation. *Cognition, 68,* 77–94.

Wilson, F. A. W., O Scalaidhe, S. P., and Goldman-Rakic, P. S. (1993). Dissociation of object and spatial processing domains in primate prefrontal cortex. *Science, 260,* 1955–1958.

Yaremko, R., and Butler, M. (1975). Imaginal experience and attenuation of the galvanic skin response to shock. *Bulletin of the Psychonomic Society, 5,* 317–318.

8

Plasticity and Health

Social Influences on Gene Expression and Neural Development

MICHAEL J. MEANEY

Our studies have taken us along a path that, I hope, will contribute to an understanding of how parental care can influence neural development. The objective is to examine gene×environment interactions with respect to specific genes and functions and thus understand how environmental events interact with the genome to produce development. Nestled within this interactionist perspective is a never-ending source of frustration for us, in the futile debate over nature and nurture, which are referred to as competing forces, vying for their share of the spotlight; this proposal is advanced by many with what often appear to be deeply personal motives. Perhaps such oppositional thinking is an inevitable property of human nature. But perhaps it is also because, thus far, we lack models sufficiently powerful and definitive to sweep the nature versus nurture debate from the intellectual landscape. Herein lies a substantial virtue of animal research: it can provide a detailed understanding of the processes of neural development. When it comes to understanding human development, the details may differ, as they would with an attempt to generalize from one species to another, but rules will remain the same. And one rule prevails: It is biologically nonsensical to separate nature from nurture or gene from environment.

A Few Short (I Promise) Biographical Notes

I began my trek in the life sciences as an undergraduate with a primary interest in general biology. My favorite course, by far, was developmental biology. Hence,

I was first introduced to the nature versus nurture quagmire under a different guise. In the 1970s, for developmental biologists, the issue was "regulated versus mosaic" development. Do fully formed, functional limbs or organs emerge from some fixed, inherited program, or is there some guidance derived from the extracellular milieu (the environment)? For my professor, this was always a question of degree. The idea of complex patterns of development emerging exclusively from one or the other was too absurd to merit serious consideration. How could any program of development operate independent of the context in which it occurred? In debates, each student could call on examples of transplant experiments with sea urchins or salamanders that seem to favor one position or the other. But we inevitably landed within the vicinity of the same conclusion as our professor: development was not a question of mosaic versus regulated development, but an emergent property of these two forces in constant interaction.

Some time later, as my interests drifted into psychology, I attended a lecture of Professor Donald Hebb of McGill University. Here the issue was fully cloaked in the nature/nurture gown: all dressed up, with everywhere to go. Hebb's comment on this issue was both simple and brilliant. When asked what contributed more to the development of personality, nature or nurture, he likened the question to that of asking what contributes more to the area of a rectangle, the length or the width?

The genius of this comment was lost on me for many years, since my biology professor had long since convinced us of the merits of the idea. It all seemed so obvious. Thus, thanks to efforts of such wonderful teachers, the nature/nurture controversy was resolved very early in my academic youth. Development emerged from a constant dialogue between gene and environment. The central questions, then, concerned the nature of the dialogue. And so, while my peers were apparently satisfied to move beyond the gene×environment equation, I became obsessed with a slightly more pedestrian concern: What the hell does that "×" *mean*?

What, Then, Is the Question?

I was eventually exposed to psychology through a course that today would be referred to as developmental psychobiology, which was taught by Pat Dundas, a recent graduate of the University of Wisconsin. Further exposure to psychology courses led me to conclude that while biologists had fantastic models, psychologists had the more interesting questions. My career in classical biology was doomed. I was seduced by the greatest intellectual temptation science has to offer: individual differences. No longer was I interested in why wolves hunted in packs. I wanted to know why some wolves go after the neck of the prey, while others always attack the hind limbs (which, by the way, is actually true).

I had landed on the question of individual differences through coursework, but its expression was a matter of chance. Wondering through the stacks in the library I found a book on psychosomatic medicine.

Here, in my mind, lay the expression of every question that would
come to preoccupy me unto this day:

What is the nature of our biological responses to stress? How and why
do they differ between individuals?

What is the relationship between our responses to stress and the degree
to which they affect our health?

Do individual differences in biological responses to stressors serve as
a basis for variations in vulnerability/resistance to disease?

Could the early environment thus influence the health of an individual?

It is rather easy to understand my preoccupation with such questions. I grew up
in Montreal, the scientific home of Hebb, Selye, Jasper, and Penfield. Given that
intellectual milieu, it is not hard to understand how I could have emerged as a scientist interested in how the early environment influences the development of brain
regions that regulate behavioral and endocrine responses to stress. If you add my
subsequent training in the lab of Bruce McEwen at the Rockefeller University, one
of the best mentors in any area of science, and the recent developments in molecular biology to the recipe, then the ultimate direction of my work becomes
rather obvious: Early environmental regulation of genes that regulate stress responses. What follows is a description of the landmarks along this path.

Early Rearing and Health in Adulthood

The quality of the early family environment can serve as a major source of vulnerability in later life. Individuals who are the victims of physically or sexually
abusive families are at considerably greater risk for mental illness in adulthood
(e.g., Bifulco, Brown, and Adler, 1991; Brown and Anderson, 1993). Perhaps somewhat surprisingly, persistent emotional neglect or conditions of harsh, inconsistent
discipline serve to increase the risk of depression and anxiety disorders to a level
comparable to that observed in more obvious cases of abuse (Holmes and Robbins,
1987, 1988). Indeed, low scores on parental bonding scales, reflecting cold and
distant parent-child relationships, also significantly increase the risk of depression
in later life (e.g., Canetti, Bachar, Galili-Weisstub, De-Nour, and Shalev, 1997;
Parker, 1981). Children need not be beaten to be compromised. And the risk is not
unique to mental health. Russak and Schwartz (1997), in a 35-year follow-up of
populations in the Harvard Stress Mastery Study, found that by midlife those
individuals who as undergraduate students rated their relationship with parents as
cold and detached had a 4-fold greater risk of chronic illness, including depression
and alcoholism, as well as heart disease and type 2 diabetes.

Individual differences in parental care are related to the health of the offspring. My colleagues and I have argued that this effect is, in part at least, mediated

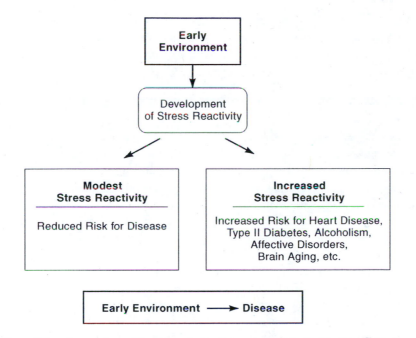

Figure 8.1. A summary of the rationale for the research described in this application.

by parental influences on the development of the neural systems that underlie the expression of behavioral and endocrine responses to stress (Figure 8.1). Parental rearing that results in enhanced reactivity to stress serves to increase the risk for illness in later life. The cornerstone of this argument is the fact that increased levels of stress hormones, notably the glucocorticoids and catecholamines, can promote the development of multiple forms of chronic illness (see Chrousos and Gold, 1992; McEwen, 1998).

Stress and Health

Obviously the ability to understand the relevance of individual differences in stress responses for the health sciences depends on some clear understanding of how stress influences health. This is the classical challenge for developmentalists: You must be an expert not only on development but also on the basic and clinical science within your field of interest. If you want to study the development of a certain system, you have to know the system.

Herein lies the first order of the business of scientific collaboration—becoming an expert in the study of a particular system. My ability to perform studies on the topic of stress and health vis-à-vis specific systems is derived from two major sources: first, my training at Rockefeller University during the 1980s with Professor

Bruce McEwen and lab mates such as Robert Sapolsky; second, my participation in many workgroups, often in the form of MacArthur Foundation Networks, during the 1980s and 1990s. Here I learned about epidemiology (from Lisa Berkman, Michael Marmot, and Burt Singer, for example), behavioral medicine (from Sheldon Cohen, Karen Matthews, Tom Pickering, and Red Williams), social psychology (from John Cacciopo, Carol Ryff, Teresa Seeman, and Shelley Tayor), and personality psychology (from Richie Davidson and Jerome Kagan). Moreover, it was often my great blessing to be paired in such groups with the best stress physiologists on the planet, Mary Dallman and George Chrousos. It is simply not possible to spend time with such incredible people and not learn something about how the environment can alter neural function, and thus about responses to stressors. I cannot overstate the importance of having participated in such networks.

Stress is a risk factor for several forms of illness. Interestingly, the effects of stress on health appear to be mediated by the activation of the same systems that ensure survival. For example, the hypothalamus-pituitary-adrenal (HPA; Figure 8.2) response to stress is a basic adaptive mechanism in mammals; it governs the metabolic and cardiovascular responses to the slings and arrows of everyday life, as well as to the more challenging conditions that prevail during chronic stress. And yet these same HPA hormones, when released at elevated levels for long periods of time, can promote the development of chronic illness. Herein lies the dilemma: The

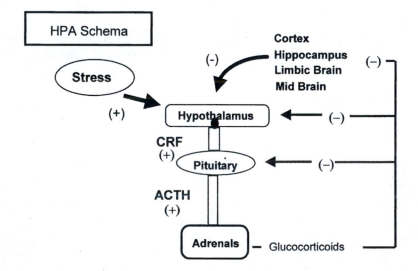

Figure 8.2. A schema of the hypothalamic-pituitary-adrenal (HPA) axis, reflecting the effect of stress on corticotropin-releasing factor (CRF) release from the hypothalamus and the subsequent activation of pituitary adrenocorticotropin (ACTH) and adrenal glucocorticoids. Note the negative feedback component to HPA function, in which the glucocorticoids act via glucocorticoid receptors to inhibit CRF expression and release. Among the primary sites for such feedback inhibition are extrahypothalamic regions such as the hippocampus.

same stress hormones that permit survival during stress can ultimately lead to disease (McEwen, 1998).

Yet the influence of stress can only be fully appreciated when we factor into the equation an understanding of the individual's response to stress. Not all individuals are equally affected by stress, and questions concerning the basis for such individual differences are central to understanding the etiology of chronic disease. The hypothesis that guides our research focuses on the role of early life events in determining individual differences in vulnerability to stress-induced illness. Very simply, we propose that early life events influence the development of individual differences in neural responses to stress, and, in turn, such individual differences influence vulnerability/resistance to stress-induced illness. If true, this formulation could provide a biological basis for the link between early life trauma and illness in later life that has been so commonly revealed in epidemiological studies.

Early Rearing and the Development of Stress Responses

The basic elements of this developmental hypothesis were actually established many years ago. Try to imagine that you are a young student full of questions concerning development on the one hand and the relationship between stress and health on the other. At this point (back in the 1970s), your professor starts to tell you about studies performed by Seymour Levine, Victor Denenberg, and their colleagues showing that rudimentary defensive responses to stress, including those of endocrine systems, could be permanently influenced by the early environment. Moreover, as Denenberg showed, these effects could then be passed onto the next generation. For those who were not around at the time, I should tell you that these findings generated remarkable excitement (almost all of the major papers on this topic in the 1960s were published in *Nature or Science;* Denenberg, 1963; Levine, 1957). Thank you very much; now I know what I want to do for the rest of my life—I want to find out how all of this happens. And that, should anyone ask, is what I have been doing for the past 20 or so years.

How Postnatal Handling Influences the Development of HPA and Behavioral Responses to Stress

Levine, Denenberg, and their contemporaries showed that early postnatal handling alters the development of behavioral and endocrine responses to stress. The handling procedure most commonly involves removing the pups from the mother and the nest site for a period of about 10–15 minutes, once per day, for the first 2–3 weeks of life. Postnatal handling decreases the magnitude of pituitary ACTH and adrenal corticosterone responses to stress in adulthood (Levine, 1975; Meaney, 2001). The beauty of this model is that it embodies the two critical features of an early environmental effect. First, there is a distinct critical period for the effect of handling on HPA development, occurring during the first week of life. Second, the effects of handling on HPA responses to stress endure throughout the life of the animal. For a neurobiologist, the postnatal handling model provides an opportunity to examine the cellular and molecular events that underlie such developmental phenomenon.

The central CRF systems are a critical target for these handling effects. This is not surprising, considering the seminal role of these systems in mediating both behavioral and HPA responses to stress (Gray and Bingaman, 1996; Lavicky and Dunn, 1993; Nemeroff, 1996; Plotsky, 1991; Plotsky, Cunningham, and Widmaier, 1989; Valentino, Curtis, Page, Pavcovich, and Florin-Lechner, 1998.) Also, as adults, neonatally handled (H, vs. NH, nonhandled) rats show decreased fearfulness in the face of novelty and more modest HPA responses to stress; these effects are related to altered CRF gene expression (Ladd et al., 2000; Plotsky and Meaney, 1993; Viau, Sharma, Plotsky, and Meaney, 1993) and decreased CRF content in the locus. Also, H animals show lower CRF receptor levels in the locus coeruleus than do NH rats. Together, these findings suggest that there would be increased CRF-induced activation of the locus coeruleus during stress in the NH animals. This is a critical effect. CRF activates the release of noradrenaline from locus coeruleus neurons (Valentino et al., 1998), and noradrenaline activates behavioral and HPA responses to stress. Thus, H rats show more modest noradrenaline responses to stress (Liu, Caldji, Sharma, Plotsky, and Meaney, 2000).

There is also evidence that postnatal handling also affects systems that regulate CRF activity (Meaney, Aitken, Sharma, Viau, and Sarrieau, 1989; Viau et al., 1993). Glucocorticoids exert a negative-feedback effect over CRF activity at the level of the hypothalamus. Handled animals show greater glucocorticoid feedback efficacy. In turn, this effect is related to the increased glucocorticoid receptor levels in the hippocampus and frontal cortex (Meaney and Aitken, 1985; Meaney et al., 1989; O'Donnell, Larocque, Seckl, and Meaney, 1994; Sarrieau, Sharma, and Meaney, 1988; Viau et al., 1993), regions that are involved in the inhibitory effects of glucocorticoids over CRF synthesis in PVNh neurons (de Kloet, 1991; Jacobson and Sapolsky, 1991). Interestingly, glucocorticoids also serve to dampen stress-induced noradrenergic responses in the PVNh (Pacak, Palkovits, Kopin, and Goldstein, 1995). Importantly, the increase in hippocampal glucocorticoid levels in the handled animals is critical: experimental manipulations that reverse the difference in hippocampal glucocorticoid receptor levels eliminate the differences between handled and nonhandled animals in HPA responses to stress (Meaney et al., 1989).

The Mechanism of Action for Handling on Glucocorticoid Receptor Development

The handling paradigm provides a model for understanding the mechanisms by which environmental stimuli can regulate neural development. This model is somewhat unique, since many other paradigms, involving alterations in either environmental or hormonal conditions, have focused on changes in either synapse formation or neuron survival. In contrast, handling affects neurochemical differentiation in the hippocampus, specifically altering the sensitivity of hippocampal cells to corticosteroids, via an effect on glucocorticoid receptor gene expression and thus receptor levels. Such variations in neuronal differentiation likely underlie important individual differences in tissue sensitivity to hormonal signals and thus represent a biochemical basis for environmental programming of neural systems.

The handling effect on the development of glucocorticoid receptor density in the hippocampus shows the common characteristics of a developmental effect. First, there is a specific "critical period" during which the organism is maximally responsive to the effects of handling. Second, the effects of handling during the first 21 days of life on glucocorticoid receptor density endure throughout the life of the animal. Third and finally, there is substantial specificity to the handling effect. Handling alters the glucocorticoid, but not the mineralocorticoid, receptor gene expression despite the fact that both glucocorticoid and mineralocorticoid receptors are co-expressed in virtually all hippocampal neurons. Thus, the handling effect on gene expression is really quite specific.

The handling model provides a clear opportunity to examine gene × envi-environment interactions at the level of the relevant DNA sites. The question, then, is what are the relevant DNA sites? This implies identifying the DNA targets for the handling effect. Our assumption here is that handling affects glucocorticoid receptor gene expression by regulating the transcriptional rate of gene expression. Sitting just up from the coding sequence of the gene there lies an enormous region of DNA that serves to regulate glucocorticoid receptor gene activity, or expression. The task is (1) characterize this sequence and (2) define its relevance for the handling effect on hippocampal glucocorticoid receptor gene expression.

Now I think that the key to doing multidisciplinary research is not simply the ability to perform various techniques, it is to perform them properly and to be able to troubleshoot protocols and interpret data. I am obsessive about this. Whenever we import a new technique, I attempt to use the data in a paper that is sent to the best journals in the field. I try to let my peers have a go at what we are doing, and if it survives this acid test, then I can proceed with some confidence. Hence, the first paper we published with hippocampal cell cultures appeared in the *Journal of Neuroscience*. The ability to simply perform an assay is not sufficient. The techniques are not all that hard—if they were, I sure as hell wouldn't have mastered them; what is challenging is to develop the necessary expertise. I have seen this in psychoneuroendocrinology, where individual master steroid assays fail to grasp the theory behind the assay or to develop the appropriate knowledge of the larger neuroendocrine picture. Thus, biological psychiatry "dexamethosone-suppressed" us to stupor because many of the individuals using the technique did not really understand glucocorticoid negative-feedback. Compare that to the work of Rachel Yehuda, whose wonderful studies on posttraumatic stress disorder (PTSD) have evolved because this scientist has taken the time to truly understand the

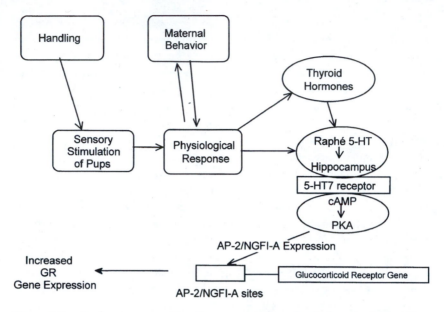

Figure 8.3. A schema summarizing the processes through which postnatal handling or maternal care are thought to regulate hippocampal glucocorticoid receptor gene expression. From Meaney et al. (2000).

steroid-receptor interactions that underlie feedback. Now I am preaching, and despite my efforts, I have not always been without fault on this issue. But herein lies a potential pitfall in the multidisciplinary approach: the collaboration can be used to overcome deficits in the technical, but not the theoretical, domains. Ultimately, the challenge is to master and not simply to import a technique. This requires time, and often the best way to master a technique is to play with it: try to improve on the existing protocols, encourage your personnel to work collectively, and to publish methods papers.

Over several years we were able to develop a model that explained, to some measure, the pathways by which handling altered the activity of the gene that produced the glucocorticoid receptor (Figure 8.3). Briefly, handling increases the production of thyroid hormones which, in turn, increase the release of serotonin in the hippocampus. Serotonin acts via a specific receptor, the serotonin 7 receptor, to increase intracellular levels of cAMP (cyclic adenosine monophosphate), a classical secondary messenger. cAMP alters gene expression by increasing the production of a class of proteins known as transcription factors—proteins that bind to specific DNA sequences and alter gene transcription. Two such transcription factors are thus increased in the hippocampus by handling: nerve growth factor-inducible factor A (NGFI-A) and activator protein 2 (AP-2). Interestingly, NGFI-A has been linked to hippocampal synaptic development, while AP-2 is associated with the regulation of glucocorticoid receptor activity in the liver.

Our findings to that point had suggested that handling permanently altered glucocorticoid receptor gene expression. Since these findings provided us with a target gene, we could begin to relate environmental events to gene expression, safe in the belief that the gene under study was functionally related to the changes in HPA activity. Recall the results of an earlier study showing that reversing the differences in hippocampal glucocorticoid receptor levels eliminated the differences in HPA responses to stress between handled and nonhandled animals (Meaney et al., 1989). We were now in a position to directly examine gene × environment interactions that mediated the development of individual differences in stress reactivity. While identifying the relevant gene is one thing, being able to directly study its expression requires that you have sequenced and characterized not only the gene but also the regulatory DNA sequences that sit upstream from the gene and determine its level of expression (or activity). The rat glucocorticoid receptor gene had been cloned some years ago, but little was known about relevant sites of regulatory control. It had to be characterized. A friend once said that if you want to get into molecular biology, clone something. Here was our chance. I spent a sabbatical year in Scotland with friend and colleague Jonathan Seckl, whose lab had cloned and studied the expression of steroid-metabolizing enzymes. (Jonathan has been a major contributor to the 11 fl-hydroxysteroid dehydrogenase story.) We began to clone what we assumed was the 5' regulatory sequence of the glucocorticoid receptor gene using cDNA libraries from rat hippocampus. We could have taken sequences that had been partially cloned from rat liver and extended them in the hope that liver and hippocampus would not differ. It would have saved considerable time, but we risked finding out one day that the hippocampal situation was different in some very important way. We did not take the chance. The experience got us into PCR (polymerase chain reaction) technology and basic DNA work. I should add that technically this was not all that great a leap. I had spent most of my post-doc in the McEwen lab studying nuclear steroid receptor proteins. Again, this reflects the benefits of multidisciplinary training at the outset. The problem was conceptual. Although I had trained in biochemistry some 15 years earlier, think of the advances in molecular biology over that period.

After that year in Scotland, we transplanted the technology into our group, with help from the strong molecular biology community at McGill. Such techniques, and many more, are now routine in our lab. A final note on the development of multidisciplinary techniques concerns the need to continually update procedures. What many behavioral scientists fail to appreciate about biochemistry is exactly what biochemists fail to appreciate about behavioral paradigms: there is no single ideal, perfect way to measure a particular event. Procedures in all disciplines evolve. Researchers develop better procedures and better interpretations of existing procedures. It is essential that labs dedicate a considerable effort to understanding the limitations of existing protocols: I have many more students who can perform Western blotting than students who really *understand* protein biochemistry. Some of this is inevitable, but it is worth trying to get every student and postdoctoral fellow to publish at least one methods paper. In the long run, this is the challenge for those launching multidisciplinary programs. You really need to become an expert in many areas. Herein lies the great advantage of working in a setting, like McGill, that offers such a rich and supportive environment. I am perfectly at ease exposing my ignorance within my native environment. And it is certainly preferable to having it uncovered at meetings or in the context of a peer-review session.

Eventually the Seckl and Meaney groups managed to clone the relevant promoter regions of the glucocorticoid receptor from rat hippocampus (McCormick et al., 2000) and to identify one region that contained binding sites for NGFI-A and that was apparently used more frequently in driving gene transcription in handled than in nonhandled animals. The relevant site, known as exon 17, appears to be the region that is affected by handling. The relevant DNA target was at hand. We then also found that handling increased the binding of NGFI-A to this exon 17 sequence, and this fact suggested that the endpoint of the model described in Figure 8.3 is the direct activation of glucocorticoid receptor gene activity through the binding of NGFI-A to a specific promoter sequence.

While interesting, this models fails to address what is really the most fascinating question: How do these effects result in the long-term changes in the expression of the glucocorticoid receptor gene in hippocampal neurons?

Our current studies on this topic focus on a process known as DNA methylation. DNA methylation is a very active process in early development that appears to be associated with the inactivation of genes, a process whereby gene expression is rendered tissue specific (Strobl, 1990). Biochemically, the process is simple: a methyl group is added onto a specific nucleotide site, a cytosine, which silences that sequence of DNA. Methylated sites are inactivated. Of course, some of these silenced sequences normally serve as binding sites for enhancers, such NGFI-A. If, during early development, the binding of these factors is enhanced, then methylation at these sites could be attenuated by the presence of the protein-DNA binding. You cannot add a methyl group if a protein already occupies the site. This would than leave these sites as unmethylated and available in later life to activate glucocorticoid receptor gene expression in response to signals, like NGFI-A. The idea here is simply this: use it in early life, and it remains available as an option in adulthood; don't use, and it is lost. This would afford a greater number of potential sites in the promoter for enhancing gene expression. At the very least, this hypothesis allows us to imagine how such processes might permanently alter the character of neuronal populations. Indeed, our findings support these ideas (Weaver et al., 2001). In collaboration with Moshe Szyf at McGill, a legend in the field of DNA methylation, we found that handling does indeed decrease the methylation of the exon 17 sequence and unmethylated sites are better able to bind NGFI-A. In nonhandled animals, the same sequence is almost completely methylated and unable to bind NGFI-A and increase glucocorticoid receptor gene activity. Thus, these animals produce fewer glucocorticoid receptors.

What Are the Critical Features of These Environmental Manipulations?

Handling increases the efficacy of neural systems that serve to restrain CRF production in the hypothalamus and amygdala, and thus to dampen behavioral and endocrine responses to stress. The handling procedure imposes a brief (15-minute) period of separation between mother and pups. Upon reunion, there is an intense period of maternal care that lasts for about an hour or more, during which time mothers remain on their nests and show frequent licking of pups. Several years ago Seymore Levine suggested that this enhanced maternal care was actually responsible for the handling effect: Handling increased maternal care, which then altered the development of neural systems, which regulated the expression of stress responses (Levine, 1975). This idea received at least indirect support from recent studies on the effects of prolonged (180-minute) periods of maternal separation (Plotsky and Meaney, 1993; Ladd et al., 2000). As adults, animals exposed to daily periods of maternal separation for the first two weeks of life show lower glucocorticoid receptor levels and higher CRF production than controls. Predictably, maternal separation increases both behavioral and endocrine responses to stress.

The decreased mother–pup contact resulting from long periods of maternal separation seems likely to be a critical variable in understanding how this procedure increases behavioral and HPA responses to stress. Perhaps, as Levine first suggested, handling exerts its effects by increasing the intensity of mother–pup interactions. But does this imply that under normal conditions maternal care actively contributes to the development of neural systems that mediate stress responses, or simply that the absence of the mother is so disruptive to pup physiology that it affects the development of these systems? If maternal care is relevant, then what are the relevant features of mother–pup interactions, and how do they influence neural development? And what of the handling effects: Do these findings bear any relevance for understanding the normal development of behavioral and endocrine responses to stress in response to natural variations in maternal care?

I have always benefited from some outstanding colleagues such as Barbara Woodside at Concordia University. Barb and husband Jim Jans have studied maternal behavior and pup development for years, and their thinking on such matters has reached an impressive level of clarity. There are several obstacles to establishing multidisciplinary research programs, but none more perilous than that of simply being able to conduct research in a manner that reflects some conceptual sophistication. If your work is to have credibility, it is essential that it reflect a solid grasp of the central issues and concepts within all areas. It is impossible to overstate the importance of great colleagues. This is crucial not only for the principal investigator, but for students and postdoctoral fellows. In this case, our goal here was to move beyond the simple handling procedure and to begin to identify the critical features of the manipulation—to directly link variations in maternal care to phenotype.

The handling paradigm has been useful in allowing us to examine the re- markable plasticity that exists within neural systems that mediate responses to stress, and to understand how individual differences in vulnerability to stress- related disease might emerge in response to early life events (see Seckl and Meaney, 1994). At the same time, the artificial and nonspecific nature of the handling paradigm is unsettling (see Alberts, 1994; Daly, 1973). Normal development in a rat pup occurs in the rather dark, tranquil confines of a burrow, where the major source of stimulation is that of the mother and littermates: There is little here that resembles the disruption associated with human handling. However, as mentioned, several authors, including Barnett and Burn (1967) and Levine (1975), have argued for the role of mother–pup interactions in mediating the effects of handling. And handling the pups does alter the behavior of the mother toward the offspring (Bell, Nitschke, Gorry, and Zachman, 1971; Lee and Williams, 1974, 1975).

We began our studies on the influence of maternal care with a brilliantly direct approach developed by Michal Meyers at Columbia (Meyers et al., 1989). We simply observed mothers with their litters for eight hours per day, with the hope of being able to identify stable, naturally occurring individual differences in maternal behavior. Briefly, we found that one behavior, maternal licking of pups, served to distinguish mothers and that such individual differences in maternal licking were stable over the first eight days of lactation. Interestingly, handling increases and maternal separation decreases the frequency of maternal licking. The obvious question, then, is whether maternal licking might alter the development of neural systems that mediate the expression of endocrine and behavioral responses to stress.

We (Liu et al., 1997) split the animals into two groups based on the behavior of all mothers within the cohort: offspring of mothers that showed high (> 1 SD above the mean) or low (<1 SD below the mean) levels of pup licking. Note, there were no differences between these groups in the overall amount of time in contact with pups (Caldji et al., 1998). Differences in the frequency of licking do not occur simply as a function of time in contact with pups. The logic here is simple. If handling-induced differences in pup licking are relevant for the effects on HPA development, then the offspring of high-licking mothers should resemble the H animals. This is exactly what was found (Liu et al., 1997). As adults, the offspring of high-licking mothers showed lower plasma ACTH and corticosterone responses to restraint stress. These animals also showed significantly higher hippocampal glucocorticoid receptor mRNA expression, enhanced glucocorticoid negative feedback sensitivity, and lower hypothalamic CRH mRNA levels than the offspring of low-licking mothers. In each case, these effects mimic those observed in H versus NH animals. Moreover, the magnitude of the corticosterone response to acute stress was significantly correlated with the frequency of maternal licking ($r = -.61$) during the first 10 days of life, as was the level of hippocampal gluco- corticoid receptor mRNA and hypothalamic CRH mRNA expression (all $rs < .70$;

Liu et al., 1997). These studies suggest that the critical feature for the handling effect on HPA development involves an increase in maternal licking and grooming. The results of these studies suggest that the behavior of the mother toward her offspring can "program" neuroendocrine responses to stress in adulthood. Moreover, as you would expect, maternal licking also serves to regulate NGFI-A activity and methylation of the exon 17 sequence of the glucocorticoid receptor gene in the hippocampus.

The offspring also differed in behavioral responses to novelty (Caldji et al., 1998). As adults, the offspring of the low-licking mothers, like NH animals, showed increased fear in a novel environment. These animals also showed higher CRF receptor levels in the locus coeruleus and lower GABAA receptor levels in the basolateral and central regions of the amygdala, as well as in the locus coeruleus (Caldji et al., 1998) and higher CRF mRNA expression in the amygdala than offspring of the high-licking mothers (Francis, Diorio, and Meaney, unpublished). Since GABA normally acts to inhibit CRF release, lower GABA receptor activity would result in higher CRF activity, higher noradrenaline release, and enhanced fear. Predictably, stress-induced increases in noradrenaline levels were higher in the offspring of the low-licking mothers (Caldji et al., 1999). These differences map perfectly onto the differences in H and NH animals and provide further support for the idea that the effects of handling are mediated by changes in maternal behavior.

It may surprise the reader that rather subtle variations in maternal behavior have such a profound effect on development. However, for a rat pup, the first weeks of life do not hold a great deal of stimulus diversity. Stability is the theme of the burrow, and the social environment in the first days of life is defined by the mother and littermates. The mother, then, serves as a primary link between the environment and the developing animal. It seems reasonable that variations in mother–pup interaction would serve to carry so much importance for development. This seems to be particularly true for tactile stimulation. Tactile stimulation derived from the mother serves to dampen HPA activity, protecting the animal against the catabolic effects of stress hormones (Levine, 1994) and to foster growth-hormone release in the young (Schanberg, Evoniuk, and Kuhn, 1984). Obviously, these effects serve to promote growth and development. Such stimulation also seems to alter the development of stress reactivity in adulthood. Indeed, in subsequent studies we found that maternal care also influences the synaptic development of the hippocampus and can thus influence the development of cognition (Liu et al., 2000).

The Transmission of Individual Differences in Maternal Care to the Offspring

The results of these studies suggest that individual differences in behavioral and neuroendocrine responses to stress are, in part, derived from naturally occurring variations in maternal care. Mothers that show increased arched-back nursing and pup licking and grooming beget offspring with more modest responses to stress. It is easy to see how such effects might serve as a possible mechanism by which selected traits might be transmitted from one generation to another. However, before we make this leap, it is important to show that the individual differences in maternal behavior show intergenerational transmission. To study this question, we simply mated the offspring of high-licking versus low-licking mothers: male and female offspring of high-licking mothers and the male and female offspring of low-licking mothers. The female offspring of high-licking mothers showed significantly more licking than did the female offspring of low-licking mothers (Francis, Diorio, Liu, and Meaney, 1999). Hence, the differences in maternal behavior are transmitted from one generation to the next.

The intergenerational transmission of parental behavior has also been reported in primates. In rhesus monkeys, there is clear evidence for family lineages expressing child abuse (Maestripieri, 1999). There is also evidence for transmission of individual differences in parental styles falling within the normal range. Fairbanks (1989) found that daughters who were reared by mothers that consistently spent a higher amount of time in physical contact with their offspring became mothers who were similarly more attentive to their offspring. In rhesus monkeys, Berman (1990) found that the rate of rejecting the infant by mothers was correlated with the rejection rate of their mothers. In primates, such individual differences in maternal behavior may be revealed in juvenile, nulliparous females. Thus, we found that among juvenile female vervet monkeys, time spent in proximity to nonrelated infants was associated with the maternal behavior of their mothers (Meaney, Aitken, and Sapolsky, 1991). In all cases these findings were independent of the social rank of the mother. Equally impressive findings exist in humans, where Miller, Kramer, Warner, Wickramaratne, and Weissman (1997) found that scores on parental bonding measures between a mother and her daughter were highly correlated with the same measures of bonding between the daughter and her child. These findings suggest a perhaps common process of intergenerational transmission of maternal behavior. The next question concerns the mode of transmission: genomic or nongenomic?

High-licking mothers are less fearful and beget less fearful offspring. The question here is whether these characteristics in the offspring occur as a function of genomic-based inheritance. Are the offspring of high-licking mothers less fearful as a function of genetic transmission of traits that determine fearfulness? If this is the case, then the differences in maternal behavior may be simply an epiphenomenon, and not causally related to the development of individual differences in behavioral and neuroendocrine responses to stress. This is certainly a possibility since maternal behavior in the rat is related to fearfulness (see "Individual Differences in Maternal Behavior" below), and selective breeding studies have suggested that variations in genotype can contribute to the development of fear-related behavior.

This question also can be expressed in terms of maternal behavior. The female offspring of high-licking mothers are, as adults, high-licking mothers. Likewise, the female offspring of low-licking mothers become low-licking mothers. The trait is stable. Thus, the individual differences in maternal behavior are transmitted from one generation to the next. The question is, how?

The issue here is not one of inheritance, that much seems clear. The question concerns the mode of inheritance. We (Francis et al., 1998) addressed this question using a variation of the study in which we mated the male and female offspring of high-licking and low-licking mothers, highs with highs and lows with lows. The pups of the female offspring were then either handled or nonhandled during the first two weeks of life. Again, the offspring of the high-licking mothers showed significantly more licking and grooming and arched-back nursing of pups than did the offspring of low-licking mothers. As expected, handling the pups of these mothers increased maternal licking and grooming and arched-back nursing. Interestingly, handling affected the maternal behavior only of the female offspring of the low-licking-derived mothers. Low-licking mothers with handled pups showed significantly more licking and grooming and arched-back nursing of pups than did the low-licking-derived mothers of nonhandled pups. This finding was predictable, based on earlier studies (Lee and Williams, 1974, 1975; Liu et al., 1997). What was interesting is that handling had no affect on the maternal behavior of the high licking-derived females. Thus, handling pups did not increase maternal behavior in those animals that naturally show high levels of licking and grooming and arched-back nursing.

We allowed the pups to grow to maturity. As adults, the animals showed the predictable differences in behavioral and HPA responses to stress. The handled offspring of low-licking mothers did not differ from either the handled or non-handled offspring of high-licking mothers on measures of plasma corticosterone responses to stress or behavioral fearfulness under conditions of novelty. They were, after all, handled pups. Predictably, the nonhandled offspring of low-licking mothers showed significantly higher HPA responses to stress and higher fearfulness in response to novelty.

The critical part of the study concerns the maternal behavior of these animals. If the differences in maternal behavior are transmitted only through genetic inheritance, then the prediction is that the offspring of low-licking mothers should also be low-licking mothers regardless of whether or not they were handled in early life. A behavioral mode of transmission would suggest that the maternal behavior of the handled offspring of low-licking mothers should resemble that of high-licking mothers, which is in character with the maternal behavior if not the genetic background of their mothers.

The answer was clear. The handled offspring of low-licking-derived mothers did not differ from the offspring of high-licking-derived mothers in their frequency of licking/grooming or arched-back nursing. The nonhandled offspring of low-licking-derived mothers were, as we would expect, low-licking mothers themselves. These findings provide evidence for a nongenomic mechanism of inheritance.

The same can be said for the effects on fearfulness. As adults, the offspring of the handled licking mothers, beneficiaries of high levels of maternal licking/

grooming that they are, resembled the offspring of either H or NH, high-licking mothers on measures of fearfulness. The offspring of nonhandled licking mothers, as we would expect, showed greater fearfulness in novel surroundings. Hence, the handling experience was transmitted to the next generation via the alteration in maternal behavior.

Thus, it appears that individual differences in maternal behavior can be transmitted from one generation to the next through a behavioral mode of transmission. In support of this conclusion we (Francis, Diorio, Liu, and Meaney, 1999) recently found that, as adults, the biological offspring of low-licking mothers which were cross-fostered onto high- licking mothers are indistinguishable from the natural progeny of high-licking mothers on behavioral measures of fearfulness. Moreover, in the adult females maternal behavior was typical of high-licking mothers. Likewise, the adult offspring of high-licking mothers reared by low-licking dams resembled the normal offspring of low-licking mothers.

These findings suggest that specific environmental events can alter the trajectory of development, not only in the affected offspring but also into the next generation. In the early 1960s Victor Denenberg's group provided evidence for such nongenomic transmission. These researchers compared the offspring of handled-handled matings with those of nonhandled-nonhandled matings and found that, as adults, the offspring of the handled parents were significantly less fearful in response to novelty than were the offspring of nonhandled parents, thus providing evidence for a transgenerational effect. For reasons that I have never understood, despite being published in *Nature*, the results of this remarkable study have remained almost ignored. Our contribution to this story is to have identified maternal behavior as a potential mediator for such transgenerational effects.

Our findings are also consistent with the results of other labs using the cross-fostering technique as a test for maternal-mediation hypotheses (McCarty, Cierpial, Murphy, and Lee, 1992). And in a recent collaboration with Hymie Anismanís's group in Ottawa, we have examined the potential effects of maternal behavior on the development of behavior and endocrine responses to stress in BALBc mice. The BALBc is normally a strain that is very fearful and shows elevated HPA responses to stress. However, BALBc mice cross-fostered to another strain, C57 mothers, are significantly less fearful, with lower HPA responses to stress (Zaharia, Shanks, Meaney, and Anisman, 1996). Importantly, C57 mothers lick and groom their pups about twice as frequently as do BALBc mothers (Anisman, Zaharia, Meaney, and Merali, 1998). If the genetic influence were paramount, then we would expect no such relationship between maternal behavior and phenotype. Comparable findings have emerged with rat strains, findings that are consistent with a behavioral transmission hypothesis. The nexus of this hypothesis is not to underestimate the importance of genetic-based inheritance, but to underscore the potential for traits to move from one generation to another via a behavioral mode of transmission that involves variations in maternal behavior.

Under normal circumstances, of course, BALBc mice are reared by BALBc mothers. The genetic and environmental factors conspire to produce an excessively fearful animal. This is usually the reality of nature and nurture. Genetic and environmental factors work in concert and are often correlated. Because parents provide both genes and environment for their biological offspring, the offspring's environment is therefore, in part, correlated with their genes. The offspring's genes are correlated with those of the parents', and the parents' genes influence the environment they provide for the offspring. The reason many epidemiological studies based on linear regression models often find that the epigenetic factors, such as parental care, do not add predictive value above that of genetic inheritance is because of this correlation. The environment the parent provides commonly serves to enhance the genetic differences: they are redundant mechanisms. The knowledge of an animal's BALBc pedigree is sufficient to predict a high level of timidity in adulthood. Additional information on maternal care would statistically add little to the predictability: the two factors work in the same direction. But this is clearly different from concluding that the maternal care is not relevant, and the results of the cross-fostering studies attest to the importance of such epigenetic influences.

Redundancy is also a key feature of development in the brain: the brain has multiple routes to the same endpoint. What is the value of this process? It can provide for diversion. If the genetically determined trajectory is not adaptive for the animal, then the ability to move in the direction of the current environmental signal would be of adaptive value. This is why there is so much room for the influence of postnatal factors and why they can override earlier influences. Thus, we can completely alter the phenotype of the BALBc mouse if it is reared in the care of a C57 mother. Hence, environment can alter the genetically influenced trajectory. This, after all, is the adaptive value of plasticity.

Individual Differences in Maternal Behavior

Individual differences in parental care can influence the development of stress reactivity and thus, we think, vulnerability for chronic illness in later life. But what accounts for such variations in parental care? Human clinical research suggests that the social, emotional, and economic context are overriding determinants of the quality of the relationship between parent and child (Eisenberg, 1990). Human parental care is disturbed under conditions of chronic stress. Conditions that most commonly characterize abusive and neglectful homes involve economic hardship, martial strife, and a lack of social and emotional support (see Eisenberg, 1990). In turn, such homes breed neglectful parents. Perhaps the best predictor of child abuse and neglect is the parents' own history of childhood trauma. More subtle variations in parental care also show continuity across generations. Scores on the Parental Bonding Index, a measure of parent-child attachment, are highly correlated across generations of mothers and daughters (Miller et al., 1997). In nonhuman primates, there is also strong evidence for the transmission of stable individual differences in maternal behavior (Berman, 1990; Fairbanks, 1996).

Individual differences in behavioral and endocrine responses to stress in the rat are associated with variations in maternal care during infancy (Liu et al., 1997; Caldji et al., 1998). The adult offspring of mothers that exhibited a low frequency of pup licking/grooming and nursing in the arched-back or crouched posture showed increased HPA responses to stress and increased fearfulness in comparison to the offspring of high-licking mothers. These individual differences in maternal care were very reliably transmitted from one generation to the next. As mothers, the daughters of high-licking mothers show significantly more licking than do the daughters of low-licking mothers. Moreover, we have provided evidence for the idea that the inheritance of individual differences in maternal care can occur via a behavioral mode of transmission.

The stress responsivity of the offspring mirrors that of their mothers. Low-licking mothers are more fearful than are high-licking dams (Francis, Champagne, and Meaney, 2000), and likewise their offspring are more fearful and timid than are those of high-licking mothers. We believe that, in fact, this is a crucial point in understanding the basis for the transmission of individual differences in parental behavior. In the rat, maternal behavior emerges as a resolution of an interesting conflict (Rosenblatt, 1994). Female rats, unless they are in late pregnancy or lactating, generally show an aversion toward pups. The novelty of the pups is a source of aversion for females, typical of the generally neophobic adult rat. Habituation to the novelty results in an altered set of responses toward pups. Thus continuous exposure to the novel pups renders females more likely to exhibit maternal behavior. For responsive females the positive cues associated with pups emerge from tactile, gustatory, and auditory cues (Stern, 1997). Thus, pup stimuli can either be aversive, eliciting withdrawal, or positive, eliciting approach. The onset of maternal behavior clearly depends on decreasing the negative withdrawal tendency that is associated with neophobia and increasing the positive-approach responses. Amygdaloid lesions, which dampen fearful reactions to novelty, also increase maternal responsivity in nulliparous females. Interestingly, a hormonal regimen that facilitates the expression of maternal behavior in the rat (Bridges, 1994) also reduces the animals fear of novelty (Fleming, Cheung, Myhal, and Kessler, 1989). Such findings may apply to the human condition. Fleming (1988) reported that many factors contribute to the quality of the mother's attitude toward her newborn, but none was correlated more highly than the women's level of anxiety. Mothers who felt depressed and anxious were, not surprisingly, less positive toward their baby (see also Field, 1998). Behaviorally, more fearful, anxious mothers, such as the low LG-ABN dams, appear to be less maternally responsive toward their offspring.

Under natural conditions, and the sanctity of the burrow, rat pups have little direct experience with the environment. Instead, conditions such as the scarcity of food, social instability, and low dominance status directly affect the status of the mother and, thus, maternal care. The effects of these environmental challenges on the development of the pups are then mediated by alterations in maternal care (see Figure 8.4). Variations in maternal care can thus serve to transduce an

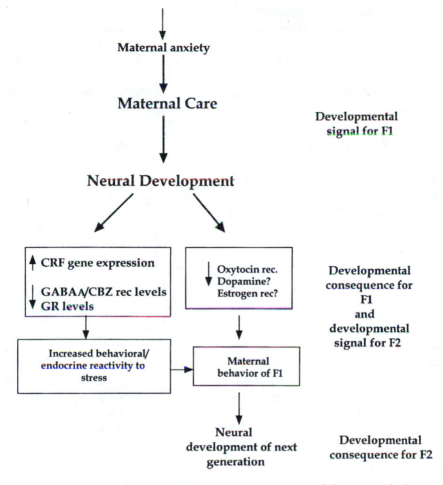

Figure 8.4. A schema representing the potential outcomes of the proposed relationship between environmental adversity and infant care. Thus variations in maternal care affect the development of neural systems that mediate stress reactivity, which may then serve to influence maternal behavior.

environmental signal to the pups. The environmentally driven alterations in maternal care then influence the development of neural systems that mediate behavioral and HPA responses to stress (see Figure 8.2). These effects can thus serve to increase or decrease stress reactivity in the offspring. We propose that more fearful, anxious animals, such as the low-licking mothers, are therefore more neophobic and lower in maternal responsivity to pups than are less fearful animals. Hence, these effects then serve as the basis for comparable patterns of maternal behavior in the offspring (F1) and for the transmission of these traits to the subsequent generation (F2; see Figure 8.4).

These individual differences are transmitted to the offspring in terms of effects on the development of neural systems mediating the expression of fearfulness. Perhaps the pivotal finding is that maternal care in infancy regulates the development of central CRF systems, which serve to activate behavioral, endocrine, and autonomic responses to stress. Variations in maternal care in the infant rat also influence the development of neural systems, such as glucocorticoid and GABAA receptor systems, which provide an inhibitory tone over CRF synthesis and release.

In addition, we propose that there are also effects of maternal care on neural systems mediating attraction to pup-related stimuli. We found evidence for reduced oxytocin receptor levels in the amygdala and medial preoptic area of the low-licking mothers, as well as alterations in ascending dopamine systems. Both systems have been implicated in the expression of maternal behavior in the rat (for reviews, see Bridges, 1994; Pederson, 1995; Stern, 1997). Importantly, central infusion of an antagonist of the oxytocin receptor completely eliminates the group differences in maternal behavior (Champagne, Diorio, Sharma, and Meaney, 2001). Individual differences in maternal care appear to be derived from early environmental effects on the development of the neural systems that mediate fearfulness, as well as those involved in maternal responsivity. Together, in turn, these effects provide the basis for stable individual differences in stress reactivity and maternal behavior in the offspring.

Perhaps the most compelling evidence for the process outlined in Figure 8.4 emerges from the studies of Rosenblum and colleagues (for a review, see Rosenblum and Andrews, 1994). Bonnet macaque mother–infant dyads were maintained under one of three foraging conditions: low foraging demand (LFD), where food was readily available; high foraging demand (HFD), where ample food was available, but required long periods of searching; and variable foraging demand (VFD), a mixture of the two conditions on a schedule that did not allow for predictability. At the time that these conditions were imposed, there were no differences in the nature of mother–infant interactions. After a number of months of these conditions, however, there were highly significant differences in mother–infant interactions. The VFD condition was clearly the most disruptive. Mother–infant conflict increased in the VFD condition. Infants of mothers housed under these conditions were significantly more timid and fearful. These infants showed the same signs of depression that are commonly observed in maternally separated macaque infants—remarkably, even while the infants were in contact with their mothers. As adolescents, the infants reared in the VFD conditions were more fearful and submissive and showed less social play behavior.

More recent studies have demonstrated the effects of these conditions on the development of neurobiological systems that mediate the organism's behavioral and endocrine/metabolic response to stress. In collaboration with Nemeroff's group (Coplan et al., 1996, 1998), Rosenblum and Coplan showed that, as adults, monkeys reared under VFD conditions showed increased CSF levels of CRF. Increased central CRF drive would suggest altered noradrenergic and serotonergic responses to stress, and this is exactly what was seen in adolescent VFD-reared animals. It will be interesting to see if these traits are then transmitted to the next generation.

These patterns of transmission likely reflect very adaptive patterns of development. Children inherit not only genes from their parents but also an environment (West and King, 1987): Englishmen inherit England, as Francis Galton remarked. We believe that these are adaptive patterns of development. Under conditions of increased environmental demand, it is commonly in the animal's interest to enhance its behavioral (e.g., vigilance, fearfulness) and endocrine (HPA and metabolic/cardiovascular) responsivity to stress. These responses promote detection of potential threat, avoidance learning, and metabolic/cardiovascular responses that are essential under the increased demands of the stressor. Since the offspring usually inhabit a niche that is similar to their parents, the transmission of these traits from parent to offspring could serve to be adaptive. It is thus perhaps understandable that parents occupying a highly demanding environment would transmit to their young a high level of stress reactivity. Farrington's research (Farrington, Gallagher, Morley, St Ledger, and West, 1988) on young males growing up in a low socioeconomic and high-crime environment in London provides an excellent illustration of this point. In this environment, the males who were most successful in avoiding the pitfalls associated with such a "criminogenic" environment were those who were shy and somewhat timid. Under such conditions, a parental rearing style that favored the development of a greater level of reactivity to threat would be adaptive. The obvious conclusion is that there is no single ideal form of parenting: different environments demand different traits in the offspring.

A final issue concerns the cost of such increased stress reactivity. The shy and timid child in the London slum may be at an advantage with respect to the demands of the immediate environment. The question is whether such traits would later also confer an increased risk for stress-induced illness. I would argue that it does, and that this risk reflects the cost of adaptation to a high level of environmental demand, such as a low socioeconomic environment, in early life. In my mind it is clear that if we are to address these questions and to contribute to a greater understanding of how such environmental factors influence health, we must continue to participate in multidisciplinary groups. If we are to formulate better questions, we must continue to remain in touch with trends in behavioral and social sciences. We must also remain at the cutting age of the biological sciences in search of more effective ways to address these questions.

Some Final Thoughts

I am a good old general biologist. I am not a molecular biologist or a biochemist; I am not even all that sophisticated in the behavioral sciences (at least not to the degree that I would like). I should not pretend to be otherwise. I am at my best when I ask questions of general biology derived from theory in psychology. I do solid molecular and cellular biology, but no one is going to confuse me with Crick and Watson. It is great fun developing new techniques, and even adding to the process of perfecting these techniques. But I'm guided by one maxim: don't forget what got you into this business in the first place. Regardless of how sophisticated one becomes in the technical sphere, the merit of the science is first and foremost derived from the quality of the questions posed, not the techniques deployed to answer them. No collaborations, no technical wizardry will ever match the importance of a damn good question. I say this to you-the-reader, because I often find that I need to repeatedly say it to myself.

Postscript

As I re-read the original version of the published chapter I am struck by my persistent reference to the importance of excellent colleagues and collaborators. As you will see from the following postscript, nothing has changed.

Our principle contribution to the field of developmental psychobiology lies in the ability to examine the cell and molecular mechanisms for gene × environment interactions. We have moved to newer genomic targets, but a principle focus has been on the regulation of glucocorticoid receptor gene expression.

Molecular mechanisms for maternal effects on hypothalamus–pituitary–adrenal responses to stress

Several years of research using both in vivo and in vitro (hippocampal neuronal cultures) models suggest that maternal care, specifically the licking of pups, alters glucococorticoid receptor levels in the hippocampus through a signalling pathway that begins with serotonin (5-HT) binding to a type 7 serotonin receptor on hippocampal neurons and the activation of intracellular pathways that lead to an increase in the levels of the transcription factor, nerve-growth factor–inducible factor-A (NGFI-A). Transcription factors are the nexus of gene x environment interactions. These proteins respond to extracellular signals, like serotonin, and are capable of binding to and altering the activity, or expression, of genes. Given that the critical extracellular signals are regulated by environmental events, such as social interactions, the transcription factors sit at the interface of environment and gene.

The next advance was in the identification of a relevant region of the DNA: where might NGFI-A act to regulate glucocorticoid receptor gene expression. Our cloning studies with Jonathan Seckl's group identified a regulatory region of the glucocorticoid receptor gene, a so-called promoter, that was more active in the adult animals reared by high compared with low licking mothers. This exon 17 promoter appears to be brain specific since it is only detected in samples that contain neurons. Importantly, the exon 17 promoter contains an NGFI-A binding site. And this is where the colleagues come in—once again.

Approximately 5 years ago we began a partnership with Moshe Szyf, a Cancer Biologist at McGill with an international reputation for innovation and very keen scientific mind. Moshe's group taught us an assay, chromatin immunoprecipitation assays, that allow scientists to examine the interactions in vivo between a specific protein, in this case NGFI-A, and a specific region of the DNA—exon 17 promoter. Together with Szyf, we found that indeed maternal licking increases NGFI-A binding to the exon 17 promoter and activates the glucocorticoid receptor in the pup (Meaney, Diorio, Francis, Widdowson, LaPlante, Caldji, Sharma, Seckl, and Plotsky (1996).

These findings suggest that NGFI-A might increase glucocorticoid receptor (GR) expression in hippocampal neurons and provide a mechanism for the effect of maternal care over the first week of life. However, while there are striking differences in NGFI-A expression in the neonatal offspring of high and low LG mothers, there is no effect of maternal care on hippocampal NGFI-A expression in the adult. We then asked whether the increased NGFI-A—exon 17 interaction in the pups of high LG mothers might result in an epigenetic modification of the exon 17 sequence that alters NGFI-A binding and might serve to maintain the maternal effect into adulthood.

The Epigenome; chromatin structure and DNA methylation

Epigenetics refers to modifications to the genome that *(1)* do not involve a change in sequence and *(2)* alter genomic function. The importance of epigenetics lies in the structural organization of genes. Most DNA is tightly packaged into nucleosomes and wrapped around a core of histone proteins. The histone–DNA configuration is maintained by electrostatic bonds between positively-charged histones and negatively-charged DNA, and regulates gene expression. This 'closed' chromatin structure precludes transcription factor binding to DNA and underscores the importance of enzymes that modify histone–DNA interactions. One class of such proteins, histone acetyltransferases (HATs), catalyze the acetylation of selected positively-charged histone tails, opening chromatin and facilitating transcription factor binding to DNA and gene expression. Thus, histone acetylation is a marker of active gene transcription. The opposing force is comprised of the histone deacetylases (HDACs) that block histone acetylation and suppress gene transcription. Intracellular signals can regulate gene expression through downstream effects on HATs or HDACs, and thus modify chromatin structure. Such histone modifications are transient, however, and cannot directly explain enduring early environmental programming effects such as those of maternal care on glucocorticoid receptor expression. A more likely, highly stable candidate may involve a modification of the genome itself.

DNA is covalently modified by DNA methyltransferases that transfer a methyl group to cytosine. The carbon–carbon bond between the methyl group and cytosine is a stable, enduring "epigenetic" mark. DNA methylation patterns are thought-established during early embryonic development, and then faithfully maintained through life. Mature, postmitotic cells such as neurons were considered beyond subsequent alteration (you can see where this is headed).

DNA methylation promotes gene silencing through effects on chromatin structure. One such silencing mechanism links DNA methylation to inactive, closed chromatin structure. A region of methylated DNA attracts different members of a family of methylated DNA-binding proteins, such as MeCP2, which recruit HDACs that block histone acetylation and result in inactive chromatin.

Epigenetic programming of hypothalamus–pituitary–
adrenal stress responses

The critical question was whether the exon 17 promoter was differentially methylated in the adult offspring of high and low LG mothers. In collaboration with Moshe's lab, we examined the methylation status of individual cytosines in the exon 17 sequence. The results revealed significant differences in cytosine methylation within the NGFI-binding region. One site, referred to as the $5'$ CpG, is almost always methylated in the offspring low LG mothers, and rarely methylated in those of high LG dams. Cross-fostering reverses the differences in the methylation of the $5'$ CpG site and suggests a direct relation between maternal behavior and DNA methylation changes within the exon 17 GR promoter. Maternal care in early postnatal life can actually alter the chemistry of the DNA.

Differences in NGFI-A expression between the offspring of high and low LG mothers in early postnatal life are no longer apparent in adulthood. Instead it appears that the methylation of the NGFI-A biding site interferes with NGFI-A binding to the glucocorticoid receptor exon 17 promoter in the offspring of low LG mothers. Indeed, ChIP assays indicate a threefold greater binding of NGFI-A protein to the hippocampal exon 17 GR promoter in the adult offspring of high compared with low LG mothers. These findings suggest that an "epimutation" at a single cytosine within the NGFI-A binding alters NGFI-A binding and might explain the sustained effect of maternal care on hippocampal GR expression and HPA responses to stress.

Reversal of maternal effects on glucocorticoid receptor expression
and hypothalamus–pituitary–adrenal stress responses

These findings suggest that an "epimutation" at a single cytosine within the NGFI-A binding alters NGFI-A binding and might explain the sustained effect of maternal care on hippocampal GR expression and HPA responses to stress. We then found a way to directly test this hypothesis. One way that cytosine methylation suppresses gene transcription is through the binding of methylated DNA binding proteins that attract a collection of proteins referred to as a repressor complex. At the heart of the repression are the HDACs, that prevent histone acetylation and thus transcription factor binding. We infused adult offspring of high or low LG mothers with a compound, trichostatin A (TSA), which inhibits HDACs and thus enhances histone acetylation. TSA infusion directly into the brain increased histone acetylation and NGFI-A binding in the adult offspring of low LG mothers, to levels comparable to those normally observed in the offspring of high LG mothers. Predictably, the increased NGFI-A binding in the offspring of low LG mothers reversed the differences in glucocorticoid receptor expression and in HPA responses to stress. These findings confirmed that DNA methylation suppresses gene expression through histone modifications. Somewhat surprisingly, we then found that the enhanced NGFI-A binding to the exon 17 promoter in the offspring of the low LG mothers also resulted in a demethylation of the 5'cytosine in the NGFI-A binding site in the low LG offspring. The maternal effect on DNA methylation was reversed.

Alteraiton of the methylation state was also observed in a subsequent study in which adult offspring of high and low LG mothers were infused with L-methionine, which increases levels of S-adenyl-methionine (SAM). SAM is the endogenous methyl donor. Elevations of SAM were associated with an increased level of methylation at the 5'CpG of the NGFI-A binding site in the offspring of high LG mothers. Predictably, in the offspring of high LG mothers this effect was associated with a decreased histone acetylation and NGFI-A binding, reduced hippocampal glucocorticoid receptor expression, and increased HPA responses to stress. Once again the maternal effect was reduced in adult animals.

Neither TSA nor boatloads of L-methionine are likely therapeutic interventions. Both are crude pharmacological tools. But the results do reveal that the maternal effect on DNA methylation can be effectively reversed in the fully mature hippocampal neurons of adult animals. These cells obviously bear the machinery to reverse the methylation state of promoters. This state presumably reflects the ability of these cells to trigger such adaptations in relation to naturally occurring signals. The critical question, then, concerns the nature of these signals.

How does maternal care alter DNA methylation?

In one of the more obvious studies, we simply examined the age at which the difference in the methylation of the 5'CpG appears over development. To our surprise, we found that the newborn offspring of high and low LG mothers show high levels of methylation of the 5'CpG, but that over the first week of life there is a demethylation of the site in the pups reared by high LG mothers. This, of course, is precisely the period of the differences in maternal LG.

We are intensively examining the mechanisms for the demethylation. The evidence to date suggests that the 5-HT–cAMP–NGFI-A cascade that is activated in hippocampal neurons in response to maternal LG is critical fort he demethylation of the 5'CpG site within the NGFI-A binding site. What impresses us, is that these findings suggest the maternal behavior, a social signal, actively targets the alteration of the methylation state at specific regions of the DNA.

Epigenetics

I think my collaborator, Moshe Syzf, puts it best when he says that epigenetic modifications, such as DNA methylation, sit at the interface between a dynamic environment and a fixed genome. Epigenetic marks reflect the environmental conditions prevailing during development. The social interactions of early life are thus biologically embedded.[1] The assumption, and it is simply that, is that such modifications serve as the basis for sustained and adaptive alterations in phenotype that allow the developing animal, as it becomes increasingly independent of parental support, to "prepare" for the demands of the local environment.

RECOMMENDED READINGS

Coplan, J. D., Andrews, M. W., Rosenblum, L. A., Owens, M. J., Friedman, S., Gorman, J. M., and Nemeroff, C. B. (1996). Persistent elevations of cerebrospinal fluid concentrations of corticotropin-releasing factor in adult nonhuman primates exposed to early-life stressors: Implications for the pathophysiology of mood and anxiety disorders. *Proceedings of the National Academy of Sciences of the USA 93*, 1619–1623.

Francis, D. D., Diorio, J., Liu, D., and Meaney, M. J. (1999). Nongenomic transmission across generations in maternal behavior and stress responses in the rat. *Science, 286,* 1155–1158.

Higley, J. D., Haser, M. F., Suomi, S. J., and Linnoila, M. (1991). Nonhuman primate model of alcohol abuse: Effects of early experience, personality, and stress on alcohol consumption. *Proceedings of the National Academy of Sciences of the USA, 88,* 7261–7265.

Liu, D., Diorio, J., Day, J. C., Francis, D. D., Mar, A., and Meaney, M. J. (2000). Maternal care, hippocampal synaptogenesis and cognitive development in the rat. *Nature (Neuroscience) 3,* 799–806.

McEwen, B. S., and Steller E. (1993). Stress and the individual: Mechanisms leading to disease. *Archives of Internal Medicine, 153,* 2093–2101.

REFERENCES

Ader, R., and Grota, L. J. (1969). Effects of early experience on adrenocortical reactivity. *Physiology and Behavior, 4,* 303–305.

Alberts, J. R. (1994). Learning as adaptation of the infant. *Acta Paediatrica Suppl 397,* 77–85.

Anisman, H., Zaharia, M. D., Meaney, M. J., and Merali, Z. (1998). Do early life events permanently alter behavioral and hormonal responses to stressors? *International Journal of Developmental Neuroscience, 16,* 149–164.

Barnett, S. A., and Burn, J. (1967). [Title.] *Nature, 213,* 150–152.

Bell, R. W., Nitschke, W., Gorry, T. H., and Zachman, T. (1971). Infantile stimulation and ultrasonic signaling: A possible mediator of early handing phenomena. *Developmental Psychobiology, 4,* 181–191.

[1]As a last testament to the merits to multidisciplinary groups, I have shamelessly ripped off the phrase "biologically embedded" from Clyde Hertzman.

Berman, C. M. (1990). Intergenerational transmission of maternal rejection rates among free-ranging rhesus monkeys on Cayo Santiago. *Animal Behavior, 44,* 247–258.

Bifulco, A., Brown, G. W., and Adler, Z. (1991). Early sexual abuse and clinical depression in adult life. *British Journal of Psychiatry, 159,* 115–122.

Bridges, R. S. (1994). The role of lactogenic hormones in maternal behavior in female rats. *Acta Paediatrica Suppl, 397,* 33–39.

Brown, G. R., and Anderson, B. (1993). Psychiatric morbidity in adult inpatients with childhood histories of sexual and physical abuse. *American Journal of Psychiatry, 148,* 55–61.

Caldji, C., Tannenbaum, B., Sharma, S., Francis, D., Plotsky, P. M., and Meaney, M. J. (1998). Maternal care during infancy regulates the development of neural systems mediating the expression of behavioral fearfulness in adulthood in the rat. *Proceedings of the National Academy of Science U.S.A., 95,* 5335–5340.

Canetti, L., Bachar, E., Galili-Weisstub, E., De-Nour, A. K., and Shalev, A. Y. (1997). Parental bonding and mental health in adolescence. *Adolescence, 32,* 381–394.

Champagne, F., Diorio, J., Sharma, S., and Meaney, M. J. (2001). Variations in maternal care in the rat are associated with differences in estrogen-related changes in oxytocin receptor levels. *Proceedings of the National Academy of Science, 98,* 12736–12741.

Chrousos, G. P., and Gold, P. W. (1992). The concepts of stress and stress system disorders. *JAMA, 267,* 1244–1252.

Coplan, J. D., Andrews, M. W., Rosenblum, L. A., Owens, M. J., Friedman, S., Gorman, J. M., and Nemeroff, C. B. (1996). Persistent elevations of cerebrospinal fluid concentrations of corticotropin-releasing factor in adult nonhuman primates exposed to early-life stressors: Implications for the pathophysiology of mood and anxiety disorders. *Proceedings of the National Academy of Sciences of the USA, 93,* 1619–1623.

Coplan, J. D., Trost, R. C., Owens, M. J., Cooper, T. B., Gorman, J. A. M., Nemeroff, C. B., and Rosenblum, L. A. (1998). Cerebrospinal fluid concentrations of somatostatin and biogenic amines in grown primates reared by mothers exposed to manipulated foraging conditions. *Archives of General Psychiatry, 55,* 473–477.

Daly, M. (1973) Early stimulation of rodents: A critical review of present interpretations. *British Journal of Psychology, 64,* 435–460.

DeBellis, M. D., Chrousos, G. P., Dom, L. D., Burke, L., Helmers, K., Kling, M. A., Trickett, P. K., and Putnam, F. W. (1994). Hypothalamic pituitary adrenal dysregulation in sexually abused girls. *Journal of Clinical Endocrinolology Metabolism, 78,* 249–255.

De Kloet, E. R. (1991). Brain corticosteroid receptor balance and homeostatic control. *Front. in Neuroendocrinology, 12,* 95–164.

Denenberg, V. H. (1964). Critical periods, stimulu input, and emotional reactivity: A theory of infantile stimulation. *Psychological Review, 71,* 335–351.

Eisenberg L. 1990. The biosocial context of parenting in human families. In N. A. Krasnegor and R. S. Bridges (Eds.), *Mammalian Parenting: Biochemical, Neurobiological, and Behavioral Determinants* (pp. 9–24). New York: Oxford University Press.

Fairbanks, L. M. (1996). Individual differences in maternal style. *Advances in Study Behavior, 25,* 579–611.

Fairbanks, L. Y. (1989). Early experience and cross-generational continuity of mother-infant contact in vervet monkeys. *Developmental Psychobiology, 22,* 669–681.

Farrington, D. A., Gallagher, B., Morley, L., St Ledger, R. J., and West, D. J. (1988). Are there any successful men from criminogenic backgrounds? *Psychiatry, 51,* 116–130.

Field, T. (1998). Maternal depression effects on infants and early interventions. *Preventive Medicine, 27,* 200–203.

Fleming, A. S. (1988). Factors influencing maternal responsiveness in humans: Usefulness of an animal model. *Psychoneuroendocrinology, 13,* 189–212.

Fleming, A. S., Cheung, U., Myhal, N., and Kessler, Z. (1989). Effects of maternal hormones on *Timidity* and attraction to pup-related odors in female rats. *Physiology and Behavior, 46,* 449–453.

Francis, D. D., Champagne, F., and Meaney, M. J. (2000). Variations in maternal behaviour are associated with differences in oxytocin receptor levels in the rat. *Journal of Neuroendocrinology, 12,* 1145–1149.

Francis, D. D., Diorio, J., Liu, D., and Meaney, M. J. (1999). Nongenomic transmission across generations in maternal behavior and stress responses in the rat. *Science, 286,* 1155–1158.

Gray, T. S., and Bingaman, E. W. (1996). The amygdala: Corticotropin-releasing factor, steroids, and stress. *Critical Review of Neurobiology, 10,* 155–168.

Holmes, S. J., and Robins, L. N. (1987). The influence of childhood disciplinary experience on the development of alcoholism and depression. *Journal of Child Psychology and Psychiatry and Allied Disciplines, 28,* 399–415.

Holmes, S. J., and Robins, L. N. (1988). The role of parental disciplinary practices in the development of depression and alcoholism. *Psychiatry, 51,* 24–36.

Jacobson, L., and Sapolsky, R. M. (1991). The role of the hippocampus in feedback regulation of the hypothalamic-pituitary-adrenal axis, *Endocrinology Review, 12,* 118–134.

Ladd, C. O., Huot, R. L., Thrivikraman, Nemeroff, C. B., Meaney, M. J., and Plotsky, P. M. (2000). Long-term behavioral and neuroendocrine adaptations to adverse early experience. *Progress in Brain Research, 122,* 79–101.

Lavicky, J., and Dunn, A. J. (1993). Corticotropin-releasing factor stimulates catecholamine release in hypothalamus and prefrontal cortex in freelymoving rats as assessed by microdialysis. *Journal of Neurochemistry, 60,* 602–612.

Lee, M. H. S., and Williams, D. I. (1974). Changes in licking behaviour of rat mother following handling of young. *Animal Behavior, 22,* 679–681.

Lee, M. H. S., and Williams, D. I. (1975). Long term changes in nest condition and pup grouping following handling of rat litters. *Developmental Psychobiology, 8,* 91–95.

Levine, S. (1957). Infantile experience and resistence to physiological stress. *Science, 126,* 405–406.

Levine, S. (1962). Plasma-free corticosteroid response to electric shock in rats stimulated in infancy. *Science, 135,* 795–796.

Levine, S. (1975). Psychosocial factors in growth and development. In L. Levi (Ed.), *Society, Stress and Disease* (pp. 43–50). Oxford: Oxford University Press.

Levine, S. (1994). Maternal behavior as a mediator of pup adrenocortical function. *Annals of the New York Academy of Science, 746,* 260–75.

Levine, S., Haltmeyer, G. C., Karas, G. G., and Denenberg, V. H. (1967). Physiological and behavioral effects of infantile stimulation. *Physiology and Behavior, 2,* 55–63.

Liu, D., Caldji, C., Sharma, S., Plotsky, P. M., and Meaney, M. J. (in press). The effects of early life events on in vivo release of norepinepherine in the paraventricular nucleus of the hypothalamus and hypothalamic-pituitary-adrenal responses during stress. *Journal of Neuroendocrinology.*

Liu, D., Tannenbaum, B., Caldji, C., Francis, D., Freedman, A., Sharma, S., Pearson, D., Plotsky, P. M., and Meaney, M. J. (1997). Maternal care, hippocampal glucocorticoid receptor gene expression and hypothalamic-pituitary-adrenal responses to stress. *Science, 277,* 1659–1662.

Lupien, S., and Meaney, M. J. (1998). Stress, glucorticoids, and hippocampus aging in rat and human. In E. Wang and S. Snyder (Eds.), *Handbook of Human Aging* (pp. 19–50). New York: Academic Press.

Maestripieri, D. (1999). The biology of human parenting: Insights from nonhuman primates. *Neuroscience and Biobehavioral Review, 23,* 411–22.

McCarty, R., Cierpial, M. A., Murphy, C. A., Lee, J. H. (1992). Maternal involvement in the development of cardiovascular phenotype [Review]. *Experientia, 48,* 315–322.

McCormick, J. A., Lyons, V., Jacobson, M. D., Noble, J., Diorio, J., Nyirenda, M., Weaver, S., Ester, W., Yau, J. L. W., Meaney, M. J., Seckl, J. R., and Chapman, K. E. (2000). 5'Heterogeneity of glucocorticoid receptor messenger ribonucleic acid is tissue-specific: Differential regulation of variant transcripts by early life events. *Molecular Endocrinology, 14,* 506–517.

McEwen, B. S. (1998). Stress, adaptation, and disease. Allostasis and allostatic load. *Annals of the New York Academy of Science, 940,* 33–44.

Meaney, M. J., and Aitken, D. H. (1985). The effects of early postnatal handling on the development of hippocampal glucocorticoid receptors: Temporal parameters. *Developments in Brain Research, 22,* 301–304.

Meaney, M. J., Aitken, D. H., and Sapolsky, R. M. (1991). Environmental regulation of the adrenocortical stress response in female rats and its implications for individual differences in aging. *Neurobiology of Aging, 12,* 31–38.

Meaney, M. J., Aitken, D. H., Sharma, S., Viau, V., and Sarrieau, A. (1989). Postnatal handling increases hippocampal type II, glucocorticoid receptors and enhances adrencocortical negative-feedback efficacy in the rat. *Neuroendocrinology, 51,* 597–604.

Meaney, M.J., Diorio J., Francis D., Widdowson J., LaPlante P., Caldji C., Sharma S., Seckl J.R., and Plotsky P.M. (1996). Early environmental regulation of forebrain glucocorticoid receptor gene expression: implications for adrenocortical responses to stress. *Developmental Neuroscience, 18,* 49-72.

Meyers, M. M., Brunell, S. A., Shair, H. N., Squire, J. M., and Hofer, M. A. (1989). Relationship between maternal behavior of SHR and WKY dams and adult blood pressures of cross-fostered pups. *Developmental Psychobiology, 22,* 55–67.

Miller, L., Kramer, R., Warner, V., Wickramaratne, P., and Weissman, M. (1997). Intergenerational transmission of parental bonding among women. *Journal of the American Academy of Child and Adolescent Psychiatry, 36,* 1134–1139.

Nemeroff, C. B. (1996). The corticotropin-releasing factor (CRF) hypothesis of depression: New Findings and new directions. *Molecular Psychiatry, 1,* 336–342.

O'Donnell, D., Larocque, S., Seckl, J. R., and Meaney, M. J. (1994). Postnatal handling alters glucocorticoid, but not mineralocorticoid mRNA expression in adult rats. *Molecular Brain Research, 26,* 242–248.

Pacak, K., Palkovits, M., Kopin, I., and Goldstein, D. S.(1995). Stress-induced norepinepherine release in hypothalamic paraventricular nucleus and pituitary-adrenrocortical and sympathoadrenal activity: In vivo microdialysis studies. *Frontiers in Neuroendocrinology 16,* 89–150.

Parker, G. (1981). Parental represnetations of patients with anxiety neurosis. *Acta Psychiatria Scandinavia, 63,* 33–36.

Plotsky, P. M. (1991). Pathways to the secretion of adrenocorticotropin: a view from the portal. *Journal of Neuroendocrinology, 3,* 1–9.

Plotsky, P. M., and Meaney, M. J. (1993). Early, postnatal experience alters hypothalamic corticotropin-releasing factor (CRF) mRNA, median eminence CRF content and stress-induced release in adult rats. *Molecular Brain Research, 18,* 195–200.

Plotsky, P. M., Cunningham, E. T., and Widmaier, E. P. (1989). Catecholaminergic modulation of corticotropin-releasing factor and adrenocorticotropin secretion. *Endocrine Review, 10,* 437–458.

Rosenblatt, J. S. (1994). Psychobiology of maternal behavior: Contribution to the clinical understanding of maternal behavior among humans. *Acta Paediatrica Suppl, 397,* 3–8.

Rosenblum, L. A., and Andrews, M. W. (1994). Influences of environmental demand on maternal behavior and infant development. *Acta Paediatrica Suppl, 397,* 57–63.

Rosenblum, L. A., Coplan, J. D., Friedman, S., Bassoff, T., Gorman, J. M., and Andrews, M. W. (in press). Adverse early experiences affect noradrenergic and serotonergic functioning in adult primates. *Biological Psychiatry.*

Russak, L. G., and Schwartz, G. E. (1997). Feelings of parental care predict health status in midlife: A 35 year follow-up of the Harvard Mastery of Stress Study. *J Behav Med 20,* 1–11.

Sarrieau, A., Sharma, S., and Meaney, M. J. (1988). Postnatal development and environmental regulation of hippocampal glucocorticoid and mineralocorticoid receptors in the rat. *Developmental Brain Research, 43,* 158–162.

Schanberg, S. M., Evoniuk, G., and Kuhn, C. M. (1984). Tactile and nutritional aspects of maternal care: specific regulators of neuroendocrine function and cellular development. *Proceedings of the Society for Experimental Biology and Medicine, 175,* 135–146.

Seckl, J. R., and Meaney, M. J. (1994). Early life events and later development of ischaemic heart disease. *Lancet, 342,* 1236.

Stern, J. M.(1997). Offspring-induced nurturance: Animal-human parallels. *Developmental Psychobiology,31,* 19–37.

Valentino, R. J., Curtis, A. L., Page, M. E., Pavcovich, L. A., and Florin-Lechner, S. M. (1998). Activation of the locus cereulus brain noradrenergic system during stress: Circuitry, consequences, and regulation. *Advances in Pharmacology, 42,* 781–784.

Viau, V., Sharma, S., Plotsky, P. M., and Meaney, M. J. (1993). The hypothalamic-pituitary-adrenal response to stress in handled and nonhandled rats: Differences in stress-induced plasma ACTH. *Journal of Neuroscience, 13,* 1097–1105.

West, M. J., King, A. P. (1987). Settling nature and nurture into an ontogenetic niche. *Developmental Psychology, 20,* 549–62.

Wilson, M. A. (1996). GABA physiology: modulation by benzodiazepines and hormones. *Critical Reviews in Neurobiology, 10,* 1–37.

Zaharia, M. D., Shanks, N., Meaney, M. J., and Anisman, H. (1996). The Effects of postnatal handling on Morris water maze acquisition in different strains of mice. *Psychopharmacology, 128,* 227–239.

POSITIVE HEALTH

What Nourishes Who Flourishes?

Domain Introduction

CAROL D. RYFF

A half century ago the World Health Organization defined health as a "state of complete physical, mental, and social well-being and not merely the absence of disease or infirmity" (World Health Organization, 1948, p. 28). In the ensuing years, however, this enlightened formulation had surprisingly little effect on health assessment, treatment, or research. The monitoring of our nation's health, for example, focuses on chronic and acute health conditions, activity and mobility limitations, and physical and psychological impairments (National Center for Health Statistics, 1974). But a broader perspective can be seen in the National Population Health Survey of Canada (Stephens, Dulberg, and Joubert, 1999), where measures of positive mental health are tabulated side by side with measures of ill health. Indeed, Statistics Canada views mental health as "a set of affective/ relational and cognitive attributes that permit individuals to carry out valued functions with reserve capacity and resilience and thus to cope effectively with challenges to both mental and physical functioning" (p. 118).

Nonetheless, health research in the United States has been overwhelmingly oriented toward illness, as illustrated by the largely disease-specific foci (e.g., cancer, heart disease, neurological disorders and stroke, drug abuse) of the institutes that comprise the National Institutes of Health. The behavioral and social sciences have growing presence in scientific agendas across these institutes (Singer and Ryff, 2001), but the emphasis again is largely negative, emphasizing the role of maladaptive behaviors, psychological and emotional disorders, or social isolation in unfolding trajectories of morbidity and mortality.

Positive health offers a much-needed counterpoint to the prevailing emphasis on illness and maladjustment. It begins with the observation that true human health and well-being involve having access to the "criterial goods" that make life worth living (Ryff and Singer, 1998). These include not just the material conditions necessary to sustain life but higher-order qualities, such as leading a life of purpose and meaning, having quality ties to others, and demonstrating positive self-regard. These levels of functioning have frequently been relegated to philosophical, humanistic, and non-health sides of the human condition, but a positive health perspective challenges this view and argues, instead, that such psychosocial goods are fundamental ingredients of health construed not simply as the absence of illness but as the *presence of wellness*. What is largely unknown and what thus constitutes a key challenge for science in the present era is *how* these features of human flourishing influence biology and, thereby, possibly both quality and length of life.

The social and behavioral sciences are essential to advancing knowledge of positive health. They bring much-needed conceptualizations of and assessment tools for measuring human strengths. That is, the disciplines of psychology, sociology, and anthropology offer extensive formulations of what it means to be fully developed and optimally functioning, whether the focus is on effective management of life roles and tasks or on realization of personal capacities, ability to regulate self and emotion, and willingness to care for, and be cared for, by others. These realms embody the "upside" of the human experience, and while they are increasingly recognized as important influences on mental health, their import for physical health has only recently received serious scientific attention. The central question therein is whether psychological and social strengths are *protective*—that is, do they help the organism fend off disease and maintain optimal physiological functioning?

There are multiple routes through which such protective effects might occur (see Ryff and Singer, 2000). First, psychological and social well-being might contribute to *disease resistance*, particularly in contexts of high risk (genetic or environmental). That is, it is known that many who carry genetic risk for particular disease outcomes (e.g., type 1 diabetes), or who are exposed to severe environmental risk (e.g., parental alcoholism or mental illness, extreme poverty), do *not* succumb to disease or become maladjusted. What accounts for such resistance or resilience in the face of known risk is a major challenge, indeed, a major opportunity, for scholars working at the interface between scientific disciplines.

Second, psychosocial strengths can play pivotal roles in *recovery processes* and, hence, contribute important differences to length of survival once disease or illness has occurred. For example, mounting evidence points to the role of hope and optimism, meaning-making in the face of loss, and social and emotional support in promoting recovery from cancer, heart disease, and AIDS (see Ryff and Singer, 2000). Because the mechanisms through which these psychosocial factors influence disease processes are still poorly understood, they constitute vital directions for future research. It is likely that such mechanisms cover a wide territory that includes the import of psychosocial strengths on positive health behaviors, as well as salubrious neurophysiological substrates.

Third, and relatedly, those who possess the criterial goods of life may evidence strong profiles of *positive health promotion*. This involves going beyond primary prevention, the cornerstone of good public health, which is fundamentally about avoiding the negative—that means, the prevention of disease. The positive health perspective calls for more in its argument that good health goes beyond knowing what health-compromising behaviors and high-risk environments to avoid. It also encompasses knowing what to embrace, seek out, and promote in order to keep the mind and body well. This again is a realm in which the social and behavioral sciences have important contributions to make in identifying the experiences—psychological, social, emotional, and spiritual—that make lives rich, vibrant, and meaningful. How these same encounters affect biology and subsequent behavior, particularly in enduring and long-term ways, is the crux of the positive health agenda.

Advancing knowledge of positive health will require integrative research that brings social and behavioral scientists together with biomedical researchers. The former provide conceptual formulations and operational definitions of psychosocial strengths, as well as knowledge of their distribution in diverse populations. Biomedical researchers bring the requisite expertise to specify possible neurophysiological mechanisms through which psychological and social factors contribute to maintenance of physiological systems and functional capacities and, thereby, to reduced or delayed onset of illness and disease.

All three chapters in this domain reach toward such integration. While each focuses on somewhat different human "strengths," all emphasize the potential of psychosocial factors to promote positive health, and all are concerned with the mechanisms—behavioral and social, as well as neurological, endocrinological, and immunological—through which such effects occur.

Chapter 10, by Ryff and Singer, addresses the topic of human resilience, which is defined as the capacity to maintain or regain health and well-being in the face of adversity. How such resilience is shaped by broad sociodemographic processes, and how it may be consequential for biology, is addressed in a series of multidisciplinary investigations, including work that links psychosocial strengths to reduced physiological stress, particularly in the face of cumulative economic adversity. Chapter 11, by Seeman, addresses the protective effects of psychological strengths, social ties, and social support on health, drawing on social epidemiology on the one hand and on neuroendocrinology on the other. This work builds physiological pathways through which social experiences are translated to life-course health outcomes, such as physical and cognitive functioning, incident cardiovascular disease, and mortality. Chapter 12, by George, examines new lines of inquiry connecting religion and spirituality to health. Findings from the Duke University multidisciplinary collaboration, emphasizing links between religious involvement and recovery from physical and mental illness as well as length of survival, are reviewed and future research directions are described.

Collectively, these cross-disciplinary agendas portray rich, new scientific terrain that follows from efforts to connect positive psychological, social, and spiritual phenomena to health. Apart from summarizing emergent findings, each collaborative agenda also includes a rich life history of the personal and institutional factors that nurtured and facilitated the building of bridges across disciplinary boundaries. Obstacles and limiting factors are also described. Still, integrative science about the salubrious rather than pathological side of human health remains an uphill climb. It is an ascent that will require serious and sustained interplay between those who map and measure human strengths with those who seem to understand the substrates of such strengths in the workings of cells, neurons, and molecules.

To reiterate, positive health is a multidisciplinary agenda focused on the nature, antecedents, and consequents of human flourishing. It requires formulation and measurement of the "goods" that comprise quality living, including the strengths that enable some to prevail in the face of adversity. It also necessitates understanding how these positive qualities are shaped by broad, macro-level forces that either provide or prohibit access to resources and opportunities in life, as well as by proximal, micro-level influences within one's own constitution and surrounding world. Most important, positive health requires linking psychosocial ingredients of flourishing to underlying processes within the brain and the body. It is this nexus between what makes life good, rewarding, and fulfilling and the attendant neurophysiology that points the way forward to understand health not as the absence of illness but as the presence of mind/body wellness.

Postscript

The postscripts added to each chapter in this section of the book speak to the rapid pace and expansive content of advances occurring in research on positive health. Ryff and Singer (1998), for example, highlight the veritable explosion of interest in positive psychology, which, in turn, has led to refinements in how human well-being is conceptualized and measured as well as how it might be integrated with abundant past research on maladjustment and illness. Their specific work now documents links between psychological well-being and neural circuitry as well as array of biological markers—areas that were promissory notes in the prior chapter. How such inquiry might incorporate genetic influences has also been examined. A significant new development, fostering the continued investigation of biopsychosocial linkages was the funding of such research in the MIDUS (Midlife in the United States) national survey by the National Institute on Aging.

As described in her Chapter 11 Postscript, new work by Seeman and colleagues (which sometimes include Singer and/or Ryff) also expands the linkages between factors and expanded biomarkers, such as levels of inflammation and oxytocin, as well as offering more refined scoring systems for allostatic load. Cultural differences in such linkages have been examined via the MacArthur and Taiwan Aging Studies, and plans to ethnic differences are underway. Seeman has also become a key collaborator in the above MIDUS study as well as in the CARDIA (Coronary Artery Risk Development in Young Adults) study. An important new collaboration will focus on the Experience Corps, which posits beneficial health effects on multiple levels, for providing older adults with meaningful, socially valuable, generative roles. The National Institute on Aging is also funding a randomized trial of this program in the Baltimore City schools.

Finally, the collaborative work of George and colleagues (Chapter 12 Postscript) on the topic of religion and health has also grown in numerous directions since the prior chapter was written, although the lack of progress with regard to theory development was noted. Although much prior research has been focused on the protective or preventive roles of religious involvement on health, new inquiries have shown that religious participation is also implicated in recovery from illness. The health outcomes studied by these researchers have also been expanded (e.g., acute care hospitalization, nursing home utilization, reports of pain). Further refinements pertain to whether multiple forms of religious participation (attending services, private religious practices, intrinsic religious motivation) contribute, multiplicatively, to better health outcomes. With regard to subgroup differences, George summarizes growing evidence (based on studies that allow for valid subgroup analyses) that the effects of religious participation on health are stronger for women than men and for African Americans than whites. Spirituality, despite definitional challenges, has become a more prominent focus in these investigations.

REFERENCES

National Center for Health Statistics (1974). Limitations of activity and mobility due to chronic conditions: United States, 1972. *Vital and Health Statistics* (Series 10, No. 96, DHEW Pub. No. HRA-75-1523). Rockville, MD: U.S. Department of Health, Education, and Welfare.

Ryff, C. D., and Singer, B. (1998). The contours of positive human health. *Psychological Inquiry, 9,* 1–28.

Ryff, C. D., and Singer, B. (2000). Biopsychosocial challenges of the new millennium. *Psychotherapy and Psychosomatics, 69,* 170–177.

Singer, B. H., and Ryff, C. D. (Eds.) (2001). *New Horizons in health: An Integrative Approach.* Washington, DC: National Academy Press.

Stephens, T., Dulberg, C., and Joubert, N. (1999). Mental health of the Canadian population: A comprehensive analysis. *Chronic Diseases in Canada, 20,* 1–12.

World Health Organization (1948). World Health Organization Constitution. In *Basic Documents.* Geneva: Author.

10

Thriving in the Face of Challenge

The Integrative Science of Human Resilience

CAROL D. RYFF and BURTON SINGER

What do we know about human resilience? The primary answer is surprisingly little, compared with what is known about human illness, dysfunction, and disorder. Scientific advances on the positive side of human functioning—understanding what constitutes human flourishing and how it comes about—lag woefully behind strides on the negative side of the health research ledger. Nonetheless, an emerging literature is documenting the remarkable capacity of some individuals, from early life through old age, to prevail in the face of life's challenges (Garmezy, 1991; Glantz and Johnson, 1999; Klohnen, 1996; Rutter, 1990; Ryff, Singer, Love, and Essex, 1998; Staudinger, Marsiske, and Baltes, 1995; Werner and Smith, 1992). Our work builds on and extends this literature, giving particular emphasis to illuminating human resilience as a *biopsychosocial process.* That is, our goal is to bring the scientific disciplines together to clarify the defining features of resilience, as well as to probe the mechanisms and processes that underlie it.

What has been learned thus far? At the outset, we underscore the importance of adopting a conception of human resilience that encompasses more than the *absence of illness* (mental or physical) vis-à-vis the exigencies of life. Our studies thus measure resilience as the *presence of wellness* in the face of adversity: that is, the capacity to flourish, develop, and function effectively, despite challenging circumstances or events. The work builds on a conceptual and empirical formulation of well-being developed by C. Ryff that includes multiple dimensions of positive functioning (Ryff, 1989; Ryff and Keyes, 1995). These dimensions have been studied in numerous cross-sectional and longitudinal studies, as well as in national surveys to examine how well-being varies by age, gender, culture, and socio-economic status (Ryff and Singer, 1996, 1998c).

Other investigations conducted by ourselves and our colleagues have documented that, indeed, there are individuals who, when confronted with difficult life events or enduring hardship, are able to maintain, or regain, high levels of well-being (Ryff et al., 1998; Singer and Ryff, 1997, 1999; Singer, Ryff, Carr, and Magee, 1998). Moreover, these studies have clarified the contributions of various "protective" factors (e.g., self-concept flexibility, coping orientations, social comparisons) in maintaining high well-being (e.g., Heidrich and Ryff, 1993a,b; Kling, Ryff, and Essex, 1997; Kling, Seltzer, and Ryff, 1997). Recently, via the prior research interests and expertise of B. Singer, we have incorporated biology into the resilience agenda. This work has been guided by the overarching question, What are the neurobiological substrates of human flourishing, and what is their role in promoting positive human health (Ryff and Singer, 1998a, b)?

These questions presuppose multidisciplinary collaboration, as they demand integration of what is known about salubrious psychological and social experience with the neural circuitry that underlies such well-being and its downstream implications for endocrine and immune function, particularly in the context of life challenge. Emergent findings from recent investigations point to biological benefits that are associated with psychosocial flourishing. For example, we have shown that *allostatic load*, a summary index of cumulative stress physiology that predicts incident cardiovascular disease, cognitive and functional impairment, and mortality (Seeman, Singer, Rowe, Horwitz, and McEwen, 1997) is linked with prior life adversity. Those who have experienced enduring economic hardship are more likely to have high allostatic load than those having more fortunate economic histories. However, underscoring the theme of resilience, we have further shown that among individuals with persistently low socioeconomic standing, those who possess quality ties to others (a key feature of well-being) are notably less likely to have high allostatic load (Singer and Ryff, 1999) than are those who lack such social connections.

In this chapter we provide an overview of this broad-based agenda on human resilience. A first section reviews why comprehensive understanding of resilience requires a multidisciplinary approach. We summarize key contributions from different disciplines and domains of inquiry. In the second section, we elaborate the findings and insights from the resilience agenda, briefly sketched above. These include not only substantive results but also the development of innovative methods for integrating data from diverse psychosocial, experiential, and biological realms. In the third section, we provide a more personal, inside look at the story of our collaboration. Before working together, each of us had a marked penchant for asking questions that required a multidisciplinary perspective. Despite parallel leanings in intellectual style, our scientific travels had nonetheless been in quite separate domains. Thus, this collaboration led each of us into notably new territories. Our historical account also includes discussion of external factors that facilitated building an integrative agenda on human resilience, as well as consideration of obstacles and constraints encountered along the way. Finally, we conclude with a forward look as to where this collective enterprise is headed. Our vision underscores the future benefits, scientific and societal, that follow from putting together psychosocial and neurobiological knowledge to understand human flourishing.

Bringing Resilience into Focus

Interest in resilience, thriving, flourishing, and more positive aspects of human functioning is at an all-time high in the social and behavioral sciences (Glantz and Johnson, 1999; Ickovics and Park, 1998; Ryff and Singer, 1998a,b; Seligman and Csikszentmihalyi, 2000). In part, heightened emphasis on the positive reflects growing awareness of the dramatic imbalance in scientific research on the side of disease, dysfunction, and pathology, relative to programmatic inquiries about human health and well-being. The latter agendas have much to contribute to the science of health promotion and primary prevention (Raczynski and DiClemente, 1999). We believe that significant strides in understanding resilience necessitate blending together social science with biology, as the former brings the requisite theories and tools to assess human strengths and challenges, while the latter provides the mechanisms for understanding *how* psychological and social factors play a role in preventing, or delaying, the onset of illness, and thereby, extending years of quality life.

Comprehensive understanding of human resilience thus requires assembling an expansive puzzle, the pieces of which come from different domains of scientific expertise. First, the agenda requires theories and measures of what it means to thrive, flourish, and be well. Second, because resilience is fundamentally about the capacity to maintain, or regain, well-being in the face of adversity, there must also be conceptual and empirical formulations of life challenges. Third, to map the physiological substrates of flourishing necessitates the linking of psychosocial well-being with diverse biological systems (cardiovascular, neuroendocrine, metabolic, immunologic). In the following discussion, we sketch how our program of studies has progressively encircled this wide territory. Along the way, we identify key ingredients of resilience as reflected in our own research, individually and jointly. In a later section, we summarize key scientific findings from studies probing the contours of resilience.

What does it mean to thrive and be well?

We endorse a conception of well-being that delineates specific components of positive psychological functioning. This approach stands in marked contrast to the prevailing models of mental health that, at best, leave the organism in neutral (i.e., free of depression, anxiety, or other disorders). To be free of the negative, however, is no guarantee that one possesses the positive. What then is the positive? In an effort to define the key features of well-being, Ryff integrated multiple conceptions of optimal functioning put forth in developmental, clinical, and humanistic psychologies (see Ryff, 1989c). Viewed from a distance, this was an *integrative task* in itself that brought together views of ego development (Erikson), individuation (Jung), self-actualization (Maslow), maturity (Allport), meaning and life purpose (Frankl), full-functioning (Rogers), and other positive criteria of mental health (Jahoda) (see Ryff, 1985, 1989a for detailed descriptions).

While offering diverse formulations of what it means to be healthy and well, these perspectives revealed notable points of convergence and overlap. Specifically, six key elements of well-being were repeatedly emphasized:

Autonomy—the capacity for self-determination

Environmental mastery—the ability to effectively manage one's life
and surrounding world

Personal growth—the realization of personal potential and continued
development

Positive relations with others—the possession of close, rewarding ties
with others

Purpose in life—the capacity to find life meaningful and have goals
in living

Self-acceptance—holding a generally positive view of one's self and
past life

Together, these dimensions encompassed a breadth of wellness that was notably lacking in the extant empirical arena. The primary stumbling block was an absence of tools to measure these diverse aspects of well-being.

Ryff thus constructed structured self-report procedures to measure positive psychological functioning, in much the same way that psychologists had developed tools to assess values, attitudes, personality traits, and coping strategies. Her early work focused extensively on the psychometric properties of the well-being scales—their reliability, validity, and factorial structure (Ryff, 1989, 1995; Ryff and Keyes, 1995). These investigations also described how avowed well-being varies according to sociodemographic characteristics, such as age, gender, class, and culture (for summaries, see Ryff and Singer, 1996, 1998c). Illustrating the recent surge of interest in positive human functioning, these measures have been adopted by many investigators across diverse social scientific and health fields, which includes the translation of the scales into18 different languages. Their widespread use underscores the contemporary commitment to advance knowledge of the positive aspects of the human condition.

Tools to assess psychological well-being have been particularly valuable to the study of resilience because they provide empirical procedures to document both the avoidance of psychopathology or maladaptive behaviors in the face of adversity (Luthar and Cushing, 1999; Rutter, 1985) and the capacity to thrive and flourish. Although there is increasing interest in the latter (e.g., Carver, 1998; Glantz and Sloboda, 1999; Staudinger et al., 1995; Tedeschi, Park, and Calhoun, 1998), the absence of empirical instruments to operationalize such positive qualities has been a notable limitation in prior studies.

Previous studies have also suffered from a blurring of *what resilience is* (i.e., how to define thriving in the face of adversity) and *how it comes about* (i.e., what biological, psychological, and social factors contribute to sustained well-being vis-à-vis challenge?) (Kaplan, 1999). Our approach sought to clarify these matters by defining resilience as the capacity to either maintain or regain multiple aspects of positive psychological functioning in the face of difficult life circumstances or demanding transitions. We have also attempted to account for resilience through a separate array of biopsychosocial protective factors (Ryff et al., 1998). These have the further advantage of broadening the study of resilience to incorporate influences from other scientific disciplines, particularly biology.

Resilience vis-à-vis challenge, transitions, and cumulative adversity

Our studies and numerous others have tracked individuals dealing with naturally occurring life challenges, such as normative transitions, critical and unexpected events, and chronically occurring difficulties. The guiding resilience question across these inquiries is, Who stays well in the face of challenging events? To illustrate, Ryff and colleagues studied the experience of having and raising children (i.e., the challenges of being a parent) to assess its effect on the well-being of parents (Ryff, Lee, Essex, and Schmutte, 1994; Ryff and Seltzer, 1996). Other studies focused on the physical health challenges that accompany aging and how they influence multiple aspects of well-being (Heidrich and Ryff, 1993a,b, 1996). Another primary focus has been on specific life transitions (studied longitudinally), such as community relocation in the later years and how it affects subsequent psychological well-being, as well as physical health (Kling, Ryff, and Essex, 1997; Kling, Seltzer, and Ryff, 1997; Smider, Essex, and Ryff, 1996). Still others, using the well-being measures, have examined the challenges of caregiving (Li, Seltzer, and Greenberg, 1999; Marks, 1998), marital transitions (Marks and Lambert, 1998), work aspirations and achievements (Carr, 1997), and goal pursuits (McGregor and Little, 1998).

Regarding unexpected and adverse experiences, we have also studied how growing up with an alcoholic parent (Tweed and Ryff, 1991) or having a child with down syndrome (Van Riper, Ryff, and Pridham, 1992) influences well-being. And, drawing connection to the growing literature on social inequalities, we have examined how position in the socioeconomic hierarchy—in particular, persistent educational and economic disadvantage—is tied to psychological well-being (Marmot, Ryff, Bumpass, Shipley, and Marks, 1997; Ryff, Magee, Kling, and Wing, 1999). Finally, in recent work with the Wisconsin Longitudinal Study, we have examined the influence of cumulative life adversity (and advantage) on well-being

(Singer et al., 1998; Singer and Ryff, 1999). These studies go beyond the focus on single life challenges to assessment of the effect of cumulative experience in multiple life domains.

The examples illustrate the variety of naturally occurring life challenges that have been studied to advance understanding of resilience. What we have learned about the human capacity to maintain or regain well-being when faced with challenging events and experiences is summarized in a subsequent section on empirical findings. While most of this work describes the prior research of Ryff, we note that Singer also brought to the collaboration prior interest in naturally occurring life challenges. For example, Singer previously studied individuals dealing with narcotics addictions, and he worked with intervention programs designed to rehabilitate chronic heroin users (Dole and Singer, 1979; Singer, 1985). This realm underscored his views about the importance of positive life purpose as a critical supplement to pharmacological treatment. In addition, he previously tracked careers of women in science, where the impact of repeated professional "hits"—or adverse events—on their scientific achievements was assessed (Cole and Singer, 1991). This work was singularly instrumental in Singer's contributions to our life history agenda that has assessed cumulative adversity and advantage over a 40-year period among members of the Wisconsin Longitudinal Study.

Links to neurobiology and physical health: Probing the substrates of flourishing

Full explication of the resilience agenda requires understanding the biology that lies beneath the capacity to thrive, flourish, and be well, particularly in the face of adversity. In a lengthy essay, we outlined the scope of the "positive health" agenda, arguing that true human health is more than not being ill—it is about possessing key features of what makes life good, such as having quality ties to significant others and an abiding sense of purpose in life (Ryff and Singer, 1998a). We argued that these qualities, central to previous work on psychological well-being, could play an important role in preventing illness or delaying its onset, and thereby extend periods of quality living. The scientific challenge is to test the empirical validity of such claims *and* identify the neurobiological processes that connect positive psychosocial experience to salubrious health outcomes. Numerous investigators from diverse fields wrote commentaries in response to this call to reconceptualize the meaning of human health. Their input pushed us to further refine the positive health formulation (Ryff and Singer, 1998b), one key feature of which is the task of advancing new research directions to map the neurobiology of human flourishing. We described multiple avenues for connecting psychosocial well-being, such as having an abiding sense of purpose in life and quality ties to others, to processes within the brain and the body (Ryff and Singer, 1998d; Ryff, Singer, Wing, and Love, 2001).

A first route pertains to cumulative wear and tear on numerous physiological systems, referred to as *allostatic load*. This construct is derived from the notion of allostasis, referring to the ability to adapt to change in the environment while maintaining physiological systems within normal operating ranges (McEwen and Stellar, 1993). Chronic overactivity or underactivity of these physiological systems creates allostatic load. Singer had been part of a collaborative team providing initial operational definitions of such load, via multiple indicators from the autonomic nervous system, the hypothalamic-pituitary-adrenal (HPA) axis, and cardiovascular and metabolic systems (Seeman et al., 1997). Assessment of these indicators in a longitudinal investigation of aging had shown that high allostatic load subsequently (seven years later) predicted incident cardiovascular disease, decline in cognitive and physical functioning, and mortality (Seeman, et al., 1997; Seeman, McEwen, Rowe, and Singer, 2001). How then does allostatic load relate to the resilience agenda? Primarily, it is by asking whether positive psychological and social factors can be instrumental in preventing high levels of allostatic load or, alternatively, in promoting optimal allostasis, particularly in the face of cumulative stressful experience.

Another factor possibly implicated in the physiological substrates of flourishing is *immune function*. The large and growing literature on psychoneuroimmunology (Cohen and Herbert, 1996; Maier, Watkins, and Fleshner, 1994) has shown that stress and negative psychological and social factors influence both cellular and humoral indicators of immune status and function. The counterpoint question is whether high profiles of well-being contribute to more positive profiles of immune function. Operationally, we have targeted assessments of antibody response to influenza and hepatitis A vaccine to probe these questions, as prior research on the stress of later life caregiving has shown differences in antibody response between caregivers and matched controls (Kiecolt-Glaser, Glaser, Gravenstein, Malarkey, and Sheridan, 1996). The question of resilience in this arena is whether having good psychosocial resources in the face of such life stress might afford protective benefits in the form of immune competence.

Another bridge to biology pertains to neural circuitry, specifically the growing literature on *cerebral activation asymmetry* in emotional reactivity (Davidson, 1992, 1995). Positive and negative affective experiences have been strongly associated with asymmetrical activation in the anterior (frontal and anterior temporal) regions of the cerebral hemispheres. Individual differences in asymmetric anterior activation, particularly decreased left prefrontal activation, are associated with increased vulnerability to depression. Alternatively, increased activation in this region is associated with dispositional positive affect and effective coping (Sutton and Davidson, 1997; Tomarken, Davidson, Wheeler, and Doss, 1992). From the perspective of brain function, resilience may thus involve capacities to activate approach-related affective processes in the face of negative environmental stressors. Via ongoing collaborative investigations with R. Davidson, we are pursuing this question.

Our summary of empirical findings in the next section focuses primarily on the first of these three bridges to biology. We nonetheless sketch the full scope of the resilience agenda to underscore the scientific breadth required to investigate positive human health as a *biopsychosocial process*. Different parts of this collaborative mosaic have been implemented in multiple empirical investigations (e.g., the Wisconsin Longitudinal Study; the Wisconsin Study of Community Relocation; and the MacArthur Midlife National Survey, known as MIDUS). The scientific fields that have been integrated by these collaborative endeavors include demography, endocrinology, epidemiology, immunology, neuroscience, psychology, psychiatry, and sociology. The following section highlights key scientific findings from this evolving work.

From Behavior and Phenomenology to Physiology: Findings and Insights from the Resilience Agenda

We will highlight three categories of scientific results. The first pertains to what our research has shown with regard to the human capacity to maintain (or recover) well-being vis-à-vis life adversity. What is the evidence that such resilience exists, either in the context of single life challenges or in cumulative profiles of adversity? What factors facilitate or contribute to such resilience? While these findings reflect prototypically psychological investigations, a second category of results takes resilience in demographic, epidemiological, and sociological directions, via research on socioeconomic inequalities in health. This work allows us to draw attention to individuals at the low end of the socioeconomic hierarchy who nonetheless flourish and have high well-being. They illustrate resilience in the face of economic hardship and limited opportunity. In the third section, we summarize our recent findings linking one aspect of well-being—positive social relationships—to one aspect of biology: allostatic load. This work intersects with the class and health agenda by probing the protective role of high-quality social relationships in offsetting the adverse consequences of low economic standing. A final section draws attention to the methodological innovation required to put the diverse and complex pieces of the resilience puzzle together. Singer's contributions to our "person-centered" analytic techniques are summarized therein.

Numerous collaborators are included in the studies described next. From a disciplinary perspective, an interesting feature of those with whom we have been privileged to work is the ever-widening territory of scientific fields they represent. Ryff's initial collaborative studies reached across different subfields of psychology (development/aging, personality, social) to formulate well-being, and then moved progressively into realms of demography, epidemiology, and sociology to track its distribution among different age, gender, and socioeconomic groups. Singer's collaborative history has been particularly wide-ranging, but reflects, on the one hand, recurrent themes of biology and health such as genetic transmission of disease susceptibility (Risch et al., 1995), malaria transmission dynamics (Cohen and Singer, 1979; Cross and Singer, 1991), and aging and disability (Manton, Singer and Suzman, 1993) and, on the other hand, issues of research design and methodology such as designs for social experiments (Fienberg, Singer, and Tanur,

1985), clinical inquiries to guide management of individual patients (Horwitz, Singer, Viscoli, and Makuch, 1996), grade of membership models (Singer, 1989), and a combinatorial theory of randomness (Pincus and Singer, 1996, 1998; Singer and Pincus, 1998).

What motivates the casting of such a wide scientific net? This we will examine in greater detail in our narrative of the life history of this collaboration. For now, we note that such a penchant for multidisciplinary work, in part, likely reflects the intellectual style of those involved—an inclination to embrace diverse territories in search of connections among them. In addition, however, it has become increasingly evident that such wide scope is *required* by the core questions we ask: namely, what is human health and how is it maintained over time?

Evidence for sustained well-being in the face of challenge

Prior studies by Ryff and collaborators have shown that, indeed, some individuals maintain, or even enhance, their well-being in encounters with life challenges. For example, a longitudinal study of community relocation among aging women has documented that some individuals sustain high levels of well-being, or actually improve, over the course of this transition (Ryff et al., 1998). These studies have also clarified that those who show *gains* in multiple aspects of well-being following relocation are persons with flexible self-concepts (Kling, Ryff, and Essex, 1997) and effective coping strategies (Kling, Seltzer, and Ryff, 1997). We have further documented that having psychological resources prior to the move (i.e., pre-move levels of well-being) clarifies who will show positive emotional reactions shortly after the move (Smider et al., 1996).

In other aging studies, both cross-sectional and longitudinal, we have shown that some individuals are able to maintain high levels of well-being in the face of increased chronic health conditions (Heidrich and Ryff, 1993a,b, 1996). The respondents' levels of social integration and their effective use of social comparisons have helped differentiate those who sustain high well-being from those who do not. These aging studies intersect with Singer's epidemiological research on later life profiles of disability (Singer and Manton, 1998). A key finding in this work has been that rates of later life disability are, at the population level, *declining*.

The complementarity between these agendas is significant: the psychosocial studies of Ryff and colleagues lack broad population generalizability, but provide clues to the kinds of psychological and social factors that contribute to the maintenance of health and well-being in the later years. Alternatively, Singer and colleagues document the population prevalence of chronic conditions and functional capacities among the elderly. These show trends toward better health, but lack formulation and assessment of factors to account for such change, as investigated in the prior studies of well-being. Both agendas, we note, underscore the theme of positive health and well-being in later life.

Other studies by Ryff and colleagues have targeted more atypical and unexpected life challenges such as having a child with mental retardation or growing up with an alcoholic parent (Seltzer and Ryff, 1994; Tweed and Ryff, 1991; Van Riper et al., 1992). These studies document that many parents of children with disabilities do, in fact, have high well-being, at levels comparable to matched parents of nondisabled children, and that many adult children of alcoholics also show numerous psychological strengths. Still other investigations of parenting, in both the normative and nonnormative cases, have clarified how particular psychosocial processes (e.g., coping strategies, social comparisons, attributional processes) differentiate between parents who do and do not have high well-being vis-à-vis the challenges of parenting (Kling, Seltzer, and Ryff, 1997; Ryff et al., 1994; Ryff, Schmutte, and Lee, 1996).

Most of the findings described above have explored the impact of single events or specific experiences on well-being. A key contribution of Singer has been to shift the focus to more *cumulative* profiles of life adversity and advantage (Singer et al., 1998). Such questions emerged from his previous work on career trajectories of women in science, where the cumulation of negative events was a guiding theme in explaining differential achievement patterns (Cole and Singer, 1991). Thus, he brought to the Wisconsin Longitudinal Study (WLS) conceptual and methodological expertise to quantify cumulative experience in a life history framework. We applied these tools to a particular version of resilience—namely, the recovery of high well-being after the experience of major depression. Our question was, What are the life histories of such individuals, in terms of their prior experiences of adversity, which were likely implicated in the onset of depression, but also of advantage, which possibly contributed to their recovery from it?

Our analyses of such resilient women in the WLS used person-centered life history techniques to identify multiple life pathways to midlife recovery of high well-being. Some of these individuals had experienced adverse events early in life (e.g., parental alcoholism, death of parent, limited parental income or education), but these difficult beginnings were accompanied by later experiences of advantage (e.g., upward occupational mobility, close ties to spouse). Others experienced major adversity in adult life (e.g., unemployment, single parenting, spousal drinking, caregiving), but their challenges were offset by good starting resources (e.g., high school abilities, parental income and education) (for details of four primary pathways of histories, see Singer et al., 1998).

Taken as a whole, this broad collection of studies provides extensive evidence that resilience can be effectively assessed in the context of naturally occurring life challenges. Such inquiry requires distinguishing between those who are able to maintain (or regain) high well-being in the face of challenge (i.e., the resilient) and those who show low (or declining) well-being as they deal with adversity (i.e., the vulnerable). These distinctions are critical for subsequent neurobiological agendas as they identify group differences on which to test hypotheses about underlying mechanisms. Specifically, do the resilient, compared to the vulnerable, show benefits in the brain circuitry that underlies their emotional responses, or in how their bodies react to stress, or how their immune systems function? Before considering select findings from this agenda, we first consider another instance of resilience—that is, the maintenance of high well-being despite educational disadvantage and lack of economic opportunity.

Resilience in the class and health agenda

Most of Ryff's initial research on well-being revealed a largely unidisciplinary, psychological focus. Although individual differences were of interest, they were examined via other psychosocial phenomena, such as how individuals compare themselves with others, how they cope, or to what they attribute outcomes in their lives. Missing from the agenda were variations in well-being that ensue from more macro-level, social structural influences, such as position in the socioeconomic hierarchy. These questions took both Ryff and Singer into new collaborative territories. For her, the new directions came through the MacArthur Research Network on Successful Midlife Development. For him, it was through the MacArthur Class and Health Network.

In the Midlife Network, Ryff was a participant in cross-disciplinary collaboration involving multiple large datasets, including the MacArthur National Survey (MIDUS), the National Survey of Families and Households (NSFH), the Wisconsin Longitudinal Study (WLS), and the Whitehall Study of British Civil Servants. This work put her psychological perspective together with those from fields of demography, epidemiology, and sociology. These collaborative endeavors added further support for socioeconomic gradients in health (Marmot et al., 1997, 1998). Thus, using diverse samples and measures, these investigations documented the increased probability of adverse health outcomes among those of lower educational, economic, and occupational standing.

The addition of psychological well-being to these class and health studies (via Ryff's measurement tools) clarified that those of lower socioeconomic standing *also* have *decreased odds* of having positive psychological experiences, such as feeling good about themselves, having quality ties to others, leading lives of purpose, and experiencing continued growth and development. As such, they are more likely to lack the psychological strengths that may serve as important protective factors when they are confronted with adversity. Bringing further psychological insight to these processes, Ryff and colleagues also showed that social inequalities have their pernicious effects on well-being, in part through how people compare themselves and their *perceptions* that life has been unfair to them (Ryff et al., 1999). Such work on "perceived inequalities" underscores the phenomenological routes through which socioeconomic disparities have their adverse effects.

These investigations, as well as Singer's involvement in the MacArthur Class and Health Network, drew attention to the fact that there is *wide variability within* educational, occupational, and income groups. That is, many individuals, at both the high and low ends of the socioeconomic hierarchy, defy the predicted gradients in mental and physical health. For example, a collaborative study of racial and ethnic inequalities in health illustrated the remarkable resilience of some individuals in the face of overwhelming adversity, abject poverty, and rampant racism

(Singer and Ryff, 1997). This line of thinking led us to consider more carefully those who lack educational or economic advantage, but nonetheless have rich and fulfilling lives. These are the resilient vis-à-vis social injustice, deprivation, and inequality.

To advance this line of thinking, we probed case examples of resilience, such as the life of Mark Mathabane under the oppressive system of apartheid in South Africa (Singer and Ryff, 1997). We also drew on large-sample surveys to clarify factors that might account for the psychological resilience of those who lacked educational advantage. Two factors emerged as part of the "protective resources" that promote resilience, particularly among men: having *persistently* positive ties to significant others (parents, spouse, friends), and having *sustained* religious/spiritual orientations (Ryff, Singer, and Palmersheim, in press). Additional inquiry, via collaborative work with Hazel Markus in the MIDMAC Network used qualitative methods to portray the strengths of those with low educational attainment who nonetheless possess high well-being (Markus, Ryff, Curhan, and Palmersheim, in press). The prominence of social relational ties, as well as religion and spirituality, were dominant themes in these lives as well.

Linking resilience to biology: What protects against high allostatic load?

In the context of various longitudinal studies, we are assessing multiple parameters of neurobiology (cerebral activation asymmetry, allostatic load, immune function). The guiding question has been whether those who possess high levels of well-being show biological advantage, such as lower allostatic load, stronger vaccine antibody response, and greater left prefrontal activation (Ryff and Singer, 1998a,d) compared to those with lower profiles of well-being. A first in-depth realm for investigating these questions pertains to quality relationships with others, a central dimension of positive human functioning. With the MIDUS national survey, we have shown that individuals who report better quality ties to spouse, family, and friends have more positive mental and physical health profiles (Ryff et al., 2001). These findings converge with the growing literature on the health-enhancing, life-promoting aspects of interpersonal flourishing (Ryff and Singer, 2000).

Using the biological subsample from the Wisconsin Longitudinal Study, we created positive and negative relationship pathways (based on combined assessments of quality ties to parents in childhood, as well as to spouse in adulthood). We found that those on the positive relationship pathway were less likely to have high allostatic load than were those on the negative relationship pathway (Ryff et al., 2001). The effects were evident for both men and women, although the differences were more prominent among males.

To sharpen the focus on resilience, socioeconomic histories were added to these inquiries (Singer and Ryff, 1999). Those with more adverse cumulative income profiles, as predicted, were more likely to have high allostatic load, compared to those who had persistent economic advantage. However, among individuals with adverse economic histories, we found that those on the positive relationship pathway were less likely to show high allostatic load than were those on the negative relationship pathway (Singer and Ryff, 1999). Such findings strengthen the evidence that high-quality social ties may afford protective benefits, particularly in the context of economic disadvantage.

Methodological innovation in the resilience agenda

Putting together the expansive information that comprises a biopsychosocial approach to resilience (i.e., sociodemographic characteristics, experiential life histories in multiple domains, diverse indicators of mental and physical health, psychosocial protective factors, endocrine and immune assessments, neural circuitry) requires novel methodological approaches. That is, the agenda demands analytic techniques that are capable of identifying multiple complex pathways through which these realms are connected. Responsive to this need, we have emphasized the use of person-centered strategies, as illustrated in our analysis of the life history pathways of resilient women (Singer et al., 1998). These pathways differ in the nature and timing of the life challenges (adversities), as well as the nature and timing of protective factors in the women's lives.

Our integration of biology into these life histories will continue to draw on person-centered techniques, as well as other methodological innovations (e.g., recursive partitioning, grade of membership analyses) advanced by Singer in his work with other collaborators (e.g., Berkman, Singer, and Manton, 1989; Zhang and Singer, 1999). The joint use of quantitative and qualitative data sources (Singer and Ryff, 2001b) is a further novel aspect of the larger research agenda; our collaborative papers have frequently drawn on biographical accounts and personal documents (poetry, letters, essays) to expand their understanding of the phenomenology of individual life struggles (Ryff et al., 2001; Singer and Ryff, 1997). This broad methodological scope is a key feature of the recently funded Center for Mind/Body Interaction at the University of Wisconsin, which includes the above-described resilience agenda.

Interventive significance: Can resilience be promoted?

A central question from the standpoint of health promotion (both mental and physical) is whether positive human functioning—well-being and resilience—can be nurtured and facilitated. That is, can interventions be designed to increase individuals' capacities for experiencing high well-being, particularly in the face of life adversity? Here the resilience agenda is notably advanced by the work of Giovanni Fava (Fava, 1999; Fava, Rafanelli, Grandi, Conti, and Belluardo, 1998), who has developed "well-being therapy" to prevent relapse among individuals suffering from major depression. Those who have experienced major depression represent particularly challenging cases for the promotion of well-being, given their high risk of relapse. Fava argues that during the residual phase of treatment, when major symptoms have subsided but well-being is not fully regained, there is need for a different form of psychotherapy. In particular, such individuals need assistance in experiencing positive life qualities, what Paul Meehl has referred to as "hedonic bookkeeping" (see Fava, 1999). To accomplish this, Fava's well-being therapy uses daily diary techniques, similar to other forms of cognitive therapy. However, a fundamental difference is that diaries are used to sharpen awareness of positive, rather than negative, experience. Clients are encouraged to see and seek positive experiences in their lives, framed by Ryff's multidimensional model of well-being. Recent findings showed that those in well-being therapy had dramatically better remission profiles than did those who received standard clinical treatment (Fava et al., 1989). These findings offer encouraging news that even in contexts of notable adversity—recurrent depression—interventions can be implemented to promote higher levels of well-being.

Summary of advances

What, broadly speaking, has such multidisciplinary integration accomplished? The sociological, demographic contribution to the overall enterprise has been to bring *better samples,* with their greater variability and representativeness, to the investigation of psychological, social, and biological processes. The longitudinal studies have contributed rich information on naturally occurring, real-life challenges. The psychological contributions have been tools for assessing mental health, giving particular emphasis to positive functioning and related protective factors. The biological contribution has been to provide intervening mechanisms, such as allostatic load, immune function, and neural circuitry, that potentially serve as linkages between the sociodemographic factors, experiential histories, and well-being profiles and the ultimate health outcomes. Taken together, the blend of these separate components represents an integrated biopsychosocial approach to understanding unfolding profiles of morbidity and mortality. Finally, the interventive contribution, well-being therapy, shows that positive psychological functioning can, in fact, be promoted, even among individuals who suffer from notable adversity, namely, major depression.

A Life History of the Resilience Collaboration

Our multidisciplinary collaboration has been actively evolving over the last decade and involves numerous scientists besides ourselves. The core ingredients of the enterprise are the talents and enthusiasm of a rich array of scholars, all of whom share a commitment to building bridges between their own areas of expertise and those brought to the scientific table by others. Many of these individuals have had the good fortune to benefit from sustained dialogue and exchange via cross-disciplinary research networks supported by the MacArthur Foundation. Such networks have played a pivotal role in nurturing innovative and integrative scientific agendas.

The scientific questions pursued have been dynamic, going through continual refinement as insights and novel directions have been added by new collaborators. Nonetheless, over time, the phenomenon of human resilience—the capacity to flourish vis-à-vis the exigencies of life—has provided an ever more valuable unifying theme for focusing the multidisciplinary mosaic. Comprehensive understanding of resilience demands a biopsychosocial approach, with different disciplines providing only part, albeit essential pieces, of the larger task of explaining positive health and well-being, particularly in the face of life's challenges.

Many of the core players in our collaboration initially crossed paths via MacArthur research networks. While the substantive foci of the networks vary, those selected to participate in such endeavors tend to score high on the "MacReach" quotient. That is, they possess an intellectual proclivity for reaching out to connect their own area of expertise with other, sometimes distant, realms of inquiry. In the Network on Successful Midlife Development (MIDMAC), directed by Orville Gilbert Brim, a subgroup of sociologists, psychologists, demographers, and epidemiologists (Larry Bumpass, Nadine Marks, Hazel Markus, Michael Marmot, Carol Ryff) came together to collaborate on various datasets (WLS, Whitehall, National Survey of Families and Household, MIDUS). The general aim was to broaden the scope of the scientific disciplines involved in understanding social inequalities in health. The import of this collaboration for the evolving resilience agenda was to connect the study of well-being, previously pursued by Ryff as a largely psychological enterprise, to macro-level social structural influences. In so doing, the representativeness of the samples on which well-being was measured was improved dramatically. The more diverse samples, in turn, brought to the fore the wide variability of well-being, particularly within socioeconomic strata.

A critical feature of this merging of demographic, epidemiological, sociological, and psychological agendas was the need for intellectual and methodological flexibility. Specifically, the psychological priority of depth-of-measurement had to be balanced against the demographic priority of sampling scope. Paradoxically, this required *reduction* in the length of the well-being instruments, at the same time that it necessitated notable *expansion* in the type and number of measures included in these large surveys to measure positive mental health (for a discussion of these trade-offs, see Ryff et al., 1999).

The biological contributions to the larger resilience agenda involved other MacArthur Networks. The Successful Aging Network, directed by Jack Rowe, and the Class and Health Network, directed by Nancy Adler, brought together another subgroup of epidemiologists, neuroendocrinologists, and physicians (Bruce McEwen, Ralph Horwitz, Jack Rowe, Teresa Seeman, Burt Singer) who collaborated in the conceptualization and operationalization of allostatic load, in itself an integrative, cross-disciplinary construct. The Mind/Body Network, directed by Robert Rose, nurtured exchange among those working at the intersections of many aspects of biology (e.g., affective neuroscience and immunology: Richard Davidson, John Sheridan, David Spiegel).

Via cross-network exchanges, many of the above-mentioned researchers attended each others' network meetings, and new collaborations were forged. Presumably, the network-specific experiences had honed among these individuals a commitment to, and belief in, the power of cross-disciplinary inquiry. Building on this foundation, new "trans-network" connections took shape. We (Ryff and Singer) began collaborating on the topic of "positive health" (Ryff and Singer, 1998a,b), which, more than anything, pushed to the fore the challenge of mapping the neurobiological substrates of flourishing. Our repeated query has been whether psychosocial well-being is protective, and if it is, what are the underlying biological mechanisms that explain how such protection occurs? In pursuing these questions, we also embarked on new agendas designed to broaden the window of time and experience that precedes assessment of particular health outcomes (mental and physical). Our life history approach, in turn, has required new ways of thinking about multiple life domains and how to put them together to create pathways of resilience (Singer et al., 1998).

Research funding for these new activities came from various sources. First, we (Ryff and Singer) obtained a grant from the National Institute on Aging to study resilience in the Wisconsin Longitudinal Study. Along the way, we had frequent discussions with Richard Davidson, also at Wisconsin and leading a major program of research on affective neuroscience. This led to new directions regarding the collection of biological data on a subsample of the WLS. The synergy at this juncture was significant and pivotal, involving an integration of multiple separate lines of inquiry (i.e., class and health, well-being, allostatic load, affective neuroscience) in the context of a large, well-characterized sample that had been studied for more than 40 years (Hauser et al., 1992). Ultimately, the Class and Health Network provided support to Singer and Ryff, and the Mind/Body Network provided support to Davidson to facilitate a new phase of data collection by incorporating the separate pieces of the resilience agenda described in this chapter.

Building on our respective network training, the new collaborative team (Davidson, Ryff, Seeman, Singer, plus Daniel Muller, who brought expertise in immunology from the UW-Madison Department of Medicine) was further facilitated by an institutional environment that strongly encouraged the reaching out across disciplinary boundaries. In fact, our investigation began at the same time that the UW-Madison Chancellor David Ward was promoting a "university without walls," in which faculty from diverse departments were encouraged to actively engage each other in the pursuit of important scientific questions. We undoubtedly benefited from this institutional climate. For example, much of our data collection was greatly facilitated by the General Clinical Research Center (GCRC) in the UW Medical School. Our collaboration, in turn, brought social science into the GCRC, hitherto a largely biomedical domain. Recently, our multidisciplinary work was featured as a key protocol in the site visit, and ultimate renewal, of the GCRC.

We underscore that implementation of this research requires working out a complex data collection plan, in which a subsample of WLS respondents were brought to the University of Wisconsin–Madison campus for the first time to participate in multiple biological assessments, including extensive data collection in Davidson's affective neuroscience laboratory. This was an unprecedented step: bringing members of a sample conceived in another discipline (sociology) for other purposes (to study social stratification) into the realm of biology. What was the pay-off for this blending of disciplines and prior agendas? Primarily, it was powerful complementarities that enabled all players to benefit from what others brought to the scientific table. That is, the various aspects of neurobiology could be studied in an extremely valuable sample that combined comprehensive assessment of well-being and multidomain life history data. In turn, this combination offered entirely new biological and health outcomes of the social stratification processes that had originally guided the study. Thus, the neurobiologists gained access to much richer life course information that could be analyzed as antecedent influences on their key variables. And the social psychological, demographic investigators gained a host of new biological and health variables to analyze as outcomes of their psychosocial and social structural variables.

What have been the key ingredients to making this overall collaboration work? The significance of the MacArthur route into the joint venture cannot be under-estimated. Such network experiences provided the critical ingredient of *time*—time to listen, *repeatedly*, to researchers outside one's discipline and thereby gain sufficient understanding of the different domains required to forge integrative agendas. Another key ingredient has been *scientific give and take*: a willingness to make trade-offs, for example, between sampling and measurement priorities (see the preceding discussion about adding assessments of psychological well-being to several national surveys). Such flexibility has also been evident in generating scientific papers from these collaborations, through which different investigators bring different priorities and approaches to the task of analyzing and interpreting data. Working together in an atmosphere of *mutual respect* is thus critical to fostering a spirit in which each investigator gives a little to make the larger enterprise work. The willingness to *take risks*—that is, to reach out into uncharted territories—is also a key facilitating factor, undoubtedly enhanced by beginning with those high on the MacReach quotient. As noted here, our collaboration has also been facilitated by a *receptive and supportive institutional environment*, in which faculty are encouraged to connect the scientific disciplines.

But most important of all was the passion, held by each member of the scientific team, *for reaching out to encircle ever wider territories*. In this regard, it is no accident that we, as collaborators, found each other. The prior MacArthur network experience had generated in some an unquenchable thirst for building innovative agendas that bring together scientific expertise to understand important questions in living. The networks, however, have finite life spans. Thus, among those most committed to continuing and expanding this integrative form of science, new collaborations took shape to carry the challenge forward. Ours is such a story.

What have been the major obstacles to the forward momentum and success of this multidisciplinary enterprise? Paradoxically, while time has been a critical facilitating factor, time is also a limiting factor. That is, putting complex biopsychosocial ingredients together in a single study takes *far longer* than any investigation conducted solely within the confines of a single discipline. The scientific products from the collaboration are thus sometimes frustratingly slow because every step of the process—from conceptualization and design, to data collection, analysis, and write-up—takes more time than in typical (more delimited) investigations.

Regarding the logistics of data collection, complex biopsychosocial studies also pose new challenges regarding *respondent burden;* that is, participants are asked to contribute a great deal of time and effort to complete interviews, questionnaires, laboratory experiments, and tests. These demands, we believe, can be effectively managed. In fact, our respondents have frequently reported back to us that they very much enjoy being in the study. Such good will requires new levels of staff attentiveness and care in maintaining and interacting with the sample.

With regard to the *peer review system*, in publishing findings and obtaining funds to conduct research, multidisciplinary inquiry faces other obstacles. Reviewers used to highly focused investigations are frequently critical of broad, integrative agendas, where the main objective is not to zero in on specific causal processes or mechanisms but, rather, to bring multiple, interacting levels of analysis together. Covering wide scientific territory also increases the likelihood that the research will be caught in the *cross-fire of conflicting criteria* for judging scientific quality. A prime example we have experienced pertains to the tensions between maximizing sampling scope and representativeness (key aims in demographic, epidemiological, and sociological studies) versus obtaining comprehensive, in-depth, carefully controlled assessments (key aims in much psychological and biomedical research). Thus, it is a persistent challenge to work within a peer review system that is entrenched in disciplinary-specific standards and is skeptical of broad, integrative research.

Fortunately, however, the winds are changing, as evident by the recent NIH funding of five Centers of Mind/Body Interaction, all aiming to advance multidisciplinary research. We were fortunate to receive funds for such a center at University of Wisconsin–Madison that includes many of the above-mentioned researchers: Richard Davidson (principal investigator), Christopher Coe, Ned Kalin, Nadine Marks, Daniel Muller, Carol Ryff, and Burt Singer. Significantly, our prior collaborative work, as described in this chapter, allowed us to demonstrate that we are already up and running with regard to integrative science. Using data from the WLS biology subsample, for example, we provided preliminary findings on links between psychological well-being and three aspects of biology (allostatic load, immune function, cerebral activation asymmetry). The new funds will allow us to apply the full profile of biological assessments to a longitudinal sample of aging women (the relocation project). Using four previous waves of data, we have distinguished between those who have been mentally and physically resilient over the course of this transition and those who show greater vulnerability. The new mind/body data collection will map the neurobiological substrates of these dynamic health trajectories.

As we move the resilience agenda forward, a major benefit of our multidisciplinary collaboration pertains to the students (undergraduate, graduate, postdoctoral) who have been brought into our endeavor. The goal is to nurture a new generation of researchers who have the requisite depth and training in their respective fields, but who also have acquired, via the opportunity to work alongside senior scholars who continually put their heads together in pursuit of important questions, the capacity for moving across disciplinary boundaries. The study of human resilience provide an invaluable forum for advancing this scientific synergy.

Future Implications of Integrative Studies of Resilience

There are significant implications for the sciences of health promotion and primary prevention (Raczynski and DiClemente, 1999), and thereby, societal well-being, for understanding human resilience. Putting together knowledge of the psychological strengths that afford resilience in the face of challenge with an understanding of the biology that underlies such flourishing offers a new approach to human functioning. It is fundamentally *a biopsychosocial synthesis of the ingredients in, and pathways to, positive health* (Singer and Ryff, 2001a). Moreover, as noted here, current interventive work is actively promoting positive psychosocial experience in contexts where it is sorely needed. As such, the broad agenda provides a promising and powerful new venue to prevent (or delay) the onset of multiple mental and physical health problems. At the core of this endeavor is an abiding belief that the ultimate goals of health and well-being will come more closely within reach, not just by fending off the negative in the human experience but by actively promoting the positive.

Although separate pieces of our collaborative enterprise represent well-documented areas of scientific inquiry, the blending of these realms places us on decidedly new ground. Ours is thus a nascent integration of multifaceted domains and expertise. As such, much work remains to be done to achieve the comprehensive understanding of human resilience that we seek. Carrying these objectives forward, we have been mindful of the following admonition: "There has never been a better time for collaboration between those meeting in the borderlands between biology, the social sciences, and the humanities. We are approaching a new age of synthesis, when the testing of consilience is the greatest of all intellectual challenges" (Wilson, 1998, p. 11). The study of human resilience resides in those borderlands and thus captures the spirit and promise of the new collaborative era.

Postscript

We put forth human resilience as a key organizing theme in our previous summary of how to put psychosocial and biological factors together in explaining trajectories of positive health. This thematic focus remains central in our ongoing cross-disciplinary research. Advances have taken place on multiple fronts since 2003. Below we summarize four ways in which the science has moved forward.

Bringing human strengths into focus: The dialectic between positive and negative experience

Growing interest in positive psychology (Aspinwall and Staudinger, 2003; Keyes and Haidt, 2003; Snyder and Lopez, 2002) has made our previous call to understand the neurophysiological substrates of flourishing, something we referred to as "positive health" (Ryff and Singer, 1998a), all the more salient. As the social and behavioral sciences probe more deeply into the meaning of well-being, there is heightened recognition that it is not simply possessing an abundance of happiness, joy, and contentment, along with a paucity of sadness, distress, and anxiety. This bifurcation of positive and negative psychological experience misses fundamental features of the human condition (see also Held, 2004). These ideas were elaborated in an essay on "Ironies of the Human Condition" (Ryff and Singer, 2003), in which we first commented on the historical blinders of the positive psychology movement (i.e., its curious obliviousness to extensive prior formulations [in philosophy and psychology] on the upside of the human experience). Arguing that the positive and the negative must be thought about together, we extracted from William James' (1902/1958) eloquent depiction of healthy mindedness and the sick soul. He wrote "the sanguine and healthy-minded live habitually on the sunny side of their misery-line," while "the depressed and melancholy live beyond it, in darkness and apprehension" (p.117). The happy souls, he elaborated, seem "unspeakably blind and shallow" (p.137) to those who live in darkness, while to the healthy-minded, the way of the "sick soul seems unmanly and diseased. With their grubbing in rat-holes instead of living in the light; with their manufacture of fears, and preoccupation with every unwholesome kind of misery, there is something almost obscene about these children of wrath" (p.137).

We observed nonetheless that from James to the present there has been little progress in putting the darkness and light together—that is, studying human experience as the dynamic blend of positive and negative experience that it is. That brought us to the theme of irony, and indeed, one of the great ironies of the human condition—namely, that human strengths are frequently born in encounters with difficult life challenges. We further emphasized that these ideas are embedded in the various aspects of psychological well-being (Ryff, 1989) that have been the focus of our empirical research. Self-acceptance, for example, involves recognizing one's failings and limitations, while purpose in life is often honed in unwanted, some-times horrific, life circumstances (e.g., Frankl and Lasch, 1992). Similarly, traumatic and adverse experiences are often the route through which significant personal growth occurs (Tedeschi, Park, and Calhoun, 1998). Even interpersonal well-being, as illustrated with our juxtaposition of "elective affinities and uninvited agonies" (Ryff, Singer, Wing, and Love, 2001), is fundamentally about the blends of positive and negative experience that comprise our most significant of human relationships. We thus summarized that "wellness comes from active encounters with life's challenges, setbacks, and demands, not from blissful, conflict-free, smooth sailing. Those who would advance a social scientific understanding of human strengths must recognize this dialectic between pain and pleasure, between what is high-minded and inspiring and what is painful, debasing, and cause for despair. Human well-being is fundamentally about the joining of these two realms." (p.279). We have tried to incorporate this insight into our empirical studies as well (see next topic below).

In another recent essay on well-being, we re-examined original writings of Aristotle, who emphasized that the highest of all human good is the realization of one's true potential, something he referred to as "eudaimonia" (Ryff and Singer, in press). Aristotle was thus strongly opposed to conceptualizing happiness as the satisfying appetites, something he likened to a "life suitable to beasts" (Aristotle/Ross, 1925, p.6), or of money-making, or of political power, or even amusement and relaxation. His vision of the highest good rather was "activity of the soul in accord with virtue" (p.11), and virtue for him was "the best thing in us" (p.236). Brought back to the present, we argue that contemporary scientific research on human well-being must incorporate eudiamonic indicators, rather than rely ex-clusively on hedonic assessments of feeling happy, contented, or satisfied with life (see also Ryan and Deci, 2001). These differing conceptions of well-being sub-stantially enrich core conceptions of human flourishing and how they are linked with health, as described below.

Neurophysiological substrates of well-being

The central hypothesis of our formulation of positive health is that human flourishing has neurophysiological correlates that promote effective regulation of multiple biological systems within the body as well as contribute to efficient re-covery from external challenges. This assertion points to a large scientific agenda, for which empirical tests have only begun to emerge. We note some of our own recent findings, along with related advances by others.

With regard to neural circuitry, considerable prior work has implicated asymmetric activation of the prefrontal cortex in approach–withdrawal motiva-tion and emotion, particularly anxiety and depression. With a study of middle-aged adults, we have demonstrated that EEG asymmetry is also correlated with well-being (Urry et al., 2004), measured with both eudaimonic and hedonic assessments. As hypothesized, we found that greater left than right superior frontal activation was associated with higher levels of both forms of well-being. However, after reports of approach-related positive affect were covaried out, multiple frontal asymmetry scores continued to predict eudaimonic, but not hedonic, well-being. Thus, EEG asymmetry explains variation in eudaimonic well-being, understood as purposeful engagement in life, having quality ties to others, and an accepting view of one's self, beyond that which is accounted for by approached-oriented positive affect, although the same is not true for hedonic well-being, understood as life satisfaction.

Moving to biological correlates, in a separate sample of aging women, we found that those with higher levels of eudaimonic well-being (especially purpose in life, personal growth, and positive relations with others) had lower levels of daily salivary cortisol, lower pro-inflammatory cytokines (soluble receptor of interleukin-6, measured from plasma), lower cardiovascular risk (weight, waist/hip ratio, cholesterol, glycosylated hemoglobin), and longer duration of REM sleep than those showing lower levels of eudaimonic well-being (Ryff, Singer, and Love, 2004). Hedonic well-being, in contrast, showed minimal linkage to the same biomarker assessments. A subsequent study incorporating an expanded set of assessments of both psychological well-being and ill-being (depression, anxiety, anger) in the same investigation to assess whether the two have mirrored, or distinct biological correlates (Ryff et al., 2006). Mirrored correlates would mean that well-being and ill-being are correlated with similar biomarkers, but show opposite directional signs, while distinct means the two have largely different biological signatures. Our findings, again on a sample of aging women, showed that outcomes for seven biomarkers (cortisol, norepinephrine, DHEA-S, HDL cholesterol, total/HDL cholesterol, systolic blood pressure, and waste/hip ratio) supported the distinct hypothesis, while only two biomarkers (weight and glycoslyated hemoglobin). We called for population-based inquiries to extend this line of analysis to larger and more heterogeneous samples.

Other recent investigations, also with the above sample of aging women, have probed how various psychosocial and behavioral factors work together to account for differing biomarker profiles. For example, Friedman et al. (2005) looked at the interplay of the women's social engagement (the quality of the social relationships) and the quality of their sleep (measured both subjectively and objectively) to account for levels of plasma interleukin-6 (IL-6), an inflammatory factor linked with numerous health outcomes (Alzheimer's, osteoporosis, rheumatoid arthritis, cardiovascular disease, and some forms of cancer). After controlling for a variety of factors, we found that women with the highest levels of IL-6 were those with both poor social relationships and poor sleep efficiency (measured objectively). However, those with low sleep efficiency but compensating quality relationships as well as those with poor relationships but high sleep efficiency had IL-6 levels comparable to those with both good social ties and good sleep.

Such findings underscore how positive psychological or behavioral factors can offset the adverse impact of negative factors.

Beyond these empirical advances, we have also identified promising new areas of research designed to test mechanistic pathways through which psychosocial strengths contribute to good health. The first pertains to genetics (Ryff and Singer, 2005), where growing evidence documents the importance, of not only susceptibility genes for diverse diseases, but also the often neglected fact that many with such genes never progress to disease status. We suggested that protective proactive social environments may play an important role in understanding why susceptibility genes are not expressed in some individuals. This necessitates greater empirical focus on social environmental phenotypes, both positive and negative, and how they interact with diverse genotypes implicated in health outcomes. We focused explicitly on the social environment in this paper, given the extensive prior literature linking the social world to health (mental and physical) as well as to intervening biological systems. A further related study (Singer, Friedman, Seeman, Fava, and Ryff, 2005) emphasized the important crosstalk between human and animal studies that could help explain reduced disease risk. Case examples involved the prevention of recurrent depression and dendrite remodeling as well as positive social relationships, brain activity, and allostatic load.

New research opportunities: Psychosocial factors and neurobiology in midlife in the United States II

In our original chapter in this volume, we emphasized that one of the central obstacles to launching innovative multidisciplinary research is that the scientific peer review system as well as funding agencies frequently do not prize such work. Happily, this impediment seems to be on the decline. A notable for instance in our world has been the awarding of a large grant from the National Institute on Aging to study biopsychosocial pathways to health and illness via a longitudinal follow-up of MIDUS (Midlife in the United States), which is a large national survey (over 7000 respondents, including twins, ranging in age from 25 to 74) begun in 1994. This initial study, funded by the John D. and Catherine T. MacArthur Foundation, has become a major forum for publishing "integrative studies" that cross disciplinary lines in the effort to understand age-related variation in health and well-being (see publications at www.midus.wisc.edu). NIA's support of the investigation has permitted, not only that we carry out longitudinal follow-up on the original survey, but also that we add comprehensive new biomarker assessments as well as measures of neural circuitry. Details of the five projects that comprise the new program project (P01) are also summarized at the above website. This dataset brings together 40 investigators from around the United States, whose collective expertise spans many scientific fields. We note that resilience and vulnerability, both of which demand an integrated biopsychosocial perspective if they are to be understood, were key themes in articulating the potential of MIDUS II. We anticipate it will be a major forum for integrative science in the years to come.

Implications for practice: Strategies for promoting well-being

Our formulation of positive health has, from the beginning, emphasized that well-being is something that can be nurtured and promoted, even among those who most lack it. To illustrate this point, we have frequently drawn on the work of Dr. Giovanni Fava and colleagues who have developed an intervention, known as well-being therapy, they use with those who suffer from recurrent depression. (This work was described in the section on "interventive significance" above.) Here, we note an important new finding from the Fava research group—that their interventions to prevent recurrent depression have been shown to be effective over a six-year period (Fava, Ruini, Rafanelli, Finos, Conti, and Grandi, 2004). Thus, well-being can not only be promoted; the effects can also be long-lasting. It is because of this kind of evidence that we have advocated a focus on dendrite remodeling, perhaps via animal models, to understand how these well-being promoting interventions affect the brain (Singer, Friedman, Seeman, Fava, and Ryff, 2005).

RECOMMENDED READINGS

Fava, G. A., Rafanelli, C., Grandi, S., Conti, S., and Belluardo, P. (1998). Prevention of recurrent depression with cognitive behavioral therapy. *Archives of General Psychiatry,* 55, 816–821.

Ryff, C. D., and Singer, B. (1998). The contours of positive human health. *Psychological Inquiry,* 9, 1–28.

Ryff, C. D., Singer, B., Love, G. D., and Essex, M. J. (1998). Resilience in adulthood and later life. In J. Lomranz (Ed.), *Handbook of Aging and Mental Health* (pp. 69–94). New York: Plenum.

Seeman, T. B., McEwen, B. S., Rowe, J. W., and Singer, B. H. (2001). Allostatic load as a marker of cumulative biological risk: MacArthur studies of successful aging. *Proceedings of the National Academy of Sciences,* 98, 4770–4775.

Singer, B., and Ryff, C. D. (1999). Hierarchies of life histories and associated health risks. *Annals of the New York Academy of Sciences,* 896, 96–115.

Singer, B., and Ryff, C. D. (Eds.). (2001). *New Horizons in Health: An Integrative Approach.* Washington, DC: National Academy Press.

REFERENCES

Aristotle (1925). *The Nicomachean Ethics* (D. Ross, Trans). New York: Oxford University Press.

Aspinwall, L. G., and Staudinger, U. M. (Eds.) (2003). *A Psychology of Human Strengths: Perspectives on an Emerging Field.* Washington, D.C.: American Psychological Association.

Berkman, L., Singer, B., and Manton, K. (1989). Black/white differences in health status and mortality among the elderly. *Demography,* 26, 661–677.

Carr, D. (1997). The fulfillment of career dreams at midlife: Does it matter for women's mental health. *Journal of Health and Social Behavior, 38,* 331–344.

Carver, C. S. (1998). Resilience and thriving: Issues, models, and linkages. *Journal of Social Issues, 54,* 245–266.

Cohen, J. E., and Singer, B. (1979). Malaria in Nigeria: Constrained continuous-time Markov models for discrete-time longitudinal data on human mixed-species infections. In S. Levin (Ed.), *Some Mathematical Questions in Biology: Lectures on Mathematics in the Life Sciences* (vol. 12, pp. 69–133). Providence: American Mathematical Society.

Cohen, S., and Herbert, T. B. (1996). Health psychology: Psychological factors and physical disease from the perspective of human psychoneuroimmunology. *Annual Review of Psychology, 47,* 113–142.

Cole, J. R., and Singer, B. (1991). A theory of limited differences: Explaining the productivity puzzle in science. In H. Zuckerman, J. R. Cole, and J. Bruer, *The Outer Circle* (pp. 277–310) New York: W.W. Norton.

Cross, A. P. and Singer, B. (1991). Modeling the development of resistance of plasmodium falciparum to anti-malarial drugs. *Transactions of the Royal Society of Tropical Medicine and Hygiene, 85,* 349–355.

Davidson, R. J. (1992). Emotion and affective style: Hemispheric substrates. *Psychological Science, 3,* 39–43.

Davidson, R. J. (1995). Cerebral asymmetry, emotion, and affective style. In R. J. Davidson and K. Hugdahl (Eds.), *Brain Asymmetry* (pp. 361–387). Cambridge, MA: MIT Press.

Dole, V. P. and Singer, B. (1979). On the evaluation of treatment programs for narcotics addiction. *Journal of Drug Issues, 2,* 205–211.

Fava, G. A. (1999). Well-being therapy: Conceptual and technical issues. *Psychotherapy and Psychosomatics, 68,* 171–179.

Fava, G. A., Rafanelli, C., Grandi, S., Conti, S., and Belluardo, P. (1998). Prevention of recurrent depression with cognitive behavioral therapy. *Archives of General Psychiatry, 55,* 816–821.

Fava, G., Ruini, C., Rafanelli, C., Finos, L., Conti, S., and Grandi, S. (2004). Six-year outcome of cognitive behavior therapy for prevention of recurrent depression. *American Journal of Psychiatry, 161,* 18721–18876.

Fienberg, S., Singer, B., and Tanur, J. (1985). Large scale social experimentation in the U.S.A. In A. Atkinson and S. Fienberg (Eds.), *International Statistical Institute Centenary Volume: A Celebration of Statistics* (pp. 251–290). New York: Springer-Verlag.

Frankl, V. E., and Lasch, I. (1992). *Man's search for meaning: An introduction to logotherapy.* Boston, MA: Beacon Press. Original published in 1959.

Friedman, E. M., Hayney, M. S., Love, G. D., Urry, H. L., Rosenkranz, M. A., Davidson, R. J., Singer, B. H., and Ryff, C. D. (2005). Social relationships, sleep quality, and interleukin-6 in aging women. *Proceedings of the National Academy of Sciences, 102,* 187571–188762.

Garmezy, N. (1991). Resiliency and vulnerability of adverse developmental outcomes associated with poverty. *American Behavioral Scientist, 34,* 416–430.

Glantz, M. D., and Johnson, J. L. (1999). *Resilience and Development: Positive Life Adaptations.* New York: Plenum.

Glantz, M. D., and Sloboda, Z. (1999). Analysis and reconceptualization of resilience. In M. D. Glantz and J. L. Johnson (Eds.), *Resilience and Development: Positive Life Adaptations* (pp. 109–128). New York: Kluwer Academic/Plenum Press.

Hauser, R. M., Sewell, W. H., Logan, J. A., Hauser, T. S., Ryff, C. D., Caspi, A., and MacDonald, M. M. (1992). The Wisconsin Longitudinal Study: Adults as parents and children at age 50. *IASSIST Quarterly, 16,* 23–38.

Heidrich, S. M., and Ryff, C. D. (1993a). Physical and mental health in later life: The self-system as mediator. *Psychology and Aging, 8,* 327–338.

Heidrich, S. M., and Ryff, C. D. (1993b). The role of social comparison processes in the psychological adaptation of elderly adults. *Journal of Gerontology, 48,* P127–P136.

Heidrich, S. M., and Ryff, C. D. (1996). The self in later years of life: Changing perspectives on psychological well-being. In L. Sperry and H. Prosen (Eds.), *Aging in the Twenty-first Century: A Developmental Perspective* (pp. 73–102). New York: Garland.

Held, B. S. (2004). The negative side of positive psychology. *Journal of Humanistic Psychology, 44,* 94–97.

Horwitz, R. I., Singer, B., Viscoli, C., and Makuch, R. (1996) Can treatment that is helpful on average be harmful to some patients? A study of the conflicting information needs of clinical inquiry and drug regulation. *Journal of Clinical Epidemiology, 49*(4), 395–400.

Ickovics, J. R., and Park, C. L. (Eds.). (1998). Thriving: Broadening the paradigm beyond illness to health. *Journal of Social Issues, 54* (2), 237–244.

James, W. (1958). *The Varieties of Religious Experience.* New York: New American Library. (Original work published in 1902).

Kaplan, H. B. (1999). Toward an understanding of resilience: A critical review of definitions and models. In M. D. Glantz and J. L. Johnson (Eds.), *Resilience and Development: Positive Life Adaptations* (pp. 17–84). New York: Kluwer Academic/Plenum Publishers.

Keyes, C. L. M., and Haidt, J. (Eds.) (2003). *Flourishing: Positive Psychology and the Life Well-Lived.* Washington, D.C.: American Psychological Association.

Kiecolt-Glaser, J. K., Glaser, R., Gravenstein, S., Malarkey, W. B., and Sheridan, J. (1996). Chronic stress alters immune response to influenza virus vaccine in older adults. *Proceedings of the National Academy of Science, 93,* 3043–3047.

Kling, K. C., Ryff, C. D., and Essex, M. J. (1997). Adaptive changes in the self-concept during a life transition. *Personality and Social Psychology Bulletin, 23,* 989–998.

Kling, K. C., Seltzer, M. M., and Ryff, C. D. (1997). Distinctive late life challenges: Implications for coping and well-being. *Psychology and Aging, 12,* 288–295.

Klohnen, E. C. (1996). Conceptual analysis and measurement of the construct of ego-resiliency. *Journal of Personality and Social Psychology, 70,* 1067–1079.

Li, L. W., Seltzer, M. M., and Greenberg, J. S. (1999). Change in depressive symptoms among daughter caregivers: An 18-month longitudinal study. *Psychology and Aging, 14,* 206–219.

Luthar, S. S., and Cushing, G. (1999). Measurement issues in the empirical study of resilience: An overview. In M. D. Glantz and J. L. Johnson (Eds.), *Resilience and Development: Positive Life Adaptations* (pp. 129–160). New York: Kluwer Academic/Plenum Publishers.

Maier, S. F., Watkins, L. R., and Fleshner, M. (1994). Psychoneuroimmunology: The interface between behavior, brain, and immunity. *American Psychologist, 49,* 1004–1017.

Manton, K. G., Singer, B., and Suzman, R. (1993). *Forecasting the Health of Elderly Populations.* New York: Springer-Verlag.

Marks, N. F. (1998). Does it hurt to care? Caregiving, work-family conflict, and midlife well-being. *Journal of Marriage and the Family, 60,* 951–966.

Marks, N. F., and Lambert, J. D. (1998). Marital status continuity and change among young and midlife adults: Longitudinal effects on psychological well-being. *Journal of Family Issues, 19,* 652–686.

Markus, H. R., Ryff, C. D., Curhan, K. B., and Palmersheim, K. A. (in press). In their own words: Well-being among high school and college-educated adults. In O. G. Brim, C. D. Ryff, and R. C. Kessler (Eds.), *How Healthy Are We? A National Study of Well-Being at Midlife.* Chicago: University of Chicago Press.

Marmot, M. G., Fuhrer, R., Ettner, S. L., Marks, N. F., Bumpass, L. L., and Ryff, C. D. (1998). Contributions of psychosocial factors to socioeconomic differences in health. *Milbank Quarterly, 76,* 403–448.

Marmot, M., Ryff, C.D., Bumpass, L.L., Shipley, M., and Marks, N.F. (1997). Social inequalities in health: Converging evidence and next questions. *Social Science and Medicine, 44,* 901–910.

McEwen, B., and Stellar, E. (1993). Stress and the individual. *Archives of Internal Medicine, 153,* 2093–2101.

McGregor, I., and Little, B. R. (1998). Personal projects, happiness, and meaning: On doing well and being yourself. *Journal of Personality and Social Psychology, 74,* 494–512.

Pincus, S., and Singer, B. (1996). Randomness and degrees of irregularity. *Proceedings of the National Academy of Sciences, 93,* 2083–2088.

Pincus, S., and Singer, B. (1998). A recipe for randomness. *Proceedings of the National Academy of Sciences, 95,* 10367–10372.

Raczynski, J. M., and DiClemente, R. J. (Eds.). (1999). *Handbook of Health Promotion and Disease Prevention.* New York: Kluwer Academic/Plenum Publishers.

Risch, N., DeLeon, D., Ozelius, L., Kramer, P., Almasy, L., Singer, B. Fahn, S., Breakfield, X., and Bressman, S. (1995). Genetic analysis of idiopathic torsion dystonia in Ashkenazi Jews and their recent descent from a small founder population. *Nature Genetics, 9,* 152–159.

Rutter, M. (1985). Resilience in the face of adversity: Protective factors and resistance to psychiatric disorder. *British Journal of Psychiatry, 147,* 598–611.

Rutter, M. (1990). Psychosocial resilience and protective mechanisms. In J. Rolf, A. S. Masten, D. Cicchetti, K. H. Neuchterlein, and S. Weintraub (Eds.), *Risk and Protective Factors in the Development of Psychopathology* (pp. 181–214). New York: Cambridge University Press.

Ryan, R. M., and Deci, E. L. (2001). On happiness and human potentials: A review of research on eudaimonic well-being. *Annual Review of Psychology, 52,* 1411–1466.

Ryff, C. D. (1985). Adult personality development and the motivation for personal growth. In D. Kleiber and M. Maehr (Eds.), *Advances in Motivation and Achievement: Motivation and Adulthood* (Vol. 4, pp. 55–92). Greenwich, CT: JAI Press.

Ryff, C. D. (1989). Happiness is everything, or is it? Explorations on the meaning of psychological well-being. *Journal of Personality and Social Psychology, 57,* 1069–1081.

Ryff, C. D. (1995). Psychological well-being in adult life. *Current Directions in Psychological Science, 4,* 99–104.

Ryff, C. D., and Keyes, C. L. M. (1995). The structure of psychological well-being revisited. *Journal of Personality and Social Psychology, 69,* 719–727.

Ryff, C. D., and Seltzer, M. M. (Eds.). (1996). *The Parental Experience in Midlife.* Chicago: University of Chicago Press.

Ryff, C. D., and Singer, B. (1996). Psychological well-being: Meaning, measurement, and implications for psychotherapy research. *Psychotherapy and Psychosomatics, 65,* 14–23.

Ryff, C. D., and Singer, B. (1998a). The contours of positive human health. *Psychological Inquiry, 9,* 1–28.

Ryff, C. D., and Singer, B. (1998b). Human health: New directions for the next millennium. *Psychological Inquiry, 9,* 69–85.

Ryff, C. D., and Singer, B. (1998c). Middle age and well-being. In H.S. Friedman (Ed.), *Encyclopedia of Mental Health* (pp. 707–719). San Diego: Academic Press.

Ryff, C. D., and Singer, B. (1998d). The role of purpose in life and personal growth in positive human health. In P. T. P. Wong and P. S.Fry (Eds.), *The Human Quest for Meaning: A Handbook of Psychological Research and Clinical Applications* (pp. 213–235). Mahwah, NJ: Lawrence Erlbaum Associates.

Ryff, C. D., and Singer, B. (2000). Interpersonal flourishing: A positive health agenda for the new millennium. *Personality and Social Psychology Review, 4,* 30–44.

Ryff, C. D., and Singer, B. H. (2003) Ironies of the human condition: Well-being and health on the way to mortality. In L. G. Aspinwall and U. M. Staudinger (Eds.), *A psychology of human strengths* (pp. 2712–2788). Washington, D.C.: American Psychological Association.

Ryff, C. D., and Singer, B. H. (2005). Social environments and the genetics of aging: Advancing knowledge of protective health mechanisms. *Journals of Gerontology: SERIES B, 60B,* 122–123.

Ryff, C. D., and Singer, B. H. (in press). Know thyself and become what you are: A eudaimonic approach to psychological well-being. *Journal of Happiness Studies.*

Ryff, C. D., Lee, Y. H., Essex, M. J., and Schmutte, P. S. (1994). My children and me: Mid-life evaluations of grown children and of self. *Psychology and Aging, 9,* 195–205.

Ryff, C. D., Love, G. D., Urry, H. L., Muller, D., Rosenkranz, M. A., Friedman, E. M., Davidson, R. J., and Singer, B. (2006). Psychological well-being and ill-being: Do they have distinct or mirrored biological correlates. *Psychotherapy and Psychosomatics, 75,* 85–95.

Ryff, C. D., Magee, W. J., Kling, K. C., and Wing, E. H. (1999). Forging macro-micro linkages in the study of psychological well-being. In C.D. Ryff and V. W. Marshall (Eds.), *The Self and Society in Aging Processes* (pp. 247–278). New York: Springer.

Ryff, C. D., Schmutte, P. S., and Lee, Y. H. (1996). How children turn out: Implications for parental self-evaluation. In C. D. Ryff and M. M. Seltzer (Eds.), *The Parental Experience in Midlife* (pp. 383–422). Chicago: University of Chicago Press.

Ryff, C. D., Singer, B., Love, G. D., and Essex, M. J. (1998). Resilience in adulthood and later life. In J. Lomranz (Ed.), *Handbook of Aging and Mental Health* (pp. 69–94). New York: Plenum.

Ryff, C. D., Singer, B., and Palmersheim, K. A. (in press). Social inequalities in health and well-being: The role of relational and religious protective factors. In O. G. Brim, C. D. Ryff, and R. C. Kessler (Eds.), *A Portrait of Midlife in the U.S.* Chicago: University of Chicago Press.

Ryff, C. D., Singer, B., Wing, E., and Love, G. D. (2001). Elective affinities and uninvited agonies: Mapping emotion with significant others onto health. In C. D. Ryff and B. Singer (Eds.), *Emotion, Social Relationships, and Health* (pp. 133–175). New York: Oxford University Press.

Ryff, C. D., Singer, B. H., and Love, G. D. (2004). Positive health: Connecting well-being with biology. *Phiosophical Transactions of the Royal Society of London B, 359*, 1383–1394.

Seeman, T. E., McEwen, B. S., Rowe, J. W., and Singer, B. H. (2001). Allostatic load as a marker of cumulative biological risk: MacArthur studies of successful aging. *Proceedings of the National Academy of Sciences, 98*, 4770–4775.

Seeman, T. E., Singer, B. H., Rowe, J. W., Horwitz, R. I., and McEwen, B. S. (1997). The price of adaptation: Allostatic load and its health consequences: MacArthur Studies of Successful Aging. *Archives of Internal Medicine, 157*, 2259–2268.

Seligman, M. E. P., and Csikszentmihalyi, M. (2000). Positive psychology: An introduction. *American Psychologist, 55*(1), 5–14.

Seltzer, M. M., and Ryff, C. D. (1994). Parenting across the life span: The normative and nonnormative cases. In D. L. Featherman, R. M. Lerner, and M. Perlmutter (Eds.), *Life-Span Development and Behavior* (Vol. 12, pp. 1–40). Hillsdale, NJ: Erlbaum Associates.

Singer, B. (1985). Self-selection and performance-based ratings: A case study in program evaluarion. In H. Wainer (Ed.), *Drawing Inferences from Self-Selected Samples* (pp. 29–49). New York: Springer-Verlag.

Singer, B. (1989). Grade of membership representations: Concepts and problems. In T. W. Anderson, K. B. Athreya, and D. Iglehart (Eds.), *Probability, Statistics and Mathematics: Papers in Honor of Samuel Karlin* (pp. 317–334), Orlando: Academic Press.

Singer, B., and Manton, K. G. (1998). The effects of health changes on projections of health service needs for the elderly population of the United States. *Proceedings of the National Academy of Sciences, 95,* 15618–15622.

Singer, B., and Pincus, S. (1998). Irregular arrays and randomization. *Proceedings of the National Academy of Sciences, 95,* 1363–1368.

Singer, B. H., and Ryff, C. D. (1997). Racial and ethnic inequalities in health: Environmental, psychosocial, and physiological pathways. In B. Devlin, S. E. Fienberg, D. Resnick, K. Roeder (Eds.), *Intelligence, Genes, and Success: Scientists Respond to the Bell Curve* (pp. 89–122). New York: Springer-Verlag.

Singer, B., and Ryff, C. D. (1999). Hierarchies of life histories and associated health risks. *Annals of the New York Academy of Sciences, 896,* 96–115.

Singer, B., and Ryff, C. D. (2001a). *New Horizons in Health: An Integrative Approach.* Washington, D.C.: National Academy Press.

Singer, B., and Ryff, C.D. (2001b). Understanding aging via person-centered methods and the integration of numbers and narratives. In R. H. Binstock and L. K. George (Eds.), *Handbook of Aging and the Social Sciences,* 5th edition (pp. 44–65). San Diego, CA: Academic Press.

Singer, B., Friedman, E., Seeman, T., Fava, G. A., and Ryff, C. D. (2005). Protective environments and health status: Cross-talk between human and animal studies. *Neurobiology of Aging, 26S,* S113–S118.

Singer, B., Ryff, C. D., Carr, D., and Magee, W. J. (1998). Life histories and mental health: A person-centered strategy. In A. Raftery (Ed.), *Sociological Methodology, 1998* (pp. 1–51). Washington, DC: American Sociological Association.

Smider, N. A., Essex, M. J., and Ryff, C. D. (1996). Adaptation to community relocation: The interactive influence of psychological resources and contextual factors. *Psychology and Aging, 11,* 362–371.

Snyder, C. R., and Lopez, S. J. (Eds.) (2002). *Handbook of Positive Psychology*. New York: Oxford University Press.

Staudinger, U. M., Marsiske, M., and Baltes, P. B. (1995). Resilience and reserve capacity in later adulthood: Potentials and limits of development across the life span. In D. Cicchitti and D. J. Cohen (Eds.), *Developmental Psychopathology*: Vol. 2. *Risk, Disorder, and Adaptation* (pp. 801–847). New York: Wiley.

Sutton, S. K., and Davidson, R. J. (1997). Prefrontal brain asymmetry: A biological substrate of the behavioral approach and inhibitor systems. *Psychological Sciences, 8,* 204–210.

Tedeschi, R. G., Park, C. L., and Calhoun, L. G. (Eds.). (1998). *Posttraumatic Growth: Positive Changes in the Aftermath of Crisis*. Mahwah, NJ: Lawrence Earlbaum Associates.

Tomarken, A. J., Davidson, R. J., Wheeler, R. E., and Doss, R. C. (1992). Individual differences in anterior brain asymmetry and fundamental dimensions of emotion. *Journal of Personality and Social Psychology, 62,* 676–687.

Tweed, S., and Ryff, C. D. (1991). Adult children of alcoholics: Profiles of wellness and distress. *Journal of Studies on Alcohol, 52,* 133–141.

Urry, H. L., Nitschke, J. B., Dolski, I., Jackson, D. C., Dalton, K. M., Mueller, C. J., Rosenkranz, M. A., Ryff, C. D., Singer, B. H., and Davidson, R. J. (2004). Making a life worth living: Neural correlates of well-being. *Psychological Science, 15,* 367–372.

Werner, E. E., and Smith, R. S. (1992). *Overcoming the Odds: High Risk Children from Birth to Adulthood*. Ithaca, NY: Cornell University Press.

Wilson, E. O. (1998). *Consilience: The Unity of Knowledge*. New York: Alfred A. Knopf.

Van Riper, M., Ryff, C. D., and Pridham, K. (1992). Parental and family well-being in families of children with down syndrome: A comparative study. *Research in Nursing and Health, 15,* 227–235.

Zhang, H., and Singer, B. (1999). *Recursive Partitioning in the Health Sciences*. New York: Springer-Verlag.

11

Integrating Psychosocial Factors with Biology

The Role of Protective Factors in Trajectories of Health and Aging

TERESA E. SEEMAN

This case study outlines the development of a program of interdisciplinary research that focuses on understanding the physiological mechanisms through which the sociocultural and socioeconomic environments, as well as personal social and psychological experience, affect health trajectories. Within this framework, the focus has been on understanding the protective effects of social and cultural factors on health and aging—especially the effects of social ties, social support, and psychological resources (e.g., beliefs about one's own efficacy and personal mastery). The first section of this chapter outlines how a program of research evolved from an initial starting point within the tradition of social epidemiology into a broader research approach that encompasses aspects of neuroendocrinology and clinical geriatrics, as well as concepts from sociology and social psychology. The second section outlines major findings from this research. The third section discusses how the initiation and groundwork for this program of research resulted from a unique opportunity when I was a new Ph.D. to participate in an interdisciplinary research network, and how this initial exposure prompted my own further efforts toward enhanced interdisciplinary training and skills, particularly in the area of neuroendocrinology. The final portions of the chapter outline how these efforts to gain additional training in disciplines other than epidemiology resulted in a network of interdisciplinary collaborators: a network that now serves as the core of a program of "transdisciplinary" research focusing on questions concerning the physiological pathways through which the individual's social and psychological experiences are translated into trajectories of health and functioning over the life course.

Interdisciplinary Features, Form of the Work, New Findings and Insights

During the past decade, I have developed a program of interdisciplinary research that seeks to understand the biological mechanisms that would explain previously observed relationships between individuals' social and psychological experiences and differentials in health. This research grew out of an initial interest in the role of social relationships in health and aging. By the late 1980s, a considerable and generally consistent body of epidemiological research had documented more favorable health outcomes for people who reported a greater degree of social integration— that is, those with more reported social ties with family, friends, and other formal and informal social groups (for reviews, see Broadhead et al., 1983; House, Landis, and Umberson, 1988; Seeman, 1996). My own research suggested that these observed protective effects of social relationships were not explained by differences in other known risk factors, including lifestyle behaviors like exercise, smoking, and diet. I became intrigued by the question of how, precisely, social relationships affected health outcomes, particularly the question of how such relationships "got inside the body," and I began to explore the idea of possible direct effects of such social relationships on internal physiology. It became necessary, then, to consider the possible cognitive and emotional pathways through which the experiences associated with social relationships might affect physiology, and, as a consequence, I became more interested in the role of psychological factors as well.

The program of research that developed from this interest in understanding biological pathways for psychosocial effects on health has resulted in the development of several new conceptual approaches to understanding these relationships and has produced a variety of empirical analyses that document the hypothesized relationships between social and psychological features of individuals' lives and differences in patterns of biological regulation. Conceptual developments have included elaboration of a multilevel, biopsychosocial model (see Figure 11.1), linking social and psychological characteristics to biology and health within a longitudinal, life-span context. Recently, this has led to the elaboration of a new concept of biological risk, allostatic load, that takes a cumulative, multisystems and life-span view of biological risks (see further discussion of this concept later in this chapter). The elaboration of this biopsychosocial model has evolved from various collaborations, including, as noted below, a series of cumulative review articles. The program of research that derives from this model has two major themes. First, there is a focus on integrating information both across and within the various domains outlined in Figure 11.1 (e.g., demographic, social, psychological, behavioral, and biological) in order to develop more comprehensive (and more accurate) models of health and aging. Second, there is a life-course component that focuses on questions concerning how the various interrelationships within and across domains play out over the life course, including issues of reciprocal relationships between these various domains over time.

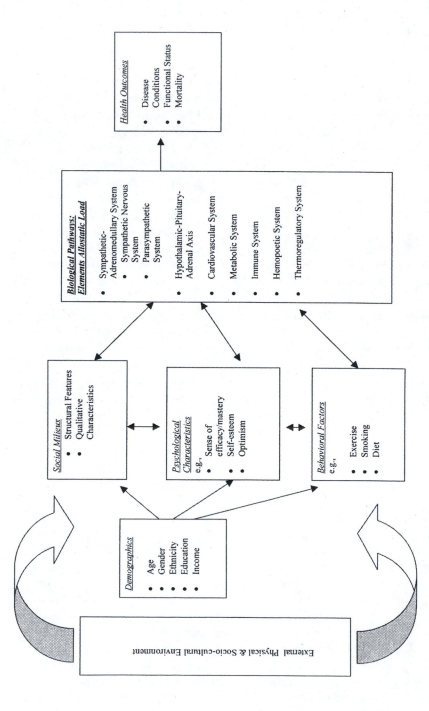

Figure 11.1. Biopsychosocial model of health and aging. Relationships presented are considered to operate at the level of the individual within a life span, cumulative effects framework. Relationships are hypothesized to be influenced by broader environmental effects of the sociocultural and physical environments within which the individual lives during his or her life span.

The earliest work that contributed to the development of this model was a literature review undertaken in collaboration with Bruce McEwen; we focused on evidence that linked aspects of the social environment to patterns of neuroendocrine regulation (Seeman and McEwen, 1996). The primary thrust of our assessment was to emphasize the breadth of evidence linking various aspects of social relationships to physiology. Importantly, we also highlighted the dual nature of this physiological association, documenting not only the potential of social relationships to reduce physiological activation but also their potential for augmenting patterns of physiological reactivity, depending on the quality of the social interaction: more positive interactions tend to result in reductions in physiological reactivity, while negative interactions carry the potential for heightening physiological reactivity. This latter point has largely been ignored in much of the literature on social ties and health where the focus has been on documenting the health-promoting effects of such ties. We suggested the need for more balanced investigation of both the positive and negative physiological effects of social relationships. The combined expertise brought to bear here in psychosocial epidemiology and neuroendocrinology provided the background for more detailed evaluation and discussion of both sides of the relationship of interest—that is, aspects of social relationships and their neuroendocrine correlates.

Two additional reviews, recently completed in collaboration with Shelley Taylor and Rena Repetti (both social psychologists), have taken a broader approach to understanding how the social environment affects health. The first of these reviews examined the pathways through which-socioeconomic status may affect health—including social, psychological and behavioral pathways, in addition to explicit discussion of biological pathways (Taylor, Repetti, and Seeman, 1997). The second review examined in more detail the importance of early family experiences for children's short-term and long-term health outcomes (Repetti, Taylor, and Seeman, 2002). Again, the focus is on integrating information from various disciplinary domains to provide a more comprehensive understanding of the factors that may affect health outcomes. Thus, the review focuses both on nonbiological factors such as the development of social competence and self-regulatory skills, and on possible underlying biological mechanisms through which family environments may affect health, such as increased dysregulation of hypothalamic-pituitary-adrenal or serotonergic pathways.

The interdisciplinary conceptual efforts outlined here have been paralleled by a number of empirical data analyses designed to test various aspects of the models and hypotheses derived from the conceptual orientation. The first major focus of empirical work was an explicit effort to explore relationships between psychosocial factors and patterns of physiological regulation, the inference being that such regulation is a mechanism that mediates the well-known psychosocial effects on health. Our initial work in this area focused on relationships between social network characteristics and neuroendocrine activity. Using data from the MacArthur Study of Successful Aging, my colleagues and I examined the hypothesis that social integration and support are associated with lower levels of endocrine activity. As hypothesized, we found negative associations between social integration and levels of social support on the one hand and levels of hypothalamic-pituitary-adrenal (HPA) axis and sympathetic nervous system (SNS) activity on the other (Seeman, Berkman, Blazer, and Rowe, 1994), a pattern of association that is consistent with the hypothesized biological pathways through which social integration and support have been postulated to protect against negative health outcomes. As outlined in this chapter, our current research is focused on extending these initial findings on associations between the person's social milieu and individual endocrine parameters to a more comprehensive model of biological health as reflected in the concept of allostatic load.

The endocrine (and other biological) data from the MacArthur Study of Successful Aging provide a "snapshot" view of the biological status of individuals at a single point—a single blood sample or, in the case of the HPA axis and SNS assessments, a single, integrated urinary assessment of total HPA axis and SNS activity over a 12-hour period of time. Current theories of health and development, however, frequently emphasize the role of more dynamic patterns of biological response to challenge in the generation of pathophysiological risks (for discussions of these issues, see, e.g., McEwen and Stellar, 1993, Seeman and Robbins, 1994). Thus, as a complement to the community-based data from the MacArthur Study of Successful Aging, a second set of empirical studies was initiated, using laboratory-based challenge paradigms to investigate the influence of individual differences in psychosocial factors on the dynamics of neuroendocrine regulation under conditions of psychosocial challenge. These studies (blending epidemiological, biological and social psychological interests) were funded through the MacArthur Network on Successful Aging and a Special Emphasis Research Career Award from the National Institute on Aging, and their major focus has been to clarify the influence of age, gender, and psychosocial factors in shaping patterns of biological regulation in response to life's circumstances and challenges.

One of the first such studies employed a driving simulation challenge that I developed. Subjects had to steer a car through a series of simulated driving situations reflecting those regularly confronting drivers (e.g., changing lanes, turning corners), as well as several more stressful situations in which a rapid response is required to avoid an accident (e.g., car in front stops suddenly or cuts into lane in front of you). Among other physiological parameters, HPA axis reactivity was measured in terms of levels of plasma cortisol and adrenocorticotrophin (ACTH) based on repeated blood sampling before, during, and after the driving simulation. Sixteen older men and women, aged 70 to 79, were enrolled in the study, and patterns of response to the challenge were examined.

The results from this study clearly demonstrated wide variation in patterns of HPA axis reactivity, even within this small sample of older adults; some individuals exhibit little response, others exhibit moderate response and relatively quick return to baseline, and a third group exhibit very large responses and very slow return to baseline even after a two and one-half- hour recovery period. Analyses have clearly shown that these different patterns of endocrine response are related to individual difference characteristics. Gender was one of the characteristics that predicted differential response to the challenge: women were more reactive than men. This finding was somewhat surprising in light of previous research in college-aged populations, which showed a generally consistent pattern of greater response among men (for discussion, see Seeman, Singer, and Charpentier, 1995).

We have since developed two additional studies to test the hypothesis that there is, in fact, a gender differential in patterns of age-related change in HPA axis regulation and that the apparent greater age-related increase in women's reactivity is associated with their declining levels of estrogen after menopause. In one study, we assessed patterns of HPA axis response to a standardized cognitive challenge in younger and older men and women. In this case, the challenge consisted of a series of cognitive tasks, presented under time constraints and with experimenter high-lighting of any errors that were made. Results of this study clearly document an age-by-gender interaction, with women showing a greater age-related increase in reactivity (Seeman, Singer, Wilkinson, and McEwen, 2001). More recently, we completed a study of HPA axis responses to challenge in postmenopausal women who are and are not on hormone-replacement therapy (HRT) using a somewhat different public speaking challenge. Women were asked to give a speech designed to convince a panel of two "evaluators" that they would be good candidates for a job teaching in an elementary school. Results from this study were consistent with the hypothesis that older women's increased HPA axis reactivity is related to their lower estrogen levels after menopause: women on HRT exhibited less response to the challenge.

In addition to these observed differences in reactivity associated with age and gender, our research has focused on the possible effect of psychological charac-teristics, such as self-esteem and perceptions of control—both of these being concepts of known importance in social psychology—on patterns of response to challenge. Our interest in these characteristics relates, at least in part, to hypo-thesized social influences on these characteristics (e.g., that those who are socially integrated within a supportive social milieu will tend to enjoy better self-esteem and may have a greater sense of personal efficacy and control). Data from the driving challenge study provide support for our hypothesis that individuals characterized by a stronger sense of self-esteem are less reactive to the challenge (Seeman, Berkman, et al., 1995). In a separate challenge study, we have examined the effect of control beliefs on patterns of cardiovascular response to an experimental manip-ulation that made salient the uncontrollable, controllable, or neutral features of the college environment. Findings from this study indicated that those with higher initial personal mastery beliefs exhibited less physiological reactivity to the ma-nipulation, as measured by blood pressure and pulse (Pham, Taylor, and Seeman, 2001). There was also a main effect for environmental controllability—those ex-posed to the controllable environmental manipulation exhibited lower blood pressure and pulse reactivity. A newly funded collaborative project with Shelley Taylor, a social psychologist at UCLA, will augment these earlier protocols with manipulations of social characteristics of the challenge situation (e.g., presence of either a socially supportive or a nonsupportive confederate), moving this laboratory-based research toward a more comprehensive test of our biopsychosocial model of health and development.

As indicated, a second area of interdisciplinary conceptual development involves our efforts to operationalize and further develop the concept of allostatic load. The concept of allostatic load, first introduced by McEwen and Stellar (1993) and further developed in McEwen (1998), has been proposed as a measure of the cumulative physiological toll that may be exacted on the body through attempts at adaptation to life's demands: "The strain on the body produced by repeated ups and downs of physiologic response, as well as by the elevated activity of physiologic systems under challenge, and changes in metabolism . . . that can predispose the organism to disease" (McEwen and Stellar, 1993, p. 2094). This idea is derived from Sterling and Eyer's concept of allostasis, meaning "the ability to achieve stability through change" (Sterling and Eyer, 1988). Allostasis emphasizes the physiological imperative that, in order to survive, "an organism must vary parameters of its internal milieu and match them appropriately to environmental demands" (Sterling and Eyer, 1988, p. 638). Healthy functioning requires ongoing adjustments of the internal physiologic milieu, with physiologic systems exhibiting fluctuating levels of activity as they respond and adapt to environmental demands. Importantly, allostasis emphasizes that while healthy functioning requires ongoing fluctuation in physiological systems, these fluctuations should remain within optimal *operating ranges* of the physiologic systems. The concept of allostatic load embodies the idea that physiological regulatory systems experience wear and tear when they operate outside optimal ranges and that the cumulative effect of such wear and tear across multiple physiological systems results in increased health risks. To date, there has been substantially more theoretical discussion of this concept than actual empirical testing; our research group has been one of the first to attempt actual empirical evaluation of allostatic load as a more integrative view of biological risk.

Using data from the MacArthur Study of Successful Aging, we developed an initial operational definition of allostatic load as a multisystem, cumulative measure of biological risk. We then sought to test the construct validity of our measure of allostatic load through examination of its ability to predict health outcomes in this cohort of older men and women. Our initial measure of allostatic load was developed using available data on 10 biological parameters, including systolic and diastolic blood pressure (SBP and DBP), relative weight (as measured by waist-hip ratio; WHR), HDL and total cholesterol, glucose metabolism, hypothalamic-pituitary-adrenal (HPA) axis and sympathetic nervous system (SNS) activity, and levels of dihydroepiandrosterone sulfate (DHEA-S; purported to be a functional antagonist to HPA axis activity). A measure of allostatic load was developed by summing the number of different parameters for which the individual's score fell into the highest risk quartile. Using this measure of allostatic load, we have shown that it predicts subsequent health outcomes, including risks for decline in physical and cognitive functioning, incident cardiovascular disease, and mortality; in all cases, higher allostatic loads are associated with increased risk (Seeman, Singer, Horwitz, Rowe, and McEwen, 1997).

In a second set of analyses, we sought to extend these initial findings and to enhance our understanding of the concept of allostatic load through more in-depth examination of the relative predictive ability of allostatic load as compared with other models of biological risk. The latter include models of the metabolic syndrome, Syndrome X (as measured by a subset of 6 of our 10 allostatic load components: high SBP and/or DBP, high WHR, high total cholesterol, low HDL cholesterol, and high glucose), as well as models based on subsets of traditional, individual risk factors. Results from these analyses provide further evidence to support the hypothesis that allostatic load, as a more comprehensive model of biological risk, is the best predictor of health outcomes (Seeman, Singer, Rowe, and McEwen, 2001). The developmental and analytic work related to allostatic load has involved (and continues to involve) active input from a psychosocial epidemiologist (Seeman), a statistician/social scientist (Burt Singer), a neuro-scientist (Bruce McEwen), and a geriatrician (Jack Rowe). This combined expertise has allowed us to develop an operational definition of allostatic load based on McEwen and Stellar's original theoretical formulation, and to demonstrate the construct validity of our measure in a series of detailed analyses using a substantial community-based population.

Our group is currently working on two further areas of conceptual devel-opment related to allostatic load. The first involves an effort to devise more com-prehensive measures of allostatic load, based on more extensive biological data from studies other than the MacArthur Aging Study. Examples of this work in-clude ongoing analyses of data from the Wisconsin Longitudinal Study (WLS) and proposed analyses of data from the Coronary Artery Risk Development in Young Adults Study (CARDIA). Each of these studies includes a broader range of bio-logical parameters than those included in the original MacArthur Study—for example, measures of immune function and cerebral asymmetry are available in the WLS substudy. These additional studies will yield opportunities to examine alternative formulations of allostatic load and their relationships to health, as well as to socioeconomic and psychosocial characteristics. In the context of this on-going effort to refine the operational definition of allostatic load, a second area of developmental work involves the use of several newer analysis techniques to ex-amine possible nonlinear models of allostatic load—for example, using categorical and regression trees (CART) and grade-of-membership (GOM) techniques.

Another thrust in both conceptual and data analytic work has focused on relationships between the concept of allostatic load and psychosocial characteristics of individuals' lives. We are currently conducting a series of analyses exploring the relationship between psychosocial characteristics and levels of allostatic load, as well as the possibility that allostatic load (as a comprehensive, multisystems measure of biological risk) will prove to be a significant mediator of psychosocial effects on health. This latter work has been enriched through collaboration with Carol Ryff and colleagues at the University of Wisconsin–Madison, on a substudy of participants in the WLS. Approximately 100 of the WLS participants have been assessed for all components of the original allostatic load measure developed from the MacArthur Aging Study. With these data, it is possible to use the extensive, longitudinal WLS data on experiences of psychosocial advantage (e.g., supportive social relationships, higher socioeconomic status) versus disadvantage (low socio-economic status, nonsupportive relationships) to examine how such prior psy-chosocial experiences relate to current levels of allostatic load and to explore the mediating physiological processes that explain the health effects of social experience.

The sophistication of these analyses is greatly enhanced by the collaborative input from a social psychologist (Ryff), a statistician/social scientist (Singer), and a psychosocial epidemiologist (Seeman). Recently completed analyses from both the WLS and the MacArthur Aging Study suggest strongly that individual differences in psychosocial profiles are associated with differences in allostatic load: those with more advantaged psychosocial profiles (e.g., more positive social relationships, greater psychological resources) exhibit lower allostatic loads (Seeman, Singer, Ryff, and Levy-Storms, 2002). These findings are paralleled by additional analyses from the MacArthur Aging Study, suggesting that levels of social support are associated with a slower accumulation of allostatic load over a two and one-half-year follow-up (unpublished data).

Major Consequences of This Work

The program of research outlined here has provided opportunities to address questions that bridge the disciplines of psychosocial epidemiology, social psy-chology, demography, and neuroendocrinology. One clear result, seen in the cited publications, is greater insight into the biological pathways through which psy-chosocial factors influence health outcomes. The sophistication and depth of the work is enhanced by the availability of expertise covering community-based epi-demiological methods, assessment and interpretation of social and psychological factors and of biological parameters, and advanced statistical methodology.

Another consequence is the ongoing development of additional collaborative projects, building on previous conceptual and analytic work. There is, for example, a recently funded collaborative NSF project with Shelley Taylor that will integrate assessments of biological parameters into her prior work on psychological re-sponses to challenge. We propose to examine individual differences in biological reactivity to challenge, in the context of differences in psychological characteristics and social settings. The new community-based work in Taiwan adds a cross-cultural component to the research program; and the evolving integration of epidemiological and demographic research methods promises to develop more comprehensive models of population health dynamics.

The most recent extension of my research, a collaboration with Gail Green-dale in the Division of Geriatrics of the School of Medicine, examines the health consequences of hormone-replacement therapy (HRT) for postmenopausal women. We propose to test the hypothesis that HRT protects such women against cognitive decline through HPA axis regulation. This research is in its early stages, and our current focus is on demonstrating links between biological parameters and our outcome, cognition. The longer-range goal is to broaden the research perspective to incorporate consideration of the effect of sociocultural and psychosocial factors on observed relationships—considering, for example, whether the potential benefits of HRT are moderated by various person or environmental characteristics.

My interest in this area of research grew out of earlier work related to stress reactivity and cognition. The earlier analyses of MacArthur data examined the relationship between levels of cortisol activity and patterns of cognitive decline. The impetus for this work developed from extensive discussion in the Neuroendocrine Laboratory at Rockefeller University of various animal models showing the effect of high cortisol on the hippocampus, a primary brain region that is involved in memory and learning. Based on these discussions, we decided to test for a relationship between higher cortisol and poorer cognitive function in our human data. Using the longitudinal MacArthur data, we were able to show that patterns of increasing cortisol activity over a two and one-half-year period were associated with significantly increased risks for decline in memory ability in older women (Seeman, McEwen, Singer, Albert, and Rowe, 1997).

My interest in this problem was further piqued by the analysis of gender differences in patterns of cortisol response to our driving simulation challenge (Seeman, Singer, and Charpentier, 1995). As noted here, we found that older women exhibited significantly greater and more prolonged responses than did the men—a finding that was somewhat surprising since most of the existing literature on gender and reactivity suggested that men were more reactive. Our study confirmed an age-by-gender interaction with respect to patterns of HPA axis response to challenge: men are more reactive in the younger group (aged 30–45) while women are more reactive in the older group (aged 70+) (Seeman, Singer, Wilkinson, et al., 2001). An obvious candidate for potential explanation of such a gender-by-age interaction in patterns of HPA axis reactivity was estrogen, since levels of this hormone are one factor that changes dramatically from premenopause to postmenopause. The hypothesis is that postmenopausal reductions in estrogen in women lead to their greater age-related increase in HPA axis reactivity.

Exploring this hypothesis has resulted in two exciting collaborative projects. The first developed as a result of my association with Dr. Caleb (Tuck) Finch at the Andrus Gerontology Center (University of Southern California), who proposed a program project (P01) grant on estrogen, stress, and cognition. The proposed program of research was a fascinating combination of three projects involving animal and molecular level research and three projects involving human studies, all focused on questions related to the hypothesized role of estrogen in cognitive aging and the potential mediating role of cortisol. Although reviewers were enthusiastic about the interdisciplinary nature of the proposal, particularly the linkages between animal and human research on a common question, the total budget was seen as prohibitive, and it was suggested that the animal and human studies be pursued separately. The animal projects were funded as a smaller P01; the human studies are under development as separate projects. This was, I believe, a missed opportunity for a truly integrated set of projects on a common question. It seemed that reviewers were generally favorable, but ultimately they felt "safer" with a more traditional separation of the animal and human research.

In seeking to pursue the estrogen-cortisol-cognition relationship, focusing in particular on a comparison of HPA axis reactivity in postmenopausal women who are or are not on estrogen-replacement therapy, I became engaged in the collaboration with Gail Greendale, who specializes in questions related to women's aging and menopause. We have embarked on a series of research projects examining the effect of estrogen on HPA axis regulation at older ages and the potential relevance of this for women's cognitive aging. What all of these projects document is the interdisciplinary advantage of engaging the complementarity of a range of disciplines: epidemiology, neuroendocrinology, clinical geriatrics, demography, statistics, and health and social psychology.

Origins and Life Course of the Collaboration

How does one become engaged and committed to interdisciplinary work? A "traditional" epidemiologist by training, I began my career with a focus on cardiovascular disease (CVD) but moved relatively quickly to a broader focus on health and aging, with a particular interest in questions related to "successful aging." This shift toward a broader focus was largely the result of two factors. First, many of those who had CVD were older adults with other comorbidities, and I became dissatisfied with focusing on only one specific aspect of their health status. Second, given the projections regarding the significant increase in the population of older adults, there was growing awareness of the importance of the heterogeneity in patterns of aging. These circumstances made it more urgent to discover what factors might protect against declines in health and functioning and whether these might be factors that were modifiable so that one could develop programs and policies to promote more "successful aging." My disciplinary interest as an epidemiologist focused on the effect of social and psychological factors as either protective or risk-inducing factors for various health and functional outcomes. The interdisciplinary nature of my work evolved from the necessity of understanding the biological pathways through which social and psychological factors affect health. Thus, the evolution of my research made it necessary to expand my repertoire of conceptual and methodological approaches in areas of interest— chiefly, physiology/endocrinology/neuroscience, psychophysiology, and health psychology—and to seek out scientists from the referent disciplines for collaboration on projects of mutual interest.

The impetus for my interdisciplinary development was my participation in the MacArthur Research Network on Successful Aging. This network was established in 1984 by the John D. and Catherine T. MacArthur Foundation Health Program, with the explicit goal of fostering interdisciplinary research on successful aging. The network itself was chaired by John W. Rowe and included 15 scientists from quite diverse disciplines, including geriatricians, neuroscientists, geneticists, epidemiologists, neuropsychologists, neurologists, sociologists, and psychologists. As a new Ph.D. in epidemiology, I was asked to supervise a multisite longitudinal cohort study, one of multiple research projects undertaken by the network in seeking to understand the factors that influence patterns of aging.

From the very beginning, it was clear that the central research question to be addressed by the network (i.e., "What leads to more successful aging?") required an interdisciplinary research approach. In my initial capacity as the project director for the longitudinal cohort study, I had the opportunity to attend all network meetings and to be exposed, early in my career, to the wide-ranging discussions that led to the development of the network's interdisciplinary program of research. As a direct result of this exposure, I developed an interest in exploring more comprehensive models of aging that would include not only the more familiar social and psychological variables from my training in psychosocial epidemiology but would attend to biological pathways as well. The network discussions were crucial to the development of my interdisciplinary approach to research, as they provided exposure to ideas and methods from multiple disciplines and, importantly, opportunities for direct discussion with scientists from these other disciplines. Through my participation in this network, I learned that such research was not only desirable (i.e., that it offered unique opportunities to address questions that could not be addressed through more narrowly focused disciplinary approaches) but, more important, that such research was in fact "do-able," because we were doing it.

How, specifically, did that process work? In developing the network's longitudinal cohort study, for example, all network members contributed to the development of protocols. As a result, the study incorporated a broad range of protocols that had not previously been used in community-based research—including extensive assessments of both cognitive and physical performance, as well as collection of both blood and urine samples. As the project director, I was responsible for implementing the various protocols, and this necessitated working closely with members of the network from neuropsychology, neurology, and clinical geriatrics. I found that I not only liked stretching to understand these other disciplines and their concepts but also enjoyed the challenge of finding ways to integrate the various disciplinary concerns and approaches into an epidemiological community-based study. The end result, as illustrated in the next section of this chapter, was a project that was enriched by its incorporation of concepts and measurements from different disciplines, with the explicit goal of examining relationships among these different concepts as a means of gaining greater understanding of the aging process.

While my own "stretching" as a researcher was primarily reflected in this effort to incorporate the work of biologically oriented clinicians and neuroscientists into our community study, there were notable examples where network research using animal models was influenced by discussions of the human data. One striking example of the evolution of such cross-discipline influences was the development (by Dr. Carl Cotman, a neuroscientist) of an animal model experiment to examine individual differences in exercise behavior and its possible impact on brain function. The idea for this study grew directly from network discussions of findings from our human cohort study, which showed that individuals who engage in more strenuous physical activity are less likely to show cognitive declines (Albert et al., 1995). Carl and his colleagues at the University of California, Irvine, designed a study in which rats were given free access to running wheels for 0 (control group), 2, 4, or 7 nights and their duration of physical activity was recorded. The study demonstrated that there were increased levels of brain-derived neurotrophic factor (BDNF), a factor postulated to enhance neuronal capacity for growth and repair in response to injury, in response to the physical exercise: animals with more nights of exposure to treadmill exercise showed greater up-regulation of brain-derived neurotrophic factor (BDNF) mRNA in the hippocampus, and mean distance run per night was positively correlated with BDNF mRNA levels (Neeper, Gomez-Pinillia, Choi, and Cotman, 1995). Thus, among the network's members, there was a reciprocal flow of ideas and concepts between the "bench" and "field" scientists.

But a career in interdisciplinary research requires investment, as well as mere positive experience. For myself, this involved the decision to "invest" in additional training in endocrinology in order to facilitate interdisciplinary collaboration exploring the biological mechanisms underlying psychosocial effects on health. This decision grew out of my network involvement in laboratory-based, experimental models of physiological aging and from growing appreciation for the potential that might be realized through integration of such methods with those from my background in epidemiology.

Thus, in 1991, I sought and obtained five years of funding for career development through a National Institute on Aging Special Emphasis Research Career Award (SERCA). SERCA awards were specifically designed to provide scientists with opportunities to obtain additional training in one or more disciplines other than their area of initial specialization. Through the SERCA funding, I was able to develop a program of training in neuroendocrinology to enhance my ability to explore models of development that focused on postulated biological mechanisms through which psychosocial factors affect trajectories of health and functioning. This SERCA funding was crucial to my ultimate ability to pursue an interdisciplinary research program. First, the funding provided the necessary "protected time" to pursue the additional training that has enabled me to communicate more easily and fruitfully on issues related to physiology, particularly neuroendocrinology. Second, through the mentoring provisions of the SERCA award, I developed incredibly valuable working relationships with senior researchers in disciplines other than epidemiology—in particular, neuroendocrinology (Bruce McEwen), statistics (Burt Singer), and physiology and clinical geriatrics (John Rowe).

As one might expect, the success of this SERCA training program depended on the initiative and commitment of senior researchers. The director of the MacArthur network (Jack Rowe) provided invaluable advice and professional contacts—in particular, contact with Bruce McEwen, who became a primary mentor for the SERCA award involving weekly tutorials, directed reading, and participation in his neuroendocrinology laboratory meetings at Rockefeller University. Bruce became a valued colleague, as well as a research collaborator.

A second mentor and collaborator was Burt Singer, a former colleague at Yale in the School of Public Health. As I began my SERCA training, I realized that I would also need special training in appropriate statistical methods, and Burt agreed to serve as a mentor on such statistical methodology—a role that quickly expanded to include collaboration on the full range of conceptual issues arising in our varied work on community studies, laboratory-based challenge studies, and empirical development of the concept of allostatic load.

In retrospect, it is clear that my transition from a more or less traditional program of epidemiological research to interdisciplinary work would have been almost impossible without the good fortune of connecting with senior colleagues who were willing to serve as mentors and collaborators when funding for their time was not available. Their dedication in this way is an object lesson regarding professional commitment and responsibility as a resource for interdisciplinary progress.

Since increased breadth of vision is the hallmark of interdisciplinary research, the scope of the work appears inevitable to expand. Thus, I was asked to join another MacArthur network focusing on socioeconomic status and health seeking to understand the psychological and biological pathways through which socioeconomic status affects health. The network is involved in a range of interdisciplinary studies using the resources of psychology, neuroscience, sociology, epidemiology, and the health sciences. For example, we have developed a series of interdisciplinary proposals for analysis in connection with the CARDIA study (involving Tony Earls's Chicago project) to examine psychological and biological mediation of socioeconomic effects in cardiac disease; an examination of the association between neighborhood social characteristics and adult mortality (in collaboration with Ichiro Kawachi in Public Health at Harvard and sociologist David Williams at Michigan); and analysis of rich array of psychological data from the Wisconsin Longitudinal Study (collaborating with Carol Ryff and her colleagues) to further the work on the psychosocial profiles associated with allostatic load.

The interdisciplinary collaborations extend to demographers as well. One such collaboration, with demographers at Georgetown University (Maxine Weinstein) and Princeton (Noreen Goldman), involves cross-cultural research on a cohort of older men and women living in Taiwan. These data will be used to explore the consistency or divergence of biopsychosocial models of aging in a sociocultural context that differs significantly from that in the United States. Another initiative integrating demography and epidemiology has been developed in conjunction with

Eileen Crimmins, a demographer at the Andrus Gerontology Center at the University of Southern California. This two-pronged project, funded by an R01 from the National Institute on Aging, centers, on investigation of biological mediators of the effects of socioeconomic status, first, on health and, second, on the establishment of an interdisciplinary UCLA/USC Center on Demography and Health that will provide a forum for the integration of epidemiological and clinical risk information with population-based methods of demography. The goal of our center is to develop more accurate population models of health that incorporate the kind of risk information that is commonly developed from epidemiological and clinical research but that has heretofore largely been absent from demography models.

These various research engagements represent a range of truly collaborative and increasingly "transdisciplinary" research endeavors (Rosenfield, 1992). In its current form, my research draws on methods and concepts from traditional epidemiology (e.g., community-based cohort study designs and "risk factor" assessment), from health psychology (e.g., laboratory-based research on physiological dynamics under varied social and psychological conditions), and from neuroscience/endocrinology (e.g., physiological parameters thought to impact importantly on health and protocols for assessment of these parameters). Further, this basic triad is clearly informed by exchange with themes and perspectives that derive from demography, sociology, and statistics. The fundamental biopsychosocial model that guides these interdisciplinary efforts is captured in Figure 11.1.

Factors That Have Facilitated and Constrained the Work

Five factors in particular have facilitated the development of this program of interdisciplinary research. They include, in order of importance:

1. *Direct exposure, as a new Ph.D., to the possibilities of interdisciplinary research.* My work with the MacArthur Successful Aging Network set me on a path of interdisciplinary research from the very beginning of my career. Through this exposure, I saw a group of highly skilled and successful senior researchers who were actively seeking to make links between their "home" discipline and the other disciplines represented around the table. It quickly became clear that such research had the potential to address complex questions in ways that would be impossible through a strictly disciplinary approach. Thus, I became aware of the potential gain from having additional training in neuroendocrinology, an investment that led to the development of a network of multidisciplinary, collaborative relationships and a variety of interdisciplinary projects focusing on the biological mechanisms through which psychosocial factors influence health and aging.

2. *Protected time for training in neuroendocrinology through an NIA-SERCA grant.* The five years of funding provided by the SERCA grant provided crucial protected time for training and research, resulting not only in the development of new skills and knowledge but also in the development of collaborative ties that have continued to enrich my research, long after the end of the SERCA funding.

3. *Interdisciplinary mentors.* Through the MacArthur Research Network on Successful Aging and the SERCA grant, I developed an incredible set of mentors, chiefly Jack Rowe, Bruce McEwen, and Burt Singer. Their investment of time and energy in mentoring provided access to disciplines outside my existing epidemiologic training, encouraging growth that incorporates aspects of clinical geriatrics, neuroendocrinology, and statistics into my program of research. Each was, in fact, committed to the idea that interdisciplinary research was the way to go. And each continues to serve as a valued mentor, as well as an integral collaborator.

4. *Foundation funding.* Funding through the NIH has sometimes been a struggle. However, facilitating the development of our program of research has been the support available through two of the MacArthur Health Program research networks (Successful Aging and, more recently, Socio-Economic Status and Health). Each of these networks has been committed to the proposition that interdisciplinary research can provide significant advances in understanding the processes that affect health outcomes over the life course.

5. *Seniority of collaborators.* My own personal growth and productivity were initially fostered by the fact that all of my mentor/collaborators were senior, established investigators who generously allowed me to take the lead on the various projects that developed out of our initial collaborations. More important than the emerging first-author publications was the fact that I was encouraged to assume primary responsibility for ensuring that the proposed research and data analyses were done correctly and at the same time collaboratively. All of this fostered the development of my conceptual, methodological, and analytic skills, and I have been fortunate to retain these mentors as valued co-investigators on various projects.

Three important factors have had the greatest effect as constraints on the interdisciplinary feature of the research.

1. *Funding of interdisciplinary research* has been relatively difficult through the traditional NIH funding mechanism. One problem has been the difficulty of "fitting" such research within more narrowly defined NIH study sections (defined frequently on the basis of more traditional disciplines or outcomes, such as "cancer" or "heart disease"). Such standing committees often lack the breadth of expertise needed to review particular interdisciplinary applications; they may also lack experience with such research approaches. The recent restructuring of some NIH study sections to incorporate a more multidisciplinary structure is encouraging in this regard.

2. Less problematic, but also a constraining factor, is the *geographic dispersion of collaborators.* With collaborators located on the East and West Coasts, as well as in the Midwest, direct face-to-face contacts are intermittent, and the vast majority of the collaboration necessarily occurs through phone, fax, and e-mail contacts. The success of these efforts can be seen in the record of collaborative publications and the current ongoing projects described here. Nonetheless, the pace of the research is always enhanced through actual face-to-face meetings, and greater funding for such opportunities is important.

3. Finally, there is the ever-present issue of *time constraints*. All of the participants in this program of collaborative research are actively engaged in multiple research endeavors, as well as in teaching and training responsibilities at their respective institutions. Despite the clear and consistent evidence of interest and commitment to our collaborative, interdisciplinary research, the reality is that these other responsibilities serve to limit the available time for the collaborative efforts.

What Are the Important Implications of the Work?

The interdisciplinary goal of this research is to increase our understanding of how aspects of individuals' social and psychological experience over the life course impact on their patterns of health and aging. Specifically, the focus is on elucidating the physiological mechanisms through which the broader socioeconomic and sociocultural environment in which individuals live, as well as their more personal social and psychological experiences, "get under the skin" and are reflected in varying profiles of physiological activity with consequences for physical and mental health over the life course.

In coming years, interdisciplinary research has the potential to provide researchers with the means to flesh out the biopsychosocial model in Figure 11.1. For example, one can envision research projects that provide more complete and longitudinal information on sociodemographic, psychosocial, and behavioral characteristics of people's lives, along with more comprehensive information on the biological parameters that reflect the major regulatory systems. Such data would be useful in developing integrative models of interrelationships both within and across social, psychological, behavioral, and biological domains, and models of how these interrelationships impact on trajectories of health and functioning over time. Another area of exciting new opportunities lies in incorporating genetic information into our models of health and aging. In my own case, given the focus on elucidating and understanding protective factors related to health and aging, a key interest would lie in likely gene × environment interactions. We are just now undertaking analyses that incorporate initial genotype information into our biopsychosocial model, looking explicitly for hypothesized gene × environment interactions in which lifestyle factors may protect against risks deriving from genetic inheritance. With developments in technology, it seems likely that there will be greatly expanded opportunities for collecting and integrating a rich array of such biological data, in addition to information on social, psychological, and behavioral characteristics, through longitudinal, population-based studies of health and aging.

Such knowledge has the potential to test the hypothesized relationships in our biopsychosocial model, as well as to enhance our ability to develop and implement more effective health and social policy interventions in several ways. First, developing a body of evidence showing the ways in which social and psychological factors impinge on internal physiology and affect health risks provides a stronger evidence base from which to develop health and social policy interventions. Thus, such evidence might well facilitate the implementation of interventions to influence the more "upstream" factors—as in the case of social policy interventions that affect aspects of the sociocultural and socioeconomic environment or the more individually oriented interventions to reduce health risks. By augmenting our understanding of the links between social and psychological factors, physiology, and trajectories of health, this program of research can also affect more individual-level health policy through insights regarding potential targets both for primary interventions to prevent health problems and for secondary and tertiary interventions to alleviate existing problems.

There are currently few actual training programs for such interdisciplinary research (and, it might be added, the experience of earlier programs—for example, at Harvard and Michigan—was not especially sanguine). We continue largely to train our Ph.D. and M.D. candidates in relatively "discipline-specific" programs, with the occasional course taken in an "outside" department. Personal experience, however, suggests that just as discipline-specific success requires that training include "hands-on" research experience, there needs to be more opportunity for junior researchers to see interdisciplinary research in action and to participate in it.

Conclusion

Finally, it is well to remember that, despite the current upsurge of interest, the idea of interdisciplinary work is not new and has been encouraged for some time by scientific bodies like the Social Science Research Council and the Health Program of the John D. and Catherine T. MacArthur Foundation. Two processes may help make the practice of interdisciplinary work more prevalent and more productive: first, there is need for a constant effort to overcome the built-in rigidities of disciplinary boundaries that are so evident in academic life; second, there is need for a constant effort, as explored in this volume, to specify the precise gains that interdisciplinary work can provide.

In an elliptical way, the kinds of gains that are involved, and are illustrated in the research outlined in this chapter, can be described as follows:

1. Increased *conceptual richness:* for example, the common single risk-factor approach that typifies the epidemiological literature is enriched through use of the more complex concept of allostatic load derived from neuroscience.

2. *Reciprocal disciplinary benefits:* for example, the ideas generated from epidemiological human studies provide the basis for animal model replication.

3. Deeper probing of the *mechanisms of effects:* for example, discerning the physiological pathways for environmental effects on health outcomes.

4. Increasing *external validity:* for example, the use of community-based epidemiological studies to test laboratory-derived physiological and psychological principles.

5. Encouraging *methodological creativity:* for example, the development of new demographic methods through integration with epidemiological approaches.

6. Integration of different *levels of analysis:* for example, developing models that appropriately specify the relation between environments and persons.

7. Providing *conceptual depth:* for example, developing statistical procedures that allow for and can grasp the complexity of personal histories as related to health outcomes.

8. Developing *alternative models* of behavior: for example, a coordinated biopsychosocial model of health, or models of positive health rather than absence of illness.

These are large tasks, and they can only be mastered through continued progress in developing interdisciplinary research.

Postscript

Since the original edition of this volume was published, my program of research has grown in both breadth and depth, including: *(1)* extension of work on biopsychosocial links, *(2)* exploration of new methodological approaches to understanding relationships between our psychosocial experiences, their biological substrates, and the consequences of this for health and aging, and *(3)* initiation of significant new interdisciplinary projects involving a wide range of collaborators. These developments have served to confirm my view that interdisciplinary work represents a powerful approach to understanding health and social behavior, and that such interdisciplinary approaches are a productive and, indeed, invaluable path for future research on the role of social–psychological factors in health and aging.

Extension of work on biopsychosocial links

Over the past decade, analyses of data from the MacArthur Studies of Successful Aging have continued to provide insights into the links between psychosocial experience and biology, including evidence linking social integration to levels of inflammation (at least in men) (Loucks et al, in press) and to overall allostatic load (in both men and women) (Seeman, Singer, Ryff, and Levy-Storms, 2002). Through a collaboration with colleagues involved in a large national survey in Taiwan, I was also able to implement the same set of biological protocols used in our MacArthur Aging Study. Interestingly, data from the Taiwan study do not show the same significant gradients in cumulative biological risk (allostatic load) either by level of social integration or social support (Seeman, Glei, Goldman, Weinstein, Singer, and Lin, 2004), possibly, as we speculate in the article, due to important sociocultural differences in the patterning and meaning of social interactions in this Asian country as compared with the United States. Indeed, the surprisingly different findings for Taiwan versus the United States highlight the significant contribution that cross-cultural, interdisciplinary work can make to our understanding of the contextual effects of such cultural differences.

Another area of research, continuing my collaboration with Shelley Taylor, has focused on the role of oxytocin (OT) in relationships between social experience and biological responses to situational experiences. Previous research had suggested that OT was related to more relaxed, calm psychological states (McCarthy, 1995), suggesting that it might be related to positive social experiences. However, other research suggested that elevated OT might be a marker of psychological or social stress, or both, being positively related to reports of relationship stress in young women (Turner, Altemus, Enos, Cooper, and McGuinness, 1999). We sought to examine these opposing hypotheses as part of a pilot study of psychophysiological reactivity in 73 postmenopausal women. Results from our study indicate that elevations in ocytocin are associated with indices of relationship stress (e.g., reporting of problems or gaps in social relationships, including less positive relationship with a primary partner) (Taylor, Lehman, Kiefe, and Seeman, 2006). We have recently received funding for a larger study, incorporating manipulation of social support before and during a challenge condition, which will further examine relationships between past and current social experience, oxytocin, and stress reactivity to the challenge condition.

Examination of area-level effects on biopsychosocial relationships represents a third area of expansion. This work has involved two new collaborations—one with Dr. Ana Diez-Roux (an epidemiologist whose work focuses on more macro-level [e.g., neighborhood] effects on health) and the other with fellow investigators in the RAND Center on Health Disparities. In collaboration with Ana Diez-Roux, I am currently working on a substudy within the larger Multi-Ethnic Study of Atherosclerosis (MESA). Our study, based at two of the MESA sites in Los Angeles and New York involves the collection of a broad range of biological markers of stress as well as area-level measures of the neighborhoods in which the participants live. Planned analyses will examine both main and interaction effects of area-level characteristics on profiles of biological risk. In collaboration with colleagues in the RAND Center on Health Disparities, we are currently examining area-level effects on profiles of biological risk based on nationally-representative National Health and Nutrition Examination Survey (NHANES) III data.

Methodological work

In collaboration with Burt Singer and Arun Karlamangla, I have continued to explore the concept of allostatic load—a multisystems view of biological risk. Since our initial work focusing on extremely simple "counting" algorithms to operationalize allostatic load from data on biological activity in various major regulatory systems, we have explored a variety of more complex scoring strategies, including use of canonical correlation techniques (Karlamangla, Singer, McEwen, Rowe, and Seeman, 2002) and scoring based on multivariable logistic models (Karlamangla, Singer, and Seeman, 2006). We have also recently used structural equation modeling to test various hypothesized models of allostatic load (Seeman, et al., in preparation). Most recently, Burt Singer has taken the lead in the use of recursive partitioning analyses to explore the utility of models that allow for a more fine-tuned assessment of higher-order interactions and nonlinearities in biological risk profiles (Singer, Ryff, and Seeman, 2004; Gruenewald, Seeman, Ryff, Karlamangla, and Singer, 2006). These various analyses have indicated that more complex scoring algorithms that allow for greater use of the full range of information contained in the raw biological data generally show stronger relationships to outcomes than did the original counting algorithm. In particular, the recursive partitioning work points to important non-linearities in risk profiles, with both lower and higher values for various biological parameters (e.g., blood pressure and cortisol) conferring increased risks for mortality (Gruenewald, Seeman, Ryff, Karlamangla, and Singer, 2006).

New interdisciplinary projects and collaborations

Mid-Life in the United States (MIDUS)—I am currently part of a large, interdisciplinary team of investigators representing health psychology, psychophysiology, neuroscience, sociology, epidemiology, and medicine who are collaborating on a program project (P01) grant, led by Dr. Carol Ryff, and funded through the Behavioral and Social Research Program at the National Institute on Aging (NIA). This project involves follow-up of a national sample of adults originally interviewed in 1995. The current P01 includes re-interviewing all members of the cohort on a wide range of health, behavioral, and psychosocial topics (Project 1). In addition, cohort members are completing a telephone cognitive battery (Project 3) and subsets of the cohort are participating in more detailed biomarker assessments (Project 4), a 7-day daily diary study of daily events (with accompanying assessment of diurnal cortisol activity) (Project 2) and functional MRI evaluations of emotion regulation (Project 5). Though still in data collection, the ultimate database will offer an incredibly rich array of information for analyses of biopsychosocial linkages, possible gender and/or age-related differences in these relationships, and their association with health outcomes.

Coronary Artery Risk Development in Young Adults (CARDIA)—In conjunction with my membership in the MacArthur Research Network on Socio-economic Status and Health, I have been the lead investigator on a substudy within the larger CARDIA study to investigate the development of allostatic load in young adults, with particular interest in the role of socio-economic status, gender, and ethnicity. A collaboration with Dr. Richard Sloan (a psychophysiologist with expertise in heart rate variability) resulted in the addition of a heart rate variability assessment to our battery of study protocols—in addition to the range of assessments originally incorporated into the MacArthur Successful Aging Study. Analyses to date have documented the presence of SES gradients in these relatively young (35–42 years old) adults for major biological systems and parameters, including heart rate variability (Sloan, Huang, Sidney, Liu, Williams, and Seeman, 2005), metabolism (Karlamangla, Singer, Williams, Schwartz, Matthews, Kiefe, and Seeman, 2005), HPA activity (Cohen, Schwartz, Epel, Kirschbaum, Sidney, and Seeman, 2006), and inflammation (Gruenewald, Seeman, Ryff, Karlamangla, and Singer, 2006). Recent work using structural equation modeling has further documented that the structure of overall allostatic load is similar for black and white men and women, and that allostatic load shows the expected SES gradient in all groups except black men (Seeman et al., in preparation). This work extends our earlier work in older adults, showing that SES gradients in biological risk become manifest much earlier in the life course and are seen in most major gender–ethnic groups. Future analyses will focus on the role of social relationships and psychological characteristics such as optimism and perceived mastery as mediators of relationships between SES and biological risk.

In conjunction with work on the CARDIA project, Shelley Taylor and I have also collaborated on development of a measure of "risky" family environments—a concept that grew out of our work with Rena Repetti on factors in early life that may have long-term impacts on health and well-being (Repetti, Taylor, and Seeman, 2002). As hypothesized, analyses of data based on this measure have yielded evidence linking exposure to childhood environments characterized by lack of warmth and disorganization to both poorer psychological and biological profiles in young adults (Lehman, Taylor, Kiefe, and Seeman, 2005; Taylor, Gonzaga, Klein, Hu, Greendale, and Seeman, 2006).

Experience Corps (EC)—Perhaps most exciting is a recent collaboration with Linda Fried and colleagues at Johns Hopkins on an intervention study to test the potential of the Experience Corps, a program that involves placing older adult volunteers in elementary schools to assist in improving educational outcomes for the children, and to improve cognitive, physical and psychosocial outcomes for older adults. The EC program represents an attempt to design meaningful, socially-valuable, generative roles for older adults that will: *(1)* attract a large proportion of the older population; *(2)* demonstrate the potential benefits of an aging society in addressing unmet societal needs (e.g., improving elementary school education); *(3)* be a vehicle for enhancing the physical, cognitive, social, and psychological health of older adults; and *(4)* provide a visible intervention to revise our social conceptions of appropriate roles and responsibilities at older ages. The program was initially developed by Linda Fried and Marc Freedman of Civic Ventures, and its feasibility has been shown in two successful national demonstrations in U.S. cities (Fried, Freedman, Endres, and Wasik, 1997).

The EC program represents a model of senior service designed to provide meaningful, socially-valued roles for older adults—bringing their time, experience, and wisdom to bear to improve academic and behavioral outcomes of children in public elementary schools—while simultaneously serving as a vehicle for health promotion by designing a program that encourages physical, cognitive, and social activity. The EC places teams of 7–10 older adults in public schools, with each older adult serving at least 15 hours per week during the school year.

Based on pilot data demonstrating initial support for the hypothesized social, psychological, cognitive, and physical benefits of participation in the EC program (Fried et al., 2004), our research group has recently received funding from the

Behavioral and Social Research Program at the NIA to conduct a randomized trial of the EC program in the Baltimore City schools. The proposed randomized trial will capitalize on the plans of the City of Baltimore to scale the EC program up across Baltimore City schools, and the City's agreement to allow us to conduct a randomized trial of the impact of this program on older adults' health and function (Project 1, "Impact on Disability, Falls and Memory in Older Adults"; Project 3, "Effects on Cognitive & Neural Pathways," and Project 4, "Social & Psychological Benefits of EC Participation"), as well as assessing the program's impact on schools and children (Project 2, "Intergenerational Benefits of EC—Impact on Children & Schools"). For the proposed trial involving older adults, men and women 60 years and older ($N = 1046$) who volunteer and are eligible for the program will be randomly assigned to participate in the EC program or to a control group involving referral to more standard, low intensity (and less structured) volunteer service opportunities through the City Commission on Aging and Retirement Education (CARE). Those assigned to the EC intervention will serve in any of 24 intervention schools for a 2-year period. Intervention and control groups will be evaluated at baseline and at 3, 12, and 24 months postenrollment. This randomized trial has begun, with the first older adults randomized to the schools in Fall 2006.

We believe that this trial represents an exciting opportunity to test a uniquely multifaceted intervention we hypothesize will benefit older adults across a wide range of important domains, including physical, cognitive, and psychosocial functioning, with a resulting enhancement of their quality of life and likely longevity. The added, and not inconsequential, benefit is that the efforts of these older adults are anticipated to benefit future generations by improving educational outcomes for young children. Indeed, we are currently working to secure supplementary funding to conduct cost–benefit analyses of the potential long-term value of the EC program in fostering greater longer-term educational and associated occupational success for children who benefit from this program in elementary school.

Summary

In sum, since the publication of the original volume my research has expanded along several new, exciting, and fruitful avenues of collaboration and investigation, including development of new methodological approaches to the operationalization of complex constructs such as allostatic load, investigation of new biological parameters such as oxytocin, inclusion of broader area-level factors in models of biopsychosocial effects on health and aging, and most recently, testing of a social–behavioral intervention for older adults.

Finally, I am also encouraged by the many signs of growth in interest in biopsychosocial research not the least of which can be seen in the many large, NIH-funded studies that have requested assistance in adding biological assessments to their range of protocols (e.g., Health and Retirement Study, Panel Study of Income

Dynamics). Inclusion of such biological data in these studies will offer expanded opportunities to study, and hopefully come to better understand, the complex relationships between social and psychological experiences, their biological substrates and sequelae, and the ultimate impact of these relationships on trajectories of health and well-being across the life course.

ACKNOWLEDGMENTS

Work on this chapter was supported by NIA grants AG-00586, AG-17056, and AG-17265 (to T.E.S) and by the MacArthur Research Network on Successful Aging and the MacArthur Research Network on Socio-Economic Status and Health through grants from the John D. and Catherine T. MacArthur Foundation.

RECOMMENDED READINGS

McEwen, B. S. (1998). Protective and damaging effects of stress mediators. *New England Journal of Medicine, 338,* 171–179.

McEwen, B. S., and Stellar, E. (1993). Stress and the individual: Mechanisms leading to disease. *Archives of Internal Medicine, 153,* 2093–2101.

Seeman, T. E., and McEwen, B. S. (1996). Social environment characteristics and neuroendocrine function: The impact of social ties and support on neuroendocrine regulation. *Psychosomatic Medicine, 58,* 459–471.

Seeman, T. E., Singer, B., Horwitz, R., Rowe, J., and McEwen, B. S. (1997). The price of adaptation: allostatic load and its health consequences: MacArthur studies of successful aging. *Archives of Internal Medicine, 157,* 2259–2268.

Singer, B. S., and Ryff, C. D. (1999). Hierarchies of life histories and associated health risks. In N. E. Adler, M. Marmot, B. S. McEwen, and J. Stewart (Eds.), *Socioeconomic Status and Health in Industrial Nations: Social, Psychology, and Biological Pathways* (pp. 96–115). New York: Annals of the New York Academy of Science.

Taylor, S. E., Klein, L. C., Lewis, B. P., Gruenewald, T. L., Gurung, R. A., and Updegraff, J. A. (2000). Biobehavioral responses to stress in females: Tend-and-befriend, not fight-or-flight. *Psychological Review, 107,* 411–429.

Taylor, S. E., Repetti, R. L., and Seeman, T. E. (1997). What is an unhealthy environment and how does it get under the skin? *Annual Review of Psychology, 48,* 411–447.

REFERENCES

Albert, M. S., Jones, K., Savage, C. R., Berkman, L., Seeman, T., Blazer, D., and Rowe, J. W. (1995). Predictors of cognitive change in older persons: MacArthur Studies of Successful Aging. *Psychology and Aging, 10,* 578–589.

Broadhead, E. W., Kaplan, B. H., James, S. A., Wagner, E. H., Schoenbach, V. J., Grimson, R., Heyden, S., Tibblin, G., and Gehlbach, S. H. (1983). The epidemiologic evidence for a relationship between social support and health. *American Journal of Epidemiology, 117,* 521–537.

Cohen, S., Schwartz, J., Epel, E., Kirschbaum, C., Sidney, S., and Seeman, T. (2006). Socioeconomic Status, Race, and Diurnal Cortisol Decline in the Coronary Artery Risk Development in Young Adults (CARDIA) Study. *Psychosomatic Medicine, 68,* 41–50.

Fried, L. P., Freedman, M., Endres, T. E., and Wasik, B. (1997). Building communities that promote successful aging. *Western Journal of Medicine, 167,* 216–219.

Fried, L. P., Carlson, M., Freedman, M., Frick, K. D., Glass, T. A., Hill, J., McGill, S., Rebok, G.W., Seeman, T., Tielsch, J., Wasik, B. A., and Zeger, S. (2004). A Social Model for Health Promotion for an Aging Population: Initial Evidence on the Experience Corps Model. *Journal of Urban Health: Bulletin of the New York Academy of Medicine. 81,* 64–78, March.

Gruenewald, T. L., Seeman, T. E., Ryff, C. D., Karlamangla, A. S., and Singer, B. H. (2006). Combinations of Biomarkers Predictive of Later Life Mortality. *Proceedings of the National Academy of Sciences, 103*(38), 14158–14163.

House, J. S., Landis, K. R., and Umberson, D. (1988). Social relationships and health. *Science, 241,* 540–545.

Karlamangla, A., Singer, B. S., Williams, D. R., Schwartz, J., Matthews, K., Kiefe, C. I., and Seeman, T. E. (2005). Impact of Socio-economic Status on Longitudinal Accumulation of Cardiovascular Risk in Young Adults: The CARDIA Study. *Social Science & Medicine, 60,* 999–1015.

Karlamangla, A. S., Singer, B. S., and Seeman, T. E. (2006). Reduction in Allostatic Load is Associated with Lower All-Cause Mortality Risk in Older Adults: MacArthur Studies of Successful Aging. *Psychosomatic Medicine, 68,* 500–507.

Karlamangla, A. S., Singer, B. S. McEwen, J. W. Rowe, and Seeman, T. E. (2002). Allostatic lead as a predictor of functional decline: MacArthur Studies of Successful Aging. *Journal of Clinical Epidemiology, 55*(7), 696–710.

Lehman, B. J., Taylor, S. E., Kiefe, C. I., and Seeman, T. E. (2005). Relation of Childhood Socioeconomic Status and Family Environment to Adult Metabolic Functioning in the CARDIA Study. *Psychosomatic Medicine, 67*(6), 846–854.

Loucks, E. B., Berkman, L. F., Gruenewald, T. L., and Seeman, T. E. (in press). Relation of Social Integration to Inflammatory Marker Concentrations in Men and Women 70–79 Years. *American Journal of Cardiology).*

McCarthy, M. M. (1995). Estrogen modulation of oxytocin and its relation to behavior. In R. Ivell and J.A. Russell (Eds.). *Oxytocin: Cellular and Molecular Approaches in Medicine and Research.* New York: Plenum Press.

McEwen, B. S. (1998). Protective and damaging effects of stress mediators. *New England Journal of Medicine, 338,* 171–179.

McEwen, B. S., and Stellar, E. (1993). Stress and the individual: mechanisms leading to disease. *Archives of Internal Medicine, 153,* 2093–2101.

Neeper, S. A., Gomez-Pinillia, F., Choi, J., and Cotman, C. (1995). Exercise and brain neurotrophins. *Nature, 373,* 109.

Pham, L. B., Taylor, S. E., and Seeman, T. (2001). The effects of environmental predictability and mastery on self-regulation and physiological reactivity. *Personal and Social Psychology Bulletin, 27,* 611–620.

Repetti, R. L., Taylor, S. E., and Seeman, T. E. (2002). Risky families: Family social environments and the mental and physical health of offspring. *Psychology Bulletin, 128,* 330–336.

Rosenfield, P. L. (1992). The potential of transdisciplinary research for sustaining and extending linkages between the health and social sciences. *Social Science and Medicine, 35,* 1343–1357.

Seeman, T. E. (1996). Social ties and health. *Annals of Epidemiology, 6,* 442–451.

Seeman, T. E., and McEwen, B. S. (1996). Social environment characteristics and neuroendocrine function: The impact of social ties and support on neuroendocrine regulation. *Psychosomatic Medicine, 58,* 459–471.

Seeman, T. E., and Robbins, R. J. (1994). Aging and hypothalamic-pituitary-adrenal response to challenge in man. *Endocrine Reviews, 15,* 233–260.

Seeman, T. E., Berkman, L. F., Blazer, D., and Rowe, J. (1994). Social ties and support and neuroendocrine function: MacArthur Studies of Successful Aging. *Annals of Behavioral Medicine, 16,* 95–106.

Seeman, T. E., Berkman, L. F., Gulanski, B., Robbins, R., Greenspan, S., Charpentier, P., and Rowe, J. (1995). Self-esteem and neuroendocrine response to challenge: MacArthur Successful Aging Studies. *Psychosomatic Research, 39,* 69–84.

Seeman, T. E., Glei, D., Goldman, N., Weinstein, M., Singer, B., and Lin, Y-H. (2004). Social Relationships and Allostatic Load in Taiwanese Elderly and Near Elderly. *Social Science & Medicine, 59,* 2245–2257.

Seeman, T. E., Gruenewald, T. L., Schwartz, J., Sidney, S., Liu, K., McEwen, B., and Karlamangla, A. Modeling multi-system biological risk in young adults: Coronary Artery Risk Development in Young Adults Study (CARDIA) (manuscript in preparation).

Seeman, T. E., McEwen, B. S., Singer, B., Albert, M., and Rowe, J. W. (1997). Increase in urinary cortisol excretion and declines in memory: MacArthur Studies of Successful Aging. *Journal of Clinical Endocrinology and Metabolism, 82,* 2458–2465.

Seeman, T. E., Singer, B., and Charpentier, P. (1995). Gender differences in HPA response to challenge: MacArthur Studies of Successful Aging. *Psychoneuroendocrinology, 20,* 711–725.

Seeman, T. E., Singer, B., Horwitz, R., Rowe, J., and McEwen, B. S. (1997). The price of adaptation—allostatic load and its health consequences: MacArthur studies of successful aging. *Archives of Internal Medicine* 157, 2259–2268.

Seeman, T. E., Singer, B., Rowe, J., and McEwen, B. (2001). Exploring a new concept of cumulative biological risk—Allostatic load and its health consequences: MacArthur studies of successful aging. *Proceedings of the National Academy of Sciences USA, 98*(8), 4770–4775.

Seeman, T. E., Singer, B., Ryff, C., and Levy-Storms, L. (2002). Psychosocial factors and the development of allostatic load. *Psychosomatic Medicine, 64,* 395–406.

Seeman, T. E., Singer, B., Wilkinson, C., and McEwen, B. (2001). Gender differences in age-related changes in HPA axis reactivity. *Psychoneuroendocrinology, 26,* 225–240.

Singer, B., Ryff, C., and Seeman, T. E. (2004). *Operationalizing Allostatic Load.* In J. Schulkin (Ed). *Allostasis, Homeostasis, and the Costs of Physiological Adaptation* (pp 1131–1149). New York: Cambridge University Press.

Sloan, R. P., Huang, M. H., Sidney, S., Liu, K., Williams, O. D., and Seeman, T. (2005). Socioeconomic status and health: Is parasympathetic nervous system activity an intervening mechanism? *International Journal of Epidemiology, 34,* 309–315.

Sterling, P., and Eyer, J. (1988). Allostasis: A new paradigm to explain arousal pathology. In S. Fisher and J. Reason (Eds.), *Handbook of Life Stress, Cognition and Health* (pp. 631–651). New York: Wiley and Sons.

Taylor, S. E., Gonzaga, G. C., Klein, L. C., Hu, P., Greendale, G. A., and Seeman, T. E. (2006). Relation of Oxytocin to Psychological Stress Responses and Hypothalamic-Pituitary-Adrenocortical Axis Activity in Older Women. *Psychosomatic Medicine, 68,* 238–245.

Taylor, S. E., Lehman, B. J., Kiefe, C. I., and Seeman, T. E. (2006). Relationship of early life stress and psychological functioning to adult c-reactive protein in the Coronary Artery Risk Development in Young Adults Study. *Biological Psychiatry, 60*(8):819–824.

Taylor, S. E., Repetti, R. L., and Seeman, T. E. (1997). What is an unhealthy environment and how does it get under the skin? *Annual Review of Psychology, 48,* 411–447.

Turner R. A., Altemus M., Enos T., Cooper B., and McGuinness T. (1999). Preliminary research on plasma oxytocin in normal cycling women: investigating emotion and interpersonal distress. *Psychiatry, 62,* 97–113.

12

Religion, Spirituality, and Health

The Duke Experience

LINDA K. GEORGE

During the past 10 to 15 years, possible links between religious participation and health have become a "hot" topic in both scientific circles and popular culture. Although writers for the general public and some scientists have significantly extended discussion beyond what is scientifically documented, the research base is growing rapidly in both size and sophistication. It is now commonly assumed that the effects of religion on health can be studied scientifically—a contention that was highly controversial a mere quarter century ago. And the research base has generated sufficient knowledge that the general thrust of the field has moved from the question of whether there is a robust relationship between religion and health to that of what mechanisms can account for that relationship.

Religious participation is fundamentally a social activity. Religion is a major social institution and its effect on cultural, even secular, values is profound. Religion is typically practiced in communities of faith—communities characterized by complex patterns of interaction, belief, and social process. Although health is appropriately studied in a multitude of ways, it is ultimately the clinicians and basic biological scientists who have the last word. No investigation of health can affect medical care or medical education unless it is respected by physicians, other clinicians, and biological scientists. In efforts to understand the effects of religion on health, other disciplines are playing significant roles, especially psychology which in this area, as in many others, elucidates many of the links that tie social factors to health outcomes. In short, a variety of scientific disciplines contribute to the study of religion and health. And the most comprehensive and methodologically strongest investigations are those in which scientists from multiple disciplines work together.

This chapter has two purposes. The first emphasis is on the state-of-the-science with regard to what is known about the links between religion and health. I review the major questions guiding the field, progress to date in answering those questions, and important directions for future effort. Throughout this review, I highlight the contributions of our research team at Duke University to this area of inquiry; we hope that both the quantity and the quality of our contributions will demonstrate that we have been major players in this rapidly developing field. A second purpose of the chapter is to describe our interdisciplinary research program on religion and health. I briefly chronicle the history of our research program and describe the nuts and bolts, opportunities, and constraints to interdisciplinary research at Duke University. I have participated in interdisciplinary research for nearly 30 years and am convinced of its value and importance. But we are not typically trained to work in interdisciplinary teams and environments. If the volume of interdisciplinary research is to accelerate in the future, the fundamentals of effective interdisciplinary collaboration need to be articulated. This is the first time that I have been asked to describe not just what we find in our research but also how we do it and with what costs and rewards. It is a story that I'm delighted to tell.

Religion and Health: Our Scientific Agenda

There is a common perception that scientific investigation of the links between religion and health, and the mechanisms on which those links rest, is a "hot, new topic" (also, occasionally, as a "flash in the pan" that will burn quickly to ash). Although there has been a resurgence of interest in this topic, it has deep intellectual routes in multiple disciplines. In psychiatry, Freud and Jung saw religion as powerful, but they disagreed about its effects: Freud viewed religion as the repository of unhealthy cognitions and emotions (Freud, 1927/1961); Jung was convinced that religion and spiritual commitments are at the very nexus of mental health in adulthood (Jung, 1955). In sociology, Emile Durkheim demonstrated strong relationships between religion and survival itself and documented multiple prosocial functions of religion (Durkheim, 1897/1951, 1915). Another sociologist, Karl Marx, is perhaps best known for his declaration that "religion is the opium of the people." Few people seem to have read Marx, however, for the full quote reads: "Religion is the opium of the people; nevertheless, it is the heart in a heartless world, the soul in a soulless world" (cited in Valliant, 1983, p. 76). And physicians are credited with the saying that "physicians treat, God heals." In a more recent review that played an important role in reigniting interest in the health implications of religion, Levin (1994) identified more than 400 studies that examined the relationships between religion and morbidity and mortality, although they were seldom the major focus of those studies. By now, the research base has probably doubled in size.

For our purposes, the most relevant period is the last 15 to 18 years, for it was in the mid-1980s that new, scientifically rigorous studies of the links between religion and health began to emerge. During this period, three research issues have dominated and continue to dominate scientific inquiry: Is there a (nonspurious) relationship between religious participation and health? What are the mechanisms that account for the relationship between religious participation and health? What are the implications of the relationship between religion and health for medical care? These issues provide a framework for understanding the state-of-the-science with regard to this research field, for highlighting the efforts of our research team to contribute to this research field, and documenting the importance of interdisciplinary efforts for answering those questions.

Relationship between religion and health

The obvious first step in this emerging research field is to demonstrate that there are robust associations between religious participation and health outcomes. Phrased in these simple terms, it appears that only correlational data would be needed to answer this question. But investigators have appropriately cast a much wider net in documenting the relationships between religion and health. This complexity plays out in four primary ways.

First, religious participation is a multidimensional concept, encompassing multiple types or dimensions of religious experience. It is important to determine whether some types of religious participation are more strongly related to health than others because such differences can provide clues to the mechanisms underlying the links between religion and health. For example, if public religious participation (e.g., attending religious services) is more strongly associated with health outcomes than are private devotions (e.g., private prayer), the social and communal aspects of public religious participation may account, in part, for this pattern of results. The primary dimensions of religious experience examined in research to date include denomination or affiliation, public religious participation (especially frequency of attending services), private religious practices (typically, prayer, meditation, and reading of sacred texts), and religious coping. Our research team also has examined use of religious mass media (television and radio) because of its potential importance to chronically ill older adults.

Second, a comprehensive knowledge of the links between religion and health requires examination of multiple health outcomes. It is possible that religious participation has stronger protective effects for some health outcomes than for others. For example, multiple investigators suggest, on theoretical grounds, that religion may have stronger effects on mental health than on physical health. (This is a variant of the "comfort hypothesis," which was one of the first used to examine the links between religion and well-being; see Glock, Ringer, and Babbie, 1967.) In research to date, the major health outcomes examined include physical health (including both specific illnesses and overall physical health status), mental health, disability, and mortality. Our research team also has examined blood pressure and specific biomarkers of immune functioning. (A related body of research, not included in this review, examines the links between religious participation and subjective well-being.)

Third, relationships between religious participation and health may vary across stages of the disease process. For example, the health benefits of religious participation may affect only or primarily the prevention or postponement of illness onset; alternatively, they may be most important during recovery from illness. Unfortunately, the illness phase is ambiguous in most studies of the religion-health relationship as a result of reliance on cross-sectional data. Nonetheless, there now are longitudinal studies that have examined several specific illness phases: prevention of illness onset, recovery from physical and mental illness, and maintenance of functioning and life quality during chronic and terminal illness. Our research has focused on both illness onset and recovery from illness.

Fourth, establishing meaningful relationships between religious participation and health requires demonstration that those relationships are not spurious (i.e., not an artifact of one or more other variables). Demonstrating this requires that the relationships between religion and health be estimated with other factors associated with religion and health statistically controlled. In our research, we routinely control the effects of basic demographic variables (age, sex, race and ethnicity, marital status), socioeconomic status (education, occupation, labor force participation, income), and both acute and chronic stressors. As described later in this chapter, health behaviors and measures of social support and interaction also are included in our models, albeit as potential mediators of the relationships between religion and health. And in all of our longitudinal work, the effects of religious involvement on subsequent health have been examined with the effects of baseline health and disability statistically controlled. Studies based on large representative samples also help rule out spuriousness, and most of our research is based on large, representative samples of community-dwelling adults or on large clinical samples.

Substantial progress has been made in investigating and estimating the relationships between religious participation and health outcomes, and our research team has figured prominently in these efforts. Perhaps the strongest evidence of the health benefits of religious participation is found in studies of the effects of frequency of attending services on mortality. Results from national and regional samples uniformly indicate that persons who regularly attend religious services live substantially longer than those who do not (Hummer, Rogers, Nam, and Ellison, 1999; Koenig et al., 1999; Oman and Reed, 1998; Rogers, 1996; Strawbridge, Cohen, Shema, and Kaplan, 1997). Indeed, in our study of a representative sample of older adults in five North Carolina counties, regular attendance at religious services was associated with an eight-year survival advantage, compared to never or rarely attending religious services (Koenig et al., 1999). Bryant and Rakowski (1992) report similar results for a sample of older African Americans. Recently, we found that private religious practices (prayer, Bible study) predicted lower risk of mortality for healthy but not disabled older adults (Helm, Hays, Flint, Koening, and Blazer, 2001). We also have found significant mortality advantages among those who attended religious services in a clinical sample of 1010 older veterans hospitalized for serious physical illness (Koenig, Larson, et al., 1998). It is important to note that, in all of these studies, the effects of religious service attendance were estimated with relevant demographic, social, and, especially important, health characteristics statistically controlled.

There have been few studies of the relationships between religious participation and the onset of physical illness. Interestingly, most of these studies focused on the effects of religious affiliation on physical illness, examining the health and longevity advantages experienced by two specific denominations with strong proscriptions and prescriptions with regard to health practices: Mormons and Seventh-Day Adventists (Gardner, Sanborn, and Slattery, 1995; Phillips, 1975; Phillips, Kuzma, Benson, and Lotz, 1980). Although these studies suggest that those denominations experience health benefits, especially for specific forms of cancer, over and above those experienced by other denominations, denominational differences are not observed in large, representative studies (e.g., Hummer et al., 1999; Koenig et al., 1999; Strawbridge et al., 1997).

Our research team has devoted considerable effort to examining the effects of religious participation on recovery from physical illness. Our results suggest that both attending religious services (Koenig et al., 1998) and using religion to cope with the challenges of physical illness (Koenig, Pargament, and Nielsen, 1998) are associated with quicker and more complete recovery. In a similar study, Oxman, Freeman, and Manheimer (1995) found that, among cardiac surgery patients, taking strength and comfort in religion was associated with better recovery and with survival itself. Again, these relationships were observed with potential confounding factors statistically controlled.

Idler and colleagues extensively studied the relationships between religious participation and disability. In initial studies, cross-sectional relationships between attending religious services and decreased prevalence of disability were observed (Idler, 1987; Idler and Kasl, 1997a). Longitudinal data subsequently demonstrated that the course of disability differed, depending on frequency of attending religious services. Those who attended services regularly were more likely to improve or stay the same (rather than experiencing additional declines in disability) than those who did not attend religious services (Idler and Kasl, 1997b). Documenting the course of disability with longitudinal data is especially important since many have argued the reverse temporal order: that disability precludes religious service attendance.

Our early research in this field focused on the cross-sectional relationships between religious participation and a variety of mental health outcomes among a representative sample of community-dwelling adults (age 18 and older) (Koenig, Ford, George, Blazer, and Meador, 1993; Koenig, George, Blazer, Pritchett, and Meador, 1993; Koenig, George, Meador, Blazer, and Ford, 1994; Meador et al., 1992). Our results consistently documented significant relationships between attending religious services (and, occasional, but not consistent relationships with other dimensions of religious experience) and decreased prevalence of mental illness. Potential confounding variables were statistically controlled in these analyses, but causal or temporal order was unclear.

Similar results, also based on cross-sectional data, have been reported by other investigators, although the measures of mental illness consisted of depressive symptom and psychological distress scales (rather than specific psychiatric disorders, which were the mental health measures used in our studies) (e.g., Braam, et al., 1998; Brown, Gary, Greene, and Milburn, 1992; Ellison, 1995).

We later conducted two longitudinal studies of the effects of religious participation on recovery from major depressive disorder: one was based on a sample of depressed psychiatric patients; the other was based on a sample of medically ill, hospitalized patients with comorbid major depression. In both studies, attending religious services was associated with quicker and more stable recovery from depression (Koenig and George, 1998; Koenig, George, and Peterson, 1998; Koenig et al., 1995). Religious coping also was associated with better course and outcome of depression in the sample of individuals with comorbid physical illness and depression (Koenig and George, 1998).

In addition to these conventional health outcomes, we examined the relationship between religious participation and other health-related characteristics. Specifically, we found that frequent church attendance was associated with lower blood pressure (Koenig, George, Cohen, et al., 1998; Steffen, Hinderliter, Blumenthal, and Sherwood, 2001) and better immune function (as indexed by interleukin-6 and d-dimers) (Koenig, Cohen, et al., 1997). Again, the effects of potential confounding variables were statistically controlled.

Thus far, only positive associations between religious participation and health outcomes have been reported. This is true in our research and that of other investigators. The failure to find evidence that there are conditions under which religious participation can harm health is of concern, however. Most scientists in this field hypothesize that certain types of religious experiences will be associated with poorer health outcomes. It appears that, on average, in representative samples, the effects of religion on health are positive. This does not mean, however, that there are not specific conditions under which, or subgroups for whom, religion harms health.

Although the research base is limited, there appear to be three conditions under which religion is associated with negative health outcomes. First, the largest volume and best quality research concerns the distinction between "positive" and "negative" religious coping, a distinction conceptually and operationally defined by Pargament (e.g., Pargament, 1997). Positive religious coping consists of perceptions of alliance with and support from God or a higher power; negative religious coping involves feelings that one is sinful and that God (or a higher power) has abandoned or is punishing one. There is now considerable longitudinal evidence that negative religious coping is associated with poorer health outcomes (Koenig, Pargament, and Nielsen, 1998; Pargament, 1997), including mortality (Pargament, Koenig, Tarakeshwar, and Hahn, 2001).

Second, members of religious denominations that prohibit medical care appear to die younger, on average, than members of other denominations and persons who are not religious (e.g., Asser and Swan, 1998; Simpson, 1989).

Third, our research suggests that, unlike other dimensions of religiousness, high levels of exposure to religious programs on television and radio do not protect health and are associated, in cross-sectional data, with higher levels of depressive symptoms (Hays et al., 1998; Koenig, Hays, George, and Blazer, 1997). However, either causal or temporal order needs to be established to understand these findings: we do not know whether religious media use increases depression or whether more depressed persons turn to religious media.

Is there a nonspurious relationship between religious participation and health? We largely know the answer to that question. Attendance at religious services is consistently associated with a variety of health outcomes: mortality, disability, physical illness, and mental illness—as well as, perhaps, with biomedical parameters such as blood pressure and immune function. Positive religious coping is strongly associated with recovery from both physical illness and depression. Evidence about private religious practices is scant in volume, but one study finds these practices to be associated with decreased risk of mortality. Religious affiliation or denomination is the dimension of religious participation least related to health outcomes, although members of denominations with strict guidelines about health practices may be advantaged relative to their peers in other denominations. We also know that certain religious practices are probably linked to poorer health outcomes, although this affects only a small proportion of the population. Very importantly, we know that these relationships are not spurious. They remain strong and largely unchanged, when the full range of other known risk factors are statistically controlled.

There is more work to be done to fully answer this question. There are neither equally plentiful nor equally good data that examine the full range of combinations and permutations of the relevant dimensions of religious experience, health outcomes, and stages of the illness process. Nonetheless, it is clear that the relationships are sufficiently strong to generate scientific interest in identifying the mechanisms by which religious participation exerts its (typically) salubrious effects on health.

Explaining the relationship between religion and health

The primary and most exciting focus of current research in this field is the search for the mechanisms by which religion promotes health. This issue is important for several reasons. First, from a basic science perspective, knowledge that a relationship exists is insufficient; we also need to understand the explanation for that relationship. Second, identifying the explanations for the links between religious participation and health or longevity will yield an understanding of the conditions under which religion does and does not promote health. Third, if we can identify the "active ingredients" in religion, it may be possible to package them in other ways; this is an important issue because not everyone will find religion a palatable form of health promotion. At this point, four possible mechanisms by which religious participation affects health have been proposed—and tested to varying degrees.

HEALTH PRACTICES   One potential mechanism by which religious participation promotes health and longevity is health practices. Religious participation may encourage effective health practices (e.g., avoidance of tobacco, alcohol in excess, illegal drugs, promiscuous sexual activity), which, in turn, result in better health. As noted previously, initial support for this hypothesis is observed in studies that compare rates of illness and mortality between denominations with and without strong, articulated prescriptions regarding health practices. It also is possible, however, that religious participation, regardless of denomination, encourages positive health habits because religion typically includes respect for the body and exhortations to protect and care for it.

Empirical evidence concerning the extent to which health practices mediate or explain the relationships between religious participation and health outcomes has been mixed. For example, five studies examined the degree to which health practices explained the relationship between attending religious services and mortality. Three of the studies report that health practices explained a modest, but statistically significant, proportion of that relationship (Hummer et al., 1999; Oman and Reed, 1998; Strawbridge et al., 1997). In our studies, however, health practices failed to significantly reduce the strength of the service attendance-mortality relationship (Koenig et al., 1999; Koenig, Larson, et al., 1998). Despite differences in the statistical significance of the findings, results across the five studies are quite consistent: health practices explain, at best, only a small amount of the protective effects of attending religious services on longevity.

Idler and colleagues examined the extent to which health practices explained the relationship between public religious participation and disability. In all three studies, health behaviors explained a small, but significant proportion of this relationship (Idler, 1987; Idler and Kasl, 1992, 1997a). Only one of the three studies was based on longitudinal data, however, rendering this conclusion tentative.

Evidence also is scant and ultimately inconclusive for the relationship between attending religious services and depression. Three studies have addressed this issue. Two report that health practices explain a small, but significant proportion of this relationship (Idler, 1987; Musick, Blazer, and Hays, 2000); the other study did not find the mediating effects of health practices to be statistically significant (Koenig, Hays, et al., 1997). Two of these three studies are based on cross-sectional data, limiting confidence in the conclusions.

Although the potential mediating effects of health practices on the relationships between religious participation and health merit further investigation, evidence to date suggests that this possible mechanism plays only a small explanatory role. Clearly, other mechanisms are at work.

SOCIAL TIES   Another possible explanation for the relationships observed between religious participation and health is social ties. "Social ties" is a multidimensional concept, and any or all of its dimensions may be relevant. Three dimensions have received theoretical attention in attempts to understand the processes by which religion promotes health: social support, social interaction, and social integration. Social support refers to the tangible and intangible forms of assistance, comfort, and information provided by friends and families. Social interaction refers to the amount of time spent in the company of friends and family and is especially important for older adults who often are retired and may live alone. Social integration refers to links to community structures, such as memberships in voluntary organizations. Public religious participation itself is a form of social integration. It also is possible, however, that one of the ways that religious participation promotes health is by encouraging congregationalists to participate in other community organizations. It is well documented that all three forms of social ties, especially social support, are robustly related to health and longevity (for recent reviews, see Krause, 2001; Turner and Turner, 1999). Empirically, investigation of the possible explanatory role of social ties in the linkages between religion and health has been restricted to social support and social interaction.

Evidence to date rather convincingly suggests that, contrary to expectation, social ties do not mediate the protective effects of religious participation on health. In particular, there is no evidence that social interaction mediates these relationships. Six studies, one of them ours, have investigated the extent to which social interaction explains the relationship between attending religious services and mortality. In all six studies, social interaction did not mediate this relationship (Bryant and Rakowski, 1992; Goldman, Korenman, and Weinstein, 1995; House, Robbins, and Metzner, 1982; Hummer et al., 1999; Koenig et al., 1999; Oman and Reed, 1998). Similar results, albeit on a much smaller volume of research, have been found for the relationship between attending religious services and disability (Idler, 1987; Idler and Kasl, 1992).

The findings with regard to social support as an explanatory factor are nearly as uniform. Three studies, two of them ours, examined the extent to which social support mediates the relationship between religious participation and mortality. Social support failed to have a significant mediating role in all three studies (Hummer et al., 1999; Koenig et al., 1999; Koenig, Larson, et al., 1998). Seven studies, three of them by our research team, examined the extent to which social support mediates the relationship between attending religious services and depression among community-dwelling adults. Two of the studies are longitudinal; five are cross-sectional. Only one study reported that social support explained a significant proportion of the link between service attendance and depression (Sherkat and Reed, 1992). Social support did not have a significant mediating effect in the other six studies (Braam et al., 1998; Commerford and Reznikoff, 1996; Ellison, 1995; Koenig, Hays, et al., 1997; Musick et al., 2000; Musick, Koenig, Hays, and Cohen, 1998;). Our research team also has examined the extent to which social support mediates the effects of religious participation on recovery from depression and from serious medical illnesses in clinical samples. Although we found social support to be a significant predictor of recovery in these studies, it did not explain a significant proportion of the relationship between religion and illness recovery (Koenig and George, 1998; Koenig, George, and Peterson, 1998).

Again, the search for mechanisms strongly implicated in the relationships between religion and health remains elusive. Although social interaction and, especially, social support are strong independent predictors of mortality, disability, and depression, they do not explain why attending religious services promotes health and longevity. Certainly not all possible links between religion and health have been examined, but the strongest links (i.e., with service attendance) have been.

PSYCHOLOGICAL RESOURCES   A third possible mechanism for explaining the relationships between religion and health is psychological resources such as self-esteem, a sense of mastery or self-efficacy, and feelings of optimism and hope. Substantial research evidence demonstrates that these psychological resources have beneficial effects on health, especially mental health (e.g., George, 2001; Mirowsky and Ross, 1989). Several investigators have hypothesized that religious participation and beliefs may foster these psychological resources, which, in turn, promote health.

Although this possible explanation has received considerable theoretical attention, it has had little empirical scrutiny. To date, three studies have examined the extent to which psychological resources mediate the relationships between various dimensions of religious participation and depression or psychological distress. None of these studies used longitudinal data, so conclusions must be viewed as tentative. Two of the studies report that psychological resources explained small, but statistically significant, proportions of the relationship between religion and depression or distress (Commerford and Reznikoff, 1996; Krause, 1992); the other did not (Braam et al., 1998). Clearly this issue requires further research before confident conclusions can be reached about the potential mediating role of psychological resources.

WORLDVIEWS   A fourth possible mechanism by which religion exerts salubrious effects on health has received considerable theoretical attention, but has not, as yet, been tested empirically. Worldviews refer to the basic cognitive and affective structures that form the taken-for-granted assumptions upon which our understanding of the world rest. As such, they are fundamental bedrocks of our beliefs, understandings, and identities. Antonovsky's (1980) construct, sense of coherence, for example, focuses on the extent to which our basic beliefs generate a sense that the world is predictable, manageable, and meaningful. Sense of coherence has been shown to predict better health. It is possible that one of the ways in which religion promotes health is by fostering and sustaining worldviews that emphasize meaning, purpose, and hope. I am enthusiastic about this hypothesis. It seems to me that in today's society, religion may well be the only social institution that promotes an integrated worldview that offers meaning to what would otherwise be meaningless and answers questions that are otherwise unanswerable (i.e., Marx's "heart in a heartless world, . . . soul in a soulless world").

To date, there are no tests of the extent to which worldviews or sense of coherence mediate the links between religion and health, although there is evidence that religion promotes sense of coherence (e.g., Bjarnason, 1998; Kark, Carmel, Sinnreich, Goldberger, and Friedlander, 1996). Clearly, this is an important issue for future research in this field.

OTHER POSSIBLE MECHANISMS   Two other types of potential mechanisms, substantially different from the psychosocial factors described above, merit brief note. First, there may be biological mechanisms that underlie the links between religion and health (e.g., religious participation may enhance immune function or reduce cortisol levels). Research on biological mechanisms is scant at this point, and none of the studies to date have tested biological parameters as mediators of the religion-health relationship. It also should be noted, however, that there are disciplinary differences in what constitutes an explanatory mechanism. Biologists seek evidence that religion has an effect on biological processes known to affect health. Social and behavioral scientists respect that desire, but do not view it as valid evidence of a mechanism. They want to identify what it is about religion that affects both biological processes and health.

Second, certain dimensions of religious experience may explain the health-promoting effects of more "distal" dimensions of religious experience. For example, religious coping has been hypothesized to explain in whole or in part the relationship between attending religious services and health (Pargament, 1997). This line of reasoning reminds us that there may be something unique about religion that promotes health, rather than religion serving solely as a vehicle for social, psychological, or biological resources that are potentially independent of religion.

Implications for medical care

Of the three issues that dominate the field of research on the links between religious participation and health, this one is the least developed. This is true for the field as a whole and for our research team in particular. Indeed, many investigators, including this author, feel that until there is more definitive evidence about the mechanisms linking religion to health, it is premature to use available knowledge as the basis for medical intervention. Nonetheless, this is an expanding research focus. Two primary streams of research focus on the implications of religious participation for medical care.

First, the most visible—and controversial—research stream is what can be called "spiritual interventions." The most compelling studies in this area consist of clinical trials examining the effects of prayer on recovery from illness or injury (e.g., Byrd, 1988; Harris et al., 1999; Propst, Ostrom, Watkins, Dean, and Mash-burn, 1992). Various forms of prayer are under investigation, including peti-tionary prayer, prayerful meditation, and prayer at a distance. Thus far, the most promising form of prayer seems to be intercessory prayer, in which strangers pray for ill or injured persons. Study of intercessory prayer also is the most method-ologically valid option for this research because patients and medical professionals can be "blinded" to the identities of the patients receiving the prayer intervention. Despite some promising results, the scientific and medical fields are reluctant to accept evidence supporting the health benefits of intercessory prayer. Unless and until the mechanism by which intercessory prayer promotes health can be iden-tified, this is likely to remain a controversial research topic, met with skepticism by the medical and scientific communities.

Variants of spiritual intervention research include interventions such as prayer-based stress-reduction programs and even the familiar 12-step programs, now commonly used for many kinds of behavior change (i.e., 12-step programs typically include recognition of and surrender to a higher power). Research results also are promising for these forms of intervention, and certainly the efficacy of 12-step programs for many individuals with a variety of health-threatening be-haviors is well documented (e.g., Benson, 1996; Gorsuch, 1995). Results of these kinds of interventions have been well received in the medical and scientific com-munities. Thus, at this point, we know much more about the effectiveness of interventions in which religious or spiritual content is part of a multidisciplinary program than we do about the power of prayer to heal.

The second stream of research on the implications of religion for medical care tackles subtler and, in my opinion, more promising issues—at least in the short run. This research focuses on the extent to which it is helpful and health promoting for clinicians to recognize the religious or spiritual needs of their patients and to ex-plicitly acknowledge those needs (e.g., Marwick, 1995; Matthews, 1997). The types of issues investigated under this rubric include the role of chaplains in health care, the willingness of physicians to listen to spiritual concerns, and the provision of appropriate resources (e.g., opportunities for privacy and the conduct of religious rituals) so that patients can engage in valued religious practices in inpatient settings.

Our research team has focused much less on this issue than the previous ones because most of us believe that the research base is not yet sufficient to justify empirically tested recommendations for the delivery of health care. Harold Koenig is an exception to this pattern and has written several pieces on this issue. Topics that he has addressed include research documenting differences in the religious perspectives of health care providers (doctors and nurses) and patients and their families (Koenig, Hover, Bearon, and Travis, 1991), translating research findings in ways useful to pastoral counselors and clergy (Koenig, 1993; Koenig and Weaver, 1997, 1998), and opportunities for clinical collaboration between clergy and health care providers (Weaver, Koenig, and Larson, 1997).

As this review of the field in general and our work in particular has dem-onstrated, investigating the effects of religious participation on health is best performed using the theories and methods of multiple disciplines. Social and psychological studies have been dominant to date, but the best studies available also incorporate the contributions of clinicians. And the biological correlates of religious participation are a rapidly growing area of investigation. Virtually all of our efforts to document the relationships between religious participation and health, and to identify possible mechanisms that can account for those relationships, have involved multiple investigators from multiple disciplines.

The Center's Life Story

Because so much is gained, in this and other fields, by interdisciplinary efforts, it is useful to understand the conditions under which such research flourishes or, alternatively, withers or never comes into being. In this section of this chapter, I describe basic structural, scientific, and practical issues that permit our interdisciplinary research team to succeed in terms of scientific productivity and career development.

The environment at Duke

To understand the development of the Center for the Study of Religion, Spirituality, and Health, it is necessary to know a bit about the larger Duke environment, especially its emphasis on interdisciplinary research. As at most, if not all universities, the major academic units at Duke are discipline-based departments. It is within departments that faculty members have their appointments, receive tenure and promotions, and do their teaching. A large proportion of all research, especially externally funded research, however, is based in centers.

Space limitations preclude a listing of the centers at Duke, but there are many of them.

All centers at Duke involve faculty from multiple disciplines—they are designed to be places where scholars investigating the same research topic can meet, exchange ideas, and, most important, perform collaborative research. It is difficult to imagine performing interdisciplinary research without such centers. Without centers, it would be difficult to identify scholars outside of one's department who share research interests. Moreover, centers provide a level of research infrastructure that is unavailable in academic departments. This infrastructure includes everything from special equipment to research personnel (technicians, statisticians) to assistance with grant preparation and management. Finally, centers help to avoid many of the administrative problems of interdisciplinary research (e.g., where will a project be housed, what department will get credit for the indirect costs).

Although Duke University encourages their development, centers are not given the kind of financial support that departments receive. In essence, centers are self-supporting—they exist only if there are externally generated funds to support them. And, indeed, centers come and go, depending on their success in generating external funds. There are both advantages and disadvantages to this method of funding. On the positive side, centers are given substantial autonomy, and the need to secure funds is a practical incentive for being productive and staying at the cutting edge of science. On the negative side, centers are always short of funds—especially for infrastructure and research activities that cannot be charged against grants (e.g., pilot studies, career development investments). Also, the constant demand to generate grants is wearing and is sometimes at odds with some of the basic tenets of excellent scholarship.

Developing a program of research on religion and health

I have spent my academic life based in the Center for the Study of Aging and Human Development (henceforth, Aging Center), which is one of Duke's largest and most distinguished research centers. My faculty appointment has always been in a department, but the Aging Center has been my real academic home, and I have directed its social and behavior programs for the past 15 years. Without the Aging Center, it is unlikely that our program and, later, the Center for the Study of Religion, Spirituality, and Health would have been possible.

Until 1986, when Harold Koenig entered our Geriatric Fellowship Program, no one at the Aging Center had performed systematic research on religion and health. Koenig came to us with an inextinguishable commitment to studying the relationship between religion and health. His interest in this topic reflected his observations, as a family practice physician, of the large, unrecognized extent to which patients relied on religion for comfort, as well as the role of religion in his own life. His intensity and the time he devoted to this topic were extraordinary.

The first era of Koenig's research consisted of using a variety of datasets archived at the Aging Center to investigate the links between religion and health to the extent possible. The pickings were pretty slim because we had never studied religion and health. But we did have more than 100 datasets available, and he scoured them for items on religion. He even recoded a set of 100 interviews from a qualitative study I had done of stress and coping. Study participants often talked about religion, but that was not what I had focused on, so Koenig had to start from scratch. The result of this era was approximately a half dozen publications on the links between religion and health. Because none of the datasets had been designed to investigate this topic, the results were less compelling than those that were to come.

During the three years of Koenig's fellowship training, he developed a set of collegial relationships that later became the core faculty for the Center for the Study of Religion, Spirituality, and Health. I served as Koenig's research mentor during his fellowship. He sought out Dan Blazer, a prominent geriatric psychiatrist and epidemiologist, who was open to Koenig's interests. Harvey Cohen, a distinguished oncologist and director of both the Aging Center and the Geriatric Fellowship Program was impressed with Koenig's energy and productivity and began to groom him for an academic home at Duke. Keith Meador, a psychiatrist and masters-level theologian, shared research interests with Koenig. Importantly, among his network members were three well-respected senior faculty members with administrative roles and, hence, the ability to open doors and make resources available to him.

The second and primary era of Koenig's research began once he'd joined the faculty. It differed from the first era in many ways other than his academic status. First, during the first era, Koenig primarily pursued independent research; the second era was and is truly collaborative. There was now a small cadre of us who had become committed to exploring the links between religion and health.

Second, and most important, we no longer were content to try to "salvage" data from previous studies. We'd accomplished about all that one could by that method, and that work was ultimately unsatisfying. We were tired of using other people's inadequate measures of religious participation (and often health outcomes as well). As a result, we became frankly opportunistic and looked for every possibility to incorporate measures of religion into other major studies. Indeed, this might be called the "piggyback era," as our primary strategy was to piggyback our measures of religion and the possible mechanisms by which it affects health into as many studies as possible. This strategy proved to be immensely valuable. The five most valuable studies in which this strategy was applied are described in Table 12.1. Note that none of these studies had an explicit focus on religion and health. Indeed, for most of them, there was no mention of religious variables in the grant applications that led to funding. After funding, however, batteries of religious variables were added to the interview schedules.

The above projects have been the major data sources for our research on religion and health. We have published more than 60 papers on the links between religion and health from them. The total cost of the five studies exceeds $20 million. By piggybacking measures of religion onto these large-scale, carefully crafted studies of health in late life, we have been able to do an impressive amount of research in the absence of any funding for that purpose.

From program to center

In the transition from informal program to formal center, we profited from the resurgence of interest in the links between religion and health in the broader scientific community. Of particular importance, I think, were the establishment of two scientific panels to assess the state-of-the-science with regard to religion and health. Duke faculty were intimately involved in both panels. The first was a panel convened by the National Institute for Healthcare Research, under contract to the Templeton Foundation, to evaluate the state of evidence regarding the effects of religion on physical health, mental health, substance abuse, and neurological processes. The panel also assessed opportunities and constraints in this research field and recommended high-priority topics for future research. Forty scientists participated in the panel; three of them were from Duke: Harold Koenig, Harvey Cohen, and me. The panel had multiple meetings and worked diligently for a year and a half, with their efforts culminating in a major report (Larson, Swyers, and

Table 12.1. Projects to Which Religious Variables Were Added

Project Title	Funding	Purpose	Sampling Frame Source	Sample Size
Epidemiologic Catchment Area Study	NIMH	Estimate incidence and prevalence of psychiatric disorders; identify social risk factors	Adults age 18 and older living in 5 North Carolina counties	3800
Depression among Medically Ill Older Veterans	VA	Study relationship between physical health and depression	Adults age 65 and older inpatients in VA hospital	341
Center for the Study of Depression in Late Life	NIMH	Study the course and outcome of major depression among the elderly	Adults age 60 and older diagnosed with major depression	1100
Established Populations for Epidemiologic Studies of the Elderly	NIA	Identify social and biological risk factors for morbidity and mortality	Adults age 65 and older living in 5 North Carolina counties	4162
Elderly Research Career Development Award	NIMH	Study the course and outcome of major depression among medically ill older adults	Adults age 65 and older who are inpatients on the medical wards of Duke Hospital	660

NIA, National Institute on Aging; NIMH, National Institutes of Mental Health; VA, Veterans Administration

McCullough, 1997). For our program, I view this panel as especially important because it brought Harvey Cohen into our work at a much higher and more enthusiastic level than previously. Indeed, after his participation on the panel, Cohen began the process of turning our informal collaborative group into an official center—and I doubt we could have done that without his sponsorship.

The second panel was a much smaller group of eight social and behavioral scientists who established a workgroup with the missions to evaluate measures of religious participation in all relevant dimensions, identify those measures most useful for research on health, and develop a battery of measures that would be recommended to investigators studying religion and health. This workgroup was jointly sponsored by the National Institute on Aging and the Fetzer Foundation. I was a member of that group. We also worked for a year and a half to accomplish our goals. The primary product resulting from our work is a major report that reviews what is known about measuring religion in ways appropriate for studying health and both long and short batteries of recommended instruments (Fetzer Institute/NIA Working Group, 1999). In addition, however, we persuaded the Fetzer Foundation to pay for adding a religion module to the 1998 General Social Survey. As a result, we have, for the first time, normative data on the religion battery we recommended for a representative sample of American adults.

Our participation in these panels helped our collaborative group at Duke to gain new visibility and convinced other scientists and administrators at Duke that we were pursuing research that was esteemed externally, in "high places." This visibility played a vital role in our ability to become a center.

Although our center was technically in place before it received major funding, the single event that coalesced our efforts was a grant obtained from the John Templeton Foundation in 1998. We were awarded a four-year, $1 million grant to develop the infrastructure necessary for a successful Center for the Study of Religion, Spirituality, and Health. This funding was a vital resource in becoming a fully-functioning center. No research was directly supported by the Templeton grant. The funds were used exclusively for infrastructure and for expenses needed to attract scientists internal and external to Duke to the study of religion and health.

Very importantly, with this funding, we began to write grant applications that focused specifically on the links between religion and health. Our hit rate for these applications is certainly not 100%, but we have been successful, particularly with private foundations. We have responded to grant proposal solicitations from the Templeton Foundation and the Fetzer Foundation for specific research projects and have obtained funding from both. More recently, the Vitas Foundation has funded center investigators to train parish nurses in integrating spiritual issues with palliative care for terminally ill adults and to do research on the implications of religious and spiritual issues for the provision of palliative care.

Thus, at this time, we are a young center but a real one. The development of this center is a prime illustration of what sociologists call an interaction between individuals and their environments. This center would not exist were it not for Duke's encouragement and successful history of interdisciplinary research. There were a myriad of potential institutional obstacles that we were able to avoid simply because they have been handled routinely for years. On the other hand, the center also would not exist were it not for the commitment—both to the topic of religion and health and to investigating it with the contributions of multiple disciplines—of the core investigators who now comprise the center.

The pleasures and problems of our interdisciplinary center

In my experience, the pleasures of interdisciplinary research far outweigh any problems it poses or obstacles it faces. But of course, I've never lived any other way, so I may not be in the best position to evaluate such issues. I think it takes a specific mind-set to appreciate and, in fact, thrive on interdisciplinary research. First, one must believe that other disciplines can make important contributions to the research topic. I, for one, cannot imagine that sociology could explain anything in its entirety. Still, I also don't believe that there are many phenomena that aren't affected to a significant degree by social factors. A common characteristic of my interdisciplinary colleagues is the conviction that the perspectives from multiple disciplines are needed to even begin to understand complex realities. Second, it's helpful if one likes to be challenged and forced to "sell" the potential contributions of his or her discipline. I get great pleasure from demonstrating to scientists from other disciplines that sociology matters. Some of my fondest professional memories are of studies in which social factors proved to be more important predictors of clinical outcomes than treatment, diagnosis, or any of the other things clinicians felt would be most important. Third, it takes incredible patience to participate effectively in interdisciplinary research. I've sat through at least 100 lectures on the biological components of our interdisciplinary aging research—lectures in which I was lost after the first sentence. But they sit through my lectures on the "soft, squishy stuff"—and besides, it's nice once in a while to have a molecular or cellular kind of guy stare at you open-mouthed when you remind him of the gender differences in the age-gradient of monoclonal gammopathies.

There have been no internal intellectual or interpersonal problems at our center. We work well together, and our biggest problem is freeing up sufficient time to do all that we would like. I've witnessed no concerns about getting appropriate credit for one's contributions or a desire to "hoard" one's ideas. We give each other ideas all the time, realizing that there are a hundred great studies waiting to be done. We respect each other's disciplines, and we respect each other as distinguished, hard-working members of those disciplines.

We have faced one issue in this collaborative work that I haven't confronted in my interdisciplinary work on aging or psychiatric illness: our topic is controversial. I substantially underestimated the extent to which much of the scientific community "knows"—in the absence of research and despite some high-quality research—that there is not and cannot be a meaningful link between religion and health. Another small group "knows" that religion is bad for health. David Larson has gathered impressive data on the "career problems" of investigators who have attempted to focus a large part of their research on the scientific study of the effects of religion. Indeed, he refers to such research as an "anti-tenure factor."

The topic of religion and health has posed no internal problems at Duke University. But we have had some negative experiences in broader scientific circles. Our research has been published in top tier journals in psychiatry, internal medicine, sociology, and aging—and the reviews we received from those journals were appropriate. We have had very different experience with journals like *Journal of the American Medical Association and the New England Journal of Medicine*. We have had multiple papers that were positively reviewed and recommended for publication by reviewers but rejected by the journal editors because of "lack of interest in the topic among journal readership."

We are highly concerned about the possibility of federal funding as well. Because of our piggybacking strategy, we have had limited experience with review of grant applications focused explicitly on religion and health at federal agencies. It is my impression that the institutes of the National Institutes of Health are highly variable in their openness to research linking religion and health. Of even more concern is the openness of their study sections to research on this topic. Of special concern is the extent to which research on religion and health is viewed as a variant of behavioral medicine or alternative medicine. This research is a different beast; its closest analog is social and epidemiologic research—and, indeed, it is facing the same obstacles (e.g., being too "soft," the problems with accounting for selection effects) that social support faced two decades ago.

Overall, we believe that our center is doing well. We are excited about our research and its contributions to our understanding of health. We like what we do and are confident that we will be able to sustain a productive and rigorous body of research. Most important for our purposes here, we cannot imagine embarking on this research program without the contributions of multiple disciplines and genuine interdisciplinary collaboration.

Future Directions

There are a number of directions that we intend to pursue in future research. My highest priority is continuing to search for the mechanisms by which religion exerts its salubrious effects on health. The "obvious suspects" of health behaviors and social support and integration cannot account for these relationships. Pilot work is under way to develop methods of assessing the worldviews associated with religion. In later research, we will examine these as possible mediators of the relationship between religion and health.

We recently had a grant from the Fetzer Foundation to develop a measure of religious history. This measure will be used in future research to determine the extent to which various trajectories of religious participation are differentially related to late life health. Judith C. Hays and I are the primary investigators on this topic.

Koenig was recently awarded a new grant from the National Institute of Mental Health to examine long-term patterns of joint physical and mental illness and factors associated with the favorable treatment outcomes. He is collecting data about religious participation, and those data will permit him to examine the relationships between religious involvement and long-term patterns of illness course and outcome.

A joint endeavor of the Duke University Divinity and Medical Schools generated $13.5 million from private foundations to establish a new Duke Institute on Care at the End of Life. Keith Meador of our center will be directing the research and educational programs of that Institute. Members of our center met with foundation officers in support of this institute, and joint research projects are in the planning stages.

Beyond these specifics, we have broad interests in studying the ways that religion may buffer the effects of stress, the biology and neuroscience of religious involvement (e.g., brain imaging studies of prayer/meditation), and using religious content to make behavioral, social, and clinical interventions more culturally congruent for specific groups of health care consumers.

Conclusions and Implications

Faculty affiliated with the Center for the Study of Religion, Spirituality, and Health are happy scientists. We are able to do the research that we want in an environment in which our research focus, which is considered controversial and nonviable at many institutions, is welcomed. Moreover, we work in an environment that appreciates and fosters interdisciplinary research.

This is not to say that our work is easy. Interdisciplinary research of any kind remains a small component of the nation's research portfolio. It is, I believe, still harder to obtain support for interdisciplinary research, given the organization of funding agencies, than for conventional discipline-based research. In addition, the most prestigious academic journals remain largely discipline-based, restricting the number and stature of publication outlets. When the interdisciplinary research topic is relatively new, less developed than mainstream topics, and controversial—as is the case for research on religion and health—all of these barriers are magnified. Given this, the commitment of the research investigators and the openness of their work environments are essential to a successful research program.

Postscript

During the few years since this original chapter was written, the religion and health field has changed relatively little in focus, although the volume of research evidence continues to grow. As is true of the chapter as a whole, I am referring here to naturalistic studies of the links between religion and health. Efforts to identify the mechanisms by which religion exerts its salubrious effects on health continue, but investigators have not yet been successful. The long-standing hypotheses that health behaviors, social support, and psychological resources (e.g., mastery) can explain the health benefits of religious participation are clearly incorrect. At this point, the biggest obstacle to progress in identifying the mechanisms that link religious participation to health is a lack of new theories.

Progress is being made, however, on other fronts. Although these advances are less dramatic than earlier research establishing the strong effects of religion on health, they provide a more fine-grained, nuanced understanding of the conditions under which various forms of religious participation affect health. I will briefly describe five themes that characterize much of the recent work in the field; our Center has contributed to each of them. My final comments will be a brief update about the status of our Center.

Increased emphasis on recovery from illness

Most naturalistic research on religion and health is based on community samples and focuses on the *preventive* or *protective effects* of religious involvement on a variety of health outcomes. This research has, without question, made important contributions to our understanding of the links between religion and health. A different question, however, is whether religious participation promotes recovery from illness—what might be called the *therapeutic role* of religion. Answering this question requires large samples of physically or mentally ill respondents who are followed over time. In other words, clinical rather than community-based samples are needed.

Although some of the early work on the links between religion and health was based on clinical samples in which the health outcome was illness course or recovery or both (e.g., Koenig, George, and Peterson, 1998; Oxman, Freeman, and Manheimer, 1995), the volume of research on clinical samples suffering from a variety of physical conditions has increased greatly in the last few years. Based on a large sample of older adults with physical illnesses requiring hospitalization at baseline, our research indicates that religious participation at baseline predicts improvements in physical health and depressive symptoms with a wide range of potential confounding variables statistically controlled (Koenig, George, and Titus, 2004; Pargament, Koenig, Tarakeshwar, and Hahn, 2004). A variety of specific types of religious participation are associated with better illness course and outcome over 21–24 months, although religious attendance is the strongest predictor—as is consistently observed in studies of the protective effects of religious involvement. There is one dimension of religious involvement, however, that is associated with poorer illness course: frequent use of religious media (i.e., television and radio) (Koenig, George, and Titus, 2004)—a pattern that we also observed in a study of the protective effects of religious participation in a community-based sample (Hays, Landerman, Blazer, Koenig, Carroll, and Musick, 1998).

Expanding the range of health outcomes

In previous research, the major outcomes examined were morality, disability, physical illness, and mental illness, especially depression. As described above, religion is associated with all of these outcomes to varying degrees. Some of our recent research has focused on other health outcomes. To our knowledge, we are the only investigators to investigate them. Based on a sample of older adults suffering a variety of physical illnesses, Koenig and colleagues investigated the effects of religious involvement on acute care hospitalization and nursing home utilization over a 21-month follow-up interval (Koenig, George, Titus, and Meador, 2004). Religious participation was unrelated to hospitalization, but was a significant, albeit a modest predictor of nursing home utilization (both the occurrence of institutionalization and days spent in a nursing home).

Harrison and colleagues examined the effects of religious participation on reports of pain among a clinical sample of African Americans suffering from sickle dell disease (Harrison, Edwards, Koenig, Bosworth, Decastro, and Wood, 2005). Controlling for age, gender, and disease severity, religious attendance was associated with lower levels of self-reported pain. In contrast, private religious practices (i.e., prayer and reading sacred texts) and intrinsic religious motivation were unrelated to pain. Unfortunately, this is a cross-sectional study; thus temporal order of service attendance and self-reported pain is unclear. The results suggest, however, that the relationship between religious involvement and pain is worthy of further investigation.

Differential effects for demographic subgroups

A question that received attention in the past, but is of increasing prominence in the field is whether the effects of religious involvement differ for population subgroups. The comfort hypothesis—one of the oldest in the field—posits that religion is most important to and beneficial for marginal subgroups including women, racial and ethnic minorities, and the economically deprived (Glock, Ringer, and Babbie, 1967). Research evidence is accumulating rapidly that the effects of religious participation on health are stronger for women than for men and for African Americans than for whites. Unfortunately, methodologically sound analyses comparing whites to racial and ethnic minorities other than African Americans are lacking.

Demographic differences in the importance of religion for health have characterized the field throughout its history. In earlier studies, however, gender and racial differences were generally reported in an off-hand manner and many studies did not test for possible race or gender interactions. Over the past several years, however, explicit attention to subgroup differences in the relationships between religion and health has become the rule rather than the exception. A strength of the data that we collected from both community-based and clinical samples is the large proportion of African Americans (e.g., 37% of Durham County residents are African American), facilitating black–white comparisons. And our research continues to support the conclusion that the effects of religion on health are stronger for women and African Americans than for their counterparts. For example, Koenig, George, Titus, and Meador (2004) found that for the total sample, religious involvement had a significant but modest effect on nursing home utilization. More fine-grained analyses revealed, however, that religion had strong protective effects against institutionalization for women and African Americans, but was not significant for men and for whites.

Increasing use of spirituality measures

A complex issue that resists resolution and consensus is appropriate conceptual and operational definitions of spirituality. Despite a lack on consensus, recent research is much more likely to include measures of spirituality, along with measures of religious participation, than in the past. Two measures of spirituality are used most often. First, many studies now include a question assessing the extent to which respondents describe themselves as spiritual. This approach is based on the assumption that we, as scientists, may not be able to define spirituality, but people have implicit definitions of spirituality and know the extent to which they "fit" those definitions. Second, many investigators are now using the Daily Spiritual Experiences Scale (Underwood and Teresi, 2002). This scale yields a simple count of the frequency with which respondents perform spiritual practices on a daily basis. Scale items range from specific behaviors (e.g., taking time to enjoy the beauty of nature) to cognitions (e.g., feeling a sense of gratitude).

Results across studies that investigate the effects of spirituality on health are inconsistent. This is especially true in studies that incorporate measures of both spirituality and religious involvement. That is, in the absence of religious measures, spirituality is typically a significant predictor of health. When religious measures are included in the analysis along with spirituality, however, results are inconsistent across studies. Our recent research exhibits this pattern of results. The study of the effects of religious participation on nursing home utilization, described above, also included a measure of self-rated spirituality (Koenig, George, Titus, and Meador, 2004). Spirituality was significantly related to nursing home use at the bivariate level, but was rendered nonsignificant when religious attendance was added to the model. In our study of recovery among physically ill older adults, however, self-rated spirituality, intrinsic religious motivation, and service attendance were all significant predictors of depression symptoms, physical illness severity, disability, and self-rated health. As usual, however, the effects of religious attendance were stronger than those for intrinsic religiosity and spirituality. Finally, in a study based on Canadian data from more than 70,000 respondents, religious attendance was associated with fewer depressive symptoms (Baetz, Griffin, Bowen, Koenig, and Marcoux, 2004). In contrast, self-rated spirituality was not significantly related to depressive symptoms in bivariate or multivariate analyses. Thus, the relative strength of relationships between spirituality and health vary across samples and as a function of the other variables in the models tested. It seems, however, that these analyses beg the most interesting question regarding the effects of spirituality on health: In the absence of religious involvement, does spirituality convey health benefits comparable to those of religion?

Do multiple forms of religious participation make a difference?

To date, a major focus of research that examines multiple dimensions of religious involvement has been to estimate the relative strength of those dimensions as predictors of health outcomes. As noted above, evidence has consistently indicated that religious attendance is a more powerful predictor of health than of private religious practices, intrinsic religious motivation, and other forms of religious or spiritual involvement. An implicit assumption in many studies examining multiple forms of religious experience has been that because religious attendance is the most powerful predictor of health, it may not be useful or important to include other religious variables in future analyses. I contend that this would be a premature decision.

To fully understand the full range of possible effects of various forms of religious participation on health, the potential interactive effects of religious variables need to be investigated. An interaction hypothesis would posit that the effects of multiple forms of religious involvement are multiplicative rather than additive. I am aware of only one study that has explored the interactive effects of religious participation. Parker and colleagues examined the direct and interactive effects of religious attendance, private religious practices, and intrinsic religious motivation on depressive symptoms and a global measure of mental health (Parker, Lee, Klemmack, Koenig, Baker, and Allman, 2003). Results in the direct effects model were similar to those in other studies: religious attendance was the strongest predictor of both outcomes. Private religious practices and intrinsic motivation were not significant predictors of depression and mental health when religious attendance was in the model. Interactive effects among the religious variables were substantial, however. Three-way interactions among the religious variables were significant predictors of both outcomes. Thus, depressive symptoms and a broader set of psychiatric symptoms were lowest among respondents who attended services regularly, pursued private religious practices, and reported intrinsic motivation for their religious involvement. These results clearly merit replication in other samples and with other health outcomes. Nonetheless, evidence to date suggests that participation in multiple forms of religious involvement reinforce each other to yield health benefits.

Our center: A brief update

The most obvious change in our Center is its name. We are now the Center for the Study of Spirituality, Theology, and Health; our previous name was the Center for Religion, Spirituality, and Health. For the most part, the name change is only cosmetic; our basic research agenda remains the same: to understand the links between religion/spirituality and health—and to do so with naturalistic studies of people in their social, cultural, and religious contexts.

Two factors are responsible for the name change—one external and one internal. The external factor was, as might be expected, the preferences of our funding agencies. Most of our research has been funded by the National Institutes of Health, but we have relied on grants from private foundations for infrastructure support. Those foundations are much more comfortable—as apparently are their boards of directors—with the term spirituality than with the term religion. The internal factor involved in the name change was our increasing integration with the Theology and Medicine program that is sponsored jointly by our medical and divinity schools. Our colleagues in the divinity school believe that theology is more specific to their interests and activities than is religion. It also was pointed out that including theology in the title makes it clear that our center has not abandoned the study of the effects of religion on health.

Analysis of large data sets remains the single largest activity of our center, but we are branching out from our own community-based epidemiologic surveys to a variety of other data sources. We have collected extensive longitudinal data from two clinical populations: older adults diagnosed with major depressive disorder and older adults who are hospitalized at baseline because of medical (rather than psychiatric) conditions. As described above, a large proportion of our studies now focus on illness course and outcome. We also are increasingly collaborating with investigators from other universities who bring their own data sets to the analytic table.

Individually, the primary investigators affiliated with our Center also have expanded the scope of their activities. Harold Koenig is now very involved in translating what is known about the links between religion and health in ways that can affect medical care. I am involved in a research project in which we are studying approximately 20 congregations in North Carolina and South Carolina. The purpose of this project, directed by Keith Meador, is to determine the extent to which congregational factors ranging from the demographic mix and size of the congregation to its health-related and other programs affect the health of church members. Because religious attendance has such a powerful effect on health outcomes, we believe the time is ripe for better understanding what it is about public religious participation that promotes health.

In summary, both the field of religion and health and our Center remain active and productive. We remain committed to interdisciplinary efforts to understand the links between religion and health. We are pleased with the payoff to date and look forward to continuing to contribute to this vital field.

RECOMMENDED READINGS

Benson, H. (1996). *Timeless Healing.* New York: Scribner.

George, L. K., Larson, D. B., Koenig, H. G., and McCullough, M. E. (2000). Spirituality and health: What we know, what we need to know. *Journal of Social and Clinical Psychology, 19,* 102–116.

Koenig, H. G. (1997). *Is Religion Good for Your Health? Effects of Religion on Mental and Physical Health.* New York: Haworth Press.

Koenig, H. G., McCullough, M. E., and Larson, D. B. (2000). *Religion and Health: A Century of Research Reviewed.* New York: Oxford University Press.

Levin, J. (2001). *God, Faith, and Health.* New York: John Wiley & Sons.

Pargament, K. I. (1997). *The Psychology of Religion and Coping: Theory, Research, and Practice.* New York: Guilford.

REFERENCES

Antonovsky, A. (1980). *Stress, Health, and Coping.* San Francisco: Jossey-Bass.

Asser, S. M., and Swan, R. (1998). Child fatalities from religion-motivated medical neglect. *Pediatrics, 101,* 625–629.

Baetz, M. Griffin, R., Bowen, R. Koenig, H. G., and Marcoux, E. (2004). The association between spiritual and religious involvement and depressive symptoms in a Canadian population. *Journal of Nervous and Mental Disease, 192,* 818–822.

Benson, H. (1996). *Timeless Healing.* New York: Scribner.

Bjarnason, T. (1998). Parents, religion, and perceived social coherence: A Durkheimian framework of adolescent anomie. *Journal for the Scientific Study of Religion, 37,* 742– 734.

Braam, A. W., Beekman, A. T. F., Knipscheer, C. P. M., Deeg, J. H., van den Eeden, P., and van Tilburg, W. (1998). Religious denomination and depression in older Dutch citizens: Patterns and models. *Journal of Aging and Health, 4,* 483–503.

Brown, D. R., Gary, L. E., Greene, A. D., and Milburn, N. G. (1992). Patterns of social affiliation as predictors of depressive symptoms among urban blacks. *Journal of Health and Social Behavior, 33,* 242–266.

Bryant, S., and Rakowski, W. (1992). Predictors of mortality among elderly African-Americans. *Research on Aging, 14,* 50–67.

Byrd, R. B. (1988). Positive therapeutic effects of intercessory prayer in a coronary care unit. *Southern Medical Journal, 81,* 826–829.

Commerford, M., and Reznikoff, M. (1996). Relationship of religion and perceived social support to self-esteem and depression in nursing home residents. *Journal of Psychology, 130,* 35–50.

Durkheim, E. (1897/1951). *Suicide: A Study in Sociology.* J. A. Spaulding and G. Simpson, translators. New York: Free Press.

Durkheim, E. (1915). *The Elementary Forms of Religious Life.* New York: Free Press.

Ellison, C. G. (1995). Race, religious involvement, and depressive symptomatology in a southeastern U.S. community. *Social Science and Medicine, 40,* 1561–1572.

Fetzer Institute/National Institute of Aging Working Group (1999). *Multidimensional Measurement of Religiousness/Spirituality for Use in Health Research,* rev. ed. Kalamazoo, MI: John E. Fetzer Institute.

Freud, S. (1927/1961). *The Future of an Illusion.* New York: Norton.

Gardner, J. W., Sanborn, J. S., and Slattery, M. L. (1995). Behavioral factors explaining the low risk for cervical carcinoma in Utah Mormon women. *Epidemiology, 6,* 187–189.

George, L. K. (2001). The social psychology of health. In R. H. Binstock and L. K. George (Eds.), *Handbook of Aging and the Social Sciences,* 5th ed. (pp. 217–237). San Diego: Academic Press.

Glock, C. Y., Ringer, B. B., and Babbie, E. R. (1967). *To Comfort and to Challenge.* Berkeley: University of California Press.

Goldman, N., Korenman, S., and Weinstein, R. (1995). Marital status and health among the elderly. *Social Science and Medicine, 40,* 1717–1730.

Gorsuch, R. L. (1995). Religious aspects of substance abuse and recovery. *Journal of Social Issues, 5,* 65–83.

Harris, W. W., Gowda, M., Kolb, J. W., Strychacz, C. P., Vacek, J. L., Jones, P. G., Forker, A., O'Keefe, J. H., and McCallister, B. D. (1999). A randomized, controlled trial of the effects of remote, intercessory prayer on outcomes in patients admitted to the coronary care unit. *Archives of Internal Medicine, 159,* 2273–2278.

Harrison, M. O., Edwards, C. L., Koenig, H. G., Bosworth, H. B., Decastro, L., and Wood, M. (2005). Religiosity/spirituality and pain in patients with sickle cell disease. *Journal of Nervous and Mental Disease, 193,* 250–257.

Hays, J. C., Landerman, L. R., Blazer, D. G., Koenig, H. G., Carroll, J. W., and Musick, M. (1998). Aging, health, and the "electronic church." *Journal of Aging and Health, 10,* 458–482.

Helm, H., Hays, J. C., Flint, E., Koenig, H. G., and Blazer, D. G. (2001). Effects of private religious activity on mortality of elderly disabled men and nondisabled adults. *Journal of Gerontology: Medical Sciences, 55A,* M400–M405.

House, J. S., Robbins, C., and Metzner, H. L. (1982). The association of social relationships and activities with mortality: Prospective evidence from the Tecumseh Community Health Study. *American Journal of Epidemiology, 116,* 123–140.

Hummer, R. A., Rogers, R. G., Nam, C. B., and Ellison, C. G. (1999). Religious involvement and U.S. adult mortality. *Demography, 36,* 273–285.

Idler, E. L. (1987). Religious involvement and the health of the elderly: Some hypotheses and an initial test. *Social Forces, 66,* 226–238.

Idler, E. L., and Kasl, S. V. (1992). Religion, disability, depression, and the timing of death. *American Journal of Sociology, 97,* 1052–1079.

Idler, E. L., and Kasl, S. V. (1997a). Religion among disabled and nondisabled persons: I. Cross-sectional patterns in health practices, social activities, and well-being. *Journal of Gerontology: Social Sciences, 52B,* S294–S305.

Idler, E. L., and Kasl, S. V. (1997b). Religion among disabled and nondisabled persons: II. Attendance at religious services as a predictor of the course of disability. *Journal of Gerontology: Social Sciences, 52B,* S306–S316.

Jung, C. J. (1955). *Modern Man in Search of a Soul.* New York: Harcourt, Brace, Jovanovich.

Kark, J. D., Carmel, S., Sinnreich, R., Goldberger, N., and Friedlander, Y. (1996). Psychosocial factors among members of religious and secular kibbutzim. *Israeli Journal of Medical Science, 32,* 185–194.

Koenig, H. G. (1993). Trends in geriatric psychiatry of relevance to pastoral counselors. *Journal of Religion and Health, 32,* 131–151.

Koenig, H. G., and Weaver, A. J. (1997). *Counseling Troubled Older Adults: A Handbook for Pastors and Religious Caregivers.* Nashville, TN: Abingdon Press (Academic Books).

Koenig, H. G., and Weaver, A. J. (1998). *Pastoral Care of Older Adults.* Minneapolis, MN: Augsburg-Fortress.

Koenig, H. G., Cohen, H. J., Blazer, D. G., Kudler, H. S., Krishnan, K. R. R., and Sibert, T. E. (1995). Cognitive symptoms of depression and religious coping in elderly medical patients. *Psychosomatics, 36,* 369–375.

Koenig, H. G., Cohen, H. J., Blazer, D. G., Pieper, C., Meador, K. G., Shelp, F., Goli, V., and DiPasquale, R. (1992). Religious coping and depression in elderly hospitalized medically ill men. *American Journal of Psychiatry, 149,* 1693–1700.

Koenig, H. G., Cohen, H. J., George, L. K., Hays, J. C., Larson, D. B., and Blazer, D. G. (1997). Attendance at religious services, interleukin-6, and other biological indicators of immune function in older adults. *International Journal of Psychiatry in Medicine, 27,* 233–250.

Koenig, H. G., Ford, S., George, L. K., Blazer, D. G., and Meador, K. G. (1993). Religion and anxiety disorder: An examination and comparison of associations in young, middle-aged, and elderly adults. *Journal of Anxiety Disorders, 7,* 321–342.

Koenig, H. G., George, L. K., Blazer, D. G., Pritchett, J., and Meador, K. G. (1993). The relationship between religion and anxiety in a sample of community-dwelling older adults. *Journal of Geriatric Psychiatry, 26,* 65–93.

Koenig, H. G., George, L. K., Cohen, H. J., Hays, J. C., Blazer, D. G., and Larson, D. B. (1998). The relationship between religious activities and blood pressure in older adults. *International Journal of Psychiatry in Medicine, 28,* 189–213.

Koenig, H. G., George, L. K., Meador, K. G., Blazer, D. G., and Ford, S. M. (1994). The relationship between religion and alcoholism in a sample of community-dwelling adults. *Hospital and Community Psychiatry, 45,* 225–231.

Koenig, H. G., George, L. K., and Peterson, B. L. (1998). Religiosity and remission from depression in medically ill older patients. *American Journal of Psychiatry, 155,* 536–542.

Koenig, H. G., George, L. K., and Titus, P. (2004). Religion, spirituality, and health in medically ill hospitalized older patients. *Journal of the American Geriatrics Society, 52,* 554–562.

Koenig, H. G., George, L. K., Titus, P., and Meador, K. G. (2004). Religion, spirituality, and acute care hospitalization and long-term care use by older patients. *Archives of Internal Medicine, 164,* 1579–1585.

Koenig, H. G., Hays, J. C., George, L. K., and Blazer, D. G. (1997). Modeling the cross-sectional relationships between religion, physical health, social support, an depressive symptoms. *American Journal of Geriatric Psychiatry, 5,* 131–143.

Koenig, H. G., Hays, J. C., Larson, D. B., George, L. K., Cohen, H. J., McCullough, M. E., Meador, K. G., and Blazer, D. G. (1999). Does religious attendance prolong survival? A six-year follow-up study of 3,968 older adults. *Journal of Gerontology: Medical Sciences, 54A,* M370–M376.

Koenig, H. G., Hover, M., Bearon, L. B. and Travis, J. L. (1991). Religious perspectives of doctors, nurses, patients and families: Som interesting differences. *Journal of Pastoral Care, 45,* 254–267.

Koenig, H. G., Larson, D. B., Hays, J. C., McCullough, M. E., George, L. K., Branch, P. S., Meador, K. G., and Kuchibhatla, M. (1998). Religion and survival of 1010 male veterans hospitalized with medical illness. *Journal of Religion and Health, 37,* 15–29.

Koenig, H. G., Pargament, K. I., and Nielsen, J. (1998). Religious coping and health outcomes in medically ill hospitalized older adults. *Journal of Nervous and Mental Disorders, 186,* 513–521.

Krause, N. (1992). Stress, religiosity, and psychological well-being among older blacks. *Journal of Aging and Health, 4,* 412–439.

Krause, N. (2001). Social support. In R. H. Binstock and L. K. George (Eds.), *Handbook of Aging and the Social Sciences,* 5th ed. (pp, 273–294). San Diego: Academic Press.

Larson, D. B., Swyers, J. P., and McCullough, M. E. (1997). *Scientific Research on Spirituality and Health: A Consensus Report.* Rockville, MD: National Center for Healthcare Research.

Levin, J. S. (1994). Religion and health: Is there an association, is it valid, and is it causal? *Social Science and Medicine, 38,* 1475–1482.

Marwick, C. (1995). Should physicians prescribe prayer for health? Spiritual aspects of well-being considered. *JAMA, 273,* 1561–1562.

Matthews, D. A. (1997). Religion and spirituality in primary care. *Mind/Body Medicine, 2,* 9–19.

Meador, K. G., Koenig, H. G., Turnbull, J., Blazer, D. G., George, L. K., and Hughes, D. C. (1992). Religious affiliation and major depression. *Hospital and Community Psychiatry, 43,* 1204–1208.

Mirowsky, J., and Ross, C. (1989). *Social Causes of Psychological Distress.* New York: Aldine de Gruyter.

Musick, M., Blazer, D. G., and Hays, J. C. (2000). Religious activity, alcohol use, and depression in a sample of elderly Baptists. *Research on Aging, 22,* 91–116.

Musick, M., Koenig, H. G., Hays, J. C., and Cohen, J. C. (1998). Religious activity and depression among community-dwelling elderly persons with cancer: The moderating effect of race. *Journal of Gerontology: Social Sciences, 53B,* S218–S227.

Oman, D., and Reed, D. (1998). Religion and mortality among the community-dwelling elderly. *American Journal of Public Health, 88,* 1469–1475.

Oxman, T. E., Freeman, D. H., and Manheimer, E. D. (1995). Lack of social participation or religious strength and comfort as risk factors for death after cardiac surgery in the elderly. *Psychosomatic Medicine, 57,* 5–15.

Pargament, K. I. (1997). *The Psychology of Religion and Coping.* New York: Guilford Press.

Pargament, K. I., Koenig, H. G., Tarakeshwar, N., and Hahn, J. (2001). Religious struggle as a predictor of mortality among medically ill elderly patients: A two-year longitudinal study. *Archives of Internal Medicine, 161,* 1881–1885.Pargament, K. I., Koenig, H. G., Tarakeshwar, N., and Hahn, J. (2004). Religious coping methods as predictors of psychological, physical, and spiritual outcomes among medically ill elderly patients: A two-year longitudinal study. *Journal of Health Psychology, 9,* 713–730.

Parker, M., Lee, R. L., Klemmack, D. L., Koenig, H. G., Baker, P., and Allman, R. M. (2003). Religiosity and mental health in southern, community-dwelling older adults. *Aging and Mental Health, 7,* 390–397.

Phillips, R. L. (1975). Role of lifestyle and dietary habits in risk of cancer among Seventh Day Adventists. *Cancer Research, 35,* 3513–3522.

Phillips, R. L., Kuzma, J. W., Benson, W. L., and Lotz, T. (1980). Influence of selection versus lifestyle on risk of fatal cancer and cardiovascular disease among Seventh Day Adventists. *American Journal of Epidemiology, 112,* 296–314.

Propst, L. R., Ostrom, R., Watkins, P., Dean, T., and Mashburn, D. (1992). Comparative efficacy of religious and non-religious cognitive-behavioral therapy for the treatment of clinical depression in religious individuals. *Journal of Consulting and Clinical Psychology, 60,* 94–103.

Rogers, R. G. (1996). The effects of family composition, health, and social support linkages on mortality. *Journal of Health and Social Behavior, 37,* 326–338.

Sherkat, D. E., and Reed, M. D. (1992). The effects of religion and social support on self-esteem and depression among the suddenly bereaved. *Social Indicators Research, 26,* 259–275.

Simpson, W. F. (1989). Comparative longevity in a college cohort of Christian Scientists. *JAMA, 262,* 1657–1658.

Strawbridge, W. J., Cohen, R. D., Shema, S. J., and Kaplan, G. A. (1997). Frequent attendance at religious services and mortality over 28 years. *American Journal of Public
Health, 87,* 957–961.

Steffen, P. R., Hinderliter, A. L., Blumenthal, J. A., and Sherwood, A. (2001). Religious
coping, ethnicity, and ambulatory blood pressure. *Psychosomatic Medicine, 63,*
523–530.

Turner, R. J., and Turner, J.,B. (1999). Social integration and social support. In C. S.
Aneshensel and J. C. Phelan (Eds.), *Handbook of the Sociology of Mental Health* (pp.
301–320). New York: Kluwer Academic/Plenum Publishers.

Underwood, L. and Teresi, J. (2002). The Daily Spiritual Experiences Scale: Development,
theoretical description, reliability, exploratory factor analysis, and preliminary construct validity using health-related data. Kalamazoo, MI: The Fetzer Institute.

Valliant, G. E. (1983). *The Natural History of Alcoholism: Causes, Patterns, and Paths to
Recovery.* Cambridge, MA: Harvard University Press.

Weaver, A. J., Koenig, H. G., and Larson, D. B. (1997). Marriage and family therapists and
the clergy: A need for clinical collaboration, training, and research. *Journal of Marital
and Family Therapy, 23,* 13–25.

IN SEARCH OF METHUSELAH

*Population Perspectives on Health
and Longevity*

Domain Introduction

LINDA WAITE

Some people live long and healthy lives, some short lives marked by illness and disease. Some *groups* of people lead longer, healthier lives than other *groups*. The processes leading to good health and long lives—or poor health and short lives—are partly biological but are also social, cultural, economic, and psychological. Those with more resources tend to be healthier than those with few; the rich, the highly educated, and those with high social status suffer from fewer diseases and medical conditions than do the poor, those with little education, and those facing discrimination.

At the same time, the *biology* of human life creates the conditions under which the *social* affects health and longevity. The biodemography of aging examines the consequences for human (and other) populations of the biological foundations of disease and death generally. We can understand senescence in individuals by using the same biological logic that also can explain and predict the pattern of mortality in populations. In brief, we age because our bodies cannot completely and perfectly repair the damage done by the constant barrage of small injuries that we sustain in the course of living. This makes it important for populations to continually replace old and damaged members with new ones, through the birth of the latter and the death of the former. At the same time, genetic mutation produces changes in genes, most of which are harmful. Genes that reduce the chances that their bearer will reproduce successfully have tended to be eliminated from the population, although the same genes would remain if they increased mortality *after* reproduction, especially if they conferred some early advantage. Senescence is the consequence of the accumulation of such genes with harmful effects that appear relatively late in life (Kirkwood, 1977; Medawar, 1952).

So, all living things are programmed by natural selection to age and die, but only after they have successfully reproduced. In most settings for most organisms, mortality is so high that very few individuals live much past the age of reproduction, and genes with deleterious effects late in life have little opportunity to be expressed. But as with the case for humans in most of the world today, when survival past the end of the reproductive period becomes common, so will senescence and senescent-related diseases and disorders (Hamilton, 1966). Population aging is the result of our ability to alter the forces of natural selection that have been operating for thousands of years to allow a substantial majority of people to live well past the age of reproduction. In fact, Robert Fogel and his colleagues have argued that advances in nutrition and public health have led to fundamental nongenetic chances in human physiology, a process that he calls *technophysio evolution* (Fogel and Costa, 1997). So, in a world with low mortality from violence, malnutrition, and disease, how long can people live? And how long can cohorts of people live? Countries from Italy to Sweden to China understand the social and economic implications of this question, as they plan for a rapid aging of their populations over the next 50 years. The theoretical and analytic tools and evidence of the biodemography of aging are being brought to bear on this fundamental problem.

Our interest in the consequences for health and the longevity of social, cultural, economic, and psychological resources is part and parcel of our interest in how long human beings can live under ideal—or even typical—modern circumstances. Contemporary societies differ dramatically in the amount of social and economic inequality among people, with explicit government policies often focused on the distribution of resources. We have come to understand that it is difficult and perhaps impossible to provide people with equal chances of a long and healthy life if they differ dramatically in their access to education, income, and social standing (Department of Health, 1999).

Although the outlines of socioeconomic differentials in health and mortality have been apparent for decades, their details have been less clear, and the mechanisms by which they are produced have remained obscure. Clearly, health and long life are universal goals, which those with more resources are better able to attain. In countries with little public health care, those with higher income can purchase more and better medical care. In poor countries, those with resources more often have safe and nutritious food and water. But even in countries such as the U.K., that have a high material standard of living, with excellent public health and nutrition, and a national health care system, those with more resources tend to live longer, healthier lives (Black, Morris, Smith, Townsend, and Whitehead, 1999). Why is this the case?

Part of the explanation lies in health behaviors, like smoking and exercise; those with more education (Ross and Wu, 1995), more income, and higher social standing tend to engage in healthier behaviors than those with less. This, of course, raises the question of why these differentials in health behaviors exist. In addition, certain diseases such as coronary heart disease tend to become progressively more common as one descends the social hierarchy (Marmot et al., 1991), although the reasons for this gradient are not clear. The environment in which one lives tends to be more salubrious for those with more resources; both illness and mortality are generally higher in poor neighborhoods than in others (Rogers, Hummer, and Nam, 2000). And differences in stress for those at various positions in the social hierarchy have been suggested as one pathway to social differentials in health and longevity (Preston and Taubman, 1994). But the biological mechanisms through which these social factors either inhibit or encourage disease and death remain more speculative than demonstrated. Exploration of the ways that the social "gets under the skin" represents the next frontier in our understanding of the link between biology, medicine, and the social world.

This domain presents the intellectual histories of two research programs that merged approaches, perspectives, theories, and data from the biological, medical, and social sciences to address fundamental—and fundamentally cross-disciplinary—questions. In Chapter 14, Michael Marmot, a physician, asks why in a group of men who are all well educated and well paid, those with higher status live longer, on average, than those below them on the totem pole. How do social resources affect biological functioning, illness, and length of life? In Chapter 15, demographer Jay Olshansky and biologist Bruce Carnes ask, Why do we age (and why are we not immortal)? How do we age? What are the biological mechanisms that cause all living things to age and, ultimately and unavoidably, to die? Why do different species age and die along characteristic, distinctive trajectories? Why do human populations differ in their pattern of mortality? And is there a biological limit to life?

Both of these intellectual histories point to the merging of questions, theories, and approaches from natural and social sciences as an *essential* step in the process of scientific advancement. Both point to a fundamental *melding* across disciplines, rather than a simple joint venture. And both describe major advances in our thinking about the nature of health and longevity.

Postscript

Since the publication of the original introduction to this section much has changed. We have made significant progress in understanding the links between social, behavioral, psychological, and physiological factors in producing health. And we have seen organizational and intellectual changes that make interdisciplinary research both more productive and easier to carry out.

First, as Michael Marmot points out, recent research has clearly pointed to key ways that social standing affects health. As one example of a very specific mechanism in this process, education seems to affect the efficacy with which people with disease use medications and other interventions to manage both symptoms and disease progression (Goldman and Smith, 2002). But education seems to have more wider and more general effects, changing the way that people gather and evaluate information, changing their sense of control over the circumstances of their lives and thus their ability and willingness to take actions to maintain and improve their health, changing their access to work that is fulfilling and creative, and potentiating and amplifying other health-improving attitudes and behaviors (Ross and Mirowsky, 2003). Fulfilling and creative work, and the sense of control that comes with autonomy at work, seem to affect health through physiological processes. Steptoe et al. (2003) found differences by socioeconomic status in the blood pressure and cortisol of employed men and women, which they conclude may reflect stress-related activation of biological pathways that contribute to variations in disease risk.

We also know more about the links between wealth and health now than we did when the first volume of this book was published; Smith (2005) finds that new serious health events have a substantial negative effect on work, income, and wealth. Wealth has little impact on future health events, however, although higher education *does* reduce chances of future negative health events.

Second, as Olshansky, Carnes, and Marmot point out in their postscripts, the organizations that evaluate and fund the scientific enterprise have become more supportive of efforts that involve researchers and research infrastructure from quite disparate fields. Olshansky and Carnes point to the "Roadmap" initiative of the National Institutes of Health, conceived of and supported at the level of the Office of the Director of NIH and itself an interdisciplinary effort. The efforts of NIH to recognize multiple principal investigators on a single grant also makes it easier to put together large interdisciplinary teams, each with its own leader, to work on a complex problem. Of course, researchers still have to face the challenges of publishing research that crosses disciplinary boundaries. This is especially the case for junior scholars whose primary appointment is located in an academic department; their promotion may depend heavily on publications read by others in the same department and little on publications outside their field. But these recent changes give reason for optimism.

REFERENCES

Black, D., Morris, J. N., Smith, C., Townsend, P., and Whitehead, M. (1999). *Inequalities in Health: The Black Report; The Health Divide.* London: Penguin Group.

Department of Health (1999). *Saving Lives: Our Healthier Nation.* London: Stationery Office.

Fogel, Robert W., and Costa, Dora L. (1997). A theory of technophysio evolution, with some implications for forecasting population, health care costs, and pension costs (in economic consequences of aging for populations and individuals). *Demography, 34*(1), 49–66.

Goldman, D. P., and Smith, J. P. (2003). Can patient self-management help explain the SES health gradient? *Proceedings of the National Academy of Sciences, 99*: 10929–10934.

Hamilton, W. D. (1966). The moulding of senescence by natural selection. *Journal of Theoretical Biology, 12*, 12–45.

Kirkwood, T. B. L. (1977). Evolution of aging. *Nature, 270*, 301–304.

Marmot, M. G., Davey Smith, G., Stansfeld, S. A., Patel, C., North, F., Head, J., White, I., Brunner, E., and Feeney, A. (1991). Health inequalities among British civil servants: The Whitehall II study. *Lancet, 337*, 1387–1393.

Medawar, P. B. (1952). *An Unsolved Problem of Biology.* London: Lewis.

Preston, S., and Taubman, P. (1994). Socioeconomic differentials in adult mortality and health status. In L. Martin and S. Preston (Eds.), *Demography of Aging* (pp. 279–318). Washington, DC: National Academy Press.

Rogers, R. G., Hummer, R. A., and Nam, C. B. (2000). *Living and Dying in the USA: Behavioral, Health, and Social Differentials of Adult Mortality.* San Diego: Academic Press.

Ross, C., and Mirowsky, J. (2003). *Education, Social Status and Health.* New York: Aldine De Gruyter.

Ross, C. E., and Wu, C. (1995). The links between education and health. *American Sociological Review, 60,* 719–745.

Smith, J. P. (2005). Unraveling the SES-health connection. In L. Waite (Ed.), *Aging, Health, and Public Policy: Demographic and Economic Perspectives.* Supplement to *Population and Development Review* vol. 30, pp. 108–132. New York: Population Council.

Steptoe, A., Kunz-Ebrecht, S., Owen, N., Feldman, P. J., Willemsen, G., Kirschbaum, C., and Marmot, M. (2003). Socioeconomic status and stress-related biological responses over the working day. *Psychosomatic Medicine, 65,* 461–470.

14

Social Resources and Health

MICHAEL MARMOT

Research on the social, economic, cultural, and psychological determinants of health and the biological pathways by which they operate has to be interdisciplinary. This chapter explores a history of how one such research program was initiated, developed, and carried out. It dealt with the inevitable resistance to interdisciplinary research by, initially, breaking it up into small nonthreatening chunks and only later attempting to prove that the whole was greater than the sum of parts. A particular problem was that the research was addressing social inequalities in health. When the political climate was unfavorable, such research was seen to be, at best, irrelevant and, at worst, threatening. When the political climate in Britain changed, yesterday's pure academic research became today's applied science.

From Research to Policy in Only Two Decades

In 1999 the British Government published its White Paper on Health Strategy for England: *Saving Lives: Our Healthier Nation* (Department of Health, 1999). Figure 6.6 from the chapter on coronary heart disease and stroke in that report is reproduced here as Figure 14.1. It shows the social gradient in coronary heart disease mortality from the first Whitehall study of British civil servants. It is worth quoting in full a section of paragraph 6.20 from the heart disease chapter of the White Paper:

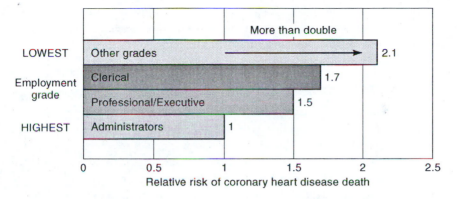

Figure 14.1. Unequal risk of heart disease death at different employment levels in the public sector, even after allowing for risk factors. Controlling for age, smoking, systolic blood pressure, plasma cholesterol, height, and blood sugar. Adapted from Marmot, Shipley, and Rose (1984).

> Tackling underlying social, economic and environmental conditions is vital. Those factors operate independently as well as through the specific lifestyle factors. So health inequality can be reduced only by giving more people better education; creating employment so that people can achieve greater prosperity; building social capital by increasing social cohesion and reducing social stress by regenerating neighbourhoods and communities; and tackling those aspects of the workplace which are damaging to health. (Pp. 81–82)

This chapter recounts some of the story of how, in the end, the findings from the two Whitehall studies found their way into a government policy document. It shows how interdisciplinary research developed around the Whitehall findings. Results from these and a number of other studies in North America and Europe informed an Independent Inquiry into Inequalities in Health and hence a government policy document. In one sense, then, this long tear-stained trail of interdisciplinary research has a happy ending. The happiest ending, of course, would be not that it influenced a government policy statement but that it reduced inequalities in health. But journeys have several steps.

Lest this sound too triumphalist, a British version of *Mr Smith Goes to Washington* except that "Washington" here is a fantasyland of enlightened and reasoned discussion, let me reassure the reader that the nature of the health debate in Britain is recognizably "normal." Scientists and the media are dazzled by the glittering successes of molecular biology and the Human Genome project; the public is daily regaled with problems of health service funding and delivery. The social determinants of health are not mainstream for either the research councils and charities or for the press. If the feeling of being an embattled outsider is a necessary stimulus for creative work, then I am pleased to say that this gift of marginality has been available in abundance. Nevertheless, starting from a straightforward epidemiological study of risk factors and cardiovascular disease (Whitehall), we have built a program of interdisciplinary research, the results of which have found their way into policy discussions.

In a book on interdisciplinary research, perhaps a word is required as to the relevance of beginning this chapter with the link with policy. First, as a physician-scientist, the aim of my work is not only rising to the scientific challenge of understanding but also making things better. As a public health physician making things better implies not treating individual patients but social action to improve health and prevent disease. This leads to the second point of relevance of policy for a book on interdisciplinary research. Just as understanding the social determinants of health requires going beyond biomedical research into understanding of economic, social, and psychological processes, so improving health of the public requires action beyond the health sector. I belong to that naïve school of thought that believes that intersectoral action on the wider determinants of health should be informed by interdisciplinary research on the determinants of health.

Of course, social action to change anything, including health, will excite political argument and prejudice, maneuvering and special interests. I make no special claim to understanding the intricacies of political action, nor has that been part of our interdisciplinary collaboration. I will, however, comment briefly on some of the political reaction to research on the social determinants of health.

From Psychosocial Factors to Social Determinants

As a physician schooled in the biological basis of disease who then became centrally concerned with the social determinants of health, I do, at times, have the sensation of passing social scientists going in the other direction. The cognitive psychologist Steven Pinker in the introduction to his excellent book *The Language Instinct* praises Noam Chomsky, in whose tradition he follows, for challenging the social science model that gives prominence to the surrounding culture in shaping the human psyche. In the case of language, Pinker's argument is that we have underestimated the fundamental contribution of the biological determinants of language and, hence, its genetic underpinning. Evolutionary psychology argues that we have underestimated the role of biological evolution in shaping human behavior. From a different perspective, behavioral geneticists emphasize the genetic underpinnings of individual differences in psychological attributes and, indeed, the contribution these attributes may make to shaping the environment.

No one who has been through a traditional medical school education, as I have in Sydney, Australia, has difficulty in recognizing the saliency of the genetic determinants of human physiology and its responses to the environment. What is less obvious is how to recognize the importance of the environment in causing human disease.

One of the clearest demonstrations of the influence of environment, in the general sense of nurture rather than nature, is the experience of migrants. When people migrate, their pattern of disease initially reflects that of the country from which they came and, subsequently, over time, comes to resemble that of the country of destination. My own introduction to this came at the University of California, Berkeley. Using specially tabulated mortality statistics, it was shown that among men of Japanese ancestry in Japan, Hawaii, and California, there were opposing trends across the Pacific. Stroke mortality, high in Japan, was lower in Hawaii and lower still in California. Coronary heart disease (CHD) mortality rates, low in Japan, showed a clear trend the other way: increasing from Japan to Hawaii and then California, and higher still among white Americans (Marmot and Syme, 1976).

Whatever differences in genetic endowment there may be between men of Japanese ancestry and white Americans, they cannot account for the low rates of CHD in Japan compared to the United States; this is because when Japanese migrate, their CHD rates move toward those of the host country. Nor can one have simple recourse to gene-environment interactions as an explanation. The findings on serum cholesterol illustrate this point. Serum cholesterol is a major risk factor for CHD, and the relation is continuous: the higher the level, the higher the risk. Mean serum cholesterol level is higher among Japanese in California than among Japanese in Japan. Detailed observation shows that it is not simply that there are more hypercholesterolemics in California than in Japan, but the whole distribution of serum cholesterol is shifted to the right.

This distinction is important. If the higher average cholesterol levels among the California Japanese were the result of a greater prevalence of individuals with risky levels of serum cholesterol, one could account for this as the changed environment bringing out a genetic predisposition to high levels of cholesterol. Given that the whole distribution moves to the right, it suggests that there is a changed environment that affects everyone.

One obvious candidate for this changed environment is increased dietary intake of saturated fat. Predictably, increased intake of saturated fat would be related to a shift to the right in the distribution of serum cholesterol level. That, in turn, would be related to increased rate of CHD. Clearly important, this did not seem to be the whole story. At equivalent levels of serum cholesterol, the California Japanese had a higher rate of CHD than the Japanese in Hawaii.

My supervisor in Berkeley was Leonard Syme, a sociologist turned epidemiologist. He said that one reason that he, a sociologist interested in health, moved from sociology to epidemiology was that he wanted to have at least one variable that could be measured precisely—"hard" health outcomes. The hypothesis that we pursued in the Japanese migrant study was that culture was important in influencing disease risk, but it did not only act through an influence on diet or smoking. The thesis was that as men acculturated to the Western way of life, they lost the protection provided by the cohesive nature of traditional Japanese society. The underlying notion was a stress hypothesis. We did not call it that as the word "stress" provoked too many antibodies in skeptical scientists, let alone intense disagreements among true believers. Rather, the task was to operationalize and measure the relevant psychosocial factors. We did indeed have evidence to support the thesis (Marmot and Syme, 1976).

This work, product of a collaboration between a physician epidemiologist, Marmot, and a sociologist epidemiologist, Syme, was perhaps not interdisciplinary in that we were both doing epidemiology, but it did bring different bodies of knowledge to bear on the problem. In particular, it was part of a relatively small corpus of work, at that time, bringing psychosocial factors into epidemiology. There is, of course, a long tradition of psychosomatic medicine that has had as an aim breaking down mind-body dualism. In my experience, it has had little impression on the mainstream of medical research. As a distinguished senior colleague put it to me: I am a gardener, I watch the trees and other plants get diseases; psychological factors cannot be important. It is true that when ecologists speak of a species decreasing 10-fold in numbers, one thinks of environmental toxins, nutrition, climate change, and predators before thinking of psychosocial factors. But when a population of nonhuman primates, in the wild or in captivity, show a social gradient in markers of cardiovascular disease, psychosocial factors become plausibly important. Similarly, among civil servants who are not exposed to toxins that could double their mortality rate and are adequately nourished—and if they have predators to deal with, they are symbolic—psychosocial factors are more plausible.

Plausibility, however, is not the only issue. Ability to deal with the scientific skepticism may turn on measurement and on the relation of psychosocial factors to relevant biological pathways. In the Japanese case, we put some considerable effort into the measures of acculturation that turned out to be related to CHD (Marmot and Syme, 1976).

Syme got me, a physician, to read Durkheim. Syme used to pose the question of why when the individuals change, the disease rate is still a function of the society. Social class differences in smoking persist, even though the individuals studied are different. Culture and the social environment seemed important in the explanation of changing disease rates among Japanese migrants and their offspring, but we put little effort into examining socioeconomic status in the Japanese.

I can remember reading only four articles on socioeconomic status and cardiovascular disease during my years at Berkeley, from 1971 to 1976. One was by John Cassel, who at the time of publication of the results from the Evans County cardiovascular disease study was commenting on the changing social distribution of coronary heart disease (Cassel, 1971). I probably did not pay as much attention to this as I should, because the second, a review from the mid-1960s by Smith (1965), was confusing; it appeared to detect no consistent pattern. The third, by Antonovsky (1967), did show a changing pattern. Syme and Berkman (1976) reviewed literature that suggested there was a relation between social class and a number of different causes of morbidity and mortality. At the time, I remember seeing this as a contribution to the Syme/Cassel thesis of general susceptibility rather than specific illness as being the appropriate focus of study. I did not read it as having import for the social distribution of disease.

From Good Housekeeping to Social Determinants: The Whitehall Studies

I then moved from Berkeley to take up a junior faculty post in epidemiology at the London School of Hygiene and Tropical Medicine. This was the home of careful epidemiology. Donald Reid had developed measurement instruments for chronic bronchitis and Geoffrey Rose for cardiovascular disease, and Rose and Blackburn had written the standard text on cardiovascular survey methods. Reid and Rose had set up the Whitehall study of British civil servants to be a British Framingham. The first Whitehall study was a cohort (longitudinal) study of 18,000 men working in the British Civil Service who had a medical examination in the late 1960s and were then followed until death. Reid and Rose saw it as a carefully conducted screening study of standard risk factors for cardiovascular and respiratory disease, with a mortality follow-up. Reid and Rose's papers from Whitehall at that time had related to the value of screening, as well as smoking and other risk factors, for CHD mortality and the predictive value of the Rose questionnaire for cardiovascular disease and ECG abnormalities.

Reid and Rose had both had some background in psychiatry in the Royal Air Force and were open to the idea of social and psychological factors being important in disease causation, but this was not their research interest. Rose was looking at data from the five-year mortality follow-up of the Whitehall study. As good housekeeping, he had looked at mortality rates by employment grade. There was an awareness within epidemiology that social class should be controlled for in analyses as it could be a confounder. He suggested that as I had an interest in the social side of health, I might want to look at these data. The data showed an inverse association between grade of employment and CHD mortality (Marmot, Rose, Shipley, and Hamilton, 1978) and mortality from other diseases (Marmot, Shipley, and Rose, 1984): the lower the grade, the higher the mortality rates.

I should emphasize that when I began to explore the analyses on the relation to mortality rates of employment grade as an indicator of socioeconomic position, I did not have a prior theory about social inequalities and health. Quite the contrary. Work at Berkeley and elsewhere had suggested a stress hypothesis as a contributory cause of coronary heart disease (CHD). The Type A behavior findings had a great deal of currency at that time. It appeared to describe the hard-driving businessman, impatient and pressed for time. It accorded with conventional wisdom, which had it that men in high-status occupations were under more stress and, hence, had higher risk of CHD. To discover that this was not the case in Whitehall prompted the thought that civil servants were atypical. Hence, we made a comparison with national data.

National data showed evidence that the social class distribution of heart disease mortality had changed (Marmot, Adelstein, Robinson, and Rose, 1978). Between 1951 and 1971 in England and Wales, rates had gone from being higher in social classes I and II to being higher in classes IV and V. (Between 1971 and 1991, the gap continued to widen to the disadvantage of those lower down; Drever and Whitehead, 1997.) Whitehall data were therefore typical of the situation in the country as a whole, except that the gradient in Whitehall was steeper.

There were three other striking findings from Whitehall, the first two of which gave rise to the next two decades of research. The third would not appeal to research councils. First, mortality rates followed a social gradient. It is an inadequate description to say that mortality rates were high in the deprived and low in the nondeprived. Among civil servants, a group of men in stable office-based employment, the higher the social position, the lower the mortality rate across the whole social range. I was at first tempted to describe this, with reference to pharmacology, as a dose-response relation. This implies that position in the hierarchy entails a corresponding "dose" of something good or bad. It may not. Position in the hierarchy may relate not to a dose but to relative position. It is not immediately obvious that it is helpful to think of relative dominance or submissiveness in terms of dose.

The research endeavor since has related to understanding not only how material deprivation affects health, but also how position in the social hierarchy in those who are not deprived in the usual sense, affects health.

To understand the second important finding, remember that Whitehall was set up as a risk factor study. At the time, and still in much of epidemiology, the approach was to identify individual risk factors for chronic disease. Whitehall included smoking, blood pressure level, plasma total cholesterol, body mass index, physical activity, and plasma glucose level after a standard glucose load. Either singly or in combination, however, these risk factors could account for no more than one-third of the social gradient in CHD mortality. Some doubt this statement, assuming that if we allowed for measurement imprecision, we could explain the gradient. To express it differently therefore: there was only a shallow social gradient in blood pressure and body mass index; the gradient went the other way for plasma total cholesterol; and we saw a similar mortality gradient by grade of employment in never smokers to that seen in smokers.

The research endeavor has therefore asked two types of question: What are the reasons for the social gradient in established risk factors such as smoking? And what else could be responsible for the gradient?

The third finding was that the gradient applied to all the major causes of death. This is not a popular finding with medical researchers. A notion of general susceptibility tends to attract the opprobrium, "lack of focus," which relates to the difficulties of getting interdisciplinary work funded. It is easy to see why coronary heart disease can be studied. There are theories as to its pathogenesis, risk factors that can be studied, biochemical and physiological measures to explore, candidate genes that can be investigated. But general susceptibility? "A chimera" was the description I was given. Not a suitable topic for medical research. It remains an interesting challenge—out with our grant applications.

A Research Program on the Social Determinants of Health

The Whitehall findings of an inverse social gradient in mortality, and those from related studies, have generated a number of trenchant criticisms over the years. In part, the interdisciplinary research program that we have undertaken has been in response to these criticisms raised by ourselves and others. Two comments are relevant. First, in science, one thing leads to another. We showed, in Whitehall, that there was a social gradient in a range of diseases. This led to two types of endeavors: negative and positive. The negative was to show that it could not be explained away as artifact or in terms of conventional understanding. The positive was to pursue hypotheses to show that the explanation for the gradient may indeed lie where we believed. This leads to the second comment: in order to pursue the hypothesis that relative deprivation was important and, hence, psychosocial hypotheses played a crucial role, we needed to go beyond conventional risk-factor epidemiology. We did not set out to do interdisciplinary research. It was a consequence of the one-thing-leads-to-another research program. We needed to go beyond our medical discipline because by itself it was inadequate to the research task.

Criticisms of the findings of the social gradient in health

As mentioned, Whitehall and related findings demonstrating the social gradient in mortality rates, have sparked off a number of criticisms that have recurred over the years. They may be summarized:

- Surely there must be some mistake in the way these figures are calculated for there to be such a general finding of lower status, higher disease rate.
- It was widely believed that people in high-status occupations had higher risk of coronary heart disease because of the stress of work. This implies that our findings of higher rates as one descends the social ladder must be wrong, or civil servants are atypical, or the stress hypothesis is wrong.
- Could the findings not more plausibly be accounted for by "health selection"? In other words, is it not likely that people with worse health will end up lower in the social hierarchy, and that the findings therefore represent the effect of health on social and economic fortunes, not the social determinants of health?
- A variant of this argument is that there may be some biological "fitness," the possession of which leads people to become of high status and of good health. Conversely, its lack leads to lower status and worse health. There is not therefore a causal link from social status to health

status. The apparent association is the result of some common third variable causing both. Might the differences between social classes not be genetic? Particularly in Britain with its rigid class structure and presumed lack of social mobility, could there not have been segregation of genetic endowment among social classes? (This has resonance with the genes–IQ debate.)

- Suppose the findings are not artifactual or the result of health selection, is not the social gradient in health simply the result of worse medical care the lower someone is in the social hierarchy?
- Even if the findings are real and not due to medical care, is the social gradient not because health education has been less successful for people lower in the social hierarchy? People lower down do not look after themselves properly—hence, they smoke, eat too many fish and chips and pastries, and are slothful and overweight.
- So, the poor have worse health. The poor are always with us and will always have worse health. Attempting to do something about this would lead to a fundamental change in society that may well make things worse. Apply the trickle-down theory of economics to the problem of poverty and health. Set the wealth creators free, and everyone in society will benefit as a result.
- Why would a medical researcher want to be drawn into politically sensitive issues about the nature of society? The way to improve health for the whole population is by applying the findings of the new biology. The human genome will be sequenced, and the potential for health improvement will come from improved understanding of the fundamental nature of disease processes and the genetic basis of disease.

The last comments show clearly the link between science and policy—or, more particularly, politics. If it is not to remain simply an academic exercise, research on the social determinants of health quickly enters the realm of policy application. This was illustrated by recent history in Britain. In 1978, Richard Wilkinson, who subsequently became a founding member of the International Centre for Health and Society, wrote an open letter to the British Secretary of State for Health asking him what he was going to do about inequalities in health. A high-level committee was set up under the prestigious chairmanship of Sir Douglas Black, who had held most of the senior posts in medicine in Britain. The committee addressed the question of why, after 30 years of a National Health Service in Britain (founded in 1948), that provided state-funded health care to all free at the point of use, there were growing social inequalities in health (Black, Morris, Smith, Townsend, and Whitehead, 1988). The Black committee reviewed the research then extant and concluded that inequalities in health were not the result of artifact, selection, lifestyle, or lack of access to medical care but were the result of material causes in society.

Our research program's response to critics

Many of the issues dealt with by Black have recurred, both the criticisms and the question of how social position is linked to health and hence what can be done about it. This and related questions of the social determinants of health have been the major focus of our work. In response to the criticisms we have:

- Endorsed the Black committee conclusions that inequalities in health are not primarily the result of artifact, health selection, or medical care
- Shown that differences in health behaviors form part of the explanation, but to the extent that they do, this shifts the question as to why there are social differences in health behaviors
- Confirmed that coronary heart disease is now more common, progressively so, as the social hierarchy is descended (Whitehall II study) (Marmot et al., 1991; Marmot, Bosma, Hemingway, Brunner, and Stansfeld, 1997)
- Produced evidence that this does not negate a stress hypothesis—it entails a new approach to what constitutes stress (Bosma, Peter, Siegrist, and Marmot, 1998)
- Shown that the social inequality in health problem is not confined to worse health among those in poverty, but that it is a social gradient that runs across the whole of society
- Pointed to the fact that the slope of this gradient changes within a society over time and varies across societies, suggesting that it may perhaps be changed by conscious policy—it is an incorrect formulation of the problem to state that the poor are always with us
- Drawn on findings that show that social inequalities in health are as strong in apparently "classless" societies such as the United States as they are in class-ridden Britain; social mobility is considerable in Britain, and the relation between class and health is not fixed
- Set up an attempt to demonstrate the biological pathways that link social and psychological processes to health and disease and, hence, plausibly underlie social inequalities in health (Brunner, Shipley, Blane, Davey Smith, and Marmot, 1999)

This work has required people with a variety of disciplinary backgrounds, skills, and approaches. It has necessitated borrowing from different fields. For much of the time, it has entailed keeping heads low and attracting research grants to work on focused pieces of the puzzle without drawing too much attention to the interdisciplinary nature of the work or its potential implications for society. In fact, more or less every time we stuck our heads above the parapet, and admitted to the interdisciplinary nature of the work, we were met with a fusillade (see the later discussion in this chapter).

As stated in the opening to this chapter, there has been at least the positive experience of our research findings having been taken seriously in recommendations to the government in the UK aimed at reducing inequalities in health (Acheson, 1998).

Developing the Whitehall II Study and Blending Disciplines

It ought to be the case that epidemiologists have little difficulty collaborating with other disciplines. An important part of epidemiology studies the causes of distribution of disease in populations. As these may be multiple in kind and varied in nature, one might imagine that an epidemiologist could not move without, at the least, consulting someone who was an expert in a particular field. This would be likely to be true whether the expert was required to help define an exposure or a biological effect.

Epidemiologists have disparate concerns. At first blush, it may seem odd that people concerned with lowering plasma cholesterol to reduce cardiovascular disease should have much in common with those investigating whether leukemia is associated with exposure to power lines, let alone those concerned with the social, economic, and cultural causes of disease and how they may act through psychological pathways. Yet all these investigators come together under the rubric of epidemiology. It should, of course, be basic to a book on interdisciplinary research to define a discipline. I shall leave that delicate task to others. In practice, epidemiologists behave like members of other disciplines: they have meetings, journals, clubs, associations, presidents, and membership secretaries.

There was not a single point at which I took the conscious decision to go beyond epidemiology. In investigating the Whitehall findings, one thing led to another. There were two crucial decisions. The first was not to treat socioeconomic status (SES) as a confounder for the "real" risk factors: individual behaviors, such as smoking or diet; or physiological markers, such as plasma cholesterol. The second, related to the first, was to treat the social gradient in disease as a manifestation of social forces. The distribution of disease in society told us something about society. Without quite knowing it, this brought us into a sociological tradition of inquiry. In a sense, this meant focusing upstream of disease pathogenesis on the social structures and processes that cause disease.

Complementary to this upstream focus was a need to focus downstream. If the Whitehall findings, described in this chapter, led to the conclusion that conventional risk factors could not account for the social gradient, a plausible model of how social forces were affecting disease required some understanding of how they might be translated into biological processes.

With a mixture of intention and happenstance, in the Whitehall II study we appear to be pursuing three different models of interdisciplinary work:

- People from different disciplines work on the same problem or study in such a way that it is hard to recognize their parent discipline.

- People from different disciplines pursue their disciplinary investigation—each taking their own approach to solving the scientific problem at hand; that is, they may be working on the same general problem, but their study design and methods are recognizably those with which they started out.
- There is a perception of what the scientific problem is that is shared by the different disciplines. They work genuinely together, using whatever method is needed.

These different methods did not start all at once. The first question, nontrivial, was how to set up a new cohort study on the social determinants of health. At the most general level, the question was what aspects of the way people live and work affects their health in ways that are not reflected in standard risk factors. Had I gone to a research council with a request for several million pounds to answer this question by setting up a new cohort study, the answer would have been swift and clinical. The negative response would have been helped by the fact that the Whitehall I work was done with almost no research funding. As with getting a credit card you need debt before people will lend you money, so with research grants you need to have them before people will give them to you.

The solution came through the back door or at least the side entrance. With Chandra Patel, a general practitioner, we had been conducting trials of biofeed-back-aided relaxation in reducing high blood pressure. We were awarded a modest grant to conduct a further study of relaxation using the civil service as the occupational setting. In order to find people with elevated blood pressure and other risk factors to come into a trial, we had to screen. We then obtained small grants, one from the British Medical Research Council and one from the National Heart Lung and Blood Institute, to add questionnaires to the initial screen and to analyze the cross-sectional data. Subsequently, a program grant from the British Heart Foundation supported our investigation of biochemical pathways linking social factors to cardiovascular disease, and a grant from the Health and Safety Executive allowed us to focus on the psychosocial work environment. Whitehall II had now taken off, although the aircraft was in the air before we knew we had the fuel to keep it flying. We had a pretty good sense of where we wished to fly the plane, but not precisely how we were to get there.

The funding strategy continued as it began. In the early phases, we had no core support for Whitehall II. We obtained discreet amounts of funding for specific research questions. The approach to the funders was that, given the existence of Whitehall II already, we could answer a research question at modest cost. In the first 10 years of its existence (it began in 1985), we had approximately 25 research grants to support Whitehall II. I am much in favor of scientists having to justify their existence in order to obtain public money to support their research. The peer review system with all its manifold deficiencies is certainly one way of ensuring intense scrutiny of the work. But being peer reviewed 25 times in 10 years for one study! While this was a huge extra burden, it perhaps had a bright side. Relatively small discreet research grants were safe for the funders. Not only can you not be very interdisciplinary in a grant that employs few people, there isn't much for the funder to lose.

At the beginning, we had to make the case that we would learn something from the cross-sectional findings. Initially, we did not request funds for a cohort study. Reviewing the history, the next piece is wondrous to behold. Our first paper on the cross-sectional findings from Whitehall II, showing the social gradient in morbidity and potential explanations (Marmot et al., 1991) was published six years after the study began. Six years, and our funders stuck with us! Somehow, preliminary analyses of these cross-sectional data were sufficient to convince the funders that they should continue support and fund a second round of clinical examinations.

We have now completed five phases of the longitudinal study. Phases 1, 3, and 5, five years apart, have been clinical examinations. Phases 2 and 4 were postal questionnaires. Our original funders appear to be pleased that their original faith was justified, as they continue to support the study at an enhanced level: a further 25 grants since 1995.

Over the years, the study team consisted of epidemiologists who came from psychiatry, medicine, biochemistry, and statistics, along with statisticians and, more recently, people from psychology, demography, sociology, and neuroendocrinology.

The study was essentially epidemiological. Initially, therefore, whatever our backgrounds, my colleagues and I were doing epidemiology. When we had results to present, we presented them either to cardiology-type meetings or epidemiology/public health meetings. I suppose my tacit assumption was that, because I had read Durkheim, had heard of the big five personality dimensions, and knew what an adrenal gland was, we did not really need to work with other disciplines. I was open to people from other disciplines joining with us, but, in a way, they were expected to become social epidemiologists, psychological epidemiologists, nutritional epidemiologists, biochemical epidemiologists, and so on.

From Blending Disciplines to Interdisciplinary and Cross-Group Research

Beyond the discipline

Gradually, three things happened. First, I found that I personally was less interested in reporting results to my discipline. I was interested in inequalities in health, more than I was in epidemiology or cardiology. If we were trying to make advances scientifically, it was not in epidemiology as a discipline but in the social determinants of health. The audience for such research was decidedly interdisciplinary.

Beyond conventional explanations

Second, we needed the expertise that came from outside our discipline. As long as we were measuring established risk factors, we did not have particular need of biochemists or sociologists. The standard way was to take the risk factor, put it into the study, and analyze it in a multivariate model. That system works, provided that the standard risk factors are the relevant mediators. When we came to the view that we were trying to construct plausible pathways as to how social influences affect biology to affect health, it was clear that conventional understanding would not do.

I must confess to a prejudice here, which developed when I was doing the research on the Japanese and has stayed with me. We know that smoking is bad for health. As a corollary, where rates of smoking vary, it is likely to make a substantial contribution to variations in health. That part we know, and it is a crucial policy issue on which sustained action is needed. That is not the end of the story. Smoking is not all there is to health. Our investigations are aimed at the "other"—those causal pathways that go beyond conventional risk factors. When we find results that do not fit with a conventional risk factor explanation, we look for alternative explanations.

What, then, is the prejudice to which I confess? It is that the nature of society influences disease rates in a way that cannot be summed up by lifestyle or individual risk factors. Prejudice of this sort also goes by the name of research program (following Lakatos). Scientists with a different prejudice assume that the only reason we have not explained the social distribution of disease in the conventional way is that we have not done justice to the conventional risk factors. We have either not accounted for measurement imprecision, regression dilution bias, duration of exposure, time lags, or interactions. Had we done so, there would be nothing left unexplained.

This argument is clearly not going to be settled by arguing about the proportion of variance unexplained. What is needed is a positive demonstration that social forces do have an influence on health risks, independent of conventional individual risk factors. This was our task in the Japanese studies. It is our task in Whitehall II and in our other studies in Central and Eastern Europe.

Formulation of psychosocial hypotheses, the measurement task, and biological understanding all required seeking help from outside our own areas of knowledge and expertise.

Interdisciplinary Research Arrangements and Formation of the International Centre for Health and Society

I moved in 1985 to University College London (UCL) to head a small department of epidemiology and public health, which has been my base for pursuing research

on the social determinants of health. After nine years, with the enthusiastic support of the head of UCL, we brought together our in-house work and existing
networks under the rubric of the International Centre for Health and Society. It
was launched in 1994 as an interdisciplinary center with the following aims:

- To study the extent of variations in health and disease within and
  between societies: methods will be improved to study social, ethnic,
  geographic, and gender inequalities in health, within and between
  countries
- To determine the social, economic, and cultural causes of these differences
- To study the ways these social environmental causes might operate: including behavior and biological effects, throughout the life
  course
- Apply these findings to the development of policy, public and private,
  relevant to health
- Evaluate those policies

Two people were particularly influential in the development of the center: Fraser
Mustard, then president of the Canadian Institute of Advanced Research, and Sir
Derek Roberts, then provost (president) of University College London.

I was aware that in the 1980s in Britain, social inequalities in health was not a
popular subject. Margaret Thatcher, famously, had offered the opinion that there
was no such thing as society—hence, there could be no societal determinants of
health. Social inequalities sounded like socialism and would not be tolerated. To
be more accurate, social inequalities could easily be tolerated. It was the drawing of
attention to them that found disfavor. I tended to frame my research proposals for
Whitehall II in terms of biological mechanisms for social variations between
groups. In our grants there was a lot about fibrinogen, insulin, and lipids, something about psychosocial factors, and very little about inequalities. We emphasized
the detail of what we were actually doing and proposing to do, and did not labor the
social implications of the research. It did not seem politic to remind the Medical
Research Council that we were trying to understand how society generated social
inequalities and how these were translated into inequalities in health. (As I write
this in 2001, I note that things have changed, and the same research is now seen as
fitting in with government priorities.)

Mustard's diagnosis of what we were doing was insightful and simple. In his
view, this emphasis on mechanisms was why we were successful in gaining research
support from established sources. The demonstration of a social gradient in disease
that cut across standard diagnoses was too radical scientifically and socially to
garner support. Too radical scientifically, said Mustard, because it did not fit into
the standard disease-based paradigm of one cause, one disease. Too radically socially because the social gradient suggested that the whole of society was affected by
inequalities, not just those at the bottom. Mustard's view was that establishing an

International Centre for Health and Society would give visibility to the work and help change the framework of understanding.

It is worth dwelling a little further on Mustard's role. He was a distinguished research scientist, who had been a pioneer in the study of clotting processes and cardiovascular disease and the consequent use of platelet-active agents to prevent disease. He was a foundation professor at McMasters Medical School and subsequently the vice-president for health sciences. He had thus seen the system both as a distinguished scientist and as an academic leader. He founded the Canadian Institute of Advanced Research as a way around the rigidities of university research establishments. He "discovered" our Whitehall findings around 1987/1988 and became a great advocate for what we were trying to do. This advocacy took many forms, for nearly all of which I am extremely grateful. One of the most important for us was for him to call on the provost of University College London to tell him how important the people of Canada found our work. History does not record how the provost reacted internally to this unusual (and un-British) approach, but it certainly caught his attention. In a more-or-less direct line, it led to the provost agreeing to set up and support the International Centre for Health and Society.

The International Centre consists of researchers who have a primary affiliation to the department of epidemiology and public health at UCL, and a network of researchers from other institutions: Richard Wilkinson from Sussex, David Blane from Imperial College in London, Chris Power from the Institute of Child Health. The principal research groups represented in the center and department are as follow:

- The Whitehall Study Group: this now includes the work on Central and Eastern Europe (directed by Michael Marmot).
- Medical Research Council National Survey of Health and Development: the 1946 birth cohort (directed by Mike Wadsworth)
- The Psychobiology Research Group (directed by Andrew Steptoe)
- The Imperial Cancer Research Fund Health Behaviour Unit (directed by Jane Wardle)
- Dental Public Health (director, Aubrey Sheiham)
- Eurodiab Research Group, examining the complications of diabetes internationally (directed by John Fuller)
- A newly developing Environmental Health Group (directed by Mark McCarthy)

In addition, we have two joint centers with other institutions, and we are part of three networks:

- Joint Health Surveys Unit, with the National Centre for Social Research (co-directed by Michael Marmot and Roger Jowell)
- Joint Centre for Longitudinal Research, a cooperative arrangement between the Centre for Longitudinal Studies at the Institute of Edu-

cation (directed by John Bynner), the International Centre for Health
and Society at UCL, and the National Centre for Social Research
(directed by Roger Jowell). The Joint Centre has responsibility for the
1958 and 1970 birth cohorts and the new Millennium Birth Cohort.
- European Science Foundation network on social inequalities in health
  (directed by Johannes Siegrist, Hilary Graham, Johann Mackenbach,
  Tores Theorell, and Michael Marmot)
- Macarthur Foundation research networks on successful midlife development (directed by Bert Brim) and socioeconomic status and
  health (directed by Nancy Adler)
- Canadian Institute for Advanced Research Population Health Program
  (directed by Clyde Hertzman)

The general approach of the International Centre for Health and Society is laid out
in Figure 14.2. The disciplines represented in these various groupings include epidemiology (both of the more medical and the more social types), statistics, sociology, social survey methodology, social psychology, psychobiology, psychiatry,
dentistry, economics, biochemistry and nutrition, neuroendocrinology, and educational psychology. The "International" in the center's title refers to the fact that we
are closely linked with networks in Canada, the United States, and Japan and with
coordinated networks of researchers in western, central, and eastern Europe.

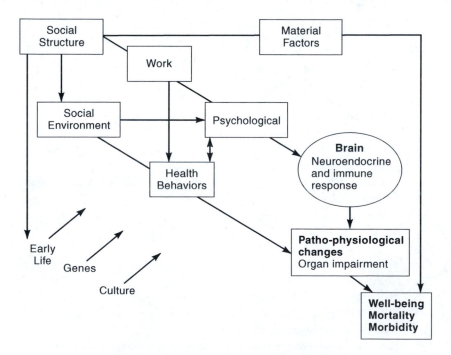

Figure 14.2. Social determinants of health.

Representative Research Findings

The type of research findings that led to setting up the center, and which have been produced by its members, are summarized here. Those of you who wish to skip this section describing our results can move on to the next section, where the interdisciplinary story continues.

Socioeconomic differences in health within and between countries

- Mortality and morbidity rates, in particular from coronary heart disease (CHD) and diabetes, show an inverse social gradient, which cannot be accounted for by known risk factors such as cholesterol level, BP, and smoking. There is a threefold difference in mortality rates in the Whitehall study of British civil servants: higher rates occurring with progressively lower positions in the social hierarchy. The fact that the gradient is present between groups throughout the whole social hierarchy, not simply in the poorer groups, indicates that relative differences in social position are crucial.
- Among rich countries, life expectancy is related not to overall levels of wealth but to income distribution. A more egalitarian distribution of income (e.g., as in Sweden and Japan) is associated with longer life expectancy than is true, for example, in the UK, United States, and Germany, again indicating that relative differences in wealth may be more important than absolute levels.
- A similar association is seen among the states of the United States. Migrant studies show that rates of disease change when people change environment.
- To an important extent, psychosocial factors may underlie the divergence in life expectancy between western Europe and the countries of central and eastern Europe—due to the dramatic rise in mortality from CHD, from accidents and violence, from other alcohol-related deaths, and from tobacco-related cancer.
- In the 1960s Japan had lower life expectancy than the UK. In 25 years, life expectancy in Japan increased by 7.5 years, despite a doubling of fat intake and a prevalence of smoking higher than 60% in men. There is circumstantial evidence that this is related to social, working, and economic conditions in Japan.
- The magnitude of the differences in all cause mortality between ends of the social hierarchy varies over time and in different populations, suggesting environmental causes. CHD mortality shows a shifting socioeconomic distribution. CHD rates among South Asians in Britain have increased more rapidly in nonmanual social classes than in manual. In South Asians, the CHD rate is now higher in higher

socioeconomic groups, like the situation in England and Wales in the 1930s. Gene-environment interactions are likely to be important.

Psychosocial factors and their importance in disease occurrence

- New evidence derived from Whitehall II, and from studies in Sweden and Germany, suggests that psychosocial factors are important determinants of the pattern of occurrence of coronary heart and other diseases in society.
- People in jobs characterized by low control over tasks have increased CHD risk.
- Independent of degree of control of tasks, people whose work is characterized by imbalance between efforts and rewards (much effort, little reward) have increased CHD risk.
- Workers whose degree of support outside work is low have increased disease risk.
- Two categories of mechanism may mediate these effects: psychosocial factors may act via health behaviors—that is, there may be differences in smoking, eating, drinking, and preventive health behavior. More challenging to scientific explanation, psychosocial risk factors such as those mentioned here may act on the cardiovascular system through the neuroendocrine system, for example, the hypothalamic pituitary adrenal axis or sympatho-adrenal medullary pathways.

How exposures from early life affect adult disease risks

- The "Barker hypothesis" has had profound impact on knowledge of times of life at which social environmental exposures can affect incidence of disease in adulthood. For example, Barker and Hales (Barker 1998) have produced convincing evidence that non-insulin-dependent diabetes risk may relate to exposures in utero that affect the beta cells of the pancreatic islets. It is likely that this early exposure needs later circumstances, such as the development of obesity in adulthood, for the diabetes to become clinically manifest.
- For development of mental disorder, Rutter and colleagues (Rutter 1989) demonstrate that it is not a single unfavorable exposure that is important but a pattern of repeated psychosocial events and circumstances throughout the life course.
- Data from the 1946 and 1958 birth cohort studies suggest that cumulation of advantage and disadvantage through the life course may be important for physical disease. Both cohorts show the importance of socially conditioned exposures (Wadsworth, 1997; Power and Hertzman, 1997).

Biological Pathways

If social and psychological factors are important, there must be biological pathways by which they operate. A number of promising lines of investigation are
coming from studies of: neuroendocrinology and its links with immune and cardiovascular function; insulin and lipid metabolism; hemostasis; endothelial dysfunction. Relevant findings are set out in the following sections.

Epidemiological studies

- A social gradient in some markers suggest insulin resistance; these are
  glucose tolerance, plasma insulin, waist to hip ratio, HDL cholesterol,
  and plasma triglycerides. This same set of factors appears to mediate
  the high rates of CHD in South Asians.
- In civil servants in Whitehall II there was an inverse social gradient in fibrinogen. Fibrinogen may be important because of its role
  in hemostasis and thrombosis but also because it is an acute phase
  protein. What mediates the relation between social position and
  fibrinogen?

Animal studies (not done by our group)

- Female rhesus macaques in captivity show a social gradient in waist to
  hip ratio and atherosclerosis: there are higher rates in submissive animals. Male monkeys show a similar social gradient. However, in a time
  of social disruption, dominant males, fighting to maintain their position in the hierarchy and access to females, have adverse responses of
  the cardiovascular system that appear to be mediated by overactivity
  of sympathetic-adrenal medullary pathways.
- Baboons show a similar social hierarchy in HDL cholesterol to that
  observed in civil servants. Low-status baboons have higher basal
  plasma cortisol levels, which correlate inversely with HDL levels,
  pointing to the importance of the hypothalamic-pituitary-adrenal
  axis. Sapolsky (Sapolsky, Romero, and Munck, 2000) posits a stress
  neuroendocrine pathway.
- Seckl has shown that high levels of circulating cortisol in pregnant rats,
  and low levels of inactivation by feto-placental oxidation, relate to
  development of hypertension in the offspring when they mature. This
  suggests that cortisol may mediate the effect of maternal factors on the
  development of hypertension in offspring.
- Postnatal stimulation (handling) of rats stimulates the HPA axis to
  respond successfully to challenges when the animal matures. Postnatal

events, if very stressful, adversely program the HPA axis (Meaney, 1988).

- Spontaneously hypertensive rats, which are genetically predisposed to hypertension, do not develop hypertension if the pups are cross-fostered with Kyoto Wistar rats. This suggests that genetic predisposition and maternal nurturing are necessary for the development of hypertension as they mature (Cierpial and McCarthy, 1987).
- Psychosocial stress in cynomolgus monkeys appears to increase rates of endothelial cell damage and replication, and chronic stress impairs endothelium-dependant (nitric oxide–mediated) vasodilatation. The mechanism is not known, but may include increased sympathetic activity, along with cytokine release. Several cytokines, including interleukin-6, appear to be under regulation of neural and endocrine responses to stress.

Human psychophysiology and clinical studies

- Acute mental stress results in transient increases in platelet aggregation and adhesion, disturbances in lipid metabolism, and alterations in cell-mediated and humoral immunity. This appears to involve several pathways from the brain: sympathetic activation, release of ACTH and cortisol, and modifications of β-endorphin secretion.
- Mental stress constricts coronary arteries of people with endothelial dysfunction and dilates normal vessels.
- Bjorntorp shows psychological attributes are related to central adiposity, and he suggests that it may be mediated by the hypothalamic-pituitary-adrenal axis.
- Glucocorticoids and stress increase free fatty acids, which stimulate hepatic glucose production. The metabolic syndrome of central obesity, lipid disturbances, and hyperglycemia is similar in pattern to Cushing's syndrome.
- Low birth weight is correlated with increased plasma cortisol levels in adulthood.
- Cellular sensitivity to glucocorticoids varies widely and correlates strongly with elevated blood pressure, insulin resistance, and some aspects of hyperlipidemia. The metabolic syndrome may relate not to excess of plasma cortisol but to increased tissue sensitivity or to reactivation of inert corticoids in tissues.

One formulation of how these strands might tie together is that early life events program the HPA axis and may importantly influence sensitivity to later threats. A socially disadvantaged environment may activate this further, thus amplifying neuroendocrine and metabolic risk factors. In addition, there may be genetic influences on sensitivity to HPA stimulation. HPA and sympathetic pathways may influence endothelial function, which, in turn, influences atherosclerosis.

Bringing Interdisciplinary Research into the International Centre for Health and Society

The provost of UCL, Sir Derek Roberts, appreciated what we were doing. As an engineer by background, he felt we were taking a systems approach to health, which was exactly what was needed. He was excited by the mix of the social, psychological, and biological. He supported us handsomely in terms of new posts, new accommodation, and profile within and outside UCL. The provost became chair of our advisory committee, and Fraser Mustard became vice chair. Subsequently, Sir Donald Acheson, former chief medical officer, became chairman of the center.

Our initial assumption was that the center would operate in three ways:

- We would continue to gain grant support for specific studies.
- We would develop support for one or more grand research projects that would involve center members in a collaboration.
- We would gain support for the center as a center.

Assumption one was correct, but not the others. Members of the center were and continue to be successful in gaining research support. They came together not because of lack of success but because the center provided colleagues who were also deeply concerned with research on the relation of health to society. This was more important to them than developing a new grand research proposal. A new grand proposal was not what they were looking for. Each member of the center had gained a reputation for the research that he or she developed and led. Each had an active program of work that they were pursuing and wished to continue. A new grand proposal contained the threat of loss of individuality and personal control over the research, as well as time taken away from what they were doing. The center had to provide something positive for each scientist involved, not ask them to make sacrifices in the service of a greater good. Any perceived loss of identity or freedom of action would weaken the benefit to them of involvement in the center.

This is not to suggest that there was no cooperation. There have been numerous joint activities among members of the center. Joint research papers are published, and members of the center are extremely willing to give of their time and effort in organizing seminars, meetings, newsletters, and books. Such cooperation is particularly valuable when one realizes that the third assumption was wrong. We had assumed that we would raise money as a center. We had hoped that this would provide tangible benefit to members' research activities, provide for new scientific staff, and provide seed money to develop new projects that could attract funding from elsewhere.

The responses we had to approaches for funding for the center were consistent with Mustard's view that while each piece of the center's activities may be attractive to funders, the full range of activities was not. The same organizations that refused to fund us a center, however, funded us for specific projects and programs.

Perhaps I should spell out in a little more detail the problems of pursuing interdisciplinary research. By the usual criteria of attracting research grant support, peer-reviewed publications, books, ratings of research excellence, invitations to international meetings, and so on, individuals within the center have been highly successful. There is even reason to believe that some of our research findings may have had some impact. The center, however, has been singularly unsuccessful in attracting research funds, *qua* center. The failure has been quite indiscriminate: it has failed with the research councils, with the charities and foundations, and with the corporate sector. We had a small grant from one foundation, but the parent company, an old established merchant bank, was brought to financial ruin by a rogue trader on the markets. He was put in prison, and our support dried up.

There may be a reader of this volume who has never had a grant application refused. The likelihood is that such a person is a Nobel laureate (even then it is doubtful—Lord Florey was refused a grant to develop penicillin because the gray heads thought the future lay in synthetic antibiotics), or has never applied. For the rest of us, there is the familiar litany of response to failure, which range from intense feelings of worthlessness, through smug feelings of satisfaction of being ahead of one's time, to anger at the sheer mediocrity of the committee process.

Let us examine the case of the International Centre for Health and Society at UCL. For simplicity, let us divide the reasons for refusal into two: proposers and funders. Take proposers: the grant may be refused because of the low quality of the work of the applicants or their inability to translate an idea into a credible proposal. The applicants, of course, are the least convincing witnesses in this trial. Are there facts in the case of the International Centre for Health and Society to decide between proposers and funders? The department of epidemiology and public health at UCL, which houses the center, consisted of about seven people in 1985. It now consists of 125, the great majority of whom are grant funded. The activity grew by securing sizeable grants and by attracting well-funded research groups to join us. There is, therefore, a prima facie case that we are able to formulate a research proposal, convince funders to support us, and carry out the work. If it's not us, perhaps it's them.

Why then has the center been as spectacularly unsuccessful in raising money as a center as we have been successful in attracting research funds for specific programs? One occurrence could be chance: twice a coincidence, three times a trend. Against our record of fund raising, failures are statistically significantly different from the trend. Fifty grants for Whitehall; none for the center. Chance is unlikely. As described earlier, every time we have stuck our heads above the parapet and admitted that we were doing interdisciplinary research, we were greeted with a fusillade. There were, to be sure, variants of the answer: not enough social science, not enough biology, second-rate immunology, insufficient focus (good word, focus; it sounds as though the committee has happened on a fatal flaw), the proposal is too ambitious (how do you do good science without ambition?). A consistent response appears to relate to turf (or territory, in the old language of the ethnobiologists). An epidemiologist straying into endocrinology or social science has to be doing poor-quality endocrinology or social science. Similarly, a social scientist who is doing applied work with, of all people, doctors, cannot be doing good psychology or economics. Private donors are more likely to give to a hospital that promises to relieve a child's suffering from cancer than to a research center whose aim is to improve society.

This, then, is my interdisciplinary tale. Frame the research in a certain limited way, and publish papers in the *Lancet*, the *British Medical Journal*, and *Social Science and Medicine*, and the research funds flow. Articulate that each specific focused piece of research, along the lines of the five aims listed here earlier, fits into a grander design that has the aim of improving the nature of the society in which we live and work, and the argument is lost.

Developing the Interdisciplinary Activity

I suggested that there were three models of interdisciplinary activity that we had followed. At the start, Whitehall II followed the first: people from different disciplines worked on the same problem or study in such a way that it was hard to recognize their parent discipline. As the activities and individuals associated with the International Centre for Health and Society in the department of epidemiology and public health increased, the other two modes developed: people from different disciplines, working alongside each other, pursue their disciplinary investigation, maintain a shared perception of what the scientific problem is, and work together, using whatever method is needed.

The epidemiologists and statisticians are currently working alongside six other disciplines, each with its own distinctive contribution to understanding the social, economic, cultural, and psychological determinants of health and the biological pathways by which they operate. These are sociology, social psychology, psychobiology, neuroendocrinology, economics, and molecular genetics. Collaboration with each discipline is at different stages, but we are confident that our interdisciplinary research collaboration will enhance and contribute to the knowledge base of the social determinants of health, and that this will eventually lead to a reduction in inequalities in health.

A Conclusion

No. I think not. It is tempting, but too inaccurate, to draw conclusions from our specific experience. There are at least two notes of caution that should be sounded. First, the dominant thrust of medical research continues, perhaps even more so, to be at fundamental biology. It is exciting, dazzling even. After Watson and Crick and the discovery of the double helix structure of DNA, the development of gene cloning and other new techniques, and within one generation the whole human genome has been sequenced. Whether or not those of us involved in the social determinants of health agree, there is a pervasive judgment that this is the way forward to improving population health.

Second, reviewers of grants are likely to continue to look with disdain at research that is not at the cutting edge of their discipline. The fact that by taking research from different disciplines, the research may be at the cutting edge of science will not carry weight with reviewers who will see it as mixing second-rate social science with second-rate biology and not being at the cutting edge of anything.

Let me finish on a more positive note, however. The New Labour Government set up an Independent Inquiry into Inequalities in Health under the chairmanship of Sir Donald Acheson, former government chief medical officer and chairman of our center (Acheson, 1998). Twenty years after the Black committee report was dismissed by the previous government, the inquiry was asked to make recommendations on how inequalities in health could be reduced. Thirteen members of our center contributed to the report (I was a member of the Scientific Advisory Group), and our research is well represented in the 39 recommendations made to the government. The whole thrust of the report was interdisciplinary. It was that the determinants of health lie outside the health service sector, and therefore our recommendations were to the whole of government: environment, transport and the regions, education and employment, the Treasury, the Ministry of Agriculture, Fisheries, and Food, and social security, as well as health.

Whereas two decades earlier the Black report had been buried by Mrs. Thatcher's conservative government, the report of the Acheson inquiry was welcomed by the new Labour government. Hence, the result with which this chapter began. The recommendations of the Acheson inquiry were largely incorporated into the government's health strategy document published in 1999 (Department of Health, 1999). An important next phase of the work is using an interdisciplinary approach to monitor how changes in the wider determinants of health might influence social inequalities in health. If researchers are to be kept on their toes by scrutiny of how they use public money, so should governments be evaluated for their performance.

As a postscript, I was knighted in the New Year 2000 Honours list "for services to epidemiology and understanding health inequalities"—an embarrassing award for someone who has shown that low status is related to poor health.

Postscript

In the five years since this was penned much has happened, although the messages about interdisciplinary research and its discontents remain.

First, there have been continued developments in the research described in the chapter.

- The Whitehall II study continues to flourish with another 10 or so grants to add to the 50 reported in the chapter. We have completed phase 6, a postal questionnaire, phase 7, a clinical examination, and are half way through phase 8, a postal questionnaire, while planning (and raising grants) for phase 9, a clinical examination.
- New cohort studies have been established in the Central and Eastern European countries of the Czech Republic, Poland, and Russia; and a fourth is to be added in Lithuania.
- Andrew Steptoe has established his psychobiology group in our Centre. Among his key aims are to examine psychobiological differences in stress responses by socioeconomic position, to understand the Whitehall findings and the effects of aging.
- Jane Wardle's Health Behaviour Unit is a leading centre for studying smoking, diet, and response to screening.

Second, it is perhaps instructive to highlight three new developments relevant to the interdisciplinary theme.

The English Longitudinal Study of Ageing (ELSA)

This study was conceived as both multidisciplinary and interdisciplinary. It is a Longitudinal Study of a representative sample of the English population aged 50 and above. It was planned in consultation with investigators who run the Health and Retirement Study (HRS) in the United States. From the beginning ELSA was planned to have major content in economics, health—clinical, biological and health care—and its determinants, social participation, and cognitive psychology. The scientists who manage ELSA and analyze its data represent those disciplines (Marmot, Banks, Blundell, Lessof, and Nazroo, 2003).

The Principal Investigator of ELSA (me) is an epidemiologist, but because of the key involvement of the other disciplines the intention has been to gather high quality data in each area. This is a different approach than the usual. For example, in the Whitehall II study we decided that wealth and income were important, so we added questions but because of competing priorities kept them to a minimum. They may have been sufficient for our purposes, which were to relate income and wealth to health. There is always the worry, however, that lack of association may be due to measurement imprecision. In ELSA our economists wanted to be able to use wealth and income in their economic analyses. This required a greater degree of precision than is the case in Whitehall II and most health surveys. It may well be that this greater precision of measurement will be of importance as we examine the relation of income, wealth, and consumption to health.

This much is multidisciplinary—different disciplines pursuing their interests in one study. We now have a flourishing interdisciplinary environment. For example, as described in the chapter, there is the usual debate as to whether health leads to socioeconomic position or socioeconomic circumstances lead to health. Collaboration between biological scientists and economist in ELSA show that both are true. People with illness are more likely to leave the workforce than those without. Social position predicts future health. One fruitful collaboration between epidemiology and economics resulted in a comparison of the social gradients in health in ELSA and HRS, i.e. in English and American white men and women aged 55–64 (Banks, Marmot, Oldfield, and Smith, 2006). We showed that there were, indeed, social gradients in a number of major diseases in both countries. Surprisingly, Americans had more illness than English; not only reported illness but also biological markers of health disadvantage. While it has been difficult to stimulate public discussion of the social gradient in health in the United States, this finding of Americans being sicker than the English appeared to strike a sensitive nerve. There has been much interest in potential explanations. My favorite focuses on the circumstances in which people live and work—the social determinants of health.

The International Centre becomes International Institute for Society and Health (IISH)

We changed the name of the International Centre for Health and Society. The change in name reflects two other key changes: the direct involvement of other academic departments in IISH, and a more international focus.

The first sounds boringly administrative but, like most things that sound thus, it has meaning to those involved. In the International Centre we pursued interdisciplinary work within one academic department. In IISH, other departments are key stakeholders, in particular anthropology, economics, child health and Medicine in addition to the Department of Epidemiology and Public Health.

The international focus has also expanded. Within the International Centre we had active international collaborations in relation to studies of cardiovascular disease in a number of countries. Within IISH, the focus is more global: economists evaluating income transfer programs and child health in Latin America; child health specialists evaluating community involvement in reducing infant and child mortality in Nepal, India and Africa; dealing with manpower issues in the third world; concern with migration and health; and our continued focus on noncommunicable disease, but expanding the area of concern to lower income countries.

IISH also embraces the other interdisciplinary work described in the chapter.

Further developing the policy focus

Several members of IISH are involved in policy development in their own particular areas of academic expertise. We are not ivory tower scientists. One new area that grows directly out of the interdisciplinary work described is the Commission on Social Determinants of Health (CSDH). This was established by the World Health Organization with the aim of marshalling the evidence and stimulating action on the social determinants of health worldwide. I chair the Commission and the secretariat is shared between WHO Geneva and IISH at University College London. The Commissioners, from every region of the world, have expertise in a number of areas apart from health. A major aim of CSDH is to convince governments and others that planning for health has to involve sectors other than "health"; and to convince other sectors that policies that they pursue have vital importance for health.

We plan to report in 2008. It will be of more than passing interest to see what impact interdisciplinary research has on policies for health globally!

ACKNOWLEDGMENTS

Professor Sir Michael Marmot is supported by an MRC Research Professorship and by the John D. and Catherine T. MacArthur Foundation Research Network on Socio-economic Status and Health. Professor Marmot would like to thank Mandy Feeney for editorial assistance.

RECOMMENDED READINGS

Acheson, D. (1998). *Independent Inquiry into Inequalities in Health Report.* London: Stationery Office.

Black, D., Morris, J. N., Smith, C., Townsend, P., and Whitehead, M. (1988). *Inequalities in Health: The Black Report; The Health Divide.* London: Penguin Group.

Marmot, M. G., and Syme, S. L. (1976). Acculturation and coronary heart disease in Japanese Americans. *American Journal of Epidemiology, 104,* 225–247.

Marmot, M. G., Adelstein, A. M., Robinson, N., and Rose, G. (1978). The changing social class distribution of heart disease. *British Medical Journal, 2,* 1109–1112.

Marmot, M. G., Shipley, M. J., and Rose, G. (1984). Inequalities in death: Specific explanations of a general pattern. *Lancet, 1,* 1003–1006.

Marmot, M. G., Davey Smith, G., Stansfeld, S. A., Patel, C., North, F., Head, J. et al. (1991). Health inequalities among British Civil Servants: The Whitehall II study. *Lancet, 337,* 1387–1393.

Marmot, M. G., Bosma, H., Hemingway, H., Brunner, E., and Stansfeld, S. (1997). Contribution of job control to social gradient in coronary heart disease incidence. *Lancet, 350,* 235–239.

Marmot, M. G., and Wilkinson, R. G. (Eds.) (1999). *Social Determinants of Health.* New York: Oxford University Press.

REFERENCES

Acheson, D. (1998). *Inequalities in Health: Report of an Independent Inquiry.* London: Stationery Office.

Antonovsky, A. (1967). Social class, life expectancy and overall mortality. *Millbank Memorial Fund Quarterly, 45,* 31.

Banks, J., Marmot, M, G., Oldfield, Z., and Smith, J. P. (2006). Disease and disadvantage. *Journal of the American Medical Association, 295*, 2037–2045.

Barker, D. J. P. (1998). *Mothers, Babies, and Health in Later Life.* Edinburgh: Churchill Livingstone.

Bjorntorp, P., and Rosmond, R. (2000). Obesity and cortisol. *Nutrition, 16*, 924–936.

Black, D., Morris, J. N., Smith, C., Townsend, P., and Whitehead, M. (1988). *Inequalities in Health: The Black Report; The Health Divide.* London: Penguin Group.

Bosma, H., Peter, R., Siegrist, J., and Marmot, M. G. (1998). Alternative job stress models and the risk of coronary heart disease. *American Journal of Public Health, 88*, 68–74.

Brunner, E. J., Shipley, M. J., Blane, D., Davey Smith, G., and Marmot, M. G. (1999). When does cardiovascular risk start? Past and present socioeconomic circumstances and risk factors in adulthood. *Journal of Epidemiology and Community Health, 53*, 757–764.

Cassel, J. C. (1971). Summary of the major findings of the Evans country cardiovascular studies. *Archives of Internal Medicine, 128*, 887–889.

Cierpial, M. A., and McCarthy, R. (1987). Hypertension in SHR rats: Contribution of maternal environment. *American Journal of Physiology 253*, H980–H984.

Department of Health (1999). *Saving Lives: Our Healthier Nation.* London: Stationery Office.

Drever, F., and Whitehead, M. (1997). *Health Inequalities: Decennial Supplement.* Series DS No.15. London: Stationery Office.

Marmot, M. G., and Syme, S. L. (1976). Acculturation and coronary heart disease in Japanese Americans. *American Journal of Epidemiology, 104*, 225–247.

Marmot, M. G., Adelstein, A. M., Robinson, N., and Rose, G. (1978). The changing social class distribution of heart disease. *British Medical Journal, 2*, 1109–1112.

Marmot, M. G., Banks, J., Blundell, R., Lessof, C., and Nazroo, J. (2003). *Health, Wealth and Lifestyles of the Older Population in England. The 2002 English Longitudinal Study of Ageing.* London: Institute for Fiscal Studies.

Marmot, M. G., Bosma, H., Hemingway, H., Brunner, E. J., and Stansfeld, S. A. (1997). Contribution of job control and other risk factors to social variations in coronary heart disease incidence. *Lancet, 350*, 235–239.

Marmot, M. G., Davey Smith, G., Stansfeld, S. A., Patel, C., North, F., Head, J., et al. (1991). Health inequalities among British Civil Servants: The Whitehall II study. *Lancet, 337*, 1387–1393.

Marmot, M. G., Rose, G., Shipley, M., and Hamilton, P. J. S. (1978). Employment grade and coronary heart disease in British civil servants. *Journal of Epidemiology and Community Health, 32*, 244–249.

Marmot, M. G., Shipley, M. J., and Rose, G. (1984). Inequalities in death: Specific explanations of a general pattern. *Lancet, 1(8384)*, 1003–1006.

Meaney, M., Aitken, D., Bhatnager, S., van Berkel, C., and Sapolsky, R. M. (1988). Effect of neonatal handling on age-related impairments associated with the hippocampus. *Science 239*, 766.

Power, C., and Hertzman, C. (1977). Social and biological pathways linking early life and adult diseases. In M. G. Marmot and M. E. J. Wadsworth (Eds.), Fetal and early childhood environment: Long-term health implications. *British Medical Bulletin, 53*, 210–222.

Rutter, M. (1988). Pathways from childhood to adult life. *Journal of Child Psychology and Psychiatry, 30*, 23–51.

Sapolsky, R. M., Romero, M., and Munck, A. U. (2000). How do glucocorticoids influence stress responses? *Endocrine Review, 21*(1), 55–89.

Smith, T. (19 65). Factors involving sociocultural incongruity and change: A review of empiri. *Milbank Memorial Fund Quarterly, 45*(2), 23–39.

Syme, S. L., and Berkman, L. F. (1976). Social class, susceptibility, and sickness. *American Journal of Epidemiology, 104*, 1–8.

Wadsworth, M. E. J. (1977). Changing social factors and their long-term implications for health. In M. G. Marmot and M. E. J. Wadsworth (Eds.), Fetal and early childhood environment: Long-term health implications. *British Medical Bulletin, 53*, 198–209.

15

A Journey through the Interdisciplinary Landscape of Biodemography

S. JAY OLSHANSKY and BRUCE A. CARNES

The biodemography of aging explores the population consequences of the biological etiology of disease and death for individuals. As a consequence, biodemographic research is inherently interdisciplinary—using theory and methodology from numerous disciplines to better understand and reveal the interwoven forces that are responsible for creating and shaping the biological, demographic, and social attributes that define a species. The primary purpose of this chapter is to describe the formation of our interdisciplinary collaboration and explain how this collaboration has allowed us to make scientific contributions to the emerging field of biodemography. We identify personal and professional challenges that emerge from collaborations in general and interdisciplinary research in particular. We then describe how we have attempted to resolve these problems over the course of a collaboration that is long-term and ongoing. A detailed examination of issues that arise from collaborations and research that are interdisciplinary is the underlying theme of this book. Nevertheless, we thought that it was important to also present a brief description of the intellectual foundation of biodemography, a short summary of our biodemographic research, a demonstration of the relevance that biodemography has to important issues of public policy, and a discussion of the ongoing expansion of biodemographic research across disciplines within the scientific community.

The Big Questions about Aging

Although an enormous amount of research on aging has been conducted, only a handful of truly big questions have emerged from this intensive effort. *Why do we age*—or, asked another way, why are we not immortal? *How do we age*—that is, what are the biological mechanisms that cause a fertilized egg to proceed along a path of growth and development that invariably leads to the effects of aging that can be seen in the mirror and a death that cannot be avoided? *When do we age*— that is, why do aging, disease, and death occur when they do, and why do they exhibit variation within a population?

The *why* question of aging has been the focus of research in the fields of evolutionary biology and genetics for over a century. The *how* question of aging has been actively pursued by scientists from a variety of disciplines, including epidemiology, genetics, histology, medicine, pathology, and molecular biology. The *when* question of aging has been addressed by actuaries, biostatisticians, demographers, and epidemiologists who have developed numerous methods of quantitative analysis for population data containing ages at death and information on the diseases and disorders that precede it.

The question of *how we age* often overshadows the *why* and *when* questions, particularly when it comes to public opinion and the policy decisions that arise from that opinion. Virtually everyone wants answers to the *how* question because of the universal desire to control the consequences of aging. As a result, the biomedical sciences devote an enormous effort to identifying age-related health effects and developing methods of intervention that either prevent or delay the expression of these effects. Physicians also have a keen interest in the *how* question because they are the ones who must deal with the consequences of an aging population on a daily basis.

By its very nature, the biodemography of aging is an interdisciplinary approach to the study of aging. Our contributions to the ongoing development of biodemography involved the development of answers to the *why* and *how* questions for individuals in order to address the question of *when* mortality occurs in populations, and to explore comparisons of age patterns of mortality across species. In seeking answers to these questions, we have combined traditional demographic analysis with theoretical and experimental elements from a variety of disciplines in which research relevant to aging has been conducted: anthropology, ecology, embryology, epidemiology, evolutionary biology, genetics, molecular biology, pathology, and population genetics. Two bodies of historic literature have had a particularly profound influence on the development of our conceptual framework for the biodemography of aging: the search for a "law of mortality" by actuaries, chemists, and biologists, and the attempts to answer the question of why we age that arose from within the field of evolutionary biology.

The Search for a Law of Mortality

The intellectual origin of our biodemographic perspective on aging can be traced to observations made by the British actuary Benjamin Gompertz (1825). In the beginning of the nineteenth century, Gompertz noticed that the age distributions of death for various human populations and time periods looked remarkably similar. In fact, the pattern of high early age mortality, a rapid decline in the risk of death from birth to sexual maturity, and an exponential rise in the death rate from sexual maturity to about age 60, was so invariant that Gompertz believed there must be some "force" responsible for this phenomenon. Gompertz speculated that the exponential rise in the risk of death that he observed following sexual maturity was the result of a "law of mortality," or state of nature, characterized by "a deterioration, or an increased inability to withstand destruction" as one grows older. Gompertz's speculations on the biological forces responsible for his demographic "law of mortality" make him an excellent candidate for being considered the intellectual father of biodemography.

In a series of articles published later in the nineteenth century, the famous actuary William Makeham (1860, 1867, 1872, 1889, 1890) noted that some "diseases depending for their intensity solely upon the gradual diminution of the vital power" (1867, p. 335) fit the Gompertz equation far more closely than a mortality schedule based on all causes of death combined (i.e., total mortality). Medical science, however, was not sufficiently advanced at that time to permit the partitioning of total mortality into its constituent elements (Makeham, 1867). Makeham modified the Gompertz equation by including a parameter that was intended to account for environmental forces of mortality that were unrelated to those associated with aging. Makeham's refinement of the Gompertz equation and his quantitative development of what he called partial forces of mortality are the origins of what today is called competing risk theory.

Early in the twentieth century, scientists began looking at patterns of mortality for species other than humans to determine whether they also conformed to Gompertz's law. Their goal was to extend the Gompertz law for humans to a universal law of mortality that applied to all living things. Their assumption was that mortality differences among species were simply a function of scale that were compressed within short time periods for some and expanded for others.

Several scientists in the early part of the twentieth century made insightful speculations on factors that could determine whether there is a law of mortality. For example, biologists Jacque Loeb and J. H. Northrop (1916, 1917a,b) theorized that a species' lifespan was determined either by the depletion of important biological substances or through the toxic buildup of damaging by-products of living. Biochemist Samuel Brody (1924) speculated on a biochemical basis for a law of mortality after demonstrating that several biological processes related to senescence could be described by an equation used to quantify changes in chemical reactions over time. These early researchers were among the first to suggest that growing old was an intrinsically biological phenomenon.

The first scientist to empirically assess the pattern of death for more than one species was biologist Raymond Pearl. In a series of articles, Pearl and his colleagues (Pearl, 1921, 1922; Pearl and Minor, 1935) asserted that a fundamental biological law of mortality would be revealed if differences in lifespan were removed by superimposing two biologically comparable points within the life cycles of humans and *Drosophila* (fruit flies). After two decades of research using this scaling approach on an expanded repertoire of species, Pearl and Minor (1935) eventually declared that a universal law of mortality did not exist because the death curves for the animals studied remained different, even after adjusting for lifespan differences. In discussing their unanticipated failure, Pearl and Minor recognized what Makeham (1867) had identified 68 years earlier as the main problem with this effort: the inability to partition total mortality into its intrinsic and extrinsic causes of death. While Makeham's development of the theory of partial forces of mortality was designed to show how Gompertz's law would apply consistently among different subgroups of the human population, Pearl and Minor declared that partitioning total mortality into its constituent elements would extend Gompertz's law to other species. As you will see, the insights by Makeham and Pearl on why they failed to discover evidence for the universal law of mortality they believed must exist were fundamental to the contributions that we have made to the biodemography of aging.

After Pearl gave up his search in 1935, scientists shifted their focus to the development of mathematical models that more reliably characterized patterns of mortality (for example, see Deevey, 1947; Heligman and Pollard, 1980; Perks, 1932; Pollard and Streatfield, 1979; Pollard and Valkovics, 1992). Although these efforts advanced the understanding of the mathematics of mortality, biological explanations for why death occurs in a Gompertzian pattern for many forms of life (the *when* question about senescence) remained a mystery. Interestingly enough, the question of *why* senescence occurs (or perhaps more appropriately, why humans and other animals are not immortal) dates back to the pioneering work of evolutionary biologists; these theoretical developments took place independently at about the same time the law of mortality was being discussed by actuaries in the late nineteenth century.

Evolutionary Theories of Senescence

Evolutionary biologists from Darwin through the present have speculated on the biological origin of senescence, but they did this independent of knowledge of research on aging in the actuarial/demographic sciences that had taken place decades earlier. When we realized that these two groups of scientists were working on closely related questions of aging completely independent of each other for

more than a century, the first pieces of the puzzle of our work on the biodemography of aging fell into place. A brief summary of the evolutionary literature on
aging will make it clear what led us down a particular theoretical and methodological path.

The origin of modern evolutionary theories of senescence dates back to the
theory of aging set forth by biologist August Weismann (see Weismann, 1891).
According to Weismann, the one aspect of life that could not be avoided was the
inevitable exposure of the individual to external forces, which produced a constant
barrage of small injuries to the body. Because the perfect repair of these injuries is
not realistically possible, it became self-evident why older individuals should be
replaced by new ones. This was the rationale supporting both the need for reproduction and the importance of death. Thus, even if immortality theoretically
were possible, it could not be realized in the real world where the external force of
injury was ubiquitous and unavoidable.

The modern evolutionary theory of aging was provided by Nobel laureate Sir
Peter Medawar (1952), who was able to make extensive use of Mendelian genetics
in his arguments. Like Weismann, Medawar invoked the importance of the ever-
present external force of mortality, which was acknowledged to be the primary
reason that most members of a population were unable to live long enough to
experience senescence. Medawar's unique contribution to the evolutionary theory
of senescence was the argument that genes arising from mutation and whose
expression is related to time would affect a different number of people, depending
on when in the lifespan it was expressed. If the gene was expressed early in the
lifespan, a large number of individuals would be affected while only a few would be
influenced if it was expressed later in the lifespan. By implication, natural selection
would favor and bring early into the lifespan those genes that were advantageous,
while figuratively pushing genes with damaging effects into later portions of the
lifespan where fewer individuals would normally be affected. Under his paradigm,
senescence arises from the accumulation of genes with damaging effects that have
been pushed by natural selection into the postreproductive period of life (which
Medawar referred to as the "genetic dustbin"), and the extended survival of individuals (through protection from external sources of mortality) into an age
range where these diseases have the opportunity to be expressed. Williams (1957)
provided an important extension of Medawar's view of aging when he hypothesized that some of the genes that have damaging effects later in the lifespan may
have positive effects early in the lifespan. This made senescence a product not just
of deleterious genes expressed later in life, but an inadvertent consequence of
selection-favoring genes with early adaptive functions and late-acting damaging
effects (referred to as pleiotropic genes).

One of the most recent extensions of the evolutionary theory of senescence
appears in a series of articles published by Thomas Kirkwood and colleagues (see
Kirkwood, 1977, 1992; Kirkwood and Holiday, 1979; Kirkwood and Rose, 1991).
Like Weismann and Medawar, Kirkwood argues that the inevitable force of external mortality plays a crucial role in the timing of senescence. However, in this

case, the logic supporting the existence of senescence is based more on its proximate causes of differential energy investments in somatic and germ cells, with the time-dependent decline in somatic maintenance and repair serving as the underlying mechanism. Thus, species under the influence of high external forces of mortality would benefit from greater investment in early reproduction and lower investment in somatic maintenance. Species facing less pressure from external forces of mortality (such as humans, animals domesticated by humans, whales, elephants, and a few other species) could afford to delay their reproductive efforts. Under this paradigm, senescence is viewed as a product of accumulated damage to somatic cells that is managed biologically at a level that depends on the intensity of external forces of mortality that are present in the environment of an organism.

In summary, the argument that selection alters the genetic composition of a population through the differential reproductive success of individuals is a basic tenet of modern evolutionary biology. According to Medawar (1952) and Williams (1957), opportunities for selection to alter gene frequencies should be greatest before individuals begin reproduction, diminish as the cumulative reproductive potential of individuals is achieved, and become weak or nonexistent once reproduction has ceased. This age-based gradient for the effectiveness of selection permits the potential lifespan of organisms to be partitioned into biologically meaningful time periods: the prereproductive, reproductive, and postreproductive periods.

The modern evolutionary theory of senescence is based on the premise that selection is most effective in altering gene frequencies in the prereproductive period. When the normally high force of external mortality is controlled and survival beyond the end of the reproductive period becomes a common occurrence, senescence and senescent-related diseases and disorders have the opportunity to be expressed. If gene expression in the postreproductive period—whether favorable or deleterious—is beyond the reach of natural selection, then a genetic basis for either immortality or senescence resulting from the direct action of selection is not possible. Under this paradigm, senescent-related diseases and disorders observed in organisms not molded by selection for extended survival (beyond the genetically defined reproductive period) is an inadvertent consequence of selection pressures that shape the reproductive biology of species (Hamilton, 1966). As a consequence, investments in the biochemical machinery necessary to maintain the integrity of the organism should diminish as the reproductive potential of the individual is achieved. This is the fundamental biological explanation for why individuals senesce, and it is a critical element in our work on the biodemography of aging.

The Formation of a Scientific Collaboration

Our contribution to modern developments in the biodemography of aging began inadvertently in 1989. At that time we were working in different divisions at

Argonne. National Laboratory (ANL), a research complex that originated with the Manhattan Project and is now managed by the University of Chicago and funded primarily by the Department of Energy (DOE). Olshansky was the director of the social sciences section in the environmental studies group, where he worked on large-scale environmental projects. For example, he was responsible for estimating population growth rates and levels near a proposed high-level nuclear waste facility in Nevada; he explored the demographic and health consequences of building the super-conductor super-collider in Texas; he used census data and worked with meteorologists to estimate levels of human exposure to noise at Air Force bases throughout the United States; and he estimated human death rates associated with accidental releases of chemical agents at chemical weapons facilities in the United States. Because Olshansky had access to vital statistics data from the United States through the ANL library system, he was also able to maintain an active research program in the field of aging during his spare time. As a demographer, his research interest was focused entirely on humans.

In 1989, Carnes was a staff scientist (biologist/statistician) in the division of biological and medical research at ANL, where he was conducting research on the biological consequences of exposure to radiation. Most of his time was spent using mortality data for exposed populations of either laboratory mice (Carnes, Grahn, and Thomson, 1989; Grahn, Lombard, and Carnes, 1992) or beagles (Carnes and Fritz, 1991, 1993) in order to develop quantitative models for the prediction of radiation-induced mortality risks. His ultimate goal was to develop a quantitative method of interspecies extrapolation for predicting the age-specific risks of radiation-induced mortality in humans from the Argonne animal data. Carnes took a significant step toward achieving this goal when he and his colleagues demonstrated that age-specific radiation-induced mortality in exposed populations of the beagle could be accurately predicted from a simple scaling of the hazard models used to describe the mortality experience of exposed mice (Carnes, Olshansky, and Grahn, 1998). The mortality and pathology data used by Carnes came from an extensive database developed and maintained at ANL for radiation biology studies conducted there between 1953 and 1992. These data include approximately 70,000 mortality records for 20 strains of laboratory mice (Grahn, 1994; Grahn, Wright, Carnes, Williamson, and Fox, 1995), detailed histopathology data for around 800 beagles (Carnes and Fritz, 1993), and an epidemiological study of humans (Carnes, Groer, and Kotek, 1997).

Olshansky developed an interest in the question of how long humans can live after he attended an interdisciplinary conference on "Estimating the Upper Limits to Human Life Expectancy" sponsored by the National Institute on Aging in 1988. Soon thereafter, he developed a simple mathematical approach that involved a unique twist to the traditional way that the question of limits to human life expectancy had been addressed in the past: a reverse engineering model designed to evaluate the magnitude of the reduction in death rates that would be required to raise life expectancy at birth from current levels to 120 years. Upon learning that life tables and survival analysis were the focus of research conducted by Carnes,

Olshansky proposed a collaboration in conjunction with Dr. Christine Cassel, a physician/geriatrician from the University of Chicago. The result of this initial collaboration was a lead article in *Science* (Olshansky, Carnes, and Cassel, 1990), international attention from the scientific and lay press, and the beginning of a debate among scientists about prospective increases in human life expectancy that continues to this day.

Shortly after the publication of our *Science* article and following discussions with colleagues in the biological sciences, we developed a strong interest in searching for the underlying biology that we believed must be driving the statistics of a life table. However, this required a dedicated full-time research and training effort that neither of us could pursue while working at Argonne. At that time, Olshansky decided to make research on aging a full-time job. The best outlet that simultaneously permitted him to leave Argonne and work on the question of biology in the life table was a Special Emphasis Research Career Award (SERCA) (K01) from the National Institute on Aging (NIA). He submitted a K01 proposal to the NIA that was funded in 1992. The purpose of the SERCA was twofold: it enabled Olshansky to leave Argonne and move to the University of Chicago in order to make research on aging a full-time career, and it enabled him to pursue an independent course of study in the fields of evolutionary biology, molecular biology, epidemiology, and statistics as each field relates to aging. The SERCA and the research and training opportunities it created were instrumental in helping Olshansky and his colleagues contribute to the emerging field of biodemography.

Carnes received his formal training in general biology, population biology, theoretical ecology, and biostatistics. Because we worked closely together after our first collaboration in 1990, Carnes's background in the biological sciences was instrumental in helping Olshansky in his training program under the SERCA. It was from these first interactions that we developed the theoretical and methodological elements of our research on the biodemography of aging. Early in 1992, it became evident to us that our research involved a unique merging of the demographic and biological disciplines, something we had not seen very often in the historical literature. We began to view our research as contributing to the development of a new interdisciplinary approach to aging. Initially, we referred to our approach as *evolutionary demography* because it was from these two disciplines (evolutionary biology and demography) that our research hypotheses were primarily derived. We quickly realized, however, that the conceptual framework we were trying to create encompassed a far broader range of biological reasoning than was implied by the restrictive term *evolutionary demography*. After settling on *biodemography* as a more accurate description of our work, we searched the scientific literature to determine whether the term had already been used. Our search revealed that the term *biodemography* appeared in a 1948 article by the ecologist G. Evelyn Hutchinson and that it had also appeared in a paper written by the geneticist Ken Weiss (1990). We also discovered that several theoretical antecedents of the biodemography of aging appeared sporadically in the scientific literature between 1825 and 1925 (for details, see Olshansky and Carnes, 1997).

The Biodemography of Aging: From
Individuals to Populations

Our initial effort to understand the biology of the life table led us to examine the forecasts of mortality and life expectancy that official government agencies like the Social Security Administration (SSA) and the Census Bureau had been making for decades. We wanted to see whether the numerical methods they used to make their forecasts were similar to ours, and whether they ever brought a biological perspective to their forecasts. We discovered that their approaches to forecasting relied primarily on the extrapolation of past mortality trends (observed during selected time periods) into the future. Although both agencies made assumptions about future trends for specific diseases, their decision-making process was not influenced by a biological understanding of aging and death.

The empirical, or nontheoretical, approach to forecasting death rates and life expectancy has been unreliable in both the short-term and long-term because the time periods used as a frame of reference for the projections led to both underestimates and overestimates of the future course of life expectancy as a consequence of trends in death rates that have been both volatile and unpredictable during the last half of the twentieth century (Olshansky, 1988). The main problem that we saw with the extrapolation method was that projected death rates must eventually approach zero when time frames with favorable mortality trends are used as a basis for extrapolating over long time periods. In our opinion, the death rates resulting from this extrapolation approach for long-term forecasts are both theoretically and biologically indefensible.

We set out to find a way to bring a biological understanding of aging and senescence to official forecasts of mortality and life expectancy. Specifically, we suggested that once death rates decline to the point where most members of a population have the opportunity to experience senescence, the biology of why and when senescence occurs must be incorporated into demographic and actuarial methods of forecasting mortality. The findings from our *Science* article led us to believe that this point had already been reached in the United States and other low mortality populations where the rise in life expectancy at birth had already begun to decelerate.

We came to realize that the theories of aging and senescence developed by evolutionary biologists contained a rationale that could be used to explain the consistent age patterns of death that researchers working independently within the actuarial sciences were trying to describe quantitatively. By combining theory with data, we thought it should be possible to test the mortality implications of evolutionary theories of senescence. Like many people working within the actuarial and demographic sciences, we had access to data on humans. However, we also possessed a truly unique data resource, the mortality data for laboratory animals used by Carnes. These data and our interdisciplinary collaboration made it possible for us to pursue a research path that simply was not available to other researchers.

What is the link between these two independent bodies of scientific research devoted to aging, and how can this link be used to make biologically defensible forecasts of life expectancy? It was our contention that the common age pattern of mortality first noticed for humans by Benjamin Gompertz in 1825, and subsequently identified for other organisms by other scientists early in the twentieth century, makes sense when the evolutionary theory of senescence is extended from individuals to populations. Evolutionary biologists did not make this linkage because the focus of their research was almost exclusively at the level of genes, sometimes individuals, rarely populations, and almost never applied to humans. The scientists working in the actuarial/demographic sciences were unable to make this linkage because *(1)* their attention was focused on finding empirical evidence for a law of mortality, *(2)* they were operating without knowledge of the evolutionary theories of senescence that had been developed during the previous 100 years, and *(3)* they admittedly did not have the appropriate data needed to test their hypotheses. It is only when these two bodies of literature are brought together that it becomes possible to understand how the ideas and concepts from one discipline may be used to explain a phenomenon (common age patterns of mortality across species) observed by scientists in other disciplines. In this case, evolutionary biology provides the biological rationale that Gompertz, Makeham, Pearl, and others believed was present to explain why consistent age patterns of death exist across species. What follows is a summary of how we merged the research of these disciplines, formed a series of testable research hypotheses, and in so doing contributed to the emergence of the biodemography of aging.

We hypothesized that the logic from evolutionary biology that establishes links between natural selection and reproduction and between reproduction and senescence for individuals has a direct bearing on *when* senescent mortality should occur in a population. The logic is as follows. The timing of genetically determined processes such as growth and development are driven by a reproductive biology that evolved under the direct force of natural selection, molded by the necessity for early reproduction, which, in turn, is driven by the normally high external force of mortality. If individual senescence is an inadvertent consequence of these developmental processes as predicted from the evolutionary theory of senescence, then patterns of *intrinsic* (biologically related) causes of death in a genetically diverse population should also be calibrated to element(s) of a species' reproductive biology. Furthermore, given that a hostile environment is the critical driving force of natural selection for most species, the linkage between reproduction and the timing of death in a population should be consistent across species. Although individuals within a population are responding to a common set of hostile evolutionary pressures, we suggest that genetic heterogeneity among individuals and a stochastic "environmental" component of senescence should inevitably lead to a distribution of senescent-related deaths across the age structure. In other words, populations of all sexually reproducing species are composed of individuals with a wide range of inherent and acquired senescent mortality risks that lead to early mortality for some and late mortality for others.

If the genetic composition of a population remains stable over time, then we predict that an age pattern of senescent (intrinsic) mortality should exist for every species that remains invariant, even under conditions where mortality pressures from extrinsic causes of death differ. We called this consistent age pattern of death an *intrinsic mortality signature* because it is believed to be as characteristic of a species as the more traditional morphological traits used by taxonomists. However, changes in the intrinsic mortality signature of a population would be expected when forces of selection acting to maintain the genetic composition of a population are disrupted (e.g., environmental challenges such as modified reproductive schedules; see, Luckinbill et al., 1984; Rose, 1984), or indirectly by "manufacturing" survival time through (among other means) medical interventions that extend life for some individuals who have approached or reached their potential lifespan. In the published literature we have suggested that this has already occurred in low mortality populations (Olshansky, Carnes, and Grahn, 1998).

We then hypothesized that the full array of potential senescent processes, their consequences, and the intrinsic mortality signature itself can be revealed only under the "unnatural" condition of survival beyond the age of sexual maturity by a significant proportion of a birth cohort—a scenario that Medawar (1952) suggests is necessary to observe the senescence of individuals. This rarely happens for animals living in the wild because, as evolutionary biologists emphasize, death almost always precedes senescence in a hostile environment. However, for species living under controlled environments where extrinsic (nonbiologically related) causes of death are dramatically reduced (e.g., humans, household pets, and zoo and laboratory animals), we suggest that each species' intrinsic mortality signature should become visible for the first time. Since there are common forces (extrinsic mortality) responsible for molding the reproductive biology of species, a common pattern of intrinsic mortality—*an evolutionary imprint*—may also become visible when species are compared on a biologically comparable time scale. These are the basic hypotheses that we initially set forth in our work on biodemography, they are the main hypotheses we subsequently proposed to test under funding from the Social Security Administration, and in the end, this is the point at which evolutionary arguments for why senescence exists can be used to test for the existence of the Gompertz/Makeham/Pearl law of mortality. The evolutionary theory of why senescence occurs at the level of individuals may also be used to provide a biological rationale for explaining why there are age patterns of intrinsic mortality in humans and other species—that is, the "vital force" in Gompertz's rationale.

Earlier it was noted that the SSA had a tradition of forecasting mortality that dates back to the origin of the Social Security trust fund in 1935 (Olshansky, 1988). The SSA's predictions about age patterns of death in populations have public policy implications that are not just theoretical, but applied. When life expectancy at birth approaches higher levels as large proportions of birth cohorts have the opportunity to survive to older ages, the main force influencing death rates will be biomechanical features of the human body that influence the expression of fatal diseases (Olshansky, Carnes, and Butler, 2001). If this is true, then forecasting models and the assumptions that drive them would benefit from a biological perspective. Specifically, the presence of an intrinsic mortality signature would suggest that there are biological forces that influence how high life expectancy can rise, and if the SSA forecasts death rates that are below these levels, then strong justification must be provided for why this will occur.

Based on the evolutionary theory of senescence, we developed the following testable research hypotheses:

1. The age of lowest intrinsic mortality will always be at puberty.
2. The intrinsic death rate at puberty will serve as the launching point for exponentially rising death rates throughout most of the age structure.
3. The rate of increase in death rates from intrinsic causes following puberty will be calibrated to the length of the reproductive period.
4. Age patterns of intrinsic mortality will remain largely unchanged across time and population subgroups.
5. Attributes of intrinsic mortality will be present across sexually re-producing species (universal law of mortality).

The last of these hypotheses, if confirmed, represents evidence for species-specific intrinsic mortality signatures and biologically related limits to declines in death rates and a rise in life expectancy.

The main problem that scientists have faced in testing for the presence of a law of mortality ever since Gompertz involves stringent requirements on data. Both Gompertz in 1825 and Pearl in 1935 recognized the importance of distinguishing between intrinsic and extrinsic causes of death, but both realized they did not have the data that would permit such partitions. Makeham modified the original Gompertz formula as a way to partially take into account the important force of extrinsic mortality, but even his modification was not actually based on observed differences in causes of death among people. Evolution biology has based its theory of senescence on the ever-present high force of extrinsic mortality that shapes reproduction, and indirectly, death, but scientists in this field have had no need to perform a partition of mortality in a real population. In order to empirically test for the existence of a universal law of mortality, accurate information on cause of death is needed for more than one species.

We soon realized that Carnes worked with and was responsible for what was perhaps one of the only sources of mortality data in the world that was intentionally designed for making mortality comparisons between species. Mortality data for control populations of humans, dogs, and dozens of strains of mice had been carefully collected and maintained. Most individuals in these studies were autopsied by veterinary or human pathologists in order to determine why death occurred. In addition, like humans, the laboratory animals were raised within controlled living environments that limited extrinsic causes of death. In other words, the conditions had been met for observing and analyzing senescence in different species. It was our expectation that the quantitative attributes of the intrinsic mortality signatures for the three species that we studied would be relatively insensitive to assumptions made about future changes of total mortality (derived either from empirical or epidemiological models).

For this chapter, it is not important to provide details about the results of the research funded by the Social Security Administration and the National Institute on Aging. Those details are provided in most of our scientific papers published since 1995. For now, it is important to emphasize that the biodemographic paradigm of aging and mortality provides scientific evidence supporting the existence of a law of mortality as originally proposed by Gompertz/Makeham/Pearl; it led to practical public policy implications for forecasting mortality that were used by the Social Security Administration; it led to a series of testable research hypotheses on the biodemography of aging (Carnes, Olshansky, and Grahn, 1996) that are being evaluated by other investigators and graduate students in the United States and abroad who have acquired an interest in this field; and it has spawned a series of new research projects that incorporate elements of other scientific disciplines such as molecular biology and anthropology.

Key Findings, Conclusions, and Implications

A number of key findings follow from the interdisciplinary perspective provided by the biodemography of aging. In a manuscript we published in *Scientific American* entitled "The Aging of the Human Species," we described how population aging, a traditionally demographic phenomenon, could and should be examined and understood within the context of evolutionary biology (Olshansky, Carnes, and Cassel, 1993). In the light of evolution biology, population aging is the product of an acquired ability to alter the forces of natural selection that have been operating on humans for thousands of years, resulting in an experiment in life that extends survival well beyond the reproductive period for a significant portion of successive birth cohorts. The public policy implications of this perspective were immediately obvious to the scientists and trustees of the Social Security Administration (SSA), who then invited Olshansky and other demographers to participate in a debate about the future course of human mortality. When our research was subsequently funded by the SSA, that was the first time any government agency had formally supported research devoted exclusively to work on the biodemography of aging. Numerous scientific publications were the direct products of this research (Bennett and Olshansky, 1996; Carnes and Olshansky, 1997; Carnes et al., 1996, 1998; Olshansky and Carnes, 1997; Olshansky et al., 1998, 2001). The SSA-funded project served as the launching point for a series of scientific publications and research that continues to this day.

The first explicit mention of biodemography in the scientific literature after Weiss (1990) was in a pair of articles that we published in *Population and Development Review* (Carnes and Olshansky, 1993; Olshansky and Carnes, 1994). In our 1993 article, we set out to describe the evolutionary theories of senescence to the demographic community and to present the literature from evolutionary biology that had, for more than half a century, focused on issues of human aging and longevity from a perspective that social scientists were not generally familiar with. In our follow-up to that article published in the next issue of *Population and Development Review* in early 1994, we then applied reasoning from evolutionary biology to examine the plausibility of various demographic methods of forecasting mortality that led some investigators to conclude that life expectancy at birth in the United States will rise above 100 years. Our conclusion was that some methods of forecasting mortality currently in use by scientists and government agencies include assumptions that, from a biological perspective, yield forecasts that are mathematically correct but are biologically implausible.

The full development of the biodemography of aging that we originally proposed included a detailed discussion of its theoretical and empirical roots, the specification of 10 testable research hypotheses, and the results of our efforts to empirically test several of these hypotheses—all of which was published in an article in *Population and Development Review* (Carnes et al., 1996). This article was the main product of the SSA-funded project on biodemography in which we provided empirical evidence favoring the existence of a "law of mortality." Findings from this research imply that there are consistent biological forces that operate in largely the same way across species that regulate age patterns of death in genetically heterogeneous populations. Unless these biological forces of mortality are altered, there is reason to believe that death rates cannot decline significantly below the intrinsic mortality schedule for a species—a finding that has a direct bearing on forecasts of mortality and life expectancy made by actuaries at the Social Security Administration.

After publication of our 1996 paper outlining the biodemography of aging, some researchers rejected the idea that there is an "intrinsic" (or biologically based) force of mortality. Instead, it was their belief that nearly all causes of death are inherently modifiable by altering either behaviors or the environments within which humans live. The suggestion that there is no such thing as intrinsic mortality was surprising, given that scientists from a variety of disciplines had recognized the distinction between intrinsic and extrinsic mortality for more than a century. In response to the initial rejection by some of the importance of intrinsic mortality or the 170-year old search for a "law of mortality," we published two separate manuscripts that were designed to address these issues head on. In the first (Olshansky and Carnes, 1997), a history of biodemographic thinking dating back to a detailed discussion of Benjamin Gompertz and the century-long debate about a "law of mortality" was presented. In the second (Carnes et al., 1999), we summarized the historical reasoning developed independently from within several biological disciplines that supports the presence of intrinsic mortality. The main problem among scientists who reject the idea that intrinsic mortality exists is a tendency to equate intrinsic mortality with an unmodifiable risk of death (i.e., if it is intrinsic, they reason, then it is biologically determined and therefore unmodifiable). We suggest that intrinsic mortality is inherently modifiable because

there can be no genetically determined death programs fashioned by natural selection. However, the fact that intrinsic mortality can be modified does not mean
that it does not exist.

Elements of the biodemographic paradigm in one form or another has made
its way into all of the publications resulting from our interdisciplinary collaborations (Bennett and Olshansky 1996; Carnes and Olshansky, 1997; Carnes et al.,
1996, 1998; Olshansky and Carnes, 1997; Olshansky et al., 1998, 2001). It is not
necessary to go into further detail at this point on exactly how the biodemography
of aging has appeared in all of our subsequent research and writing. The relevant
papers are referenced in this article and the reader is invited to explore these
publications in depth.

Modern Biodemography

The rebirth of biodemography in the early 1990s was an important development.
The work of Gavrilov and Gavrilova (1991) was initially focused on a general
examination of age patterns of death across species, but has since narrowed in on
the link exclusively in humans between parental age at conception and adult onset
of age-related diseases in offspring. The work of Weiss and colleagues was focused
more narrowly on the genetics behind age patterns of death in humans, although
Weiss (1990) should be credited with merging elements of demography and anthropology and bringing back the notion of biology contained within the life table
as originally theorized by Gompertz.

Our collaboration that resulted in the development of the biodemographic
paradigm of aging ignited a spirited debate among scientists in the social and
biological sciences. Although the debate about human longevity continues to this
date, perhaps what is more important is that the biodemography of aging surfaced
at a time when other successful collaborations between biologists and social scientists also had been established. As it turns out, during the decade of the 1990s, a
number of different research teams were conducting research in what is now
known as biodemography, although the term itself was not initially associated with
their work. In the paragraphs that follow, we describe how our own research program on biodemography has developed from the initial ideas developed in 1992, to
a much more broadly defined program that is being embarked on today. In addition, we discuss how biodemography has since branched out well beyond the
study of aging and mortality to include other critically important elements of the
life cycle of humans.

Several important developments have been made on the biodemography of
aging since the publication of our initial findings. When we demonstrated in 1996
that the age patterns of death overlapped for different species, we noticed that at
very old ages humans fared better than the laboratory animals. At first this was
puzzling, given our prediction that the mortality schedules would overlap perfectly, but it later became clear why this occurs. The laboratory animals were

permitted to die from life-threatening conditions. In other words, no heroic medical measures were used to extend their lives. By contrast, humans go through considerable effort to extend life through biomedical interventions. We concluded that humans are capable of "manufacturing" survival time for enough people to increase life expectancy marginally beyond its biologically related limits. Details of this hypothesis are presented in Olshansky et al. (1998).

A second development in our biodemographic work involves an extension of our previous research to evaluate other attributes of the mortality schedule of humans. For example, Medawar (1952) theorized about the age when inherited diseases should be expressed and how they should accumulate within the post-reproductive period of the lifespan. Although his theories have not been tested in vertebrates, information coming from the human genome project offers intriguing opportunities to study the demography of inherited diseases. We believe that this work has important implications for public policy because it will enable us to define our previously identified intrinsic mortality schedule with far greater pathologic specificity. Efforts to get this work funded have not met with success for reasons that will be discussed in the next section. Despite these setbacks, we are persisting in our struggle to merge scientific disciplines in order to address both scientific and public policy issues.

A third development in our biodemographic work involves an effort to bring molecular biology directly into our research paradigm. We have proposed to work with a molecular biologist to establish a transgenic mouse model for the purpose of exploring the role of antioxidants in the aging process, and to use this animal model to test predictions from biodemography regarding the onset and age progression of intrinsic mortality. In this unique example of interdisciplinary collaboration, we will establish the research protocol, and a colleague (molecular biologist, Alan Diamond) would produce a genetically engineered strain of mouse that produces elevated levels of a specific antioxidant (the cytosolic form of selenium-dependent glutathione peroxidase, or Gpx). In effect, this project would test for changes in the "rate of aging" at the molecular level in relation to attributes of the species' reproductive schedule—a phenomenon that we have explored indirectly through our use of mortality statistics for populations.

These are just three of many examples of how our work on the biodemography of aging has already led to several other research projects that involve scientists from other disciplines. In addition to these projects, we have worked with a postdoctoral student from France on the concept of manufactured time; we are working with an epidemiologist from Australia (and his graduate student) to refine our definition of intrinsic mortality using data from their country; and we are working with a geneticist and anthropologist to explore a possible association between longevity of offspring and parental age at conception.

One particularly important development in biodemography is that it is no longer restricted to the study of aging. In an excellent book entitled *Between Zeus and the Salmon* (Wachter and Finch, 1997), a number of authors discuss interdisciplinary collaborations involving the application of biodemography to other attributes of the life cycle. For example, geneticists Thomas Johnson and David Shook combine evolutionary theory and demography as they explore how genes are associated with longevous phenotypes. Entomologists James Carey and Catherine Greunfelder use data from nonhuman species to develop a theoretical and empirical foundation for their argument that the elderly of many species contribute more to reproductive fitness than is currently believed. Evolutionary biologist Steven Austad explores how menopause and postreproductive survival in species other than humans can influence the behavior of offspring. Economist Ronald Lee explores the economic flow of resources and knowledge between generations as a basis for explaining the utility of a postreproductive population; this is a particularly novel approach that links longevity to intergenerational transfers.

As it turns out, many other forms of biodemography have appeared throughout the literature during the past 170 years, although the term "biodemography" was never directly associated with these projects. These include studies based on biochemistry (Brody, 1924; Brownlee, 1919; Greenwood, 1928; Loeb and Northrop, 1916), interspecies comparisons of age patterns of mortality (e.g., see Deevey, 1947; Pearl, 1922; Pearl and Minor, 1935), physiologically based models that were at times based on the experimental use of senescence accelerators (e.g., see Brues and Sacher, 1952; Failla, 1958; Lorenz, 1950; Mildvan and Strehler, 1960; Sacher, 1956; Sacher and Trucco, 1962; Szilard, 1959), medical and demographic models that use multiple risk factor simulations for human populations (e.g., see Manton, Stallard, and Tolley, 1991), studies of age patterns of mortality of nonhuman species (e.g., see Brooks, Lithgow, and Johnson, 1994; Carey, Liedo, Orozco, and Vaupel, 1992; Fukui, Xiu, and Curtsinger, 1993), and life history models from the fields of ecology and evolutionary biology (e.g., see Orzack and Tuljapurkar, 1989; Tuljapurkar, 1990).

Obstacles to the Biodemography of Aging

Pursuing research on an interdisciplinary subject like biodemography requires collaboration between scientists. These collaborations can be extremely beneficial because the interactions between researchers from different disciplines often generate novel insights that would not have been revealed had the scientists been conducting the same research on their own—a synergy that can most easily be observed in the enhanced quality of publications. Although the participating scientists benefit from these collaborations, the greatest beneficiaries are the graduate students who are being exposed to the broader perspective offered by interdisciplinary research.

Initially, technical communication was the biggest problem that we had to overcome. Although both of us worked with life tables, numerous misunderstandings arose over the different terminology and mathematical formulas that we use to describe the same life table concepts. Although the problem was initially frustrating, the universal language of mathematics made this a relatively easy problem to solve. The technical jargon of biology also created communication problems at first. Fortunately, the SERCA award from NIA gave Olshansky the time and freedom to pursue training in the biological sciences, greatly accelerating his learning curve. Within a relatively short time, he was able to read classic papers on aging from journals in the biological sciences and then discuss them with Carnes. At the same time, Olshansky provided Carnes with key papers on aging from the demographic/social sciences. This creative and interactive research environment would have been nearly impossible to achieve without the intellectual freedom that was made possible by the SERCA award from NIA.

A potential problem that we never faced in our collaborations was how to initiate research projects and carry them through to the publication of manuscripts. Olshansky is skilled at visualizing the broad implications of a research problem, and Carnes excels at seeing interconnections between the technical details of a research problem. Olshansky often generates the first draft of manuscripts and proposals. However, once Carnes weaves in his independent views, the expanded second draft usually bears little resemblance to the initial draft. After numerous iterations, a final document emerges that completely blends our individual contributions. Invariably, our collaborative papers are broader in scope and more clearly written than any document that either of us could have produced on our own. Although we have become progressively more interdisciplinary in our thinking and writing, we still depend on each other to ensure the substantive accuracy of information content from our respective disciplines of biology and demography.

Our collaborative team has been able to develop a cooperative and equal partnership within a working environment of mutual trust. Without this trust, we would not have been able to maintain a collaboration that has persisted for over a decade. Maintaining collaborations even over a short term requires overcoming serious obstacles, especially when the collaborations involve scientists. The generation of grant money and publications are key measures of productivity that are often used to make salary, tenure, or promotion decisions for scientists. This means that problems can easily arise over such issues as "ownership" of ideas, distribution of effort, professional recognition (within an organization, as well as among peers), distribution of senior authorship on papers, identifying a principal investigator on proposals, and the distribution of grant money.

Interpersonal issues are a challenge, but the greatest impediments to creating and sustaining a successful collaboration are publishing papers and obtaining funds, especially when the collaboration is interdisciplinary. Both impediments have a common cause. Review panels at journals and funding agencies usually do not have an interdisciplinary composition. As a consequence, papers and proposals of an interdisciplinary nature easily can be misunderstood, criticized, and put at a severe competitive disadvantage relative to their more traditional counterparts.

By definition, interdisciplinary research and the manuscripts generated from this research will involve subject matter from different disciplines—disciplines that may not share theories, methodology, technical jargon, or literature. Although expanded intellectual scope is a real strength of interdisciplinary research, it also causes problems when trying to publish interdisciplinary research papers. Most professional societies, the journals they spawn, and the people chosen to review manuscripts come from either a single discipline or a fairly narrow range of related disciplines. This means that an interdisciplinary manuscript is likely to contain some subject matter that goes beyond the technical expertise of any reviewer. We have routinely experienced reviews at journals in the social sciences where one or more of the reviewers did not appear to know or understand the biological terms, concepts, or literature needed to properly review the submitted manuscript. Our solution to this problem has been to submit large manuscripts with a careful definition of terms, extensive background information, and a large literature citation section. Despite these precautions, almost every biodemography paper that we have tried to publish in the demography literature has been an exhausting and often frustrating process—although every paper submitted has been published.

Funding is by far the biggest impediment that we face in trying to maintain our interdisciplinary collaboration, and this problem continues to this day. Just as with journals, study sections or their equivalents at funding agencies are invariably composed of reviewers who come almost entirely from a single discipline. Once again, a lack of familiarity with technical language, concepts, and literature has been a serious problem. Our colleagues in the biological sciences who have considerable experience serving on study sections will often give the biological components of our biodemography proposals a strong positive endorsement, just as our colleagues in the demographic and actuarial sciences will endorse the demography components. However, when submitted to a social sciences study section, the proposals have come under severe criticism. We have tried to counter this problem by pursuing an active agenda of publishing peer-reviewed papers that address the specific issues raised by the reviewers. This has obviously been time consuming, and, as yet, this strategy has been only partially successful—each of us has received Independent Scientist Awards (K02) from the NIA, but neither of us has yet had a biodemography R01 funded. The only real solution to developing and maintaining a biodemography program will be for funding agencies like the National Institutes of Health and the National Science Foundation to create interdisciplinary study sections to review and fund interdisciplinary grant proposals.

Postscript

Expanding the Boundaries of Health and Social Science: Case Studies in Interdisciplinary Innovation was published in 2003. The primary motivation for producing the book was not only to discuss the benefits of interdisciplinary collaborations, but also to describe the formidable barriers that make it difficult to implement and sustain these collaborations. In response to the paucity of literature on these issues, the editors enlisted successful collaborative research teams to tell their personal stories in order to reveal how they were able to achieve their success.

The end result of their efforts was a landmark contribution that has become both a catalyst and guiding light for interdisciplinary research in the future.

Two years after publication, the National Institutes of Health (2005a) and the National Academy of Sciences (2005) emphasized the importance of developing and using interdisciplinary approaches for answering critical scientific questions. For example, according to the NIH Roadmap "Health research traditionally has been organized much like a series of cottage industries, lumping researchers into broad areas of scientific interest and then grouping them into distinct, departmentally based specialties. But, as science has advanced over the past decade and the molecular secrets of life have become more accessible, two fundamental themes are apparent: the study of human biology and behavior is a wonderfully dynamic process, and the traditional divisions within health research may in some instances impede the pace of scientific discovery." To address this concern, the NIH set out to lower the organizational barriers to interdisciplinary science by establishing awards that make it easier for scientists to conduct interdisciplinary research. These awards included, among other advances, additional funding for the training of interdisciplinary scientists and the creation of specialized centers to help scientists forge new and more advanced disciplines from existing ones.

In the demographic and population sciences, the NIH promoted the development of interdisciplinary science by soliciting planning centers through the P20 mechanism (http://grants.nih.gov/grants/guide/rfa-files/RFA-RM-040–04.html) as a way to encourage research consortia to develop new interdisciplinary approaches to solving complex and important biomedical research problems. One important NIH program announcement that emerged recently that relates directly to our collaboration in biodemography was the call to support and enhance interdisciplinary research opportunities that focus on determinants of population size, growth, composition, distribution, and on the determinants and consequences of population processes. Included in the description of the announcement was a focus on the antecedents and impacts of changing social, demographic, economic, and health characteristics of the population.

In response to this RFA, Olshansky submitted a proposal to NICHD to create a training program in the School of Public Health at the University of Illinois at Chicago for young scientists to foster interdisciplinary research—with a focus on enhancing opportunities to work with population scientists, disseminating the use of existing data sets in the population sciences, and advancing the development and adoption of quantitative and qualitative methodologies. Olshansky's goal is to create a permanent addition to the curriculum in the School of Public Health that would engage students of epidemiology at early stages in their graduate education in interdisciplinary training in the population sciences. The idea is to expose new graduate students who are seeking advanced degrees in public health (e.g., the Ph.D., Dr.PH, and MPH) to new concepts, theories, challenges, sources of data, role models for interdisciplinary collaboration, and research on public health in the population sciences as a way to enhance and encourage epidemiologists just entering the field, to subsequently develop interdisciplinary research collaborations with population scientists and conduct interdisciplinary research. The topics to be covered address a broad range of issues in the health and population sciences including (but not limited to) fertility, mortality, migration and health; genetics, stress, and heart disease; population genetics; marriage, divorce, and health; affective neuroscience; social influences on gene expression and neural development; genetic epidemiology; psychosocial effects on biology; the health of centenarians; the biodemography of aging; and sources of data in the population sciences. The proposed educational training program is expected to become a permanent part of the core curriculum in the graduate program in the School of Public Health. The content of the course will be updated annually to reflect new interdisciplinary collaborations and opportunities that involve the health and population sciences and the availability of new sources of data that encourage such collaborations. What is particularly unique about the proposed training course is that the lectures will be given by the two authors of this article, and a number of invited faculty consultants from interdisciplinary research teams that have already successfully bridged the gap between scientific disciplines—including many of those representing research teams that appear in this book. As part of their training, students will be required to formulate and draft a 10-page grant proposal for an interdisciplinary research idea of their choosing using the R03 mechanism that is now commonly used at NIH. This training program is expected to yield a number of interdisciplinary scientists who might not otherwise choose this pathway to scientific research, and it will serve as a catalyst for interdisciplinary research for years to come.

Carnes responded to the same NIH request to promote interdisciplinary population research by proposing a permanent course to be added to the curriculum of the University of Oklahoma Health Sciences Center (OUHSC). The proposed course will be offered to students from all colleges within OUHSC, targeting those who are in the early stages of their health care training. The course will introduce to students the concepts, theories, methods, and resources of population science as applied to the health sciences. Interdisciplinary topics and approaches will be emphasized by involving instructors from a variety of health-related fields who are engaged in interdisciplinary research, and who will offer students an opportunity to participate in their research. In doing so, these role models are expected to influence some students to become interdisciplinary population biomedical scientists, and provide others (e.g., M.D.s) with the knowledge needed to develop effective collaborations with interdisciplinary population scientists.

The overall content of the courses to be offered at the OUHSC and the UIC School of Public Health will overlap considerably since both Carnes and Olshansky (Olshansky, Butler, and Carnes, 2007) are involved in the development of both educational programs, and each will serve as instructors at both institutions. The initial review of the grant proposals submitted by both Olshansky and Carnes have been very positive, and we expect these interdisciplinary training courses to have begun in the Fall of 2007.

Three formidable obstacles to sustaining interdisciplinary collaborative research were identified in the initial publication: *(1)* the inability of NIH to recognize co-principal investigators, *(2)* the penalties imposed by promotion and tenure committees on individuals who participate in collaborative activities (e.g., co-investigator on grants and co-authorships on papers or books), and *(3)* departmental concerns in academic settings over effort spent on activities traditionally viewed as being within the purview of other departments other disciplines, or both. Although these obstacles still exist, there are harbingers of positive change for interdisciplinary collaborative research ventures. Foremost among these have been the decision by NIH to support interdisciplinary "team science" (Fox, 2006; Zerhouni, 2006), and the movement by NIH to formally recognize "multiple Principal Investigators" (National Institutes of Health, 2006). The former change will have a big impact on departmental perceptions of interdisciplinary research, and the latter will not eliminate but should hopefully lessen the penalties on collaboration imposed by promotion and tenure committees. In other words, it is change at NIH that ultimately drives the perceptions and generates the support for interdisciplinary collaboration at universities and departments, not the other way around.

ACKNOWLEDGMENTS

Funding for this work was provided by the National Institutes of Health/National Institute on Aging for Dr. Olshansky and Dr. Carnes (AG13698-01, AG00894-01), the National Aeronautics and Space Administration (98-HEDS-02-257 for Dr. Carnes), and the Social Security Administration (Grant No. 10-P-98347-5-01 for Dr. Olshansky).

RECOMMENDED READINGS

Carnes, B. A., and Olshansky, S. J. (1993). Evolutionary perspectives on human senescence. *Population and Development Review, 19*(4), 793–806.

Carnes, B. A., Olshansky, S. J., and Grahn, D. (1996). Continuing the search for a law of mortality. *Population and Development Review, 22*(2), 231–264.

Kirkwood, T. B. L. (1992). Comparative life-spans of species: Why do species have the life spans they do? *American Journal of Clinical Nutrition,* 55, 1191S–1195S.

Medawar, P. B. (1952). *An Unsolved Problem of Biology.* London: Lewis.

Olshansky, S. J., and Carnes, B. A. (2001). *The Quest for Immortality: Science at the Frontiers of Aging.* New York: Norton.

Olshansky, S. J., Carnes, B. A., and Grahn, D. (1998). Confronting the boundaries of human longevity. *American Scientist, 86*(1), 52–61.

Pearl, R. (1922). A Comparison of the laws of mortality in *Drosophila* and in man. *American Naturalist, 56,* 398–405.

Wachter, K. W., and Finch, C. E. (Eds.) (1997). *Between Zeus and the Salmon: The Biodemography of Longevity.* Washington, DC: National Academy Press.

Williams, G. C. (1957). Pleiotropy, natural selection, and the evolution of senescence. *Evolution, 11,* 298–311.

REFERENCES

Bennett, N. G., and Olshansky, S. J. (1996). Forecasting U.S. age structure and the future of social security: The impact of adjustments to official mortality schedules. *Population and Development Review, 22*(4), 703–727.

Brody, S. (1924). The Kinetics of Senescence. *Journal of General Physiology, 6*, 245–57.

Brooks, A., Lithgow, Gordon J. and Johnson, Thomas E. (1994). Mortality rates in a genetically heterogeneous population of *Caenorhabditis elegans. Science, 263*, 668–671.

Brownlee, J. (1919). Notes on the biology of a life-table. *Journal of the Royal Statistical Society, 82*, 34–77.

Brues, A. M., and Sacher, George A. (1952). Analysis of mammalian radiation injury and lethality. In J. J. Nickson (Ed.), *Symposium on Radiobiology* (pp. 441–465). New York: Wiley.

Carey, James R., Liedo, P., Orozco, D., and Vaupel, James W. (1992). Slowing of mortality rates at older ages in large medfly cohorts. *Science, 258*, 457–461.

Carnes, B. A., Grahn, D., and Thomson, J. F. (1989). Dose-response modeling of life shortening in a retrospective analysis of the combined data from the JANUS program at Argonne National Laboratory. *Radiation Research, 119*, 39–56.

Carnes, B. A., and Fritz, T. E. (1991). Responses of the beagle to protracted irradiation: I. Effect of total dose and dose rate. *Radiation Research, 128*, 125–132.

Carnes, B. A., and Fritz, T. E. (1993). Continuous irradiation of beagles by gamma rays. *Radiation Research, 136*, 103–110.

Carnes, B. A., and Olshansky, S. J. (1993). Evolutionary perspectives on human senescence. *Population and Development Review, 4*, 793–806.

Carnes, B. A., Olshansky, S. J., and Grahn, D. (1996). Continuing the search for a law of mortality. *Population and Development Review, 22*(2), 231–264.

Carnes, B. A., and Olshansky, S. J. (1997). A biologically motivated partitioning of mortality. *Experimental Gerontology, 32*, 615–631.

Carnes, B. A., Groer, P. G., and Kotek, T. (1997). Dial workers: Dose-response and modeling issues. *Radiation Research, 147*, 707–714.

Carnes, B. A., Olshansky, S. J., Gavrilov, L., Gavrilova, N., and Grahn, D. (1999). Human longevity: Nature vs nurture–Fact or fiction. *Perspectives in Biology and Medicine, 42*(3), 422–441.

Carnes, B. A., Olshansky, S. J., and Grahn, D. (1998). An interspecies prediction of the risk of radiation-induced mortality. *Radiation Research, 149*, 487–492.

Carnes, B. A., Grahn, D. and Hoel, D. (2003). Mortality of Atomic bomb survivors predicted from laboratory animals. *Radiation Research, 160*, 159–167.

Carnes, B. A., Olshansky, S. J., and Grahn, D. (2003). Biological evidence for limits to the duration of life. *Biogerontology, 4*, 314–5.

Carnes, B. A., Holden, L. R., Olshansky, S. J., Witten, T. M. and Siegel, J. S. (2006). Mortality partitions and their relevance to research on senescence. *Biogerontology, 7*, 183–198.

Curtsinger, J. W., Fukui, H., Townsend, D., and Vaupel, J. W. (1992). Demography of genotypes: Failure of the limited life-span paradigm in *Drosophila melanogaster. Science, 258*, 461–463.

Deevey, E. S. Jr. (1947). Life tables for natural populations of animals. *Quarterly Review of Biology, 22*, 283–314.

Failla, G. (1958). The aging process and cancerogenesis. *Annals of the New York Academy of Sciences, 71*, 1124–1140.

Fox, R.J. (2006). Translational and Clinical Science: To the Editor. *New England Journal of Medicine, 354*(9), 978.

Fukui, H. H., Xiu, L., and Curtsinger, J. W. (1993). lowing of age-specific mortality rates in *Ddrosophila melanogaster. Experimental Gerontology, 28,* 585–99.

Gavrilov, L. A., and Gavrilova, N. S. (1991). *The Biology of Life Span: A Quantitative Approach.* Switzerland: Harwood Academic Publishers.

Gompertz, B. (1825). On the nature of the function expressive of the law of human mortality and on a new mode of determining life contingencies. *Philosophical Transactions of the Royal Society of London, 115,* 513–585.

Grahn, D. (1994). *Studies of Acute and Chronic Radiation Injury at the Biological and Medical Research Division, Argonne National Laboratory, 1953–1970: Description of Individual Studies, Data Files, Codes, and Summaries of Significant Findings.* ANL-94/26. Argonne, IL: Argonne National Laboratory.

Grahn, D., Lombard, L. S., and Carnes, B. A. (1992). The comparative tumorigenic effects of fission neutrons and cobalt-60 ? rays in the B6CF1 mouse. *Radiation Research, 129,* 19–36.

Grahn, D., Wright, B. J., Carnes, B. A., Williamson, F. S., and Fox, C. (1995). *Studies of Acute and Chronic Radiation Injury at the Biological and Medical Research Division, Argonne National Laboratory, 1970–1992: The Janus Program: Survival and Pathology Data.* ANL-95/3. Argonne, IL: Argonne National Laboratory.

Greenwood, M. (1928). Laws of mortality from the biological point of view. *Journal of Hygiene, 28,* 267–94.

Hamilton, W. D. (1966). The moulding of senescence by natural selection. *Journal of Theoretical Biology, 12,* 12–45.

Heligman, L., and Pollard, J. H. (1980). The age pattern of mortality. *Journal of the Institute of Actuaries, 107,* 49–80.

Hutchinson, G. E. (1978). *Introduction to Population Ecology.* New Haven, CT: Yale University Press.

Kirkwood, T. B. L. (1977). Evolution of aging, *Nature, 270,* 301–304.

Kirkwood, T. B. L. (1992). Comparative life-spans of species: Why do species have the life spans they do? *American Journal of Clinical Nutrition, 55,* 1191S–1195S.

Kirkwood, T. B. L., and Holliday, R. (1979). The evolution of ageing and longevity. *Proceedings of the Royal Society of London B: Biological Sciences, 205,* 531–546.

Kirkwood, T. B. L., and Rose, M. (1991). Evolution of senescence: Late survival sacrificed for reproduction. *Philosophical Transactions of the Royal Society of London B: Biological Sciences, 332,* 15–24.

Loeb, J., and Northrop, J. H. (1916). Is there a temperature coefficient for the duration of life? *Proceedings of the National Academy of Sciences, 2,* 456–457.

Loeb, J., and Northrop, J. H. (1917a). On the influence of food and temperature upon the duration of life. *Journal of Biological Chemistry, 32,* 102–121.

Loeb, J., and Northrop, J. H. (1917b). What determines the duration of life in metazoa? *Proceedings of the National Academy of Sciences, 3,* 382–386.

Lorenz, E. (1950). Some biologic effects of long-continued irradiation. *American Journal of Roentgenol Radium Therapy, 63,* 176–185.

Luckinbill, L. S. et al. (1984). Selection for delayed senescence in *Drosophila melanogaster. Evolution, 38,* 996–1003.

Makeham, W. M. (1860). On the law of mortality and the construction of annuity tables. *Journal of the Institute of Actuaries, 6,* 301–310.

Makeham, W. M. (1867). On the law of mortality. *Journal of the Institute of Actuaries, 13,* 325–358.

Makeham, W. M. (1872). Explanation and example of a method constructing mortality tables with imperfect data; and of the extension of Gompertz's theory to the entire period of life. *Journal of the Institute of Actuaries, 16,* 344–354.

Makeham, W. M. (1889). On the further development of Gompertz's law. *Journal of the Institute of Actuaries, 28,* 152–160, 185–192.

Makeham, W. M. (1890). On the further development of Gompertz's law. *Journal of the Institute of Actuaries, 28,* 316–332.

Manton, K. G., Stallard, E., and Tolley, H. D. (1991). Limits to human life expectancy. *Population and Development Review, 17*(4), 603–637.

Medawar, P. B. (1952). *An Unsolved Problem of Biology.* London: Lewis.

Mildvan, A., and Strehler, Bernard L. (1960). A critique of theories of mortality. In B. L. Strehler, J. D. Ebert, H. B. Glass, and N. W. Shock (Eds.), *The Biology of Aging.* Pub. No. 6. Washington, DC: American Institute of Biological Sciences.

National Academy of Sciences (2005). Committee on facilitating interdisciplinary research. http://www7.nationalacademies.org/interdisciplinary/

National Institutes of Health (2005a). NIH Roadmap: Accelerating Discovery to Improve Health. http://nihroadmap.nih.gov/index.asp

National Institutes of Health (2005b). NIH Roadmap: Accelerating Discovery to Improve Health. http://nihroadmap.nih.gov/interdisciplinary/

National Institutes of Health (2006). Multiple principal investigators: an overview. http://grants2.nih.gov/grants/multi_pi/overview.htm.

Olshansky, S. J. (1988). On forecasting mortality. *Milbank Quarterly, 66*(3), 482–530.

Olshansky, S. J., and Carnes, B. A. (1994). Demographic perspectives on human senescence. *Population and Development Review, 20*(1), 57–80.

Olshansky, S. J., and Carnes, B. A. (1997). Ever since Gompertz. *Demography, 34*(1), 1–15.

Olshansky, S. J., and Carnes, B. A. (2000). *The Quest for Immortality: From Folklore to Science—Aging, Health and Longevity in the 21st Century.* New York: Norton.

Olshansky, S. J., Carnes, B. A., and Butler, R. (2001). If humans were built to last. *Scientific American,* March, pp. 70–75.

Olshansky, S. J., Carnes, B. A., and Cassel, C. (1990). In search of Methuselah: Estimating the upper limits to human longevity. *Science, 250,* 634–640.

Olshansky, S. J., Carnes, B. A., and Cassel, C. (1993). The aging of the human species. *Scientific American,* April, pp. 46–52.

Olshansky, S. J., Carnes, B. A., and Grahn, D. A. (1998). Confronting the boundaries of human longevity. *American Scientist, 86*(1), 52–61.

Olshansky, S. J., Butler, R. N., and Carnes, B. A. (2007). Re-engineering Humans. *The Scientist, 21*(3), 28–31.

Orzack, S. H., and Tuljapurkar, S. (1989). Population dynamics in variable environments: VII. The demography and evolution of iteroparity. *American Naturalist, 133,* 901–923.

Pearl, R. (1921). Experimental studies on the duration of life. *American Naturalist, 55,* 481–509.

Pearl, R. (1922). A comparison of the laws of mortality in *Drosophila* and in man. *American Naturalist, 56,* 398–405.

Pearl, R., and Minor, J. R. (1935). Experimental studies on the duration of life: XIV. The comparative mortality of certain lower organisms. *Quarterly Review of Biology, 10,* 60–79.

Perks, W. (1932). On some experiments in the graduation of mortality statistics. *Journal of the Institute of Actuaries, 63,* 12–57.

Pollard, J. H., and Streatfield, K. (1979). Factors affecting mortality and the length of life. Presented at the Joint Convention of the Institute of Actuaries of Australia, Christchurch, New Zealand.

Pollard, J. H., and Valkovics, E. (1992). The Gompertz distribution and its applications. *Genus, 48,* 15–27.

Rose, M. R. (1984). Laboratory evolution of postponed senescence in *Drosophila melanogaster. Evolution, 38,* 1004–1010.

Sacher, G. (1956). On the statistical nature of mortality, with especial reference of chronic radiation mortality. *Radiology, 67,* 250–257.

Sacher, G. A., and Trucco, E. (1962). The stochastic theory of mortality. *Annals of the New York Academy of Sciences, 96,* 985–1007.

Szilard, L. (1959). On the nature of the aging process. *Proceedings of the National Academy of Sciences, 45,* 30–45.

Tuljapurkar, S. (1990). *Population Dynamics in Variable Environments.* Berlin: Springer-Verlag.

Vaupel, J. W., Manton, K. G., and Stallard, E. (1979). The impact of heterogeneity on individual frailty on the dynamics of mortality. *Demography, 16,* 439–454.

Wachter, K. W., and Finch, C. E. (Eds.) (1997). *Between Zeus and the Salmon: The Biodemography of Longevity.* Washington, DC: National Academy Press.

Weismann, A. (1891). *Essays upon Heredity and Kindred Biological Problems.* Oxford: Clarendon Press.

Weiss, K. (1990). The biodemography of variation in human frailty. *Demography, 27,* 185–206.

Williams, G. C. (1957). Pleiotropy, natural selection, and the evolution of senescence. *Evolution, 11,* 298–311.

Zerhouni, E. A. (2006). Translational and Clinical Science: A Reply To the Editor. *New England Journal of Medicine, 354(9),* 978–979.

A TALE OF TWO CITIES

Prevention and Management of HIV/AIDS

Domain Introduction

NEIL SCHNEIDERMAN

This section consists of two case studies, each describing how multidisciplinary teams of investigators working in culturally diverse metropolitan locations, San Francisco (Bay Area) and Miami (Miami–Dade County), set out to confront HIV/AIDS in two major epicenters of the disease. At the outset it should be recognized that HIV/AIDS is a global pandemic, and that the two case studies can therefore provide only a glimpse of the bio-psycho-social perspectives that are evolving in the prevention and management of this highly communicable disease. By the end of the last millennium, HIV/AIDS, whose early cases began to be reported in 1981, had affected 33.6 million people worldwide (National Institute of Allergy and Infectious Diseases, 1999). More than two-thirds of these people were located in sub-Saharan Africa, with another 18% in Southern Asia. Nearly a million people are believed to be infected with HIV in the United States.

Within the United States, most of the early HIV/AIDS cases occurred among men who have sex with men and to a lesser extent among injection drug users. More recently, another wave of HIV/AIDS has occurred among women sex partners of injection drug users, bisexual men, and heterosexually active persons. Thus between 1995 and 1999 the percentage of women AIDS cases in the United States increased from 11% to more than 20% (Centers for Disease Control and Prevention, 1999). The change in HIV/AIDS demographics has also seen an increasing percentage of African Americans afflicted. In 1993 whites accounted for 48% of AIDS deaths in the United States, whereas blacks accounted for 34% and Hispanics 17%. By 1998 blacks accounted for 49%, whites 32%, and Hispanics 18% of AIDS mortality. These changes in HIV/AIDS demographics have required the development of innovative prevention and management strategies for dealing with increasingly hard to reach at-risk and HIV-infected populations. The two centers described as case studies in this section have spent much of their efforts tracking the HIV/AIDS epidemic and responding to these demographic changes and the consequential challenges.

The Center for AIDS Prevention Studies (CAPS) in San Francisco that is the focus of the Chapter 18, by Chesney and Coates, was founded in 1986 with a principal emphasis on primary prevention. One of the first findings reported by the group was that after a diagnosis of HIV seropositive, men either in nonmonogamous relationships or not in a relationship reported substantial reductions in high-risk but not low-risk sexual behaviors (Coates, Morin, and McKusick, 1987). Another early finding was that the use of recreational drugs during sex, the number of drugs used, and the frequency of combining sex and drugs were all positively associated with risky sexual activity (Stall, McKusick, Wiley, et al., 1986).

As the HIV/AIDS epidemic progressed, CAPS expanded its realm of study to those persons already infected with HIV. One study found that depression predicted a rapid decline in CD4 lymphocyte counts in HIV-seropositive men and that that association was not attributable to differences in alcohol or drug use or to differences in perceived somatic symptoms (Burack et al., 1993). Another study observed that neither caregiving for an HIV-infected partner nor the stress of bereavement was associated with hastening HIV disease progression (Folkman, Chesney, Cooke, Boccellari, and Collette, 1994). More recently, Chesney, Ickovics, Hecht, Sikipa, and Rabkin (1999) have identified important variables associated with medication nonadherence in HIV-seropositive patients as alcohol use, stresses of daily living, and psychological distress. Based on these and other research findings, the CAPS investigators have collaborated with a number of community-based organizations to disseminate AIDS-prevention information in ways that can affect public health practices and policy.

In contrast to the approach taken by CAPS in San Francisco, the Miami group responsible for the studies reported in Chapter 17, by Schneiderman and Antoni, has largely focused on group-based, cognitive behavioral stress management (CBSM) interventions among HIV-infected individuals. Initially, such intervention was aimed exclusively at gay men, but over time it expanded to provide CBSM for women and for men with a history of drug abuse. The studies have typically examined the effects of CBSM on psychosocial variables such as depressed affect, coping skills, and perceived social support, as well as on subclinical markers of disease (Schneiderman, Antoni, Saab, and Ironson, 2001). By now there is strong epidemiological evidence that psychosocial factors are associated with immune status (e.g., Ickovics et al., 2001) and mortality in HIV/AIDS (e.g., Leserman et al., 2000).

As a corollary, and as Schneiderman and Antoni point out in their chapter, the development of combination therapy and protease inhibitors has brought about a change of emphasis in HIV treatment from palliative care to chronic disease management. Although the new medical treatments seem able to prolong good health in HIV-infected patients, medication adherence remains a major unsolved problem, with ominous implications for public health. Improving medication adherence is thus important for the good health of individual patients, as well as for those having sexual relationships with them. For one thing, lack of medication adherence may increase the likelihood of infecting those who are not diseased. For another, lack of adherence can increase the risk of infecting those with or without HIV with a drug-resistant variant of the virus. Medication adherence is thus important for primary and tertiary prevention, as well as for patient management. More generally, from the point of view of public health issues surrounding medication adherence, successfully addressing these issues will require behavioral and social science attention.

The two case studies in this part are intended to provide cogent examples of how a range of behavioral and social science approaches have, in fact, been used to tackle one of our most important public health problems. It is clear that the deployment of the behavioral and social sciences to combat HIV/AIDS must occur at multiple levels and requires the application of different skills, both within and across levels. These levels range from the interpersonal, as exemplified by the Miami program, to the broader social levels embraced by CAPS, including interventions with organizations such as schools and community centers, social marketing, development of media messages, and the engagement in advocacy aimed at legislation and changes in public policy.

It is important to note that the behavioral/social science research carried out in Miami and San Francisco did not occur independently from research occurring elsewhere and at various levels. Although the Miami group focused on HIV-infected individuals at the interpersonal level, other studies have focused on decreasing the high-risk behaviors that promote HIV transmission. For example, in one study using individual counseling, fewer sexually transmitted diseases (STDs) were observed in those who received counseling than in those who received only didactic messages (Kamb et al., 1998). At the community and institutional level, a program developed for the Royal Thai Army is illustrative and important (Celentano et al., 2000). The program was carried out in small groups at the company level and was designed to increase condom use, to reduce alcohol consumption and brothel patronage, and to improve sexual negotiation and condom skills. Incident STDs were seven times less frequent among men assigned to the intervention than in the control group, and incident HIV was 50% less in the intervention group. And at the public policy level, the passage of a syringe law in Connecticut in 1992 permitted the purchase of up to 10 nonprescription syringes in pharmacies. A study of the results of this law found that, whereas 52% of intravenous drug users reportedly shared needles before the law was passed, this number subsequently dropped to 31% (Groseclose et al., 1995). Further, a large number of studies of syringe-exchange programs worldwide has shown that such programs lead to reductions in HIV risk behavior without a concomitant increase in drug use (DesJarlais and Friedman, 2001). It would thus appear that interventions conducted at multiple levels can have an effect on high-risk behaviors for HIV, as well as the well-being of HIV patients.

The two chapters in this part describe somewhat different approaches to the HIV/AIDS epidemic and involve different organizational structures. Although the approaches are complementary, their institutional similarities and differences are worth noting. The University of Miami HIV/AIDS Program Project, sponsored by the National Institute of Mental Health (NIMH), is nested within the university's Behavioral Medicine Research Center (BMRC), directed by psychologist Neil Schneiderman. The BMRC, in turn, is under the governance of the College of Arts and Sciences and the School of Medicine and consists of a team of multidisciplinary investigators who have adopted a common interpersonal approach to chronic disease management of cancer, chronic fatigue syndrome, coronary heart disease, diabetes, and HIV/AIDS. This center is physically located within a large academic medical complex that provides ready access to patients, physician specialists, nurses, clinics, medical expertise, and biomedical laboratory resources. With its multiple NIH-funded center and program project grants, multiple research training grants, and cadres of biomedical and social science personnel, the BMRC is positioned to provide leadership in research at the interpersonal level involving the patient management of HIV/AIDS.

In contrast, CAPS—sponsored by the NIMH and directed by psychologist Tom Coates—has an exclusive involvement in HIV/AIDS prevention. Housed at the University of California, San Francisco and under the umbrella of the AIDS Research Institute (ARI) led by Coates, the center coordinates and fosters the university's research and training in HIV/AIDS. In essence, through its collaboration with Bay Area institutions outside of the university (including health department and community-based organizations), CAPS serves as the central node in linking more than 200 San Francisco Bay Area investigators with expertise in epidemiology, behavioral medicine, biostatistics, biomedical and basic sciences, survey research, substance abuse, ethics, public health, international health, and health policy research and analysis. CAPS is thus uniquely positioned to use multidisciplinary, multilevel approaches to combat the spread of HIV/AIDS. Overall, then, these chapters provide valuable insight into the origin and development of two multidisciplinary programs that have confronted the HIV/AIDS epidemic in somewhat different ways.

Postscript

Changes in the HIV/AIDS epidemic related to the introduction of protease inhibitors and highly active antiretroviral therapy (HAART) have brought the San Francisco and Miami programs closer together in terms of their perspectives and strategies. Instead of being looked upon as a death sentence requiring palliative care, HIV/AIDS has come to be considered a chronic disease that requires both pharmacological and behavioral management. In that context, CAPS scientists conducted some of the first research on adherence to HIV medications (Chesney, Ickovics, Hecht, Sikipa, and Rabkin, 1999) and the Miami group demonstrated the impact of psychosocial factors on both medication adherence and HIV viral load (Weaver et al., 2005), as well as the influence of adherence training and CBSM on HIV viral burden (Antoni et al., 2006).

Although successful HAART treatment has led to dramatic reductions in AIDS-related morbidity and mortality in the United States (Centers for Disease Control and Prevention, 2003), patients on HAART who are nonadherent to their medication regimen can develop drug resistant strains of HIV. These can undermine the effectiveness of medications, thereby producing a major threat to public health. With the recent and ongoing development of one tablet per day HAART, distribution of such medications worldwide is becoming feasible as a result of the efforts of international governmental support and the Gates Foundation. Hence, CBSM and adherence interventions such as those being developed in Miami, and international information dissemination programs such as those being developed by CAPS, should facilitate the creation of more effective means of promoting HIV/AIDS medication adherence while minimizing the threat of drug resistance.

As CAPS and the Miami BMRC program in HIV/AIDS have developed, they both have continued their emphasis upon multidisciplinary research. The UCSF Center for AIDS research (CFAR), directed by Drs. Paul Volberding, M.D. and Warner Greene, M.D., Ph.D., is funded by the National Institute of Allergy and Infectious Diseases. Similarly, in 2007 the University of Miami was awarded a Developmental CFAR under the direction of Dr. Savita Pahwa, M.D. Both CFARs support a multidisciplinary environment that promotes basic, clinical, epidemiological, behavioral, and translational research in the prevention, detection, and treatment of HIV/AIDS. Further, both CAPS and the Miami program have used the CFAR mechanism to bring together behavioral researchers, biomedical scientists, and public health investigators to work on important problems.

In similar fashion, investigators at both CAPS and the University of Miami have expanded their programs to other countries. CAPS scientists, for example, have developed important HIV/AIDS programs in Zimbabwe, Uganda, India, and Latin America. Meanwhile, the University of Miami's NIH Fogarty International Center's AIDS and TB Training and Research Program, under the direction of Dr. Gail Shor-Posner, prepares scientists to conduct significant biomedical, behavioral and epidemiological-prevention projects in the Dominican Republic, Colombia, Peru, and Guyana. Such training has encompassed a very large number of problems associated with HIV/AIDS, and has included programs in CBSM and medication adherence under the direction of Schneiderman and Antoni.

As one reads our tale of two cities it will become apparent that the success of both programs has been intimately related to the development of multidisciplinary cooperation and the visualization of interdisciplinary solutions to complex problems. The individual investigators, who came to important problems with both an open mind and a willingness to cooperate across disciplinary, professional, departmental and school boundaries, deserve a large measure of credit. So too do the administrators of the University of California, San Francisco and the University of Miami as well as community leaders and organizations who, seeing the need to work together, have offered their continued cooperation. As important, in the two decades that CAPS and the BMRC have been engaged in HIV/AIDS research, we have also seen a sea change in the NIH, which has moved from a more insular, institute approach toward research to an emphasis on a multidisciplinary approach that transcends disciplinary and professional affiliation. The clear result has been an improvement in the research enterprise.

For many years CAPS has been a leader in assessing HIV prevention policies, while its policy and ethics research has grown significantly during the past decade. CAPS has also taken the lead in assessing evidence-based policies for access to optimum HIV treatment. Based upon the kind of research that has been conducted during the past 20 years in both Miami and San Francisco, policy making agencies are beginning to find themselves in a better position to understand and evaluate options for the prevention and management of HIV/AIDS. There is still no cure for HIV/AIDS, and the pandemic is not yet under control, but the strategies needed to manage HIV/AIDS as a major health problem have advanced considerably in the past decade and even in the years since the original edition of this volume appeared.

REFERENCES

Antoni, M. H., Carrico, A. W., Durán, R. E., Spitzer, S., Penedo, F., Ironson, G., Fletcher, M. A., Klimas, N., and Schneiderman, N. (2006). Randomized clinical trial of cognitive behavioral stress management on human immunodeficiency virus load in gay men treated with highly active antiretroviral therapy. *Psychosomatic Medicine, 68,* 143–151.

Burack, J., Barrett, D., Stall, R., Chesney, M., Ekstrand, M., and Coates, T. J. (1993). Depressive symptoms and CD4 lymphocyte decline among HIV-infected men. *Journal of the American Medical Association, 270,* 2568–2573.

Celentano, D. D., Bond, K. C., Lyles, C. M., Eiumtrakul, S., Go, V. F., Beyrer, C., and Chiangmai, C. (2000). Preventive intervention to reduce sexually transmitted infections. *Archives of Internal Medicine, 160,* 535–540.

Centers for Disease Control and Prevention (1999). *HIV/AIDS Surveillance Report, 1999, 11*(1), 3–36.

Centers for Disease Control and Prevention (2003). Increases in HIV diagnosis. *Morbidity and Mortality Weekly Report, 52,* 1145–1148.

Chesney, M. A., Ickovics, J., Hecht, F. M., Sikipa, G., and Rabkin, J. (1999). Adherence: A necessity for successful HIV combination therapy. *AIDS, 13* (Suppl. A), S271–S278.

Coates, T. J., Morin, S., and McKusick (1987). Behavioral consequences of AIDS antibody testing among gay men. *JAMA, 258,* 1988.

DesJarlais, D. C., and Friedman, S. R. (2001). Strategies for preventing HIV infection among injecting drug users: Taking interventions to the people. In N. Schneiderman, M. A. Speers, J. M. Silva, H. Tomes, and J. H. Gentry (Eds.), *Integrating Behavioral and Social Sciences with Public Health.* Washington, DC: American Psychological Association.

Folkman, S., Chesney, M. A., Cooke, M., Boccellari, A., and Collette, L. (1994). Caregiver burden in HIV-positive and HIV-negative partners of men with AIDS. *Journal of Consulting and Clinical Psychology, 62,* 746–756.

Groseclose, S. L., Weinstein, B., Jones, T. S., Valleroy, L. A., Fehrs, L. J., and Kassler, W. J. (1995). Impact of increased legal access to needles and syringes on practices of injecting-drug uses and police officers—Connecticut, 1992–1993. *Journal of Acquired Immune Deficiency Syndromes and Human Retrovirology, 10,* 82–89.

Ickovics, J. R., Hamburger, M. E., Vladhou, D., Schoenbaum, E. E., Schuman, P., Boland, R. J., and Moore, J. (2001). Mortality, CD4 count decline, and depressive symptoms among HIV- seropositive women. *JAMA, 285,* 1466–1474.

Kamb, M. L., Fishbein, M., Douglas, J. M., Rhodes, F., Rogers, J. et al. (1998). Efficacy of risk-reduction counseling to prevent human immunodeficiency virus and sexually transmitted diseases: A randomized controlled trial. *Journal of the American Medical Association, 200,* 1161–1167.

Leserman, J., Petitto, J. M., Golden, R. N., Gaynes, B. N., Gu, H., Perkins, D. O., Silva, S. G., Folds, J. D., and Evans, D. L. (2000). Impact of stressful life events, depression, social support, coping, and cortisol on progression to AIDS. *American Journal of Psychiatry, 157,* 1221–1228.

National Institute of Allergy and Infectious Diseases (December, 1999). *HIV/AIDS Statistics.* Fact Sheet. Bethesda, MD: NIAID.

Schneiderman, N., Antoni, M. H., Saab, P. G., and Ironson, G. (2001). Health psychology: Psychosocial and biobehavioral aspects of chronic disease management. *Annual Review of Psychology, 52,* 555–580.

Stall, R., McKusick, L., and Wiley, J. (1986). Alcohol and drug use during sexual activity and compliance with safe sex guidelines for AIDS: The AIDS behavioral research project. *Health Education Quarterly, 13,* 359–360.

Weaver, K. E., Llabre, M. M., Durán, R. E., Antoni, M. H., Ironson, G., Penedo, F. J., and Schneiderman, N. (2005). A stress and coping model of medication adherence and viral load in HIV positive men and women on highly active antiretroviral therapy (HAART). *Health Psychology, 24,* 835–892.

Learning to Cope with HIV/AIDS

NEIL SCHNEIDERMAN and MICHAEL ANTONI

In early 1986 Carl Eisdorfer, M.D., Ph.D., was preparing to become chair of the department of psychiatry at the University of Miami, Michael Antoni was about to receive his Ph.D. in psychology at the same institution, and Neil Schneiderman, Ph.D., learned that his application for an NIH program project in cardiovascular behavioral medicine was about to be funded. While discussing the allocation of new research space for the program project, Bernard Fogel, M.D., dean of the School of Medicine, shared with Schneiderman his fear that Jackson Memorial, the University's major teaching hospital could soon become almost exclusively an acquired immunodeficiency syndrome (AIDS) hospital. He suggested that Schneiderman should meet with Mary Ann Fletcher, Ph.D., director of the School of Medicine's E. M. Papper Clinical Immunology Laboratory and with Eisdorfer to consider developing a comprehensive interdisciplinary research program to fight human immunodeficiency virus (HIV/AIDS). A meeting between Schneiderman and Fletcher was arranged by Gail Ironson, M.D., Ph.D., who was then one of Schneiderman's postdoctoral fellows. When Eisdorfer arrived at the university, he applied to the NIMH for a Center for the Biopsychosocial Study of AIDS, which was funded in October 1986. One project, co-led by Schneiderman and Fletcher, studied stress responses and behavioral management in individuals infected with HIV.

The first cases of AIDS had been reported in 1981 (Centers for Disease Control [and Prevention], 1981), and by 1984 several research groups had reported isolation of its causative agent, HIV (Barre-Sinoussi et al., 1983; Levy et al., 1984; Popovic, Sardgadharan, Read, and Gallo, 1984). Although there were no known or potential cures for HIV/AIDS, tests were soon developed to detect antibodies to the virus

(Centers for Disease Control [and Prevention], 1985). By 1986, almost 100,000 cases of AIDS had been reported in 132 countries (Centers for Disease Control [and Prevention], 1986) and another 5 to 10 million people were believed to be asymptomatic carriers of HIV (Mahler, 1988). In the United States, most HIV-infected individuals were either gay men or intravenous (IV) drug users (or both).

Against this backdrop, the Schneiderman and Fletcher group decided to study HIV/AIDS as a chronic disease. Because there was no cure on the horizon, the strategy we adopted was to try and learn how to keep people healthy as long as possible during the clinical latent period (i.e., before HIV-infected persons showed AIDS symptoms) and to improve quality of life by reducing stress. One of our underlying hypotheses was that psychosocial stressors, particularly those that persistently increase distress and depress mood, exacerbate the course of HIV/AIDS by adversely influencing the immune system. Conversely, we hypothesized that psychosocial interventions that reduce persistent distress, depressed mood, and emotional arousal favorably impact the immune system, thereby attenuating disease progression. We assumed that the impact of psychosocial variables on the immune system is mediated by stress hormones. With these thoughts in mind, we realized that to develop a research program, we would need to recruit a multidisciplinary team with expertise in psychosocial assessment and interventions, endocrinology, immunology, and clinical medicine.

This chapter provides a brief introduction to the common language that has allowed our research team to share and integrate basic concepts. We then discuss how psychosocial variables that affect quality of life in individuals with HIV can influence the subclinical markers of disease that are associated with disease progression and mortality. This is followed by discussion of the revolution in HIV patient management brought about by combination therapy and the advent of protease inhibitors. Whereas our initial psychosocial interventions focused on improving quality of life and subclinical markers of HIV spectrum disease, the revolution in HIV/AIDS treatment has meant that our present intervention studies have also had to deal with preventing drug resistance and its consequences. This has caused us to focus on medication adherence and the need to help decrease illicit drug use and risky sex in HIV-infected individuals. As the HIV epidemic has progressed, it has increasingly infiltrated poor minority communities. Because Miami is one of the epicenters of the HIV epidemic, we have had to learn to deal with complex issues involving diverse groups of people within our community who have become infected via various routes of transmission. In order to show how we have adjusted to the rapidly changing AIDS scene, we have included a brief description of our program infrastructure.

Learning to Talk to Each Other

A major challenge posed by the development of a multidisciplinary research program was for investigators to become facile with a common language that would allow collaborators to understand each other's concepts. The biomedical scientists and physicians, for example, had to learn that psychosocial variables can be rigorously defined and assessed in precise terms and that the biological changes to be studied are modulated by a sociocultural context that also needs to be evaluated. Conversely, the psychosocial scientists had to become conversant with a whole new language that is based on major biological concepts. Most important, both the psychosocial and biomedical scientists had to learn to think in terms of relationships between psychosocial variables and pathobiology.

At the outset, everyone in the research group had to understand that AIDS is caused by a virus, HIV, and is characterized by a breakdown of the body's immune defenses. For this reason, it is important to know about the body's immune defenses and how HIV attacks the immune system.

The immune system has two functional systems involving lymphocytes, which are small white blood cells that are paramount in immune defense. A first line of defense (nonspecific, or innate, immunity) is importantly safeguarded by natural killer (NK) cells. In contrast, once first-line defenses are breached, specific immunity is provided by B cells and T cells, which learn to recognize specific infectious agents. For this reason the B cells and T cells are said to constitute an adaptive immune system. The B cells produce antibodies (memory cells) that "cleanse" body fluids, whereas T cells "cleanse" body tissues. Although the cells of the innate and adaptive immune systems have their own specific functions, they work together closely. Some lymphocytes are killers such as NK cells or cytotoxic-T (CD8) cells, whereas other subtypes such as the T helper (CD4) cells recognize and activate the cells that oppose disease-causing agents. In our work with long-term survivors of AIDS, we have observed that nonspecific cellular immunity involving NK cells appears to protect the health of these HIV-infected patients even though they have very low CD4 counts (Ironson et al., 2001).

HIV attacks T helper (CD4) cells. The virus invades the cell and uses the machinery inside the cell to multiply and kill the cell before moving on to kill other CD4 cells. Because these CD4 cells are critical to T cell and B cell function, their destruction permits microorganisms to cause infections, including those that are normally held under control such as cytomegalovirus. These infections will finally kill the host. Because psychosocial stressors were thought to contribute to immunosuppression, we set out to document such suppression in HIV-infected (HIV+) individuals and to determine whether psychosocial interventions can attenuate this suppression.

Psychosocial Factors and Immune Status in Asymptomatic Gay Men

We decided to begin studying asymptomatic HIV+ individuals as soon as possible after they became infected, because their immune systems would be reasonably intact. We reasoned that this would maximize our ability to keep these HIV+ people healthy for as long as possible. With this in mind, we sought at-risk gay men who thought they might be infected and wished to be tested and counseled anonymously for HIV. Because there were few places in the community where such testing could be done and because of the potential stigma involved, it was relatively easy to find individuals who wished to be tested anonymously. Initial recruitment was from a gay men's organization and through recruitments in a local newspaper. We were substantially helped by an HIV+ gay nurse, John Simoneau, who was a valuable member of our research team and was a member of the gay men's organization.

The basic strategy used in the first studies was to invite gay and bisexual men to be tested for HIV. These men were told that we would take psychological, immune, and health profiles on them immediately. Then within the next 10 weeks, as scheduling would permit, we would conduct the HIV antibody test. We would provide the results and appropriate counseling three days later, then examine the men periodically for the remainder of the 10-week period. In actuality, all participants were tested after five weeks so that we were able to study the anticipation and consequences of diagnosis.

One of the more striking findings in the study was the initial impairment in immune status noted at baseline, for individuals who subsequently turned out to be uninfected (HIV–) (Ironson et al., 1990). Specifically, the HIV– men, who did not know their HIV status initially, appeared to enter the five-week anticipatory period displaying impairments in number of CD4 helper cells in the peripheral circulation, reduced functional lymphocyte responses, and NK cell activity (relative to matched laboratory controls) with these markers returning to normal values over the five-week period (Klimas et al., 1991). These immune system changes suggested that the decision to enter a study in which the at-risk men would learn their HIV antibody status was a key stressor in the study. This was further supported by the findings that at study entry, both distress scores and responses of the stress hormone cortisol were elevated in the HIV– men (Antoni, August, et al., 1990).

The second key stressor in this study was HIV status notification in the HIV+ men. In response to an HIV+ diagnosis, these individuals showed significant increases in state anxiety, as well as intrusive thoughts and avoidant responses as assessed by the Impact of Event Scale (Horowitz, Wilner, and Alvarez, 1979). In contrast, the people who turned out to be HIV– revealed no such changes. The HIV+ men also showed a significant decrease in NK cytotoxicity following HIV+ diagnosis that was related to their anxiety responses at the time of diagnosis (Ironson et al., 1990).

In a two-year follow-up of the HIV+ men, we found that level of distress at diagnosis and excessive denial (five weeks postdiagnosis minus prediagnosis score) were significant predictors of two-year disease progression (Ironson et al., 1994). Briefly, magnitude of distress in response to the HIV+ diagnosis, magnitude of increase in distress before and after diagnosis, and denial increase before and after notification, were each positively and significantly correlated with disease progression to symptoms. The relationship between denial increase and symptoms was maintained, even after controlling for CD4 helper cell number at entry into the study. An increase in denial before and after notification was a significant predictor of disease progression to AIDS, even after controlling for CD4 number at entry into the study. We also examined and found that magnitude of increase in denial before and after diagnosis was significantly correlated with one-year immune status. Thus, increase in denial correlated with CD4 helper cell number and with lymphocyte function (i.e., ability of lymphocytes to multiply when stimulated). We also found that, in turn, one-year immune status was reliably correlated with two-year disease progression in terms of both symptoms and AIDS.

The investigation by Ironson et al. (1994) was the first published study to report significant relationships between psychological variables on the one hand and both changes in immune measures and HIV disease progression on the other. Previous studies that had attempted to relate psychosocial variables to immune status or disease progression in HIV+ subjects produced inconsistent results. There are several reasons these various studies did not find a relationship between psychosocial factors on the one hand and both immune changes and disease progression on the other. These include heterogeneity in the disease stage of subjects, too-limited a selection of immune markers, and failure to assess individual differences in transactional variables such as coping strategies used to deal with specific stressors. In contrast, in the Ironson et al. (1994) investigation, we studied participants who were asymptomatic and relatively homogeneous with regard to age and source of infection and examined transactional factors such as denial and active coping strategies, which extended the range of psychosocial factors studied, in addition to the mood dimension. We also examined important psychological (i.e., distress, denial) and immune (e.g., CD4) responses to a potent stressor (i.e., HIV status notification). Finally, by selecting a sample of men who were healthy and knew neither their HIV status nor their CD4 counts, we were able to disentangle the potential problem posed in prospective studies of not knowing which is causal in the constellation of having symptoms, immune system changes, and depression.

In summary, our initial HIV studies in gay and bisexual men led to several interesting findings. First, we found that anticipation of a diagnosis of HIV was a stressor that could lead to psychological, stress hormone, and immune system changes. Second, we observed that an HIV+ diagnosis could lead to somewhat different psychological, endocrinological, and immunological stress responses in infected and noninfected individuals. Third, we learned that psychological responses to an HIV+ diagnosis could predict long-term immune changes and disease progression.

Group-Based Psychosocial Interventions before the Advent of Protease Inhibitors

At the time we began our studies on HIV/AIDS, pharmacological treatments for the disease were primitive and often associated with undesirable physiological (e.g., bone-marrow suppression, anemia, neutropenia) and psychological side effects. Then, as now, there was no cure for AIDS, and only a tiny percentage of HIV-infected patients worldwide were likely to benefit from pharmacological treatment. Then, as now, it was also evident that the management of HIV spectrum disease necessarily involves both psychosocial and biomedical considerations. Studies such as those conducted by Ironson et al. (1990) indicated that although the early asymptomatic stage after HIV diagnosis was stressful, the level of distress in these gay men was somewhat lower than might be expected. Thus, the level of psychological distress in asymptomatic HIV+ gay men was higher than in healthy noninfected norm groups, but was considerably less than is commonly found in psychiatric patients. Similar low levels of depressive symptoms or syndromal psychiatric disorder in asymptomatic HIV+ gay men were reported elsewhere (Rabkin, Williams, Neugebauer, Remien, and Goetz, 1990).

In spite of the above-mentioned qualifications, we knew that the anticipation and impact of HIV antibody testing could be highly stressful (Ironson et al., 1990). We also learned that this stress was related to an increase in the incidence of psychiatrically diagnosed emotional and adjustment disorders (Jacobsen, Perry, and Hirch, 1990). And, according to one report, the rate of suicide in HIV+ individuals was 36 times that of age-matched uninfected men (Marzuk et al., 1988). Given the psychological climate of the time, there was a need to develop psychosocial interventions to help infected individuals cope with the emotional aspects of their situation.

In our initial HIV research we had conceptualized the infection and its sequelae as a long-term disease whose clinical course might be influenced by many factors. We reasoned that because HIV infection is associated with increased distress (Antoni, Schneiderman, et al., 1990), which, in turn, has adverse effects on the immune system (Ironson et al., 1990), psychosocial interventions that decrease distress might beneficially affect immune status and thereby slow the course of disease.

The psychosocial intervention approach that we chose to use with HIV-infected individuals was based on group-based cognitive-behavioral stress management (CBSM). Our CBSM treatment included the use of relaxation skills training, cognitive restructuring, instruction in self-monitoring of environmental stressors, and social skills training (Lichstein, 1988). In terms of psychosocial adjustments, our CBSM intervention was designed to help stressed individuals become aware of and reduce anxiety and distress, learn coping skills, and appropriately negotiate interpersonal situations.

It is important to note that the psychosocial intervention we chose was conducted in a group format that emphasized interpersonal interaction. Thus, in addition to skills learning, the members of the group received social support from each other as they shared personal experiences, fears, and hopes and learned to communicate better with one another. Thus, both experiential factors and skills learning were important factors in our group-based CBSM intervention.

The goal of our initial group-based CBSM study was to examine the stress-buffering effects of our intervention on anxiety, depression, and immune system status in asymptomatic gay and bisexual men learning of their antibody test results (Antoni, et al., 1991). Participants were enrolled at study entry into either a CBSM group or to an assessment-only control condition. Those participants in the CBSM condition met twice weekly for 10 weeks in groups of four to six men led by two cotherapists. One 90-minute weekly session was devoted to cognitive restructuring and behavior change strategies. These sessions also provided basic information concerning psychological, social, and physiological aspects of stress responses. Participants were also instructed about the nature of HIV transmission and associated behaviors, as well as about safer sex behaviors. The participants were also encouraged to generate examples of recently experienced stressors and to demonstrate the use of CBSM in dealing with stressors by means of behavioral role play with other group members. A second session held each week lasted 45 minutes and was devoted to training and practice in progressive muscle relaxation and imagery.

HIV antibody testing and notification of serostatus occurred between weeks five and six and was given by a licensed clinical social worker, who had received extensive training in pretest and posttest counseling. It is important to note that this counseling was given to both our intervention *and* control participants. Within the intervention groups, however, participants worked on the anticipation of their test results for the first five weeks, and on adjusting to their status and life-style needs during the next five weeks. Psychological distress and immune measures were assessed in all participants at study entry and several times after study onset.

Men in the control group who learned that they were HIV positive revealed significant increases in anxiety and depressed affect between pre- and post-HIV status notification. In contrast, among men who participated in the CBSM group, neither anxiety nor depression changed reliability during the pre- to post-HIV notification period. The immunological results tended to mirror the psychological findings. Thus, the men in the control group who were informed that they were HIV+ revealed significant decreases in helper lymphocyte (CD4) and NK cell counts, as well as in lymphocyte function (i.e., ability to proliferate) when given an HIV+ diagnosis. These effects were buffered among the HIV+ men in the intervention group.

In a parallel study conducted on asymptomatic gay and bisexual men, we examined the effect of aerobic exercise training as a buffer of the affective distress and immune changes that accompany an HIV+ diagnosis (LaPerriere et al., 1990). Briefly, asymptomatic gay men with a cardiovascular fitness level of average or below were randomly assigned either to an aerobic exercise training program or to a no-contact control condition. After five weeks of training, at a point 72 hours before HIV status notification, psychometric, fitness and immunological data were collected on all participants. Psychometric and immunological measures were again collected one week after HIV status notification and counseling. The HIV+ control participants revealed significant increases in anxiety and depressed affect, as well as decrements in NK cell number after notification, whereas, HIV+ exercisers showed no similar changes and, in fact, resembled participants in the control or exercise groups who turned out to be HIV–. These findings suggest that concurrent changes in some affective and immunological measures in response to an acute stressor might be attenuated by an experimentally manipulated aerobic exercise training intervention. A caveat is in order, however, because the exercise was conducted in a small-group format. Thus, the study did not attempt to resolve the issue of the extent to which social support may have interacted with exercise per se to bring about beneficial results.

In any event, the data that we have presented suggest that both CBSM and exercise can attenuate the distress associated with an HIV+ diagnosis and buffer some of the immune changes associated with the distress response (Antoni, et al., 1991; LaPerriere et al., 1990). We have also examined the feasibility of using CBSM and aerobic exercise to exert improved cellular control over latent herpesvirus activation under these same conditions in HIV-infected persons (Esterling et al., 1992). The two herpesviruses that we studied were Epstein-Barr virus (EBV) and human herpesvirus 6 (HHV-6).

Usually EBV is under adequate control by the immune system, which restricts the ability of EBV-infected lymphocytes to multiply (Miller, 1980). Because HIV binds to CD4 helper lymphocytes (Klatzmann et al., 1985), findings that EBV-infected B cells also have the attachment site for HIV (Alsip, Ench, Sumaya, and Boswell, 1988) is of interest. This is particularly the case because HIV can infect and multiply in EBV-infected but not in normal B cells (Montaganier et al., 1984). Thus EBV-infected B cells may represent a potentially important reservoir for HIV, especially considering the capacity of these host cells to multiply (Rosenberg and Fauci, 1991). Our goal then, was to determine whether CBSM could help shrink the reservoir.

Basically, we investigated separately the effects of aerobic exercise and CBSM on EBV and HHV-6 antibody modulation in gay men in the five weeks preceding and following notification of their HIV status. Among HIV+ and HIV– participants, respectively, those randomized to either behavioral intervention (i.e., exercise or CBSM), had significant decreases in both herpesvirus antibody titers over the course of the intervention, as compared with the assessment-only HIV+ and HIV– controls. It therefore appears that both the CBSM and aerobic exercise interventions can help to normalize immunological control over certain herpesviruses in both healthy individuals and in asymptomatic persons infected with HIV.

Symptom emergence in HIV often presents a second major crisis of adjustment after that of diagnosis. Increased depression and anxiety commonly accompany symptom onset (e.g., Belkin, Fleishman, Stein, Piette, and Mor, 1992) and are due in part to anticipation of uncontrollable and unpredictable stressors, such as uncertain disease course, HIV-related deaths of friends, and stigmatization by acquaintances and family. In fact, symptomatic HIV+ men may experience even more depression and anxiety than those with full-blown AIDS because of uncertainty of the eventual disease course (Tross and Hirsch, 1988). Consequently, we tested the effects of a 10-week group-based CBSM intervention on mood and immunological parameters in HIV+ gay men who were pre-AIDS, but whose disease had progressed to a symptomatic stage (Lutgendorf et al., 1997).

In the Lutgendorf et al. (1997) study, HIV+ men were randomized to either CBSM or a modified wait list control group. The latter condition consisted of an optional one-day didactic and experimental stress management seminar given after the 10-week wait list period. Another modification that we made in our protocol, at the request of participants, was to substitute one longer session per week for the two shorter sessions per week used previously. This was readily accepted by our participants. We found that the CBSM intervention significantly decreased self-reported dysphoria, anxiety, and total distress. The intervention group also showed decreases in genital herpes (herpes simplex virus type 2) antibody titers, whereas the control group showed changes neither in mood nor antibody titers. In subsequent work we found that the CBSM intervention decreased the 24-hour output of the stress hormone cortisol, and that decreases in depressed mood paralleled the cortisol reduction (Antoni, Cruess, Cruess, Kumar, et al., 2000).

We have also examined the relative contributions of changes in coping skills and social support during the intervention period to reductions in dysphoria, anxiety, and distress-related symptoms (Lutgendorf et al., 1998). Briefly, we found that the CBSM, but not the control group, showed significant improvement in cognitive coping strategies involving positive reframing and acceptance, and in social support involving attachment and alliance formation. Importantly, analyses indicated that changes in social support and coping skills mediated our observed decreases in distress noted during the intervention.

In recent work we have examined the effects of our CBSM intervention on relationships among anxiety, 24-hour output of norepinephrine (another stress hormone), and changes in cytotoxic T (CD8) cells over time in symptomatic HIV+ gay men (Antoni, Cruess, Cruess, Lutgendorf, et al., 2000). As before, symptomatic HIV+ men were randomized to either the CBSM condition or a 10-week modified wait list condition. Men assigned to the CBSM condition showed significantly lower posttreatment levels of self-reported anxiety, anger, total mood disturbance, and perceived stress than did men in the wait-list control condition. The men in the CBSM condition also revealed less output of the stress hormone norepinephrine than did the controls. At the individual level, anxiety decreases were significantly correlated with decreases in norepinephrine, and greater decreases in norepinephrine predicted less of a decline in cytotoxic T (CD8) cells at follow-up 6 to 12 months later. Thus, it appears that the long-term immunological effects of CBSM were mediated in part by decreases in the stress hormone norepinephrine that were associated with intervention-induced reductions in tension and anxiety.

We have also recently examined the effects of our CBSM intervention on relationships among depressed affect, 24-hour output of the stress hormone cortisol, and changes in naive T cells (i.e., T cells that do not yet have memory for a prior infection) over a 12-month period in symptomatic HIV+ gay men (Antoni et al., 2002). The HIV+ participants were randomized to either the CBSM condition or a

10-week modified wait list condition. Men assigned to the CBSM condition revealed significantly lower posttreatment levels of depressed affect and the stress hormone cortisol. An analysis of covariance controlling for postintervention levels of naive T cells revealed at one-year follow-up a significantly greater number of naive T cells among those who participated in CBSM than in those assigned to the control condition. Whereas CBSM participants showed a small increase over this period, the control participants revealed more than a 25% decline. Using path analysis models, we provided evidence that both decreases in depressed mood and cortisol partially mediated the long-term effects of CBSM on the maintenance of the naive T cells over time.

The findings by Antoni et al. (2002) suggest that reductions in the stress hormone cortisol and depressed mood during a stress-reduction intervention are related to the ability of the immune system to reconstitute naive T cells over time. Although it would be premature to conclude that this is reflected in health benefits to HIV+ persons, reconstitution of naive T cells could be related to the normalization of cell-mediated immune responses to novel antigens (i.e., substances recognized by the immune system) and greater protection against opportunistic infections. It is of further interest that the intervention and control groups did not differ in HIV viral load either before or after the intervention, suggesting that changes in immune system reconstitution that occurred during the one-year follow-up period were not due to differences in viral burden.

Alterations in endocrine functions occurring during the course of HIV infection include a progressive decrease in free testosterone, which can ultimately lead to decreased muscle mass or wasting (Coodley, Loveless, Nelson, and Coodley, 1994). In our research, we have shown that symptomatic HIV+ gay men randomized into a CBSM condition showed significant increases in testosterone that were associated with distress reduction (Cruess et al., 2000). In contrast, participants in the modified wait-list control condition showed significant decreases in testosterone. Follow-up data suggest that the CBSM intervention helped maintain testosterone levels within the normal clinical range.

In summary, our studies conducted on asymptomatic gay men with HIV infection indicate that CBSM can buffer distress and some measures of immune function associated with notification of a positive HIV diagnosis. More recent studies conducted on symptomatic pre-AIDS men with HIV infection have indicated that CBSM can (a) ameliorate dysphoria-, anxiety-, and distress-related symptoms; (b) decrease cortisol and norepinephrine levels while increasing testosterone level; and (c) decrease antibody titers of EBV, HHV-6, and genital herpes (HSV-2), as well as maintain the number of T cytotoxic/suppressor (CD8) and naive T helper/inducer (CD4) lymphocytes. The studies examining relationships among psychosocial factors, stress hormones (norepinephrine, cortisol), and CD4 and CD8 cells have demonstrated relatively long-term effects of relatively brief CBSM intervention. Also, the increase in testosterone level induced by the intervention suggests that CBSM may help prevent hypogonadal function in HIV+ men. Because these studies were conducted before the widespread use of combination therapy and protease inhibitors, they have important implications for the millions of HIV+ people worldwide who lack access to these medications.

The Revolution in HIV Patient Management: Combination Therapy and the Advent of Protease Inhibitors

Between 1986 and 1996, most participants in our studies were not on antiretroviral medication, and only a tiny fraction were on combination therapy. The first antiretroviral medication, zidovudine (AZT), was approved by the Federal Drug Administration (FDA) in 1986, but modest results, uncomfortable side effects, fear of drug toxicity, contemporary norms for physician practice, and the high cost of medications resulted in few of our participants receiving antiretroviral therapy.

Although new antiretroviral drugs were approved by the FDA beginning in 1991, it was not until 1995 that lamivudine (3TC) was approved for use in combination with AZT. Both AZT and 3TC are nucleoside reverse transcriptase inhibitors (NRTIs). Once HIV enters a CD4 cell, HIV uses the reverse transcriptase enzyme to convert its RNA into DNA. The NRTIs act by incorporating themselves into the DNA of the virus, thereby preventing the DNA from creating a new virus. Whereas AZT belongs to a thymidine subgroup of NRTIs, 3TC belongs to a non-thymidine subgroup. In any event, when drugs from these two subgroups are used together, synergistic effects are observed in terms of CD4 cell counts, viral load, and disease progression (Staszewski, Bartlett, Hill, Katlama, and Johnson, 1997).

Toward the end of 1995, the FDA approved saquinavir as the first protease inhibitor. In contrast to the NRTIs, which work on the early stage of viral replication within the infected CD4 cell, protease inhibitors block the protease enzyme at the last stage of the reproductive cycle. Thus, protease inhibitors prevent HIV from being assembled and released from the HIV-infected CD4 cell. When saquinavir was used in conjunction with NRTIs, patients rapidly showed dramatic improvement in HIV viral load and CD4 count. Unfortunately, saquinavir is not well absorbed, and the reported side effects include nausea, diarrhea, and abdominal discomfort.

Some newer protease inhibitors are better tolerated than saquinavir. Consequently, by the end of 1997 the U.S. panel of the International AIDS Society was able to publish a consensus statement in the *Journal of the American Medical Association (JAMA)*. This consensus statement recommended that for all HIV-infected patients with detectable HIV RNA in plasma, physicians should consider prescribing two NRTIs and a protease inhibitor as triple combination therapy (Carpenter et al., 1997). By late 1997, when we submitted our most recent program project renewal application to the National Institute of Mental Health (NIMH), it was apparent that a revolution was under way in the United States in terms of the management of AIDS patients.

The nature of the HIV treatment revolution was that, for the first time, therapeutic focus shifted from palliative care to the maintenance of health. Before the treatment revolution, emphasis was placed on attempting to delay the onset of symptoms and opportunistic infections, improve quality of life on a time-limited basis, and prepare the individual to confront his or her mortality. With the advent of the treatment revolution, emphasis shifted to maintaining health. It now appeared that, for the first time, medications were becoming available, which, if they did not cure the disease, could at least keep people healthy.

One of the key factors in the HIV treatment revolution was that public funds became available to support HIV care. The major public programs that support this care are Medicaid, the Ryan White Care Act, and the AIDS Drug Assistance Program. Medicaid is a federal and state government program that insures individuals, Ryan White supplies funds to hard-hit cities and funnels monies through states to pay for pediatric care, and the AIDS Drug Assistance Program supplies federal funds supplemented by state monies to buy pharmaceuticals for uninsured HIV patients with modest incomes. Based on these programs, the vast majority of HIV+ individuals in the United States have access to combination therapy and monitoring. The cost for therapy and monitoring exceeds $12,000 per year for each patient.

The promise of highly effective antiretroviral therapy in 1997 depended entirely on adherence to regimens that required at least 18 pills or capsules—some requiring refrigeration—taken on structured time lines, with food in some instances and on an empty stomach in others. Initial studies of adherence to antiretroviral therapy focused largely on adherence to AZT. In nondrug-dependent populations, AZT adherence ranged from 26% to 94% (Cortese, Chung, Stoute, and Oster, 1993; LoCaputo, Maggi, Buccoliero, and Federico, 1993; Muma, Ross, Parcel, and Pollard, 1995), with most studies reporting less than 75% adherence. Several factors were associated with the less than adequate adherence rates observed for AZT. These included its unpleasant side effects, perceptions of toxicity, and the extended duration of its prescription (Wall et al., 1995). Moreover, patients expressing skepticism about the efficacy of AZT turned out to be less adherent (Muma et al., 1995) Nonadherent intravenous drug users receiving AZT showed improved adherence when under directly observed therapy, involving onsite medication consumption (Wall et al., 1995). However, the gains in adherence remained significantly increased only during periods of direct supervision.

As might be expected, adherence to combination antiretroviral HIV therapy, which involves taking multiple drugs, has also been found to be problematic, ranging from 17% to 80% among various populations (Malow et al., 1998).

In a preliminary study, we observed that among 290 HIV+ individuals seen at the Miami Veterans Administration Medial Center (VAMC), only 17% of patients filled each of their prescriptions over a six-month period (Malow et al., 1998). The likelihood of actually taking these medications was certainly less. Consequently, we decided to examine the effects of a short behavioral intervention among the men who had not refilled their prescriptions of antiretroviral medications and other drugs to prevent opportunistic infection. More than half also had a history of current or recent substance abuse; most lived alone, and a quarter were homeless.

At an initial visit, each HIV+ patient met individually with a doctoral-level pharmacist who provided a multicomponent weekly pill container and counseling. During this visit, patients were taught to fill the pill container and were asked to role play a day with their medication schedule. Patients' compliance, measured as monthly refills obtained for all medications, increased from 48% before counseling to 75% after counseling, while clinic visits increased from 66% to 76%. Furthermore, viral load reductions of 0.5 logs or greater (often used by physicians as a criterion for clinical significance) occurred in 50% of patients. These findings suggest that individual counseling, coupled with consistent follow-up, can significantly increase at least one measure of adherence among HIV+ individuals who do not adhere to medication regimens using usual standards of care.

Although the improvement of refills from 48% before counseling to 75% after counseling was significant, it is not good enough. First, amount of refills represents the maximum amount of medications likely to be taken; it does not account for prescriptions filled but drugs not taken due to drug holidays, forgetfulness, and so on. Second, virologic success on a population level requires greater than 95% adherence to protease inhibitors. Thus, for example, in one study reporting a significant association between adherence and virologic suppression, 81% of those with greater than 95% adherence had complete viral suppression (Paterson et al., 1999). In contrast, only 50% of those with 80% to 90% adherence and 6% of those with less than 70% adherence had complete viral suppression.

The HIV treatment revolution has brought about important improvements in the health care of HIV+ patients in some technologically advanced countries (Lewin, 1996). But the revolution also has a dark side. For once patients go on highly active antiretroviral therapy, including protease inhibitors, missing surprisingly few doses can rapidly lead to viral escape and mutations that result in drug resistance and ineffective therapeutic response (Van Hove, Shapiro, Winters, Merigan, and Blaschke, 1996). The replication rate of HIV is very high, with as many as 10^{10} viral particles produced each day (Perelson, Neuman, Markowitz, Leonard, and Ho, 1996). This is particularly important because HIV reverse transcriptase is error prone, causing a high level of genetic mutations (Coffin, 1995). The high rate of mutation, in the presence of high levels of replication, leads to the rapid development of resistance. This is particularly problematic in the presence of selective pressure by antiretroviral therapies. For example, a specific protease inhibitor may select for mutations within the gene for HIV protease, leading to structural changes in the enzyme and subsequent drug resistance to the particular protease inhibitor.

A strain of the virus that becomes resistant to one drug also may become resistant to other drugs in the same class. This is referred to as "cross-resistance" and means that a patient who is resistant to a medication that he or she is taking may also be resistant to other drugs in the same class. For example, in the case of NRTIs, an HIV viral strain resistant to 3TC may be cross-resistant to other members of the nonthymidine subgroup, such as didanosine (ddI) and zalcitabine (ddC). Similarly, an HIV viral strain resistant to the protease inhibitor indinavir may be cross-resistant to the protease inhibitor ritonavir. Although the exact clinical implications of specific mutation patterns are currently under study, it is clear that the development of resistance in patients taking combination therapy can dramatically narrow the range of treatment options for the patient. The development of drug-resistant strains of HIV is also a potential major public health problem, because drug-resistant strains of HIV can be passed from one person to another, even within monogamous relationships. Thus, highly active antiretroviral combination therapy, which can keep HIV+ people healthy and active interpersonally, has an Achilles' heel: in nonadherent patients it can lead to the spread of disease-resistant strains of HIV.

In summary, it appears that the introduction of highly active antiretroviral medications has dramatically changed the emphasis of HIV treatment from palliative care to chronic disease management. Although pharmacologic tools have been developed that appear to be able to prolong health in HIV-infected patients, lack of medication adherence remains a major unsolved problem, with ominous implications for public health. It is of some interest that until the advent of highly active antiretroviral therapy, many physicians did not believe that the behavioral and social sciences had much to offer in the way of patient management. Since then, however, problems of medication management and drug resistance have made strong allies of AIDS physicians and behavioral/social scientists.

New Behavioral Approaches to the Management of HIV/AIDS

Toward the end of 1997, our HIV research team prepared a competitive renewal application to the NIMH for continued funding of our ongoing program project entitled "Behavioral Management and Stress Responses in HIV/AIDS." Briefly, a program project consists of a number of closely related research projects (e.g., behavioral management and stress response studies in HIV-infected women, gay men, and recovering substance abusers), which share logistical support from common core unit facilities (e.g., administration, health assessment, psychosocial assessment, endocrinology, immunology, and data management and statistics). The use of core units makes it possible to assemble an interdisciplinary team (in our case, AIDS physicians, a biochemist, clinical psychologists, computer analysts, an endocrinologist, immunologists, nurses, pharmacists, psychophysiologists, a psychiatrist, and statisticians), who are able to work cooperatively on multiple, closely related research projects.

In the months preceding preparation of our program project renewal application, our research team considered the implications of the HIV treatment revolution that was beginning to unfold. We felt that an important focus in our research should be on medication adherence, which in part would be based on the experience we had accumulated in terms of patient management. Recall that at the outset of our investigations in 1986 we had suspected that the potential exists in HIV spectrum disease for patients to remain free of symptoms for a prolonged period and that appropriate patient management could delay the onset of AIDS and ameliorate its course. For these reasons, we believed it would be useful to view HIV as a chronic disease and that CBSM might play an important role in both improving quality of life and slowing symptom onset and disease progression.

Our initial research had been predicated on the hypothesis that CBSM could improve the HIV+ person's quality of life by decreasing the distress and depressed affect associated with having a chronic and likely fatal disease, increasing the use of acceptance and positive reframing strategies, and increasing or maintaining social support. We also suspected that a CBSM intervention including relaxation training might be able to attenuate the effect of stressors on an already compromised immune system and in so doing might slow the course of immune decline that is observed in HIV spectrum disease. Finally, we believed that our psychosocial intervention would facilitate adherence to good health practices and appropriate utilization of the health care system by decreasing the use of avoidance and denial as coping strategies and using problem-focused rather than emotion-focused coping in situations where problem-solving skills could be useful. Now, based on more than 10 years of research experience involving psychosocial interventions with HIV+ people, we hypothesized that CBSM protocols that provide information, skills, and social support to patients could facilitate both adherence to medication protocols and harm reduction (e.g., promote safe sex practices).

Before designing the studies for our program project renewal application, we called on two members of our research team to brief our group extensively on issues in HIV medication adherence. These collaborators were Shvawn Baker, Pharm.D., who for several years has specialized in counseling HIV-infected patients on medication adherence and Nancy Klimas, M.D., who is director of AIDS research and codirector of the AIDS Clinical Research Unit at the VAMC. Based on their input, our team's previous experience conducting group interventions with HIV+ individuals, along with a careful search of the literature, we initiated separate focus groups over multiple sessions with HIV+ women, gay men, and veterans with a history of drug abuse, all of whom were on highly active retroviral therapy.

The findings from our focus groups appear to be consistent with previous reports from published medication adherence studies that lack of social support (Morse et al., 1991), depressed affect (Blumenfield, Milazzo, and Wormser, 1990) and illicit substance and alcohol use (Broers, Morabia, and Hirschel, 1994) are associated with poor medication adherence. Other factors associated with self-reports of poor medication adherence were not believing in drug efficacy, side effects, financial problems, not understanding doctor or nurse instructions, forgetfulness, conflicts with routines, difficulty in maintaining confidentiality, dissatisfaction with health care providers, and not understanding the consequences of failing to take medications exactly as prescribed.

In the studies we designed for the program project renewal, both our intervention *and* control groups receive a session of medication adherence counseling just prior to randomization, immediately after the assessments following the 10-week intervention period, and again after 6-month and 12-month assessment follow-ups. Adherence coping strategies are also part of each session in our 10-week group-based psychosocial intervention protocol and subsequent monthly maintenance sessions. The sessions include physician-patient role plays, skills training in negotiation, a description of patient responsibilities (e.g., asking questions, keeping scheduled appointments), and patient strategies. Participants, for example, are instructed to take a notebook to their medical appointments and write down, or have the health care provider write down, the treatment specified. In addition, the group intervention sessions deal with the manner in which negative emotional affect, poor coping skills, erroneous health beliefs, poor self-efficacy, and lack of social support are issues.

Another focus of our interventions is on sexual risk behavior and substance use. Among the important factors influencing such risk-taking behavior is the use of alcohol and drugs during sex (Lollis, Johnson, Antoni, and Hinkle, 1996; Stall, McKusick, and Wiley, 1986). Depressive symptoms also appear to be more likely to occur in men and women who abuse alcohol and illicit drugs (Walker, Howard, Lambert, and Suchensky, 1994). Thus chronic depressive symptoms, substance abuse, and unprotected sexual behavior appear to be related to one another, as well as to poor medication adherence. Our CBSM intervention was designed to modify these phenomena concurrently.

Our group-based psychosocial intervention studies are necessarily multimodal in design. Figure 17.1 is a schematic diagram of the variables we incorporated into our group-based psychosocial intervention studies in the new program project studies. Fortunately, statistical techniques such as structural equation modeling and other methods of path analysis exist for assessing mediation in multimodal treatment interventions. Thus, for example, it will be of interest to determine whether the learning of adaptive coping skills leads directly to medication adherence and thereby to decreased viral load, as opposed to increases in adaptive coping and social support leading to decreased distress, which, in turn, leads to increased medication adherence and reduced viral burden. Similarly, we shall be able to examine the roles that adaptive coping, changes in cognitive appraisal, and decreased distress play in reducing illicit drug use and risky sexual behavior.

One of the interesting outcomes of the use of highly active antiretroviral therapy is that aside from leading to undetectable levels of the virus in the peripheral blood, lymph nodes, and semen, there appears to be some reconstitution of the immune system. Nevertheless, there is now evidence that the new population of T helper (CD4) cells is different from those that existed before HIV infection, such that T cytotoxic (CD8) and naive CD4 cells are conspicuously absent, indicating a loss of immunologic repertoire and impaired ability to respond to new antigens (Klimas, Maher, Dickinson, and Fletcher, 1997). Consequently, one of the

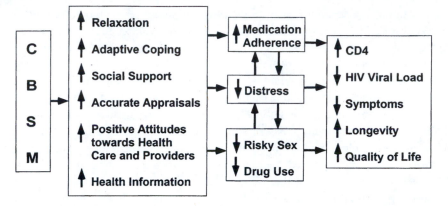

Figure 17.1. Conceptual diagram describing some possible pathways by which elements of the cognitive behavioral stress management (CBSM) intervention may influence proximal (distress, medication adherence, substance abuse, risky sex) and distal (HIV disease progression) endpoints. Adapted from Schneiderman (1999).

objectives of our current research is to assess the functional status of CD4 cells as a function of HIV infection and our CBSM intervention. Our previous findings that CBSM buffers decrease in CD8 and naive CD4 lymphocytes suggest that some synergy could exist between highly active antiretroviral therapy and CBSM. Another objective based on the laboratory psychophysiological studies of Barry Hurwitz, Ph.D., is to look at changes in immune responses to stressors occurring in HIV+ individuals as a function of stage of disease and CBSM training.

When our program project renewal application was funded in early 1998, the intervention projects included separate CBSM studies on gay men and women. The study on women followed extensive piloting, which was supported by a supplement to our existing NIMH program project from the NIH Office on Research on Women's Health (ORWH). This two-year pilot project was awarded in 1995 and was designed to develop a culturally and gender-sensitive behavioral intervention for HIV+ African American women. At the time we requested the supplement, women were the fastest-growing AIDS risk group and accounted for over 11% of known AIDS cases (Centers for Disease Control and Prevention, 1995); by 1999 that number exceeded 20% (Centers for Disease Control and Prevention, 1999). Although African Americans accounted for only 19% of the women in the United States in 1995, they constituted 53% of all female cases of AIDS; by 1999 that figure reached 62%. In both 1995 and 1999, Florida had the second highest AIDS rate in the United States for women, with the greatest number being in Miami–Dade County. Most are poor women of childbearing age who have contracted HIV either heterosexually or through illicit drug use.

The HIV-infected African American women appear to suffer more losses and psychosocial stressors, and a faster decline in their immunity and health, than do their gay white male counterparts (Mays, and Cochran, 1988). Because they are poor, they also face major challenges when interacting with the medical community, including overburdened public clinics (e.g., long waits for appointments), lack of transportation, and inaccessibility to child care (Quinn, 1993). Our group also has found that psychosocial factors such as pessimism are associated with poorer NK cell cytotoxicity and lower T cytotoxic (CD8) cell counts in HIV+ African American women (Byrnes et al., 1998).

Before we developed a group-based psychosocial intervention for HIV+ African American women, we conducted focus groups in an attempt to understand these women's life situations and needs in terms of the intervention. Our approach to these focus groups was in part derived from insights gleaned from Miami AIDS anthropologist Bryan Page. At the outset of our inquiry, we were fortunate to have as members of our research team two African American women, Debra Greenwood, Ph.D., R.N., and Constance West-Edwards, Ph.D. Greenwood is a clinical psychologist and was a member of the psychology department faculty; West-Edwards was then a graduate student in the health clinical psychology program.

Greenwood and West-Edwards found that because the HIV+ women they interviewed were poor and burdened with domestic responsibilities, their recruitment and retention into our studies would depend on our providing child care, transportation, and even lunch for the women and their children. We observed that we also had to be flexible in terms of time arrangements. Thus, for example, even though the women attempted to be punctual to our sessions, the taxi companies with whom we arranged for transportation in poor neighborhoods tended to be less reliable than those we have worked with in more affluent areas.

Because the women interviewed by Greenwood and West-Edwards were generally less literate than the men we had previously studied, the interviewers found that our questionnaires were better given as face-to-face interviews. They also found, in developing our protocol, that whereas our HIV+ gay men tended to complete homework assignments satisfactorily, the women did better when we substituted in-session work for homework. There were several reasons for this, including the women's inexperience with doing homework; a lack of privacy, quiet, and convenience in the home; and a cultural tradition that sees working with others as the most meaningful way to solve problems. Similarly, we found that issues of spirituality and religion tend to be more important to African American women than to white (including Hispanic) gay men. For this reason, we tended to use spirituality and religion as potential resources in the development of our protocols.

In terms of content, we identified many issues that were uniquely relevant to women, including reproductive decisions dealing with children with or without AIDS, and past and current physical abuse. Whereas it is a rather straightforward matter to deal with safe-sex issues with HIV+ gay men, the situation is more complex with HIV+ African American women. Numerous women indicated to us that they would risk physical abuse if they were suddenly to request that their primary sexual partner wear a condom.

Based on the information obtained from focus groups, our team developed a therapist manual and participant workbook. Extensive piloting of these materials by West-Edwards and another advanced graduate student, Deidre Byrnes-Pereira, resulted in changes being made in the intervention. These included a "check-in" period at the start of each session, which allows participants to summarize their most recent stressors, intervention adherence issues, and current life happenings. Other changes included making the icons in the manual, handouts, and overheads gender and race appropriate and introducing idioms that are appropriate in the African American community. References to key African American figures were also included in the intervention. For example, Tina Turner was used as a well-known survivor of severe domestic violence, who successfully and radically changed her life by tapping her inner personal and spiritual strength via the use of meditation. Similarly, the coping module incorporates "The Serenity Prayer" to demonstrate the importance of applying the appropriate coping (problem-focused vs. emotion-focused) responses to stressors. Therefore, based on our experience, we believe that the tailoring of our interventions should be based not only on adjustments for socioeconomic status, but also on considerations of sociocultural and gender contexts.

Once the manual and participant workbook were developed, a pilot study was conducted with several dozen HIV+ African American women. Qualitatively, we observed that CBSM was well tolerated, some relaxation exercises were enjoyed and practiced regularly, and attendance at sessions was, for the most part, quite good. Our participants often indicated that they wished the intervention protocol was longer than 10 weeks in duration, and they looked for ways to maintain contact with other members of the group after the intervention. Most of the women we initially studied in our protocol were not receiving antiretroviral drugs. We observed that both our intervention and control participants showed a decrease in CD4 cell counts, but the decline was steeper in the control group (West-Edwards, Pereira, Greenwood, Antoni, and Schneiderman, 1997). The control group also showed a significant increase in depressed mood across the 10-week intervention, whereas the intervention group did not. Similarly, the control group showed a reliable increase in avoidant thoughts on the Impact of Events Scale, whereas the intervention group experienced a decrease.

To determine if our intervention would generalize from a university-based setting to the more "real-world" setting of community mental health centers, we applied to the NIMH for a research grant with Stephen Weiss, Ph.D., serving as principal investigator. Jonathan Tobin, Ph.D., who is executive director of the clinical directors network of Region II (including New York and New Jersey), became an important collaborator. Briefly, the study sought to examine the effects of our intervention on quality of life and psychosocial and health status indices in a randomized clinical trial conducted in the Bronx, New York, and Newark, New Jersey, as well as in Miami. The HIV+ women participants were assigned to either the group-based intervention condition or to a contact-control condition in which participants received equivalent information via videotape in an individual-based format. Preliminary data analysis conducted for the 432 representative AIDS patients has indicated that women in the group-based condition showed greater improvements in quality of life, decreased distress, and improved coping skills than women enrolled in the contact-control condition (Weiss et al., 1999).

Based on our experience examining HIV+ women, we included a parallel investigation to the HIV+ gay men's intervention study in our program project renewal. Both studies emphasize medication-adherence counseling and harm-reduction strategies, as well as increasing social support and adaptive coping while decreasing distress (see Figure 17.1).

After our NIMH program project competitive renewal was funded, the Office of AIDS Research (OAR) at the NIH awarded us a supplementary grant to develop culturally and linguistically sensitive interventions for Spanish-speaking women and men living with HIV/AIDS. The rationale for this is that many HIV+ Hispanic men and women either speak only Spanish or are more comfortable expressing themselves in Spanish. In the initial two-year period after the state of Florida began tracking HIV infections in July 1997, 57% of HIV+ individuals were black men and women, compared with 29% Hispanics and 14% white non-Hispanics.

The project leader for our supplement was Ronnie Franco Durán, Ph.D., a clinical psychologist on the faculty of our department of psychology. He was assisted by Hernan Rincón, M.D., a psychiatrist and Fogarty Fellow from Cali, Colombia, and by Lt. Commander Luis Fernandez, Ph.D., ABPP, who is a clinical psychologist attached to us by the United States Navy.

The first step in developing a valid, linguistically and culturally sensitive CBSM intervention for Spanish-speaking individuals involved translation of our intervention materials. The procedures used to translate the intervention materials involved (a) minimizing aspects of language (e.g., jargon) that would be difficult to translate; (b) using a professional translating service for the "first pass" translation from English to Spanish; (c) reviewing the Spanish translation—without aid of the English version—to determine appropriateness of language; (d) "back translating" (on audiotape) the Spanish version from Spanish to English; and (e) comparing the English back translation with the English original and adjusting discrepancies on the Spanish version by committee. Our translation "committee" consisted of seven bilingual/bicultural individuals from diverse Spanish-speaking cultures—Colombia, Cuba, Mexico, and Spain.

After translating our materials, we conducted focus groups with Spanish-speaking men and women living with HIV, as well as with community leaders and frontline mental health workers. This was done to determine the appropriateness of the CBSM in the target population, receive feedback on the best ways to present material, determine appropriateness of language, and inform key community gatekeepers and frontline workers about the project.

As of January 1, 2000, a 150-page participant manual outlining the 10-week CBSM intervention was completed, a Medication Adherence Training Interview (MATI) manual designed to enhance HIV medication adherence was also developed, and the lengthy multisession focus groups were conducted. In addition, several cohorts of Spanish-speaking men and women were run in parallel with our HIV+ African American women and white gay men's projects.

During the summer of 1999, we moved many operations of our HIV/AIDS program project to the Miami VAMC. In addition to providing us with increased space and research facilities, the move allowed us greater opportunity to interact with both clinical service providers and researchers. For example, the Miami VA AIDS unit expressed interest in collaborating with our research team to ensure that all HIV+ patients at the Miami VAMC recommended for highly active anti-retroviral therapy would first receive our Medication Adherence Training Interview and also be offered the opportunity to be randomized into our research protocols. To facilitate this research, the National Institute of Drug Abuse (NIDA) provided us with a two-year supplement to our NIMH program project to carry out a study entitled "Managing Adherence in HIV+ Men with Drug Abuse History." The project leader for this study is clinical psychologist and associate professor of psychiatry Robert Malow, Ph.D., and the project co-leader is assistant professor of psychology Frank Penedo, Ph.D. Other investigators include Nancy Klimas, M.D., and Gordon Dickenson, M.D., who is professor of medicine and acting chief of the Division of Infectious Diseases at the University of Miami and clinical director of the Special Immunology (AIDS) Unit at the Miami VAMC.

Another collaboration with our program project that deserves note is with Paul Costa, Ph.D., who is chief of the Laboratory of Personality and Cognition at the Gerontology Research Center in the National Institute of Aging (NIA). Briefly, the NIA has been able to provide us with Medication Event Monitoring System (MEMS) Caps that allow us either to monitor medication adherence using a microchip fitted into the cap of a medication bottle (Track Caps) or provide this monitoring *and* a signal (Smart Caps) that prompts participants to take their medication. Costa, an expert in personality theory, is interested in determining whether conscientiousness as one of five basic factors of personality (McCrae, Costa, Del Pilnar, Rolland, and Parker, 1998) can predict medication adherence in diverse HIV+ individuals.

In any event, both the MEMS Track Caps and Smart Caps record over several months each time that the pill bottle is opened, providing the time and date that the most salient drug (usually a protease inhibitor) is taken. In addition, the Smart Cap has both a reminder beeper and a visual aid to remind the patient of the last dose and total number of doses taken so far that day. We also use several other measures of adherence in our studies and compare each of them with HIV viral load. The other measures of adherence that we use are (a) the AIDS Clinical Trials Group (ACTG) adherence interview questionnaire, (b) pill counts at each health assessment, and (c) pharmacy fill dates.

Construction of Program Infrastructure

During preparation of the present volume, the authors, editors, and advisors met in the office of the Social Sciences Research Council to review draft manuscripts. Among the criticisms of our draft was that it provided little insight into how the authors, particularly Schneiderman, had managed to build a large multidisciplinary team of productive biomedical and social/behavioral scientists. The comment was of particular interest because Schneiderman and Antoni are both Ph.D. psychologists, and the program is housed in an institutional setting in which one might expect leadership in AIDS research to come from the medical establishment.

Although it is not possible to provide a definitive response to these comments, several points deserve mention. The initial iteration of the present program structure developed within the context of an NIMH P50 center directed by a psychiatrist, Carl Eisdorfer. Both Schneiderman and Fletcher, who jointly directed a major project in the center, were already senior faculty and well-established in the university community. They attracted a nucleus of scientists, including Antoni, Hurwitz, Ironson, LaPerriere, Klimas, and Kumar. Antoni and LaPerriere had been students in the department of psychology, and Hurwitz and Ironson had been postdoctoral fellows with Schneiderman. Nancy Klimas had received her immunology research training with Fletcher, and Mahendra Kumar, who is a Ph.D. biochemist-endocrinologist, had been recruited to Miami by Eisdorfer.

When it became apparent that the P50 center would not be funded beyond its initial five years, the HIV/AIDS group working with Schneiderman and Fletcher decided to apply for an NIMH P01 program project grant. Schneiderman was the likely choice to serve as program director for several reasons. First, he already had experience organizing and administering NIH program projects and training grants. Second, his research experience spanned both clinical and basic science, as well as the biomedical and social sciences. Third, he had extensive experience as an NIH consultant and study section member. Fourth, as director of the university's Behavioral Medicine Research Center (BMRC), he had experience working under the joint governance of the Medical School and College of Arts and Sciences.

The HIV/AIDS program project and ancillary studies are nested in the BMRC. This BMRC also houses interdisciplinary NIH centers, program projects, investigator-initiated projects, multicenter trials, and training grants in the areas of AIDS, cancer, cardiovascular disease, chronic fatigue syndrome, and diabetes. Liaison among projects is considerable. For example, besides their HIV/AIDS research, Michael Antoni is program director of a large NIH mind-body center on psycho-oncology, and Neil Schneiderman is the long-time director of an NIH program project on cardiovascular disease. Similarly, Nancy Klimas is program director of an NIH-supported chronic fatigue center. Almost all of our investigators work in more than one area, and almost all have independent R01 grants.

There are distinct advantages for the HIV/AIDS and other BRMC projects to be housed jointly between the Medical School and the College of Arts and Sciences. One advantage is that the Medical Center offers access to patients, physicians, nurses, clinics, biomedical expertise, and biomedical laboratory resources. Another advantage is that the College of Arts and Sciences, particularly the department of psychology, offers access to social scientists and graduate students. In particular, the Division of Health Psychology, which includes a large program in

Health Clinical Psychology and is directed by Schneiderman, provides access to outstanding research-oriented graduate students whose interests span the social/behavioral and biomedical sciences.

An important aspect of the HIV/AIDS program project research is that it is interdisciplinary, as well as multidisciplinary. By *multidisciplinary* is meant that all of our projects require input from people recruited from a variety of disciplines. By *interdisciplinary*, we mean that individual scientists must know not only the vocabulary used by their collaborators but also basic aspects of the methods, concepts, and literature from more than one discipline. Thus, in our interdisciplinary framework, both the investigators and trainees are expected to be familiar with sociocultural, psychosocial, behavioral, and biomedical approaches to research. They are expected to become versed in pathobiology, as well as in biology and the social sciences, and in clinical investigation, as well as basic science. Consequently, it is not surprising that Michael Antoni is an expert in clinical psychology and psychoneuroimmunology; that Gail Ironson, who is board certified in psychiatry, is also an expert in psychometrics and psychoneuroimmunology; and that Nancy Klimas is an expert in infectious diseases, immunology, medical treatment, and medication adherence.

Our interdisciplinary NIMH training grant entitled "Biopsychosocial Research Training in Immunology and AIDS" has provided a successful bridge across schools and disciplines. At the postdoctoral level, the training grant has trained physicians, clinical immunologists, and psychologists; predoctoral trainees consist of graduate students in the health clinical psychology program within the department of psychology. Both pre- and postdoctoral trainees conduct rotations and research that expose them to biomedical, psychosocial, and sociocultural approaches to HIV/AIDS investigations. The training and research of our pre- and postdoctoral fellows is closely related to our program project research. Moreover, most of our fellows become highly competent in more than one venue. Thus, for example, Dean Cruess, Ph.D., was equally comfortable either working in the endocrinology laboratory of Professor Mahendra Kumar, Ph.D., or leading CBSM groups.

A key feature of our HIV/AIDS research is that it has taken place within a multiethnic community that mirrors the nationwide HIV/AIDS pandemic. The participants in our research have consisted of people who have contracted HIV through drug abuse or through heterosexual or homosexual activity. They differ from one another in terms of age, culture, family structure, gender, language, race, sexual orientation, and socioeconomic status. Fortunately, through the collaboration of multiple NIH institutes and offices (NIDA, NIMH, NIA, OAR, ORWH), as coordinated by Ellen Stover, Ph.D., director of the Office on AIDS at NIMH (assisted by Willo Pequegnat, Ph.D., Dianne Rausch, Ph.D., and David Stoff, Ph.D.), we have been able to adjust our research to the rapidly changing AIDS scene.

To adapt our research to the AIDS landscape, it has been essential to develop and maintain contact with key elements of the community. Although community boards are essential for maintaining liaison with constituent HIV+ groups, one cannot overestimate the role of individual contacts. In our initial research efforts, as previously mentioned, it was an HIV+ gay nurse on our staff who facilitated the recruitment of subjects, coached us in the development of our manuals, and acted as a liaison both to our participants and to the community. Similarly, in our subsequent research with HIV+ minority women, it has been a warm, articulate HIV+ African American woman on our staff, Arnetta Phillips, who has organized recruitment and maintenance of participants, coached our staff in terms of appropriate interactions with participants, and served as an effective liaison to the minority community. The participants in our research protocols have also been an important source of recruitment and advice. To the extent possible, we have sought to provide for these participants a warm, respectful, professional atmosphere in which the entire composition of our research team reflects the rich cultural and ethnic diversity of the Miami community.

Summary and Conclusions

Beginning in 1986, our research group developed group-based CBSM interventions for HIV+ individuals that were designed to decrease distress, improve quality of life, and, we hoped, have a relatively long-term effect on health. Our initial published studies conducted with HIV+ asymptomatic gay men indicated that CBSM could buffer distress and some measures of immune function associated with HIV+ notification. More recent published studies conducted with symptomatic pre-AIDS men who were HIV+ indicated that CBSM can (a) ameliorate dysphoria-, anxiety-, and distress-related symptoms; (b) decrease stress hormones such as cortisol and norepinephrine levels, while increasing testosterone level; and (c) decrease antibody titers of EBV, HHV-6, and genital herpes (HSV-2), as well as buffer declines in T helper (CD4) and T cytotoxic (CD8) cell numbers for up to a year. Although the next step in this research would ordinarily have been to develop a large-scale, long-term clinical trial to study whether our CBSM intervention could reduce disease progression, the revolution in HIV patient management in terms of combination therapy and use of protease inhibitors necessarily modified our research objectives. Nevertheless, because millions of HIV+ people worldwide lack access to these medications, the development of a clinical trial to study the long-term health effect of CBSM used with people who lack access to HIV/AIDS antiretroviral medications remains worthwhile.

It should be noted that in the era before the advent of highly active antiretroviral medication, the average time between infection and development of AIDS was a little over 10 years (Munoz et al., 1989), and it was difficult retrospectively to pinpoint the onset of disease. Thus, assessments of the efficacy of therapy, including behavioral treatment, promised to be a long and arduous task. In recent years, however, treatment-induced changes in HIV RNA level and the CD4 lymphocyte count, taken together, have been found to be valid predictors of

HIV-related disease (O'Brien et al., 1996) and should be useful in assessing the efficacy of both behavioral and antiretroviral interventions. Whereas HIV RNA viral load provides a valid assessment of disease severity, the CD4 count provides useful information about the trajectory of the disease (Ledergerber et al., 1999).

Perhaps the greatest benefit of our having developed the CBSM interventions for HIV+ patients is the broad applicability these interventions have for helping HIV+ patients who now have access to highly active antiretroviral medication. Thus, in addition to decreasing distress, our interventions offer promise of improving medication adherence and promoting harm reduction (e.g., decreasing risky sex and illicit drug use). This, in turn, should improve quality of life, decrease HIV viral burden, reduce opportunistic symptoms, and increase longevity. Although it was only dimly perceived when we began our research, the potential for our interventions to improve medication adherence and promote harm reduction in HIV/AIDS patients is considerable.

Based on our current research program, we foresee several future objectives. First, if our present studies can demonstrate a clinically significant increase in medication adherence and promotion of harm reduction across a broad range of risk groups, it would be appropriate for the NIH to develop a large-scale multi-center clinical trial to assess the effect of a psychosocial intervention similar to our own on morbidity and mortality. Second, because studies such as we are conducting are largely university based and involve payment of subjects and the use of highly trained personnel, as well as complex recruitment and maintenance strategies, it would be useful to move from efficacy studies to effectiveness trials based in community health centers. Third, as each of our studies demonstrates effectiveness of CBSM for particular HIV risk groups, we would like to disseminate our techniques to the practice community by making our manuals available to practitioners.

In conclusion, the development of our interdisciplinary HIV/AIDS research program has been due to the efforts of many individuals and institutions. We are, of course, obligated to the many people living with AIDS who have shared with us their time, effort, and insights. Also, we are obliged to the many community leaders who have given freely of their time and advice. A very large number of scientists at the University of Miami have worked collaboratively for many years, learned new scientific languages, and taught each other the basic concepts of each others' disciplines. The university administration, and the chairs of the departments of psychology (Rod Wellens, Ph.D.), medicine (Laurence Gardner, M.D.), and psychiatry and behavioral sciences (Carl Eisdorfer, Ph.D., M.D.) have been uniformly helpful. Our program project staff has been incredibly hardworking and loyal. Finally, the graduate students and the pre- and postdoctoral fellows have provided an inordinate amount of intellectual stimulation and hard work. We are happy that together we have all been able to make some contribution to HIV/AIDS research, but we believe that our greatest contribution has been to provide the infrastructure for important new research.

Postscript

In the previous summary of our research group's work on "Learning to Cope with HIV/AIDS," we emphasized how, beginning in 1986, we developed group-based CBSM interventions for HIV+ individuals that were designed to decrease distress, improve quality of life, and, we hoped, have a relatively long-term effect on health. We concluded our report by suggesting that the greatest benefit of our having developed the CBSM interventions for HIV+ patients is the broad applicability these interventions have for helping HIV+ patients who now have access to highly active antiretroviral therapy (HAART). We felt that, in addition to decreasing distress, our psychosocial interventions offered promise of improving medication adherence, which in turn would decrease viral burden, improve health, and increase longevity.

Subsequent research has produced findings that, in part, reinforce these assumptions. Thus, in men and women receiving HAART we found that greater negative mood and lower social support were related to greater use of avoidance (denial) coping strategies. This, in turn, was related to poorer medication adherence and higher viral load among HIV+ men and women using avoidance coping strategies (Weaver et al., 2005). The situation may be a little more complicated, however, as we also found that while depressed mood and feelings of hopelessness predicted poorer adherence, decreased CD4 count and increased viral load, the relationship between psychosocial variables and viral load persisted even after controlling for medication adherence (Ironson et al., 2005a).

These Ironson et al. (2005a) findings imply that at least in some patients, adherence training alone might not completely control HIV viral load if patients are highly distressed. We confirmed and expanded on this hypothesis in the recent trial conducted by Antoni et al. (2006) in which we tested whether a CBSM intervention in combination with medication adherence training (MAT) influences HIV viral load burden more than MAT alone. In brief, we found that among HIV+ men on HAART who had detectable HIV viral load at baseline, those who were randomized to CBSM+MAT showed significantly greater decreases in viral load than those randomized to MAT. The greater decreases in HIV viral load in the CBSM+MAT condition were associated with greater decreases in depressed affect, suggesting that at least in some HIV+ individuals, complete viral suppression may require an alleviation of distress.

In a related initiative, based upon the extensive HIV medication adherence literature including our own studies, as well as our focus group experiences, we responded to an invitation to write an article about our development and implementation of a medication adherence training instrument for persons living with HIV (McPherson-Baker, Jones, Duran, Klimas, and Schneiderman, 2005). This article—which describes the medication adherence training instrument (MATI) developed under the leadership of an experienced PharmD and expert in HIV medications, Shawn McPherson-Baker and a distinguished HIV/AIDS physician, Nancy Klimas—now serves as one of the pillars of our behavioral interventions in the era of HAART.

In more general terms, research over the past few years establishes that the introduction of HAART has led to dramatic reductions in AIDS-related morbidity and mortality in the United States (Centers for Disease Control and Prevention, 2003a). Successful antiretroviral therapy is marked by suppression of HIV viral load to near undetectable levels and may be accompanied by immune reconstitution including increases in the number of CD4 lymphocytes. At one stage in the renewal of our program project we tested a structural model on 322 (58% men, 42% women; 60% African American, 23% nonHispanic White, 13% Latino/Hispanic) participants who received HAART across a 15-month period (Weaver et al., 2005). The model incorporated participants' age, time since diagnosis, perceived social support, coping, and negative mood (e.g., depressed affect) as predictors of medication adherence as well as HIV viral load. Medication adherence was assessed by both electronic monitoring (MEMS caps) and by self-report. Results from the model indicated that greater negative mood and lower social support were related to a greater use of avoidance coping strategies. Use of these coping strategies by the patients on HAART was related to poorer medication adherence and higher viral load.

Recently members of our group (Ironson et al., 2005a) examined psychosocial factors predicting viral load and CD4 change across 24 months for 177 HIV+ women and men from a completely different but demographically similar cohort than that studied by Weaver et al. (2005). Unlike the Weaver et al. study, however, which included both HIV+ and AIDS patients who were all on HAART therapy, Ironson et al. (2005a) looked only at nonAIDS HIV+ patients, a little more than half of whom were on HAART therapy with the remainder on combination therapy or no antiretroviral medication. Ironson et al. found that both baseline and cumulative depressed affect and hopelessness predicted poor adherence, decreased CD4 count and increased viral load, but that the relationship between psychosocial variables and viral load persisted even after controlling for medication adherence. This Ironson et al. finding, that psychosocial variables are related to HIV viral load after controlling for adherence, is consistent with our important recent observation that a psychosocial intervention including CBSM can reduce HIV viral load even after controlling for adherence (Antoni, et al., 2006; Ironson et al. 2005b; LaPerriere et al., 2005).

Also as part of our program project Antoni et al., (2006) tested whether a CBSM intervention in combination with antiretroviral medication adherence training (MAT) influences HIV viral load more than MAT alone. We initially found no difference as a function of CBSM+MAT versus MAT-alone conditions in 130 randomized participants. In the 101 men with detectable viral load at baseline, however, those randomized to CBSM+MAT showed significantly greater decreases in viral load than those randomized to MAT. Decreases in depressed mood, which were significantly greater in the CBSM+MAT condition, explained the differences between groups. Thus it may be that in patients with detectable

HIV viral load who do not respond to adherence training alone, a psychosocial intervention such as CBSM may be required in order to maintain optimum health.

One of our most important findings, of course, has been that in patients with detectable HIV viral load, the combination of CBSM+MAT appears to be considerably better than MAT alone in decreasing viral load to undetectable levels (Antoni et al., 2006). This finding may have important implications for the treatment of HIV. Although successful HAART treatment has led to dramatic reductions in AIDS-related morbidity and mortality in the United States (Centers for Disease Control and Prevention, 2003b), patients on HAART with detectable viral load can develop resistant strains of HIV, which can undermine the effectiveness of these medications thereby producing a major threat to public health. Currently up to 10% of new HIV cases show evidence of drug resistance (Pillay, 2001). For patients with undetectable viral load, regular treatment by their AIDS physicians appears to be sufficient. Patients, however, who have detectable viral loads not directly attributable to drug resistance may benefit from medication adherence training. Finally, those patients who still have detectable viral load after adherence counseling may require the combination of MAT and an intervention such as CBSM in order to achieve an undetectable viral burden.

Thus after a decade of HAART implementation and evaluation, it now appears that people living with HIV/AIDS can be kept alive and in relatively good health if given proper treatment. The advent of single tablet per day medication, in place of taking 30 or more pills per day, has been an important development. It now appears that many people with HIV/AIDS can live healthy, normal lives if they scrupulously take their medications and follow preventive medicine guidelines. For some patients who have detectable HIV viral load, simple medication adherence training by a qualified health professional in a doctor's office may be insufficient to get these individuals on track. However, in instances where this is not the case, and where the elevated viral load is not due to pharmacological resistance, CBSM may be a necessary component of the treatment regimen. Thus, as pharmacologic treatment becomes more available worldwide, there will be an increased need to develop culturally sensitive, behavioral interventions providing medication adherence training as well as treatments that can alleviate distress.

ACKNOWLEDGMENTS

Our research described in this chapter was largely supported by grants P50 MH4355, P01 MH49548, and T32 MH18917. We thank Leonard Mitnick, Ph.D., who from the beginning challenged us to imagine the future.

LIST OF ABBREVIATIONS

3TC   lamivudine

ACTG   AIDS Clinical Trials Group

AIDS   Acquired Immunodeficiency Syndrome

AZT   zidovudine

BMRC   Behavioral Medicine Research Center

CBSM   cognitive-behavioral stress management

CD4+   T-helper cells

CD8   cytotoxic-T cells

ddC   zalcitabine

ddI   didanosine

EBV   Epstein Barr Virus

FDA   Federal Drug Administration

HAART   Highly Active Antiretroviral Therapy

HHV-6   Human Herpes Virus-6

HIV–   HIV uninfected individuals

HIV   Human Immunodeficiency Virus

HIV+   HIV infected individuals

HSV-2   genital herpes

IV   intravenous drug

MAT   Medication Adherence Training

MATI   Medication Adherence Training Interview

MEMS   Medication Event Monitoring System

NIA   National Institute of Aging

NIDA   National Institute of Drug Abuse

NIMH   National Institute of Mental Health

NK   natural killer

NRTI   nucleoside reverse transciptase inhibitors

OAR   Office of AIDS Research

ORWH   NIH Office of Research on Women's Health

VAMC   Veterans Administration Medical Center

RECOMMENDED READINGS

Alsip, G. R., Ench, Y., Sumaya, C. V., and Boswell, R. N. (1988). Increased Epstein-Barr virus asymptomatic human immunodeficiency virus infections. *Journal of Infectious Diseases, 157,* 1072–1076.

Antoni, M., and Schneiderman, N. (1998). HIV/AIDS. In A. Bellack, and M. Hersen (Eds.), *Comprehensive Clinical Psychology* (pp. 238–275). New York: Elsevier Science.

Carpenter, C. C. J., Fischl, M. A., Hammer, S. M., Hirsch, M. S., Jacobsen, D. M., Katzenstein, D. A., Montaner, J. S. G., Richman, D. D., Saag, M. S., Schooley, R. T., Thompson, M. A., Vella, S., Yeni, P. G., and Volberding, P. A. (1997). Antiretroviral therapy for HIV infection in 1997: Updated recommendations of the International AIDS Society–USA Panel. *Journal of the American Medical Association, 277*, 1962–1969.

Kuby, J. (2000). *Immunology*, 4th ed. New York: W. H. Freeman.

Pantaleo, G., Graziosi, C., and Fauci, A. S. (1993). The immunopathogenesis of human immunodeficiency virus infection. *New England Journal of Medicine, 328*, 327–335.

Schneiderman, N., Antoni, M. H., Ironson, G., Klimas, N., Hurwitz, B., Kumar, M., LaPerriere, A., Brownley, K., and Fletcher, M. A. (1999). Psychoneuroimmunology and HIV/AIDS. In M. Schedlowski, and U. Tewes (Eds.), *Psychoneuroimmunology: An Interdisciplinary Introduction* (pp. 487–507). New York: Kluwer Academic/Plenum.

REFERENCES

Antoni, M. H., August, S., LaPerriere, A., Baggett, H. L., Klimas, N., Ironson, G., Schneiderman, N., and Fletcher, M. A. (1990). Psychological and neuroendocrine measures related to functional immune changes in anticipation of HIV–1 serostatus notification. *Psychosomatic Medicine, 52*, 495–510.

Antoni, M. H., Baggett, L., Ironson, G., August, S., LaPerriere, A., Klimas, N., Schneiderman, N., and Fletcher, M. A. (1991). Cognitive behavioral stress management intervention buffers distress responses and immunologic changes following notification of HIV–1 seropositivity. *Journal of Consulting and Clinical Psychology, 59*, 906–915.

Antoni, M. H., Carrico, A. W., Durán, R. E., Spitzer, S., Penedo, F., Ironson, G., Fletcher, M. A., Klimas, N., and Schneiderman, N. (2006). Randomized clinical trial of cognitive behavioral stress management on human immunodeficiency virus load in gay men treated with highly active antiretroviral therapy. *Psychosomatic Medicine, 68*, 143–151.

Antoni, M. H., Cruess, S. E., Cruess, D. G., Kumar, M., Lutgendorf, S., Ironson, G., Dettmer, E., Williams, J., Klimas, N., Fletcher, M. A., and Schneiderman, N. (2000). Cognitive behavioral stress management reduces distress and 24-hour urinary free cortisol output among symptomatic HIV-infected gay men. *Annals of Behavioral Medicine, 22*, 29–37.

Antoni, M. H., Cruess, D. G., Cruess, S. E., Lutgendorf, S., Kumar, M., Ironson, G., Klimas, N., Fletcher, M. A., and Schneiderman, N. (2000). Cognitive behavioral stress management intervention effects on anxiety, 24-hour urinary norepinephrine output, and T-cytotoxic/suppressor cells over time among symptomatic HIV-infected gay men. *Journal of Consulting and Clinical Psychology, 68*, 31–45.

Antoni, M. H., Cruess, D. G., Klimas, N., Maher, K., Cruess, S. E., Kumar, M., Lutgendorf, S., Ironson, G., Schneiderman, N., and Fletcher, M. A. (2002). Stress management and immune system reconstitution in symptomatic HIV-infected gay men over time: Effects on transitional naive T-cells. *American Journal of Psychiatry, 159*, 143–145.

Antoni, M. H., Schneiderman, N., Fletcher, M. A., Goldstein, D., Ironson, G., and LaPerriere, A. (1990). Psychoneuroimmunology and HIV–1. *Journal of Consulting and Clinical Psychology, 58*, 38–49.

Barre-Sinoussi, F., Chermann, J., Rey, F., Nugeyre, M., Chameret, S., Gruest, J., Dauguet, C., Axler-Blin, C., Vezinet-Brun, F., Rouzioux, C., Rosenbaum, W., and Montagnier, R. (1983). Isolation of a T-lymphotropic retrovirus from a patient at risk of acquired immunodeficiency syndrome (AIDS). *Science, 220,* 861–871.

Belkin, G. S., Fleishman, J. A., Stein, M. D., Piette, J., and Mor, V. (1992). Physical symptoms and depressive symptoms among individuals with HIV infection. *Psychosomatics, 33,* 416–427.

Blumenfield, M., Milazzo, J., and Wormser, G. (1990). Non-compliance in hospitalized patients with AIDS. *General Hospital Psychiatry, 12,* 166–169.

Broers, B., Morabia, A., and Hirschel, B. (1994). A cohort study of drug users' compliance with zidovudine treatment. *Archives of Internal Medicine, 154,* 1121–1127.

Brunet, J. B., and Ancelle, R. A. (1985). International occurrence of the acquired immunodeficiency syndrome. *Annals of Internal Medicine, 103,* 670–674.

Byrnes, D., Antoni, M.H., Goodkin, K., Efantis-Potter, J., Asthana, D., Simon, T., Munjai, J., Ironson, G., and Fletcher, M.A. (1998). Stressful events, pessimism, natural killer cell cytotoxicity, and cytotoxic/suppressor T cell in women at risk for cervical cancer. *Psychosomatic Medicine, 60,* 714–722.

Carpenter, C. J., Fischl, M. A., Hammer, S. M., Hirsch, M. S., Jacobsen, D. M., Ketzenstein, D. A., Montaner, J. S. G., Richman, D. D., Saag, M. S., Schooley, R. T., Thompson, M. A., Vella, S., Yeni, P. G., and Volberding, P. A. (1997). Antiretroviral therapy for HIV infection in 1997: Updated recommendations of the International AIDS Society. USA panel. *Journal of the American Medical Association, 277,* 1962–1969.

Centers for Disease Control [and Prevention] (1981). Kaposi's sarcoma and *Pneumocystis* pneumonia among homosexual men: New York City and California. *Morbidity and Mortality Weekly Reports, 30,* 250–252.

Centers for Disease Control [and Prevention] (1985). Screening donated blood and plasma for antibody to the virus causing acquired immunodeficiency syndrome. *Morbidity and Mortality Weekly Reports, 34,* 1–4.

Centers for Disease Control [and Prevention] (1986, April). *HIV/AIDS Surveillance Report,* 1–18.

Centers for Disease Control and Prevention (1995). *HIV/AIDS Surveillance Report, 7,* 1–27.

Centers for Disease Control and Prevention (1999). *HIV/AIDS Surveillance Report, 11,* 1–25.

Centers for Disease Control and Prevention (2003a). *HIV/AIDS Surveillance Report 2002, 15,* 1–25.

Centers for Disease Control[and Prevention] (2003b). Increases in HIV diagnoses. *Morbidity and Mortality Weekly Report, 52,* 1145–1148.

Coffin, J. M. (1995). HIV population dynamics in vivo: Implications for genetic variation, pathogenesis, and therapy. *Science, 267,* 483–489.

Coodley, G. O., Loveless, M. O., Nelson, H. D., and Coodley, M. K. (1994). Endocrine function in the HIV wasting syndrome. *Journal of Acquired Immune Deficiency Syndrome, 7,* 46–51.

Cortese, L., Chung, R., Stoute, J., and Oster, C. (1993). Zidovudine usage: Patient compliance and factors. *International Conference on AIDS, 9*(1), 507.

Cruess, D. G., Antoni, M. H., Schneiderman, N., Ironson, G., McCabe, P., Fernandez, J. B., Cruess, S. E., Klimas, N., and Kumar, N. (2000). Cognitive-behavioral stress management increases free testosterone and decreases psychological distress in HIV–seropositive men. *Health Psychology, 19,* 12–20.

Esterling, B. A., Antoni, M. H., Schneiderman, N., Ironson, G., LaPerriere, A., Klimas, N., and Fletcher, M. A. (1992). Psychosocial modulation of antibody to Epstein-Barr viral capsid antigen and herpes virus type-6 in HIV–1 infected and at-risk gay men. *Psychosomatic Medicine, 54,* 354–371.

Horowitz, M., Wilner, N., and Alvarez, W. (1979). Impact of event scale: A measure of subjective stress. *Psychosomtic Medicine, 41,* 209–218.

Ironson, G., Balbin, E., Solomon, G., Fahey, J., Klimas, N., Schneiderman, N., and Fletcher, M. A. (2001). Relative preservation of natural killer cell cytotoxicity and number in health AIDS patients with low CD4 cell counts. *AIDS, 15,* 2065–2073.

Ironson, G., Friedman, A., Klimas, N., Antoni, M., Fletcher, M. A., LaPerriere, A., Simoneau, J., and Schneiderman, N. (1994). Distress, denial, and low adherence to behavioral interventions predict faster disease progression in HIV–1 infected gay men. *International Journal of Behavioral Medicine, 1,* 90–105.

Ironson, G., LaPerriere, A., Antoni, M. H., Klimas, N., Schneiderman, N., and Fletcher, M. A. (1990). Changes in immune and psychological measures as a function of anticipation and reaction to news of HIV–1 antibody status. *Psychosomatic Medicine, 52,* 247–270.

Ironson, G., O'Cleirigh, C., Fletcher, M. A., Laurenceau, J. P., Balbin, E., Klimas, N., Schneiderman, N., and Soloman, G. (2005a). Psychosocial factors predict CD4 and viral load change in men and women with human immunodeficiency virus in the era of highly active antiretroviral treatment. *Psychosomatic Medicine, C7,* 1013–1021.

Ironson, G., Weiss, S., Lydston, D., Ishii, M., Jones, D., Asthana, D., Tobin, J., Lechner, S., LaPerriere, A., Schneiderman, N., and Antoni, M. (2005b). The impact of improved self-efficacy on HIV viral load and distress in culturally diverse women living with AIDS: The SMART/EST Women's Project. *AIDS Care, 17,* 222–236.

Jacobsen, P., Perry, S., and Hirsch, D. (1990). Behavioral and psychological responses to HIV antibody testing. *Journal of Consulting and Clinical Psychology, 58,* 31–37.

Klatzmann, D. E., Champagne, E., Chouret, S., Grunest, J., Guetart, D., Hercend, T., Gluckman, J. C., and Montaganier, L. (1985). T lymphocyte T4 molecule behaves as the receptor for human retrovirus LAV. *Nature, 312,* 767–770.

Klimas, N., Caralis, P., LaPerriere, A., Antoni, M., Ironson, G., Simoneau, J., Ashman, N., Schneiderman, N., and Fletcher, M. A. (1991). Immunologic function in a cohort of HIV–1 seropositive and negative healthy homosexual men. *Journal of Clinical Microbiology, 29,* 1413–1421.

Klimas, N., Maher, K., Dickinson, G., and Fletcher, M. A. (1997, May). T cell phenotypes following effective anti-retroviral treatment. Presented at the Spring Symposium on Immunomodulation, Vail, CO.

LaPerriere, A., Antoni, M. H., Schneiderman, N., Ironson, G., Klimas, N., Caralis, P., and Fletcher, M. A. (1990). Exercise intervention attenuates emotional distress and natural killer cell decrements following notification of positive serologic status for HIV–1. *Biofeedback and Self-Regulation, 15,* 125–131.

LaPerriere, A., Ironson, G., Antoni, M. H., Pomm, H., Jones, D., Ishii, M., Lydston, D., Lawrence, P., and Grossman, A. (2005). Decreased depression up to one year following CBSM+ intervention in depressed women with AIDS: The SMART/EST women's project. *Journal of Health Psychology, 10,* 223–231.

Ledergerber, B., Egger, M., Erard, V., Weber, R., Hirschel, B., Furrer, H., Battegay, M., Vernazza, P., Bernasconi, E., Opravil, M., Kaufmann, D., Sudre, P., Francioli, P., and

Telenti, A. (1999). AIDS-related opportunistic illnesses occurring after initiation of potent antiretroviral therapy. *Journal of the American Medical Association, 282,* 2220–2226.

Levy, J., Hoffman, A., Kramer, S., Landis, J., Shimabukaro, J., and Oshiro, L. (1984). Isolation of lymphocytopathic retroviruses from San Francisco patients with AIDS. *Science, 225,* 840–842.

Lewin, D. (1996). Protease inhibitors: HIV–1 summons a darwinian defense. *Journal of the National Institutes of Health Research, 8,* 33–35.

Lichstein, K. (1988). *Clinical Relaxation Strategies.* New York: Wiley.

LoCaputo, S., Maggi, P., Buccoliero, G., and Federico, M. (1993). Antiretroviral therapy with zidovudine: Evaluation of the compliance in a cohort of HIV positive patients. *International Conference on AIDS, 9*(1), 489.

Lollis, C., Johnson, E., Antoni, M. H., and Hinkle, Y. (1996). Characteristics of African Americans with multiple risk factors associated with HIV/AIDS. *Journal of Behavioral Medicine, 19,* 55–70.

Lutgendorf, S., Antoni, M. H., Ironson, G., Klimas, N., Kumar, M., Starr, K., McCabe, P., Cleven, K., Fletcher, M. A., and Schneiderman, N. (1997). Cognitive behavioral stress management decreases dysphoric mood and herpes simplex virus-type 2 antibody titers in symptomatic HIV–seropositive gay men. *Journal of Consulting and Clinical Psychology, 65,* 31–43.

Lutgendorf, S., Antoni, M. H., Ironson, G., Starr, K., Costello, N., Zuckerman, M., Klimas, N., Fletcher, M. A., and Schneiderman, N. (1998). Changes in cognitive coping skills and social support mediate distress outcomes in symptomatic HIV–seropositive gay men during a cognitive behavioral stress management intervention. *Psychosomatic Medicine, 60,* 204–214.

Mahler, H. (1988). Opening address. Presented at the International Congress of AIDS, Paris.

Malow, R. M., McPherson, S., Klimas, N., Antoni, M. H., Schneiderman, N., Penedo, F. J., Ziskind, D., Page, B., and McMahon, R. (1998). Adherence to complex combination antiretroviral therapies in HIV+ drug abusers. *Psychiatric Services, 49,* 1021–1024.

Marzuk, P. M., Tierney, H., Tardiff, K., Gross, E. M., Morgan, E. G., Hsu, M. A., and Mann, J. (1988). Increased risk of suicide in persons with AIDS. *Journal of the American Medical Association, 259,* 1333–1337.

Mays, V., and Cochran, S. (1988). Issues in the perception of AIDS risk reduction activities by Black and Hispanic/Latina women. *American Psychologist, 43,* 949–957.

McCrae, R. R., Costa, P. J., Jr., Del Pilar, G. H., Rolland, J. P., and Parker W. D. (1998). Cross-cultural assessment of the five-factor model: The Revised NEO Personality Inventory. *Journal of Cross-Cultural Psychology, 29*(1), 171–188.

McPherson-Baker, S., Jones, D., Durán, R., Klimas, N., and Schneiderman, N. (2005). Development and implementation of a medication adherence training instrument for persons living with HIV: The MATI. *Behavior Modification, 29,* 286–317.

Miller, G. (1980). Biology of Epstein-Barr virus. In G. Klein (Ed.), *Viral Oncology* (pp. 713–738). New York: Raven Press.

Montagnier, L., Gruest, S., Chamaret, C., Douguet, C., Axler, D., Guetard, D., Nugeyre, M. T., Barre-Sinoussi, F., Chermann, J. C., Klatzmann, D., and Gluckman, J. C. (1984). Adaptation of lymphoadenopathy associated virus (LAV) to replication in EBV-transformed B-lymphoblastoid cell lines. *Science, 226,* 63–66.

Morse, E. V., Simon, P. M., Coburn, M., Hyslop, N., Greenspun, D., and Balson, P. M. (1991). Determinants of subject compliance with an experimental anti-HIV drug protocol. *Social Science and Medicine, 32,* 1161–1167.

Muma, R., Ross, W., Parcel, G., and Pollard, R. (1995). Zidovudine adherence among individuals with HIV infection. *AIDS Care, 7,* 439–448.

Munoz, A., Wang, M., Good, R., Detels, H., Ginsberg, L., Kingsley, J., Phair, J., and Polk, R. F. (1989). Estimation of the AIDS-free times after HIV–1 seroconversion. *American Journal of Epidemiology, 130,* 530–538.

Namir, S., Wolcott, D. L., Fawzy, F. I., and Alumbaugh, M. J. (1987). Coping with AIDS; Psychological and health implications. Special issue: Acquired Immune Deficiency Syndrome. *Journal of Applied Social Psychology, 17,* 309–328.

O'Brien, W. A., Hartigan, P. M., Martin, D., Esinhart, J., Hill, A., Benoit, S., Rubin, M., Simborkoff, M., and Hamilton, J. (1996). Changes in plasma HIV–1 RNA and CD4+ lymphocyte counts and the risk of progression to AIDS. *New England Journal of Medicine,* 426–431.

Paterson, D., Swindell, S., Mohr, J., Brester, M., Vergis, E., Squier, C., Wagener, M., and Singh, N. (1999). How much adherence is enough? A prospective study of adherence to protease inhibitor therapy using MEMS caps. *6th Conference on Retroviruses and Opportunistic Infections, 6.*

Perelson, A. S. Neuman, A. V., Markowitz, M., Leonard, J. M., and Ho, D. D. (1996). HIV–1 dynamics in vivo: Virion clearance rate, infected cell life-span, and viral generation time. *Science, 271,* 1582–1586.

Pillay, D. (2001). The emergence and epidemiology of resistance in the nucleoside-experienced HIV-infected population. *Antiviral Therapy, 3,* 15–24.

Popovic, M., Sardgadharan, M., Read, E., and Gallo, R. (1984). Detection, isolation and continuous production of cytopathic retroviruses (HTLV-III) from patients with AIDS and pre-AIDS. *Science, 224,* 497–500.

Quinn, S. C. (1993). AIDS and the African American woman: The triple burden of race, class and gender. *Health Education Quarterly, 20,* 305–320.

Rabkin, J. G., Williams, J. B. W., Neugebauer, R., Remien, R. H., and Goetz, R. (1990). Maintenance of hope in HIV–spectrum homosexual men. *American Journal of Psychiatry, 10,* 1322–1326.

Rosenberg, Z. F., and Fauci, A. S. (1991). Activation of latent HIV infection. *Journal of NIH Research, 2,* 41–45.

Schneiderman, N. (1999). Behavioral medicine and the management of HIV/AIDS. *International Journal of Behavioral Medicine, 6,* 3–12.

Singh, N., Squier, C., Sivek, C., Wagner, M., Hong Nguyen, M., and Yu, V. (1996). Determinants of compliance with antiretroviral therapy in patients with human immunodeficiency virus: Prospective assessment with implications for enhancing compliance. *AIDS Care, 8,* 261–269.

Stall, R., McKusick, L., and Wiley, J. (1986). Alcohol and drug use during sexual activity and compliance with safe sex guidelines for AIDS: The AIDS behavioral research project. *Health Education Quarterly, 13,* 359–360.

Staszewski, S., Bartlett, J., Hill, A. M., Katlama, C., and Johnson, J. (1997). Reductions in HIV–1 disease progression for zidovudine/lamivudine relative to control treatments: A meta-analysis of controlled trials. *AIDS, 11,* 474–483.

Tross, S., and Hirsch, D. A. (1988). Psychological distress and neuropsychological complications of HIV infection and AIDS. *American Psychologist, 43*, 929–934.

Van Hove, G. F., Shapiro, J. M., Winters, M. A., Merigan, T. C., and Blaschke, T. F. (1996). Patient compliance and drug failure in protease inhibitor monotherapy. *Journal of the American Medical Association, 256*, 1955–1956.

Walker, R., Howard, M., Lambert, M., and Suchensky, R. (1994). Psychiatric and medical comorbidities of veterans with substance use disorders. *Hospital and Community Psychiatry, 45*, 232–237.

Wall, T., Sorenson, J., Butki, S., Delucchi, K., London, J., and Chesney, M. (1995). Adherence to zidovudine (AZT) among HIV-infected methadone patients: A pilot study of supervised theory and dispensing compared to usual care. *Drug and Alcohol Dependence, 37*, 261–269.

Weaver, K. E., Llabre, M. M., Durán, R. E., Antoni, M. H., Ironson, G., Penedo, F. J., and Schneiderman, N. (2005). A stress and coping model of medication adherence and viral load in HIV positive men and women on highly active antiretroviral therapy (HAART). *Health Psychology, 24*, 385–392.

Weiss, S. M., Schneiderman, N., Tobin, J., LaPerriere, A., Jones, D. L., Goldstein, A., and Chesney, M. A. (1999). Assisting disempowered women with AIDS. *Symposium at the annual meeting of the American Psychological Association, Boston.*

West-Edwards, C., Pereira, D., Geenwood, D., Antoni, M., and Schneiderman, N. (1997). Stress management and relaxation training for HIV+ African-American women: Preliminary findings. Presented at the annual meeting of the American Psychological Association, Chicago.

The Evolution of HIV Prevention in San Francisco

A Multidisciplinary Model

MARGARET A. CHESNEY and THOMAS J. COATES

Combating the spread of AIDS and reducing its upward trajectory of morbidity and mortality has required a response as far-reaching, adaptable, and complex as the virus itself. In San Francisco, an epicenter of the epidemic, a confluence of people, events, attitudes, and communities spawned a new and highly successful model for the prevention of AIDS that brings many fields of scientific inquiry to bear on fighting its spread.

Each evolutionary step in the battle against AIDS in San Francisco has engendered new coalitions between scientists of disparate backgrounds. Physicians, for example, first encountered the illness in the clinic. Molecular biologists and epidemiologists joined the effort, discovering the source of the disease, identifying the routes of transmission, and developing the antibody test. When these combined forces within the biomedical community reached an impasse in connecting with communities at risk for infection, they called on the skills of their colleagues in the behavioral and social sciences. These scientists shed light on the individual and societal issues surrounding the virus and its modes of transmission through populations, and they developed interventions that proved to prevent its spread and curb its morbidity. Their research, by helping to inform the decision-making of physicians, clinicians, and others on the front lines of care and treatment, brought the battle against HIV full circle.

The Center for AIDS Prevention Studies (CAPS) was founded in 1986 as part of the Department of Epidemiology and Biostatistics at the University of California, San Francisco (UCSF). It was initially funded through National Institutes of Mental Health Center grants as one of the first organized efforts to bring together investigators from such different backgrounds as anthropology, psychology, virology, and biostatistics, among many others, under one roof with a common goal. In addition to being multidisciplinary, the center is community-focused, multiethnic, multi-institutional, and dedicated to training new scientists who are passionate about ending the epidemic. From its inception, it has thrived by fostering an environment of collaboration, collegiality, and respect, in which individual investigators trade freedom to pursue their own research goals for contributions they make to the body of knowledge generated by the center. Today, CAPS research addresses questions in the areas of both primary and secondary prevention. It consists of more than 200 scientists of all disciplines and has enlarged its research agenda into the international realm. It functions as an integral part of the UCSF AIDS Research Institute (ARI), which has further spread the net of scientific inquiry by drawing in new specialists from immunology and virology, to oral health and clinical medicine.

The success of the San Francisco response to the AIDS epidemic provides ample evidence that synergy results from collaboration—a lesson that is already being applied to AIDS prevention efforts in other places around the world.

Understanding the Extent of the Problem

In 2000, HIV surpassed other pathogens to become the world's leading infectious cause of adult death (Farmer et al., 2001). The extent of the global HIV crisis is such that the predictions made a decade ago, and considered at the time "alarmist," are now revealed as sober projections (Mann, Tarantola, and Netter, 1992). In contrast, as we write this, AIDS morbidity in the United States has declined among many at-risk populations. The rise in new infections has been curbed dramatically. There is an increasingly sophisticated understanding of the basic biology of AIDS infection and progression. Treatment options have increased multifold. Behavioral strategies have been honed for coping with the stress of illness, caring for its victims, and adhering to complicated drug regimens. New societal norms have evolved around the best approaches to prevention. Granted, AIDS science has a long way to go. But the great strides made against the epidemic to date would not have been possible without the involvement of scientists from every specialty. The AIDS epidemic already had a stronghold on the San Francisco Bay Area by the time the virus was identified. Perhaps this unprecedented public health challenge inspired the scientists to cooperate with the teamwork that has characterized CAPS. How and why did a collaborative approach to AIDS prevention evolve here?

The story begins in the early days of the HIV epidemic in San Francisco. The first cases of a "gay cancer" appeared in 1981, and by 1984 several research groups had reported isolation of its causative agent, HIV, a sexually transmitted retrovirus. Beginning with the earliest cases in the United States, most HIV-infected individuals were gay men and/or intravenous drug users. Although no known or potential cures for HIV/AIDS yet existed, tests were developed in the mid-1980s to detect viral antibodies. But by 1986, almost 100,000 cases of AIDS had been reported in 132 countries, with upward of 10 million people believed to be asymptomatic carriers of HIV.

In San Francisco as elsewhere, developments in understanding the basic science and routes of transmission of the virus occurred against an intricate mosaic of gay life. A history of isolation from mainstream society and a mistrust of many of its leaders, including providers of medical care, had left the gay community vulnerable to threats to its health. Horror at the rapid decline and death of previously robust friends and neighbors, coupled with media reports suggesting that gay men had spawned an epidemic that now threatened society at large, resulted at first in a period of profound shock and denial within the community.

In this context, the discovery of the virus was a double-edged sword, raising hopes on the one hand, fears on the other. Since HIV was shown to be sexually transmitted, gay men dreaded both losing the sexual freedom that had become one defining characteristic of their community and facing further approbation by society at large. Calls for mandatory testing of at-risk populations and public reporting and isolation of those infected not only served to reinforce the worst fears of the gay community but also provided individuals with a rationale for refusing to be tested for the virus and learning their serostatus—cornerstones of any meaningful effort at prevention.

San Francisco embraced a large gay population, a substantial injection drug abuse cohort, and clearly demarcated at-risk minority communities—three demographic characteristics suggesting that prevention efforts would find fertile ground here. Of less tangible but equally important benefit, the City of Saint Francis had a history of tolerance and diversity that reflected the compassion of its namesake; a threat to the welfare of any segment of society would not go unnoticed or unchallenged.

Underpinnings of a Multidisciplinary, Community-Based Prevention Model

In many ways, this case study in multidisciplinary research is a story of individuals from different paths, who came together to address an urgent public health problem. To tell this story, we have to trace these paths. While individuals may be noted, in every case, the projects they led and the results they found are not their work alone but, rather, represent the work of many more dedicated people.

In the early 1980s, one of the authors, Thomas Coates, then associate professor of medicine at UCSF, was working with Stephen B. Hulley, professor of medicine, UCSF, on the development and implementation of community-level behavior change efforts aimed at smoking cessation as a risk reduction for cardiovascular disease. Because cardiovascular disease prevention models had been proven effective on the community level by involving sociologists, anthropologists, and psychologists in the effort, the National Heart, Lung and Blood Institute began trials to determine if interventions organized and delivered by behavioral and social scientists through existing community structures could reach smokers and convince them to quit.

Coates was also leading an effort within the Division of General Internal Medicine at UCSF, which was tasked with providing innovative teaching, clinical services, and research at the interface between behavioral and biomedical sciences. Founded in 1982, the Behavioral Medicine Unit (BMU) had a multidisciplinary staff of 15 psychologists, internists, a psychiatrist, nurses, and social workers participating in a variety of activities, including some of the community-based cardiovascular research undertaken by Coates and Hulley.

Meanwhile, one of the authors, Margaret Chesney, as director of the department of behavioral medicine at (the former) Stanford Research Institute in nearby Palo Alto, California, was also studying cardiovascular disease, with an emphasis on investigating individual strategies for coping with coronary heart disease and adhering to treatment regimens for hypertension. She also had worked with Coates on parallel RO1 grants studying hypertension and smoking cessation throughout the late 1970s and early 1980s—grants that included cardiologists and general medicine doctors as investigators in a biomedical-behavioral alliance.

By 1983, patients with compromised immune systems were appearing in increasing numbers at San Francisco General Hospital (SFGH), a teaching hospital staffed by UCSF physicians, and gay men were showing up at psychotherapy offices with symptoms of profound dysphoria. Coates and Leon McKusick, Ph.D., an assistant research psychologist at UCSF who also maintained a private psychotherapy practice with many gay clients, began comparing notes about possible behavioral links between immune dysfunction and psychological factors.

That same year, Chesney was program chair for the annual meeting of the division of health psychology at the American Psychological Association. Several papers submitted to the meeting dealt with the new, still controversial issue of AIDS. Chesney approached Coates and asked him to work with her to put together what would be the first symposium on the topic of AIDS at a national behavioral and social science meeting. Despite threats of picketing, the symposium was presented to a crowd that filled the meeting room, spilling out into the halls of the convention center.

By 1984, along with the discovery of HTLV-III (as HIV was then known), it was commonly accepted that the virus was spreading chiefly through sexual contact (and, to a lesser degree, through transfusions and injection drug use). But while clinical investigators, immunologists, and virologists had been turning their attention and resources to investigating the immune dysfunction affecting gay men, no efforts at sexual risk reduction or behavior modification had been organized. Coates and McKusick, both of whom were familiar with community-based models of behavioral intervention, contacted the National Institutes of Mental Health (NIMH) to suggest that they jump-start a behavioral approach to prevention, and the deliberate wheels of government began to turn.

Through his history of working with cardiovascular disease, Coates had developed a strong interest in whether or not psychological factors were predictive of disease progression. Since the mid-1970s, the National Institute of Allergy and Infectious Diseases (NIAID) had been funding a broad-based health research enterprise in the Bay Area: the San Francisco Men's Health Project (SFMHP). Headed up by Warren Winkelstein, M.D., M.P.H., professor of epidemiology at the University of California, Berkeley, this sero-epidemiological study had been monitoring, among other variables, the rates of venereal and bloodborne diseases among a cohort of several hundred men. Winkelstein readily agreed to let Coates investigate whether stress was a predictor for HIV disease progression among the SFMHP subjects and encouraged him to attach a supplemental grant request for NIAID funding.

McKusick, witnessing increased levels of stress in the gay community, asked Coates to join him in studying the effect of HIV on gay men from a psychological and behavioral perspective. Their early studies asked whether psychological counseling affected illness progression, and whether the psychological adaptations gay men were making in response to seeing friends grow ill were themselves affecting disease progression.

Among other findings, the pair ascertained that, while counseling reduced stress and improved the quality of life for patients with AIDS, the intervention did not change levels of immune function (Coates, McKusick, Stites, and Kuno, 1989). Another early collaborative study, led by McKusick and Coates and funded by the San Francisco Department of Public Health, concluded that knowledge of health guidelines alone was having little or no effect on sexual behavior and that sex was often used to relieve stress and express a gay identity. Firsthand knowledge of someone with AIDS, however, was shown to reduce the frequency of sexual risk-taking (McKusick, Hortsman, and Coates, 1985).

With these results in mind, Steve Morin, Ph.D., assistant clinical professor at UCSF and a private-practice psychologist, assisted his colleagues in writing a grant proposal, which was funded by the NIMH and which further investigated the effect of psychological stress on sexual behavior. The study found, among other conclusions, that subjects who knew their sero-status as positive were less likely to engage in unprotected high-risk sex, but that younger gay men were still taking the risk (McKusick, Coates, Morin, Pollack, and Hoff, 1990). Recommendations included tailoring some community risk-reduction programs specifically to young people, promoting antibody testing, and challenging peer norms. These recommendations informed evolving community-level interventions in San Francisco and nationwide.

Although it could hardly have been clear at the time, even to their participants, the above-mentioned developments in the professional lives of Coates, Hulley, Winkelstein, McKusick, and Morin formed building blocks for the first large-scale, community-based, multidisciplinary HIV prevention efforts in San Francisco.

The work of Coates and Hulley in cardiovascular disease would serve as a model for a community-centered approach to AIDS behavioral interventions. Coates's leadership of the Behavioral Medicine Unit presaged his future AIDS work that involved doctors of many disciplines, as did teaming up with McKusick, Morin, and Winkelstein on the first NIMH and NIAID grant requests. For years to come, data generated by SFMHP would prove invaluable in assessing the prevalence of infection in the general population, latency period of the virus, onset of symptoms, and morbidity. Recommendations made in the SFMHP-based studies were put to use immediately by community AIDS prevention agencies hungry for tools to use in designing risk-reduction programs. And Chesney's cross-disciplinary efforts, particularly as they related to coping with the stress of cardiovascular diseases as chronic illnesses, would inform her future research on coping with HIV and adherence to the complex regimens developed for its treatment.

Each of these scientists shared a belief that if the task of applying psychology to health—in this case, the behavioral study of HIV prevention—was to be effective, it would require the full participation of biomedical scientists in a collaborative effort. Physicians and health departments were stationed on the front lines, interfacing with at-risk populations in sexually transmitted disease clinics, methadone clinics, emergency rooms, and private practices with persons requesting to be tested for the virus. These were places to which behavioral and social scientists would have to gain access to find their first study participants, and they needed the participation of the biomedical community to act as go-between.

The biomedical community was beginning to reach the same conclusion. Treatment for both symptoms and underlying HIV disease were severely lacking, and in their absence, reducing rates of infection was seen as the best way to rein in the virus and keep people from getting sick in the first place. Behavioral science, population science, anthropological research, sociology, epidemiology, and chain intervention studies would be needed to supplement clinical and laboratory efforts in this epidemic, just as they had come to be used in the battle against cardiovascular disease through smoking cessation, nutrition counseling, and other prevention interventions.

The Formation of CAPS

Isolation of the AIDS virus and the quick development of the first antibody tests in 1984 prompted the head of the U.S. Department of Health and Human Services to declare that a vaccine would be available within a matter of years. The elation was short-lived. By 1985, epidemiological research suggested that most people who sero-converted to HIV would progress to develop AIDS. Yet no medications existed to remedy symptoms or improve underlying immune dysfunction, and AIDS remained unrelentingly fatal. Moreover, those at greatest risk—gay men—were often refusing to be tested for the virus.

Virologists were shocked and saddened that their creation of a scientific tool to identify infected individuals could not be used successfully in the field. Although instituting voluntary, anonymous testing and counseling eventually encouraged some people to submit to the test (see Kegeles, Catania, Coates, Pollack, and Lo, 1990), many in a gay community beset with distrust and denial were reluctant to be tested. Without a viable treatment, the rationale for testing was not clear. Lacking the tools to explain this behavior or to devise methods to overcome it, the biomedical community turned to behavioral scientists for assistance. Clearly, changing behavior—beginning with the behavior associated with getting tested—was going to play a critical role in stemming new infections.

Questions for behavioral scientists arose in three other areas in San Francisco as well. The city's minority communities were hit with a higher prevalence of AIDS than their proportion of the general population would suggest. Many speculated that substance abuse, both within and outside of minority communities, and not linked strictly to injection drug use, was playing a role in the spread of the virus. Simultaneously, research surveys and anecdotal evidence had uncovered a reluctance among medical professionals to talk to their patients about sexuality, risk for HIV infection, or strategies for prevention. A multifaceted prevention program in San Francisco would be needed to meet these crises.

In September 1986, the U.S. Department of Health and Human Services funded the first five-year grant to create multidisciplinary centers to study AIDS viral prevention around the United States. CAPS was tasked with creating an environment in which investigators could pursue basic, clinical, and applied research and develop strategies for coordinating and integrating activities with other centers at UCSF and other scientific and health organizations in the local community.

Under the directorship of Hulley, the center established its primary goal as preventing the spread of the AIDS epidemic into at risk-populations. To meet this goal, the center set out "to create a working environment that would bring together scientists and health care providers at the three main institutions involved with AIDS in San Francisco: academic researchers at the University of California (UCSF), county health officials at the San Francisco Department of Public Health (SFDPH), and minority health care providers at Bayview-Hunter's Point Foundation (BHPF)" (grant proposal to HHS, May 1987).

The building blocks of future collaborative research on AIDS in San Francisco can be seen in this visionary plan, which included establishing linkages among AIDS programs and investigators who had little or no contact; coordinating new multidisciplinary research projects into the mental health and substance abuse aspects of AIDS; having a multiplier effect on the growth of knowledge about the same; and enhancing the formation of local, national, and global health policy as a consequence.

The first research proposals to garner funding for the center included psychosocial, multicultural, and substance abuse components. Among them was the study entitled "Psychological and Behavioral Reactions to HIV Antibody Testing" (see Coates, Morin, and McKusick, 1987). This project sought to ascertain the effect of antibody testing on knowledge about AIDS and changes in sexual behavior and drug use. Two separate cohorts were studied: 683 gay and bisexual males from an ongoing UCSF AIDS Behavioral Research Project and a heterogenous sample of 1,000 persons volunteering for antibody testing under the California Antibody Testing Program in Alameda County. Among other findings, the study concluded that men in nonmonogamous relationships and men not in relationships reported substantial reductions in high-risk sexual behavior, but not a corresponding increase in low-risk sexual behavior. In this and future studies, knowledge of one's antibody status as positive was shown to reduce the frequency and type of sexual behavior reported—a conclusion that helped public health authorities design effective media and grass-roots prevention campaigns.

Another study supported by the center, entitled "Depressive Symptoms and CD4 Lymphocyte Decline among HIV-Infected Men" (see Burack et al., 1993), examined the relationship between depression and illness progression in a cohort of 330 men with serological evidence of HIV. This study found that overall and affective depression predicted a more rapid decline in CD4 lymphocyte counts; this association was not attributable to baseline psychological differences, perceived somatic symptoms, or differences in alcohol or drug use. Later studies showed that emotional, practical, and informational support were inversely correlated with depression in those with AIDS.

The relationship between alcohol and drug use and high-risk sexual behavior, immune dysfunction, and disease progression was the focus of another study, entitled "Alcohol and Drug Use Risk for AIDS" (see Stall, McKusick, Wiley, Coates, and Ostrow, 1986). This project found that use of particular drugs during sex, the number of drugs used, and the frequency of combining sex and drugs were all positively associated with risky sexual activity for AIDS, and the authors recommended that safer-sex education messages take these conclusions into account.

The study entitled "AIDS Prevention through Community Action Networks for Blacks and Hispanics" posed the question of how community workshops affected awareness and attitudes toward AIDS. This project found that these meetings could be effective if information was tailored to the needs of individual groups.

Center Design

The design of the Center reflected an emerging philosophy within the NIMH and the San Francisco AIDS community that the complexity of the epidemic called for multifaceted response. CAPS leadership believed that the production of excellent research on the extent and amount of behavioral change, and what it took to bring such change about, would be essential to building a reputation of respect and trust within the biomedical research community. A partnership with biomedical scientists and clinicians was recognized as critical from the start, as these groups become important gatekeepers and provide channels to the communities at risk and the individuals living with HIV. Some of the potential biomedical colleagues either had not worked with social and behavioral scientists or perceived the disciplines as less rigorous. Producing and disseminating solid data by combining the best of behavioral science with the best of epidemiology became the center's primary focus.

To meet this end, the CAPS faculty developed three major components of technical assistance, called Cores, available to all investigators:

Epidemiology and Biostatistics offered expertise in research design and data analysis, training, administration of pilot studies, and access to computer resources. Thus, an investigator with a background in clinical psychology, for example, might enlist the aid of this core to fine-tune a statistical component of a qualitative survey on condom use.

Biomedical and Basic Science provided advice on clinical laboratory measurements and coordinated biomedical interventions and follow-up care—critical components to any CAPS study that could be expected to affect the biomedical community.

Health Policy Analysis and Dissemination developed and analyzed health policy on AIDS and disseminated analyses and recommendations, together with research findings from center studies to health providers, laboratories, and the community at large, so that the results of CAPS research would not end up in a vacuum.

These three basic areas of technical assistance have survived and expanded within CAPS to the present day.

Weekly meetings of the CAPS investigators created a tight working group of scientists from different disciplines and settings. From the start, the center's directorate placed a high emphasis on collegiality, sharing of information, and ties to community and public health groups.

By early 1987, as results from the first research projects began to accumulate, the efficacy of the center's format and collaborative approach had been established. A follow-up grant application expanded existing multicultural, psychosocial, and substance abuse areas of study.

A new Multicultural Inquiry and Research on AIDS (MIRA) conducted epidemiological and prevention studies in ethnic and racial minority communities. This SFDPH collaboration included studies focusing on condom use among heterosexuals and substance abuse-related transmission, with secondary heterosexual and perinatal transmission components. A study on condom use in multiethnic neighborhoods was among the projects coordinated by the MIRA component of CAPS. This study determined, for instance, that African American and Hispanic women were less likely than Caucasian women to have sexual partners who always used condoms, but suggested that sexual communication skills were a key influence on condom use across all social strata and ethnic groups (Catania et al., 1991).

Collaboration with UCSF yielded new studies in psychosocial, ethical, and international arenas. In response to surveys showing that AIDS risk-reduction counseling among physicians was uneven and often insufficient, CAPS generated a study that determined the efficacy of a continuing educational program for health professionals in spreading messages of antibody testing and safer sex. Social learning theory and social marketing were applied to an intervention to counteract linkages between high-risk sexual behavior, drug use, and sexually transmitted diseases among adolescents. Ethics studies included interventions that encouraged the use of durable power of attorney for health care and publicized successful methods of adaptive coping. And studies in Africa and other parts of the world helped determine which prevention methods developed in this country might effectively be transplanted to foreign shores.

In addition to these NIMH-funded inquiries, CAPS investigators, demonstrating the multiplier effects of the center, began to apply for grants for AIDS research from the NIH, the University of California Taskforce on AIDS, and other entities.

CAPS also built bridges to the UCSF Institute for Health Policy Studies (IHPS) to study the efficacy and applicability of European models of IV drug-user AIDS intervention. Along with IHPS, CAPS began producing an AIDS Weekly Reader to help keep center investigators and others apprised on current developments in AIDS policy, research, and service development. Dissemination activities were supported by an extensive information development effort, including membership in national and state AIDS networks; subscriptions to international, national, state, and local newsletters, journals, and reports; receipt of monthly federal, state, and local AIDS statistics; and development of program reference files. These lines of internal communication continue to thrive at CAPS today.

Also within its first six months, CAPS convened the first Community Forum on Mental Health and Substance Abuse in AIDS, with a focus on the topic "AIDS in Minorities." This community-based forum introduced the center to local public policymakers, public health program managers, health service providers, members of the gay and ethnic minority communities, and the press. The center's emphasis on direct dissemination to the public may be traced to this first forum.

In early 1987, CAPS developed two additional faculty cores to assist investigators. The *Survey Research Resources* core supplied technical expertise and field operations to survey research on population-based cohorts, while the *Analysis and Ethical Issues* core gave assistance and training on ethical issues concerning research projects and aided investigators in extracting conclusions from their data.

CAPS expanded the range of scientists associated with the center by recruiting policymakers, anthropologists, sociologists, virologists, and experts in the ethical issues associated with AIDS prevention. A beneficial influence to CAPS' involvement of scientists from so many different backgrounds turned out to be its geographical location. At first, lacking space in the clinical epidemiology program on the main UCSF campus, the center made its home in a small former surgical suite at San Francisco General Hospital, forcing many investigators to work from home. In 1987, the center grouped investigators into a single off-campus site, which immediately fostered cross-discipline communication through the "water-cooler" effect. The location, in downtown San Francisco, was both near transit hubs, allowing easy access for members of the community, and close to the offices of the SFDPH, with which CAPS wanted to continue its close ties.

Expanding into Secondary Prevention

Once biomedical scientists began to develop treatments for AIDS and AIDS-related conditions, beginning with the discovery of the efficacy of the drug AZT at combating symptoms of the disease in 1988, efforts at secondary prevention (keeping HIV-positive individuals from progressing to death) began in earnest. Since HIV was now recognized as a chronic—though often fatal—illness, a new set of psychological, anthropological, and policy issues came to the fore.

CAPS recruited new teams of scientists who were experts in the ramifications of chronic illness, including Chesney from Stanford Research Institute and Susan Folkman, Ph.D., a research psychologist from the University of California, Berkeley, who specialized in stress and coping issues over a broad spectrum of diseases and syndromes. Ironically, Chesney, tapped in 1987 to study AIDS risk-reduction interventions for the U.S. Army base at Fort Ord (Monterey, CA), had asked Coates to assist her as a consultant to the project. He convinced her instead to join him at CAPS.

With these scientists, CAPS could expand its realm of study to include issues related to coping with the stress of living with HIV and the strain the uninfected felt at being surrounded by illness and death. CAPS scientists began examining various strategies for caregiving, both within the medical establishment and by individuals in home-care settings. Recruiting for these studies brought Chesney and Folkman into collaboration with clinical scientists, who requested their assistance with a clinical problem that was undermining clinical drug trials—namely, patients having difficulty adhering to HIV drug-treatment regimens. Chesney, having investigated adherence earlier with hypertensive patients, collaborated with clinicians Molly Cooke and Paul Volberding in the first study of adherence in HIV, funded by NIMH.

At first, some early CAPS investigators were concerned about expanding the center's target population beyond those at risk to include those who were living with HIV. They feared that resources drawn away from primary prevention might stunt the center's developing expertise at risk-reduction and end up prolonging the epidemic. Other investigators saw these new forays into secondary prevention as a means to connect clinicians, hospitals, and community-based agencies, whose patients were struggling with issues of coping, caregiving, and adherence, with the work of the center. CAPS leadership convinced both sides that prevention was not a zero-sum game and that additional resources could be brought into the center to support both approaches. This emphasis on resolving either/or disputes by developing solutions that encompassed *both* has continued to prove an effective strategy for the center.

Three early studies of secondary prevention provide examples of the center's added direction.

Positive education project

One of these studies was the Positive Education Project, a CAPS research project codirected by Chesney and Folkman in 1990 and funded by NIMH. This study tested an intervention to assist persons coping with chronic diseases such as HIV/AIDS. The intervention, Coping Effectiveness Training (Chesney, Folkman, and Chambers, 1996), represented a merger between Folkman's work in social psychology on the theory of stress and coping and Chesney's research in clinical psychology research on interventions for managing stress. The study was conducted as a clinical trial, contrasting Coping Effectiveness Training (CET) with two controls conditions: an HIV educational intervention, and a delayed treatment group. The results indicted that CET was a significantly more effective strategy for reducing psychological stress associated with HIV/AIDS than the control conditions were. The study also generated findings with implications for multidisciplinary work. It provided preliminary evidence that CET increased patients' ability to adhere to medications, which if confirmed could have major implications for the biomedical community, which was struggling with high levels of patient nonadherence to HIV medications. In addition, the study confirmed other evidence suggesting that positive morale and meaning in life are important positive components of stress and coping theory. Simply put, persons who are able to experience positive meaning, a positive outcome of CET, are better able to handle life stressors.

The results of the Positive Education Project led to a second and third study of CET and its tenets. The first is testing various strategies to enhance the maintenance of the effects of CET over time and examining the effect of CET on health care costs. The second is testing the effects of CET on adherence to care and biological health outcomes. Thus, the two new studies have taken CET into new fields, including health economics and clinical medicine.

Effects of caregiving

The second early CAPS study in the area of secondary prevention addressed the effects of caregiving for persons with HIV/AIDS. As the number of people living with HIV disease grew—at a faster pace than the development of drugs to lessen virulence or delay symptom onset—the population in need of caregiving swelled. Much of the burden for providing this care fell on the partners of those who were infected—people who where themselves HIV-positive, at risk for infection, or perhaps burdened with knowledge that their partners had become infected through sexual activity outside of the primary relationship. Many in the HIV community, in both biomedicine and the social sciences, hypothesized that the stress of caregiving might itself increase susceptibility to infection.

The largest study ever undertaken to study the effects of caregiving, entitled "Coping and Well-being in Caregivers of Persons with AIDS" (see Folkman, Chesney, Cooke, Boccellari, and Collette, 1994), brought psychologists, social psychologists, physicians in general internal medicine, and medical ethicists together to ascertain the toll the disease might be taking on those providing care. The study showed that neither caregiving nor the stress of bereavement was associated with hastening disease progression—good news for the community that had sustained numerous losses. It demonstrated that specific psychological variables existed in individuals who were able to manage caregiving and loss, including an ability to find positive meaning in caregiving.

Further research from the caregiving study delved into the sensitive realm of assisted dying of those in late-stage AIDS. The study, entitled "Informal Caregivers and the Intention to Hasten AIDS-Related Death" (see Cooke et al., 1998) concluded that the decision to hasten death was not a rare event in the lives of informal caregivers. It showed that such a decision did not result from caregiver distress, poor relationship quality, or intolerable caregiver burden; nor was it a cause of excessive discomfort in the surviving partner. The conclusions drawn from these studies, widely disseminated to affected communities, health care providers, and the public at large, helped reorient society's perceptions of people with AIDS and the gay community.

Adherence to clinical regimen

The third early CAPS study in secondary prevention responded to the alarming discovery that as many as 25% of patients in clinical trials were having difficulty maintaining their regimen of AIDS medication, threatening the integrity of clinical trials and increasing the likelihood that a potentially effective treatment might be missed. Chesney directed the study entitled "Adherence in Clinical Trials for HIV Disease" beginning in 1990 (see Chesney and Folkman, 1999). The study tested an adherence intervention in asymptomatic HIV-positive individuals enrolled in ongoing trials at SFGH, one of the sites of the AIDS Clinical Trials Group (ACTG). It brought together Chesney, professor in the departments of medicine and epidemiology and biostatistics at UCSF, with Paul Volberding, M.D., chief of the AIDS program at San Francisco General Hospital and principal investigator of ACTG. As the only public acute-care hospital in San Francisco, SFGH served and continues to serve as the most important single source of HIV-related outpatient and inpatient care.

Volberding acted as the liaison between the project and the ACTG. Molly Cooke, M.D., associate professor of clinical medicine and codirector of the project, was responsible for tracking and maintaining information about upcoming trials and developing recruitment procedures for subjects. Maria Ekstrand, Ph.D., a clinical psychologist, assisted Chesney in the development of the adherence intervention. This research project was seminal to further investigation of adherence with regard to new drugs, including protease inhibitors, as they were developed in the years to come. In particular, it confirmed that nonadherence to therapy was a serious problem that was observed in approximately half the patients on HIV medications. It also identified the leading variables associated with nonadherence, including alcohol use, the stress of daily living, and psychological distress, and pointed to the need for individually tailored interventions to increase adherence (Chesney, Ickovics, Hecht, Sikipa, and Rabkin, 1999).

Following this formative adherence project, the new highly active antiretroviral therapies, known as "drug cocktails," became available and offered more effective management of the disease. Once these newer therapies became available, the biomedical community soon realized the paramount importance of addressing the issue of adherence. Not only were patients having difficulty taking over 20 medications per day, but when they failed to do so, they increased the likelihood of incubating drug-resistant viral strains.

The importance of adherence built a stronger bridge between CAPS and the clinical research under way at SFGH. As a result of these closer connections, a new multidisciplinary team developed between Chesney; James Kahn, M.D., associate professor and director of the independent clinical trials group that performed research for pharmaceutical companies; Frederick Hecht, M.D., an assistant professor of medicine on the unit; and Robert Grant, M.D., a virologist at the Gladstone Institute of Virology and Immunology at UCSF. This team began studying persons newly infected with HIV in the hope that immediate and aggressive therapy with the new treatment regimens might arrest the progression of the disease. The multidisciplinary "Options Project" was born. The research community had doubts that the team could identify persons so early in infection and turned down requests for funds. This did not stop the team, which launched the study without funds and soon found themselves with a large number of patients who needed clinical care and counseling in adherence and stress management. An urgent appeal by Chesney to the Centers for Disease Control and Prevention led to an emergency grant to help with the project's costs. The study is now well known for the first identification of a person infected with a multidrug-resistant form of HIV. The person who transmitted the resistant virus had been nonadherent to his HIV medications (Hecht et al., 1998). Furthermore, the success of this project resulted in the National Institutes of Health funding a network of such studies throughout the country. Among the sites funded for these studies was the UCSF team, now led by the internationally renowned immunologist, Jay Levy, M.D.

Recent studies

Today, studies into AIDS risk across the United States, undertaken by CAPS with the leadership of Joseph Catania, Ph.D., are another example of cross-disciplinary collaboration. Results of the research help inform clinicians, hospitals, and caregivers, as well as policy makers on a national level about behavioral factors relating to gay male sexuality, condom use, HIV testing, partner negotiation and notification, help-seeking, and AIDS prevalence among different populations, among other topics.

Among the findings generated by Catania's CAPS research have been that HIV incidence rates among men who have sex with men (MSM) have been relatively constant since the late 1980s and at levels that are parallel to those in sub-Saharan Africa. Although many in the media and government have jumped to the conclusion that the overall increased longevity of people with HIV spells an end to the epidemic, Catania's findings prove otherwise. And while small incursions of HIV disease among heterosexuals have been seized upon and magnified by power brokers, in fact, overall HIV prevalence and related cofactors (syphilis) have declined in the highest risk heterosexual populations since 1992. In the United States, AIDS remains largely an epidemic of gay men—a finding with ramifications in public policy formation.

Defining the CAPS Multidisciplinary Model

Now entering its fourteenth year and fourth NIMH grant cycle, CAPS continues to adapt to new challenges presented by the epidemic. Through the course of its evolution, several defining characteristics of the center, particularly as they relate to its multidisciplinary approach, have been revealed.

Collaborations with other scientists and organizations

Through collaborations within UCSF and with Bay Area institutions outside of the university, including health departments and community-based organizations, CAPS links more than 200 San Francisco Bay Area investigators with expertise in epidemiology, behavioral medicine, biostatistics, biomedical and basic sciences, social science survey research, substance abuse, ethics, public health, international health, and health policy research and analysis. We will highlight three of these links: to UCSF–SFGH, to the San Francisco Men's Health Project, and to the San Francisco Department of Public Health.

As director of the AIDS clinical programs at SFGH, Volberding was eager to involve social and behavioral scientists in the creation and improvement of care and treatment models. Since AIDS was clearly spread by behavior, studying behavior became an overarching imperative. Discovering ways to encourage testing and counseling required both social marketing and counseling standards that were the forte of behaviorists. In addition, on SFGH wards and in outpatient clinics, Volberding and others encountered patients suffering from psychological strain over issues of coping and quality of life on a daily basis. Behavioral and social scientists, in turn, had developed a keen respect for AIDS doctors with few tools at their disposal outside of a positive attitude.

Beginning in 1990, when Chesney began collaborating with Volberding, she was invited to attend meetings at the Center for AIDS Research (CFAR) to provide technical expertise in the areas of recruitment and retention of subjects, adherence and quality of life. When the CFAR was re-competed, Volberding included a small "subcore" within the center's Clinical Core, to provide support for "Behavioral Science." In 1997, CFAR converted the subcore into a full-standing core devoted to Behavioral Science and Epidemiology, with Chesney as the director and Frederick Hecht as codirector. The philosophy of "bench to bedside" was quickly transformed into "bench to bedside to behavior."

Links to the San Francisco Men's Health Project, the defining study in terms of the natural history of HIV, have also continued to bear fruit, in one case playing a pivotal role in understanding the prevalence of Kaposi's sarcoma among HIV-infected individuals. The disproportionate occurrence of this cancer suggested that an additional factor, besides HIV, was responsible for its development. Once the HHV-8 virus was discovered, Martin and Osmond of CAPS, collaborating with Ganem's laboratory at UCSF, were the first to perform a well-controlled longitudinal study of HHV-8 (Martin et al., 1998). For this study, they used the banked sera and well-considered behavioral questions from the original SFMHP study, which determined that infection with the virus temporally precedes and is independently associated with the development of Kaposi's Sarcoma in MSM. This study, and similar ones that followed it, served as the basis for the inference that HHV-8 is a necessary causal agent for Kaposi's sarcoma.

CAPS scientists have teamed with the San Francisco Department of Public Health since the first center grant, sharing resources and data, serving together on local and state AIDS panels, and developing community-based strategies for prevention. In 1999 a comprehensive set of research projects focusing on transmission dynamics, prevention of infection among individuals recently exposed to HIV, and disease progression was developed jointly by UCSF and SFDPH. The programs include NIH Grants to Jay Levy et al. in the area of primary HIV infection; an NIH Grant to Tom Coates (with Kahn and Katz) in the area of postexposure prevention; the Options Project (Kahn, Chesney, Hecht, and Grant), dealing with treatment and risk reduction for primary HIV infection; the AIDS Clinical Trials Group study of primary HIV Infection (Volberding et al.); and a University of California grant to James O. Kahn et al. (in collaboration with UCLA and UCSD) to identify sources and offer partner services.

Community collaborations

Dramatic behavioral changes observed among gay and bisexual men in San Francisco have been attributed to a shift in community norms that resulted from the design and implementation of multifaceted community-level HIV risk-reduction programs. Many of these programs were designed after qualitative, anthropological surveys determined that information, motivation (especially a heightened sense of personal threat—"I, too, can become infected"—and the perception that safe sex can be enjoyable), skill training, and modification of peer norms could contribute to behavioral change.

The first CAPS community collaboration, with the Bayview-Hunter's Point Foundation (BHPF), was an example of the benefits and challenges of such pairings. As a community agency in a predominantly African American, socially disadvantaged section of San Francisco with higher-than-average rates of intravenous drug use, BHPF was a logical partner in implementing risk-reduction interventions, and CAPS set up an independent research group located on site. Since treatment and care needs in the community were great, however, the primary focus for BHPF was securing services to those in distress, while CAPS investigators were intent on accessing a pool of at-risk individuals from which they could draw methodologically rigorous data.

These conflicting goals left neither partner entirely satisfied. CAPS clinical investigators provided as much care for patients as the study allotted, but no more; BHPF provided as much support and scientific tracking as their resources allowed, but no more.

CAPS took away from the BHPF experience a firm resolve not to split its investigative team up by placing investigators in community settings; dividing the team geographically was found to reduce the intellectual critical mass at CAPS and to hamper cross collaboration and communication among scientists. Although the alliance with BHPF has not survived to the present day, the data gathered on intravenous drug use and related cross-infection into heterosexual populations, and access to care, has informed clinicians, hospitals, and policy makers of issues unique to this studied population and has been used as a model for interventions with other inner-city populations.

A longer-lasting relationship has been sustained with San Francisco's Stop AIDS Project, which has partnered with CAPS since 1989. This agency sends volunteer survey takers into gay neighborhoods to provide an ongoing series of data snapshots about condom use, exposure, safe sex practices, psychological issues around partner notification, and other behavioral issues. CAPS investigators design the questionnaires, tabulate data, and interpret results, which are then recycled into improved surveys and disseminated to other community organizations, health care providers, and policy makers.

In 1996, the San Francisco AIDS Foundation (SFAF), in partnership with other AIDS bodies, began looking for ways to cut further the rate of new infections in the city. Although social marketing and behavioral modification methods had resulted in the largest reduction in risk-taking ever documented in response to a public health threat, and although these methods were being replicated successfully nationwide, they were not effective 100% of the time, particularly with younger gay men, who may not have had firsthand experience with the destructive power of the disease.

Finding little data to explain why some gay men were continuing to engage in high-risk sexual behavior without condoms, SFAF teamed up with CAPS' anthropologists to conduct qualitative ethnographic research of the gay community.

Analyzed by CAPS scientists, the resulting data steered SFAF toward creating Gay Life, a series of programs with a holistic approach to prevention.

Gay Life, and its constituent program, Black Brothers Esteem, acknowledge and attempt to ameliorate factors associated with the decision, conscious or unconscious, to take risks. These factors have been shown to include, among others, racism, homophobia, lack of jobs and safe housing, gay community support, depression, and substance abuse. CAPS scientists continue to evaluate Gay Life, which like earlier prevention methods, has rippled out through community-service agencies throughout the United States. Project EXPLORE, for example, now under way in six cities, is studying the processes that contribute to an individual's risk taking, with HIV incidence as the endpoint.

Through the numerous research projects in which CAPS has participated, investigators have learned a few keys to maximizing the potential of community-based collaborative research:

1. Invest time in building and maintaining collaborative relationships.
2. Invest money in supporting collaborative research.
3. Ensure that all participants are committed to the services being offered, the evaluation project, and the consortium.
4. Set appropriate expectations for research efforts and fund accordingly.
5. If possible, actively involve funders.
6. Be flexible in designing and fielding collaborative studies.
7. Learn from difficulties encountered in implementing research.

An emphasis on dissemination

CAPS interacts with community-based organizations, as well as other scientists and the general population, through its Technology and Information Exchange (TIE) Core. Finding that standard channels of scientific communication such as journals did not adequately reach service providers and policymakers, the TIE Core created innovative strategies to forge links between research and service and to disseminate prevention science in ways that provide optimum results for influencing policy and practice.

The TIE Core's goals include educating health care establishments and providers; the media; policymakers; the San Francisco Department of Health; schools; worksites; STD, family planning, and drug abuse treatment centers; community-based organizations, including churches and clubs; and antibody testing centers about HIV, how it is transmitted, and the psychology of resistance to testing.

CAPS and the TIE Core accomplish this expansive task of communication and dissemination through the CAPS Newsletter; the CAPS Internet home page, HIV In-Site (http://www.caps.ucsf.edu/capsweb); a directory of CAPS investigators; a selected bibliography of publications by CAPS scientists; and media releases and stories. CAPS also transfers research findings to the community through publications in peer-reviewed journals; presentations at local, national, and international meetings; frequent HIV prevention fact sheets, published in English and Spanish; CAPS monographs; participation on the local HIV prevention planning council and in roundtables, forums, and seminars; and editorials, feature articles, and press releases. These media guide community service providers, policy makers, other scientists, and funders to CAPS as a resource for scientific information and assistance.

Continually adapting and expanding the cores

While the original center grants stipulated the formation of cores, it left their makeup to the individual centers. The core structure at CAPS has adapted over the years to keep pace with the epidemic. The original five cores of 1987 (Epidemiology and Biostatistics, Biomedical and Basic Science, Health Policy Analysis and Dissemination, Survey Research Resources, and Analysis and Ethical Issues) have been restructured and supplemented to increase efficiency. In addition to the TIE Core, Ethics and International Cores have been added. (A new shuffling of responsibilities is currently under way.) Each core is directed by a senior scientist at the center and is staffed and budgeted according to direction provided by CAPS leadership, which bases its decisions on need and function.

While individual investigators at CAPS pursue research in their area of specialty, the core structure ensures internal collaboration. In contrast to the less flexible approach whereby scientists are assigned to individual projects with a small percentage of effort throughout a given project's period of funding, assembling scientists into a core resource enables experts to be assigned on the basis of need. Organized programs for feedback, mentoring, and lecturing grow out of the cores. And since investigators from disparate backgrounds are required to devote a portion of their time to staffing each of the cores, a healthy exchange of ideas and information results.

The Administrative core puts CAPS' multidisciplinary focus to the test by creating a structured way for social and behavioral scientists (psychologists, sociologists, anthropologists) to work with medical scientists (internists, pediatricians, obstetricians) and public health scientists (epidemiologists, health department professionals). Medical and public health specialties are represented in this core by scientists with expertise in primary and secondary prevention who consult with one another and review projects that involve medical and public health issues.

Peer review by the Administrative core, overseen by Kegeles, ensures scientific excellence and applicability across disciplines. All research proposals and manuscripts, abstracts for international meetings, comments from review committees and journal editors, and, on request, oral presentations produced by CAPS must pass through this core, which puts investigators on equal footing, regardless of their status outside of CAPS.

The core provides biostatistical consultation overseen by Professor Richard Brand, head of biostatistics at UCSF, and undertaken by partial-time CAPS biostatisticians. Scientific presentations from multiple disciplines, debates, visiting scientists' presentations, and presentations by CAPS scientists are also organized through the Administrative Core.

The Administrative Core becomes another channel through which investigators and staff educate themselves and stay abreast of developments in their separate fields. As scientists in new fields have joined CAPS, their particular theories and expertise have needed to be translated into language that can be understood by other scientists. A common, off-campus location forcing immersion into each other's languages has been essential to this understanding, as have the regular town hall meetings of the entire CAPS staff.

How might some of these cores be used in a representative CAPS study? A study of young gay men provides a case in point. In 1988, Robert Hays began hearing anecdotal reports that many young gay men were engaging in high-risk sex, despite epidemiological data showing a downturn in risk-taking behavior among gay men overall. He began working with Susan Kegeles, who was interested in the application of community-level intervention approaches used previously in coronary heart disease to HIV prevention. They collected epidemiological data and the correlates of risk-taking behavior among young gay men in three West Coast communities (Hays, Kegeles, and Coates, 1990) that documented the high level of risk taking and identified its predictors.

The pair then wrote an R01 to develop, implement, and evaluate a community-level intervention for young gay men: The Mpowerment Project (Kegeles, Hays, and Coates, 1996; Kegeles, Hays, Pollack, and Coates, 1999). During this project, they consulted with the Survey Research Resources Core regarding how to deal with issues of missing data from their longitudinal cohort (e.g., using multiple imputation methods); with the TIE core regarding development of community advisory boards and how to deal with community politics; and with the Policy Core regarding a cost-effectiveness analysis of the project. The researchers recognized the need to augment their intervention approach to focus on the emerging issue of high-risk sex in primary relationships and the application of community organizations to HIV prevention.

Upon observing epidemiological research indicating disparities in risk-taking behavior among different ethnic/racial groups, the team decided to examine the intervention's efficacy in more racially/ethnically diverse communities. A competing R01 renewal was submitted and funded by NIMH to continue this research in communities having large Latino populations. In the course of this research (which is ongoing), the TIE core has been consulted frequently about community politics and how to transfer the intervention from research to community-based organizations, which has involved working with state departments of health and community planning groups.

The Mpowerment Project remains the only community-level intervention found to be effective with young gay men and is listed as such by the CDC in their Compendium of Effective Interventions. This research team (Kegeles, Hays, and Gregory Rebchook, research specialist) has begun conducting research on replication issues to understand barriers and facilitators of effective implementation of science-based intervention programs by community-based organizations.

An emphasis on training

Recognizing that tomorrow's AIDS prevention scientists need to be conversant and expert in the wide variety of disciplines required for effective AIDS prevention research, policy, and practice, CAPS has placed a premium on training new AIDS scientists through its Traineeships in AIDS Prevention Studies (TAPS), designed by Hulley, and the Collaborating Scholars (international) programs, which works in conjunction with the joint UCSF–UC Berkeley Fogarty Center.

Today, a physician considering placing a homeless injecting drug user on highly active antiretroviral therapy (HAART), for example, has to consider the ethical issue of treating or not treating, needs to be knowledgeable about drug resistance, and should consider behavioral strategies for improving adherence to treatment if the treatment is prescribed. A behavioral scientist devising a prevention strategy that fits the realities of current therapy and prophylaxis needs to understand what is known about the effectiveness of medical advances such as HAART, post-exposure prophylaxis (PEP), and candidate HIV vaccines and how these interventions are evaluated. CAPS programs aim to be at the cutting edge of AIDS training by including the disciplines of behavioral science, medicine, epidemiology, ethics, and public policy and by addressing the ways in which the disciplines intersect and complement one another.

TAPS is a postdoctoral research training program in the areas of epidemiology, behavioral medicine, and health policy. The program is designed to prepare physicians and behavioral scientists for research and academic careers in clinical epidemiology and in the prevention of AIDS and other diseases. At the end of the two- or three-year program, each trainee has completed an MPH degree or its equivalent; taken advanced courses in research methods, statistics, and other topics relevant to his or her major field(s) of interest; participated in and led numerous seminars on research topics; participated in the formal teaching program of the department of epidemiology and biostatistics or other relevant departments; designed several research protocols; completed at least one significant research project under the direction of a faculty preceptor; made several presentations at national or international meetings; and submitted several papers for publication.

TAPS has traditionally been comprised of 50% M.D.s and 50% Ph.Ds, and has included lawyers, entrepreneurs, and other nonscientists among its ranks. Since 1989, the TAPS program has trained 42 postdoctoral fellows, 31 of whom have finished training and gone on to excellent positions in academic institutions and departments of public health. TAPS trainees have contributed substantially to the medical literature. Counting publications from their entry into the training program and afterward to 2001, they have published approximately 350 papers in peer review journals, 150 of which are first author publications, and have received funding for more than 100 grant awards.

In addition to TAPS, the CAPS International Scholars program, begun in 1987, selects scholars each year through an open application process in which scientists from any developing country may apply. To date, CAPS has chosen 50 scholars from Latin America, Asia, Africa, and Eastern Europe; of this group, 29 are physicians (clinical, laboratory, public health, and research scientists), and 21 represent the social sciences, including public health education, medical anthropology, and psychology. Applicants accepted into the program come to San Francisco to work with CAPS scientists for 10 weeks to develop their research protocols. They are immersed in CAPS' full multidisciplinary range, including behavioral and prevention science research methods, the biology of HIV disease, questionnaire development, biostatistics, and computer skills. Each scientist is also assigned a CAPS preceptor for individualized help and feedback in designing a complete research protocol for implementation in the scholar's home country.

Both of these training programs are essential to prevent CAPS scientists and science from becoming too provincial—too focused on viewing the epidemic from the perspective of San Francisco and the West Coast of the United States. One recently completed CAPS study demonstrates how far the prevention models developed at the center have spread (Voluntary HIV-1 Counseling and Testing Efficacy Study Group, 2000). Coordinated by CAPS, the study involved researchers from AIDSCAP, Family Health International, the Global Programme on AIDS of the World Health Organization, the United Nations Program on AIDS, the Kenya Association of Professional Counselors, physicians from Muhimbili Medical College in Tanzania, and Queens Park Counselling Centre in Port-of-Spain, Trinidad.

The findings of this, the first randomized trial of HIV counseling and testing in these developing countries, support the efficacy of HIV voluntary counseling and testing in promoting behavior change. Voluntary counseling and testing is an expensive intervention, compared with standard health education and other counseling strategies (Kamb et al., 1998; NIMH Multisite HIV Prevention Trial Group, 1998). Couples assigned to voluntary counseling and testing reduced unprotected intercourse with enrollment partners significantly more than couples assigned to receive basic health information. The study also found significantly greater changes for persons infected with HIV than for those not infected with HIV.

An emphasis on science that will make a difference

CAPS places a premium on producing outstanding research in the basic sciences. The core structure ensures that CAPS science is both theory-driven and relevant to the needs of the community, bridging the gap between research and practice. At San Francisco General Hospital, for instance, CAPS investigators affiliated with the CFAR can now extend the reach of scientific understanding from laboratory to outpatient clinic to behavioral research study, with each link in the chain of knowledge reinforcing the next.

The CAPS philosophy when deciding what issues warrant their research encompasses two questions: "Is it good science?" and "Will it help save lives?" CAPS investigators strive to meet three additional goals with the products of their research. It should be *timely,* reflecting changes in the epidemic. It should be *practical* in its formation, involving disciplines that stand to benefit the most from the products of the research (ethical issues and studies of condom use are two examples), and practical in its application. And it should be *readily disseminated* throughout the biomedical and behavioral communities, as well as to society at large.

The Formation of the AIDS Research Institute at UCSF

By 1997, UCSF had become an acknowledged leader in many aspects of combating AIDS, including, among others, virology under the leadership of Jay Levy, epidemiology led by Stephen Hulley, clinical and laboratory sciences headed by Paul Volberding, medical ethics chaired by Bernard Lo (who also heads the CAPS Ethics Core), policy studies at the UCSF Institute for Health Policy Studies, international training at the Fogarty center at UCSF and Berkeley, and behavioral science at CAPS.

Haile Debas, dean of the UCSF School of Medicine, recognized that competition for resources and recognition within the UCSF system had begun to channel away energy and time that could be better used to further the struggle against AIDS. When departments had worked jointly on one facet of AIDS (such as the successful collaboration between CAPS and CFAR), benefits had accrued for all parties. But these coalitions had been too random, lacking overall guidance. The situation called for a superordinate level of collaboration—an approach for which CAPS provided a ready template.

The formation of the AIDS Research Institute (ARI) at UCSF in 1998, modeled after CAPS and the UCSF Cancer Center, formalized and made more efficient exchanges of information across disciplines by bringing all aspects of AIDS under one administrative umbrella. Coates was chosen to head the new entity. The ARI mandate included fostering and maintaining collegial relationships within the AIDS community; assuming overall responsibility for AIDS program planning, with a particular emphasis on coordination of clinical and biostatistical programs; and stimulating innovative AIDS research with a particular emphasis on identifying translational, interdisciplinary scientific questions in the basic, prevention, and clinical areas.

With the creation of ARI, biomedical scientists involved in AIDS research and care at UCSF found themselves in the unique position of being led by an individual, Coates, who came from a behavioral background. Where once behaviorists at CAPS perceived linkages to biomedical science as a threat to the primacy of behavioral prevention, now the UCSF biomedical community worried that they might have a reason to fear an encroachment of behavioral science. Coates and his team quickly allayed these fears by putting the new entity's best grant-writing minds to work on finding funds for a new virology laboratory—the most pressing need of ARI as a whole, and a decidedly nonbehavioral initiative. By allocating resources according to need instead of following any personal behavioral agenda, Coates and company were able to set a standard of fairness within ARI that continues to rule. Moreover, the structure of ARI allows CAPS to maintain its identity as primarily a prevention shop with some biological components, whereas San Francisco General Hospital remains mostly a place of biology with some prevention.

To date, the initial 1997 goals developed by the committee appointed by UCSF School of Medicine Dean Haile Debas that established ARI have been met, including the following:

- Translational research was made a priority theme of UCSF–GIVI CFAR (a collaboration of UCSF and the Gladstone Institute of Virology and Immunology), successfully restructured and re-competed in 1998.
- Primary HIV infection programs were established, focusing on transmission dynamics, prevention of infection among individuals exposed to HIV, and delay of progression among those recently infected with HIV.
- Core translational laboratories were established in virology, immunology, and flow cytometry.
- Research in the delivery of care to HIV-infected patients was established to study barriers in access to care and to develop improved models for funding AIDS care.
- International HIV research was strengthened through the appointment of George Rutherford, M.D., as director of international programs and the successful re-competition of the UCB–UCSF Fogarty International Program under the direction of Art Reingold, M.D., M.P.H.
- The ARI identified funding opportunities and implemented a private development plan.
- An internal and external communication strategy was established.
- Fourteen new faculty members were recruited.

ARI continues to pursue research into new areas of AIDS prevention, basic science, clinical treatment, epidemiology, and policy research. As with CAPS, the emphasis is on science that will make a difference. Examples of recent projects and the difference they have made are summarized in Table 18.1. These projects include the discovery of a new causal factor in Kaposi's sarcoma, extension of postexposure prophylaxis to the community, development of innovative strategies to assist HIV-infected persons cope, and demonstration that voluntary counseling and testing is not only feasible, but effective in preventing HIV infection in the developing world.

Table 18.1. CAPS/ARI Projects Making a Difference

Discovery of a New Causal Factor in Kaposi's Sarcoma	Among HIV-infected men, the disproportionate occurrence of Kaposi's sarcoma had long suggested that an additional factor, besides HIV, was responsible for the development of this relatively rare form of cancer. Shortly after the discovery of human herpesvirus 8 (HHV-8), Jeff Martin and Dennis Osmond, collaborating with Don Ganem's laboratory at UCSF, were the first to perform a well-controlled long-term study that determined that infection with the human herpesvirus precedes and is independently associated with the development of Kaposi's sarcoma in men. This study was the first to point at HHV-8 as a necessary causal factor in the development of Kaposi's sarcoma. This has opened up new strategies for the prevention and treatment of Kaposi's sarcoma (Martin et al., 1998).
Post-Exposure Prophylaxis	When workers were exposed to HIV on the job, they were immediately given HIV treatment, known as post-exposure prophylaxis (PEP). Evidence that this approach to prevention was effective in lowering the risk of HIV led to the call for PEP following nonoccupational exposures in the community. CAPS performed a feasibility study of PEP in persons reporting potential exposures to HIV outside the work setting. There had been a concern that offering PEP would increase risk behaviors and serve as a "morning after pill." In the PEP study, 401 persons who reported exposures were offered four weeks of antiretroviral therapy, received risk reduction and medication adherence counseling, and were seen for follow-up for up to a year. No infections occurred in the treated participants during the follow-up, and there was no evidence that offering PEP led to an increase of risk behavior in the community.
Coping Effectiveness Training	Persons infected with HIV confront a unique set of challenges and chronic stressors, including stigmatization, alienation from family and friends, complex treatment regimens, and often debilitating side effects as they attempt to manage the psychological and physiological consequences of their condition. CAPS developed a theory-based intervention to help HIV-infected persons cope with HIV. This intervention, Coping Effectiveness Training (CET) (Chesney et al., 1996), incorporates elements of stress management interventions, and provides a framework for choosing among coping strategies to promote adaptive coping and reduce distress. In a randomized clinical trial with 149 HIV-infected persons, those who received CET showed significantly greater increases in positive morale and optimism and greater reductions in perceived stress than those who received a control condition of HIV Information. The increases in positive morale were found to be sustained over time, a finding which contributed to an important revision of coping theory (Folkman, 1977) and CET that focuses on enhancing positive meaning as well as diminishing distress.
The Voluntary Counseling and Testing Efficacy Study	With at least 9 out of every 10 new cases of HIV/AIDS occurring in the developing world, it is imperative that prevention strategies be developed and tested far beyond the UCSF environment. Many countries in the developing world did not offer voluntary counseling and testing because there was no evidence that informing persons of their HIV status would result in reductions in risk behavior. CAPS conducted a randomized clinical trial to test the efficacy of

(continued)

Table 18.1.   *(continued)*

---

voluntary counseling and testing (VCT) for prevention of HIV in Nairobi, Kenya; Dar es Salaam, Tanzania; and Port-of-Spain, Trinidad. Individuals or couples were randomly assigned to receive client-centered VCT or view a culturally appropriate health information videotape. Couple members received their test results separately and then were encouraged to come together to share their results in the presence of the counselor. The percentage of individuals reporting high-risk behavior with non-primary partners declined significantly more in those receiving VCT than in those receiving only health information. This study provided the evidence needed for states to offer voluntary counseling and testing, and for funds to support this effective prevention strategy. (The Voluntary HIV-1 Counselling and Testing Efficacy Study Group, 2000).

Challenges Arising from the Multidisciplinary Approach

The evolution of a collaborative response to AIDS in San Francisco has not been without its stumbling blocks. Specialization of scientific study, long regarded as the sine qua non of education and training in the sciences, seems on its surface to work against scientific collaboration. Instead of synergy, what if a multidisciplinary foray resulted in diffusion of focus and loss of identity? CAPS has been able to overcome such fear by demonstrating that devoting more and various minds to a problem leads to better science. Scientists who experience the positive outcomes of collaboration are more willing to engage in it again and to encourage others to do so, and a steady process of conversion has resulted. CAPS leadership has tried to demonstrate that there are more advantages to collaboration than there are in isolation, and by putting the needs of the organization first, it has promoted a fair sharing of resources.

But if the needs of the group are primary, how do individual investigators in an entrepreneurial system such as CAPS stay motivated? Collaboration among biomedical and behavioral scientists in doing research means that solo authorship of any resulting papers, for example, is almost unheard of; CAPS papers with eight or nine co-authors are not uncommon. It has been found that investigators who prefer to work alone and demand sole recognition for their efforts do not thrive in the collaborative atmosphere of CAPS, and after a short period they often seek the limelight elsewhere.

Individual scientists who take the lead in various of the multidisciplinary teams, however, gain recognition both for themselves and their teams. And the makeup of the center has been remarkably stable over time, with very little turnover. An environment of respect and collegiality, coupled with a high degree of passion for ending the AIDS epidemic, may be the primary reasons individual investigators are willing to give up some degree of personal recognition for the center's larger vision.

The breadth of work at CAPS, and the variety of angles of attack proposed to answer each research question, can result in a surfeit of information and a cacophony of voices. How can the center work democratically and honor the expertise that each person brings to a debate without slowing the pace of work or constantly drawing specialists into areas outside of their expertise? While recognizing these concerns and acknowledging that they can be a problem, CAPS core structure and executive committee leadership continually refocus the energies of the group on well-defined areas of study in an effort to overcome them.

Another potential pitfall grew out of the historical power differential between biomedical sciences and behavioral sciences at the university level. At the dawn of the epidemic, behavioral interventions to prevent illness were viewed at UCSF as secondarily important and lacking in scientific rigor, compared to more glamorous and replicable scientific endeavors such as cloning genes. How would behaviorists find the resources they needed to bring their skills to bear on AIDS prevention?

As the epidemic grew in ferocity, the leadership of the School of Medicine threw its support behind behavioral prevention efforts year after year. And, by producing strong science and publishing studies that were highly regarded in the scientific community as a whole, CAPS slowly built a reputation for excellence that resonated across disciplinary borders. As a result, a university culture once defined by its differences is now known for its coalitions, as exemplified by ARI.

Conclusion and Implications

Along the main hallway connecting the cubicles and offices of CAPS and ARI are a series of black-and-white photographs of people who have succumbed to AIDS. These close-up images of smiling faces offer both encouragement and mute witness to the work we do and remind us on a daily basis why we must continue. The personal commitment of individual investigators at CAPS cannot be undervalued in assessing the reasons why a multidisciplinary approach to AIDS prevention thrived here.

It should be noted that this multidisciplinary approach to AIDS prevention, at CAPS and elsewhere, has fostered scientific breakthroughs in areas well beyond AIDS. New knowledge of immunology, virology, and the biology of cancer, among others, has come out of the struggle to understand and combat the virus. We believe the multidisciplinary model can and should be applied in the future to other public health challenges, including sexually transmitted diseases, violence, and teenage pregnancy.

Postscript[1]

The Center for AIDS Prevention Studies (CAPS) is about to celebrate its 20th anniversary and is beginning its fifth funding cycle. Since the beginning, the Center has been themed around promoting scientific innovation and multidisciplinary approaches to the challenges posed by the HIV epidemic. Scientific innovation depends on structure, process and people (Slappendel, 1996). The center grant provides the structure to stimulate new ideas and to organize research projects into coherent research programs addressing the full range of HIV/AIDS prevention and policy issues. The Center has developed a process that encourages concepts to be developed into innovative research projects, while assuring that the design of research is the best that it can be, and that the latest technologies are used to organize, manage, and analyze data. The center grant also allows us to bring together the people—a multidisciplinary group of investigators to stimulate new thinking not limited by the boundaries of traditional disciplines. Thus, the Center is a place for sustenance of scholars devoting their careers to this effort, and for the training of new scholars, domestically and internationally, so that the field can respond to future challenges.

Over the last five years, the scientific leadership at CAPS has gradually changed. These changes have allowed us to re-examine our direction and priorities. As Center Director, Dr. Steve Morin has replaced Dr. Tom Coates, who has joined the faculty at UCLA while maintaining a joint appointment at UCSF. Dr. Margaret Chesney was on leave from UCSF until 2006 to serve as Deputy Director of the Center for Alternative and Complementary Medicine at NIH. Dr. Susan M. Kegeles, co-director of the Center, has replaced Dr. Susan Folkman, who now serves as Director of the UCSF Osher Center for Integrative Medicine. These transitions, while significant, have been smooth and represent an opportunity for the next generation of leadership to expand the vision and mission of CAPS. The former directors stay in close contact and remain committed to our success.

Several new senior faculty members bring large and important programs of research. Dr. Michael Reyes, head of the Pacific AIDS Education and Training Center (PAETC), brings a large AIDS-related training program providing education and information services to health care providers. The addition of Dr. Reyes and his group offers CAPS opportunities to examine changes in clinical care and the relationship between such changes and improved health outcomes. The Pacific AIDS Education and Training Center also brings a network of minority community-based organization (CBO) partnerships that will benefit from our prevention research dissemination efforts. These include providers in the U.S.-affiliated Pacific Jurisdictions and the United States–Mexico Border, as well as African American, Native American, Latino, and Asian/Pacific Islander populations. Through his leadership of the International Training and Education Center on HIV (I-TECH), Dr. Reyes also brings CAPS new international research opportunities.

Dr. Nancy Padian brings with her the Women's Global Health Imperative. The addition of this large and important research group, including Dr. Craig Cohen, recently recruited from the University of Washington, offers collaboration on various biomedical approaches to HIV prevention including microbicides, diaphragms, sexually transmitted infections (STI) control, and antiretroviral prevention strategies through the HIV Prevention Trials Network (HPTN) and treatment research for other STIs. This affiliation also allows us to develop a program of collaborative research with partners at the University of Zimbabwe School of Medicine. Our co-location with the Institute for Global Health (IGH) brings us new faculty, such as Dr. Thomas Novotny, with strong links to HIV prevention in Eastern Europe and Central Asia.

In 2001, CAPS IV was funded under the P30 mechanism instead of the prior P50 mechanism. This reconfiguration required refocusing the center grant around services provided to CAPS scientists that would enable higher quality and more productive science. Recognizing the growing importance and availability of a wide variety of biostatistical, qualitative, and electronic data recording methods in HIV research, we created a Methods Core to meet CAPS investigators' increasing demand for expertise in these areas. Recently, our Traineeship in AIDS Prevention Studies (TAPS) successfully competed for separately funded training grants. During this grant period, we also focused more extensively on the dissemination of science and translation of research to practice.

Our Collaborative HIV Prevention Research in Minority Communities Program has also been separately funded. The program provides education, mentoring, and technical assistance to scientists from around the United States in developing, conducting, and analyzing research on ethnic minority populations. We have recruited and worked with 37 scientists from distinguished universities in the United States and Puerto Rico. Participants have had a major impact on the literature regarding ethnic minorities and HIV/AIDS; in 2005 there were over 50 manuscripts published by past and current participants. Program participants have over 2.8 million dollars in active funding and have received over 20 million dollars in funding over the past 9 years to conduct their culturally specific research with communities of color. In addition, 3 R10s from current program participants were submitted in January 2006.

Recent accomplishments

Below we highlight some accomplishments of scientists whose work illustrates the breadth of activities and collaborative relationships that have been supported by the cores under the center grant:

- Oral Acquisition of HIV Infection: A multidisciplinary team of researchers led by Dr. Kimberly Page-Shafer from CAPS completed a five-year study on the acquisition of HIV from performing oral sex (Page-Shafer, Shiboski, Osmond et al., 2002). No cases of oral acquisition of HIV were identified, suggesting that oral sexual practices carry a very low risk for HIV acquisition. The completion of this study required different sets of expertise. CAPS experts, including Drs. Dennis Osmond, William McFarland, Dr. Steve Shiboski, and

Dr. Joyce Balls joined Dr. Page-Shafer in bringing epidemiological skills and field study experience to the effort. Drs. Caroline Shiboski and Deborah Greenspan, from the Department of Stomatology at UCSF, provided the essential expertise on oral medicine, while Dr. James Dilley from the AIDS Health Project (AHP) provided access to the community sample of participants required for the study

- Behavioral Epidemiology: CAPS scientists led by Dr. Joseph Catania developed the Urban Men's Health Study (UMHS), the first large-scale household probability survey of gay and bisexual men (Catania, Osmond, Stall et al., 2001). The study screened more than 60,000 households in New York, San Francisco, Los Angeles, and Chicago and interviewed more than 2800 gay and bisexual adult men on health and mental health issues. This study has resulted in more than 28 published papers. The study was a collaboration of health geographers, demographers, and other behavioral scientists. Together, they constructed the first maps showing the density of gay households in 26 major urban areas of the United States. This work also challenged dogma by showing that it was possible, through the use of new survey techniques, to obtain interviews with men who had not disclosed their same gender sexual behavior to family, friends, co-workers, or neighbors. In addition, UMHS provided the first real evidence that the HIV epidemic among gay and bisexual men was not over in the United States, but has continued unabated. The investigators have made their extensive datasets available to other scientists who have produced publications on a range of health problems facing gay and bisexual men including one on the impact of sexual orientation disclosure to employers on income, and the impact of expected income-loss on disclosure.

- Draw the Line/Respect the Line: Drs. Barbara Marin and Cynthia Gómez in collaboration with colleagues at ETR Associates, Inc. developed and tested a theoretically based curriculum designed to reduce risk behaviors to prevent HIV/STDs and pregnancy among middle school adolescents (Coyle, Marin, Gardner, Cummings, Gomez, and Kirby, 2003; Marin, Coyle, Cummings, Gardner, Gomez, and Kirby, 2003; Marin, Coyle, Gomez, Jinich, and Kirby, 2003) The intervention, which was tested through a randomized controlled design, delayed sexual initiation among boys, but not among girls. Boys exhibited significantly greater knowledge than comparison students, perceived fewer peer norms supporting sex, had more positive attitudes toward not having sex, had stronger sexual limits, and were less likely to put themselves in situations that could lead to sex. Girls in the program had greater knowledge at each follow-up, perceived fewer peer norms supporting sex than other girls, and reported fewer unwanted sexual advances in the past 12 months at the eighth grade follow-up (Coyle, Kirby, Marin, Gomez, and Gregorich, 2004).

- Adherence with HIV medications: CAPS scientists conducted some of the first research on adherence to HIV medications (Chesney, Ickovics, Hecht, Sikipa, and Rabkin, 1999; Chesney and Ickovics, 1997). Prior to the availability of HAART, CAPS worked closely with the UCSF Adult AIDS Clinical Trial Group (ACTG) at San Francisco General Hospital to develop adherence measures and intervention strategies for Participants in AIDS Clinical Trials (PACT). With the development of HAART, the entire Adult ACTG became interested in assessing adherence in AIDS Clinical Trials and revised the PACT adherence self-report assessment for the ACTG. Pilot data collected from ACTGs across the country with this instrument were first analyzed at CAPS. The instrument known as the ACTG Adherence Questionnaire then was developed and has now been used with thousands of clinical trial patients around the world. As part of this research program, CAPS scientists also worked closely with others at UCSF, including Drs. Frederick Hecht and David Bangsberg on studies of patients with primary HIV infection, the first study documenting that drug-resistant HIV could be transmitted, and an entire program of research on adherence to HIV medications in various populations, including the homeless, incarcerated persons, and persons living with HIV/AIDS around the globe. Copies of CAPS adherence instruments and intervention strategies have been disseminated widely through national and international meetings, in peer-reviewed journals, and on the CAPS website.
- Redesigning California ADAP: In response to rising costs and the state's economic downturn and budget deficit, teams of policy researchers at CAPS (Morin, Myers, Koester, and Charlebois), UCLA, and RAND conducted research related to the development of new short- and long-range policy, financing, and delivery strategies for the California AIDS Drug Assistance Program (ADAP). The average cost paid by state ADAPs for an HIV prescription did not relate in a statistically significant way to the manner in which the state ADAP program is organized (direct purchase vs. rebate model). Thus, there was no evidence that California could reduce its drug acquisition costs by changing the structure of its ADAP program. Nonetheless, key informant interviews with program administrators in other states indicated that renegotiating the state contract for pharmacy benefits management could generate cost savings. The University of California, San Francisco researchers modeled the proposal to cap enrollment and found that over a 10-year span, the number of excess deaths attributed to capping the program would grow to approximately 1632 while cost saving would be minimal. In addition to writing scientific

manuscripts, researchers briefed state policy makers who used these scientific findings when they redesigned state contracting policies.

- Coping with HIV: CAPS scientists lead by Dr. Margaret Chesney successfully evaluated a coping intervention, Coping Effectiveness Training (CET), designed to assist HIV-infected gay men in sustaining psychological health despite the ongoing stress associated with HIV infection (Chesney, Chambers, Taylor, Johnson, and Folkman, 2003). The study was an RCT of an innovative, theory-based coping intervention. The research questions addressed quality of life, health care utilization and adherence to medical care, and tested new advances in stress and coping theory. Coping Effectiveness Training participants demonstrated greater improvement in psychological distress and well-being (e.g., negative morale, coping self-efficacy, personal growth, and positive states of mind) than did the control group participants during the three-month intervention phase. These differences were maintained during the nine-month maintenance phase.

Policy research

While CAPS has historically been a leader in assessing HIV prevention policies, formal policy and ethics research has expanded greatly over the last five years. We now assess evidence-based policies for access to optimum HIV treatment and conduct international HIV policy analysis and research. Policymaking agencies need to evaluate options before setting a policy and to evaluate data about the impact of the policies after implementation. CAPS has an expanding role in conducting this research.

International research

In May 2006, UNAIDS estimated 2.8 million deaths due to AIDS globally, 4.1 million newly infected with HIV, and 38.6 million people living with HIV (UNAIDS, 2006). Sub-Saharan Africa alone accounts for more than two-thirds of all AIDS deaths (2.0 million). While CAPS scientists work throughout the region, we have developed concentrated programs in Zimbabwe and Uganda. With 8.3 million people in Asia estimated to be living with HIV, that region is an area of critical concern to AIDS policymakers and caregivers. CAPS has established research programs throughout the region with particular interest in India, China, and Vietnam. Latin America is also a focus of concern, with an estimated 1.6 million living with HIV. The Center for AIDS Prevention Studies programs now operate in Argentina and Peru, but our most concentrated efforts are in Brazil. Finally, the rapid emergence of HIV in Eastern Europe and Central Asia, where more than an estimated 1.5 million live with

HIV, has prompted CAPS to plan several studies in the region, with a planned partnership in Croatia.

Continued emphasis on multidisciplinary collaboration

The AIDS Research Institute (ARI), now directed by Dr. John S. Greenspan, brings together scientists from the four professional schools at UCSF (Medicine, Dentistry, Pharmacy, and Nursing), UCSF-affiliated laboratories (Gladstone Institute of Virology and Immunology, Blood Systems Research Institute, and the California State labs), the San Francisco Department of Public Health (SFDPH), and the School of Public Health at UC Berkeley. The ARI is committed to harnessing the extraordinary resources of UCSF to advance scientific discovery in the service of fighting HIV/AIDS. The University of California, San Francisco is ranked among the world's preeminent medical education and research institutions.

The University of California, San Francisco's Center for AIDS Research (CFAR) co-directors, Drs. Paul Volberding and Warner Greene, confer regularly with the CAPS director and co-directors to maintain close coordination between biomedical and behavioral research agendas. CFAR offers CAPS the potential for collaboration with biomedical and clinical colleagues, virological and immunological laboratory expertise, specimen banking, and access to clinical populations.

Conclusions

In 2005, the Center has supported the work of scientists from a variety of disciplines. Of those scientists, 47 serve as principal investigators on 56 NIH-funded projects and 57 projects funded by other agencies. Our science centers around four major themes—*(1)* rigorous theory-based research that will have the maximum impact on the theory, practice, and policy of HIV prevention; *(2)* multidisciplinary research with maximum impact on optimizing health outcomes and preventing further transmission from individuals infected with HIV; *(3)* policy research that responds to the needs of local, state, national, and international agencies to use evidence-based research findings; and *(4)* international research responding to the growing challenges posed by the global pandemic.

The Center for AIDS Prevention Studies is composed of investigators from different disciplines coming together with a common purpose. Thus, CAPS provides the platform—the intellectual environment for good work to happen. CAPS is propelled by both a center grant and a portfolio of investigator-initiated studies focusing on HIV prevention and policy studies. The center grant provides the intellectual, administrative, and physical foundation that allows our scientists to respond to an ever-changing set of research demands. The center grant is the essential foundation upon which CAPS scientists have built an impressive, diversified, and productive scientific program. Importantly, CAPS has not been content to let its science sit on the shelf. We continue to leverage resources to maximize impact on policy, practice, and training. In summary, our investigators drive the science but the Center continues to make that science better.

NOTE

1. Stephen Morin, the current Director of CAPS, was the primary author of this Postscript. As an expression of the continuity of CAPS' collaborative spirit, his contribution was welcomed by the original chapter authors and the co-editors. Chesney was serving as Deputy Director, National Center for Complementary and Alternative Medicine, National Institutes of Health when the Postscript was written.

RECOMMENDED READINGS

Chesney, M. A., Folkman, S., and Chambers, D. (1996). Coping effectiveness training for men living with HIV disease: Preliminary findings. *International Journal of STD and AIDS, 7* (suppl. 2), 75–82.

Farmer, P., Leandre, F., Mukherjee, J. A, Claude, M. S., Nevil, P., Smith-Fawzi, M. C., Koenig, S. P., Castro, A., Becerra, M. C., Sachs, J., Attaran, A., and Kim, J. Y. (2001). Community-based approaches to HIV treatment in resource-poor settings. *Lancet, 358,* 404–409.

Kegeles, S., Hays, R. B., and Coates, T. J. (1996). The Mpowerment Project: A community-level HIV prevention intervention for young gay men. *American Journal of Public Health, 86,* 1129–1136.

Mann, J., Tanantola, D. J. M., and Netter, T. J. (1992). *AIDS in the World.* Cambridge: Harvard University Press.

NIMH Multisite HIV Prevention Trial Group (1998). A randomized clinical trial of small group counseling to reduce risk for HIV. *Science, 280,* 1889–1894.

REFERENCES

Burack, J., Barrett, D., Stall, R., Chesney, M. A., Ekstrand, M., and Coates, T. J. (1993). Depressive symptoms and CD4 lymphocyte decline among HIV-infected men. *JAMA, 270,* 2568–2573.

Catania, J., Coates, T. J., Kegeles, S., Fullilove, M., Peterson, J., Marin, B., Siegel, D., and Hulley, S. (1992). Condom use in multiethnic neighborhoods of San Francisco: The population-based AMEN (AIDS in Multi-Ethnic Neighborhoods) Study. *American Journal of Public Health, 81,* 284–287.

Catania J. A., Osmond D., Stall R.D., et al. (2001). The continuing HIV epidemic among men who have sex with men. *American Journal of Public Health, 91*(6), 907–914.

Chesney, M. A., and Ickovics, J. (1997). Adherence to combination therapy in AIDS clinical trials. Annual Meeting of the AIDS Clinical Trials Group, Washington, D.C.

Chesney, M. A., Chambers, D. B., Taylor, J. M., Johnson, L. M., and Folkman S. (2003). Coping effectiveness training for men living with HIV: results from a randomized clinical trial testing a group-based intervention. *Psychosomatic Medicine, 65*(6), 1038–1046.

Chesney, M. A., and Folkman, S. (1999). The psychosocial management of HIV disease in adults. In King Holmes, P. Frederick Sparling, Per-Anders Mardh, Stanley Lemon,

Walter Stamm, Peter Piot, and Judith Wasserheit (Eds.), *Sexually Transmitted Diseases,* 3rd ed. (pp. 987–993). New York: McGraw-Hill.

Chesney, M. A., Ickovics, J., Hecht, F., M., Sikipa, G., and Rabkin, J. (1999). Adherence: A necessity for successful HIV combination therapy. *AIDS, 13*(suppl. A), S271–S278.

Coates, T. J., Morin, S., and McKusick, L. (1987). Behavioral consequences of AIDS antibody testing among gay men. *JAMA, 258,* 1988.

Coates, T. J., McKusick, L., Stites, D. P., and Kuno, R. (1989). Stress management training reduced number of sexual partners but did not improve immune function in men infected with HIV. *American Journal of Public Health, 79,* 885–887.

Cooke, M., Gourlay, L., Collette, L., Boccellari, A., Chesney, M. A., and Folkman, S. (1998). Informal caregivers and the intention to hasten AIDS-related death. *Annals of Internal Medicine, 158,* 69–75.

Coyle, K., Marin, B. V., Gardner, C., Cummings, J., Gomez, C. A,, and Kirby D. B. (2003). Draw the Line/Respect the Line: Setting Limits to Prevent HIV, STD and pregnancy. Grade 7. Scotts Valley, CA: ETR Associates.

Coyle K. K., Kirby, D. B., Marin, B. V., Gomez, C. A., and Gregorich, S. E. (2004). Draw the line/respect the line: a randomized trial of a middle school intervention to reduce sexual risk behaviors. *American Journal of Public Health, 94*(5):843–851.

Folkman, S., Chesney, M. A., Cooke, M., Boccellari, A., and Collette, L. (1994). Caregiver burden in HIV-positive and HIV-negative partners of men with AIDS. *Journal of Consulting and Clinical Psychology, 62,* 746–756.

Hays, R. B., Kegeles, S. M., and Coates, T. J. (1990). High HIV risk-taking among young gay men. *AIDS, 4,* 901–907.

Hecht, F. M., Grant, R. M., Petropoulos, C. J., Dillon, B., Chesney, M. A., Tian, H., Hellmann, N. S., Bandrapalli, N. I., Digilio, L., Branson, B., and Kahn, J. O. (1998). Sexual transmission of an HIV-1 variant resistant to multiple reverse-transcriptase and protease inhibitors. *New England Journal of Medicine, 339,* 307–311.

Kamb, M., Fishbein, M., Douglas, J., Rhodes, F., Rogers, J., Bolan, G., Zenilman, J., Hoxworth, T., Malotte, K., Iatesta, M., Kent, C., Lentz, A., Graziano, S., Byers, R. H., and Peterman, T. A. (1998). Efficacy of risk-reduction counseling to prevent human immunodeficiency virus and sexually transmitted diseases. *JAMA 280,* 1161–1167.

Kegeles, S., Catania, J., Coates, T. J., Pollack, L., and Lo, B. (1990). Many people who seek anonymous HIV testing would avoid it under other circumstances. *AIDS, 4,* 585–588.

Kegeles, S., Hays, R. B., Pollack, L., and Coates, T. J. (1999). Mobilizing young gay and bisexual men for HIV prevention: A two-community study. *AIDS, 13,* 1753–1762.

Marin, B. V., Coyle, K., Gomez, C. A., Jinich, S., and Kirby, D. B. (2003). Draw the Line/ Respect the Line: Setting Limits to Prevent HIV, STD and pregnancy. Grade 6. Scotts Valley, CA: ETR Associates.

Martin, J. N., Ganem, D. E., Osmond, D. H., Page-Shafer, K. A., Macrae, D., and Kedes, D. H. (1998). Sexual transmission and the natural history of human herpesvirus 8 infection. *New England Journal of Medicine, 338*(14), 948–954.

McKusick, L., Coates, T. J., Morin, S., Pollack, L., and Hoff, C. (1990). Longitudinal predictors of unprotected anal intercourse among gay men in San Francisco. *American Journal of Public Health, 80,* 978–983.

McKusick, L., Hortsman, W., and Coates, T. J. (1985). AIDS and the sexual behavior reported by gay men in San Francisco. *American Journal of Public Health, 75,* 493–496.

NIMH Multisite HIV Prevention Trial Group (1998). A randomized clinical trial of small group counseling to reduce risk for HIV. *Science, 280,* 1889–1894.

Page-Shafer, K., Shiboski, C. H., Osmond, D. H., Dilley, J., McFarland, W., Shiboski, S.C., Klausner, J.D., Balls, J., Greenspan, D., and Greenspan, J.S. (2002). Risk of HIV infection attributable to oral sex among men who have sex with men and in the population of men who have sex with men. *Aids, 16*(17), 2350–2352.

Slappendel, C. (1996). Perspectives on innovation in organizations. *Organizational Studies, 17*(1), 107–129.

Stall, R., McKusick, L., Wiley, J., Coates, T. J., and Ostrow, D. (1986). Alcohol and drug use during sexual activity and compliance with safe sex guidelines for AIDS: The AIDS Behavioral Research Project. *Health Education Quarterly, 13,* 259–271.

UNAIDS. (2006). Report on the Global AIDS Epidemic. Geneva: UNAIDS.

Voluntary HIV-1 Counselling and Testing Efficacy Study Group (2000). Efficacy of voluntary HIV-1 counselling and testing in individuals and couples in Kenya, Tanzania, and Trinidad: A randomized Trial. *Lancet, 356,* 103–112.

Zenilman, J., Hoxworth, T., Malotte, K., Iatesta, M., Kent, C., Lentz, A., Graziano, S., Byers, R.t H., and Peterman, T. A. (1998). Efficacy of risk-reduction counseling to prevent human immunodeficiency virus and sexually transmitted diseases. *JAMA 280,* 1161–1167.

CLOSING COMMENTARY

Fostering Interdisciplinary Research:
The Way Forward

PATRICIA L. ROSENFIELD and FRANK KESSEL

We must acknowledge that interdisciplinary spaces are hard to construct and hard to maintain. It is relatively easy to produce disciplinary versions of purportedly interdisciplinary spaces.... The real challenge is to find a way to hold the interdisciplinary and the disciplinary in view, not only as authors, but as readers, listeners, and participants in academic institutions. Only then will truly interdisciplinary work flourish.

> —Ken Wissoker, "Negotiating a Passage
> between Disciplinary Borders"

The underlying premise of this collection is that constructive approaches toward interdisciplinary science can be drawn from the practical experiences of successful research teams and that these experiences can illuminate the way forward to creative and usable findings for science and society. From the outset, the hope and promise of the project was that scholars, researchers, administrators, and practitioners who seek to meet the challenge of constructing interdisciplinary teams and programs aimed at addressing pressing problems of humanity will find guidance in such cases. The basic goal, then, was to provide a set of case studies that serve as signposts of successful interdisciplinary research linking the health and social sciences.

This collection can also be viewed as a contribution to settling the sometimes spurious debate concerning the unity of knowledge prompted most recently by Edward Wilson's *Consilience* (1998). Here Wilson claims that biology is the glue that can and should bind together all other disciplines, including the social sciences and humanities. Acknowledging that physics provides the underlying set of principles for understanding nature, he nevertheless argues that biology serves as the only meaningful conceptual and empirical framework for the synthesis of different disciplinary perspectives.

Yet this sought-after endpoint where all science and scholarship are brought together, this attempt to define the perfect web for linking disparate and diverse forms of knowledge, has tended to polarize scientists in all spheres of academic life for at least a century. (See Ceccarelli, 2001; Menand, 2001; Mudimbe and Jewsiewicki, 1996.) Indeed, arguing for the unity of knowledge has never been a purely scientific quest, neither neutral nor value-free. Whether it was Laplace and Quetelet in the nineteenth century hoping to illuminate scholarly life with the higher light of social statistics, or Wilson now claiming that biology provides the fundamental and all-embracing intellectual framework, the search parties have usually promoted the primacy of their own disciplines. All sides have selected their preferred teammates for the quest and created obstacles for others. The endpoint, it seems, has been not so much the shining light of unified knowledge but, rather, the justification of a particular theoretical or metatheoretical paradigm as irreducible bedrock for the pursuit of all future scientific agendas.

Although it is often used, or misused, as a synonym for the unity of knowledge, *interdisciplinarity* as a form or frame for scientific inquiry should not be viewed with the same skeptical eye. Since the problems confronting humanity—social, economic, cultural, educational, medical, environmental, agricultural—are rarely defined by one intellectual framework, our core assumption is that their solutions demand integrative contributions from many disciplines along a variety of intersecting dimensions. As beautifully elucidated by Leah Ceccarelli (2001), the concept of interdisciplinarity has deep historical roots and has generated both commitment and controversy over the past 200 years of European and American scholarship. More recently, in the second half of the twentieth century, Jacob Bronowski (1972), C. P. Snow (1993), and others sketched new frameworks for bringing the cultures of the social sciences and the humanities together with those of the "hard sciences" of physics, chemistry, and biology in nonreductionistic ways. As the attempt to link disciplines creatively in the search for new knowledge and practical pathways for human betterment, interdisciplinarity does share with the notion of the unity of knowledge the quality of "harmonious design" (*Merriam-Webster's Collegiate Dictionary*, 1993). But it does not presume or demand an overarching, dominant theoretical or metatheoretical framework drawn from one discipline. As illustrated by the case studies in this volume, such openness and flexibility are the essence of interdisciplinarity.[1]

The literature is filled with examples of failed attempts to build and reinforce bridges across disciplinary domains. One of the more perceptive analyses of such failures is William Sewell's "Some Reflections on the Golden Age of Interdisciplinary Social Psychology" (1989). Examining how "in the 25 years or so that began with World War II, there was a great wave of enthusiasm for interdisciplinary social psychology, which resulted in the establishment of interdisciplinary... training and research programs in some of the major universities in the United States [but how] by the mid-1960s, this seeming Golden Age had vanished" (p. 1), Sewell concluded that four main factors were at work: The threat of these programs to the traditional departmental structure of the university, particularly in light of the relatively weak position of the social sciences in that structure. The lack of adequate and appropriate funding from either university or federal sources. The lack of a major breakthrough in social and psychological theory . . . [and the fact that] advancements in research methods did not produce a greatly increased understanding of social-psychological phenomena (pp. 1–2).[2]

As John Rowe discusses in his introductory chapter to this volume, while these case studies of interdisciplinary inquiry are drawn from a particular set of experiences in a number of substantive areas relating to health, a primary criterion for their selection lay in the *success* of the associated research programs. It should thus be evident that, while they have recognized many of these sources of failure in interdisciplinary collaboration and thus underscore the continuing relevance of Sewell's discussion for the health and social sciences, the authors primarily provide illuminating examples of how various obstacles to such collaboration can be productively overcome. As a consequence, they present substantive findings that could come to be viewed as akin to the breakthroughs that led to the linking of physics and chemistry and biology in the now-flourishing field of molecular biology. At the least, we suggest that the case studies will provide rich grist for the mill of future historians and sociologists of science seeking to understand how a range of researchers, occupying different spaces in the network of the health and social sciences in the late twentieth and early twenty-first centuries, succeeded in crafting creative conversations across conventional disciplinary boundaries.

Background

These case studies of generative interdisciplinary research programs were prepared under the joint aegis of the National Institutes of Health Office of Behavioral and Social Science Research (OBBSR) and the Social Science Research Council (SSRC). Within the framework of OBSSR's overall mandate and drawing on the SSRC's long-term programmatic experience and organizational expertise, the project was run by a core working group of scientists.[3] Taking the lead in shaping and introducing the several substantive case study domains (each of which comprises a section in this collection), the working group members were responsible for recruiting additional authors for the project. What emerged from this process was a final pool of scientists who have engaged in interdisciplinary research themselves and were also eager to reflect on how the obstacles to their efforts could be constructively surmounted and to identify key factors that facilitated their work. Via the systematic and comparative study of a range of cases, the working group thus sought to document both the processes of discovery and noteworthy findings that have emerged from these integrative efforts.

Why OBSSR and SSRC? Established by Congress in 1993, OBSSR has developed an array of activities aimed at pursuing its overall mandate and responsibilities. In this context, the most relevant are: *(1)* advancing behavioral and social sciences research and training; *(2)* integrating a biobehavioral perspective across the NIH; and *(3)* improving communication among scientists and with the public (OBSSR Web site). In pursuing such a mandate, OBSSR has also sought to form productive organizational partnerships for some of its activities.[4]

OBSSR's partner in this particular endeavor, the SSRC, has a long, proven record of creating innovative interdisciplinary programs in the form of committees, working groups, and fellowship programs. Indeed, it was founded in 1923 with a mandate to reach across disciplinary and institutional boundaries and bring social researchers together to address problems of public concern. Its distinctive niche remains to innovate and incubate, to identify emergent lines of research that will be enhanced by interdisciplinary or international ties, to help scattered researchers build networks and nascent fields to achieve critical mass. Over the years, the council has thus played a major role in launching new fields of inquiry such as sociolinguistics and life-course human development. And consistent with a central feature of this particular boundary-crossing project, it has served as the institutional home for a number of initiatives at the intersection of the biological, behavioral and social sciences.[5]

Selecting and Framing the Case Studies

The process of selecting the candidate cases began with conversations among OBSSR and SSRC staff, and then took more specific shape during several meetings of members of the core working group. Three primary criteria guided the selection: *(1)* The research represented would be illustrative both in terms of bridging two or more disciplines and in yielding illuminating, even surprising findings. *(2)* In the aggregate, and particularly on the behavioral/social science side, topics would involve the blending of disciplines (e.g., psychology, sociology, demography, cognitive science). And *(3)* also in the aggregate, the focus of the cases would reach in two directions—first, over a range of health problems and issues and thus toward the biomedical sciences, and, second, across different stages in the lifecycle. The working group also considered which type of health questions and issues might be more likely to profit from interdisciplinary collaboration and provide persuasive experiences for other scholars, scientists, and practitioners.

The group also discussed the dilemma of how different terms are used to define or refer to collaboration across disciplines. As Rowe notes in his introduction, the literature contains an often confusing variation in use among "multidisciplinary," "cross-disciplinary," "interdisciplinary," and even "transdisciplinary," In the end, and in the context of guidance to the authors, the working group chose not to take a firm stance on one term to the exclusion of any other. Rather, as discussed by Marmot (Chapter 14) and Seeman (Chapter 11), as well as Rowe, it seems more important to be clear on features of the continuum along which there are degrees of melding of conceptual frameworks and methods. "Multidisciplinarity," involving the parallel and perhaps sequential collaboration of individuals but relatively little blending of disciplinary approaches, can be regarded as representing one end of the continuum. (See Chesney and Coates, Chapter 18.) At the other end of this continuum, when a new "hybrid" field of inquiry emerges from an extended period of collaborative and creative work, "transdisciplinarity" seems the appropriate term. (See Davidson, Chapter 6; Seeman, Chapter 11; also Rosenfield, 1992). And "interdisciplinarity" lies somewhere in between, when research team members explicitly bring together disciplinary perspectives and levels of analysis in interactive, potentially integrative ways or when they do not fall back on discipline authorization for theory, method, and, most fundamentally, definition of the problem. (See Berntson and Cacioppo, Chapter 2; Schneiderman and Antoni, Chapter 17; also Anderson, 1998). Recognizing that this is indeed a continuum, and that several subtleties could be introduced, we suggest that the significant central tendency of these case studies lies in the direction of an increasingly interdisciplinary paradigm for the understanding of health.[6]

In one respect, the most important "criterion" in selecting cases for study centered on the willingness of all the project participants to be reflective about the challenges of interdisciplinary research and thus willing to give time and effort to meeting and writing about those in collegial and constructive ways. The task was nonetheless challenging—and, in some respects, unusual—because the authors were asked to analyze two different dimensions: first, the findings and conclusions that emerged from the research under scrutiny; second, the history and dynamics, both substantive and organizational, of their collaborative work. (They were also asked to indicate how such findings would not have been possible without genuine collaboration at various levels within the conceptual and methodological aspects of other disciplines.) As might have been expected, these talented researchers were at ease writing about the results of their research and even disciplinary perspectives different from their own. But they found it intellectually challenging, even somewhat disconcerting, to write reflexively and thus in their own voices about the dynamic process of conducting interdisciplinary research. Our judgment is that they have met that challenge in instructive and engaging ways.[7]

Seeking to create a degree of coherence across the resulting case studies, the working group also developed a series of questions that the authors were encouraged to address. In varying degrees, and in ways that each found most congenial, they thus describe the interdisciplinary features of their work: new findings and insights generated by the research; the origins and life course of the collaboration; factors that facilitated and constrained the research; and the important implications of the research.

What, then, of the substantive fields that the group selected as "domains" for the case studies? As is evident, these include some of the most pressing issues facing our society, as well as the most innovative research seeking basic knowledge about human bio-psycho-social functioning. Cardiovascular diseases and HIV/AIDS were the main disease foci chosen; wherever the cognitive and affective neurosciences, lifespan development and longevity, and human capacity for resilience and managing stress are three fundamental domains that affect overall human functioning, both individually and socially.

Two final notes about the cases selected: First, while this volume focuses on experiences of U.S. investigators working in U.S. institutions, there have been a number of noteworthy efforts to support research linking the health and social sciences in international organizations (such as the World Health Organization) and in other countries.[8] Second, following John Rowe's lead and anticipating a major conclusion that arises from these case studies, we want to underscore that several U.S. foundations have funded interdisciplinary research and institution-strengthening activities linking the health and social sciences, notably the MacArthur Foundation, the Kellogg Foundation, the Rockefeller Foundation, the Ford Foundation, and Carnegie Corporation. These activities have led to publications on the results of such activities that complement this collection (Andreano, 2001; Farmer and Beceerra, 2001; Good, Heggenhougen, and Kleinman, 2001; Silva and Ramos-Jimenez, 1996). We are certain, however, that the kind of reflective life histories of scientific inquiry presented here—the varied descriptions of dynamic processes of disciplinary collaborations alongside discussion of their resulting theoretical and empirical contributions—amount to a distinctive contribution to the growing literature examining interdisciplinary research on health.

Signposts of Interdisciplinary Innovation: Findings and Implications of the Case Studies

In this section, we first touch on a few of the significant theoretical and empirical findings that have emerged from the research programs discussed in the chapters. We then sketch aspects of the broader framework of research processes within which such findings were produced. Following that, we attempt to tease out the main facilitating and constraining factors associated with interdisciplinary efforts. Noting again that further analysis of such factors is called for, we hope to provide some signposts for other scholars and scientists who wish to undertake such collaborative research, for university and research center administrators seeking to stimulate it, for funders keen to support it, and for policymakers and practitioners who wish to use the results of interdisciplinary inquiry.

Research results: An illustrative sampler

Given that the authors themselves discuss the findings that have emerged from their research programs in depth, and as a complement to the domain introductions, we only wish to highlight how some of these were contingent on processes of discovery that entailed theoretical and methodological perspectives stretching beyond conventional disciplines and their concomitant levels of explanation (see Table 19.1, appendix to this chapter).

- In the domains of cardiovascular functioning and neuroscience, the imaginative research reported by Berntson and Cacioppo (Chapter 2),

Light et al. (Chapter 3), and Davidson (Chapter 6), clearly—even dramatically—points to insights and benefits that emerge from a detailed explanation of the way social and psychological processes intersect in dynamic and reciprocal fashion with physiological, biological systems that are central to health.

- Specifically, Berntson and Cacioppo have contributed to shaping the new field of social neuroscience through defining principles and an analytical framework for research that has begun to identify the complex, heterarchical pathways and linkages across the autonomic and neuroendocrinological systems as these relate to human behavior. Light et al. have elucidated the effects of social stress and social environment on arterial disease, demonstrating the role of behavioral factors in the cause of the disease, even in the absence of cholesterol problems; they have also suggested related intervention strategies. And Davidson and his colleagues have been instrumental in developing the new interdisciplinary area of affective neuroscience—the study of the upstream and downstream relationships that link emotions to the brain, to biological systems, and to health and disease. Their specific findings on affective style as it relates to the prefrontal cortex and the amygdala, to mood, and to anxiety and emotional regulation seem central to a deeper understanding of how individual differences in behavior take shape and affect health.

- The lifespan analysis of aging now provides a deeper understanding of how societal and biological factors interconnect and interact to create multiple pathways, not only for disease but also for individual well-being. As an area for interdisciplinary research and as described by Ryff and Singer (Chapter 10), human resilience provides the intellectual and scientific basis for promoting the capacity to live healthfully. Also operating within a heterarchical, multilevel framework, the work done on human resilience promises to elaborate in detail the different processes and pathways that fundamentally affect human well-being.

- Drawing on the concept of allostatic load, this research provides approaches for measuring the cumulative and differential effects of bio-psycho-social stress on individuals over time (Karlamangla, Singer, McEwen, Rowe, and Seeman, 2002). It also offers preventive and therapeutic promise that can only be realized through increased interdisciplinary efforts to elucidate different developmental pathways and mechanisms; in turn, such understanding could shape social and health policies. In fact, two teams working on lifespan research have already had a specific influence on policy. Marmot and his collaborators' (Chapter 14) counterintuitive findings of the inverse relationship between status in the employment hierarchy and development of disease—based on a series of in-depth, longitudinal analyses linking biological and social processes—have been incorporated into the 1999

British Government Health Strategy White Paper. For their part, extending work on the life span of individuals to populations and, more broadly, blending the disciplines of evolutionary biology and demography, Olshansky and Carnes (Chapter 15) have helped shape the new field of biodemography. Identifying a consistent biological mechanism that operates across species and regulates age patterns of mortality, their research has influenced the actuarial calculations of the U.S. Social Security Administration.

- In the domain of HIV/AIDS, the wide-ranging case studies of Schneiderman and Antoni (Chapter 17) and Chesney and Coates (Chapter 18) illustrate the potential and actual benefits of research that ranges across psychological, interpersonal, and community levels of analysis for improved treatment and policy.

- Specifically, the CBSM (cognitive-behavioral stress management) intervention strategy—based on their prior studies of HIV-stressors, and then designed, tested, and implemented by Schneiderman and Antoni's team—has resulted in improved coping strategies, stronger social support systems, and increased immune response among patients from a range of ethnic and socioeconomic backgrounds. Chesney and Coates, in turn, describe a richly varied set of studies, including specific work on coping strategies, nonadherence to drug regimens, and HIV/AIDS clinical trials. Their team became prominent for identifying the first HIV/AIDS patient with multidrug resistance, a finding that led NIH to fund a network of such studies around the country to examine behavioral risk factors.

As each of the chapters conveys, such results are not the endpoint for these researchers. Some groups are building more complex models to fill gaps at the intersections of psychological, sociological, neurological, immunological, and genetic processes. Others are enlarging their research frameworks to move from individual- to population-based research, or from health system to broader social system analyses. Finally, several authors point to the need to increase their capacity for communicating clearly to practitioners so that their results are more likely to be used in diagnosing and treating patients or in designing effective health programs.

The collaborative research process: Central features

While the case studies demonstrate that interdisciplinary collaborations and, indeed, interdisciplinarity itself, operate in a variety of forms and at a variety of levels of scientific inquiry, we suggest that a number of features are central to extended, successful partnerships across established boundaries. Although they obviously overlap with some of the factors presented in the next section, we see merit in highlighting such features here. (For summary details of collaborative pathways and of facilitating and constraining factors, see Tables 19.2 and 19.3 in the Appendix to this chapter.)

ROLE OF THE PI   The case studies illustrate the centrality of the principal investigator (PI) in building any interdisciplinary team effort. In these cases, the role of the PI takes several forms—an individual initiator who becomes polyvalent in his or her capacity to undertake research (Kosslyn, Light, Meaney, Seeman). A two-person team where a duo from different disciplines meet (sometimes by chance) and find areas of common interest (Berntson and Cacioppo, Kaplan and Manuck, Olshansky and Carnes, Ryff and Singer). Or a mentor who creates a forum for individuals to work together in a relatively modest program (George). On occasion, such a modest program becomes the core of a larger group that, given time and resources, conducts a multitude of multidisciplinary, interdisciplinary, even transdisciplinary research projects, with a variety of individuals moving in and out of the network (e.g., Chesney and Coates, Davidson, Marmot, Schneiderman and Antoni).

SHARED STARTING POINT   As a PI initiates conversations with (potential) colleagues, the case studies suggest that it is the definition of the problem—rather than a common theoretical framework and corollary set of conceptual issues—that structures the nature of sought-after research collaboration. The focus on a problem helps orient the potential partners and provides the foundation on which the discipline-based researchers build their joint analytical and methodological frameworks. Through such a problem focus, and over time, team members see less need for discipline authorization and are able to move comfortably and coherently across each other's fields and frameworks.[9] The end result can be creative orientations for research and, via this blending of theories, concepts, and methods, new fields of inquiry as well. Where appropriate, an emergent joint framework can also build consensus on strategies for treatment and policy directed at the original energizing problem, especially if that takes the form of a social problem.[10]

ROLE OF LANGUAGE   As networks take shape around a shared problem, and beyond the initial impetus of a PI, to a significant degree, the design and conduct of successful interdisciplinary research hinges on the capacity of investigators to learn to understand and speak different disciplinary languages. The formidable challenge of learning such new languages is patently a part of the process of establishing a broad framework of communication and, hence, joint inquiry. What the case studies in this volume illustrate is that if the team is committed to the solution of a particular problem, and given sufficient time, the collaborating individuals become conversant in the language of the "other," and team members become able to communicate with each other at a variety of levels. In a direct and powerful way, absent successful communication, there can be no successful collaborative research. Thus the investment of time and interpersonal space for acquiring at least a well-informed understanding of alternative conceptual and methodological languages is a prime requirement for successful interdisciplinary initiatives.

ROLE OF THE INSTITUTION   The institutional arrangements represented in the case studies range from individual grants and projects to research programs to centers for intra-university, cross-faculty collaborations and, in some cases, interuniversity and international collaboration. The critical foundational element, however, is the degree to which the structure and functioning of the "host" institution—notably its leadership and incentive structures—provides the requisite space and time for such forms to take hold. In a variety of ways, these case studies illustrate how institutional frameworks can foster intellectual innovation.[11]

In addition to these central features, what other factors do the case study authors suggest have been at work in either facilitating and constraining their attempts to work across disciplinary boundaries? For heuristic purposes, and partly following Rowe's introductory chapter, we propose that in both categories such factors can be classified as internal (those that come primarily from within the individual) and external (those located in the social context). In the flow of everyday scientific work these interact in various dynamic ways.

Facilitating factors

INTERNAL FACTORS   The qualities of individuals involved in interdisciplinary work seem to revolve around the following: *a willingness, even desire, to work with others—that is, not being a relative loner; penetrating intellectual curiosity; and intellectual tenacity, even courage,* in branching out and creating new fields of scholarship or defining new approaches in treatment and policy. Each of the chapters illustrates the intellectual creativity and commitment of individuals who are inclined to engage in interdisciplinary collaboration; almost by definition, they are intellectual risk-takers. In addition to their demonstrated intellectual powers, those who engage in such research also exhibit a ready willingness to trust and respect other disciplines. With a basic confidence that comes from their own grounding in a specific field of knowledge, these researchers have the capacity to lead teams and to foster in others the capacity for mutual respect and trust.

Moreover, although this may fly in the face of a view of science as a purely logical and orderly enterprise, and may even undercut our own goal of guiding those who wish to "organize" interdisciplinary innovation, it is worth noting that these individuals underline *the role played by serendipity in the research process.* In many of the professional life histories reported here, serendipitous factors of timing and personality have also contributed, in nontrivial ways, to successful collaborations. For example, personal initiative led Davidson as a graduate student and both Cacioppo and Olshansky early in their postgraduate careers to seek out others who became influential in shaping their research trajectories. They were also fortunate in finding like-minded individuals in their academic institutions (some outside their departmental base). As a somewhat different example, Kaplan and

Manuck report their encountering one another by chance as faculty on their home campus, while Meaney describes how—along with courses beyond his undergraduate major (biology)—a random encounter with a text on psychosomatic medicine in the library provoked what have become for him perennial guiding questions and also prompted him to seek out scientists who provided the foundation for his interdisciplinary work.

Another fundamental internal facilitating quality, also rarely talked about but amply evident in the long-term collaborations presented in this volume, is that of *investigator perseverance*. This can take several forms: perseverance in finding the right people and building the right teams; perseverance against the intellectual challenges raised by scientific skeptics, as well as funders and publishers; perseverance in finding the supportive institutional environment and in building a new set of institutional arrangements; and, where appropriate, perseverance in achieving linkages not only across academic disciplines but also across institutions (including government agencies and nongovernmental organizations).

Perhaps perseverance and the basic quality of having an open, yet prepared, mind minimized the element of chance and increased the likelihood that these individuals would have developed collaborative activities no matter where they were in time or space. Yet here is where an astute mentor and a sympathetic institutional environment will facilitate the future work of intellectually energized graduate students or junior faculty members—by encouraging their search for others with complementary capacities and interests or steering them toward such individuals. These case studies also provide persuasive evidence that even the most enterprising and intellectually secure individual—the person who can generate and build interdisciplinary research teams—cannot function effectively for any productive length of time unless favorable external circumstances are also present.

EXTERNAL FACTORS   The institutional environment for interdisciplinary research must first be guided by the kind of *institutional leadership* that nurtures cross-boundary linkages. Such leadership is clearly evident in the universities presented by the case studies here. Prominent among them, the University of Wisconsin and Duke University are two that seem to foster support for the kind of multidimensional cross-discipline research linkages and center-building activities that provide fertile environment for vibrant interdisciplinary research.[12] As represented here, the leaders at the University of California, San Francisco; the University of California, Los Angeles; and the University of Miami have also welcomed cross-boundary research endeavors, as well as facilitated overcoming the usual institutional constraints of overhead and time allocation and tenure review to foster interdisciplinary activities. These are surely not the only academic institutions in the United States or elsewhere with such qualities, but they seem to be characterized by a culture that welcomes and nurtures such connections.[13]

However, important and essential as it is for nurturing such activity—and, indeed, for providing seed funding—university leadership often cannot provide the major long-term funding required for novel and complex collaborative research. These case studies provide ample evidence that, for interdisciplinary research in the health and social sciences to flourish, *government funding and foundation support are essential*. Federal funding, primarily through the National Institutes of Health, has been critically important in sustaining both large and small collaborative endeavors; NIH support for centers of various kinds has consolidated and sustained the infrastructure and financial support for interdisciplinary research. And the MacArthur Foundation provides an outstanding example of foundation support for these endeavors. As emphasized by several of the case study authors, in the broad interdisciplinary area of the health and social sciences in the United States, for almost two decades the MacArthur Foundation has been instrumental in fostering linkages across disciplines in a variety of health domains. The Robert Wood Johnson Foundation has also supported such work in a number of directions, including a pathbreaking study by Samuel Bloom of medical training that promotes inclusion of the social sciences in the core curriculum (Bloom, 1992; see note 17).

Nonetheless, as noted by all the case study authors and referred to in the following section, there are too few sources of *sustained support* to permit the long-term perseverance required for team building and obtaining valid results. This was, in fact, the major factor noted by Sewell (1989) that limited the capacity of interdisciplinary research in social psychology to flourish in the same way that research linking chemistry and biology did to form the new field of molecular biology. Without sustained funding, such that new findings can form the basis for the next cycle of research, it is not possible to build new fields of scholarly inquiry that will be both iterative and generative.

In many cases, as indicated earlier, another critically important external factor prompts an individual to undertake interdisciplinary research: *an astute and open-minded academic mentor*. Nearly all the members of the generation of interdisciplinary health/social science researchers in the United States present in this volume have had devoted mentors. Many of those highlighted by the case study authors— for example, Tom Carlson, Bruce McEwen, John Rowe, Leonard Syme—are drawn primarily from the health sciences and from interdisciplinary backgrounds themselves but, curiously, not from the social sciences (Syme is a sociologist turned epidemiologist). While this may be an artifact of the project's choice of case study authors or illustrative research domains, it is essential to consider how to persuade social scientists to encourage their students to think further about and engage more actively in interdisciplinary research and training. That, in turn, may entail openness to research addressing problems drawn as much from broader social concerns as from health- or discipline-specific issues.

Another significant external element facilitates effective work and often makes it possible for the innovative, intellectual risk-taker to pursue interdisciplinary endeavors: *the availability of training opportunities that move individuals across disciplinary lines*. Teresa Seeman and Jay Olshansky are outstanding examples of scholars coming from the social and behavioral sciences who, through the availability of generous postdoctoral support in the form NIH SERCA[14] grants (notably provided by the National Institute on Aging), have been able to delve deeply into the biomedical areas of greatest interest to them. That, in turn, has enabled them to become effective team members, as well as polyvalent and valued promoters of interdisciplinary collaboration.

Finally, the availability of both *new technologies and concepts* has also been vital to the success of many of these collaborations. As described in the case studies, new techniques from chemical studies of the brain, new equipment for imaging the brain and linking brain activity to social and behavioral elements, and new therapies in HIV/AIDS—all these have made it possible to focus on new sets of issues that are ripe for interdisciplinary collaboration. Further, new statistical approaches have facilitated analyses of data with difficult scale and measurement requirements. New concepts in defining and measuring stress and well-being (e.g., allostatic load as a significant case in point) have also changed the nature of collaboration and research, bringing in biostatisticians and epidemiologists who make it possible for social psychologists, immunologists, and endocrinologists to work on populations, not just individuals. In turn, this has broadened the validity, reliability, and applicability of these concepts. Such new concepts and technologies have linked field and laboratory work and have moved across the boundaries of survey research and laboratory research, as well as animal and human studies. Through new analytical and statistical approaches, such as those described by Light et al. (Chapter 3), Ryff and Singer (Chapter 10), and Schneiderman and Antoni (Chapter 17), researchers from different disciplines have been able to find ways to combine different units of analysis and to define common conceptual and analytical frameworks, and thereby undertake innovative research programs.

Constraining factors

We have sketched a range of factors that facilitate innovative interdisciplinary research. But as Norman Anderson (2000) and others have noted, there are also nontrivial internal and external factors that inhibit such research. The case studies also illustrate these—some the direct converse of facilitating factors, others not. (See Table 19.3.)

INTERNAL FACTORS   Language and status barriers are often confronted by principal investigators and individual team members. As mentioned, language barriers not only hinder understanding of the basic assumptions, concepts, and methods in a particular discipline but can also lead to a lack of agreement about the role that each discipline, and thus each investigator, plays in the research process (Shine, 2002). A major challenge in interdisciplinary research, then, is to minimize or eliminate discipline authorization and achieve a shared understanding of the nature of the problem and appropriate approaches undertaken to tackle it.

On the matter of status, social and behavioral researchers often consider themselves second-class citizens in the world of biomedical science and, indeed, are seen as such by those scientists. Moving beyond separate or even multidisciplinary research (where each discipline separately tackles different elements of the problem sequentially or in parallel) certainly requires an understanding of the fundamentals of all the relevant disciplines, and it also requires *mutual respect*. As indicated in these case studies, the research teams have respected and had confidence in the knowledge and skills brought to the program by all members of the team. But, as candidly described by Chesney and Coates, this is not the norm at the beginning of the process and can often only be achieved through dedicated time and effort.[15]

EXTERNAL FACTORS   Many external factors can constrain interdisciplinary research. From the perspective of the case study authors, the most significant are institutional arrangements, funding, peer review of grants, and peer review of publications. Indeed, our sense is that almost anyone who has engaged in interdisciplinary research will identify these as the major external barriers to undertaking and sustaining such research. While these can be overcome, they are often largely beyond the researcher's control.

Institutional *barriers* include such issues as the difficulty in finding time to move across departmental boundaries, as well as the frequently cited matter of the tenure review process, which does not encourage but, rather, discourages team research and joint publications. As several of the authors discuss, institutional barriers are found both within and outside their home institutions. Within their home institutions, nearly all report confronting obstacles to cross-departmental and cross-faculty collaboration. Berntson and Cacioppo (Chapter 2), for example, identify the issue of distinct histories, research traditions, and technical demands that may make branching out difficult, even within a given field. Such problems are obviously multiplied when reaching out across faculties and across institutions. And the issue of different traditions and criteria, allied to the fact that the kinds of interdisciplinary research reported here involve multiple responsible PIs, takes on especially consequential form in the context of promotion and tenure decisions.

Nor does the establishment of centers for interdisciplinary research bypass all barriers. While the movement to promote such centers is positive in many ways, they must often be self-supporting. As George (Chapter 12) reports, this means, in turn, that researchers affiliated with such a center must spend valuable time in fundraising. Ryff and Singer (Chapter 10) and Seeman (Chapter 11) also highlight the issue of time pressures coming from engagement in numerous research projects as well as teaching and training responsibilities. As noted by Light et al. (Chapter 3) and Schneiderman and Antoni (Chapter 17), that problem becomes more acute for researchers who have clinical responsibilities that can impede active participation in a research team.

The *preparation and peer review of interdisciplinary proposals* is another challenge noted in many of these chapters. For one thing, preparing grant applications with multiple partners from different disciplines is usually more time-consuming. For another, and perhaps constituting more of a constraint, reviewers on funding panels within NIH or foundations often do not understand the nature of interdisciplinary research and are inclined to challenge the frameworks, as well as the language used in such proposals. As described by both Marmot (Chapter 14) and Chesney and Coates (Chapter 18), the apparent lack of a tight focus relates to the difficulty of getting interdisciplinary work funded. In Marmot's case, the dominant emphasis of medical research in the United Kingdom on "fundamental" biological research led funders to regard with disdain research conducted across disciplinary lines. In the United States, this has led some research teams to identify somewhat unusual funding sources such as the Office of Naval Research or the Social Security Administration.

The same difficulty affects *publication of papers* on the results of interdisciplinary research on health. Too few journals offer a welcome home for such papers. *Social Science and Medicine* and *Culture, Medicine and Psychiatry* are among the few successful journals in this area. Both in biomedical and social science disciplines, however, publication in journals such as these tends not to be regarded as prestigious as publishing in those that are discipline-specific. And the matter of prestige, or at least acceptance, arises in another direction. As noted especially by Light et al. in Chapter 3, when therapeutic recommendations are made on the basis of research, it is especially important to publish in the appropriate medical journals in order to reach clinicians and medical researchers involved in changing practices or policies regarding interventions. Yet those journals often will not accept research when presented in the form of an interdisciplinary paper, a gatekeeping fact that authors must decide how to take into account when contemplating report preparation.

A greater understanding of the form and functional consequences of these kinds of institutional barriers will surely emerge from further work, both conceptual and empirical. Lamont and Guetzkow (2000), for example, have offered a subtle discussion of the dynamics of evaluating types of interdisciplinary work, including how these dynamics can differ across settings such as journals, department tenure committees, and federal review panels. They also cite a study of evaluation processes they are undertaking that can be regarded as part of an emerging empirical literature on particular aspects of research collaborations.[16] As we suggested in our opening section, at the least the life histories that the authors have provided should serve as rich grist for such work.

Guidance for Future Interdisciplinary Collaborations

What of the future? As scientists, academic administrators, and potential funders look toward the next generation of work on the multiple, interactive dimensions of health, we propose that the case study reflections of these researchers and their discussions of factors that facilitate and constrain interdisciplinary inquiry yield a set of four key elements, all of which must be present to effect the conduct of sustained, successful integrative research:

1. First and foremost, and perhaps paradoxically, the individual scientist is central. It is the inquiring risk-taker who provides the intellectual spark and personal passion that generates and sustains the energy for successful interdisciplinary research.

2. As a corollary, training programs that foster open and inquisitive minds are essential for promoting and sustaining interdisciplinary research. Such training programs not only shape individual outlooks and competencies but also use the research generated by previous generations of interdisciplinary researchers. This, in turn, increases the likelihood of an accumulation of knowledge and a new generation of research of greater depth across appropriately varied fields or subfields.[17]

3. Such training and allied research, in turn, require a third element: supportive academic environments that foster integrative, multilevel interdisciplinary collaboration. To create the kind of culture that attracts and nurtures individuals, both senior scientists and students, seeking to undertake interdisciplinary research, the leadership at all levels of the institution—president, deans, and department heads—must be mutually supportive. Such leadership welcomes and provides opportunities for faculty to move across disciplines, for students to be trained across disciplines, and for both individuals and the institution itself to achieve funding and recognition for interdisciplinary research.

4. Finally, for all these elements to coalesce and continue to generate creative work, sufficiently sustained long-term funding must be available from the academic institutions themselves (e.g., via their endowments), from foundations, and from public sources, most notably in the health realm, NIH.

Concluding Comments

To return to our opening discussion about the limitations of the conventional quest for unity of knowledge (see Fodor, 1998), we believe that the chapters in this volume signal vividly that theoretical and philosophical positions and oppositions do not need to be drawn along disciplinary battle lines. Rather, conceptual and methodological perspectives can be creatively blended and most fruitfully integrated when a problem-oriented, solution-driven focus predominates in scientific work. Indeed, given how such lines have been drawn over the past decade or two by proponents and opponents of disciplinarity and interdisciplinarity—of postmodernism, reductionism, and reconstruction—it seems clear to us that sustaining a vibrant intellectual atmosphere in many of our academic institutions has been the major casualty. Of course, a host of factors contribute to such a state of affairs, and there is thus no single solution, including "interdisciplinarity" (see note 11). Yet our sense is that generative institutional frameworks for academe could emerge from the kinds of scientific collaborations exemplified in this volume, as well as from further discussion of some of the conceptual innovations these scholars have been exploring.

As a significant example of such conceptual innovations, *heterarchy*—as introduced by Berntson and Cacioppo (Chapter 2)—could serve as a heuristically powerful metaphor for framing both our scientific thinking and organizational practice in the realm of human and social problems that are patently complex, multidimensional, and interactive (over time and space). The essential epistemological spirit of heterarchy is conveyed by Berntson and Cacioppo's principles of multiple, nonadditive, and reciprocal determinism. (See also Cacioppo, Berntson, Sheridan, and McClintock, 2000.) Not surprisingly, the term was first used by one of the pioneers of contemporary cognitive neuroscience, Warren McCulloch (1945), to describe forms of brain organization which, though structured, are not hierarchical. And the research programs of Cacioppo, Davidson, and their many colleagues—crossing as they do the boundaries and levels of the neural, the psychological, and the social—can be regarded as realizing in rich detail McCulloch's initial insight. Yet, as Crumley (1995) has noted, "to date [the concept of heterarchy] has had little impact on the study of society" (p. 3). More generally:

> Heterarchy may be defined as the relation of elements to one another when they are unranked or when they possess the potential for being ranked in a number of different ways. . . . Many structures, both biological and social, are not organized hierarchically. There is nothing intrinsically hierarchical about an oak tree or a symphony, yet each has undeniable structure and constitutes an orderly representation among elements. Nonetheless, few terms identify other kinds of order. Hierarchy—inasmuch as it is often a reductionist metaphor for order—has disproportionately influenced theory building in both social and natural scientific contexts. . . . This conflation of hierarchy with order makes it difficult to imagine, much less recognise, patterns of relations that are complex but not hierarchical. It is ironic that the government structure we most prize (democracy) is the ideal representation of a power *heterarchy* (pp. 2–3).

This should help convey why we sense, at a number of levels, significant metaphorical force in this concept, not least in the context of emerging interdisciplinary inquiry.

We suggest, then, that twenty-first-century institutions serving scientific research—especially relating to health—will thrive to the degree they move past territorial or ideological disputes, striving instead to invigorate intellectual creativity. And innovative contributions to knowledge, policy, and practice are all the more likely if we develop:

> . . . creative . . . interdisciplinary approaches in our liberal arts curricula in order to provide intellectual coherence through interdisciplinary themes. There is no reason why scientific, historical and literary themes cannot be taught through team-teaching as well as multiple and comparative perspectives and expertise in order to provide our students [with] knowledge not only of disciplines but also of their interconnectedness as well. . . . In addition, universities must develop strategies of enabling their faculty members steeped in different disciplines to have opportunities of interdisciplinary and multidisciplinary work and to develop a broad general education of their own (Gregorian, 1993, pp. 610–611).

Our closing conviction is that such a positive perspective—powerfully presented and represented by the contributors to this volume—is needed to identify, across conventional disciplinary boundaries, complementarities and commonalities in concepts and theories, analyses and interpretations, and in many cases, sound recommendations for action, whether in the form of scientific research and scholarly inquiry or interventions and policy aimed at improving individual health and social well-being.

As leaders in interdisciplinary research, these case study authors are communicating both a shared vision of scientific success and, as important, tangible findings. Their hard-won results, along with their self-reflective insights, should help put to rest skepticism about work at the boundaries of established disciplines.[18] More positively and importantly, the kinds of theoretical and empirical work represented here should encourage academic colleagues, policymakers, and the public to embrace interdisciplinary collaboration as vital for the well-being of science *and* society.

> The new biology cannot remain isolated from social issues. The future lies in broadening the horizon of the interplay between the biomedical and social sciences and in the transdisciplinary synthesis of science and technology with society's needs and values in a changing world.
> —V. Ramalingaswami, *"The Art of the Possible"*

Appendix

Table 19.1. Major Contributions from the Case Studies Prompted by Interdisciplinary Approaches

Case Study	Contributions
Berntson and Cacioppo (Chapter 2)	• Helped shape new field of social neuroscience: principles and analytical framework for integrated, multilevel approach linking behavior, cardiovascular disease, and health • Elaborated and applied concept of heterarchy to interdisciplinary research in social neuroscience
Light, Girdler, and Hinderliter (Chapter 3)	• Research led to basic findings on the relationship between stress, personal ties, and social isolation; confirmed findings that same behavior in different people have different effects—such as stress buffers in relationship to social support, factors influencing recovery after stress • Used new technique to elaborate individual differences to demonstrate evidence for building social support systems and reducing cardiovascular disease effects, including relationship between stress and family history of hypertension; special emphasis on gender-related effects
Kaplan and Manuck (Chapter 4)	• Demonstrated that behavioral factors establish vulnerability and resistance to arterial disease • Identified nature of male and female differences in the influence and mediation of behavioral factors on arterial disease • Identified premenopausal years as period when atherosclerotic heart disease begins in females, and naturally occurring estrogen deficiency as factor responsible for accelerating disease

(continued)

Table 19.1. *(continued)*

Case Study	Contributions
Davidson (Chapter 6)	• Helped develop new interdisciplinary area of affective neuroscience—effect of brain and body and nature of emotion; identified gap in understanding mechanics of how emotions affect health; transformed field • Team contributed to understanding mechanics of mind-body interactions • Brought together neuroscientist, psychologists, molecular geneticist, physicists, and computer scientists for the first time to analyze individual differences in these interactions • Understanding of brain as the basis of changes in emotion in health produced by traditional and nontraditional psychological interventions such as meditation
Kosslyn (Chapter 7)	• Developed theory and model of visual mental imagery based on confluence of different types of data resulting in insights into neural bases of imagery and new methods for studying it • Developed approaches for analyzing how images affect the whole body in relation to health and for using images to evoke and modify emotions and cognitive reactions
Meaney (Chapter 8)	• Demonstrated relevance of animal models for fundamental understanding of the importance of plasticity (redundancy) within the human neural system for mediating response to stress and to individual differences, especially from early life events • Developed hypothesis and model of genetic pathways to understand how handling affects genetic transmission to next generation via alterations in natural behavior • Contributed to understanding how parental care affects development of neural systems that influence behavior and endocrine response to stress; elucidated role of individual differences in vulnerabilities and resistance to stress and disease
Ryff and Singer (Chapter 10)	• Developed integrative biopsychosocial approach to understanding morbidity and mortality; demonstrated role of resilience as biopsychosocial protective factor • Identified overarching neurobiological substrate of human flourishing and role in promoting positive health • Tested concept of allostatic load as marker of cumulative stress for understanding relationship between biology and psychosocial flourishing
Seeman (Chapter 11)	• Contributed to work on how social relations affect health outcomes—how to "get inside" the body through cognitive, emotional, and biological pathways • Instrumental in advancing research on allostatic load—developed initial operational definitions of allostatic load and demonstrated ability to predict health risks • Developed new framework to elaborate concept of cumulative risk; allows integration of information across multiple domains; comprehensive model of health and aging includes examination of how different domains emerge over the life course

(continued)

Table 19.1.   *(continued)*

Case Study	Contributions
George (Chapter 12)	• Elucidated mechanisms of effects of spirituality and religion on health: examined physical, chemical, biological factors, and social ties; results showed frequency of attendance at religious services decreases mortality, decreases blood pressure, increases immune response; not clear about heart rate, social ties, psychological response, or worldviews • Examined multiple concepts of religious participation, multiple types of health outcomes, variation across disease processes; established the role of support using statistical controls
Marmot (Chapter 14)	• Ultimate result of 30 years of effort: the findings from two Whitehall studies incorporated into 1999 National Health Strategy Paper for England • Findings from two decades of research: mortality is inversely related to a social gradient, with high social position related to lower mortality; identified risk factors accounted for only one-third of social gradient; need to go beyond biological research to understand risk factors • Social and economic differences within and between social units relative to differences in social position are crucial; in rich countries, psychosocial factors are important in disease occurrence; exposure early in life and throughout life could affect adult disease risks
Olshansky and Carnes (Chapter 15)	• Revived and reinvigorated the discipline of biodemography • Extended evolutionary biology from individual to population by bringing in demography: literatures brought together showed how concepts from one discipline can be used to explain phenomena observed in others—for example, showed common age patterns of mortality across species • Examined patterns of death and the public policy implications re life expectancy; first time any government agency had formally supported work on biodemography of aging • Findings imply consistent biological focus operates in same way across species, regulating age patterns of death; death rates cannot decline significantly below intrinsic mortality schedule for a species; direct bearing on mortality and life expectancy forecast made by actuaries
Schneiderman and Antoni (Chapter 17)	• Overall application of behavioral and social science approaches—with multiple levels and different skills both within and across fields and institutions—to HIV/AIDS disease management • One main contribution: designed and applied new, group-format approach to stress management (CBSM) that emphasizes interpersonal interaction; focuses on improving coping strategies, providing social support, and medication adherence; demonstrated effect on increase in immunity (T-cells and hormones) • Developed CBSM manual and workbook; piloting new intervention with community health centers

(continued)

Table 19.1.   *(continued)*

Case Study	Contributions
Chesney and Coates (Chapter 18)	• Great strides against HIV/AIDS epidemic in San Francisco and elsewhere through involvement of scientists from every specialty; wide variety of results emerged from the CAPS interdisciplinary program and from new coalitions of social and medical scientists and practitioners, across different disciplines and backgrounds, and with public health programs and hospitals • Studied effects of caregiving and coping strategies, examined ways to maintain AIDS medication regimes, developed clinical trials examining home treatment to reduce non-adherence, pointed to individually tailored interventions from research on adherence • Multidisciplinary team involved in clinical drug trials; identified first person with multidrug resistance; led to NIH funding of network of such studies and then to multidisciplinary study of AIDS risk across the United States, focusing on behavioral factors • With NIH grants joined San Francisco Department of Health to conduct comprehensive set of research projects on disease dynamics from perspective of prevention • Developed models for funding AIDS research, identified community strategies that work, and assisted UCSF in establishing the AIDS Research Institute to bring together many different medical and social science disciplines based on CAPS model

Table 19.2.   Highlights of Collaborative Pathways Drawn from the Case Studies

Case Study	Collaboration
Berntson and Cacioppo (Chapter 2)	Two principal investigators provide the glue since 1989 • Collaboration began "by accident" • Students and colleagues change regularly • Common theme links group overtime
Light, Girdler, and Hinderliter (Chapter 3)	Principal investigator (Light) worked as behavioral scientist in interdisciplinary teams since 1976 • Runs program on stress and health with physicians and other medical students • Students/colleagues change regularly; core group composed of social scientists, medical scientists, clinicians, and grad students • Collaboration expanded to include colleagues at clinical research center with researchers worldwide • Mentoring/training important component of collaboration
Kaplan and Manuck (Chapter 4)	Two behavioral scientists meet by chance at same university • Active collaboration since 1979; survived move of one PI to another university, expanded collaboration to two universities since 1981

(continued)

Table 19.2. *(continued)*

Case Study	Collaboration
	• Each investigator brings different skills that are complementary; each suggests studies from different perceptions • Expanded to collaborate with Swedish institute
Davidson (Chapter 6)	Principal investigator encouraged as graduate student to seek collaborators outside of graduate department • Chance encounter with former colleague from graduate school led to joint paper in *Science,* 1982; series of publications followed • PI moved to Wisconsin in 1985 and worked in primate lab with NIH support; collaborated with psychoneuroimmunologist • 1990–1991 initial set of collaborative studies persuaded Wisconsin to invest in neuroimaging facility • Collaboration between Davidson, Ryff, and Singer to compete for NIH mind-body center grant
Meaney (Chapter 7)	Principal investigator originally a biologist; in 1970s, a professor introduced him to questions in psychology • By chance, in the library stacks, PI found book on psychosomatic medicine, led to interest in individual differences; sought training in Bruce McEwen's lab • Scientific collaboration in 1980s at Rockefeller University with McEwen as mentor • Participation in MacArthur working groups in 1980s and 1990s; PI met epidemiologists, social psychologists, and others • Strength of collaboration demonstrated by carrying work forward, even when networks have ended
Ryff and Singer (Chapter 10)	Two PIs: social scientist (Ryff) with tools and theories to address human strengths and challenges; biologist (Singer) with skills in epidemiology and statistics • Team asks questions requiring multidisciplinary perspectives and seeks new partners in relation to the questions • Over the last decade, developments in neuroscience community have led to bridge building • Collaboration has focused on concepts/tools to measure well-being, expanded to include demography, sociology, biology, and neuroscience and has explored both single and multiple life challenges • Both PIs participate in MacArthur networks—provide opportunity to learn about other disciplines and build mutual respect
Seeman (Chapter 11)	PI trained as traditional epidemiologist; also studied social and psychological factors in relation to health outcomes • As junior scholar in MacArthur network on aging, determined need to understand biological pathways • In 1991, received 5-year SERCA training award to study endocrinology; enabled transition from traditional program of epidemiological research to interdisciplinary research

(continued)

Table 19.2. *(continued)*

Case Study	Collaboration
	• PI has developed research collaborations that incorporate neuroendocrinologists, demographers, economists, health psychologists, and geriatric medicine
George (Chapter 12)	Since 1986, PI served as mentor, promoting collaborative work on religion and health • Duke-supported center has facilitated collaboration for PIs and others • Developed collaboration with Duke University Divinity School and Medical School and Duke Institute on Care at the End of Life
Marmot (Chapter 14)	PI started from epidemiology study of cardiovascular disease, over 30 years developed major interdisciplinary program, building a center in the process • Beginning in 1970s, developed research program with epidemiologists and researchers with various backgrounds, skills, and approaches • Encouraged by senior scientist and university provost, in 1994 established major international research center to house a wide variety of health and social science interdisciplinary research
Olshansky and Carnes (Chapter 15)	In 1989, two PIs, each in different divisions of Argonne Lab—Olshansky in human disease and demography, Carnes in biology and statistics—began to work together • In 1988, Olshansky attended interdisciplinary conference sponsored by NIA, became interested in new area of research, led to collaboration with Carnes and joint article in *Science*, 1990 • With a SERCA grant from NIA in 1992, Olshansky pursued independent course of study at University of Chicago in new fields of biology • Following Olshansky's training, team developed research program merging demography and biology
Schneiderman and Antoni (Chapter 17)	In 1986, dean asked Schneiderman to develop comprehensive interdisciplinary program to fight HIV/AIDS • Core team has enlarged over time, depending on issues being addressed; team is interdisciplinary, multidisciplinary, and multicentered • Project expanded from University of Miami to Veteran Medical Center, bringing more clinical collaborators; able to work with physicians, behavioral and social scientists, and focus groups to test new interventions and develop a multimodal program design
Chesney and Coates (Chapter 18)	In 1983, two PIs put together the first symposium on AIDS at a social/behavioral science conference • In 1986, founded CAPS, bringing together psychological and biomedical approaches to health with an emphasis on training • At CAPS, health-oriented social scientists and biomedical scientists realized they needed each other for effective research

(continued)

Table 19.2. *(continued)*

Case Study	Collaboration
	• Multidisciplinary model involves collaboration with other scientists and other organizations across the university and elsewhere in the Bay area
	• Over time, administrative core approach at CAPS structured way for social and behavioral sciences to work with medical sciences, public health services and local communities
	• Training programs at CAPS led to collaborations with counterparts in Latin America, Africa, Asia, and Eastern Europe
	• In 1998, university formed AIDS Research Institute bringing together many different medical and social science disciplines modeled after CAPS

"Long-term interdisciplinary collaborations ultimately emanate from the interests of the investigators themselves and depend on the willingness of these investigators to invest a level of energy in research collaboration comparable to that expended on behalf of other strong interpersonal relations. In this sense, in our experience, the successful collaboration more closely resembles a happy marriage than an impersonal, scientific endeavor"

(Kaplan and Manuck, Chapter. 4).

Table 19.3. Factors Facilitating and Constraining the Conduct of Interdisciplinary Research, as Described in the Case Studies

Case Studies	Facilitating Factors	Constraining Factors
Berntson and Cacioppo (Chapter 2)	• Professional and personal compatibility of the two main PIs	
	• Complementary and intersecting skills of team members essential for multilevel analysis	
	• PIs and other team members able to do independent, collaborative work outside of team	
	• Availability of longitudinal data made multilevel analysis possible	
	• Advances in ambulatory recording procedures and experience sampling methods made it possible to extend lab work to field	
	• Academic research centers help to cut across multiple levels of organization	
	• Historical barriers between fields of biology and psychology	
	• Residual discipline barriers prevented easy access of researchers—including physical location, administrative structure, differences in language, research traditions, and technical demands	
	• Funding challenge: grant review process for interdisciplinary research—panels comprised of scientists from more traditional disciplines	
Light, Girdler, and Hinderliter (Chapter 3)	• Positive attitude and training of researchers	
	• Supportive teachers and mentors	
	• Medical school location facilitated access to colleagues and NIH support	
	• Continuity of funding: NIH support for research, predoctoral fellowships, training grants	

(continued)

Table 19.3.   *(continued)*

Case Studies	Facilitating Factors	Constraining Factors
	• Advances in technology for research, including access to e-mail, enabled researchers and clinicians worldwide to communicate regularly	
		• Nature of interdisciplinary research: time-consuming, long-term and costly, often lasting beyond career of an individual researcher and original team
		• Disincentives for physicians to participate: clinical duties, teaching responsibilities, and no system to provide for reduction of responsibilities
		• Grant applications more time-consuming than usual project proposal: extensive justification to funders necessary
		• With publications, five or more coauthors often share credit, need to have separate first-authored papers for all major PIs or cannot contribute to career advancement
		• Limited influence on practitioners because publications in behavioral journals not read by physicians; can't publish paper with behavioral focus in clinical hypertension journals (no reviewers and too long)
Kaplan and Manuck (Chapter 4)	• Complementary research tradition to other investigators worked best: training was not interdisciplinary; complementary and specific skills; appreciation of each other's knowledge	
	• Mentor provided expectations, encouragement, infrastructure for both PIs	
	• Medical school location a plus—access to colleagues in other fields	
	• Advances in technology, such as e-mail, made possible daily contact between investigators, the transfer of data and analysis of manuscripts easy	
		• Early work on relation of behavior to heart disease not widely accepted
		• Institutional infrastructure not designed to facilitate interaction with other institutions
Davidson (Chapter 6)	• Mentor encouraged PI as graduate student to explore other fields within and outside home institution	
	• In-depth training in new field opened up collaboration with scientists in complementary areas	
	• As graduate student, saw limitations of behavioral sciences and work on personality	
		• Limited interest in 1970s in linking work on biology and emotion, no field called affective neuroscience
	• Early publication of research in *Science* helped build reputation	
	• Supportive academic environment: provided new technologies, established research center	
	• Advantage when medical school and school of arts and science on same campus and good relations between psychology and psychiatry	
	• Institution flexible in training and hiring new faculty	
	• Training key component for fostering interdisciplinary research, requires institutional flexibility and dedicated mentors	
	• Participation in MacArthur research networks	
	• McDonnell foundation support helped launch the domain	
	• Federal grants also important—NIMH	
	• High-level, visible meetings at White House and with congressional staff increased funding for research	

(continued)

Table 19.3. *(continued)*

Case Studies	Facilitating Factors	Constraining Factors
	• Access to new technology of brain imaging • Early on, hard to obtain grant funds because few reviewers with competence in biology and emotion research • Location of schools of arts and sciences limits ability to engage in medical science–related interdisciplinary research; for example, institutional barriers for psychologists and neuroscientist to use technologies controlled by departments of radiology	
Kosslyn (Chapter 7)	• As graduate student, able to engage in interdisciplinary research • With distinct problem focus, able to draw on many collaborators from many fields to design and test theories, access to new data, and PI able to learn new skills • Key funding from foundations (MacArthur and McDonnell Foundations) and non-health government agencies (Office of Naval Research and Air Force) • Advances in technology (new imaging techniques) opened up field	• Struggle to get early work funded and still finding resistance; was difficult to get funding for theorizing about neuroscience aspects in psychology • Too few models on how to conduct interdisciplinary research
Meaney (Chapter 8)	• Faculty mentors in graduate school provided essential guidance • PI able to learn field and system, and become multivalent expert; collaboration used to overcome deficits more in technical area rather than theoretical	• PI's early work constrained by prevalence of basic argument of nature vs. nurture • Challenge in multidisciplinary research is to master and not simply import a technique • Conceptual sophistication of all team members, not just PI but also students and post-docs
Ryff and Singer (Chapter 10)	• Supportive institutional environment that promotes collaboration within and across departments • Shared commitment of PIs to building bridges across disciplines; intellectual and methodological flexibility • Participation in cross disciplinary research networks supported by MacArthur Foundation • Unifying theme—e.g., human resilience—for focusing multidisciplinary efforts • Availability of new analytical techniques capable of identifying multiple complex social, psychological, and biological pathways • Supportive institutional environment strongly encouraged, reaching out across discipline boundaries; "university without walls" philosophy • Close ties with medical school facilitated data collection and collaboration	• Time is a major limiting factor: complex studies take longer to complete; results are slow because of process depth, logistics of data collection are more burdensome, etc. • Respondent burden—participants need to give considerable time as part of data collection

(continued)

Table 19.3.   *(continued)*

Case Studies	Facilitating Factors	Constraining Factors
		• Peer review system for funding and publication: reviewers used to highly focused investigations are critical of interdisciplinary proposals; covering broad scientific territory leads to conflicting criteria for judging scientific quality
Seeman (Chapter 11)	• Individual researcher open to stretching intellectual boundaries	
	• Participation as new Ph.D. in leadership position for MacArthur Network provided exposure to other disciplines and data sets; provided career path	
	• Training opportunity through NIA SERCA award provided time and access to senior researchers in other disciplines	
	• Participation in additional MacArthur networks expanded scope of research and collaboration	
	• Supportive university environment—established new center for interdisciplinary research	
	• Funding available from foundations and government (NIA, NSF)	
		• Funding difficult with traditional NIH funding mechanisms, difficulty with narrowly defined study sections: reviewers lack breadth to review interdisciplinary applications
		• Geographic dispersion of collaborators: lack of funding means lack of regular face-to-face meetings; slows pace of research
		• Time constraints: participants balance multiple research projects with teaching and training responsibilities, limits time available for collaborative efforts
George (Chapter 12)	• Individual scientist convinced of value and importance of interdisciplinary research, willing to encourage and mentor others	
	• Research collaborators share commitment to interdisciplinary research	
	• University support for interdisciplinary research centers	
	• Availability of interdisciplinary fellowship programs to attract key junior researchers	
	• Resurgence of interest in research area, namely religion and health, led to increased government interest, supporting scientific panels and publications (NIA, primarily)	
	• Foundation support essential (Templeton Foundation, Fetzer Foundation and Vitas Foundation)	
		• Controversial nature of research topic made it difficult to obtain funding and be published in top journals that reach practitioners
		• Early funding difficult, especially from federal government: needed to salvage data from other projects and then piggyback questions on religion and health in other studies; religion and health still considered a soft topic or variant of behavioral medicine
		• Limitations of research centers: always short of funds for infrastructure and non-grant-chargeable research activities
		• Time constraints: multiple responsibilities, especially challenge of fundraising
Marmot (Chapter 14)	• Mentor in graduate school instrumental in introducing PI to interdisciplinary research	
	• Shared understanding of scientific problem by different disciplines made it possible to work together using most relevant methods and measures	

(continued)

455

Table 19.3. *(continued)*

Case Studies	Facilitating Factors	Constraining Factors

- Supportive institutional environment: encouragement to bring together existing networks under one interdisciplinary center promoted collaboration and enabled freedom of action for individual researchers
- Funding for small-scale studies used to build interdisciplinary program
- Social determinants of disease not part of traditional medical education or mainstream medical research
- Topic of social inequalities in health was considered politically controversial
- Perceived "lack of focus" made it hard to get interdisciplinary work funded; work not seen as cutting edge by discipline-specific reviewers; dominant thrust medical research is still fundamental biology
- Rigidity of university setting limited opportunities for interdisciplinary research
- Center structure and activities: unable to attract funding for a center from government, foundations, and corporate sector
- Need to frame research in limited way to obtain research funds and be published in major journals

Olshansky and Carnes (Chapter 15)
- Complementary skills and training of two investigators reinforced interdisciplinary research capacity and enabled them to shape new field of research
- Early work on evolution and mathematics of mortality proceeded along independent lines for more than a century
- Interdisciplinary collaboration was
- Mutual trust and respect strengthened partnership
- Graduate students able to benefit from exposure to broader perspectives
- SERCA grant helped one of the researchers (Olshansky) redirect research and pursue independent course of study; SERCA research and training opportunities were instrumental for future interdisciplinary collaboration
- Availability of animal mortality data essential for broader research
- Publication of research in major journals (*Science, Population and Development Review, Scientific American*) helped build reputation of team
- Availability of funding from Social Security Administration and NIA difficult because of different traditions and technical languages
- Major work generated scientific controversy among social and biological scientists, thus affecting acceptance of findings
- Involvement of multiple investigators in projects where credit is shared—implications for salary, tenure, promotions
- Review panels for funding agencies do not have interdisciplinary composition; papers and proposals easily misunderstood, criticized, and at severe competitive disadvantage
- Narrow focus of professional society journals affect ability to publish interdisciplinary research papers; subject matter goes beyond technical expertise of reviewers

(continued)

Table 19.3. *(continued)*

Case Studies	Facilitating Factors	Constraining Factors
Schneiderman and Antoni (Chapter. 17)	• Focus on problem a major advantage for bringing together researchers with different skills from within and across fields • Developing a common language made it possible to analyze relationships between psychosocial variables and pathobiology and develop new intervention approaches • Two PIs had major responsibilities for separate centers and were able to merge research projects and programs • Significant encouragement and support from university administration for interdisciplinary research • Able to house research jointly between medical research center and college of arts and sciences • Funding from Office of AIDS Research, National Institute of Drug Abuse, and NIH for research, training, specific investigators, and center	• Lack of common language and familiarity with each other's concepts and methods • Lack of respect for contributions from different fields
Chesney and Coates (Chapter 18)	• Focus on shared problems brought together two PIs and enabled them to develop more extensive interdisciplinary research efforts • Research center location facilitated sharing of research, provided infrastructure support for investigators • Center design and philosophy encouraged individual scientists to take lead on multidisciplinary teams • School of medicine dean and university leadership supportive of interdisciplinary research • Funding from NIMH and Department of Health and Human Services essential for establishing center; NIAID, CDC, and university funding also available for research and a variety of training opportunities • Access to health department and communities enhanced scope and applicability of research and training	• Biomedical research perspective that social and behavioral sciences less rigorous; "power" differences between behavioral and biological scientists • Constant tension between scientists' motivation for collaborative work versus rewards of solo work; perception that multidisciplinary research results in diffusion of focus and loss of identity • Some critical interdisciplinary areas—secondary prevention, early identification—initially seen as unrealistic by researchers and funders • Training programs often too provincial

ACKNOWLEDGMENTS

Our various collaborators on this project deserve sincerest thanks.

• First and foremost, Norman Anderson—for his catalytic role as OBSSR director and continuing contribution to the working group discussions, and thus as coeditor of this volume.

- Ken Prewitt—for his critical support when the project was launched and his overall vision as SSRC president.
- Richard Suzman—for his imaginative organizational assistance as associate director for behavioral and social research at the National Institute on Aging.
- All the chapter authors but, as *primus inter pares*, the core working group who took responsibility for the substantive domains—for making the project much more than the sum of its parts.
- Craig Calhoun and Cora Marrett, current SSRC president and board chairman—for being willing to find the time to provide an insightful foreword.
- Catharine Carlin, editor par excellence at Oxford University Press, and her more-than-able assistant, John Rauschenberg—for significant sense, sensibility, *and* patience.
- The OUP production editor, Christi Stanforth; their copyeditor, Cynthia Garver; and several anonymous reviewers—for helping to make the manuscript better in numerous ways than it otherwise would have been.
- Molly Brunson, program assistant nonpareil at the SSRC—for priceless competence and calm, and friendship, while working on a whole host of projects, not the least of which was preparing this manuscript for the publisher.
- Taryn Drongowski, new but already much-appreciated SSRC program assistant—for commitment and creativity in helping move from copyedited manuscript to final production.

NOTES

1. As Calhoun and Marrett mention in their foreword, the idea of interdisciplinarity was given significant impetus in the earlier part of the twentieth century by the Social Science Research Council. See Sills, 1986.

2. Sewell also contrasted this picture of decline with successes in blending some areas of inquiry in the natural sciences. See note 12.

3. Chaired by Patricia Rosenfield, the core group was composed of John Cacioppo, Richard Davidson, John Rowe, Carol Ryff, Neil Schneiderman, and Linda Waite. Norman Anderson and Virginia Cain from OBSSR and Frank Kessel from the SSRC participated in all the project meetings.

4. In its critical, and successful, formative years, OBSSR was led by Norman Anderson. Raynard Kington has now assumed the role of director. For further information on OBSSR, see its Web site: http://obssr.od.nih.gov/.

5. The Committee on Bio-Social Perspectives on Parent Behavior and Offspring Development, active from 1980 to 1991, produced several volumes (e.g., Lancaster, Altmann, Rossi, and Sherrod, 1987) and provided the impetus for establishment of the "interdisciplinary, biosocial journal" *Human Nature*. And while the focus of the Committee on Culture, Health, and Human Development, established in 1991, has been more on the cultural and social dimensions of health, its projects have not ignored biomedicine (see

Lock, Young, and Cambrosio, 2000; Stone and Richards, 1993). The Council's Web site—www.ssrc.org—contains more on both its history and its current programs.

6. Among the subtleties or variations: Ryff and Singer, who were responsible for leading an examination of "an integrative approach" to health (Singer and Ryff, 2001), consistently refer to their own work as "multidisciplinary" (Chapter 10). And while we speak here of the blending of disciplinary perspectives within research teams or centers, Kosslyn (Chapter 7), Light et al. (Chapter 3), Olshansky and Carnes (Chapter 15), and Seeman (Chapter 11) represent cases in which the *individual scientist* crosses conventional boundaries. For further refinements on what interdisciplinarity does and does not (or should and should not) entail, see the set of reflections published as part of a SSRC "symposium" (Wissoker et al., 2000).

7. A primary source of the idea of presenting both the substantive and personal dimensions of a scientific story was a *festschrift* for Roger Brown (Kessel, 1988) in which prominent language development researchers—all Brown graduate students at Harvard—reflected on how their work had been shaped by his particular intellectual style.

8. Consistent with its original mission, but with increasing emphasis over the past decade or so, the SSRC is especially engaged in supporting the development of institutional bases for social science at national and regional levels and helping social researchers around the world develop stronger relationships and better communication. One focus for these efforts is its Inter-Regional Working Group on International Scholarly Collaboration (SSRC, 2000).

9. What might be called the-problematic-of-the-problem warrants further analysis since, in scientific practice, what constitutes the "problem" is often the function or expression of a particular theoretical or disciplinary paradigm. How, then, do potential collaborators from different disciplines work their way toward a definition of "the problem" that unites rather than divides them? Beyond that, critical histories of science have examined how broader social, cultural, and political contexts can shape what a discipline takes to be its appropriate problem domain and, even, its discourse. (See, for example, Danziger, 1994, 1997, on the dynamics that influenced the emergence and form of psychology as a science in the late nineteenth century.)

10. In no way neglecting the problematic of what constitutes a "significant" social problem, it can be argued that "sharing a common interest in finding answers to policy questions they consider significant, [some] social scientists are often impatient with disciplinary self-regard, preferring instead pragmatic and eclectic utilization of a variety of approaches, perspectives and methods. Disciplinary purists sometimes shudder at this promiscuity, but it serves not only to bring the insights of a variety of disciplines to bear on a pressing social problem, but also to foster mutual understanding, if not appreciation, across the disciplines" (Anderson, 2000, p. 8).

11. Whether they currently do encourage innovation relates, in turn, to a host of issues currently being debated in U.S. academic institutions. These issues go well beyond the intersection of the health and social sciences and concern matters such as undergraduate curriculum reform, the place and function of the liberal arts and "general education" in a world of hyperspecialization, the relative importance of research and teaching, and—still more broadly—what universities can and should contribute to the national intellectual infrastructure (Katz, 2002).

12. It may be worth noting that William Sewell (1989) considers how the University of Wisconsin failed to foster interdisciplinary research in social psychology in the 1960s (after initial funding from the SSRC for a cross-departmental research seminar); his discussion

falls under the heading "The Threat to the Departmental Structure" (pp. 7–8). Ironically, as an emerging interdisciplinary field in the natural sciences, molecular biology had been given great support on the Madison campus—in part because of significant federal funding—in the prior decade (p. 14).

13. The University of Chicago, the University of Michigan, and the University of California at Irvine are among other campuses where, less or more recently, interdisciplinary scholarship has been nurtured.

14. SERCA is a Special Emphasis Research Career Award.

15. It is as well not to be naive or panglossian about all aspects of academic culture: "There is something about academic training that makes people insistent that one disciplinary approach must be right and others wrong, or, at best, misguided. . . . Scholars treat interlopers from other disciplines as if they were engaged in a war for territory, as if interdisciplinarity were a zero-sum game. There are certainly some institutional contexts in which that is realistic. . . . However, the attitude surfaces on far too many occasions—in, for instance, grandstanding questions at public lectures. Such a territorial attitude belies the intellectual values that academics always trumpet: a dedication to producing new knowledge and the free exploration of ever more creative and complex ideas. Scholars who could be learning from each other spend their time knocking each other down. Territoriality is often redoubled when interdisciplinary spaces are at stake. Perhaps that is because such spaces are new, with boundaries less clear and less ritualized than in traditional disciplines" (Wissoker, 2000, p. 7).

16. Endersby (1996), for example, has examined the issue of when social science researchers are and are not given credit for multiple-authored publications. Sicotte, D'Amour, and Moreault (2002) illustrate not only how interdisciplinary collaborations are being cultivated in the context of primary health care delivery but also how such efforts can be evaluated.

17. Building partly on this project, and with the support of the Robert Wood Johnson Foundation, the SSRC has now launched a working group aimed at helping lay both the intellectual and organizational ground for a series of model joint-degree doctoral programs that would serve as a catalyst for a new generation of integrative interdisciplinary research on health. Among other steps, the group will survey past and present joint-degree efforts, articulate conceptual and methodological approaches that would be central to creative curriculum change, and identify a select number of campuses where many of the necessary conditions for institutional innovation at the intersection of the social and life sciences are in place. Bloom's (2002) most recent work on the sociology of medical education is clearly germane to this enterprise.

18. "Interdisciplinarity is not a significant end in itself. If anything, when viewed in this fashion, it becomes a significant problem, as in un-disciplined and sloppy" (Goldfarb, 2000, p. 11).

RECOMMENDED READINGS

Berkman, L. F. (Ed.) (2002). *Through the Kaleidoscope: Viewing the Contributions of the Behavioral and Social Sciences to Health*. Washington, DC: National Academy of Sciences Press.

Cacioppo, J. T., Berntson, G. G., Sheridan, J. F., and McClintock, M. K. (2000). Multilevel integrative analyses of human behavior: Social neuroscience and the complementing nature of social and biological approaches. *Psychological Bulletin, 126,* 829–843.

Singer, B. H., and Ryff, C. D. (Eds.). (2001). *New Horizons in Health: An Integrative Approach.* Washington, DC: National Academy Press.

Wissoker, K., Anderson, L., Appadurai, A., Bender, T., Goldfarb, J., Lamont, M., and Guetzkow, J. (2000). Negotiating a passage between disciplinary borders: A symposium. *Items and Issues, 1*(III–IV), 1, 5–13.

REFERENCES

Anderson, L. (2000). In K. Wissoker, L. Anderson, A. Appadurai, T. Bender, J. Goldfarb, M. Lamont, and J. Guetzkow. Negotiating a passage between disciplinary borders: A symposium. *Items and Issues, 1*(III–IV), 8.

Anderson, N. B. (1998). Levels of analysis in health science: A framework for integrating sociobehavioral and biomedical research. *Annals of the New York Academy of Sciences, 840,* 563–576.

Anderson, N. B. (2000). The untold story: Barriers and facilitators of interdisciplinary bio-behavioral collaborations. Presented at the American Psychological Association Convention, August 4, Washington, DC.

Andreano, R. (2001). *The International Health Policy Program: An Internal Assessment.* Madison: University of Wisconsin Press.

Bloom, S. W. (1992). Medical education in transition: Paradigm change and organizational stasis. In R. Q. Marston and Roseann M. Jones (Eds.), *Medical Education in Transition: Commission on Medical Education—The Sciences of Medical Practice* (pp. 15–25). Princeton, NJ: Robert Wood Johnson Foundation.

Bloom, S. W. (2002). *The Word as Scalpel: A History of Medical Sociology.* New York: Oxford University Press.

Bronowski, J. (1972). *Science and Human Values.* New York: Perennial Library, Harper & Row.

Ceccarelli, L. (2001). *Shaping Science with Rhetoric: The Cases of Dobzhansky, Schrödinger, and Wilson.* Chicago: University of Chicago Press.

Crumley, C. L. (1995). Heterarchy and the analysis of complex societies. In R. M. Ehrenreich, C. L. Crumley, and J. E. Levy (Eds.), *Heterarchy and the Analysis of Complex Societies* (pp. 1–5). Archaeological Papers of the American Anthropological Association, No. 6.

Danziger, K. (1994). *Constructing the Subject: Historical Origins of Psychological Research.* Cambridge: Cambridge University Press.

Danziger, K. (1997). *Naming the Mind: How Psychology Found its Language.* Thousand Oaks, CA: Sage Publications.

Endersby, J. W. (1996). Collaborative research in the social sciences: Multiple authorship and publication credit. *Social Science Quarterly, 77,* 375–387.

Farmer, P., and Beceerra, M. (2001). Biosocial research and the TDR agenda. *World Health Organization TDR News, 66,* 5–7.

Fodor, J. (1998). Look! Review of E. O. Wilson, *Consilience. London Review of Books, 20,* No. 21 (Oct. 29).

Goldfarb, J. (2000). In K. Wissoker, L. Anderson, A. Appadurai, T. Bender, J. Goldfarb, M. Lamont, and J. Guetzkow. Negotiating a passage between disciplinary borders: A symposium. *Items and Issues, 1*(III–IV), 11.

Good, M. D., Heggenhougen, K., and Kleinman, A. (2001). *East Africa Health and Behavior Fellowship Program in Institutional Strengthening in Social and Medical Sciences.* Boston: Department of Social Medicine, Harvard Medical School.

Gregorian, V. (1993). Education and our divided knowledge. *Proceedings of the American Philosophical Society, 137,* 610–611.

Guyer, J. I. (2001). Revitalizing area studies: The transformation of interdisciplinarity. *News and Events* (Program of African Studies, Northwestern University), *12* (1), 2–3.

Higginbotham, N, Briceño-León, R., and Johnson, N. A. (2001) *Applying Health Social Science: Best Practice in the Developing World.* London: Zed Books.

Karlamangla, A. S., Singer, B. H., McEwen, B. S., Rowe, J. W., and Seeman, T. E. (2002). Allostatic load as a predictor of functional decline: MacArthur studies of successful aging. *Journal of Clinical Epidemiology, 55,* 696–710.

Katz, S. N. (2002). The pathbreaking, fractionalized, uncertain world of knowledge. *Chronicle of Higher Education Review* (Sept. 20), B7–9.

Kessel, F. S. (Ed.) (1988). *The Development of Language and Language Researchers: Essays in Honor of Roger Brown.* Hillsdale, NJ: Erlbaum.

Lamont, M. and Guetzkow, J. (2000). In K. Wissoker, L. Anderson, A. Appadurai, T. Bender, J. Goldfarb, M. Lamont, and J. Guetzkow, Negotiating a passage between disciplinary borders: A symposium. *Items and Issues, 1*(III–IV), 1, 12–13.

Lancaster, J. B., Altmann, J, Rossi, A. S., and Sherrod, L. R. (Eds.) (1987). *Parenting across the Life Span.* New York: Aldine de Gruyter.

Lock, M., Young, A., and Cambrosio, A. (Eds.) (2000). *Living and Working with the New Medical Technologies.* Cambridge: Cambridge University Press.

McCulloch, W. S. (1945). A heterarchy of values determined by the topology of neural nets. *Bulletin of Mathematical Biophysics, 7,* 89–93.

Menand, L. (2001). *The Metaphysical Club: A Story of Ideas in America.* New York: Farrar, Straus and Giroux.

Mudimbe, V. Y., and Jewsiewicki, B. (1996). *Open the Social Sciences: Report of the Gulbenkian Commission on the Restructuring of the Social Sciences.* Stanford, CA: Stanford University Press.

Shine, K. I. (2002). Wrap-up. In L. F. Berkman (Ed.), *Through the Kaleidoscope: Viewing the Contributions of the Behavioral and Social Sciences to Health* (pp. 53–56). Washington, DC: National Academy of Sciences Press.

Ramalingaswami, V. (1986). The art of the possible. *Social Science and Medicine, 22,* 1097–1103.

Rosenfield, P. L. (1992). The potential of transdisciplinary research for sustaining and extending linkages between the health and social sciences. *Social Science and Medicine, 35,* 1343–1357.

Sewell, W. H. (1989). Some reflections on the golden age of interdisciplinary social psychology. *Annual Review of Sociology, 15,* 1–16.

Sicotte, C., D'Amour, D. D., and Moreault, M-P. (2002). Interdisciplinary collaboration within Quebec community health care centers. *Social Science and Medicine, 55,* 991–1003.

Sills, D. L. (1986). A note on the origin of "interdisciplinary." *Items, 40,* 17–18.

Silva, K. T., and Ramos-Jimenez, P. (Eds.) (1996). *Towards a Health Society: Case Studies in Health Social Science Partnerships in the Asia-Pacific Region.* Manila: De La Salle University Press.

Snow, C. P. (1993). *The Two Cultures,* rev. ed. Cambridge: Cambridge University Press.

SSRC (2000). *International Scholarly Collaboration: Lessons from the Past.* Working Paper Series, Vol. 3. New York: Social Science Research Council.

Stone, M. P., and Richards, P. (1993). Social and natural science conjoined: The view from the Africa program. *Items, 47*(2–3), 29–34.

Wilson, E. O. (1998). *Consilience: The Unity of Knowledge.* New York: Random House.

Wissoker, K. (2000). Negotiating a passage between disciplinary borders. In K. Wissoker, L. Anderson, A. Appadurai, T. Bender, J. Goldfarb, M. Lamont, and J. Guetzkow. Negotiating a passage between disciplinary borders: A symposium. *Items and Issues, 1*(III–IV), 1, 5–7.

INDEX

Academy of Finland, xi
Acetylcholine, 95, 97f
Adherence to HIV/AIDS treatment regime. *See under* HIV/AIDS
Adversity, response to. *See* Resilience
Affective neuroscience. *See also* Neuroscience
amygdala and, 116–118, 120–121
animal models, 120
approach- and withdrawal-related emotion, motivation, and, 113–114
areas of brain involved in affective processes, 113, 114f
future *vs.* immediate outcomes and, 115–116
history of field, 111–113
history of interdisciplinary research in, 112, 121–123
implications of modern research in, 126–127
left and right prefrontal regions and, 115, 119–121
MRI, fMRI, and, 112, 124–125
plasticity of neural circuitry and, 109, 126
prefrontal cortex (PFC) and, 114–116, 119–121
psychobiological basis of emotion, 111–112
Affective style, defined, 118
African Americans

HIV/AIDS infection, 351, 374–376, 400–402
hypertensive heart disease, 45, 47t, 54–57
Aging. *See* Biodemography; Longevity
Aging Center, 268
AIDS. *See* HIV/AIDS
AIDS Drug Assistance Program (ADAP), 423–424
AIDS Research Institute (ARI), 394, 425
CAPS/ARI projects, 416, 417–418t
formation, 415–416
Albrecht, Glenn, xii
Alcoholism, 202, 207. *See also* Drug use
Allostatic load, 435
psychosocial strengths and, 234–236, 247–248
resilience and, 199, 203–204, 209–210, 212
Ambulatory research, 37
Amygdala
affective neuroscience and, 116–118, 120–121
maternal behavior in rats and, 180
Anderson, Norman, xxiii, 441, 457t, 458n3
Animal models. *See also under* Atherosclerosis; Atherosclerosis, social stress (in monkeys) and; Environmental effects on gene expression and neural development
affective neuroscience and, 120

465

Animal models (*continued*)
  biodemography and, 328, 330, 333–334,
    336–337
  psychosocial strengths, estrogen studies,
    and, 237–238
  socioeconomic status, longevity, health,
    and, 311–312
  visual mental imagery and, 141–142, 149
Antoni, Michael, xiii, xvi, 358–392, 448t,
    451t, 457t
Anxiety and fear
  amygdala function and, 116–118
  environmental transmission, 175,
    176–181
  heterarchical organization of nervous
    system, autonomic control of heart,
    and, 23, 24, 26–27, 28f, 29
  prefrontal cortex (PFC) and, 114–115, 120
  psychobiology, 111
  visual mental imagery and, 150–152
Aristotle, 218
Associative memory and visual mental
    imagery, 143, 144, 147–148, 150
Asthma, 128
Asymmetrical cerebral activation
  affective neuroscience and, 115, 119–120
  resilience and, 199, 204
Atherosclerosis
  definition and description, 68–70
  premenopausal precursors of
    postmenopausal disease, 94–95
  social stress (in monkeys) and, 16, 74–75,
    76f, 76–77
    choice of animal model, 69–71, 86–87, 92
    diet and, 79–81, 84–85
    estrogen deficiency and replacement
      therapy and, 83–86, 85f, 88–89
    facilitating factors for interdisciplinary
      research on, 92–93
    in female animals, 83–86, 85f
    history of interdisciplinary research
      program, 68, 76–78, 90–93
    housing and, 79–81
    impediments to interdisciplinary
      research on, 92–93
    implications for men, 87–88
    implications for women, 88–90
    individual high stress reactivity and,
      86–87, 87f, 90
    in male animals, 79–82
    status, dominance, subordination, and,
      79–86, 81f, 85f
Attention shifting and visual mental imagery,
    144–145, 149–150

Autonomic nervous system. *See* Heterarchical
    organization of nervous system and
    autonomic control of heart;
    Neuroscience
Autonomy, 201
AZT (zidovudine), 368, 369, 403

BALBc mice, 176–177
Behavior, alternative models of, 246
Behaviorists, 35, 137
Berntson, Gary G., xiii, xiv, xviii, 21–43, 445,
    446t, 449t, 452t
Biodemography (of aging), 287–290, 322,
    340–343, 436
  animal models and, 328, 330, 333–334,
    336–337
  data sources and collection, 330, 333–334
  drawbacks of extrapolation method, 330,
    332–333, 335
  evolutionary theories, 325–327, 330–331,
    333–336
  formation of a scientific collaboration,
    327–329
  genetics and, 326, 327, 331–332
  history of field, 324–327, 336–338
  hypotheses, findings, conclusions, and
    implications, 333–336
  interdisciplinary nature of, 323
  intrinsic mortality schedule or signature
    and, 332–337
  "law of mortality" and, 323–325, 333, 335
  merging individual and population studies,
    330–334
  modern, 336–338
  molecular biology and, 337
  non-aging aspects of life cycle, 337–338
  obstacles to interdisciplinary research in,
    338–340, 343
  origins of the term, 329
  survival beyond sexually reproductive
    period and, 327, 332
Biopsychosocial model of health and aging,
    229, 230f
Biopsychosocial processes, 189, 198, 204–205,
    215, 216, 246–247
Bisexual men. *See* Gay and bisexual men and
    HIV/AIDS
Blacks. *See* African Americans
Blood pressure (BP). *See* Hypertensive heart
    disease
Blood sugar, 298
Brain imaging methods, 108–109. *See also*
    Magnetic resonance imaging
Briceno-Leon, Roberto, xii

Cacioppo, John T., xiii, xiv, xviii, 13–20, 21–43, 438, 445, 446t, 449t, 452t, 458n3
Calhoun, Craig, xxi–xxiii, 458
Canada, xii, 177
Canadian Institutes for Health Research (CIHR), xii
CAPS. *See* Center for AIDS Prevention Studies (CAPS)
Cardiography. *See under* Hypertensive heart disease
Cardiovascular health and disease, 13–17, 433, 435. *See also* Coronary disease; Heterarchical organization of nervous system and autonomic control of heart; Hypertension; Hypertensive heart disease
  socioeconomic status, psychosocial factors, and, 295–297. *See also* Whitehall studies
Cardiovascular health and disease prevention model, applied to HIV/AIDS, 395–397
Career advancement issues for interdisciplinary researchers, 7, 8, 63–64, 240–241
Caregiving, effects of, 404–405
Carnegie Corporation, 434
Carnes, Bruce A., xiii, xvi, xvii, 322–347, 448t, 451t, 456t
Case for Mental Imagery, The (Kosslyn et al.), 154
Case studies
  major contributions of, 446–449t
  selection of, 432–434
  updates on, xiii–xvii
    new methods, techniques, and findings, xiii–xiv
Catania, Joseph, 406–407
Center for AIDS Prevention Studies (CAPS), 393–394, 419–421, 425–426
  adherence to treatment regime, 423
  behavioral issues arising for, 398–400
  CAPS IV, 421
  Collaborative HIV Prevention Research in Minority Communities Program, 421
  community involvement, 395–398
  continued emphasis on multidisciplinary collaboration, 425
  core areas, 401, 410–413
  defining the CAPS multidisciplinary model, 407
    collaborations with other scientists and organizations, 407–408

  community collaborations, 408–410
  continually adapting and expanding the cores, 411–413
  emphasis on dissemination of information, 410–411
  emphasis on science that will make a difference, 414–415
  emphasis on training, 413–414
  design, 400–403
  emphasis on practicality of research, 415
  epidemiology and, 401, 411–412
  ethical issues and, 402
  expansion of programs to secondary prevention, 403–407
  faculty and scientific leadership, 420
  formation, 398–400
  funding, 421
  impediments to interdisciplinary research, 418–419
  international research, 424–425
  Methods Core, 421
  multidisciplinary, multiethnic, multi-institutional nature of, 394, 406
  policy research, 424
  racial/ethnic differences and, 401–402, 412
  recent accomplishments, 421
    adherence with HIV medications, 423
    behavioral epidemiology, 422
    coping with HIV, 424
    draw the line/respect the line, 422–423
    oral acquisition of HIV Infection, 421–422
    redesigning California ADAP, 423–424
  recent studies, 406–407
  technical assistance and dissemination of information, 401
  Technology and Information Exchange (TIE) Core, 410–411
  testing issues, 414, 417–418t
Center for AIDS Research (CFAR), 408, 425
Center for the Study of Aging and Human Development, 268
Center for the Study of Religion, Spirituality, and Health
  developing a program of research on religion and health, 268–270
  pleasures and problems of, 271–273
  from program to center, 269–271
  recent changes, 278–279
Center for the Study of Spirituality, Theology, and Health, 278–279
Cerebral activation asymmetry and resilience, 204

Challenges, response to. *See* Resilience

Chesney, Margaret A., xv, 393–428, 449t, 451t, 457t

Cholesterol levels, 13–14, 54, 295, 298

Chomsky, Noam, 294

Chronic illness
HIV/AIDS as, 352–353
resilience and, 206

Coates, Thomas J., xv, 393–428, 449t, 451t, 457t

Cognitive-behavioral stress management (CBSM), 363. *See also* Miami group-based CBSM for HIV/AIDS-positive subjects

Cognitive neuroscience. *See* Neuroscience

Communication and language issues, 359–360, 432–433, 437–438, 441

Community Alliances for Health Research (CAHR), xii

Community-based organization (CBO) partnerships, 420

Community involvement
in Miami HIV/AIDS CBSM interventions, 380–381
in San Francisco CAPS program, 395–398, 402, 408–410

Community relocation and resilience, 206

Computational modeling in neuroscience, xxiii, 16–17, 97, 139

Connecticut syringe law, 353

Connor, Linda, xii

Consilience (Wilson), 429

Cooke, Molly, 405–406

Cooper, Lynn, 138

Coping Effectiveness Training (CET), 404, 417t, 424

Coronary Artery Risk Development in Young Adults Study (CARDIA), 248–249

Coronary disease. *See also* Atherosclerosis; Cardiovascular health and disease
culture, genetics, and, 294–295
socioeconomic factors and, 292–296, 309–311. *See also* Whitehall studies
stress and, 295, 297

Corticotropin-releasing factor (CRF), 164f, 166, 171, 173, 180

Cowell, Alan, xiv

Crab-eating monkeys. *See* Macaques *(Macaca fascicularis)*

Cross-cultural studies, 241, 294–296, 309–310, 434

Crumley, Carolyn L., xviii, 445

Culture, Medicine, and Psychiatry, 443

Cynomolgus monkeys. *See* Macaques *(Macaca fascicularis)*

Daily Spiritual Experiences Scale, 277

Darwin, Charles, 35, 325

Data analysis, levels of, 246

Data sources and collection, 6, 205–207, 213–215, 231, 257–261, 268, 269, 330, 333–334

Davidson, Richard J., xiii, xiv, xv, xvi, 105–110, 111–134, 164, 204, 213, 215, 435, 438, 445, 447t, 450t, 453t, 458n3

Demographic factors. *See also* Biodemography; Evolutionary demography; Longevity
HIV/AIDS infection and, 351–352
psychosocial strengths and, 241–242

Depressive symptoms
affective neuroscience and, 115, 120
environmental effects on gene expression and neural development and, 162
HIV/AIDS and, 362–367, 373, 400
religion, health, and, 261–264

Determinism
multiple, 38
nonadditive, 39
reciprocal, 39

Diet
and cholesterol levels and coronary heart disease, 95, 295
and social stress and atherosclerosis in monkeys, 79–82, 84–85

Disability, religion, and health, 259, 262

DNA methylation, 170, 183–185
maternal care and, 185

DNA sites, gene-environment interaction at, 167–170

Drug use. *See also* Alcoholism
HIV/AIDS and, 353, 373, 378, 399, 400
religion, health, and, 262
syringe and needle exchange programs, 353

Duke University xvi. *See also* Center for the Study of Religion, Spirituality, and Health
environment at, 267–268

Durkheim, Émile, 256, 296, 304

Dyads research, 5

Echocardiography and hypertensive heart disease, 54–56

Economic status. *See* Socioeconomic status

Educational advantage/disadvantage and resilience, 208–209

Emotion, neuroscience of. *See* Affective neuroscience

Emotional reactivity. *See* Stress reactivity

Endothelial dysfunction, 94–95

English Longitudinal Study of Ageing (ELSA), 317–318

Environmental effects on gene expression and neural development, 160. *See also* Maternal care animal models
   BALBc mice, 176–177
   monkeys, 174
   anxiety, fear, and, 175, 176–181
   corticotropin-releasing factor (CRF) and, 164f, 166, 171, 173, 180
   DNA sites, gene-environment interaction, and, 167–170
   early family environment and adult health, 162–163
   early family environment and mental illness, 162
   interdisciplinary research on
      historical background to, 160–162
      impediments to, 171
   novelty response and, 173, 178
   stress, health, and, 163–165, 180–181
   stress reactivity and, 163, 165, 173–181

Environmental effects on health, mechanisms of, 245

Environmental exposure and hypertensive heart disease, 44

Environmental mastery, 201

Epidemiology, 302, 304, 311, 401

Epigenetic programming of HPA stress responses, 184–185

Epigenetics and the epigenome, 183–186

Epstein-Barr virus (EBV) activation in HIV/AIDS-positive subjects, 365

Estrogen levels and hormone replacement therapy (HRT)
   hypertensive heart disease and, 61
   psychosocial strengths and, 236–237
   and social stress and atherosclerosis in monkeys, 83–86, 85f

Ethnic/racial differences. *See also* Cross-cultural studies
   in HIV/AIDS infection, 351–352, 400–402, 412
   in hypertensive heart disease, 45, 47t, 54–57

European Science Foundation, xi, xvii

Evolutionary demography, 329

Evolutionary theories of senescence, 325–327, 330–331, 333–336

Exercise as stress buffer
   in HIV/AIDS-positive gay and bisexual men, 364–365
   and hypertensive heart disease, 58–59

Experience Corps (EC), 249–250

Fairtlough, Gerard, xviii

Fava, Giovanni, 210–211

Fear. *See* Anxiety and fear

Fetzer Foundation, 271, 273

Folkman, Susan, 403, 420

Foraging conditions for rats and maternal care, 180

Ford Foundation, 434

Foundation support, 243, 440. *See also* Funding for research

Framingham Study, 5, 297

Freud, Sigmund, 256

Frontal lobes and information shunting, 143–144

Funding for research, xvi–xvii, 6–7, 434, 439–440, 442–444
   in affective neuroscience, 125–126
   in biodemography, 340
   on HIV/AIDS, 369, 379
   on hypertensive heart disease, 63
   on psychosocial strengths, 240–243
   in religion and health, 271, 273
   on resilience, 213, 215
   in socioeconomic status, longevity, and health, 303–304, 313–314
   sustained support, 440
   on visual mental imagery, 146, 153

Gay and bisexual men and HIV/AIDS. *See also* Miami group-based CBSM for HIV/AIDS-positive subjects
   exercise as stress buffer for, 364–365
   mental health and mental illness in, 361–367
   San Francisco CAPS program and, 394–395, 407. *See under* Center for AIDS Prevention Studies (CAPS)
   San Francisco Men's Health Project (SFMHP) and, 397, 398

Gender differences. *See* Sex differences in susceptibility

Genetics. *See also* Environmental effects on gene expression and neural development; Hypertensive heart disease
   aging, longevity, and, 294–296
   biodemography and, 326, 327, 331–332
   and psychosocial strengths, 244
   sociobiology and nature *vs.* nurture, 294–296

George, Linda K., 255–284, 448t, 451t, 455t

Girdler, Susan S., 44–73, 446t, 449t, 452t

Glucocorticoid receptor (GR) development
environmental effect on, 167–170, 172–173, 312
mechanism of action for handling, 166–170

Glucocorticoid receptor (GR) expression, reversal of maternal effects on, 184–185

Gompertz, Benjamin, 324, 331–336

Government funding, 440. See also Funding for research

Grant proposals, 442–443

Group-based cognitive-behavioral stress management (CBSM). See Miami group-based CBSM for HIV/AIDS-positive subjects

Gunderson, Lance, xix

Hall, Kara, xi

Hartzog, Paul, xix

Health. See also Longevity; Positive health
defined, 193
inequalities in. See Socioeconomic status

Health promotion. See Positive health

Heart, autonomic control of. See Heterarchical organization of nervous system and autonomic control of heart

Heart health and disease. See Cardiovascular health and disease; Hypertensive heart disease

Herpesvirus activation in HIV/AIDS-positive subjects, 365

Heterarchical organization of nervous system and autonomic control of heart, 21–22, 36–40, 435
anxiety and, 23, 24, 26–27, 28f, 29
bottom-up influences, 23, 26–27, 29, 39
facilitating factors in interdisciplinary research on, 33–38
historical and current impediments to research, 35–36
history of research program, 21–22, 31–36
immune system and, 29–33
interdisciplinary training and, 38
multiple interactive neural processing levels, 21–26
multiple levels of research and analysis, 21–22, 33–39
social connection and, 14, 24–25, 31–33
stress factors and, 23–24, 27, 28f, 29–31, 30f
top-down influences, 23, 29–31, 39

Heterarchy, concept of, xviii, 444–445

Higginbotham, Nick, xii

Hinderliter, Alan L., 44–73, 446t, 449t, 452t

Hispanics and HIV/AIDS infection, 351, 377, 400, 401–402

Histone deacetylases (HDACs), 183–185

HIV/AIDS, xxii, 3, 5, 351–354, 433, 436. See also Center for AIDS Prevention Studies (CAPS); Gay and bisexual men and HIV/AIDS; Women, with HIV/AIDS infection
abbreviations and acronyms, 385–386
as chronic illness, 352–353
coping with, 424
disease process, 360
drug-resistant strains, 370–371
drug use and, 353, 373, 378, 399, 400
epidemiology, 424–425
heterosexuals and, 407. See also Women
historical background, 358–359, 393–395
interventions
Mpowerment Project, 412–413
programs aimed at high-risk behavior, 353, 373
racial/ethnic differences and, 351–352, 400–402, 412
sexual risk behavior and, 373, 397, 400, 401–402, 409–410, 412
testing issues, 361, 364–365, 398–400, 414, 417–418t
understanding the extent of the problem, 394–395

HIV/AIDS patients
effectiveness of counseling for, 397, 414, 417–418t
interventions, 353. See also Miami group-based CBSM for HIV/AIDS-positive subjects
group-based psychosocial interventions before advent of protease inhibitors, 362–368
from palliative care to chronic disease treatment, 352–353
testosterone levels, 367
treatment adherence
in Miami CBSM program, 369–373, 378, 383–385
in San Francisco CAPS program, 405–406, 423
treatment and management of, 403, 406
combination therapy and advent of protease inhibitors, 368–371
new behavioral approaches to, 371–378

Homosexual men. See Gay and bisexual men and HIV/AIDS

Hormone replacement therapy. *See* Estrogen levels and hormone replacement therapy (HRT)
Housing conditions, atherosclerosis, and social stress in monkeys, 79–81
Hulley, Stephen B., 395, 399, 415
Hypertension, socioeconomic status and, 298, 311
Hypertensive heart disease, genetic and behavioral factors in, 15–16, 65–67
  active *vs.* passive coping and, 51–52
  ambulatory blood pressure levels, 54, 56–57
  echocardiography and, 54–56
  elements of interdisciplinary research program, 46, 48–50
  environmental exposure, 44
  estrogen replacement therapy, 61
  family history of hypertension, 46, 47t, 53, 60–61
  gene variants associated with specific physiological alterations, 47t
  heart rate (HR), 45, 46, 50–51
  impedance cardiography and, 54–56
  impediments to interdisciplinary research on, 61–64
  individual susceptibility, 44–45
  initial studies of life stress exposure and blood pressure, 57–58
  interaction between genetic and behavioral traits, 45–46
  interdisciplinary elements of program, 46, 48–50
  longitudinal approaches in a small research group, 59–61
  need for composite assessment battery, 64
  potassium intake, 56–57
  racial differences in susceptibility, 45, 47t, 54–58
  salt intake, 44, 46, 56–57
  sex differences in susceptibility, 45, 56, 61
  social connection, 59
  stress factors, 44–45
    behavioral buffers, 46, 58–59
    difficulties in implicating, 51–53
    high stress responsivity, 45–46, 53–57, 59–61, 64
    history of transition to emphasis on, 50–54
    potassium intake, 56–57
    salt intake, 56–57
    "total stress burden," 63

summary of major research findings, 46, 47t
transfer to clinical practice, 62–63
Hypothalamic-pituitary-adrenocortical (HPA) activation, 31, 33, 164f, 164–166, 175, 311–313
  psychosocial strengths and, 212, 232–234, 237, 238
Hypothalamus-pituitary-adrenal (HPA) stress responses
  epigenetic programming of, 184–185
  maternal effects on
    molecular mechanisms for, 182–183
    reversal of, 184

Imagery. *See* Visual mental imagery
Immune function, 359–362. *See also* HIV/AIDS
  heterarchical organization of nervous system, autonomic control of heart, and, 29–33
  resilience and, 204
Information shunting via frontal lobes, 143–144
Institutional flexibility and freedom, 7
Institutional leadership, 439
  training, curriculum development, and, xv–xvi
Institutions, role of, 7, 438–440, 442
Integrative concepts, 441
  new, 6
Integrative field, new, xiv
Interdisciplinary collaborators
  geographic dispersion, 243
  seniority, 243
Interdisciplinary Health Research Team (IHRT), xii
Interdisciplinary research, xxi–xxiii. *See also* Interdisciplinary training; *specific topics*
  approaching, 3–9
  attitudes toward, 7
  benefits of, 245–246, 338
    reciprocal disciplinary, 245
  collaborative pathways, 449–452t
  conceptual depth, 246
  conceptual richness, 245
  defined, 4
  determinants of the success of, 5–7
  facilitating factors in, 6–7, 33–38, 92–94, 124–125, 153, 213–215, 242–244, 271–273, 452–457t
    external factors, 439–441
    internal factors, 438–439

Interdisciplinary research, (*continued*)
  fostering, 429–446t
  guidelines for future projects, 443–444
  impediments to, 35–36, 61–64, 92–93,
      124–126, 139, 153, 171, 215,
      242–244, 272, 338–340, 343, 418–419,
      452–457t
    external factors, 442–443
    internal factors, 441–442
  vs. multidisciplinarity, 4, 5, 380, 432–433
  phases in development of, 7–8
  publications, xvi, 443
  terminological issues in, xix, 432–433
  time issues in, 8, 244
  unity of knowledge and, 429–430,
      444–445
Interdisciplinary team science
  complementary initiatives, x–xiii
  recognition of the value of, x–xiii
Interdisciplinary training, xxii, 8–9, 38,
      440, 444
  affective neuroscience and, 122, 123,
      126–127
  approaches to, 8–9
  Miami CBSM interventions and, 380
  psychosocial strengths and, 228, 241,
      242, 245
  resilience and, 213
  San Francisco CAPS program and, 413–414
International Center for Health and Society,
      318
  bringing interdisciplinary research into,
      313–315
  interdisciplinary research arrangements and
      the formation of, 305–308
International Institute for Society and Health
      (IISH), 318
  further developing the policy focus, 318–319
Intrinsic mortality signature or schedule,
      332–337

Jackson, John Hughlings, 22
James, William, 111, 124, 125
John Henryism, 58
John-Steiner, Vera, xix
Johnson, Nancy, xii
Journals, 443

Kaplan, Jay R., xiii, 17, 74–110, 437, 446t, 449t
Kaposi's sarcoma, 408, 417t
Kegeles, Susan M., 412, 420
Kessel, Frank, ix–xx, xxiii, 429–446t, 458n3
Kirkwood, Thomas, 326
Klein, Julie T., xi

Kluver-Bucy syndrome, 117
Koenig, Harold, 273
Kosslyn, Stephen M., xiii, 135–159, 447t, 454t
  The Case for Mental Imagery, 154

Language and communication issues,
      359–360, 432–433, 437–438, 441.
    See also Linguistics
Latinos and HIV/AIDS infection, 351, 377,
      400, 401–402
Lesion studies. *See* Affective neuroscience
Levy, Jay, 406, 408, 415
L-GH (lymphocyte growth hormone)
      levels, 33
Life challenges, response to. *See* Resilience
Life purpose, 201
Light, Kathleen C., xiii, xiv, xvi, 44–73, 446t,
      449t, 452t
Linguistics
  sociobiology and, 294
  visual mental imagery and, 138
Longevity
  health, aging, and, 287–290, 433, 435–436.
      See also Biodemography; MacArthur
      Research Network on Successful
      Aging; MacArthur Study of Successful
      Aging
  the big questions about aging, 323
  evolutionary theories of senescence,
      325–327, 330–331, 333–336
  genetics and, 294–296
  psychosocial strengths and, 230f,
      231–233, 238–239
  reasons for aging, 323
  religion and, 268
  resilience studies and, 202, 206
  search for a law of mortality, 324–325
  socioeconomic status and, 288, 315–317.
      See also Coronary disease;
      International Center for Health and
      Society; Whitehall studies
  animal models and, 311–312
  biological pathways, 311–313
  from blending disciplines to
      interdisciplinary research, 304–305
  coronary heart disease and, 294–295
  criticisms of findings of the social
      gradient in health, 299–302
  cross-cultural studies, 294–295, 309–310
  developing the interdisciplinary activity,
      315
  early life and adult health, 311–312
  epidemiology, 302, 304, 311
  history of interdisciplinary research, 296

how exposures from early life affect disease risks, 310
HPA activation and, 311–313
mechanisms, 306–308
moving beyond conventional individual risk factors, 305
policy and research, 292–294, 300, 316
psychophysiology and clinical studies, 312–313
psychosocial factors and disease occurrence, 310
from psychosocial factors to social determinants, 294–296
research program on social determinants of health, 299–302
socioeconomic differences in health within and between countries, 309–310
Longitudinal studies
on heterarchical organization of nervous system and autonomic control of heart, 37
on hypertensive heart disease, 59–61
on psychosocial strengths, 235–236, 241
on religion and health, 260, 262, 263
on resilience, 202, 205, 206, 209, 211
with a small research group, 59–61
on socioeconomic status, longevity, and health, 304
Lymphocyte growth hormone (L-GH) levels, 33

Macaques (Macaca fascicularis), 77, 82, 311. See also Atherosclerosis
visual mental imagery processing in, 141–142, 149
MacArthur Class and Health Network, 208
MacArthur Foundation, 7, 123, 126, 208, 212, 214, 434
Research Network for the Study of Mind-Body Interaction, 123
MacArthur Research Network on Successful Aging, 238–239, 242, 243
MacArthur Study of Successful Aging, 232, 234–237
Magnetic resonance imaging (MRI and fMRI) and affective neuroscience, 112, 124–125
Makeham, William, 324, 325, 333
Manuck, Stephen B., xiii, 17, 74–110, 446t, 449t, 453t
Markus, Hazel, 209, 212
Marmot, Michael, xiv, xv, xvii, 292–321, 448t, 451t, 455t

Marrett, Cora, xxi–xxiii, 458
Marx, Karl, 229
Maternal care
and amygdala, 180
and anxiety and fear, 175, 176–181
arched-back nursing, 174, 175, 178
and DNA methylation, 185
foraging conditions for rats and, 180
individual differences in
reasons for, 177–181
transmitted to offspring, 173–181
licking and tactile stimulation, 171–175
and oxytocin and atherosclerosis, 64–66
postnatal handling and maternal separation, 165–174, 311–312
Mathabane, Mark, 209
McDonnell Foundation, 125
McEwen, Bruce, 231, 234, 241
McKusick, Leon, 396–398
Meaney, Michael J., xiii, xiv, 160–197, 447t, 450t, 454t
Medawar, Sir Peter, 326, 327, 332, 337
Medication adherence training (MAT), 383–385
Memory, associative
and visual mental imagery, 143, 144, 147–148, 150
Menopausal women. See Estrogen levels and hormone replacement therapy (HRT)
Mental health and mental illness. See also Depressive symptoms
early family environment and, 162, 311–312
in HIV-positive gay men, 361–367
religion and, 259–264
Mental imagery. See Visual mental imagery
Mentors, interdisciplinary, 243. See also Interdisciplinary training
Methodological creativity, 245
Miami group-based CBSM for HIV/AIDS-positive subjects, 358–359, 381–385, 436
adherence to treatment regime, 369–373, 378, 383–385
African American women and, 374–376
assessing functional status of CD4 cells, 373–374
communication between collaborators, 359–360
community involvement, 380–381
conceptual diagram of variables, 373, 374f
construction of program infrastructure, 378–381
drug abusers and, 373, 378

Miami group-based CBSM for HIV/AIDS-positive subjects (*continued*)
focus on asymptomatic/latent period of disease, 359–362
focus on women in, 374–377, 401–402
immune status impairment levels in uninfected subjects, 359–362
interdisciplinary training, 380
multiethnic community, 380
multiethnic study of condom use, 401–402
program after availability of drug treatments, 371–378
stress factors, 359, 373, 374–375
decision to take test, 361
hypothesis, 359
notification of positive HIV status, 361, 364–365
symptom emergence, 365–366
suicide and, 363
therapies, 368–371
Midlife-in-the-United States (MIDUS), xv
network, xv, 109, 248
Migrants, genetics, and socioeconomic factors, 294–295, 309
Mind-body interactions and visual mental imagery, 150–153
Mind-Brain-Behavior and Health Initiative, 128
Molecular biology and biodemography, 337
Monkeys, 311, 312. *See also* Atherosclerosis
maternal care and transmission of individual differences, 174
visual mental imagery processing in, 141–142, 149
Morin, Stephen F., xv, 397, 419–426
Mortality. *See under* Biodemography; Longevity
Moser, Richard, xi
Mothers. *See* Maternal care
Mpowerment Project, 412–413
Multicultural Inquiry and Research on AIDS (MIRA), 401–402
Multidisciplinary *vs.* interdisciplinary research, xix, 4, 5, 380, 432–433
Mustard, Fraser, 306–307, 313, 314
Myocardial infarction risk and cholesterol levels, 13–14

Narcotics. *See* Drug use
Nash, Justin M., xi
National Academies of Science (NAS), x
National Cancer Institute (NCI), x–xi
National Heart, Lung, and Blood Institute, 13, 37

National Institute of Allergy and Infectious Diseases (NIAID), 397
National Institute of Drug Abuse (NIDA), 378
National Institute of Mental Health (NIMH), 124, 243
HIV/AIDS and, 406
Miami CBSM interventions, 379, 380
San Francisco CAPS, 393, 397, 400
National Institute on Aging (NIA), xxiii, 5, 218, 243, 244
medication caps for adherence monitoring in HIV/AIDS patients, 378 -
National Institutes of Health (NIH), x, xi, xvii, xxiii, 6, 8, 341, 343
HIV/AIDS and, 379, 380, 408
Office of AIDS Research (OAR), 377
Office of Behavioral and Social Science Research (OBSSR), NIH, xxiii, 431–432
Office of Naval Research, 146, 443
Roadmap, xvii, 290, 341
Nature *vs.* nurture. *See* Genetics
Needle exchange programs, 353
Nerve growth factor–inducible factor A (NGFI-A), 168f, 170, 182–185
Neurobiology and psychosocial factors in midlife, 220
Neuroendocrine activity and psychosocial strengths, 231–234, 237
Neuroendocrinology, 242
Neuroplasticiy. *See* Plasticity of neural circuitry
Neuroscience, 105–110, 435. *See also* Affective neuroscience; Environmental effects on gene expression and neural development; Heterarchical organization of nervous system and autonomic control of heart; Visual mental imagery
computational modeling and, xxiii, 139
computer technology, xxiii
development of, 36–39
Novelty response, environmental effects on, 173, 178
Nucleoside reverse transcriptase inhibitors (NRTIs), 368

OBSSR. *See* National Institutes of Health
Olshansky, S. Jay., xiii, xvi, xvii, 322–347, 448t, 451t, 456t
"Options Project," 406
Organizations. *See* Institutions
OUHSC (University of Oklahoma Health Sciences Center), 342

Ovarian function and coronary disease, 97–98
  premenopausal precursors of
    postmenopausal disease, 94–95
Oxytocin (OT), 65–67, 247

Pacific AIDS Education and Training Center
    (PAETC), 420
Padian, Nancy, 420
Pain, religious participation and, 276
Paivio, Alan, 138
Panarchy, xviii
Parental care. See also Environmental effects
    on gene expression and neural
    development; Maternal care
  resilience studies, 206–207
Parietal system, 149
Patel, Chandra, 303
Pearl, Raymond, 325, 333
Peer review, 215, 411, 442–443
PEP (post-exposure prophylaxis) for HIV/
    AIDS exposure, 417t
Personal growth, 201
Personal ties. See Social connection
PFC. See Prefrontal cortex (PFC)
Pigeons and atherosclerosis, 92
Pinker, Steven, 294
Plasticity of neural circuitry. See also
    Environmental effects on gene
    expression and neural development
  affective neuroscience and, 109, 126
Plato, 136–137
Popper, Karl R., 137
Positive and negative experience, dialectic
    between, 217–218
Positive Education Project, 404. See also
    Coping Effectiveness Training
Positive health, 193–197, 218. See also
    Psychosocial strengths; Religion and
    health; Resilience; Well-being
  bringing human strengths into focus,
    217–218
  promotion of, 195
  stress and, 163–165. See also Stress
Positive Psychology, xiv
Post-exposure prophylaxis (PEP) for HIV/
    AIDS exposure, 417t
Potassium intake and hypertensive heart
    disease, 56–57
Prefrontal cortex (PFC)
  affective neuroscience and, 114–116,
    119–121
  ventromedial, 114–115
Prefrontal regions, left and right, 114–115,
    119–121

Prewitt, Kenneth, xxiii, 458
Principal investigator (PI), role of, 437
Problem, focus on the, 437
Promoting Interdisciplinary Research, xi. See
    also National Academies of Science
    (NAS)
Protease inhibitors, 368–371
Protective factors, 199. See also Psychosocial
    strengths; Resilience
Psychosocial strengths, 194–195, 228, 246,
    250–251. See also Religion and health
  allostatic load and, 234–236, 247–248
  biopsychosocial model and, 230f, 244,
    246–247
  cross-cultural studies on, 241
  demographic factors and, 241–242
  driving simulation challenge and, 232, 233
  estrogen levels, HRT, and, 236–237
  genetics and, 244
  interdisciplinary research on
    facilitating factors in, 242–244
    history of, 228, 229, 238–242
    impediments to, 242–244
  interdisciplinary training and, 228, 241,
    242, 245
  interventions and, 244–245
  literature reviews on, 231
  methodological and conceptual
    development of research program on,
    229, 231–236
  methodological work, 247–248
  neuroendocrine activity and, 231–234, 237
  new interdisciplinary projects and
    collaborations, 248–250
  psychological resources, 228, 233–234, 264
  sex differences in susceptibility, 237
  socioeconomic status and, 241
Purpose in life, 201

Racial/ethnic differences. See also Cross-
    cultural studies
  in HIV/AIDS infection, 351–352,
    400–402, 412
  in hypertensive heart disease, 45, 47t,
    54–57
Radio and television programs, religious,
    261
Reciprocal determinism, principle of, 39
Recovery processes, psychosocial promotion
    of, 194–195, 259, 275
Reflex responses and multiple neural
    processing, 22–23
Reid, Donald, 297
Relations with others, positive, 201

Religion and health. *See also* Religious
    participation
  biological mechanisms and, 265
  clinical practice and, 266–267
  data sources and collection of evidence,
      257–261, 268, 269
  differential effects for demographic
      subgroups, 276
  disability and, 259, 262
  future research directions, 273–274
  health outcomes, 257–261
    expanding the range of, 275–276
    negative, 260–261
  history of field of study, 255–257
  interdisciplinary research on
    facilitating factors in, 271–273
    impediments to, 272
  long-term patterns and, 273
  and mental health and mental illness,
      259–264
  projects adding religious variables, 270t
  psychological resources and, 264
  recovery processes and, 259, 275
  relationship between, 257–261
    explaining the, 261–265
    implications for medical care, 265–267
  social connection and, 255, 263–264
  television and radio programs and, 261
  themes in recent work in, 274–278
  therapeutic role of religion, 275
  worldviews and, 264–265
Religious activity, public *vs.* private, 257
Religious coping, positive and negative,
    260–261, 265
Religious participation
  examining multiple forms of, 277–278
  and health practices, 262–263
  and pain, 276
Relocation of community and resilience, 206
Research networks, xv, 128
Resilience, human, 433. *See also* Positive
    health; Well-being
  allostatic load and, 199, 203–204,
      209–210, 212
  as biopsychosocial process, 198, 199,
      204–205. *See also* Biopsychosocial
      processes
  cerebral activation asymmetry and, 204
  in the class and health agenda, 208–209
  data sources and collection, 205–207,
      213–215
  defined, 198
  immune function and, 204
  interdisciplinary research on

facilitating factors in, 213–215
history of, 205–206, 211–216
impediments to, 215
implications of integrative studies,
    216–217
person-centered methodology, 210
specific challenges studied, 202–203,
    206–208
interdisciplinary training and, 213
intervention to promote, 210–211
neurobiology, physical health, and,
    203–205
social connection and, 209
socioeconomic status and, 208–210
sustained well-being in the face of challenge,
    206–208
vis-à-vis challenge, transitions, and
    adversity, 202–203, 206–207
Resilience agenda
  findings and insights from the, 205–211
  methodological innovation in the, 209
Resistance to disease, psychosocial, 194. *See
    also* Psychosocial strengths; Resilience
Reyes, Michael, 420
Rockefeller Foundation, 6, 434
Rose, Geoffrey, 297
Rosenfield, Patricia L., ix–xx, xxiii, 242,
    429–446t, 458n3
Rowe, John W., 3–20, 431, 432, 458n3
Ryff, Carol D., xiii, xiv, xv, 123, 164, 193–197,
    198–227, 235–236, 241, 248, 447t,
    450t, 454t, 458n3, 459n6

Salt intake and hypertensive heart disease, 44,
    46, 56–57
SAM (sympathetic adrenomedullar)
    activation, 31
San Francisco AIDS Foundation (SFAF),
    409–410
San Francisco Center for AIDS Prevention
    Studies. *See* Center for AIDS
    Prevention Studies (CAPS)
San Francisco Department of Public Health
    (SFDPH), 399, 408
San Francisco General Hospital (SFGH), 396,
    405–407
San Francisco Men's Health Project (SFMHP),
    397, 398
Schneiderman, Neil, xiii, xvi, xvii, 351–357,
    358–392, 436, 448t, 451t, 457t, 458n3
Seckl, Jonathan, 169, 170
Seeman, Teresa E., xiv, xv, xvii, 228–254, 447t,
    450t, 455t
Self-acceptance, 201

Senescence, evolutionary theories of, 325–327, 330–331, 333–336

SERCA (Special Emphasis Research Career Award), 8, 221, 240–243, 329

Sewell, William, 430–431

Sex differences in susceptibility, 237. *See also under* Atherosclerosis

  HIV/AIDS intervention program for African American women, 374–376

  hypertensive heart disease, 45, 56, 61

Sexual risk behavior

  AIDS/HIV and, 373, 397, 400–402, 409–410, 412

  effect of firsthand knowledge of people with AIDS and, 397

  stress and, 397

Shepard, Roger, 138

Singer, Burton, xiii, xiv, xv, 123, 198–227, 241, 447t, 450t, 454t

Skin conductance response (SCR) and visual mental imagery, 152

Skinner, Burrhus F., 35

Social connection

  and cardiovascular disease, 24–25, 31–33, 59

  psychosocial strengths and, 228–229, 230f, 231–232

  religion, health, and, 255, 263–264

  and resilience, 209

Social determinants of health, 308f. *See also* Environmental effects on gene expression and neural development; Longevity, socioeconomic status and

Social neuroscience, 16–17, 36. *See also* Neuroscience

Social phobias and affective neuroscience, 115, 120

Social Science and Medicine, 443

Social Science Research Council (SSRC), xxii, 224, 431, 432

Social strengths. *See* Psychosocial strengths

Society of Heart Brain Medicine, xiv, 40

Socioeconomic status (SES). *See under* Longevity

  and cardiac disease, 295–296

  and psychosocial strengths, 241

  and resilience, 208–210

Spanish-speaking persons/Hispanics and HIV/AIDS infection, 351, 377, 400, 401–402

Spatial-properties-processing system, 148–149

Special Emphasis Research Career Award (SERCA), 8, 221, 240–243, 329

"Spiritual interventions," 265–266

Spirituality. *See* Religion and health

Spirituality measures, increased use of, 276–277

SSRC (Social Science Research Council), xxii, 224, 431, 432

Status. *See also* Socioeconomic status

  and atherosclerosis in monkeys

    female animals, 83–86, 85f

    male animals, 79–82, 81f

  as impeding factor in interdisciplinary research, 441–442

  psychosocial strengths and, 241

  resilience and, 208–210

Stokols, Daniel, xi

Stress. *See also* Allostatic load; Atherosclerosis; Exercise as stress buffer; Hypertensive heart disease; Miami group-based CBSM for HIV/AIDS-positive subjects; Resilience

  and autonomic control of heart, 23–24, 27, 28f, 29–31, 30f

  and coronary heart disease, 295, 297

  and gene expression and neural development, 163–165, 180–181

  and health, 163–165

  maternal care and, 180–181

  visual mental imagery and, 150–152

Stress reactivity, individual

  affective neuroscience and, 111, 118–121

  atherosclerosis and social stress in monkeys, 86, 87f, 90

  environmental effects on gene expression and neural development, 163, 165, 173–181

  and hypertensive heart disease, 45–46, 53–57, 59–61, 64

Substance abuse. *See* Drug use

Suicide rates in HIV-positive individuals, 363

Suzman, Richard, xxiii, 458

Syme, Leonard, 295–296

Syringe exchange programs, 353

Szyf, Moshe, 183, 186

Tactile stimulation by mother, gene expression, and neural development, 171–174

Taylor, Brandie, xi

Taylor, Shelley, 231, 233, 236, 246–247, 249

Team Science program, x. *See also* National Cancer Institute (NCI)

Technologies, new, 6, 441

Technophysio evolution, 288

Television and radio programs, religious, 261

Terminological issues in interdisciplinary
    research, 432–433
Thai army HIV/AIDS prevention program,
    353
Thatcher, Margaret, 306
Thriving. *See* Positive health; Resilience;
    Well-being
Training. *See* Interdisciplinary training
Transcranial magnetic stimulation (TMS),
    109, 140
"Transdisciplinarity," xix, 432, 433
Treatment adherence. *See under* HIV/AIDS
Type A behavior theory, 297

Unity of knowledge and interdisciplinary
    research, 429–430, 444–445
University of California, San Francisco
    (UCSF), 402. *See also* Center for AIDS
    Prevention Studies (CAPS)
    AIDS Research Institute (ARI), 394,
        415–416, 425
    Institute for Health Policy Studies (IHPS),
        402
University of Miami. *See* Miami group-based
    CBSM for HIV/AIDS-positive
    subjects
University of North Carolina (UNC) Stress
    and Health Research Program. *See*
    Hypertensive heart disease
University of Oklahoma Health Sciences
    Center (OUHSC), 342
Urban Men's Health Study, 422

Validity, external, 245
Visual mental imagery
    animal models and, 141–142, 149
    anxiety, fear, and, 150–152
    attention shifting and, 144–145, 149–150
    attention window and, 141
    computational modeling and, 139
    depictive aspect, 140–141
    dorsal system and, 142, 149
    health implications, 135, 150–153
    history of field of study, 136–138
    history of interdisciplinary research
        program on, 136, 139
    information shunting and, 143–144
    interdisciplinary research on
        facilitating factors in, 153
        impediments to, 139, 153
    linguistics and, 138
    object properties and, 141–143

protomodel, 140, 141f
reasons for, 145–146
skin conductance response (SCR)
    and, 152
spatial properties and, 141–143
stress reactivity and, 150–152
stress regulation and, 150–152
theory of, 145–146
    development of, 140–146
    revision of, 149–150
    testing the theory of processing
        components, 146–149
    top-down priming and, 144–145
    visual buffer and, 140–141, 147–150
Volberding, Paul, 405–408
von Goldammer, Eberhard, xix

Waite, Linda, xiii, 287–291, 458n3
"Water-cooler" effect, 403
Watson, J. B., 137
Weisman, August, 326
Well-being. *See also* Positive health; Resilience
    assessment of, 201–202
    elements of, 201
    nature of, 200–201
    neurophysiological substates, 218–220
    strategies for promoting, 221
Whitehall studies, 292–293, 297–299, 302–304
    developing the Whitehall II study and
        blending disciplines, 302–304
Wilson, Edward O., 216, 429, 430
Winkelstein, Warren, 397
Wisconsin Longitudinal Study (WLS)
    psychosocial strengths and, 235–236
W.M. Keck Foundation, x
Women. *See also* Estrogen levels and hormone
    replacement therapy (HRT); Ovarian
    function and coronary disease; Sex
    differences in susceptibility
    with HIV/AIDS infection
        African American, 374–376
        Hispanic/Spanish-speaking, 376–377
        multiethnic study of condom use and,
            401–402
    as role models for cynomolgus monkeys,
        97–98
World Health Organization (WHO), xv, 193,
    319, 339, 414, 434
Worldviews, religion, and health, 264–265
Wundt, Wilhelm, 137, 138

Zidovudine (AZT), 368, 369, 403